MIDDLE INCOME A

Though most conceptions of the rule of law assume equality before the law – and hence equal access to the justice system – this basic right is not being met for many low and middle income Canadians. This book focuses on the problem of civil access to justice for middle income earners – those whose household income is high enough to disqualify them from legal aid but not high enough to cover the costs of litigation.

Featuring contributions by leading Canadian and international scholars, practitioners, and members of the judiciary, this multidisciplinary collection draws on scholarship in the fields of law, social science, and public policy. There is a particular emphasis on family law, consumer law, and employment law, as these are the areas where research has indicated that unmet legal needs are highest.

Middle Income Access to Justice presents a variety of innovative solutions, from dispute resolution process reforms to the development of non-lawyer forms of assistance and new methods for funding legal expenses. In doing so, it lays the foundation for the development of a much-needed new delivery model to provide early intervention for legal services.

MICHAEL TREBILCOCK holds the Chair in Law and Economics in the Faculty of Law at the University of Toronto.

ANTHONY DUGGAN holds the Honourable Frank H. Iacobucci Chair in the Faculty of Law at the University of Toronto.

LORNE SOSSIN is Dean of Osgoode Hall Law School at York University.

Middle Income Access to Justice

Edited by Michael Trebilcock, Anthony Duggan, and Lorne Sossin

UNIVERSITY OF TORONTO PRESS
Toronto Buffalo London

© University of Toronto Press 2012
Toronto Buffalo London
www.utppublishing.com
Printed in Canada

ISBN 978-1-4426-4444-1 (cloth)
ISBN 978-1-4426-1268-6 (paper)

Printed on acid-free paper.

Library and Archives Canada Cataloguing in Publication

Middle income access to justice / edited by Michael Trebilcock,
Anthony Duggan, and Lorne Sossin.

Includes bibliographical references and index.
ISBN 978-1-4426-4444-1 (bound). – ISBN 978-1-4426-1268-6 (pbk.)

1. Legal services – Ontario.   2. Middle class – Civil rights – Ontario.
3. Justice, Administration of – Ontario.   4. Equality before the law –
Ontario.   I. Trebilcock, Michael J., 1941–   II. Duggan, Anthony J.
III. Sossin, Lorne Mitchell, 1964–

KEO175.M53M53 2012   347.7130086'22   C2012-901174-6
KF337.5.M53M53 2012

University of Toronto Press acknowledges the financial assistance to its
publishing program of the Canada Council for the Arts and the Ontario
Arts Council.

University of Toronto Press acknowledges the financial support of the
Government of Canada through the Canada Book Fund for its publishing
activities.

Contents

Part 7: Creating Change and Reform of the Judicial System

Part 8: The Options Papers

Foreword

We live in a society committed to the rule of law. We have a *Charter*, a complex and vast edifice of law (both common law and statute), a strong legal profession, and a respected judiciary. We have built, in Canada, what by world standards is an impressive justice system – one of the best in the world. This has not been easily done. It was achieved by the vision, tenacity, and sacrifice of the generations that have preceded us. We should be proud of their accomplishment. Yet the task of securing justice for Canadians is not done. Having achieved a justice system that is the envy of many countries, we face another challenge: ensuring that all Canadians – not just the rich, but the poor and those of average income as well – can actually avail themselves of the system.

It is said that every generation faces its own unique challenges. If the task of the generations that preceded us was to build an excellent justice system, then the task that falls to our generation is to ensure that every man, woman, and child has access to that system; not merely access on paper, but actual, meaningful, and substantive access to justice.

Regrettably, we do not have adequate access to justice in Canada. We have better access than in many countries, but it is still not what it should be. Among those hardest hit are the middle class. They earn too much to qualify for legal aid, but frequently not enough to retain a lawyer for a matter of any complexity or length. When it comes to the justice system, the majority of Canadians do not have access to sufficient resources of their own, nor do they have access to the safety net programs established by the government.

I believe that lack of access to civil justice represents the most significant challenge to our justice system. I am not alone in this regard. In its 2011 *Rule of Law Index*, the World Justice Project identifies access to civil justice as the area where Canada has most difficulty in terms of challenges to the rule of law.[1] With respect to access to civil justice, the index ranks Canada ninth out of twelve wealthy North American and Western European countries. Difficulties in accessing legal counsel and delay in the administration of civil justice are identified as areas of particular concern.

The problem of lack of access to justice is a complex and multifaceted one. As with most complex problems, there is no single solution that will provide the answer. There is no 'silver bullet' that will solve the problem of access to justice. What is required is a sustained multipronged attack on the problem of access to justice. If we are to have any success in improving access, a coordinated, collaborative approach among governments, lawyers, and judges is necessary.

The academy, of course, must form an integral part of this coordinated, collaborative approach. We rely on academics to research access to justice-related issues and explore and suggest potential solutions. This collection of essays presented at the Middle Income Access to Justice Colloquium held at the University of Toronto in February 2011 is a significant contribution in this respect. The topics covered read like an encyclopaedia to the access to justice problem: civil legal needs, dispute prevention, alternative service models and fee arrangements, legal aid, public legal education, unbundling of legal services, pro bono services, prepaid legal services plans, legal expense insurance, triage, court process simplification, and so on.

I commend this important collection to all those concerned about lack of access to justice. As someone who cares deeply about this issue, I thank the editors and the authors for their important contribution to a topic of great importance to our justice system.

The Right Honourable Beverley McLachlin, P.C.,
Chief Justice of Canada

---

1 M.D. Agrast, J.C. Botero, and A. Ponce, *WJP Rule of Law Index 2011* (Washington: World Justice Project, 2011), 23 and 51.

Contributors

Nicholas Bala

Nicholas Bala has been a Professor at the Faculty of Law at Queen's University since 1980 and since 2006 has also been serving as the Academic Director of the Osgoode Hall Law School Part-Time Family Law LLM Program. His main area of teaching and research expertise is Family and Children's Law and he has published widely in this field. In 2009 he was awarded the Law Society of Ontario Medal and received the Ontario Bar Association Award for Excellence in Family Law.

Nigel J. Balmer

Dr Nigel Balmer is an Honorary Senior Research Fellow in the Centre for Empirical Legal Studies, UCL Faculty of Laws. He holds a PhD from John Moores University and a BSc (Hons.) in Mathematics and Psychology from the University of Stirling. He is a Fellow of the Royal Statistical Society, a Member of the American Statistical Association, and an Honorary Fellow of John Moores University.

Jamie Baxter

Jamie Baxter is a recent graduate of the University of Toronto Faculty of Law. He has written in the areas of indigenous land reform, rural development, and access to civil justice. He holds a master's degree in Economics from McMaster University and was a Canada–U.S. Fulbright Scholar at the University of Kentucky in 2007.

Samreen Beg

Samreen Beg graduated from the University of Toronto Faculty of Law in 2010 and is now serving as Legal Counsel at the Canadian Securities Transition Office. Prior to attending law school, Samreen worked as a policy advisor in the Ontario Public Service.

Sujit Choudhry

Sujit Choudhry is Cecelia Goetz Professor of Law at the NYU Law School. He previously held the Scholl Chair at the University of Toronto Faculty of Law and from 2008 to 2011 he was Associate Dean (First Year Program). At the University of Toronto, he was cross-appointed to the Department of Political Science and the School of Public Policy and Governance. He was named a Trudeau Fellow in 2010.

The Honourable George Czutrin

The Honourable George Czutrin is a Justice of the Superior Court of Justice (Ontario) and has been based in Toronto since January 2007. From 1995 to 2006 he was a Local Administrative Justice, Hamilton Family Court. Since September 2009, he has served as Family Team Leader in Toronto, Superior Court of Justice (Ontario). Justice Czutrin is a member of the Family Rules Committee; past Chair Chief Justice's Committee on the Unrepresented Litigant; past member of the Civil Justice Review Family Law Subcommittee and the Family Law Implementation Committee; and past President of the Association of Family and Conciliation Courts.

Anthony Duggan

Tony Duggan holds the Hon. Frank H. Iacobucci Chair in Capital Markets Regulation in the Faculty of Law at the University of Toronto. He is also a Professorial Fellow in the Faculty of Law at the University of Melbourne. He has doctoral and undergraduate degrees in law from Melbourne and a master's degree in law from Toronto. He served as Associate Dean at the Faculty of Law, University of Toronto from 2002 to 2004. His main teaching and research interests are in commercial law and equity and trusts. He has published widely in the areas of secured transactions, bankruptcy law, and consumer protection.

Russell Engler

Russell Engler is a Professor of Law and the Director of Clinical Programs at New England Law in Boston. He directs New England's clinical programs, teaches the Lawyering Process and Public Interest Law Seminar and Clinic, co-teaches clinical component courses, and directs the Public Service Project of the school's Center for Law and Social Responsibility.

Stephen B. Ginsberg

Stephen B. Ginsberg is the Executive Director of the CAW Legal Services Plan. He received his BA from the University of Toronto and his LLB from the University of Western Ontario. He is a former president and current board member of the American Prepaid Legal Services Institute, funded by and affiliated with the American Bar Association, in Chicago, Illinois.

Dennis Kao

Dennis Kao obtained his JD from the University of Toronto in 2009. During 2010, he served as a full-time research assistant to professors Tony Duggan and Jacob Ziegel at the University of Toronto Faculty of Law, working on a wide range of commercial law projects. He is now employed with Sidley Austin LLP in New York City.

Justin Malbon

Justin Malbon is a professor at the Law School at Monash University in Melbourne, Australia. He has an LLM from Osgoode Hall Law School and a PhD from the University of New South Wales. He is on the board of the Queensland Competition Authority, which regulates the revenues of monopolies regarding water, gas, electricity, ports, and rail. He also sits on Financial Ombudsman Service panels, which hear consumer complaints against insurers, financial planners, and stockbrokers.

Judith McCormack

Judith McCormack is the Executive Director of Downtown Legal Services, the University of Toronto Faculty of Law's community legal clinic, and she serves as Acting Assistant Dean, Students, at the Faculty of Law. She has been a litigator, a mediator, and an adjudicator, and has extensive expertise in the areas of labour law, administrative law, and alternative dispute resolution.

Shelley McGill

Shelley McGill is an Associate Professor in the Policy and Law area of the School of Business and Economics at Wilfrid Laurier University and in the Global Governance area of the Balsillie School of International Affairs. She is an Ontario lawyer holding a Bachelor of Laws (LLB) from the University of Western Ontario and a Master of Laws (LLM) from York University. She is a Deputy Judge of the Ontario Small Claims Court, an arbitrator and mediator for the Better Business Bureau, and an author of a leading Canadian business law textbook.

Pascoe Pleasence

Pascoe Pleasence is Professor of Empirical Legal Studies and co-director of the Centre for Empirical Legal Studies at University College London. He is also an Academic and Scientific Advisor at the Legal Services Commission, where, from 1995 to 2009, he was Head of the Legal Services Research Centre. He has published widely in the field of empirical legal studies. His most influential work, a second edition of *Causes of Action: Civil Law and Social Justice* (2006: TSO), has become central to the development of access to justice policy in England and Wales.

Iain Ramsay

Iain Ramsay, LLB (Edinburgh), LLM (McGill), is Professor of Law at Kent Law School, University of Kent, Canterbury, U.K. From 1986 to 2007 he was a Professor of Law at Osgoode Hall Law School, York University, Toronto, Canada. His primary area of research is regulation of consumer markets at the national, regional, and international levels, in particular regulation of consumer credit, debt, and insolvency.

Azim Remani

Azim Remani is in the third year of the JD program at the University of Toronto.

Carol Rogerson

Carol Rogerson is a Professor at the University of Toronto Faculty of Law, where she has taught since 1983, serving as Associate Dean from 1990 to 1993. She teaches and writes in the areas of family law, constitutional law, and children and the law, and has written extensively on spousal and child support issues. She has worked with both federal and provincial governments on issues of family law reform.

Rebecca L. Sandefur

Rebecca L. Sandefur joined the American Bar Foundation in September 2010 to lead the foundation's new access to justice research initiative. Before joining the American Bar Foundation, Sandefur served on the faculty of Stanford University for nine years after receiving her PhD in sociology from the University of Chicago. In addition to being Senior Research Social Scientist at the ABF, she is Consulting Assistant Professor of Sociology at Stanford University.

Noel Semple

Noel Semple is a PhD candidate at Osgoode Hall Law School, York University. His doctoral work focuses on the legal procedures by which custody and access arrangements are made for children following the breakdown of their parents' relationships. A member of the Ontario bar, Noel Semple holds a JD degree from the University of Toronto Faculty of Law and an LLM from Osgoode Hall.

Roger Smith

Roger Smith, OBE, is the Director of the London-based human rights and law reform organization, JUSTICE. He is a visiting professor at the University of London South Bank and an Honorary Professor at the University of Kent. He has worked in a variety of non-governmental organizations since 1973. These have included law centres, the Child Poverty Action Group, the Legal Action Group, and the Law Society, where he was Director of Legal Education and Training. He has followed developments in Ontario over a number of years since first visiting the province to study its legal clinics in 1991.

Lorne Sossin

Lorne Sossin became Dean of Osgoode Hall Law School on 1 July 2010. Prior to this appointment, he was a Professor with the Faculty of Law at the University of Toronto (2002–10). He is a former Associate Dean of the University of Toronto (2004–7) and served as the inaugural Director of the Centre for the Legal Profession (2008–10). Previously (1997–2002), he was a faculty member at Osgoode Hall Law School and the Department of Political Science at York University. His teaching interests span administrative and constitutional law, the regulation of professions, civil litigation, public policy, and the judicial process.

Michael Trebilcock

Michael J. Trebilcock graduated from the University of Canterbury in New Zealand in 1962 with an LLB and completed his LLM at the University of Adelaide in 1965. In 1972 he joined the Faculty of Law at the University of Toronto, where he is now a University Professor. In 1999, Professor Trebilcock was awarded the Canada Council Molson Prize in the Humanities and Social Sciences. In 2007 he was the recipient of the Ontario Attorney General's Mundell Medal for contributions to Law and Letters. In 2010, he was the recipient of the Ontario Premier's Discovery Award for the Social Sciences. In 2008, he undertook a review of the Legal Aid Program in Ontario for the Attorney General.

Paul A. Vayda

Paul Vayda is currently the Managing Lawyer at the Oakville office of the CAW Legal Services Plan, and has been a Plan lawyer for twenty-four years. He graduated with an Honours BA from the University of Toronto, and holds an LLB from the University of Ottawa and an LLM from Cambridge University. He has taught at Mohawk College and at the Bar Admission Course. He has written articles on title insurance, family law and bankruptcy, and the New Home Warranty Program.

James Wilson

James S.F. Wilson was educated at the University of Toronto Faculty of Law, where he was an editor-in-chief of the Law Review, and Harvard College. Before attending law school, he worked as a speechwriter to the prime minister of Canada (2005–6). He has also worked in the U.S. book publishing and film industries. He is currently an associate with a Toronto law firm.

Albert Yoon

Albert Yoon is an Associate Professor at the University of Toronto Faculty of Law. Before coming to Toronto, he was Professor of Law at Northwestern University School of Law. He received his undergraduate degree from Yale and his law and doctoral (political science) degrees from Stanford. Professor Yoon's primary research areas are the legal profession, torts, judicial politics, American political development, and corporate law. In 2007 he was awarded the Ronald H. Coase Prize from the University of Chicago for the best published (co-authored) paper in Law and Economics.

PART 1

Introduction

Introduction

MICHAEL TREBILCOCK, ANTHONY DUGGAN,

AND LORNE SOSSIN

I. The Project

This volume proceeds on the fundamental assumption that access to justice is a basic right. Access to justice, as we conceive it, means the effective right of an individual to advance in appropriate *fora* legitimate legal claims or defences against claims by others.[1] Most conceptions of the rule of law assume equality before the law and hence access to law or the justice system as one of its fundamental predicates. This basic right is not being met for many low and middle income Ontarians, especially in the area of civil justice (which we take to include the full range of non-criminal legal contexts, including consumer, employment, and family law disputes).

The reasons for this are various: financial eligibility requirements for legal aid remain frozen at extremely low levels, and the range of services prioritized even within these financial eligibility requirements exclude

---

1 'While [access to justice] was once linked to concerns over how litigants could obtain affordable legal representation (which was addressed primarily through legal aid), more recent approaches have included organized pro bono, creating specialized courts (*Gladue* courts, domestic violence courts, etc.), replacing courts with tribunals, promoting ADR and Collaborative Law, replacing tort with no-fault accident compensation schemes, community and public legal education, self-help and the prevention of disputes. Access to justice is also closely linked to the promotion of equity, fairness and the elimination of barriers to justice (whether physical, psychological, financial or social). In this sense, access to justice raises questions about the degree to which the citizen has access to and can participate in the procedures by which substantive law is made.' Lorne Sossin, *Research Priorities Report: Submitted to the Board of Governors of the Law Commission of Ontario* (2007) at 3.

many areas of the civil justice system. Market rates for legal services continue to rise, and representation by legal counsel is unaffordable for many citizens. Other methods of obtaining legal services, such as through paralegals, summary advice services, or public legal information, remain uncoordinated and incomplete in their capacity to address unmet legal needs. For our purposes, when we refer to middle income earners, we are contemplating the large group of individuals whose household income is too high to allow them to qualify for legal aid, but too low, in many cases, for them to be in a position to hire legal counsel to represent them in a civil law matter. As a result of this denial of effective access to justice, we are witnessing a staggering number of individuals trying to navigate an increasingly complex civil justice system without any or adequate legal assistance and feeling increasingly alienated from the legal system. This is the crisis of access to civil justice that we face. While we are not so naive as to believe there is a simple or 'silver bullet' solution to this crisis, the essays collected in this book provide a veritable cornucopia of ideas and proposals for addressing the crisis.

This volume is the culmination of a much longer initiative. Over two years ago, one of us (Michael Trebilcock) prepared a review of Ontario's legal aid system for the Ministry of the Attorney General. One of the findings in this review was an acute lack of access to civil justice for lower and middle income earners in Ontario, manifesting itself particularly in an increasing number of unrepresented litigants. Not only was this a manifestation of injustice in itself, but it also raised major political economy problems in terms of the commitment of middle income earners to supporting a legal aid system of which they were never beneficiaries but only contributors as taxpayers, even while they faced similar denials of access to justice themselves. The attenuated commitment of middle income earners to the civil justice system is reflected in substantial increases in real *per capita* expenditures on health care and education in Ontario over recent years (both areas in which middle income earners have a significant stake), but declining expenditures on legal aid (where middle income earners have no appreciable stake). The point is that significant improvements in the delivery of public services are unlikely without the support of those who principally fund them, and that to gain this support, the improvements must be pitched to a broader constituency than those who are most obviously in need. For these reasons, this book focuses in particular on improving access to justice for middle income groups. On the other hand, while the legal problems encountered by low income and middle income individuals and families diverge in important respects, they also share many common elements, so many of the reform initiatives canvassed in the book are equally relevant to both groups.

Subsequent to this review, a team at the University of Toronto Faculty of Law set out to study and better understand the causes of the problem and potential responses to it. We began by conducting an extensive set of interviews with leading members of the judiciary, the bar, and the academy both in Canada and internationally. We oversaw the preparation of a detailed literature review to understand better the sources of the problem and responses to it in terms of a preliminary evaluation of initiatives undertaken in Canada and beyond.

We also held focus group meetings with major stakeholders in three of the highest-needs areas of civil justice identified in various civil justice needs surveys, namely, family law, employment law, and consumer and debtor/creditor law (hosted by major Toronto law firms). Following the focus group meetings, we prepared three options papers, focusing on each of these three areas and drawing on the views of stakeholders as well as comparative experience as reflected in our literature review. Finally, we reached out to many experts, Canadian and international, in the field of access to civil justice and invited them to prepare papers for a colloquium on Middle Income Access to Civil Justice held at the University of Toronto Faculty of Law, 10–11 February 2011. The essays in this volume are revised versions of the colloquium papers. The volume also includes revised versions of the three options papers mentioned above. While these initiatives had their genesis in Ontario, we believe that the issues they address have salience across Canada, as attested to by the broad national and international representation of participants and speakers at the colloquium (and authors represented in this volume).

Both the organization of the colloquium and the organization of essays in this volume follow a basic structure. First, we need to be clear on exactly what the dimensions of the problem of middle income access to civil justice are and where the most frequent and severe legal needs arise. A number of jurisdictions, including Ontario, in recent years have undertaken civil justice needs surveys of members of the population with a view to developing a more precise understanding of this question and how individuals respond (or do not respond) to problems with legal dimensions and whether demographic or socio-economic indicators can be identified that predict problem types and advice-seeking behaviours.

Second, with a better definition of the problem we are trying to solve, we then turn to what we have called front-end or proactive solutions to particular clusters of problems. We are motivated here by the metaphor of a cliff located in a highly populated area, creating a danger of accidents: there are two types of measures that can be put in place: an ambulance at the bottom of the cliff to attend to those who are injured, or a fence erected at the top of the cliff to prevent accidents. In many areas of the legal system where citizens confront legal problems or grievances that require redress, we believe that policy options are often available that would pre-empt these problems or grievances.

Third, as many civil needs surveys have made clear, not all problems or grievances are seen by individuals as requiring a lawyer's intervention, and many people would prefer, for cost or other reasons, to pursue other kinds of responses. In this respect, we need to be clear on what other resources are available or could be made available, as well as on the potential and limits of various forms of self-help, limited legal assistance, Internet and telephone call centre services, and neighbourhood advice centres such as the UK Citizens Advice Bureaux, which integrate the provision of legal advice with advice on solving other social and administrative problems.

Fourth, while we readily accept that many problems or grievances can be addressed effectively without a lawyer's intervention, it is equally clear that some legal problems do require legal representation. Hence, the question that needs to be addressed is how we can improve access to lawyers for middle income citizens. In this context, we need to be clear on exactly what barriers people confront, or perceive themselves as confronting, in seeking legal representation: is it mostly a matter of the cost of legal services, or is it a lack of reliable information on the cost, availability, and accessibility of lawyers competent to address the problem or grievance at hand? In terms of reducing the cost of access to lawyers' services, what are the potential and limits of a strategy of promoting the unbundling of lawyers' services so that individual citizens are able to retain lawyers for discrete tasks within well-specified financial parameters in a larger transaction or legal proceeding? What is the potential role for prepaid legal service plans or legal expense insurance schemes, which may address expensive legal contingencies but also through their buying power and ability to achieve volume discounts reduce legal costs for more routine and predictable matters?

Fifth, assuming that some subset of legal problems are appropriately resolved through dispute resolution processes, we need then to explore whether there are ways of reducing the cost, complexity, and protractedness of many adjudicative processes, for example, by reforming and simplifying rules of procedure, unifying family courts, and making small claims courts more accessible and effective in enforcing judgments, as well as utilizing more fully less formal alternative forms of dispute resolution, such as mediation and arbitration.

Finally, we turn to the political economy challenge of mounting an effective strategy for reform of the civil justice system, given the concentrated and largely autonomous groups of stakeholders on the supply side of the legal services market, and diffuse, heterogeneous, and unorganized consumers on the demand side of this market. Alternative reform strategies range from piecemeal or focused reform proposals, such as those set out in our three options papers focusing on family law, employment law, and consumer and debtor/creditor problems, to larger and more ambitious but perhaps less politically tractable reforms, such as a public legal insurance scheme, and various intermediate strategies between these two alternatives.

In the next part of this introductory essay, following the structure set out above, we provide brief synopses of the papers presented around each of these major themes, identifying points of convergence or divergence and unresolved questions that require further research or deliberation.

II. The Essays

A. Defining the Problem – What Are the Unmet Legal Needs?

The essay by Pascoe Pleasence and Nigel Balmer examines the empirical basis for our understanding of civil legal needs. Adopting Gillian Hadfield's reference to the 'law-thick' world in which middle income people live, Pleasence and Balmer discuss the justiciable problems which have the highest incidence (such as workplace, consumer, and family law problems) and the various surveys conducted around the world in the wake of Hazel Genn's landmark 1999 *Paths to Justice* study. Since that project, over twenty related empirical studies on civil legal needs have been undertaken, spanning thirteen countries (including Canada). These studies demonstrate both the ubiquity of legal problems and the distinct ways in which disparate jurisdictions have attempted to address those needs. Pleasence and Balmer note that these surveys have important policy implications. They demonstrate the potential of legal aid schemes to redress the difficulty people have in

obtaining the legal services they need, but also the need for policy makers to address the difficulties that middle income earners face in accessing legal services.

Pleasence and Balmer draw from both this comparative terrain and
a recent study of Civil and Social Justice carried out in 2010 in England
and Wales, in order to analyse the available data on justiciable problems
and the role of lawyers in helping people resolve those problems. The
authors highlight from this latest survey that the work undertaken by
the legal profession does not always reflect the public's experience with
justiciable issues. To take one example, Pleasence and Balmer show that
while personal injury, employment, and welfare benefits may all generate important civil legal needs, lawyers report a much higher degree of
involvement in personal injury work than in employment, and virtually
no lawyers report working on welfare benefits disputes.

In their essay, Jamie Baxter, Michael Trebilcock, and Albert Yoon
explore recent civil justice needs studies in Canada in comparative
perspective. Using the recently released data summarized in *Listening
to Ontarians,* the report of the Civil Legal Needs Project,[2] Baxter, Trebilcock, and Yoon situate this latest study within a comparative perspective, and build on the analysis presented in the essay by Pleasence and
Balmer. Baxter, Trebilcock, and Yoon note the variation found with
respect to the incidence of legal problems in the Ontario study and
speculate that it may be driven by methodological differences (e.g., in
the Ontario study, middle income respondents were asked about their
'legal needs,' whereas in the post–*Paths to Justice* studies examined by
Pleasence and Balmer, respondents from all income ranges were given
a list of justiciable events and asked if any matched their 'problems').

Beyond noting the methodological complexities of surveying legal
needs, Baxter, Trebilcock, and Yoon emphasize that the existing empirical study of legal needs remains fragmented and incomplete. They
believe that more sustained and rigorous empirical study is needed.
They note that the challenge for future research on civil legal needs
surveys will be to identify techniques that can help further explain the
underlying determinants of advice-seeking behaviour.

B. 'Front-End' Proactive Solutions

The essay by Anthony Duggan and Iain Ramsay addresses the issue

---

2 One of the editors served as the research director for the Civil Legal Needs Project.

of front-end strategies for dealing with access to justice concerns. The underlying message is that prevention is better than cure, and so, while – returning to the cliff metaphor – first aid and ambulance services may be a good idea and are probably necessary in any event, it would be a mistake to make them the only strategy. Similarly, when considering strategies for addressing the access to justice problem, it makes sense to think about ways of lowering the number of disputes and reducing the demands on the justice system. Pursuing this line of thought, the question Duggan and Ramsay address in their essay is, can we improve the design of our laws to help people steer clear of conflict in the first place?

The essay uses the consumer credit laws as the focus of its inquiry, and it identifies five main types of front-end response: (1) consumer education initiatives, aimed at helping people make better purchasing decisions; (2) statutory disclosure requirements, aimed at drawing consumers' attention to the financial details of their transactions; (3) cooling-off periods, aimed at giving consumers a limited opportunity to change their minds after signing a contract; (4) behaviour-modifying initiatives, aimed at facilitating choices that are consistent with consumers' longer-term or unrevealed preferences; and (5) substantive interventions aimed at protecting consumers from potentially welfare-reducing decisions by restricting their range of choices (examples include regulation of products, regulation of suppliers, and regulation of contract terms and conditions). The authors critically analyse these five sets of measures, identifying their relative strengths and shortcomings. The essay concludes with a list of specific suggestions for improving the consumer credit laws with the aim of heading off disputes that might otherwise lead to costly litigation. These suggestions relate specifically to consumer credit, but the authors' broader aim is to stimulate thinking about preventive strategies across the range of subject areas where the need for unmet legal services is high.

C. Non-Lawyer Forms of Assistance

Russell Engler, in his essay on non-lawyer forms of assistance for middle income earners, stresses the importance of a comprehensive strategy for promoting access to justice to ensure that steps taken to assist middle income earners are not at the expense of low income groups and also to ensure that access to justice reform does not simply take us 'down the path of second class justice.' Engler proposes a three-pronged approach to the access to justice problem at large: (1) revision of the roles of the key players in the court system, such as judges, court-connected mediators, and clerks, to include the provision of assistance to unrepresented litigants; (2) the increased use of assistance programs short of full representation paired with rigorous evaluation measures; and (3) the adoption of a civil right to counsel in cases where lesser forms of assistance are insufficient. He then seeks to demonstrate that the ideas of 'non-lawyer' and 'middle income,' reflected in the essay's title, are really just variables of the wider access to justice question.

The reform possibilities at Prong 1 include judicial guidelines and training on how to assist self-represented litigants, guidelines and training for court staff, simplified forms and self-help materials, expanded use of technology, improved case management, and flexible procedures allowing for adjustments to the level of formality depending on the size and complexity of the case. At Prong 2, the possibilities include improved public legal education and information, hotlines, technological assistance, clinics, *pro se* clerks' offices, Lawyer-of-the-Day programs, self-help centres, expansion of the role of paralegals, and allowing non-lawyers to provide legal advice in controlled circumstances. With regard to the 'middle income' variable identified above, initiatives like these are typically not means tested, so they potentially benefit low income and middle income groups alike. It is true that at Prong 3, an expanded civil right to counsel probably would be means tested, but there are other options in the access to justice armoury for giving middle income litigants access to counsel, including the unbundling of legal services. With regard to the 'non-lawyer' variable identified above, there are opportunities at all three prongs for the increased use of non-lawyers. At Prong 1, non-lawyers can play key roles in clerks' offices, self-help centres, and court information centres, while at Prong 2, the opportunities are self-evident. At Prong 3, relevant initiatives include the recognition of paralegals and lay advocates as competent to represent litigants in certain types of disputes.

Roger Smith's essay discusses the U.K. Ministry of Justice's consultation paper on reform of legal aid in England and Wales, published in November 2010, and its implications for Canada. The essay canvasses the pattern of legal aid provision in England and Wales with particular reference to pending cuts in the legal aid budget, the provision of legal advice by Citizens Advice Bureaux, and the availability of online information and call centres, noting the consultation paper's enthusiastic support for an enhanced call centre 'able to refer clients to the source of advice most appropriate to them, [acting] as a reliable one-stop shop for clients looking for legal advice [and serving] as the single gateway to civil legal aid services.' According to Smith, the features of the consultation paper most likely to interest a Canadian audience are these: (1) its support for a facility that provides at least initial advice for all inquirers on a non-means-tested basis; (2) the efforts made in the paper to identify priority areas for civil legal aid funding; (3) the absence of any mention in the paper of *pro bono* legal services as a means of compensating for cuts in the legal aid budget; and (4) the recognition the paper gives to the potential of the Internet and the phone as facilities for providing legal advice.

D. Access to Lawyers

In their paper, Samreen Beg and Lorne Sossin proceed on the assumption that there is a subset of legal problems that can only be adequately addressed by lawyers. This raises the concern that many people cannot afford to pay for full legal representation from the beginning to the end of a disputed matter (such as a family law matter). The authors point to the increasing number of unrepresented litigants in the civil justice system in Ontario, but most particularly in family law matters. While simplified legal processes and procedures can mitigate problems encountered in the formal justice system for unrepresented litigants, it is likely that, for a range of issues encountered in civil litigation, the assistance of lawyers will substantially enhance the prospects of positive outcomes for otherwise unrepresented litigants. To this end, the authors focus on one particular strategy for reducing the costs of legal assistance without dispensing with such assistance altogether: unbundled legal services.

The concept of unbundling legal services entails clients being able to retain lawyers for discrete tasks in a larger overall transactional or litigation context and negotiating well-defined fees for these discrete tasks. These tasks might include general counselling and legal advice; limited court appearances; and preparation of documents. In promoting the unbundling of lawyers' services in Canada, the authors identify a number of regulatory and ethical issues that require clear governing rules relating to interactions between the client and the lawyer, between the lawyer and the court, and between the lawyer and opposing legal counsel. The authors are confident, based on recent comparative experience, that law societies and other relevant bodies can craft an effective set of policies to mitigate potential risks associated with unbundling while maximizing the benefits from enhancing access to justice.

Rebecca Sandefur, in her essay, points to survey evidence suggesting that 'legal' problems are socially constructed. By this she means that though many problems reported by survey respondents had clear legal dimensions, respondents did not identify them as 'legal' problems and instead sought, or at least desired, non-legal forms of assistance. One exception is family law problems, which respondents did widely identify as 'legal' problems. In addition, surveys have revealed that, at least among respondents who had used lawyers in the recent past, the cost of legal services was not a major concern and thus should not necessarily be viewed as the principal impediment to wider use of lawyers' services.

Sandefur also refers to social science research suggesting that people seeking legal assistance typically identify lawyers or law firms through a variety of social networks rather than formal legal referral services. She draws two tentative conclusions from these findings: first, that one way to change how people think about their justice problems would be through campaigns for public legal education, aimed at encouraging people to seek out the assistance of lawyers for certain kinds of problems. An alternative or complementary strategy might be to ask people about the kinds of help they would favour with their own justice problems and then develop services that meet their perceived needs, even if those services turn out not to be traditional legal services. Some of these innovations may require changes in the regulation of lawyers' monopoly of legal services.

In their essay, Paul Vayda and Stephen Ginsberg argue that access to justice for people of low and moderate means can be significantly enhanced by a wide range of strategies designed to provide advice and assistance in a timely fashion. These strategies include *pro bono* provision of legal services; class actions and contingency fees; self-help; and utilization of professionals other than lawyers, such as paralegals. However, the authors focus principally on legal services plans, including prepaid legal services plans and legal expense insurance. In their view, well-designed plans can encourage the timely seeking of legal advice; lower legal costs through volume purchasing of legal services, at least for more routine matters; and provide for legal assistance in more contingent, higher-cost legal problems. While the authors note that about 5 million Canadians already participate in various kinds of legal services plans, often as an element of group employment benefits, relatively few are aware of or utilize these entitlements. Thus, a major public education program is required to promote legal services plans and sensitize the public to the importance of timely legal assistance.

One important theme running through these three papers is the appropriateness of seeking legal advice. For Sandefur, this is an open question and leaves broad scope for the provision of various kinds of non-lawyer forms of assistance. The papers by Beg and Sossin and Vayda and Ginsberg assume that for a subset of problems (e.g., family law problems), some form of legal assistance is necessary, although in a wider range of cases where individuals do not customarily seek legal advice they would be significantly advantaged by doing so. With respect to the latter two papers, it is assumed that a major reason why individuals do not seek legal assistance where it would be advantageous for them to do so is the cost of legal services; this is a proposition that Sandefur regards as far from clearly established in the social science literature. For her, attempting to turn all problems that have a legal dimension into lawyers' problems is not a strategy that the current state of social science research in this area unambiguously supports. Even where a problem is appropriately thought of as a lawyer's problem, it would be wrong to assume that costs are the principal barriers to retaining lawyers. Rather than falling back on cost minimization strategies, a more appropriate response might be facilitating access to reliable networks for identifying appropriate lawyers.

E. Reforming the Dispute Resolution Process

In the first part of his essay, Nicholas Bala identifies the main problems with the present family law justice process in Ontario and discusses ideas for reform, with particular reference to the 'Four Pillars' being implemented by the Ontario government: (1) better access to information; (2) an improved intake process ('triage'); (3) improved access to legal advice and early access to alternative dispute resolution facilities; and (4) streamlining of the court process. In the second part of the essay, Bala identifies the need for reforms beyond the Four Pillars, including these: more collaborative family law; better protection for children's interests; improved continuity and case management ('one judge for one family'); and faster progress on the establishment of Unified Family Courts (UFCs) throughout Ontario. In this last connection, Bala points out that the effective resolution of family cases depends on the availability of a range of legal and non-legal services, including parenting education, mediation assessments, child representation, legal advice, and triage services. One advantage of a single court is that it can offer the full range of these services more efficiently. Another advantage is that a single court enables judges to develop the specialized skill sets necessary for handling complex family matters. Bala laments the 'frustratingly slow pace of extending UFCs in Ontario,' stresses the 'efficiency and efficacy of a UFC compared to the present divided jurisdiction,' and concludes with the warning that 'Ontario can no longer afford a model of family justice that was developed in the nineteenth century.'

Justice George Czutrin strongly supports Bala's call for a province-wide Unified Family Court with comprehensive jurisdiction and specialized judges, arguing that a properly staffed and resourced family court would provide a solid foundation for the other changes that Bala discusses in his paper, and calling on the government to act 'within a specific and reasonably short period.' Justice Czutrin also identifies a number of other pressing issues, including the need for solutions to the problem of self-represented litigants; for the creation of a roster of lawyers in Family Court Information Centres who are willing to offer reduced rates; for more multidisciplinary research on family law issues; for more resources and better staffing for the courts; and for the establishment of Family Court Clinics to offer custody and parenting assessments. He concludes with a call for the adoption of a 'holistic effort,' with lawyers and other professionals, institutions, and government departments working together on solutions to family problems.

The Bala and Czutrin contributions address reforms to the dispute resolution process in the family law context. The next two essays focus on consumer dispute resolution. In his essay, Justin Malbon discusses three interesting Australian developments. The first is the establishment of super-tribunals, most notably the Victorian Civil and Administrative Tribunal (VCAT). VCAT has jurisdiction over a wide range of consumer-related and other matters, including residential tenancy disputes, small claims, consumer credit, domestic building disputes, motor car traders' licensing, travel agents, guardianship, and freedom of information. VCAT was established to improve efficiencies in the delivery of tribunal support services and to address the problems of varying procedures and inconsistent decision making from one tribunal to another. Malbon reports that, despite some lingering problems, VCAT has succeeded in providing low-cost access to justice across a wide variety of disputes, and that it is heavily used by the public.

The second Australian development Malbon identifies is the emergence of industry-run ombudsman schemes, including the Financial Ombudsman Service (FOS). There are industry ombudsman schemes in Canada, too, but the Australian approach, as represented by the FOS, is distinctive for its layers of compulsion: (1) financial advisers and the like must be licensed; (2) as a condition of the licence, a licensee must subscribe to an external dispute resolution scheme; and (3) any such scheme must be approved by the regulator. Third, Malbon discusses the emergence of litigation funding companies, which fund class actions for selected cases in return for a substantial share of any damages award. This development, he argues, has had positive effects on the access to justice front; but by the same token, a company's obligation to maximize returns for its shareholders is at least a potential threat to class members' interests because a company might use its bargaining power to extract excessive returns from successful cases.

In her essay, Shelley McGill, a Deputy Judge of the Ontario Small Claims Court, addresses the issue of small claims court reform. She starts with the observation that small claims courts serve a number of competing objectives, perhaps the most fundamental of which are facilitating access to the court system and delivering case outcomes that are procedurally and substantively fair. These goals are in tension because cheaper access depends on reducing the formality of proceedings, for example, by barring legal representation, taking procedural short cuts and limiting appeals. On the other hand, measures such as these all increase the risk of judicial error. The essay canvasses a number of reform options, including a 'graduated value approach,' under which there would be different levels of procedural formality depending on the amount in dispute and the complexity of the case.

In the second part of her essay, McGill discusses 'the absence of access to justice in the small claims court's post-judgment phase.' She makes the point that current procedures are little more than a mirror image of the Superior Court model and that they lack 'the easy, fast, and inexpensive features' of the pre-judgment phase. She makes a number of recommendations for reform, including these: more use of written information, as opposed to personal attendance, in judgment debtor examinations; measures aimed at enabling parties to discuss payment arrangements immediately following trial, which would reduce the number of defaults and avoid the need for subsequent court attendances; and increased powers for the court to offer debtors relief from hardship, for example, by consolidating indebtedness, imposing a single payment schedule, and suspending collection tools and interest accrual. In the final part of her essay, McGill discusses the impact on the small claims court of 'external developments,' including class actions, consumer arbitration, and the increase in representation by lawyers, paralegals, and other intermediaries such as collection agencies. She recommends allowing the joinder and consolidation of small claims, with the idea of facilitating a type of class proceeding at the small claims court level; limiting the enforceability of arbitration clauses; and procedural and other adjustments to regulate litigant representatives, including provision for orders to control the behaviour of collection agencies.

F. Creating Change and Reform of the Judicial System

Finally, the essay by Sujit Choudhry, Michael Trebilcock, and James Wilson explores the dynamics of legal expense insurance and its potential to address access to justice for middle income individuals and families in Canada. The authors argue that legal expense insurance has significant potential but requires a strong public sector impetus. The authors begin from the observation that legal aid is not working to advance access to justice, in part because its low eligibility and subject area specificity excludes many of the important needs faced by the low and middle income community. Further, they take as a point of departure the absence of a single guiding institutional 'centre' to the legal system. Various autonomous institutions (e.g., the courts, the government, the legal profession, and legal aid) make it difficult to adopt coordinated or coherent strategies to address access to justice problems. Choudhry, Trebilcock, and Wilson argue that extending the mandate of Legal Aid Ontario (LAO) to the not-for-profit legal expense insurance realm could both address urgent access to justice needs and ensure that the effort to do so remains within a public interest structure.

In order for public legal expense insurance to succeed, and to overcome the traditional barriers to such insurance schemes (including moral hazard and adverse selection), the authors advocate a model of default coverage for all, with the ability to opt out for those who wish not to be part of the scheme. Choudhry, Trebilcock, and Wilson conclude that the proposed scheme addresses the institutional, market, and political objections that might otherwise arise in the context of legal expense insurance.

III. The Policy Implications

The proposals contained in the essays that comprise this volume raise a key question as to which person, institution, or office has the responsibility and capacity to address the problem of access to justice. The inability of any single actor in the justice system to develop and implement a comprehensive policy to enhance access to justice requires both an understanding of the roles that different actors might play, and more important, a road map for how those actors might act in a coordinated and cooperative fashion. If an accessible justice system is to be achieved, the sum of these systemic efforts will have to be greater than its various parts.

The political responsibility for the justice system in Canada is shared by the federal and provincial/territorial governments. The federal government has responsibility for appointing and funding judges for what are known as s.96 courts (referring to the section of the *Constitution Act, 1867*, outlining the federal appointment power). These courts now include the superior trial courts in every province and territory, the courts of appeal in every province and territory, the federal courts, and the Supreme Court of Canada. The federal government is also responsible for the rules and administration of the federal courts and the Supreme Court. Pursuant to s.92(14) of the *Constitution Act, 1867*, the provinces and territories are responsible for 'the administration of justice,' which includes appointing and funding judges for provincial courts and justices of the peace, and for the rules and court administration of provincial courts, superior courts, and courts of appeal.

While criminal law, immigration and refugee law, and divorce law fall under federal legislative authority, legal aid for many individuals affected by these laws falls under provincial and territorial government authority. In other words, policies aimed at improving access to justice at both the 'front end' and the 'back end' of disputes may depend on federal/provincial cooperation. Indeed, the innovation of Unified Family Courts discussed in this volume arose primarily as a consequence of the cost, complexity, and delay occasioned by the laws relating to the consequences of separation falling under provincial legislative authority, including access to provincial courts, while the laws relating to divorce fell under federal legislative authority, which are supervised by superior courts. This example demonstrates that federalism may be part of the access to justice problem, but that it also has the potential to be a significant part of the solution.

Within provincial authority over 'the administration of justice,' the Attorney General, as the province's chief law officer, has primary responsibility for government justice policy, including the funding and structure of the courts, the budget for legal aid and public legal services, and the statutory framework that authorizes other justice system institutions, such as the law societies, which regulate the legal profession in the public interest; the law foundations, which fund public interest legal NGOs; and those bodies that manage and deliver legal aid. Attorneys General are finding more and more, however, that substantial increases to direct government provision of civil legal services are not realistic, especially in an environment where justice issues must compete with pressing health care and education needs for attention and resources. Indeed, the Attorney General for Ontario's major announcement of new funding in 2009 ($150 million over four years) was divided into four pillars, mostly concerned with criminal justice; the major proposal dealing with civil justice featured the diversion of family disputes *from* provincially funded courts.

On the other hand, provincial task forces undertaken by former Justice Coulter Osborne (2008 Civil Justice Reform Project), former Chief Justice Patrick LeSage, and then Professor Michael Code (2008 Review of Large and Complex Criminal Case Procedures) and Professor Michael Trebilcock (2008 Legal Aid Review), all have called for the government's leadership in achieving improved access to justice. Government leadership involves a commitment to provide sufficient resources as well as accountability for those resources, but it also includes the use of other legislative, regulatory, and administrative instruments. Indeed, relatively simple policy changes may facilitate substantial changes to access to justice. For example, the Ontario *Class Proceedings Act* (1992) and the *Access to Justice Act, 2005*, established a new model of entrepreneurial litigation funding by legalizing contingency fees in Ontario. As Choudhry, Trebilcock, and Wilson argue in their essay in this volume, a similar policy change to establish a public legal expense insurance regime could result in even more significant changes to the legal profession and to the access of middle income groups to legal services.

When considering the role of government in addressing access to justice, we should keep in mind that jurisdiction over courts, legal aid, and other aspects of the justice system comprises just one aspect of the government's role. The regulation and mitigation or prevention of civil disputes through better investigation and enforcement by public interest or industry regulators, or through the establishment of expeditious and informal dispute resolution, may have a greater impact than any court reform. For example, the regulatory decision to move to a no-fault insurance scheme in Ontario in 1989 likely had a greater impact on access to justice than any innovation in legal service delivery in the auto collision sector ever could have. As we noted above, preventing a person from falling over the cliff is a better health care strategy than even the most effective ambulance and medical response team at the bottom of the cliff.

While avoiding disputes through more effective regulation should be considered (particularly in settings such as employment and consumer law), at some point access to justice will require access to the courts. Government cannot implement justice system reform unilaterally. Coulter Osborne's Civil Justice Reform Project led to a series of changes in the Rules of Civil Procedure – for example, it enlarged the jurisdiction of Small Claims Court and simplified procedures in the civil courts – but it falls to judicial discretion and the conduct of parties to litigation (and, where relevant, their lawyers) to determine whether these changes will make a positive difference. More funding for Legal Aid Ontario's civil justice programs and clinics, if it ultimately is squandered on an inefficient court system, hardly constitutes progressive change.

Courts remain a bottleneck in the justice system; and the civil procedure rules, based on an adversarial system of advocacy and evidence, continue to drive cost, complexity, and delay in litigation. A system based on the assumption that parties will be represented by counsel, and that the quality of justice does not depend on a party's financial resources, is giving way to a system which assumes the prevalence of self-represented parties and which accepts that scarce judicial resources will have to be rationed. For example, in Ontario, courts with high family law caseloads now feature Family Law Information Centres (FLICs), while other courts have facilitated duty counsel programs, self-help centres, and *pro bono* initiatives. While courts appear more open to innovative programs than ever before, the need to remain independent and impartial means they cannot drive either government policy or advocacy on behalf of particular parties. A Chief Justice might opine that legal fees are too high or that too many parties have too little legal representation, but the ability of the courts to initiate and implement policy change is constrained.

Together, government programs and court resources may make a difference, particularly when designed in consultation with a broad

spectrum of affected interests, but together they amount to a patchwork quilt of services and supports rather than a response to the systemic problem of access to justice for low and middle income people. If
new government and court programs are necessary but not sufficient
to achieve greater access to justice, the legal profession (including in
Ontario lawyers and regulated paralegals), legal aid clinics, and *pro
bono* and public interest NGOs will have to fill many of the gaps that
remain in the civil justice system.

The law societies across Canada have embraced access to justice as
an ideal but have done little to turn that ideal into concrete realities.
Most of their efforts to date have consisted of rule changes to accommodate unbundling and *pro bono* activities, the establishment of lawyer referral services, and the sponsoring of studies, along with raising
the profile of access to justice issues. As first and foremost regulators,
law societies are wary about wading directly into legal service delivery.
The various bar associations have been more active, but often in ways
that might appear self-serving. An example is the Canadian Bar Association's 2005 litigation against the Province of British Columbia, during which it asserted a constitutional right to civil legal aid; this would
have expanded significantly the reach of public funding for private litigation (the case was dismissed by the B.C. courts on justiciability and
standing grounds).

The legal aid clinic, *pro bono,* and public interest NGO communities
are less constrained and less narrowly focused than legal professional
associations. In Ontario, these organizations (often with the funding
support of provincial law foundations) have initiated a range of small-
scale, innovative reforms, ranging from the Law Help Ontario Centres
in Toronto and Ottawa developed by Pro Bono Law Ontario (PBLO) to
CLEONet, the online legal information service offered by the Legal Aid
Ontario (LAO) funded Community Legal Education Ontario (CLEO).
While these organizations are making a positive difference for the communities and constituencies they serve, their ability to work together
and coordinate services has been limited. The Law Foundation of
Ontario (LFO) has tried to address this deficiency as part of its ambitious 2008 Rural and Linguistic Access to Justice initiative. In 2010, the
LFO circulated a call for organizations (legal aid clinics, NGOs, etc.)
to join into 'Connecting Regions' with a view to coordinated service
provision either in underserved geographic areas or for underserved
linguistic groups. In 2005, the LFO, the Law Society of Upper Canada
(LSUC), the Attorney General, and the six Ontario law schools came

together to create the Law Commission of Ontario, with a mandate to explore law reform in areas including access to justice.

The 2010 Ontario Civil Justice Needs Assessment was commissioned by the LSUC, PBLO, and LAO with a view to better informing the programs of each. It included the goal of identifying areas for further collaboration. And as initiatives like the University of Toronto Middle Income Access to Justice Colloquium demonstrate, law schools may serve as catalysts for networks of organizations with kindred goals. While it is too early to determine the success of these joint ventures, motivating organizations to create networks and to act in a coordinated fashion is a promising pathway to reform. In B.C., for example, 'Clicklaw' allows users to access a range of justice information provided by twenty-four NGOs and government organizations through a single portal (www.clicklaw.ca). This consortium approach is likely the only mechanism capable of delivering meaningful progress in the short term.

As the American Bar Foundation's (ABF) recent study concludes, while past research projects have tended to focus on single tiles in the mosaic, there is need for a holistic portrait, one that includes a range of possible solutions to unmet civil justice needs. A recent ABF project, the Civil Justice Infrastructure Mapping Project, has brought together for the first time information about different elements of the access to civil justice infrastructure.[3] In addition to examining the wide range of means that exist to deliver civil legal assistance (including government-funded legal assistance and *pro bono* initiatives), the project also explores some aspects of how market-based legal services may be provided across states. Available evidence in the United States suggests that when low income people face civil justice problems and seek out a lawyer's help, most of their contacts with attorneys are actually not with legal aid or *pro bono* attorneys, but rather with private practice lawyers and in the context of fee arrangements. The market is clearly an important source of legal services for groups eligible for civil legal assistance. As the ABF study suggests, understanding what markets can and do provide is essential to a complete picture of the access to justice infrastructure.

In Canada as well, the goal of bringing together those with legal needs

---

3 See *Access across America: First Report of the Civil Justice Infrastructure Mapping Project* (Chicago: American Bar Foundation, 2011) (draft provided on 5 August 2011 by Rebecca Sandefur).

and those with the ability to address those needs likely cannot be met by government, courts, clinics, and NGO programs alone. The private bar has a key role to play as well; in particular, it must be receptive to new methods for the delivery of legal services. For example, unbundling legal services may allow lawyers and paralegals to tap into a market for discrete legal services that did not exist before. New brokerage services (both public and private, online and in person) seek to marry those willing to provide subsidized, discounted, or even auctioned legal services with those seeking those services at acceptable quality and cost. Flat fees instead of hourly billing, and other contractual variations in how legal services are paid, when they are paid, and how risks associated with legal expenses are allocated, all can have a significant impact on middle income consumers of legal services. Expanding the market for regulated paralegals also may result in better value for legal consumers with problems that do not require the expertise of lawyers.

While all the actors and factors mentioned above must play a role, the elusive piece missing from this puzzle, as noted above, has been coordination. This goal explains in part the genesis of this volume and the colloquium out of which it has grown. Rather than initiatives that just focus on a particular area of legal reform (e.g., family law) or a venue for that reform (e.g., the courts or the legal profession), or a leader of that reform (e.g., government), we have sought in this collection to bring together multiple areas of reform, proposed through multiple venues – including all those discussed above – which will require both leadership and partnership from the various actors in the justice system in order to succeed. While many of the essays in this volume highlight the need for more research and for better empirical data to inform policy and program initiatives, we share the view expressed by several participants at the colloquium that the time is ripe for action, and for risk taking on new ideas.

IV. Acknowledgments

As indicated above, this book grew out of an international colloquium on Middle Income Access to Civil Justice held at the University of Toronto Faculty of Law, 10 and 11 February 2011. We gratefully acknowledge the contributions of the paper presenters, commentators, and moderators at the colloquium, as well as the contributions of the Chief Justice of Canada, the Honourable Beverley McLachlin; the Chief Justice of Ontario, Chief Justice Warren Winkler; and Justice Coulter Osborne, who made major presentations. We are particularly grateful to the paper presenters for revising their papers for publication in this volume subsequent to the colloquium.

We would also like to acknowledge the contributions of the Steering Committee for the colloquium: Judith McCormack, Carol Rogerson, Nikki Gershbain, Emily Orchard, Andrea Russell, and Kim Snell (in addition to the three editors of this volume) and to the Events staff led by Jennifer Tam. We are particularly indebted to Dean Mayo Moran of the University of Toronto Faculty of Law for her vision in inspiring and supporting this initiative.

We are very grateful to the following individuals for research assistance provided at various stages of this project: Azim Remani, Sam Kaufman, Khalid Janmohamed, Chantal Morton, Noel Semple, Dennis Kao, George Reid, Chris Barker, and Ryan MacIsaac. Additional thanks to George Reid and Chris Barker, who compiled the select bibliography.

Finally, we are indebted to Legal Aid Ontario and to the University of Toronto Faculty of Law for financial assistance with the publication of this volume.

PART 2

Defining the Problem – What Are the Unmet Legal Needs?

1 Caught in the Middle: Justiciable Problems and the Use of Lawyers

PASCOE PLEASENCE AND NIGEL J. BALMER

I. Introduction

The problems to which the principles of civil law apply are, to a great extent, problems of everyday life. They concern people's employment, housing, family life, consumer transactions, health, and welfare. As Hadfield has commented, we live in a 'law-thick' world.[1]

While 'not all problems are justiciable,[2] nor all justiciable events problematic,'[3] those everyday problems that are justiciable consistently result in worry,[4] frequently involve adverse health consequences, and can lead to loss of income, employment, or a home or even the break-up of a family.[5] Thus, it is a matter of general concern that people be able

---

1 Gillian Hadfield, 'Higher Demand, Lower Supply? A Comparative Assessment of the Legal Landscape for Ordinary Americans' (2010) 37 *Fordham Urban Law Journal, 129* at 133.

2 'A matter experienced by a respondent which raised legal issues, whether or not it was recognised by the respondent as being "legal" and whether or not any action taken by the respondent to deal with the [matter] involved the use of any part of the civil justice system': Hazel Genn, *Paths to Justice: What People Do and Think about Going to Law* (Oxford: Hart, 1999) at 12 [Genn, *Paths to Justice*].

3 Rebecca L. Sandefur, 'The Importance of Doing Nothing: Everyday Problems and Responses of Inaction,' in *Transforming Lives: Law and Social Process* (Norwich: TSO, 2007), ed. P. Pleasence, A. Buck, and N.J. Balmer, at 112 [Sandefur, *Transforming Lives*] [Pleasence *et al.*, 'The Importance of Doing Nothing'].

4 Just 9.5% of 'difficult to solve' problems reported through the 2004 English and Welsh Civil and Social Justice Survey did not lead to any worry.

5 Pascoe Pleasence, N.J. Balmer, A. Buck, A. O'Grady, and H. Genn, 'Civil Law Problems and Morbidity' (2004) 58 Journal of Epidemiology and Community Health 552; A. Currie, 'Civil Justice Problems and the Disability and Health Status of Canadians,' in Sandefur, *Transforming Lives, supra* note 3 at 44; and P. Pleasence, N.J. Balmer, A. Buck, M. Smith, and A. Patel, 'Mounting Problems: Further Evidence

to resolve such problems in a manner that is efficient, effective, and fair. This will not, of course, necessitate the use of lawyers. As Lewis's DIY solution for housing disrepair aptly demonstrated, there are a range of potentially appropriate routes to the resolution of justiciable problems.[6] Equally, though, there are times when the use of a lawyer is evidently the most appropriate course of action.

Since the mid-1990s, 23 national surveys of the public's experience of justiciable problems have been undertaken, across 13 countries[7] (Table 1.1).[8] Each has inquired into the incidence of problems and, among

---

of the Social, Economic, and Health Consequences of Civil Justice Problems,' in *Transforming Lives, supra* note 3 at 67 [Pleasence *et al.*, 'Mounting Problems'].

6 Philip Lewis, 'Unmet Legal Needs' in *Social Needs and Legal Action*, ed. P. Morris, R. White, and P. Lewis (Oxford: Martin Robertson, 1973) at 73. See also Rebecca Sandefur, 'Money Isn't Everything: Understanding Moderate Income Households' Use of Lawyers' Services,' *infra* this volume.

7 With the addition of a national survey in Taiwan in late 2011, these numbers will rise to 24 and 14, respectively.

8 American Bar Association, *Legal Needs and Civil Justice: A Survey of Americans* (Chicago, 1994) [ABA, *Legal Needs and Civil Justice*]; Asia Consulting Group Limited and Policy 21 Limited, *Consultancy Study on the Demand for and Supply of Legal and Related Services* (Hong Kong: Department of Justice, 2008) [Asia Consulting, *Legal and Related Services*]; A. Currie, 'A National Survey of the Civil Justice Problems of Low and Moderate Income Canadians: Incidence and Patterns,' *International Journal of the Legal Profession* (2006) [Currie, 'National Survey']; A. Currie, 'The Legal Problems of Everyday Life' in *Access to Justice*, ed. Rebecca L. Sandefur (Bingley: Emerald, 2009) at 1 [Sandefur, 'The Legal Problems of Everyday Life']; A. Currie, 'Lives of Trouble: Criminal Offending and the Problems of Everyday Life,' paper presented at the ILAG Conference, Wellington, April 2010; T. Dignan, *Northern Ireland Survey* (Belfast: Northern Ireland Legal Services Commission, 2006) [Dignan, *Northern Ireland Legal Needs*]; *Paths to Justice, supra* note 2; H. Genn and A. Paterson, *Paths to Justice Scotland: What People in Scotland Think and Do about Going to Law* (Oxford: Hart, 2001) [Genn and Paterson, *Paths to Justice Scotland*]; GfK Slovakia, *Legal Needs in Slovakia II* (Bratislava: GfK Slovakia, 2004) [GfK Slovakia, *Legal Needs in Slovakia*]; M. Gramatikov, *Justiciable Events in Bulgaria* (Sofia: Open Society Institute, 2010) [Gramatikov, *Justiciable Events in Bulgaria*]; Ignite Research, Report on the 2006 National Survey of Unmet Legal Needs and Access to Services (Wellington: Legal Services Agency, 2006) [Ignite, *Unmet Legal Needs*]; T. Maeda, 'Legal Problems and Consultations with the Legal Profession: The Viability of an Internet Survey,' *New Generation in the Sociology of Law* (Japan, 2009); E. Michelson, 'Climbing the Dispute Pagoda: Grievances and Appeals to the Official Justice System in Rural China' (2007) 72 *American Sociological Review* 459 [Michelson, 'Climbing the Dispute Pagoda']; E. Michelson, Popular Attitudes towards Dispute Processing in Urban and Rural China (Oxford: Foundation for Law, Justice, and Society, 2009); M. Murayama, 'Experiences of Problems and Disputing Behaviour in Japan' (2007) 14 *Meiji Law Journal* pinpoint [Maruyama, 'Experiences of Problems'];

many other things, whether or not people receive services from lawyers for assistance with those problems. These surveys comprise the most recent and highest-profile surveys in a tradition that dates back to Clark and Corstvet's 'test' survey of 'the needs of the community for legal service' of 412 Connecticut residents, conducted during the recession at the United States Bar in the 1930s.[9] In addition to the national surveys, various similar surveys have also been conducted at a regional level, including in at least 18 of the 50 U.S. states.[10]

All the above surveys have been intended to inform access to justice policy, generally with a focus on the needs of those who are most disadvantaged or on the lowest incomes.[11] However, there is growing interest in the predicament of those people on middle incomes who face

---

P. Pleasence, *Causes of Action: Civil Law and Social Justice,* 2nd ed. (London: TSO, 2006) [Pleasence, *Causes of Action*]; P. Pleasence, N.J. Balmer, A. Patel, and C. Denvir, *Civil Justice in England and Wales 2009: Report of the 2006–9 English and Welsh Civil and Social Justice Survey* (London: Legal Services Commission, 2010) [Pleasence *et al., Civil Justice in England and Wales 2009*]; I. Sato, H. Takahashi, N. Kanomata, and S. Kashimura, *Citizens Access to Legal Advice in Contemporary Japan: Lumpers, Self-Helpers, and Third-Party Advice Seekers,* paper presented at the Law and Society Association Conference, Berlin, July 2007 [Sato *et al., Citizens' Access to Legal Advice*]; B. Van Velthoven and C.M.K. Haarhuis, *Geschilbeslechtingsdelta 2009. Over Verloop en afloop van (potentieel) juridische van burgers* (Den Haag: WODC, 2010); B. Van Velthoven and M. Ter Voert, *Paths to Justice in the Netherlands,* paper presented at the International Legal Aid Group conference, Killarney, Ireland, 8–10 June 2005 [Van Velthoven and Ter Voert *Paths to Justice in the Netherlands*].

9 Charles Clark and Emma Corstvet, 'The Lawyer and the Public: An A.A.L.S. Survey' (1938) 47 *Yale Law Journal* 1272.

10 Legal Services Corporation, *Documenting the Justice Gap in America: The Current Unmet Civil Legal Needs of Low Income Americans* (Washington, 2007); Legal Services Corporation, *Documenting the Justice Gap in America: The Current Unmet Civil Legal Needs of Low Income Americans: An Updated Report of the Legal Services Corporation* (Washington, 2009). Reports and details of studies also available at http://www.nlada.org/Civil/Civil_SPAN/SPAN_Library/document_list?topics=000055&list_title=State+Legal+Needs+Studies:+Reports. See also Jamie Baxter, Michael Trebilcock, and Albert Yoon, 'The Ontario Civil Needs Project: A Comparative Analysis of the 2009 Survey Data,' *infra* this volume, discussing the findings of the Ontario Civil Needs Project in the context of international research data.

11 The 1993 U.S. survey excluded those on higher incomes, and the 2004 Canadian survey was limited to those on low income. Seven of the twenty-three national surveys have been funded directly by legal aid authorities. See also, for example, A. Buck, P. Pleasence, and N.J. Balmer, 'Social Exclusion and Civil Law: Experience of Civil Justice Problems among Vulnerable Groups' (2005) 39 *Social Policy and Administration* 302; and G. Mulherin and C. Coumarelos, 'Access to Justice and Disadvantaged Communities' in *Transforming Lives, supra* note 3 at 9.

justiciable problems that might best be resolved with the involvement of lawyers, especially given the increasing pressure on many legal aid budgets that is seeing legal aid eligibility rates fall and scope narrow.[12]

In this paper, we draw on findings from the 23 national surveys undertaken since 1993 to explore the experience of those on middle incomes, in terms of both justiciable problem incidence and use of lawyers. We also present new findings from the most recent English and Welsh Civil and Social Justice Panel Survey, including the results of new analyses that explore the relationship between income and the use of lawyers, controlling for problem type, problem severity, and the availability of legal aid.

II. The Surveys

All 23 of the national surveys set out in Table 1.1 have adopted broadly similar approaches and methods. In all cases, respondents were presented with details[13] of justiciable problems and asked whether they had recently experienced any of them. If respondents indicated that they had experienced problems, then they were asked about the steps they took, if any, to try to resolve them.

However, while the methods employed for the surveys have been superficially similar, significant differences are evident. Most obviously, as can be seen from Table 1.1, the mode of delivering the surveys has included face-to-face interviewing, telephone interviewing, and Internet questioning. But there are also other differences between the surveys as regards their sampling, framing, units of analysis, forms of questioning, and scope. So, for example, while the great majority of the national surveys have followed Genn's *Paths to Justice* survey practice

---

12 E.g., Michael Trebilcock, *Report of the Legal Aid Review* (Toronto: Ministry of the Attorney General, 2008); Ministry of Justice, *Proposals for the Reform of Legal Aid in England and Wales* (London: TSO, 2010). In England and Wales, Griffith has reported an almost halving of eligibility of levels for civil legal aid between 1998 and 2007, to 29%, 'with a particularly sharp decline between 2005 and 2007': A. Griffith, 'Dramatic Drop in Civil Legal Aid Eligibility,' *Legal Action,* September 2008, 10 [Griffith, 'Dramatic Drop']. For a discussion of the impact of proposed scope changes in England and Wales, see N.J. Balmer, *Research Methods for Legal Empowerment and Access to Justice,* paper presented at the symposium A Decade of Bottom-up Legal Development Cooperation: A Socio-Legal Perspective on the State of the Field,' University of Amsterdam, 7–8 February 2011.

13 Generally, lists of problems that raise legal issues.

Table 1.1. Recent national surveys of justiciable problems

Country	Study	Date	Size	Method
Australia	Australian Survey of Legal Needs	2008	20716	Telephone
Bulgaria	Access to Justice and Legal Needs Bulgaria	2007	2730	In person
Canada	National Survey of Civil Justice Problems (10 provinces)	2004	4501	Telephone
		2006	6665	
		2008	7002	
China	Popular Attitudes towards Dispute Processing	2001–2	4026	In person
England and Wales	Paths to Justice	1997	4125	In person
	Civil & Social Justice Survey (CSJS)	2001	5611	In person
		2004	5015	
		2006–9	10537	
	Civil & Social Justice Panel Survey (CSJPS)	2010	3806	In person
Hong Kong	Demand & Supply of Legal & Related Services	2006	10385	In person
Japan	National Survey of Everyday Life & the Law	2005	12408	In person
	Access to Legal Advice: National Survey	2006	5330	In person
	Everyday Life and Law	2007	5500	Internet
Netherlands	Paths to Justice in the Netherlands	2003	3516	Internet
		2009	5166	
New Zealand	Legal Advice and Assistance Survey	1997	5431	In person
	Unmet Legal Needs & Access to Services	2006	7200	Telephone
Northern Ireland	Northern Ireland Legal Needs Survey	2005	3361	In person
Scotland	Paths to Justice Scotland	1998	2684	In person
Slovakia	Legal Needs in Slovakia	2004	1085	In person
United States	Comprehensive Legal Needs Study	1993	3087	Telephone + In person

of inquiring about the experience of individuals, the Chinese survey followed the American Bar Association's *Comprehensive Legal Needs Study* approach of inquiring about experience at the aggregated household level.[14] Also of particular note, among the 23 surveys the reference period has varied between one and six years, the number of problems detailed has ranged from fewer than 30 to more that 100, there has been

---

14 Almost all of the U.S. state-level studies have followed the American Bar Association approach and taken the household, rather than the individual, as the unit of analysis.

inconsistency as to whether all problems should be reported or just problems that respondents found 'difficult to solve,'[15] and there has been inconsistency as to whether samples extend to the whole public or (as in the case of the 1993 American survey and the 2004 Canadian survey) just those in a particular income range.

Thus, though there is much continuing interest in comparing survey results, 'the differences in approach taken by differing legal needs studies makes comparisons difficult.'[16] At the very least, 'it is important to keep in mind that differences in the methodology, populations surveyed, time period, and focus of the questions produce somewhat different results.'[17] Indeed, we have conducted a series of experiments that highlight the extent to which some of these differences may affect results. These experiments have shown, for example, that the inclusion of the phrase 'difficult to solve' in problem identification questions reduces problem reporting by around one-third, and that lengthier lists of example problems significantly increase problem reporting.[18]

As a consequence, there remains great uncertainty around the extent to which the 'remarkable differences'[19] between some of the surveys' findings – for example, the extraordinary range of reported rates of problem experience (from 19% in Japan[20] to 69% in the Netherlands[21]) – are the product of differences in public experience or of different methods being applied in different jurisdictions.

III. Past Survey Findings – Income and Incidence

While caution is necessary in bringing together the findings from multiple, differently specified surveys, it is evident that the experience of justiciable problems is common 'across all social, educational and demographic boundaries.'[22] That this is so should be of no surprise.

15 This was the phrase used originally by Genn in *Paths to Justice, supra* note 2.
16 American Bar Association, *Legal Needs and Civil Justice, supra* note 8 at 43. See also Baxter *et al., infra* this volume, which makes the same point with particular reference to the results of the Ontario Civil Legal Needs Project.
17 Carol McEown, *Civil Legal Needs Research Report* (Vancouver: Law Foundation of British Columbia, 2009) at 3.
18 Pascoe Pleasence and Nigel J. Balmer, *Comparing Apples and Oranges: Methodological Issues Affecting the Comparative Analysis of the Public's Experience of Justiciable Problems* (forthcoming).
19 Van Velthoven and Ter Voert, *Paths to Justice in the Netherlands, supra* note 8 at 21.
20 Murayama, 'Experiences of Problems,' *supra* note 8.
21 Van Velthoven and Ter Voert, *Paths to Justice in the Netherlands, supra* note 8.
22 Genn, *Paths to Justice, supra* note 2 at 59.

Every member of the public engages in a range of social and economic activities, most of which have potential to bring about the 'defining circumstances'[23] through which justiciable problems can arise. Consumer problems arise from consumer transactions, employment problems arise from employment, family problems arise from family relationships, and so on. As Van Velthoven and Ter Voert have suggested, drawing on 'participation theory,' exposure to disputes can be expected to increase along with greater participation in social and economic life,[24] and overall participation in social and economic life tends to increase with income.

Thus, the 1997 New Zealand survey found that those on very low personal incomes (under NZ$10,000) were least likely to report problems, with incidence broadly going up with income.[25] Similarly, the 2003 Dutch survey found that respondents in higher-income households reported problems more frequently than others, with incidence rising with income.[26] Likewise, the 2006–9 English/Welsh survey found that those in the highest personal income bracket (£50,000 or more) reported problems more often than others. Again incidence increased broadly in line with income.[27] Also, the 1993 American survey found that moderate income households reported problems at a higher rate than low income households (52% vs 48%).[28]

However, demonstrating the 'complexity of patterns of vulnerability'[29] to justiciable problems, the 2006 New Zealand survey pointed towards a fairly flat distribution of problems by income, with those on the very highest incomes (NZ$100,000 or more) associated with the lowest incidence rate.[30] Also, the 2001 and 2004 English/Welsh surveys found problem incidence to be highest among those at both the top and the very bottom of the income scale, a reflection of the increased deal-

---

23 Pascoe Pleasence, *Causes of Action, supra* note 8 at 28.

24 Van Velthoven and Ter Voert, *Paths to Justice in the Netherlands, supra* note 8.

25 Gabrielle Maxwell, Catherine Smith, Paula Shepherd, and Allison Morris, *Meeting Legal Service Needs: Research Report Prepared for the Legal Services Board* (Wellington: Legal Services Board, 1999) [Maxwell, *Meeting Legal Service Needs*].

26 Van Velthoven and Ter Voert, *Paths to Justice in the Netherlands, supra* note 8.

27 See Pleasence *et al.*, *Civil Justice in England and Wales 2009, supra* note 8, along with supplementary descriptive analysis conducted for the purposes of this paper. The same was also found in New South Wales (C. Coumarelos, Z. Wei, and A.Z. Zhou, *Justice Made to Measure: New South Wales Legal Needs Survey in Disadvantaged Areas* (Sydney: Law and Justice Foundation of New South Wales, 2006).

28 ABA, *Legal Needs and Civil Justice, supra* note 8.

29 Pleasence, *Causes of Action, supra* note 8 at 21.

30 Findings from supplementary descriptive analysis conducted for the purposes of this paper.

ings of the latter group with public services, poor-quality housing, and the welfare benefits system.[31] In fact, those surveys, along with the 2006–9 English/Welsh survey, the 1997 and 2006 New Zealand surveys, the 2003 Dutch survey, the 2004 Canadian survey, and the 2005 Northern Irish survey, all pointed to higher incidence for respondents in receipt of welfare benefits.[32] Importantly, given the relationship between exposure to the defining circumstances of problems and their incidence, vulnerability is best understood at the level of individual problem types.

Unsurprisingly, in every country in which the analysis has been undertaken (Canada, England/Wales, New Zealand, Northern Ireland, Scotland, and the United States),[33] low income has been found to go hand in hand with increased incidence of problems related to welfare benefits. Low income has also been found to be associated with problems relating to housing (Canada and the United States),[34] though different vulnerabilities are associated with different types of tenancy. So, across the United Kingdom (England/Wales, Northern Ireland, and Scotland), problems with rented accommodation (particularly poor-quality rented accommodation) and homelessness are associated with those on low incomes.[35] Meanwhile, problems faced by owner-occupiers have been associated more with those on high incomes.[36]

As income rises, so does employment and the incidence of employment problems. Higher incidence of employment problems has been observed among people on middle incomes in Canada, New Zealand,

---

31 Pleasence, *Causes of Action, supra* note 8.

32 Pleasence *et al., Civil Justice in England and Wales 2009, supra* note 8; Van Velthoven and Ter Voert, *Paths to Justice in the Netherlands, supra* note 8; Currie, 'National Survey,' *supra* note 8; Dignan, *Northern Ireland Legal Needs, supra* note 8. For the 2006 New Zealand survey, findings are from supplementary descriptive analysis conducted for the purposes of this paper.

33 Unpublished findings from 2004 Canadian survey, supplied by Ab Currie. For New Zealand, findings are from supplementary descriptive analysis conducted for the purposes of this paper. Also, Pleasence, *Causes of Action, supra* note 8; Pleasence *et al., Civil Justice in England and Wales, supra* note 8; Dignan, *Northern Ireland Legal Needs, supra* note 8; Genn and Paterson, *Paths to Justice Scotland, supra* note 8; ABA, *Legal Needs and Civil Justice, supra* note 8.

34 Unpublished findings from 2004 survey, supplied by Ab Currie. See also ABA, *Legal Needs and Civil Justice, supra* note 8.

35 Genn, *Paths to Justice, supra* note 8; Pleasence, *Causes of Action, supra* note 8; Pleasence *et al., Civil Justice in England and Wales, supra* note 8; Dignan, *Northern Ireland Legal Needs, supra* note 8; Genn and Paterson, *Paths to Justice Scotland, supra* note 8.

36 Pleasence, *Causes of Action, supra* note 8; Pleasence *et al., Civil Justice in England and Wales, supra* note 8.

and the United States,[37] and among those on higher incomes in England/Wales, Scotland, and Slovakia.[38] However, in England/Wales, a link has also been observed between employment problems and unemployment at the time of interview, perhaps 'demonstrating the immediate economic impact that can be brought about by justiciable problems of this type.'[39]

Also, as income rises, so does consumption and the incidence of consumer problems. Higher incidence of consumer problems has been observed among people on higher incomes in Canada, England/Wales, and Scotland. However, against this, incidence was found to be flat across income bands in New Zealand[40] and between low and moderate income households in the United States.[41] Consumer problems have also been associated with receipt of welfare benefits in England/Wales, though this finding was explained by pointing to the 'greater relative value ... of routine consumer transactions'[42] for those on benefits. For example, respondents in receipt of benefits in the 2001 English/Welsh survey reported a disproportionate number of low-value consumer problems, including problems relating to unfit food products and small electrical purchases. It is probable that those on higher incomes would not regard such problems as 'difficult to solve.'

Finally, reflecting the likely greater value of assets in issue, higher incidence of problems concerning wills, estates, and directives (e.g., powers of attorney) has been associated with those on higher incomes in Canada[43] and among moderate income households (as compared to low income households) in the United States.[44]

So, while people on different incomes are evidently exposed to problems of different types, it is clear that, as Currie has observed, 'law is pervasive in the lives of all people in contemporary bureaucratic societies.'[45] Given the potentially serious impact of many types of jus-

---

37 Unpublished findings from 2004 Canadian survey. For New Zealand, findings are from supplementary descriptive analysis conducted for the purposes of this paper.

38 Pleasence *et al.*, *Civil Justice in England and Wales, supra* note 8; Genn and Paterson, *Paths to Justice Scotland, supra* note 8; GfK Slovakia, *Legal Needs in Slovakia, supra* note 8.

39 Pleasence, *Causes of Action, supra* note 8 at 41.

40 Findings from supplementary descriptive analysis conducted for the purposes of this paper.

41 ABA, *Legal Needs and Civil Justice, supra* note 8.

42 Pleasence, *Causes of Action, supra* note 8 at 39.

43 Unpublished findings from 2004 Canadian survey, supplied by Ab Currie.

44 ABA, *Legal Needs and Civil Justice, supra* note 8.

45 Currie, 'The Legal Problems of Everyday Life,' *supra* note 8 at 2.

ticiable problem,[46] the ability of people from all walks of life to deal effectively with the problems they face is therefore a matter of serious policy concern.

IV. Past Survey Findings – Income and Strategy

When faced with justiciable problems, some people will take no action to resolve them, some will try to resolve them on their own, and the remainder will seek to resolve them with the assistance of others, often lawyers. The survey evidence has consistently pointed to the 'lumping it'[47] option being the least common option, with handling alone generally the next most common option and seeking assistance from others the most common option, though estimates of rates have varied considerably.[48] Unfortunately, detailed comparison of rates is effectively precluded by the abundance of methodological differences alluded to above, which are compounded further by some surveys having asked about strategy only in relation to the most serious problems reported. Certainly, though, rates will vary between jurisdictions. For example, the relatively low rate of lawyer use observed through the 2005 and 2006 Japanese surveys is likely to be, at least in part, a reflection of 'the remarkably small population of lawyers' in that country, which has 'narrowed citizens' access to lawyers.'[49] It may also, as ter Voert and Niemeijer have argued,[50] have something to do with the low level of individualism in Japan, as reflected in Hofstede's cultural indices.[51]

---

46 Pleasence *et al.*, 'Mounting Problems,' *supra* note 5.

47 M. Galanter, 'Why the "Haves" Come Out Ahead: Speculation on the Limits of Legal Change (1974) 9 *Law and Society Review* 95 at 124 [Galanter, 'Why the "Haves" Come Out Ahead'].

48 For example, estimates of 'lumping it' have generally fallen in the 10% and 20% range, though estimates occasionally fall outside this range, such as in the case of the 2002 rural Chinese and 2007 Bulgarian surveys, which put the figure at a high 33% and 31% respectively: Michelson, 'Climbing the Dispute Pagoda,' *supra* note 8; Gramatikov, *Justiciable Events in Bulgaria*, *supra* note 8.

49 Sato, *Citizens Access to Legal Advice, supra* note 8 at 11. See also Maruyama, 'Experiences of Problems.' Japan has 1 lawyer per 4,373 population, compared to 1 per 260 in the United States, 1 per 451 in the United Kingdom, 1 per 547 in Germany, and 1 per 1,275 in France: Murayama.

50 M. ter Voert and B. Niemeijer, 'Varieties in Disputing Behaviour in Different Countries: Explanatory Strategies and Methodological Pitfalls,' paper presented at the Law and Society Conference, Berlin, 26 July 2007.

51 G. Hofstede, *Culture's Consequences* (Thousand Oaks: Sage, 2001).

Very low rates of lawyer use have also been observed in China and Hong Kong.[52] We should not expect lawyer use to be immune to market and cultural influences.

In general, rates of seeking advice rise along with problem severity. This has been demonstrated by, for example, the 2001 and 2004 English/Welsh surveys, the 2005 Northern Irish survey, and the 2006 Japanese survey.[53] When looking specifically at legal advice, it is now generally understood that the determinants of consumer behaviour are likely to extend to problem severity, people's 'perceptions and attitudes'[54] regarding problems and legal institutions, people's awareness of legal services and dispute resolution options, people's 'cognitive capacity to "name" problems and "blame" offenders,'[55] and people's personal capacity to act, including their financial resources.[56]

In respect of the last of these factors, financial resources, it might be expected that lawyer use would increase with income, lawyer use being a form of consumption. Thus, as Kritzer has recently observed, 'a central aspect of much of the debate over access to justice is the cost of legal services.'[57] Yet Kritzer pointed to empirical studies having consistently

---

52 In rural China the rate was less than 1% (Michelson, 'Climbing the Dispute Pagoda,' *supra* note 8). In Hong Kong, it was under 10%: *Legal and Related Services, supra* note 8. Overall, the range of estimates for lawyer use range from under 1% (China) to over 30% (United States): ABA, *Legal Needs and Civil Justice, supra* note 8.

53 Pleasence, *Causes of Action, supra* note 8; Dignan, *Northern Ireland Legal Needs, supra* note 8; Sato, *Citizens' Access to Legal Advice, supra* note 8.

54 Masayuki Murayama, *What Explains the Use or Non-Use of a Lawyer?*, paper presented at the workshop on Current Socio-Legal Perspectives on Dispute Resolution, Onati, Spain, 8–9 July 2010 at 1. See also P. Pleasence and N.J. Balmer, 'Horses for Courses? People's Characterisation of Justiciable Problems and the Use of Lawyers' in Legal Services Board (ed.), *The Future of The Legal Services Sector* (London: Legal Services Board, 2010) at 37 [Pleasence and Balmer, 'Horses for Courses']. See also Rebecca Sandefur, 'Money Isn't Everything: Understanding Moderate Income Housholds' Use of Lawyers' Services', *infra* this volume.

55 Michelson, 'Climbing the Dispute Pagoda,' *supra* note 8 at 462, drawing on W.L.F. Felstiner, R. Abel, and A. Sarat, 'The Emergence and Transformation of Disputes: Naming, Blaming, Claiming ...' (1981) 15 *Law and Society Review* 631.

56 E.g., Pascoe Pleasence and Nigel J. Balmer, 'Understanding Advice Seeking Behaviour: Findings from New Zealand and England and Wales' in *Empirical Studies of Judicial Systems*, Volume 9, ed. K.C. Huang (Taipei: Academia Sinica, 2009) [Pleasence and Balmer, 'Understanding Advice-Seeking Behaviour']; Sandefur, 'Money Isn't Everything,' *infra* this volume.

57 Herbert M. Kritzer, 'To Lawyer or Not to Lawyer? Is That the Question?' (2008) 5 *Journal of Empirical Legal Studies* 875 [Kritzer, 'To Lawyer or Not to Lawyer?'].

shown that income has 'at best a very small' influence on whether action is taken to resolve problems.[58] On the basis of a review of survey evidence from seven countries, he suggested that 'income has relatively little relationship with the decision to use a legal professional to deal with a dispute or other legal need', with the decision dictated more by the nature of problems and by an 'evaluation of the costs and benefits of hiring a lawyer.'[59] This is echoed in Genn's observation that, when it comes to the use of lawyers, 'problem type tends to swamp other considerations,' and that most problem types characterized by lawyer use share a likely 'importance ... to the parties and the relative intractability of the issues that might be involved' (e.g., family and housing disputes).[60]

However, the fact that lawyer use is well predicted by problem type – which we have argued elsewhere to be an unsatisfactory explanation of problem resolution behaviour, given that it likely acts as a proxy for more fundamental factors, such as the requirement of court involvement, the structure of the legal services market, cultural expectations, and people's understanding and characterization of their problems[61] – does not render unimportant other factors, such as income, that may still play a noteworthy role in behaviour within problem types.

Also, Kritzer's analysis did not account for the relatively good availability of legal aid in some of the jurisdictions under study. He may therefore have mischaracterized some of the findings as indicating 'no clear relationship between lawyer use and income,'[62] where a more nuanced relationship than that being looked for was evident. For example, it was apparent in the case of the 2006 Canadian survey that those on both high and low incomes most often accessed lawyers for problems of a type for which legal aid was likely to be available. Indeed, Currie's reporting of the 2006 Canadian survey draws attention to the general relationship between lawyer use and receipt of welfare benefits and suggests that 'it is possible that people on social assistance are more likely than others to use legal assistance because they are eligible for legal aid.'[63]

Similar to this, the 1997 New Zealand survey found that lawyer use

---

58 *Ibid.* at 878.
59 *Ibid.* at 875.
60 Genn, *Paths to Justice, supra* note 8 at 141.
61 Pleasence and Balmer, 'Horses for Courses,' *supra* note 54.
62 Kritzer, 'To Lawyer or Not to Lawyer?', *supra* note 57 at 892.
63 Currie, 'The Legal Problems of Everyday Life,' *supra* note 8 at 18.

was more common for those on higher personal incomes or, alternatively, those on welfare benefits or in unpaid work. It was concluded that 'the ability to use lawyers by those who are beneficiaries or are in unpaid work is undoubtedly a result of the availability of legal aid.' Analysis we ourselves undertook of data from the 2006 New Zealand and 2006–9 English/Welsh surveys also indicated the existence of a U-shaped distribution of lawyer use by income, though the distribution was more pronounced in New Zealand and fell short of significance in England/Wales. The 1998 Scottish survey also indicated 'a rough U-shaped distribution,'[64] and 'several respondents in qualitative interviews made reference to the plight of "those in the middle" – people who were neither wealthy enough to contemplate taking legal advice with equanimity, nor poor enough to qualify for legal aid.'[65] Again, the 2003 Dutch survey found that 'lawyer usage is highest at both ends of the income curve.'[66] All these jurisdictions just mentioned have established legal aid schemes.

Further to this – and in addition to evidence that Kritzer sets out from a range of surveys[67] that income has quite a substantial impact on lawyer use *within* those problem types most associated with lawyer use (e.g. relationship breakdown, property), and evidence from the 2007 Bulgarian survey that 'the relationship between income and legal advice is almost linear,'[68] with those on higher incomes using lawyers more often – cost has been explicitly identified as an obstacle to lawyer access across the recent national surveys of justiciable problems detailed at the outset of this paper. For example, the 2004 Slovakian survey found that the second most common reason provided for not using lawyers was that 'legal services are too expensive.'[69] Thus, a good proportion of those who felt they needed a lawyer did not instruct one.[70]

---

64 Genn and Paterson, *Paths to Justice Scotland, supra* note 8 at 105. Although the quantitative data presented in this instance were not compelling.

65 *Ibid.* at 100.

66 Van Velthoven and Ter Voert, *Paths to Justice in the Netherlands, supra* note 8 at 11.

67 Including the 1993 United States survey, the United States Civil Litigation Research Project, and the Ontario Dispute Study.

68 Analysis provided by Martin Gramatikov (personal correspondence).

69 GfK Slovakia, *Legal Needs in Slovakia, supra* note 8 at 49.

70 The proportion varied by problem type. So, for example, whereas 18% of respondents felt they needed a lawyer to deal with problems concerning government/social services and just 10% instructed a lawyer, all of the 76% of respondents who felt they needed a lawyer to help deal with a family problem instructed one.

Similarly, the 2006 Japanese survey found that 64% of those who considered using a lawyer, but did not, mentioned cost as a barrier.[71] Also, the 2006 New Zealand survey found that 'over a quarter of people with problems felt that the fear of cost had stopped them from approaching a lawyer.'[72] Even in the case of the 1997 English/Welsh survey, where no difference in lawyer use by income band was observed, cost was mentioned as a reason for 'lumping it' and 'there was a widespread feeling among many respondents that obtaining legal advice was simply not an option because of the cost.'[73]

Curiously, though, in the case of the 2005 Japanese survey, which again found no difference in lawyer use by income band, it was found, through multivariate analysis, that concern about 'how much money it would cost to resolve the problem' was a significant predictor of lawyer use; and this is perhaps a reflection of the fact that people only start to think about the cost of lawyers once they are considering using one.[74] This ties in with findings in England/Wales that people rarely explain inaction in terms of costs, but that those who consider using lawyers raise costs as an issue relatively frequently.

V. New Findings from the 2010 Civil and Social Justice Panel Survey

A. Methods

To supplement the findings we have set out above, we conducted an analysis of new data from the 2010 English and Welsh Civil and Social Justice Panel Survey, a nationally representative panel survey of 3,806 individuals aged 16 or over, living in 2,318 households in England and Wales. It is a substantially developed form of Genn's *Paths to Justice* survey and, as indicated above, provides detailed information on the nature and pattern of people's experience of justiciable problems and problem resolution strategies. The reference period was 18 months. The mean interview duration was 37 minutes, though interviews could be considerably longer if problems were identified. The household response rate was 88% and the cumulative eligible adult response rate

---

71   Sato, *Citizens Access to Legal Advice, supra* note 8.
72   Ignite, *Unmet Legal Needs, supra* note 8 at 79.
73   Genn, *Paths to Justice, supra* note 8 at 80.
74   Murayama, *Use or Non-Use of a Lawyer, supra* note 54. Thanks to Masayuki Murayama for suggesting this interpretation.

was 54%. The 14 problem categories included in the survey are listed in Figure 1.1.

In addition to questions about problem experience and problem resolution strategies, including use of lawyers,[75] all respondents were also asked for a range of details about themselves and the household in which they resided. These included details of welfare benefits received and personal income.

The purpose of the analysis undertaken was to further illustrate the different patterns of problems experienced by people on different incomes and then explore, in greater detail than before, how income and legal aid eligibility relate to use of lawyers. In particular, the analysis was intended to address these two hypotheses: (1) lawyer use increases with income, but (2) those people neither eligible for legal aid nor on high incomes are the least likely to obtain assistance from lawyers in resolving justiciable problems where legal aid is most available.

The 2010 English/Welsh survey provided a unique basis for this, as it contained newly formulated data regarding the relative seriousness of reported problems.[76] This was included in regression analyses, implemented using MLwiN version 2.19, to test the influence of income on the likelihood of respondents obtaining assistance from lawyers, controlling for problem type and the availability of legal aid.[77]

---

75 For the purposes of this paper, 'lawyers' included private practice solicitors, barristers, and those working in law centres, etc. At least 92% of all 'lawyers' were solicitors.

76 The survey incorporates a severity scale, in the form of a vertical line with two fixed reference problem types (placed near the top and bottom) indicating problems of relative high severity ('being regularly assaulted by a partner') and low severity ('purchasing a moderately expensive electrical item that proves to be faulty').

77 Multilevel binary logistic regression analysis was undertaken using MLwiN (J. Rasbash, C. Charlton, W.J. Browne, M. Healy, and B. Cameron *MLwiN Version 2.1* (Centre for Multilevel Modelling: University of Bristol, 2009) [Rabash, *MLwiN*]. Multilevel regression analysis (H. Goldstein, *Multilevel Statistical Models*, 4th ed. (Chichester: Wiley, 2011) [Goldstein, *Multilevel Statistical Models*]) was the appropriate method to correctly model the hierarchical structure of the data (problems were nested within individuals and individuals within households). Ignoring this type of hierarchical structure can result in erroneous results, notably the underestimation of the standard errors of regression coefficients (Rasbash, *MLwiN, supra*). Random intercept models were fitted to allow the probability of obtaining assistance from a lawyer to vary across respondents (to acknowledge that how a person deals with one problem may link to how that person deals with other problems) and households (to acknowledge that how one person behaves in a household may link to how other people in that household behave).

For the purpose of our analysis we created a legal aid proxy, derived from means-tested benefits status and income. All people on means-tested benefits[78] (15%) were included as eligible, plus those people with both a personal income less than £10,000 and a household income less than £25,000.[79] The legal aid proxy we used will not have directly equated to actual eligibility as, for example, it did not account for capital. However, it represented a reasonably comprehensible and transparent alternative. We then produced a composite income/legal aid eligibility variable by dividing non-eligible respondents into four groups based on personal income levels (<£15,000, £15,000–£24,999, £25,000–£39,999, and >£40,000).

B. Findings

Overall, 33.3% of respondents to the 2010 English/Welsh survey reported one or more justiciable problems, with neighbour disputes and consumer, employment, and money problems the most commonly experienced (9.4%, 8.9%, 5.5%, and 5.3% respectively). Incidence was fairly flat across income bands, though those people deemed to be eligible for legal aid (of whom almost two-thirds were in receipt of welfare benefits) were associated with a higher incidence rate, of 40.1%.

As can be seen from Figure 1.1, benefits problems, debt problems, domestic violence, and (the very few) problems relating to child welfare were more often experienced by respondents on low incomes, and problems concerning rented accommodation were associated with those on low and middle incomes, not those on high income. Conversely, problems concerning owner-occupation, consumer transactions, and injuries increased with income. Employment and money problems were more frequently reported by those on middle and high incomes.

Turning to problem resolution strategy, Table 1.2 shows that this varied significantly by income/legal aid eligibility.[80] Most notably, people tended to take action more often as income increased and, at the end of the strategy continuum, they also tended to make use of lawyers

---

78 Unemployment-related benefits, national insurance credits, income support, council tax benefit, and housing benefit.

79 Griffith put the level at 29%: Griffith, 'Dramatic Drop,' *supra* note 12 at 10. The proxy used for our analysis extended to 28.8% with a personal income cutoff of £5,000. People were excluded from the analysis where income details were not available.

80 $\chi^2_{12} = 36.71$, p< 0.001.

Figure 1.1

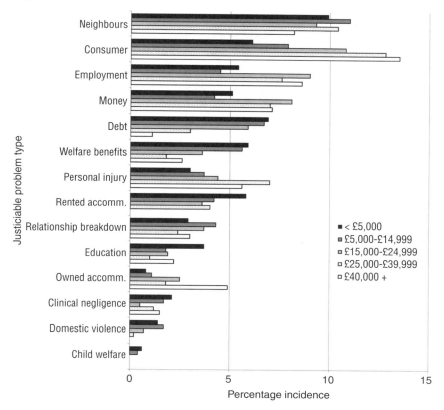

more frequently as income increased. However, in simple numerical terms this progression was interrupted in the case of those respondents deemed eligible for legal aid.

Tables 1.3 and 1.4 show that while this pattern of interruption becomes even more pronounced when looking only at problems for which legal aid is most available under the current legal scheme in England and Wales, it is absent when looking at other problems.[81]

---

81 For this purpose, availability of legal aid was assessed by reference to the number of solicitor legal aid contracts (>100) and volumes of work (>5,000) within each area of law. Problem types for which legal aid was treated as being most available

Table 1.2. Strategy by income and legal aid eligibility

Income / legal aid eligibility	Strategy				
	No action	Handled alone	Advisor (non-lawyer)	Lawyer	N=(100%)
Eligible	12.5%	56.9%	24.4%	6.3%	714
<£15,000	10.3%	64.9%	20.9%	3.8%	445
£15,000–£24,999	8.3%	62.0%	23.8%	5.9%	324
£25,000–£39,999	8.1%	56.8%	27.3%	7.7%	271
£40,000+	7.0%	69.2%	11.9%	11.9%	143
All	10.2%	60.6%	22.9%	6.3%	1,897

Table 1.3. Strategy by income and legal aid eligibility (legal aid most available)

Income / legal aid eligibility	Strategy				
	No action	Handled alone	Advisor (non-lawyer)	Lawyer	N=(100%)
Eligible	11.2%	53.0%	26.9%	8.9%	383
<£15,000	13.0%	59.6%	23.6%	3.8%	208
£15,000–£24,999	6.8%	58.8%	27.0%	7.4%	148
£25,000–£39,999	6.7%	45.6%	35.6%	12.2%	90
£40,000+	7.3%	53.7%	14.6%	24.4%	41
All	10.2%	54.8%	26.4%	8.5%	870

Table 1.4. Strategy by income and legal aid eligibility (other problems)

Income / legal aid eligibility	Strategy				
	No action	Handled alone	Advisor (non-lawyer)	Lawyer	N=(100%)
Eligible	13.9%	61.3%	21.5%	3.3%	331
<£15,000	8.0%	69.6%	18.6%	3.8%	237
£15,000–£24,999	9.7%	64.8%	21.0%	4.5%	176
£25,000–£39,999	8.8%	62.4%	23.2%	5.5%	181
£40,000+	6.9%	75.5%	10.8%	6.9%	102
All	10.2%	65.4%	20.0%	4.4%	1027

Table 1.5. Strategy by income and legal aid eligibility

Covariate	Categories	Whether advice requested		
		Estimate	Std. Error	Odds Ratio
Constant		−4.20	0.48	−
Income /	Eligible for legal aid	0.27	0.33	1.31
legal aid eligibility	<£15,000	0.00	−	−
	£15,000–£24,999	0.46	0.39	1.58
	£25,000–£39,999	**0.89**	**0.38**	2.44
	£40,000+	**1.35**	**0.42**	3.86
Severity		**0.30**	**0.10**	1.03
Problem type	Employment	0.00	−	−
	Consumer	−1.39	**0.59**	0.25
	Neighbours	**−1.24**	**0.59**	0.29
	Owned housing	0.79	0.52	2.20
	Money and benefits	−0.56	0.41	0.57
	Personal injury	**1.30**	**0.45**	3.67
	Relationship breakdown	**1.92**	**0.37**	6.82
	Other	−0.15	0.43	0.86
Household level variance		0.43	1.61	−
Person level variance		0.49	1.64	−

Of course, these patterns do not take account of the different problem types that respondents on different incomes and with different legal aid eligibility status will have experienced, and as is clear from earlier findings, strategy varies markedly by problem type.

Tables 1.5 and 1.6 set out the results of the regression analyses we undertook to control for problem type, problem severity, and the availability of legal aid. In all analyses, those with income just above legal aid eligibility were used as a reference category to which other income groups were compared. The results set out in Table 1.5 relate to an analysis that included all problems detailed in the survey (as in Table 1.2, above). As can be seen, though the coefficient indicates that those just above the legal aid eligibility threshold were less likely than those who met the eligibility criteria to instruct lawyers to assist in resolving prob-

were those concerning relationship breakdown, domestic violence, child welfare, rented accommodation, employment, debt, and welfare benefits. Figures from Legal Services Commission, *Statistical Information 2009/10* (London: Legal Services Commission, 2010).

Table 1.6. Strategy by income and legal aid eligibility, by availability of legal aid

| | | Whether advice requested | | | |
| | | Most Available | | Other | |
Covariate	Categories	Estimate	Std. Error	Estimate	Std. Error
Constant		−6.01	0.72	−5.00	0.70
Income /	Eligible for legal aid	0.74	0.46	−0.24	0.50
legal aid eligibility	<£15,000	0.00	–	0.00	–
	£15,000–£24,999	0.73	0.55	0.43	0.54
	£25,000–£39,999	**1.34**	**0.56**	0.20	0.51
	£40,000+	**2.19**	**0.64**	0.45	0.57
Severity		**0.03**	**0.01**	**0.03**	**0.01**
Problem type	Debt and benefits	–	–	–	–
(Legal aid most	Employment	**1.37**	**0.60**	–	–
available)	Relationship breakdown	**3.54**	**0.55**	–	–
	Other	**1.66**	**0.60**	–	–
Problem type	Neighbours	–	–	0.00	–
(Other)	Consumer	–	–	−0.31	0.72
	Owned housing	–	–	**2.08**	**0.66**
	Money	–	–	**1.35**	**0.60**
	Personal injury	–	–	**2.60**	**0.60**
	Other	–	–	0.62	0.73
Household level variance		0.78	0.51	0.70	0.73
Person level variance[1]		0.00	0.00	0.00	0.00

Significant findings (p <0.05) in bold
1 Incidentally, fitting models using Markov Chain Monte Carlo methods within MLwiN avoids the issue of coefficients and standard errors of zero for person level variance terms. Household variance remains non-significant and other coefficients and standard errors remain much the same.

lems, the discrepancy was not statistically significant. Moving higher up the income scale, lawyer use became more common, with those on the highest incomes significantly more likely than those falling just outside legal aid eligibility to make use of lawyers.

The results set out in Table 1.6 relate to two analyses conducted so as to also account for the availability of legal aid. The first, presented on the left, included (roughly) those problems where legal aid is most available in England and Wales, the second (roughly) other problems. As can be seen, while the coefficient for legal aid eligibility is positive when legal aid is most available, it is negative for other problems.

Though neither of the results is, on its own, statistically significant, the results taken together support the idea that legal aid acts to increase lawyer use among those eligible for legal aid for those problem types

Figure 1.2 Using a Lawyer by Income/Legal Aid Eligibility and Legal Aid
Availability

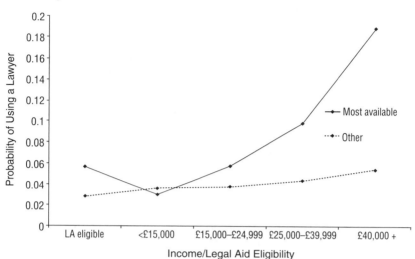

where legal aid is most available. If we combine the two models into a
single model with an 'in scope / out of scope' by income interaction, the
'legal aid eligible' by 'in scope' term is statistically significant,[82] indicating that eligibility is related to a significant increase in lawyer use for in
scope problems when compared to low middle income respondents (in
this case less than £15,000 per annum, but ineligible). For 'other' problem types, lawyer use increases with income in a fairly linear fashion,
though none of the income terms alone reach significance. The two sets
of findings are illustrated in Figure 1.2, which sets out predictions of
rates of lawyer use (obtained from the customized predictions function
of MLwiN), holding problem type and severity patterns constant, for
problems where legal aid is most available and other problems.

---

82 Using '<£15,000' as a reference category, testing the interaction term; $\chi^2_1 = 4.43$,
   p = 0.035. The model used to obtain this result was a cross-classified model
   within MLwiN (see Goldstein, *Multilevel Statistical Models, supra* note 77, for an
   introduction), with lawyer use classed by respondent (within household) and
   problem type. Further details of the model are available from the authors, on
   request.

C. Discussion

Our findings from the 2010 English/Welsh survey confirm that justiciable problems are ubiquitous and commonly experienced across all social groups. Our finding that justiciable problem incidence was not, *in general*, linked to income among respondents adds to the mixed global picture on the overall relationship between income and incidence set out earlier. However, it also demonstrates (again) that problem incidence is best understood at the problem category level, and that vulnerability to particular types of problems follows on from exposure to their defining circumstances. So, problems relating to welfare benefits and rented housing most often affect those on low incomes, and problems relating to consumer issues and owned housing those on high incomes. In respect of those on middle incomes (which in England and Wales we might take to be, for personal income, between around £11,000 and £25,000),[83] it appears that people are frequently affected by problems across the full range of those studied in national surveys to date.

Evidently, therefore, the ability of people on middle incomes to deal with justiciable problems is a matter of importance, and this includes the ability of people on middle incomes to access legal advice when necessary.

How, then, do people on different incomes go about resolving justiciable problems? Our findings from the 2010 English/Welsh survey indicate clearly that as income increases, so too does the rate at which people act to resolve problems. This ties in with earlier findings from the 1993 U.S. survey,[84] the 1998 Scottish survey,[85] the 2006 Canadian survey[86] and the 1997 and 2006–9 English/Welsh surveys;[87] though the 2001 and 2004 English/Welsh surveys uncovered no such link.

---

83 This band captures approximately the central 50% of the taxpayer population of the United Kingdom (as detailed in the most recent figures set out by HM Revenue and Customs at http://www.hmrc.gov.uk/stats/income_distribution/3-1table-jan2010.pdf).

84 Sandefur, 'The Importance of Doing Nothing,' *supra* note 3 at 115.

85 Genn and Paterson, *Paths to Justice in Scotland, supra* note 8.

86 Ab Currie, *The Legal Problems of Everyday Life, supra* note 8 at 13. This finding relates to problems where people do nothing and give a reason other than that the problem was not important enough.

87 Genn, *Paths to Justice, supra* note 8; Pleasence, *Civil Justice in England and Wales, supra* note 8. Balmer *et al.* have also pointed to income being a particular factor where people do not act because they are 'unable': N.J. Balmer, A. Buck, A. Patel, C. Denvir, and P. Pleasence, *Knowledge, Capability and the Experience of Rights Problems* (London: PLENET, 2010) at 23.

Sandefur, echoing Galanter's repeat player thesis[88] and drawing on data from a series of focus groups with low and low moderate income residents of a Midwestern American city, has suggested that people in these income groups are more likely to take no action to resolve problems because of the 'unfavourable balance of power' that exists in relation to many problems and 'the lessons of past experience,' where action will sometimes have been repeatedly unsuccessful.[89] In addition, Balmer *et al.* found that inaction among respondents to the 2006–9 English/Welsh survey was linked to lack of awareness of legal rights, and this in turn was linked to income, with knowledge of rights 'greater with higher income.'[90] This raises questions around the legal literacy of low and middle income earners. Balmer *et al.* also found that use of lawyers was linked to awareness of legal rights and of legal processes, which ties in with our finding, in line with our hypotheses, that the use of lawyers noticeably increased with income for 2010 English/Welsh survey respondents. However, this may be more a function of a simpler relationship between financial resources and lawyer use. The evidence from the 2010 English/Welsh survey adds to the increasing evidence from around the world (e.g., 1993 U.S. survey, 1997 New Zealand survey, 2003 Dutch survey, 2006 Canadian survey, 2006 New Zealand survey, 2006–9 English/Welsh survey, and 2007 Bulgarian survey)[91] that lawyer use is directly linked to income, with those on higher incomes more likely to instruct lawyers to resolve justiciable problems. Importantly, our findings in this regard account for problem type and problem severity, though it is to be noted that severity does not equate to absolute value, which could potentially vary across income bands.

Of particular interest in respect of those on middle incomes, our findings from the 2010 English/Welsh survey showed – again in line with our hypotheses – that those people just ineligible for legal aid were the least likely to obtain assistance from lawyers in resolving justiciable

---

88 Galanter, 'Why the "Haves" Come Out Ahead,' *supra* note 47.
89 Sandefur, 'The Importance of Doing Nothing', *supra* note 3.
90 Balmer *et al.*, *Knowledge, Capability, supra* note 87 at 39. See also A. Buck, P. Pleasence, and N.J. Balmer, 'Do Citizens Know How to Deal with Legal Issues? Some Empirical Insights' (2008) 37 *Journal of Social Policy* 661.
91 ABA, *Legal Needs and Civil Justice, supra* note 8; Maxwell, *Meeting Legal Service Needs, supra* note 25; Van Velthoven and Ter Voert, *Paths to Justice in the Netherlands, supra* note 8; Currie, *The Legal Problems of Everyday Life, supra* note 8; Pleasence and Balmer, 'Understanding Advice-Seeking Behaviour,' *supra* note 56. Analysis of the 2007 Bulgarian survey provided by Martin Gramatikov (personal correspondence).

problems where legal aid was most available.[92] Again, our findings are in keeping with earlier findings from around the world; especially those from jurisdictions with extensive and established legal aid schemes (e.g., 1997 New Zealand survey, 1998 Scottish survey, 2003 Dutch survey, 2006 Canadian survey, 2006 New Zealand survey, 2006–9 English/Welsh survey).[93] They also provide a framework for frequent reports of cost being an inhibitor of lawyer use (e.g., 1997 English/Welsh survey, 2004 Slovakian survey, 2006 Japanese survey).[94]

Our findings on lawyer use have a range of policy implications. They suggest that legal aid affords access to lawyers for people who would otherwise not use lawyers because of their position on the earnings scale – a key assumption of legal aid provision. Our findings also point to a need for policy makers to address the possible difficulties that middle income earners face in accessing legal services, along with the more recognized difficulties faced by those on low incomes. This is particularly so in jurisdictions, such as England and Wales at present, where legal aid is in retreat.[95]

In respect of access to traditional legal services, our findings confirm the potential value of alternative fee arrangements, such as contingent and conditional fees, which have become increasingly common around the world in recent decades.[96] The use of contingent/conditional fees is now standard in personal injury cases in countries such as Canada and England and Wales, as well as in the United States, with further

---

92 In fact, our findings may understate the difficulties faced by those on low middle incomes, as our legal aid proxy will not have been wholly accurate in distinguishing between those eligible and ineligible for legal aid, thus diluting our results.

93 Maxwell, *Meeting Legal Service Needs, supra* note 25; Genn and Paterson, *Paths to Justice Scotland, supra* note 8; Van Velthoven and Ter Voert, *Paths to Justice in the Netherlands, supra* note 8; Ignite, *Legal Needs and Access to Services, supra* note 8; Currie, *The Legal Problems of Everyday Life, supra* note 8; Pleasence and Balmer, 'Understanding Advice-Seeking Behaviour,' *supra* note 56. In the case of the 2006 New Zealand survey, respondents were asked about use of legal aid lawyers. Unsurprisingly, use of legal aid lawyers was found to be associated with low income.

94 Genn, *Paths to Justice, supra* note 8; GfK Slovakia, *Legal Needs in Slovakia, supra* note 8; Sato, *Citizens Access to Legal Advice, supra* note 8.

95 Griffith, 'Dramatic Drop,' *supra* note 12; Ministry of Justice, *Proposals for the Reform of Legal Aid in England and Wales* (London: TSO, 2010) [Ministry of Justice, *Proposals for Reform*]. See also Roger Smith, 'Middle Income Access to Justice: Implications of Proposals for the Reform of Legal Aid in England and Wales,' *infra* this volume.

96 Herbert M. Kritzer, *Risks, Reputations, and Rewards: Contingency Fee Legal Practice in the United States* (Stanford: Stanford University Press, 2004).

expansion ongoing.[97] Doubts remain about whether such fee arrangements can provide sufficient access to justice,[98] and debate continues around the best form of fee arrangement (or alternative provision) to meet this goal while maintaining professional standards.[99] Nevertheless, the (albeit limited) survey evidence presented above suggests that the availability of contingent/conditional fees is associated with low and middle income earners accessing lawyers as often as higher income earners.[100] Consistent with this, we found no apparent relationship between income and lawyer use among 2010 English/Welsh survey respondents in the case of personal injury problems,[101] though the number of problems was small. But, as Kritzer has observed, findings that income does not influence rates of lawyer use in relation to personal injuries in jurisdictions in which contingency fees are well established should not be surprising.[102]

Our findings also point to the potential value of innovation in the legal services sector – whether driven by technology, as in Susskind's vision of the future,[103] or by new types of funding mechanisms, such as legal expenses insurance,[104] or by new service delivery models, such as 'unbundling' of legal services – that increases the affordability of legal services.[105]

More broadly, our findings demonstrate the important role performed by the wider advice sector in providing support to people facing jus-

---

97 In England and Wales, the recent review of civil litigation costs resulted in a recommendation that contingency fees be allowed: R. Jackson, *Review of Civil Litigation Costs: Final Report* (London: Judiciary of England and Wales, 2010).

98 E.g., Richard Moorhead, 'An American Future? Contingency Fees, Claims Explosions, and Evidence from Employment Tribunals' (2010) 73 *Modern Law Review* 752.

99 E.g., James Sandbach, *No Win, No Fee, No Chance: CAB Evidence on the Challenges Facing Access to Injury Compensation* (London: Citizens Advice, 2004); R. Moorhead and P. Hurst, *Improving Access to Justice* (London: Civil Justice Council, 2008).

100 ABA, *Legal Needs and Civil Justice, supra* note 8; Kritzer, 'To Lawyer or Not to Lawyer', *supra* note 57.

101 $\chi^2_1 = 6.44$, p = 0.168.

102 Kritzer, 'To Lawyer or Not to Lawyer,' *supra* note 57 at 878.

103 Richard Susskind, *The End of Lawyers? Rethinking the Nature of Legal Services* (Oxford: Oxford University Press, 2008).

104 Matthias Kilian, 'Alternatives to Public Provision: The Role of Legal Expenses Insurance in Broadening Access to Justice: The German Experience' (2003) 30 *Journal of Law and Society* 31.

105 See Samreen Beg and Lorne Sossin, 'Should Legal Services Be Unbundled?', *infra* this volume.

ticiable problems in jurisdictions, such as England and Wales, where there are relatively few restrictions on the provision of legal advice. The 2010 English/Welsh survey respondents routinely sought advice from non-lawyers when faced with justiciable problems. In all, 14% of those respondents who obtained formal advice did so from an independent advice agency (most frequently a Citizens Advice Bureau), but not a lawyer. The English/Welsh advice sector (which is often free at the point of delivery) performs a key function in delivering (often legal) information and advice in cases where people cannot afford to instruct a lawyer. In this sense it acts as an essential support to the traditional legal services sector (one that is relatively absent in jurisdictions such as Canada and the United States).[106] With increasing pressure on the English and Welsh legal aid budget having led to recent proposals for substantial scope cuts,[107] the role of the advice sector looks set to become more important still. It is a matter of concern, therefore, that the future of some Citizens Advice Bureaux has been reported to be under threat as a consequence of reductions in local government financial backing resulting from budget cuts.[108]

Reflecting earlier studies, the 2010 English/Welsh survey also indicated that the use of advice services, rather than lawyers, was particularly common in the case of problems concerning, for example, debt, housing, and welfare benefits, but less common in the case of problems concerning, for example, relationship breakdown. This finding links to the universally acknowledged relationship between problem type and lawyer use. It is evident that people tend to go to lawyers in relation to some types of justiciable problem, but not others. For example, people commonly go to lawyers about family problems, but not welfare benefits problems. Why is this? One reason is that some problems (e.g., divorce) are inherently legal. Another reason is that the cost of going to a lawyer, relative to the income of people affected by problems, varies by problem type. People with problems concerning (say) welfare benefits are unlikely to have much spare disposable income. Another (but related) reason, one that we have recently demonstrated,[109] is that

---

106 See Roger Smith, 'Middle Income Access to Civil Justice: Implications of Proposals for the Reform of Legal Aid in England and Wales', *infra* this volume.

107 Ministry of Justice, *Proposals for Reform, supra* note 95.

108 A. Gentleman, Citizens Advice Services Face Closure, *The Guardian*, 27 January 2011, at http://www.guardian.co.uk/society/2011/jan/27/citizens-advice-services-face-closure.

109 Pleasence and Balmer, 'Horses for Courses,' *supra* note 54.

while people are quick to characterize justiciable problems of some types (e.g., family) as legal, they are slow to characterize problems of other types (e.g., welfare benefits) the same way. Though we live in a law-thick world, people do not generally perceive the world in this way, and this has a bearing on access to lawyers (and justice). If people do not perceive certain types of problems as legal, they are unlikely to think first of going to a lawyer when faced with problems of those types.[110] To the extent that this prevents people from achieving justice, this points to the role of public legal education and legal literacy in the access to justice sphere, in raising awareness of legal rights and directing people to appropriate support when looking to resolve justiciable problems.[111] Furthermore, as we noted earlier, awareness of legal rights is associated with income, with those on low and middle incomes less likely than those on higher incomes to be aware of their rights.

Another reason for lawyers being much more commonly used in relation to some justiciable problem types is the relative importance and economic value of the problems. People, as economically rational agents, will spend more on advice in relation to more important problems, given the equal utility of advice. Likewise, lawyers, as economically rational agents, will be more inclined to work in areas of law that are more rewarding, and potential rewards will relate to the value of the issues involved. Top law students from top law schools tend to practise in large firms specializing in corporate areas of law.[112] That is where the money is. At the other end of the spectrum, there is no great rush to practise in areas of 'poverty'[113] or 'social welfare' law.[114] Thus, the work undertaken by the legal profession in England and Wales does not reflect the public's experience of justiciable issues. While 25% of all English and Welsh solicitors' non-corporate income relates to personal

---

110 For further exploration of this point, see Sandefur, 'Money Isn't Everything,' *supra* note 6.

111 See further, Sandefur, 'Money Isn't Everything,' *supra* note 6.

112 See, for example, J.P. Heinz, R.L. Nelson, R.L. Sandefur, and E.O. Laumann, *Urban Lawyers: The New Social Structure of the Bar* (Chicago: University of Chicago Press, 2005).

113 Defined, for example, by Salinger, as the law that applies 'particularly to the financially poor in his or her day-to-day life': L. Salinger, *'Poverty Law: What Is It?' (1992)* 12 *Legal Reference Services Quarterly* 5.

114 Defined, for example, by the Legal Services Commission as including the law that applies to community care, debt, employment, housing, and welfare benefits: Legal Services Commission, *Making Legal Rights a Reality* (London: Legal Services Commission, 2006).

injury,[115] 9% relates to employment problems, and less than 1% relates to problems concerning welfare benefits,[116] the prevalence of these three problem types in the general population is similar.[117] Yet all three problem types also have a potentially serious impact on people's lives. It is a matter of public importance, therefore, that all three problem types be resolved without great difficulty on the part of those facing them.[118]

In conclusion, it is clear that justiciable problems are ubiquitous and affect people in all income groups. Yet people in different income groups appear to use lawyers to varying extents, even after controlling for problem type and severity. In broad terms, lawyer use increases with income. However, for problem types where legal aid is most available, it is those on lower incomes, but not eligible for legal aid, who are least likely to use lawyers. Our findings have clear policy implications. They demonstrate that legal aid is enabling many people on low incomes to access lawyers when they would otherwise not do so. In light of the apparent absence of a relationship between income and lawyer use where contingent/conditional fees are available, they also show the potential value of alternative fee arrangements to facilitating access to lawyers, and point to the value of other innovations – such as increased use of new technologies, alternative funding mechanisms, and new service delivery models – that increase the affordability of legal services. Finally, and especially in light of traditional legal services being relatively unavailable for many justiciable problems in the social welfare field, the varying use of lawyers by people on different incomes demonstrates the value of a broader advice sector that can provide low or no cost (legal) advice across a broad range of problem areas.

At a time when many legal aid budgets and wider advice services are under considerable pressure, these policy implications have particular resonance.

---

115 Including clinical negligence.
116 Law Society, *Solicitors' Firms* (London: Law Society, 2003).
117 In the 2010 Civil and Social Justice Survey, 4.1% of respondents reported problems concerning personal injuries, 5.5% problems concerning employment, and 4.4% problems concerning welfare benefits.
118 This last point also raises questions about the extent to which supply side factors influence the use of lawyers. As well as focusing on work that is more profitable, lawyers might also be expected to situate themselves in locations that are more accessible to more affluent clients.

2 The Ontario Civil Legal Needs Project: A Comparative Analysis of the 2009 Survey Data

JAMIE BAXTER, MICHAEL TREBILCOCK, AND

ALBERT YOON

I. Introduction

Several countries have followed the lead of British researchers since the late 1990s by using civil legal needs surveys to characterize the types of legal problems that individuals confront, their responses to these events in terms of advice-seeking behaviour, and the demographic traits and socio-economic conditions that are likely to predict patterns of problem and response. A shared approach to conducting and analysing these surveys has emerged – first among the Commonwealth jurisdictions and more recently in countries such as Belgium, the Netherlands, Japan, and China. The comparative results of these studies are now beginning to tell an increasingly nuanced story about the prevalence and consequences of legal problems and about the nature of civil justice systems as a whole. In a similar vein of research, the Ontario Civil Legal Needs Project (OCLNP) undertook a survey of low and middle income Ontarians in 2009, and released a report of its findings, *Listening to Ontarians*, in May 2010.[1] Our paper provides a further analysis of the OCLNP survey's quantitative results and situates these in the context of the international research to date.

Growing attention to civil legal needs surveys presumes a demand-oriented approach to civil justice reform based on the incidence of *justiciable events*, or 'happenings and circumstances that raise legal issues but that people may never think of as legal and with respect to which they

---

1 Ontario Civil Legal Needs Project, 'Listening to Ontarians: Report of the Ontario Civil Legal Needs Project' (Toronto, 2010) online: http://www.lsuc.on.ca/media/may3110_oclnreport_final.pdf.

may never take any legal action.'[2] This approach has also been called a 'bottom up' or 'micro-oriented' behavioural perspective.[3] As a basis for research that seeks to improve policy making aimed at improving access to justice, civil legal needs surveys provide one means to capture the preferences and expectations of participants in the legal system.

As Pleasence and Balmer observe in a recent study of advice-seeking behaviour, the 'common intellectual underpinning of the most recent surveys, based on Genn's concept of the "justiciable event," and their similar methodologies provides an unprecedented opportunity for comparative study and identification of behavioural norms.'[4] While some challenges for doing comparative work have emerged, partly as the result of methodological differences between surveys, the shared theoretical approach that links many of these studies serves as a promising starting point for work that begins to link findings across jurisdictions.

It is possible to discern a general trend in approaches to analysing the results of civil legal needs surveys. The first wave of studies was concerned with questions of identification – that is, with the nature of justiciable events and responses to these events, particularly in terms of advice-seeking behaviour. These studies have established the ubiquity of civil justice problems in jurisdictions where legal needs surveys have been carried out and have led to some general observations about commonalities in the prevalence of specific problem types and individual responses.

A second wave has now emerged with an emphasis on explanatory variables. These studies address, first, who experiences justiciable events, mainly in terms of demographic and socio-economic characteristics such as age, gender, ethnicity, and income, and second, the relationship between problem type and response, including the type of justiciable event as a predictor of individuals' likelihood of seeking legal or non-legal advice. The present paper fits squarely within this

---

2 Rebecca L. Sandefur, 'Access to Civil Justice and Race, Class, and Gender Inequality' (2008) 34 *Annual Review of Sociology* 339 at 341.

3 *Ibid.* at 343.

4 Pascoe Pleasence and Nigel Balmer, 'Understanding Advice Seeking Behaviour: Findings from New Zealand and England and Wales' in *Empirical Studies of Judicial Systems*, ed. K. Huang (Taipai: Academia Sinica, 2009), 219 at 223, http://www.iias.sinica.edu.tw/cht/index.php?code=list&flag=detail&ids=151&article_id=3259&eng=1 (accessed 28 June 2010) [Pleasence and Balmer, 'Advice Seeking'], with reference to Hazel Genn, *Paths to Justice: What People Do and Think about Going to Law* (Oxford: Hart Publishing, 1999) [Genn, *Paths to Justice*].

most recent vein of research. As such, we examine how the OCLNP survey can contribute to exploring the following two questions:

1 Which legal problems do respondents experience most frequently and what are the best individual-level predictors of these problem types?
2 Are there identifiable patterns of advice-seeking behaviour, and how significant are respondent characteristics and problem types for predicting whether these individuals will seek advice in response to recognized civil legal problems?

In brief, the OCLNP data suggest that the frequencies with which Ontarians experience particular justiciable events vary widely from those reported in other jurisdictions. Some commonalities with other studies do exist; we find, for example, that demographic variables such as age and disability status are strong predictors of the kinds of problems that individuals are likely to experience. The OCLNP data reveal, however, that income is not a predictor of most problem types, and this represents a key difference from comparable studies.[5] Because this and other outcomes may be influenced by survey design as well as by the target respondent population, we discuss the primary differences in survey design between the Ontario study and others in greater detail below.[6]

Patterns of advice-seeking behaviour in Ontario closely match studies of other jurisdictions that have examined the decision to seek legal advice. Our results support previous findings that the type of problem experienced is often an overriding predictor of advice-seeking behaviour in comparison to demographic characteristics and socio-economic factors.

In Part II of this paper, we undertake a brief overview of civil legal needs surveys internationally and compare the findings that are most relevant to these two research questions. We describe the OCLNP data in Part III, and in Part IV we map our methodology. Part V presents the results of our statistical analysis; this is followed by a discussion of these findings and our conclusions in Part VI.

---

5 See Pascoe Pleasence and Nigel J. Balmer, 'Caught in the Middle: Income, Justiciable Problems, and Use of Lawyers' *supra* this volume.
6 See Part 3, *infra*.

II. Comparative Overview of Civil Legal Needs Surveys

Our survey of the international literature reveals that no comprehensive, comparative study of national civil legal needs surveys has been undertaken to date. One multicountry study has attempted to collect and catalogue survey responses pertaining to the types of civil justice problems encountered by individuals,[7] while a few others have engaged statistical models to compare results between two or more countries on the topic of advice-seeking behaviour. Some single-country studies, which appear to contain the most in-depth analyses of survey results, aim to orient their findings with reference to surveys from other jurisdictions, but fail to provide any substantive overview or evaluation of comparative findings. While some national survey reports have developed statistical models that are likely to make comparative work fruitful – this is true especially for Canada, the U.K., New Zealand, and Australia – general insights from the growing body of empirical work on civil legal needs remain fragmented.

Many of these legal needs surveys have been heavily influenced in their design and analysis by Hazel Genn's *Paths to Justice* study conducted in England and Wales in 1999,[8] followed two years later by a companion study in Scotland.[9] The original *Paths to Justice* study was the first of its kind to capture data, on a national scale, about the incidence of justiciable events and the nature of problem resolution strategies. Genn's pioneering empirical work took place amid a period of keen attention to civil justice reforms in the wake of Lord Woolf's review of the civil justice system in England and Wales beginning in 1994 and reported through the mid-1990s. Woolf's final report presented his sweeping vision for a new kind of civil justice system, one that would emphasize access to justice based on fair, transparent, and efficient procedures and that would rationalize the current system in England and Wales and dramatically reduce costs to legal users and the public.[10] Much of the policy debate at the time, how-

---

7 M. Barendrecht, P. Kamminga, and J.H. Verdonschot, 'Priorities for the Justice System: Responding to the Most Urgent Legal Problems of Individuals' (2008) *TISCO Working Paper No. 001/20* [Barendrecht, 'Priorities for the Justice System'].

8 Genn, *Paths to Justice, supra* note 4.

9 Hazel Genn and Alan Paterson, *Paths to Justice Scotland: What People Do and Think about Going to Law* (Oxford: Hart Publishing, 2001) [Genn and Paterson, *Paths to Justice Scotland*].

10 Lord H. Woolf, 'Access to Justice: Final Report to the Lord Chancellor on the Civil Justice System in England and Wales' (London: HMSO, 1996).

ever, was occurring in the vacuum left by a lack of available empirical evidence about the kinds of legal problems, and the systemic barriers to their resolution, that individuals were actually experiencing.[11] Genn's study was a first attempt to begin filling this gap and to create a sound basis for policy developments in the area of civil justice reform.

Central to Genn's approach to civil legal needs studies was her concept of the 'justiciable event.' This concept broke away from earlier approaches to studying civil legal needs, which focused 'on the kinds of *people* who use legal services, rather than on the kinds of problems which are taken to lawyers.'[12] The 'justiciable event' was therefore an attempt to understand the basic nature of serious problems that people experienced in day-to-day life, and to give these problems – as well as responses to them – a broader characterization than conventional categories of 'legal' disputes would allow. By clarifying the nature of justiciable events that survey respondents tended to confront, *Paths to Justice* refocused the lens through which to study civil legal reform. Genn's innovative methodology now serves as the starting point for most national civil legal needs surveys as well as a useful common denominator for comparative work in this area.

There is thus ample opportunity to more closely examine the lessons and policy implications from existing surveys. Comparative work in this area is not, however, without its challenges, given that differences in survey design and delivery may bear heavily on the degree to which survey results reflect the same phenomena. This section begins with a brief inventory of the most recent civil legal needs surveys, followed by a discussion of the comparative findings relevant to our regression analysis of the OCLNP data in Parts IV and V below.

A. Inventory of Civil Legal Needs Surveys

In those jurisdictions where civil legal needs surveys have been carried out, most have produced a single national or regional survey and report. Canada and the U.K. are exceptions, with national surveys having been conducted periodically or on a continuous basis.

(i) Canada (2004–8). The Canadian Department of Justice conducted

---

11 Genn, *Paths to Justice, supra* note 4 at 2.
12 *Ibid.* at 6.

national telephone civil legal needs surveys in 2004,[13] 2006,[14] and 2008. In his most recent report, titled *The Legal Problems of Everyday Life*, Currie provides a detailed analysis of the 2006 survey results.[15] The 2008 results for Canada have not yet been released. All ten provinces were included in the 2006 survey of 6,665 individuals aged eighteen or older. Respondents were asked if they had experienced any of eighty specific justiciable events.[16] Currie's analysis of these data explicitly tracks approaches used in England and Wales, making these two surveys good candidates for comparative work.

(ii) United Kingdom (1997–2009). Hazel Genn's original *Paths to Justice* survey was carried out in England and Wales in 1997–8.[17] A second *Paths to Justice* survey was conducted in Scotland two years later, and Northern Ireland conducted its own Legal Needs Survey in 2005.[18] Since then, the Legal Services Commission (LSC) conducted the English and Welsh Civil and Social Justice Survey in 2001, following this with a second national survey in 2004.[19] From 2006 to 2009, this survey was conducted on a continuous basis, with data being reported quarterly.[20] This face-to-face survey method pioneered by Genn

---

13 Albert W. Currie, 'Legal Problems and Vulnerable Groups in Canada,' *JustResearch Edition No. 13* (2005), Department of Justice Canada, http://www.justice.gc.ca/eng/pi/rs/rep-rap/jr/jr13/p5e.html.

14 Albert W. Currie, *The Legal Problems of Everyday Life: The Nature, Extent, and Consequences of Justiciable Problems Experienced by Canadians* (Ottawa: Department of Justice Canada, 2007), http://justice-canada.net/eng/pi/rs/rep-rap/2007/rr07_la1-rr07_aj1/rr07_la1.pdf [Currie, *Legal Problems of Everyday Life*].

15 *Ibid*.

16 Seventy-six specific problems were used in the 2004 Canadian survey.

17 Genn, 'Paths to Justice,' *supra* note 4.

18 Genn and Patterson, *Paths to Justice Scotland*, *supra* note 9; Tony Dignan, *Northern Ireland Legal Needs Survey: Statistical Annex* (Belfast: Northern Ireland Legal Services Commission, 2006), http://www.nilsc.org.uk/uploads/publications/documents/NI%20Legal%20Needs%20Survey%20Statistical%20Annex.pdf.

19 For a report on first LSRC survey in 2001, see Pascoe Pleasence *et al.*, *Causes of Action: Civil Law and Social Justice* (Legal Services Commission, 2004), http://www.justice.gov.uk/downloads/publications/research-and-analysis/lsrc/Causes%20of%20Action.pdf [Pleasence, 'Causes of Action'].

20 See Pascoe Pleasence, Nigel Balmer, and T. Tam, *Civil Justice in England and Wales: Report of the 2006 English and Welsh Civil and Social Justice Survey* (London: Legal Services Commission, 2007), http://www.justice.gov.uk/publications/research-and-analysis/lsrc/research-projects/english-and-welsh-civil-and-social-justice-survey/key-facts.htm. Data for the 2004 and 2006–8 surveys are available at http://www.lsrc.org.uk/csjs.html.

contains a main and a follow-up interview. In the main interview, respondents are asked to identify whether they have experienced a difficult problem in each of eighteen distinct categories. Respondents are then asked more in-depth questions about their two most recent problems. In the most recent report from the LSC, Pleasence *et al.* have reported on the 2007 English and Welsh Civil and Social Justice Survey.[21] For that survey, 3,658 individuals aged eighteen or older were interviewed, with 27 per cent completing both the main and follow-up interviews. Beginning in 2010, the LSC will commence a panel survey to track the incidence of legal problems and resolution strategies for participants over time.

(iii) New South Wales, Australia (2003). The Law and Justice Foundation of New South Wales commenced its Access to Justice and Legal Needs research program in 2002, conducting a series of quantitative civil legal needs surveys in disadvantaged areas in 2003. Coumarelos *et al.* report on the survey findings in a study titled 'Justice Made to Measure.'[22] While respondents in most other national surveys were selected randomly, the New South Wales surveys were carried out in regions identified as being at high risk of cumulative socio-economic disadvantage. A total of 2,431 residents aged fifteen years or older were surveyed, with a response rate between 24 and 34 per cent.

(iv) New Zealand (2006). New Zealand's Legal Services Agency conducted a national civil legal needs survey in 2006.[23] The survey was carried out by telephone with 7,200 randomly selected respondents, including a 'booster' sample of 350 Māori and 150 Pacific Island people (traditionally underrepresented groups in survey samples in New Zealand). Respondents were aged fifteen years or older. The identified problem categories for this study were confined to seven distinct areas.

(v) Japan (2006). Japan's National Survey on Legal Advice Seeking

---

21 Pascoe Pleasence *et al.*, *Civil Justice in England and Wales: Report of the 2007 English and Welsh Civil and Social Justice Survey* (London: Legal Services Research Centre, 2008), http://www.justice.gov.uk/downloads/publications/research-and-analysis/lsrc/2007CSJS.pdf [Pleasence, '2007 Survey'].

22 Christine Coumarelos, Zhigang Wei, and Albert Zhou, 'Justice Made to Measure: NSW Legal Needs Survey in Disadvantaged Areas' (Sydney: Law and Justice Foundation of New South Wales, 2006), http://www.lawfoundation.net.au/ljf/site/articleIDs/B9662F72F04ECB17CA25713E001D6BBA/$file/Justice_Made_to_Measure.pdf [Coumarelos, 'Justice Made to Measure'].

23 Legal Services Agency, *Report on the 2006 National Survey of Unmet Legal Needs and Access to Services* (Wellington, 2006).

was carried out in 2006. Sato reports on the findings.[24] In all, 5,330 individuals between age twenty and seventy were surveyed, using fourteen distinct problem categories. The survey period covered problems occurring in the past five years.

(vi) Netherlands (2003). The Dutch Ministry of Justice carried out a national survey among 3,500 individuals in 2003.[25] This study was modelled explicitly on the earlier *Paths to Justice* studies in the United Kingdom. Individuals aged eighteen and over were asked whether they had experienced problems from a list of ten main categories (sixty-six distinct legal problems overall). The questionnaire asked about events covering a five-year period between January 1998 and December 2002.

(vii) Bulgaria (2007). A civil legal needs survey modelled on the U.K. surveys was conducted in Bulgaria in 2007 – apparently the first such 'justiciable events' survey conducted in a Central or Eastern European country.[26] For this survey, 2,730 adults were interviewed, aged 18 and older, about problems within the past three-and-a-half years. As with the U.K. surveys, these interviews were carried out in person.

(viii) China (2002). In 2002, researchers at Renmin University of China administered a legal needs survey of rural households in six Chinese provinces, with Michelson reporting the results of this study.[27] Local schoolteachers living and working at the survey sights were training to conduct the interviews. In all, 2,902 households were included in the survey, from thirty-seven villages selected to be representative of the six sample counties. Unlike most other studies, data from this study were reported at the household rather than individual level – that is,

---

24 Iwao Sato, 'Citizens' Access to Legal Advice in Contemporary Japan: Findings from the 2006 National Survey' (2008), Institute for Law and Social Sciences, Civil Justice Research Project, Working Papers No. 13, vol. 3, http://www.kisc.meiji.ac.jp/~ilss/english/e_workingpapers_no.1/workingpapers-vol.%203.pdf. See also Masayuki Murayama, 'Experiences of Problems and Disputing Behaviour in Japan' (2007) 14 *Meiji Law Journal* 1.

25 Ben Van Velthoven and Marijke ter Voert, 'Paths to Justice in the Netherlands: Looking for Signs of Social Exclusion' (Leiden: Leiden University Department of Economics, 2004) [Van Velthoven and Marijke ter Voert, 'Paths to Justice in the Netherlands'].

26 Martin Gramatikov, 'Multiple Justiciable Problems in Bulgaria,' Tilburg University Legal Studies Working Paper No. 16/2008 (Tilburg Institute for Interdisciplinary Studies of Civil Law and Conflict Resolution Systems, Tilburg University, 2008), http://arno.uvt.nl/show.cgi?fid=83936 [Gramatikov, 'Multiple Justiciable Problems'].

27 Ethan Michelson, 'Climbing the Dispute Pagoda: Grievances and Appeals to the Official Justice System in Rural China' (2007) 72 *American Sociological Review* 459 [Michelson, 'Climbing the Dispute Pagoda'].

interviews were conducted with household heads as representatives of their entire household.

(ix) U.S. and State-Level Studies (1994–2008). The American Bar Association (ABA) conducted a legal needs survey in the forty-eight contiguous states in 1994.[28] The sample design for this study was somewhat more complex, with three distinct sample populations being targeted: all households in the United States, low income households, and households in urban areas. Overall, telephone and in-person surveys were conducted with 1,782 low income households and 1,305 moderate income households. Respondents were asked about problems experienced within a one-year period in any one of sixty-seven problem areas. Note that, unlike other national surveys in this inventory, the ABA study was carried out prior to Genn's *Paths to Justice* study in England and Wales, though differences in methodology may amount to variations in degree rather than a divergence in their underlying theoretical approaches. For example, the ABA study appears to emphasize the narrower concept of 'legal needs' based only on problems that can be addressed through the civil legal system, rather than the more inclusive idea of a justiciable event.[29]

Hadfield reports that at least twelve state-level legal needs surveys have been carried out in the United States subsequent to the 1994 ABA study. These studies vary in their methodology. Most of them report legal needs by household, although a few report only individual-level responses. As well, according to Hadfield, '[t]he surveys differ substantially in how they report the use of legal services: some report only the use of lawyers, some report actions taken as a percentage of households, and others as a percentage of problems. Not all the surveys report whether a respondent took no action whatsoever. The list of "problems" provided to respondents was relatively consistent across states with the exception that Massachusetts included municipal and language problems that are arguably not susceptible to assistance by a lawyer.'[30] Hadfield provides a summary of key survey results on the incidence of legal needs and the steps taken to resolve problems.[31]

---

28 American Bar Association, *Legal Needs and Civil Justice: A Survey of Americans* (Chicago: American Bar Association, 1994), http://www.abanet.org/legalservices/downloads/sclaid/legalneedstudy.pdf [ABA, *Legal Needs and Civil Justice*].

29 Gillian Hadfield, 'Higher Demand, Lower Supply? A Comparative Assessment of the Legal Resources Landscape for Ordinary Americans' (2010) 37 *Fordham Urban Law Journal* 129 at 130 [Hadfield, 'Higher Demand, Lower Supply?'].

30 *Ibid.* at 140.

31 *Ibid.* at 142.

The majority of legal needs surveys included in this brief overview derive their methodology from Genn's original *Paths to Justice* studies in England and Wales and Scotland.[32] Most of these surveys, for example, supplied respondents with a finite list of everyday problems covering both conventional civil legal events such as wills and estate planning or family disputes, as well as issues that would not normally, or necessarily, be viewed by respondents as 'legal' issues, such as some consumer and debt problems. Respondents were then asked to select the problem types that applied to their specific experiences. Other aspects of survey design and delivery, however, differed among studies and may be important contributing factors towards observed differences in the results across jurisdictions. For example, the number and type of problem categories presented to survey respondents appear to vary widely between surveys. Some surveys were conducted in person, others by telephone, and others were administrated via the Internet. The nature of the sample population in each survey also varied. In most studies, respondents were selected from a random sample, but a few studies targeted specific income or other demographic groups. While we do not attempt to draw any general conclusions in this paper about how civil needs survey design can affect survey results, we do highlight some of the unique features of the OCLNP survey below and reflect briefly on these design features as possible factors in generating some of the unique results observed in Ontario.

B. Comparative Findings from Civil Legal Needs Surveys

Using the inventory of civil needs surveys discussed above, this section provides an overview of the comparative findings assembled from survey analyses and reports. We focus mainly on those findings relevant to our two research questions, which aim (1) to characterize the types of problems that individuals experience, including the influence of demographic and socio-economic factors, and (2) to identify predictors of advice-seeking behaviour.

   (i) *Problem Types – the Prevalence and Nature of Justiciable Events.* The process of characterizing legal problem types actually includes a collection of several inquiries:

---

32 But for exceptions, see Pascoe Pleasence and Nigel J. Balmer, 'Caught in the Middle: Income, Justiciable Problems, and the Use of Lawyers,' *supra* this volume, Part II.

- How prevalent are civil justice problems in general?
- Which types of problems do people encounter and at what rates?
- Which demographic and socio-economic characteristics best predict these problems?
- How and when do individuals experience multiple problems?

Take together, existing civil legal needs surveys support a general assertion that civil justice problems are ubiquitous in everyday life,[33] although the proportion of individuals who experienced one or more problems varies from 28.7 per cent in New Zealand to 67 per cent in the Netherlands.[34] Similar variation has been observed in state-level surveys from the United States. In a brief overview of these U.S. studies between 2001 and 2007, Hadfield observes that the proportion of respondent households experiencing one or more problems ranged from 45 per cent in Wisconsin to 67.5 per cent in Utah.[35]

Turning to specific types of legal problems, Barendrecht *et al.* compile the most frequent justiciable issues identified in legal needs surveys from Canada, the United Kingdom, the Netherlands, Australia, Bulgaria, China, the United States, and Germany.[36] The authors observe that problems related to consumer purchases, debt and money, and employment occur with a high frequency in the greatest number of jurisdictions. Personal injury and housing problems also occur frequently, but in fewer jurisdictions. China is flagged as an outlier, with legal problems such as water use and agricultural taxes occurring at very high rates. The authors also briefly compare the severity of problems between the United States, the Netherlands, the United Kingdom, and Canada. Personal security, employment, and personal relationship problems all emerge as the problems most frequently reported as 'severe.'[37]

---

33 Pleasence and Balmer, 'Advice-Seeking,' *supra* note 4 at 1–2.
34 The proportion of individuals experiencing one or more problems was 69.1 per cent in the Australian study, keeping in mind that this survey targeted disadvantaged groups. Other proportions are China (55 per cent), Bulgaria (46.3), Canada (44.6), UK (36), and Japan (36.5).
35 Hadfield, 'Higher Demand, Lower Supply?', *supra* note 29 at 142. Two state-level surveys conducted in Arizona and New Jersey with individual instead of household respondents revealed lower rates of experience with legal problems, at 32 and 33 per cent respectively.
36 Barendrecht, 'Priorities for the Justice System,' *supra* note 7 at 10.
37 Several different methods were used across these four different national surveys to assess the impact of problems on people's lives: *ibid.* at 12.

Table 2.1. Comparative taxonomy for legal problems, Barendrecht *et al.* (2008)

Legal Problem Category	Examples/Explanation
1 Subsistence problems	Access to basic survival needs such as food, water, heating, urgent health care.
2 Basic personal security	Crimes related to the person, unfair detention, personal injury.
3 Property rights protection	Crimes related to property, registration of property, property disputes, expropriation.
4 Identity issues and documents	Acknowledgment of identity and nationality.
5 Problems in land use relationships	Problems in relation to land use, house leases, and/or eviction.
6 Problems in employment relationships	Dismissal, employment conditions, and/or safety in the workplace.
7 Problems in family relationships	Divorce, domestic violence, exploitation of women or children.
8 Problems in neighbour relationships	Disturbances, environmental damage.
9 Problems with sellers of goods and services	Issues regarding quality of goods or services.
10 Business problems	Setting up a business, unfair regulation, unfair taxation, issues between participants in enterprise, issues with suppliers.
11 Debt problems	Unpaid debts.
12 Problems with financial services	Savings, insurance, pensions.

Barendrecht *et al.* offer a simple taxonomy for comparing identified legal problems between countries. They attempt to establish a set of twelve generalized problem categories, which they claim are capable of standardizing the different categories employed in national surveys. A main shortcoming of this approach, however, is that the authors do little to explain *why* they developed their twelve specific categories. These categories are explained briefly in Table 2.1.

Certain categories within this taxonomy will be applicable to many existing civil legal needs surveys, while others may prove less useful for comparative purposes. For example, debt, neighbourhood, employment, and family problems are all reported as basic problem types included in most surveys. 'Personal security' may also be a particularly useful aggregate category, encompassing personal injury and unfair detention, which are frequently reported as distinct problem types. Categories such as 'subsistence problems' will likely be less useful, given that this class contains a wide range of potentially ill-defined problem types.

Moving beyond taxonomical questions, some national studies have attempted to identify the best predictors of civil justice problems according to demographic characteristics. Studies by Currie (Canada), Pleasence *et al.* (England and Wales), and Coumarelos *et al.* (New South Wales) estimate predictors including age, gender, education, language, number of children, disability status, employment status, income, social assistance, ethnicity, and visible minority status.[38] In general, disability and age appear to be the two most common predictors of justiciable events across problem categories. Income and number of children, or family type, are also significant predictors of problems in several categories. In New South Wales, Indigenous status is a significant indicator in many categories. A summary of the statistically significant predictors for the most common problems is provided in Table 2.2.

Notably, Michelson's study of rural China diverges from other national studies by focusing on the social and regional/geographic factors that may influence the prevalence and nature of civil justice problems in a given county.[39] Michelson finds that controlling for household-level predictors, namely high income and education, reduces the likelihood of experiencing a problem, but he demonstrates that these are insignificant predictors once regional-level controls such as county identification, tax rates, per capita GDP, and the type of labour force are included. The strength of a household's political connections to local village leaders, however, remained a highly significant predictor, increasing the likelihood of reporting a civil justice problem.

National studies from England and Wales and Canada also address the incidence of multiple justiciable problems. Pleasence *et al.* (2004) observe three distinct trends in their analysis of the English and Welsh data. First, the likelihood of experiencing justiciable problems appears to be cumulative, meaning that '[e]ach time a person experiences a problem they become increasingly likely to experience additional problems.'[40] Problems associated with domestic violence, relationship breakdown, and homelessness increased markedly along with the number of problems reported for a given respondent. The authors note, however, that the causal relationships between problems can be

---

38 Currie, *Legal Problems of Everyday Life, supra* note 14 at 26; Pleasence, 'Causes of Action,' *supra* note 19 at 14; Coumarelos, 'Justice Made to Measure,' *supra* note 22 at 79.

39 Michelson, 'Climbing the Dispute Pagoda,'*supra* note 27 at 477.

40 Pleasence, 'Causes of Action,' *supra* note 19 at 31.

Table 2.2. Significant demographic predictors of civil justice problems in Canada, UK, and New South Wales

	Consumer	Employment	Credit and Debt	Social Assistance	Housing	Discrimination	Family	Wills
Canada[i]	Disability, age, number of children	Disability, age, employment status	Disability, age	Disability, age, income	Disability, receives social assistance, employment status, income	Disability, age, minority status	Disability, number of children	Disability, age
England and Wales[ii]	Disability, age, income, housing and tenure	Disability, age, income, housing and tenure, family type,	Disability, age, income, housing and tenure	Disability, employment status, age, income	Disability, education, income, family type	Disability, ethnicity, housing, family type, employment status	Housing type, family type, age, employment status	n/a
New South Wales[iii]	Disability, age, income	Disability, Indigenous status	Disability, age, Indigenous status	Disability, age, n/a	Disability, age, income, education	n/a	Disability, age, income, education	Age, education, income, country of birth, Indigenous status

[i]Currie (2007); [ii]Pleasence et al. (2007); [iii]Coumarelos et al. (2006).

complex, making it difficult to predict which problems are more likely to occur in isolation.

Some of these complex dynamics may be explained by 'triggering' and 'clustering' effects. First, problems may tend to 'trigger' one another in predictable ways. Pleasence *et al.* (2004) find that problems associated with domestic violence, relationship breakdown, and divorce commonly precede the occurrence of other problems.[41] Problems likely also tend to 'cluster' according to distinct patterns. In this case, the concurrence of two or more problems may be related directly to underlying factors, including demographic ones. The authors identify the following clusters: domestic violence/family problems; homelessness/unfair treatment by police; and clinical negligence/mental health/immigration.[42] Pleasence *et al.* (2004) also include an analysis of which population groups are most likely to experience these problem clusters. Reports by Currie (Canada), Coumarelos *et al.* (New South Wales), Gramatikov (Bulgaria), and the New Zealand Legal Services Agency all contain similar treatments of multiple justiciable problems.[43]

Finally, studies in several jurisdictions have noted that legal problems can lead to non-legal problems, such as physical and mental health issues. In Canada, for example, Currie reports that over 38 per cent of respondents with one or more legal problems reported experiencing a health or social issue caused by that problem.[44] These issues included drug and alcohol abuse, violence in the family, and feelings of personal insecurity and fear for their own safety. A further area of research in this respect may be to link legal problem types with specific outcomes. In England and Wales, for example, Pleasence *et al.* (2004) observe that legal problems related to self-employment and unemployment have been connected to a decline in mental health.[45]

(ii) Advice-Seeking Behaviour – Responses to Justiciable Events. A second set of issues concerns individuals' responses to justiciable events. Respondents may choose to simply do nothing, they may engage in various forms of self-help to resolve their problems, or they may seek advice from a third party, who may or may not be a lawyer. Ques-

---

41 *Ibid.* at 35.
42 *Ibid.* at 39–40.
43 Currie, *Legal Problems of Everyday Life, supra* note 14 at 42; Coumarelos, *supra* note 22 at 75; Gramatikov, *supra* note 26; Legal Services Agency, *supra* note 23 at 24.
44 Currie, *Legal Problems of Everyday Life, supra* note 14 at 73.
45 Pleasence, 'Causes of Action,' *supra* note 19 at 23.

tions related to individuals' responses to justiciable events include the following:

- What proportion of people take action to resolve civil justice problems?
- Do those who take action seek advice from a lawyer and/or from other sources?
- What demographic factors and types of problems best predict advice-seeking behaviour, and why?

Comparative survey results indicate that between 8.8 per cent and 33.1 per cent of individuals experiencing justiciable events simply 'lump it' – that is, they take no action in response to these problems. For those individuals who do respond in some way to civil legal problems, patterns of advice-seeking behaviour also vary widely. For example, New Zealanders demonstrate the lowest propensity to seek any kind of advice, at 23.6 per cent. By contrast, 51 per cent of individuals in New South Wales sought either legal or non-legal advice in response to a justiciable event. The comparable results of national surveys are summarized in Table 2.3.[46]

In a recent article, Hadfield draws attention to the apparent disconnect between the supply of and demand for legal services in the United States as well as in some other nations with supposedly well-developed formal legal systems.[47] She observes that in these 'law-thick' countries, rates of legal consumers who 'lump it' are surprisingly high: 32.8 per cent in New South Wales, 26 per cent in the United States, and 22 per cent in Canada. Hadfield argues that 'despite being one of the most law-based socio-economic systems on the planet, [the United States] arguably devotes significantly less support than most other countries – both developed and developing – to the legal markets and institutions necessary to make all this law the organizing principle in fact, not just theory, of everyday relationships.'[48] A prominent illustration of the current disconnect between supply of and demand for legal services

---

46 Data in many national surveys are also available to characterize responses to justiciable events according to problem type: Pleasence, '2007 Survey,' *supra* note 21 at 50; Van Velthoven and Marijke ter Voert, 'Paths to Justice in the Netherlands,' *supra* note 25 at 9; Coumarelos, 'Justice Made to Measure,' *supra* note 22 at 99; Currie, *Legal Problems of Everyday Life, supra* note 14 at 64.
47 Hadfield, 'Higher Demand, Lower Supply?', *supra* note 29.
48 *Ibid.* at 134.

Table 2.3. Responses to justiciable events

	Took No Action	Handled on Own	Non-Legal Advice	Legal Advice
Canada[i]	22%	44%	22.1%	11.7%
New South Wales[ii]	32.8	16	51.2	
England and Wales*[iii]	8.8	34.6	49.1	
Netherlands[iv]	9.9	46.3	44.1	
New Zealand**[v]	76.4		13.8	9.8
United States[†vi]	26	42	51	
Japan[vii]	16.6	54.9	28.5	
Bulgaria[‡viii]	n/a	n/a	n/a	n/a
China[ix]	33.1	46.8	n/a	n/a

*Study also includes statistics on individuals who tried and failed to obtain advice (1.7%) and who tried, failed, and handled the problem on their own (5.8%).
**See tabulations provided in Pleasence and Balmer (2009).
†Survey statistics are for middle-income Americans. Statistics total to greater that 100% because some respondents reported more than one type of action taken.
‡Survey statistics are not comparable, but of interest is the high incidence of respondents with justiciable problems who expected a public authority or institution to intervene (37.43%).
[i]Currie (2007); [ii]Coumarelos (2006); [iii]Pleasence et al. (2007); [iv]VanVelthoven and terVoert (2004); [v]New Zealand Legal Services Agency (2006); [vi]American Bar Association (1994); [vii]Sato (2006); [viii]Gramatikov (2008); [ix]Michelson (2002).

in respect of civil legal needs, reports Hadfield, is that an increasing majority of legal services are going to corporate clients, with an increasingly smaller share being consumed by individuals (measured as a proportion of annual expenditures). Hadfield estimates that the average number of hours of legal services per household per legal problem in the United States has declined dramatically in the past fifteen years – perhaps by as much as 60 per cent.[49] Although her calculations yield at best very rough estimates, she suggests that this overall trend may be shaped by the lack of a major role for government in overseeing and regulating the legal system.

While Hadfield concentrates on the provision of legal services by private lawyers, other sources of legal and non-legal advice may also be significant. Pleasence, Balmer, and Reimers observe that even where individuals frequently seek advice of some kind in order to solve their

---

49 *Ibid.* at 146.

legal problems, sources of advice can be very diverse and include a mix of legal and non-legal sources. For example, in the most recent survey from England and Wales, people sought formal legal advice for almost 60 per cent of difficult-to-solve justiciable issues, but that advice came from lawyers in only 13 per cent of cases.[50] 'Alternative' sources of legal advice included Citizen's Advice Bureaux, local authorities, trade unions, social workers, the police, politicians, and clerics.

Once advice-seeking behaviour has been characterized, subsequent questions arise about the underlying causes of this behaviour. In a multi-national study, Kritzer evaluates the assumption that the reluctance to utilize legal mechanisms to resolve justiciable problems is a function of the affordability of legal assistance.[51] Using survey data from Australia, Canada, the U.K., Japan, the Netherlands, and New Zealand, Kritzer compares the likelihood of respondents consulting a lawyer in each problem category identified, for high, middle, low, and very low income brackets.[52] The survey findings about advice-seeking behaviour across jurisdictions are remarkably consistent. He concludes from this comparative evidence that income has relatively little impact on decisions to seek the advice of a lawyer. Kritzer argues that the response pattern in national surveys suggests that individuals undertake a cost–benefit analysis aimed at assessing the likely benefit of consulting a lawyer. He finds that as a consequence, the type of civil justice issue or problem is a much more consistent predictor of the decision to seek legal advice. Kritzer does not, however, present any synthesis of the results of his comparisons as to which problem categories are most likely to motivate advice-seeking behaviour.

The conclusion that 'problem type tends to swamp other considerations' is supported in multivariate analyses by Genn,[53] and elaborated

50 Pascoe Pleasence, Nigel Balmer, and Stian Reimers, 'Horses for Courses? People's Characterisation of Justiciable Problems and the Use of Lawyers' in *The Future of Legal Services*, papers presented at the Future of Legal Services Conference, ed. Legal Services Board (London, 14 June 2010), at 37, http://www.legalservicesboard. org.uk/news%5Fpublications/publications/pdf/14_june_conference_papers.pdf [Pleasence, Balmer, and Reimers, 'Horses for Courses?'].

51 H.M. Kritzer, 'To Lawyer or Not to Lawyer: Is That the Question?' (2008) 5 *Journal of Empirical Legal Studies* 875.

52 Kritzer also refers to a multivariate analysis from an unpublished study comparing lawyer use in Australia and the United States, which tends to support his conclusions: *ibid.* at 898.

53 Genn, *Paths to Justice, supra* note 4 at 141.

in more detail in a recent two-country study by Pleasence and Balmer using data from England and Wales and from New Zealand.[54] In a brief survey of the international literature, Pleasence and Balmer note that family breakdown, housing problems, and wills/probate are generally associated with a high incidence of lawyer consultation. But variation also exists between national jurisdictions. For example, whereas negligent accidents are associated with seeking legal advice in Canada and the United Kingdom, this is not the case in Japan, Australia, and New Zealand.[55]

Pleasence and Balmer go on to provide statistical models of the predictors of advice-seeking behaviour in the 2006 New Zealand and 2006–7 England and Wales civil justice surveys. They find that age has an impact on the decision to seek advice, with 25 to 59 year olds more likely than 18 to 24 year olds to obtain non-legal advice (when compared to not seeking advice at all). Also, female respondents were more likely to seek any type of advice compared to men, especially non-legal advice. The same was true of respondents who were members of racialized groups. These individuals were more likely to obtain advice compared to members of non-racialized groups.

Notably, in contrast to Kritzer's finding that income has little impact on advice-seeking behaviour, Pleasence and Balmer find that income is a significant predictor, with high income individuals more likely to obtain legal advice than individuals in the middle income group. Low income individuals were also more likely to seek legal advice compared to middle income individuals – although this prediction was not found to be statistically significant.[56] Pleasence and Balmer's study therefore tentatively suggests a U-shaped distribution of advice-seeking behaviour with respect to income, with those in high and low income groups more frequently consulting lawyers compared to those in the middle income range. The authors point out that an area for future research may be to explore the influence of problem type by income interactions on advice-seeking behaviour.

Pleasence and Balmer's study also confirms prior research that problem type heavily influences the propensity to seek advice. Family, housing/land, and employment problems were the most likely problems leading to legal advice in New Zealand and England and Wales. As

---

54 Pleasence and Balmer, 'Advice Seeking,' *supra* note 4.
55 *Ibid.* at 5.
56 *Ibid.* at 9 and 11.

well, problems related to immigration, mental health, and unfair police treatment were associated with using a lawyer in England and Wales. In New Zealand and in England and Wales, problems with social assistance benefits were most likely to lead to non-legal advice seeking. Neighbourhood problems in England and Wales were also linked to seeking non-legal advice.[57]

Coumarelos *et al.* also report on advice-seeking behaviour from the 2006 civil legal needs survey in New South Wales, Australia.[58] Human rights problems were the strongest predictor of advice seeking; consumer problems, personal injury, employment, and wills and estates were also found to be statistically significant. One difference of note in the New South Wales results is that experiences of two significant problem types – consumer and human rights issues – were found to actually decrease the likelihood of an individual seeking legal advice. All significant problem types identified by Pleasence and Balmer increased the likelihood of seeking legal advice.

The demand-side picture of civil justice systems that starts to emerge from comparing legal needs surveys contains several common elements or insights, but also continues to raise key questions about the links between the kinds of problems that individuals experience, their responses to these events, and their underlying social and economic conditions and demographic characteristics. Our analysis of the Ontario survey results, below, reinforces both parts of this picture. Some of our observations are consistent with the international literature, while others diverge noticeably and add to outstanding questions about how individuals interact with and perceive access to civil justice services.

III. OCLNP Survey Data Description

During June 2009, the OCLNP contracted with Environics Research

---

57 *Ibid.* at 11. In a separate, unpublished study using Internet survey data from the United Kingdom, Pleasence tests the hypothesis that individuals' own characterizations of a problem as 'legal' or 'non-legal' will influence their decision to seek advice from a lawyer. While his findings appear to be preliminary, Pleasence finds some support for this hypothesis in the U.K. data. For example, he finds that when problems related to homeownership were characterized by respondents as 'non-legal,' 11 per cent looked to lawyers for advice, while 55 per cent looked to lawyers when these same problems where characterized as 'legal': see Pleasence, Balmer, and Reimers, 'Horses for Courses?', *supra* note 50.

58 Coumarelos, 'Justice Made to Measure,' *supra* note 22.

to collect quantitative telephone survey data from 2,000 residents of Ontario, aged eighteen or older, with household incomes less than $75,000. The OCLNP survey employed an open-ended format in which respondents were asked if they or anyone in their household experienced problems or issues for which they did or did not seek legal assistance. Respondents were then asked to identify problem types without being prompted or presented with a list of possible categories. The OCLNP survey also contained a number of questions regarding individuals' perceptions of the fairness and efficacy of the civil justice system and their satisfaction with problem resolution strategies.

Three potentially significant differences between the OCLNP data and survey data from other jurisdictions are worth noting. First, the Ontario results are restricted to low and middle income households, whereas surveys in most other countries, as well as the Canadian national survey, conducted a random sampling of households. The latter therefore contain responses from all income groups, whereas the Ontario data exclude those from households with a combined income over $75,000. An exception is the 2006 civil legal needs survey from New South Wales, reported by Coumarelos *et al.*, which targeted six disadvantaged areas within the state – three suburban areas of Sydney, a large provincial centre, a coastal rural area, and a remote rural area.[59] The survey results from the New South Wales study may therefore represent the closest analogue to our data from Ontario.

Second, the survey methodology employed in the OCLNP survey may have led to less specificity in respondents' answers when identifying and characterizing their experience of justiciable events. The OCLNP survey method diverged considerably from the one developed in the original *Paths to Justice* project. Ontarians were asked to identify justiciable events without being provided with a list of possible problem types. In other surveys, respondents were presented with a menu of justiciable events and asked to select those, if any, that matched their experience. In the 2006 Canadian survey, for example, respondents were asked to identify problems that they 'felt were serious and difficult to resolve' from a list of fifteen potential problem types.[60] Each problem type included a list of examples or descriptors to prompt the

---

59 These areas were selected using a risk score for cumulative socio-economic disadvantage: see *ibid.* at 51–2.
60 The DOJ 2006 survey also included an 'other' category for which respondents could
   specify their own problem type and description.

respondent. Similar methods were employed in the United Kingdom, New Zealand, and New South Wales. This difference in survey design likely influenced the frequency and type of justiciable events cited by respondents.

Third, the OCLNP survey asked respondents to identify justiciable events experienced either by themselves *or by someone in their household.* This aspect of civil legal needs surveys varies considerably between jurisdictions. For example, respondents in the United Kingdom were asked to report only their own experiences, whereas the Canadian national survey queried events experienced by the respondent or their partner. The Ontario survey therefore likely captured the widest range of experience by including the problems encountered by all members of a given household.

Respondent characteristics by population frequency for the OCLNP data are provided in Table 2.4.[61]

More than one-third (35 per cent) of Ontarians surveyed reported that they had experienced one or more legal problems in the three years prior to the OCLNP survey.[62] Of the total respondents, 26 per cent experienced one problem, while the number of individuals experiencing two problems (7 per cent), three problems (3 per cent), and four or more problems (1 per cent) dropped off considerably.

The frequencies with which Ontarians experienced specific problem types are summarized in Table 2.5. Problems with family relationships were by far the most prevalent, with over 12 per cent of respondents reporting issues in this category. Surprisingly, legal problems associated with money and debt, consumer issues, and neighbourhood issues were relatively infrequent. Comparing these percentages with frequencies from other jurisdictions in Table 2.6, we find that the OCLNP results are noticeably at variance with the more closely matched frequencies

---

61 Note that the frequencies reported in this table are percentages of total respondents. Columns may not total to 100 per cent as the result of some respondents declining to provide an answer to some questions regarding demographics and socio-economic characteristics.

62 These statistics represent the number of respondents who experienced one or more legal problems who either did or did not seek some form of assistance to resolve their problem. 22 per cent of respondents experienced a legal problem and actually sought some form of legal assistance: see Environics Research Group, *Civil Legal Needs of Lower and Middle-income Ontarians Quantitative Research* (Toronto: Ontario Civil Legal Needs Project, 2009) at 19.

Table 2.4. OCLNP respondent characteristics by population frequency

Characteristic	%	Characteristic	%	Characteristic	%
Gender		Marital Status		Education	
Male	43.9	Married	44.9	None	0.5
Female	56.1	Single	27.4	Elementary	9.8
		Widowed	9.5	High school	36.2
		Separated	5.5	Postsecondary	37.9
		Divorced	10.9	Postgraduate	13.8
Language (Primary)		Employment Status		Region	
English	98.8	Full-time	32.9	City of Toronto	18.5
French	1.2	Part-time	11.0	Outer GTA	19.6
		Unemployed	13.6	Eastern Ontario	15.0
		Self-employed	7.6	Central Ontario	10.0
		Student	3.8	Hamilton/Niagara	8.0
		Retired	24.1	Western Ontario	19.0
		Disability Pension	4.4	Northern Ontario	10.0
Age Category		Household Income		Country of Birth	
18 to 29	16.3	Under $10k	5.9	Canada	76.0
30 to 44	22.5	$20k-$30k	13.7	United States	1.8
45 to 59	32.2	$30k-$40k	13.9	Other	21.1
60 or older	29.1	$40k-$50k	15.8	N/A	1.2
		$50k-$60k	14.2		
		Over $60k	17.5		
Aboriginal	4.6	Disabled	17.5	Racial Minority	11.0

between legal problem types in Canada as a whole, England and Wales, and New Zealand.

A main reason for differences in the Ontario data with respect to problem type frequencies may be derived from the differences in survey design discussed above. Because the OCLNP survey did not prompt respondents with a definitive list of legal problem types, some of the more common issues in other surveys, such as consumer, money and debt, and neighbourhood problems, may not have been recognized by Ontario respondents as 'legal' problems. That observation is not, of course, intended to diminish the utility of the Ontario survey results. Each of the legal needs surveys discussed above yields results – along with their attendant policy responses – that are, to some extent, constructed by the questions they ask. We leave a rigorous exploration of these consequences to future research, but draw attention to methodo-

Table 2.5. Frequency of problem types in OCLNP data

Problem Type	Ontario (OCLNP 2009)	
	% Total Sample	N
Family relationship	12.1	242
Wills/power of attorney	5.6	103
Housing/land	4.2	83
Real estate transactions	3.5	69
Employment	3.2	63
Criminal problems	2.6	51
Personal injury	2.2	43
Money/debt	1.5	29
Legal action	1.2	23
Neighbourhood/property	1.1	22
Consumer	0.8	15
Disability-related	0.8	15
Discrimination	0.6	12
Immigration	0.6	11
Welfare/social assistance	0.5	10
Small/personal business	0.4	7
Hospital treatment/release	0.3	6

logical differences here as an aid for interpreting the OCLNP data in context of the international literature discussed earlier.

In addition to being the most frequently cited legal problem type in Ontario, family problems were identified as being the most serious issue experienced by the greatest number of respondents (30 per cent). Other problem types that were cited as the most serious by a relatively significant proportion of individuals were wills and powers of attorney (12.5 per cent), real estate transactions (8.8 per cent), and personal injury problems (6.3 per cent).

In terms of individuals' responses to legal problems, Ontarians were first asked to report if they had experienced one or more legal problems for which they had sought legal advice in the past three years, without being provided with possible definitions or sources of 'legal advice.' Individuals' responses to this question should therefore be interpreted to give 'legal advice' the broadest possible interpretation. Approximately one in seven Ontarians who experienced a civil legal problem and who recognized that they needed legal assistance did not seek any, but overall, legal advice was sought for 65.4 per cent of the

Table 2.6. Frequency of problem types in Canada, the United Kingdom, and New Zealand

Canada[i] Problem Type	%	N	England and Wales[ii] Problem Type	%	N	New Zealand[iii] Problem Type	%	N*
Consumer	22.0	1469	Consumer	13.3	748	Consumer	10.4	748
Money/debt	20.4	1356	Neighbours	8.4	471	Money/debt	8.1	583
Employment	17.8	1184	Money/debt	8.3	465	Welfare Benefits	6.7	482
Wills and powers of attorney	5.3	348	Employment	6.1	344	Housing or land	5.8	417
Relationship breakdown	3.6	239	Personal injury	3.9	217	Employment	5.4	388
Personal injury	2.9	192	Rented housing	3.8	215	Family/relationship breakdown	4.8	345
Police action	2.0	133	Owned housing	2.4	135	Immigration	0.8	57
Discrimination	1.9	130	Welfare benefits	2.3	127			
Housing	1.7	116	Relationship breakdown	2.2	124			
Hospital treatment/release	1.6	108	Divorce	2.2	122			
Other family	1.4	93	Children	1.9	108			
Welfare benefits	1.2	78	Clinical negligence	1.6	92			
Legal action	1.2	82	Domestic violence	1.6	88			
Disability benefits	1.0	66	Discrimination	1.4	80			
Immigration	0.6	40	Unfair treatment by the police	0.7	38			
			Homelessness	0.6	36			
			Mental health	0.5	26			
			Immigration	0.3	18			

*Estimated from reported frequencies and a total survey population of 7,200.
[i]Currie(2007), [ii]Pleasence et al. (2007), [iii]New Zealand Legal Services Agency (2006)

total legal problems experienced.[63] Among the individuals surveyed, three in ten respondents (29 per cent) had a legal problem for which they had sought some form of legal advice,[64] and within this group of legal advice seekers, two-thirds had engaged a private lawyer. For individuals who sought advice for a non-criminal problem only, the most popular sources of advice were private lawyers (41 per cent), a friend or relative (30 per cent), the Internet (27 per cent), and legal aid (19 per cent).

IV. Methodology

Demographic predictors of problem type have previously been modelled using results from civil legal needs surveys in England and Wales,[65] New South Wales,[66] and Canada.[67] Following these studies, we use a series of binomial logistic regressions to identify statistically significant demographic predictors for all justiciable problems together and for each type of problem individually using the OCLNP data. Each model employs problem type as a dependent binomial (yes/no) variable and includes all or a subset of the demographic predictors as independent binomial or categorical variables. All models estimated using the OCLNP data include a common set of independent variables.[68]

One significant challenge unique to the OCLNP data is the small number of observations recorded for some problem types. An option to address this challenge is to combine two or more problem type categories, using the amalgamated observations as the dependent variable. The points of overlap in these categories, however, are not immediately

---

63 That is, out of a total of 989 legal problems recorded in the survey (with some individuals experiencing more than one legal problem), legal assistance was sought in 647 instances, or 65.4 per cent of the time.

64 This figure is difficult to compare to those of other jurisdictions because interpretations of 'legal advice' likely vary between surveys; however, the Ontario figures likely correspond to the aggregate of legal and non-legal advice in Table 2.3, above, and are therefore on the lower end of the comparable results: New South Wales (51.2 per cent), U.S (51), England and Wales (49.1), the Netherlands (44.1), Canada (33.8), Japan (28.5), and New Zealand (23.6).

65 Pleasence, 'Causes of Action,' *supra* note 19.

66 Coumarelos, 'Justice Made to Measure,' *supra* note 22.

67 Currie, *Legal Problems of Everyday Life*, *supra* note 14.

68 Independent variables included in the models are age, education, marital status, economic status, minority status, Aboriginal status, disability status, recipient of social assistance, and household income.

obvious (see Appendix A for a description of each category, including examples, used in the Ontario survey). One example is to combine employment, money/debt, social assistance, and disability-related benefits into a single category. This strategy may capture a range of problems related to unemployment, personal debt and bankruptcy, and collecting benefits or applying for other forms of social assistance. We find some further support for aggregating problem types in this way from the England and Wales Civil and Social Justice Survey reported in 2004. In this survey the authors identify a cluster of problems that include issues related to social assistance benefits, money/debt, and employment.[69] Combing our four categories yields an aggregate problem type with 108 observations. A model was estimated using this aggregate category and is included in the results, below.

Advice-seeking behaviour was estimated using a mixed-effects binomial logistic regression model with fixed and random effects. This model includes both demographic characteristics of respondents and problem types as predictors of the decision to seek legal advice compared to the decision not to seek legal advice. A mixed-effects model was used to account for the possibility that the OCLNP data are correlated as a result of the fact that some respondents experienced and reported more than one legal problem. These data for justiciable events are therefore 'clustered' for participants. Mixed-effects models are designed to compensate for this type of data structure, by avoiding the false conclusion that independent variables are statistically significant predictors of the outcome when they are in fact insignificant in cases where the data are hierarchically clustered or nested.

Our model treats both demographic characteristics and problem types as fixed effects (i.e., with a fixed set of categorical values) and includes participants as random effects. The mixed-effects model allows us to account for patterns of dependence resulting from the clustered structure of the data and thereby to more accurately identify which predictors of advice-seeking behaviour are statistically significant.

Similar modelling strategies have been employed to analyse advice-seeking behaviour by Coumarelos *et al.* for the New South Wales civil

---

69 Pleasence, 'Causes of Action,' *supra* note 19 at 40. The problem cluster identified in this survey also included consumer transactions, neighbours, housing, and personal injury. Housing problems were not identified in the OCLNP, and we exclude the remaining categories to avoid an overinclusive aggregate problem type that lacks explanatory power.

legal needs survey,[70] and, more recently, by Pleasence and Balmer to compare the results of the England and Wales and New Zealand surveys.[71] We follow closely the method used in New South Wales. We were unable to include a third category of 'non-legal advice' in our outcome variable, since the OCLNP survey captured only reported problems for which a given respondent either sought legal advice or chose not to seek advice at all. By contrast, Pleasence and Balmer were able to compare both legal advice-seeking and non-legal advice-seeking behaviour in estimating their models. Future survey designs in Ontario may wish to expand the response choices to include non-legal advice.

V. Results and Analysis

A. Predictors of Problem Type

Results from the binomial logistic regression analysis used to predict problem type by demographic and socio-economic predictors are presented in Appendix B.

The most striking difference between these results and those observed in other jurisdictions (see Table 2.2, above) is that income does not appear as a significant predictor for any of the problem types in Ontario. By comparison, income was a significant predictor of legal problems in two or more countries for consumer, employment, credit/debt, social assistance, and housing problems. There may be at least three reasons for the anomalous results from Ontario. Since the OCLNP survey was conducted only within low and middle income households, income effects may be attenuated within the sample population. In other words, given a narrower income distribution in the Ontario sample, there may be less variation in problem types experienced across income groups.[72] Results from the analysis of the 2006 New South Wales survey by Coumarelos *et al.*, however, run counter to this explanation. Despite the fact that the New South Wales survey was conducted only in disadvantaged areas, income appears as a significant predictor for four different problem types. Alternatively, the differing results from Ontario with respect to income might again be explained by differences in sur-

---

70 Coumarelos, 'Justice Made to Measure,' *supra* note 22 at 292.
71 Pleasence and Balmer, 'Advice Seeking,' *supra* note 4.
72 Seven income groups were coded in the OCLNP survey data, starting with an 'under $10,000 per year' category and moving upward in $10,000 increments.

vey design. Since respondents may not have identified issues such as consumer and money/debt problems as 'legal' problems as such, these issues may have gone underreported in the OCLNP data. We speculate that if this pattern of underreporting is more prevalent for lower income groups, perhaps because of issues related to access to information or perceptions of the legal system, the Ontario sample may be biased in this respect.

A final possibility is that the small number of legal problems reported in certain categories, such as consumer and social assistance problem types, may lead to inaccurate estimations from the specified models. We note that our strategy of aggregating problem type categories may correct for these inaccuracies, although income does not appear as a significant predictor for the employment and social assistance benefits category that we specified.

B. Predictors of Advice-Seeking Behaviour

Our hierarchical model identified four significant predictors of the decision to seek legal advice, against the choice not to seek any advice. These results are reported in Appendix C. All four significant predictors are problem types – criminal, family, wills and powers of attorney, and real estate problems – while none of the demographic or socio-economic variables in our model yielded statistically significant estimates.[73] Experiencing each of the four problem types identified as significant predictors increased the likelihood that individuals would seek legal advice.

Our results are comparable to those obtained using data from New South Wales, reported by Coumarelos *et al.*, and from England and Wales and New Zealand, reported by Pleasence and Balmer. In New South Wales, accident and injury, consumer, employment, human rights, and wills and estates problems were all identified as significant predictors of the decision to seek legal advice. In New Zealand, employment, housing, money and debt, and family problems were significant, while in England and Wales predictors included welfare benefit issues

---

73 We include the criminal problem type as a predictor in our model, even though criminal problems themselves clearly fall outside the category of civil justice needs. It is worthwhile to note, for comparative purposes, that an individual's experience of criminal justice problems is one of the few significant predictors of advice-seeking behaviour overall.

as well as housing, family, personal injury, mental health, and immigration problems.

As noted above, Pleasence and Balmer were able to compare advice-seeking behaviour for legal and non-legal advice, whereas the structure of OCLNP survey made this type of analysis unavailable. Briefly, these authors found that in New Zealand, welfare benefits problems were most associated with non-legal advice, as were employment and housing problems. In England and Wales, welfare benefits and employment problems were also linked to non-legal advice. Neighbour problems were also linked to non-legal advice in this jurisdiction.

Overall, our results provide the strongest support for the hypothesis that problem type tends to be an overriding indicator of advice-seeking behaviour, compared to other studies that have considered this question. Similar to our results, Pleasence and Balmer's study found that very few demographic and socio-economic variables were significant predictors of advice-seeking behaviour once problem types were included in the model. This was, however, a more consistent finding for seeking legal advice compared to seeking non-legal advice, where age in particular appeared to be a significant predictor both in England and Wales and in New Zealand. The results from New South Wales provide somewhat less support for the hypothesis that problem type is an overriding predictor, given that age, education and Indigenous status were still found to be statistically significant predictors of advice-seeking behaviour when included with legal problem types.

VI. Conclusions

Our survey of the international literature on national and sub-national civil legal needs surveys reveals a number of common trends in kinds of problems that individuals experience, the frequency with which they experience these problems, and their responses to particular problem types. Moreover, a growing body of work that seeks to uncover some of the significant demographic and socio-economic predictors of problem types and advice-seeking behaviour has begun to shade in our picture of civil legal needs in different countries, which has been outlined in earlier empirical studies. Comparative evidence also suggests that some important puzzles – such as whether and how household income influences individuals' experiences of civil legal systems – remain unresolved. A common theoretical approach based on the demands of individual users links many of these legal needs surveys together and provides a shared foundation from which to build on lessons and experiences across jurisdictions.

We set out to address two research questions in this comparative analysis of data from the civil legal needs survey of low and middle income Ontarians. First, we asked which legal problems respondents experienced most frequently and which individual-level characteristics best predicted these problem types. The profile of the Ontario data is unique in comparison to other civil legal needs surveys, with a much higher incidence of family relationship problems and a lower incidence of problems that are common in other jurisdictions, in particular consumer, money and debt, and neighbourhood problems. This variation is likely the result of differences in survey design that made it more difficult for respondents in the Ontario survey to identify some problems as justiciable events.

The most striking finding from our analysis of problem types using individual-level predictors was the absence of income effects in almost every problem category, except for reported real estate problems and our aggregate class of employment and benefits problems. These results suggest that within the survey group of low and middle income Ontarians (under $75,000 household income per annum), variations in income level are statistically insignificant in predicting the kinds of problems these individuals experience. We are cautious, however, about extrapolating more general conclusions about the significance of household income from this analysis, given that a random population sample from all income groups may yield different results.

Second, we asked whether there are identifiable patters of advice-seeking behaviour based on respondent characteristics and the types of problems they experience. Our results support recent findings from other countries that demographic and socio-economic factors are likely to be less significant predictors of advice seeking behaviour compared to problem types. Criminal, family, wills and estates, and real estate problems were all statistically significant in estimates of the choice to seek legal advice in Ontario compared to the decision not to seek legal advice. Experiencing a problem in each of these categories increased the likelihood that an individual would seek legal advice. None of the demographic or socio-economic characteristics were found to be significant, once problem type was accounted for in our model.

The insight that 'problem type tends to swamp other considerations' is not, however, a very satisfactory explanation of advice-seeking behaviour, particularly from a policy-making perspective. As researchers from the United Kingdom have recently noted, the observation[74]

> [t]hat people who have suffered personal injuries through negligence more often go to lawyers is not explained by the fact that they have experienced personal injuries. There must be something lying beneath; something about the people who suffer personal injuries, the nature of personal injuries, people's understanding of lawyers or the law in relation to personal injuries, or the type or range of services that solicitors offer.

The challenge for future research on civil legal needs surveys will be to identify techniques that can help further explain the underlying determinants of advice-seeking behaviour. One approach suggested by research in the United Kingdom is to include survey questions that ask respondents to characterize each problem type as either 'legal' or 'non-legal.' The resulting data can then be included in statistical models as an explanatory variable that helps capture individuals' understandings about the nature of justiciable events.[75] Alternatively, there may be opportunities to develop analytical approaches that take advantage of variations in existing survey methodologies to explore how survey results differ depending on the types of questions asked and the various meanings associated with terms such as 'legal advice.'

Finally, some of the methodological challenges associated with analysing the OCLNP data reveal possible lessons for designing future surveys. We suggest that standardizing the categories of problem types – perhaps to bring them more closely in line with periodic or continuous studies being carried out in Canada nationally, in England and Wales, and elsewhere – would greatly improve researchers' opportunities to undertake comparative work. By contrast, when survey respondents are asked open-ended questions about their experiences of legal problems, which are subsequently coded or categorized by the surveyor, the resulting data may prove to be less useful for cross-national comparisons. On the other hand, we recognize that legal needs surveys are frequently designed to meet the purposes of specific policy contexts and that 'standardizing' survey designs will not be feasible in all cases.

---

74 Pleasence, Balmer, and Reimers, 'Horses for Courses?' *supra* note 50 at 38.
75 *Ibid.*

We also suggest that future surveys be designed to capture at least three distinctive responses to problems in terms of advice-seeking behaviour: the choice to seek legal advice, the choice to seek non-legal advice, and the choice not to seek any type of advice. Within these categories, it may also be possible to explore more nuanced understandings of advice-seeking behaviour – for example, by focusing on specific sources of legal and non-legal advice. Lastly, we suggest that the OCLNP may wish to follow the lead of the Legal Services Commission in England and Wales by setting a long-term agenda to implement periodic or continuous surveys, and perhaps to design a panel survey that tracks the experiences of specific individuals over time. Recognizing that panel surveys are more complex and will therefore need to be more heavily resourced, the resulting data would provide a rich source of information for future research. These and other innovations in civil legal needs surveys will undoubtedly provide valuable inputs into policy-making processes in Ontario that address the continuing challenge of improving access to civil justice for all Ontarians.

Appendix A

Problem Type Category Descriptions from the OCLNP

The following is a list of problem type categories used to code responses from the OCLNP survey.

ID	Problem type	Description/examples
1	Consumer problems	Purchasing faulty goods or appliances, receiving incorrect or misleading information, being overcharged for goods and services, etc.
2	Employment problems	Job loss, harassment, bullying or discrimination, difficulty collecting employment benefits or Employment Insurance, etc.
3	Money or debt problems	Inability to make payments, personal bankruptcy, collecting a debt, etc.
4	Welfare or social assistance problems	Seeking or obtaining benefits, reduction in benefits, difficulty with a benefit company or government agency, etc.
5	Housing or land problems	Landlord–tenant problems, eviction, foreclosure etc.
6	Immigration problems	Difficulty with government agencies, obtaining proper documents and papers, threatened deportation, etc.
7	Discrimination/harassment problems	Racial, ethnic, gender-based discrimination and/or harassment involving housing or services, etc.
8	Criminal problems	Being questioned, charged with an offence or arrested, etc.
9	Family relationship problems	Divorce or separation, child custody or access, division of property, support payments, domestic violence, etc.)
10	Wills and powers of attorney problems	Writing a will, managing the affairs of someone unable to do so on their own, managing the estate of a deceased person, etc.
11	Personal injury problems	Car accident, slip and fall, medical malpractice, a dog bite, etc.
12	Hospital treatment or release problems	Patient's rights or mental health issues, etc.
13	Legal action problems	Being sued or receiving letters threatening to sue or wanting to sue someone, etc.
14	Disability-related issues	n/a
15	Neighbourhood problems and property damage	n/a
16	Real estate transactions	n/a
17	Small or personal business issues	Issues relating to incorporation, partnerships, and sole proprietorships, copyright and intellectual property

Appendix B

Binomial Logistic Regression Results: Predictors of Problem Type

						PROBLEM TYPE				
Independent variable	Level	Wills	Personal injury	Hospital	Legal action	Disability	Neighbour	Real estate	Small business	Aggregate
		10	11	12	13	14	15	16	17	(2+3+4+14)
Age	30–44	.319	-.557	12.124	-.293	15.617	-.935	.504	-.903	.739
	45–59	.803 (0.424)**	-.653	12.154	.402	15.869	1.035	.488	-.924	1.184 (0.378)*
	60+	.135	-1.023	14.012	-.615	14.444	1.252	.090	-2.337	-.001
Education	Grades 7–8	-.754	-.161	2.681	.252	.543	-18.203	17.623	-.376	-1.467
	Grades 9–11	17.144	16.350	18.239	16.097	16.825	-.734	17.711	-.400	-1.607
	Grades 12–13	17.661	17.596	18.753	16.128	.416	-1.674	17.195	15.435	-1.694
	Some college	18.000	18.105	3.097	17.139	16.787	-.693	16.897	14.156	-1.078
	College	17.221	17.923	18.440	16.805	15.433	-1.395	17.898	14.652	-1.054
	Some university	18.350	16.714	2.639	17.103	18.241	-.940	17.320	14.931	-.346
	University	18.257	17.331	18.665	16.942	16.795	-1.223	17.491	13.540	-.934
	Postgraduate	18.099	17.174	2.470	17.284	17.381	-1.261	17.847	14.222	-1.255
Marital status	Single	.125	.027	1.977	.207	-.392	.621	.139	-1.021	.280
	Widowed	.871 (0.364)*	-.047	2.110	.225	.832	-.116	.420	-15.609	-.173
	Separated	.259	.521	-14.438	-.612	-.059	.448	.800 (0.456)**	-16.147	.310
	Divorced	-.760	-.225	1.531	-.514	.138	-.037	-.835	.168	.092
Employment	Part-time	.172	.326	-.443	.901	.725	.288	-.413	.236	.642 (0.363)**

Binomial Logistic Regression Results: Predictors of Problem Type (*concluded*)

Independent variable	Level	Wills	Personal injury	Hospital	Legal action	Disability	Neighbour	Real estate	Small business	Aggregate
						PROBLEM TYPE				
	Unemployed	.208	.953 (0.548)**	-.287	-16.207	.628	.865	-.114	-16.168	1.176 (0.341)*
	Unemployed (not seeking)	.609	.892	16.466	.278	.418	.589	.282	2.345 (0.708)*	.056
	Self-employed	-1.090	.874	14.452	1.147	1.562	.323	-.359	-15.732	1.040 (0.456)*
Income	Student	.091	-17.351	2.583	-16.628	-15.729	-16.018	.042	-16.591	.367
	Retired	.475	.383	12.701	.699	1.277	.031	.041	.180	.605
	Disability pension	1.202 (0.564)*	-1.145	15.435	1.245	.894	-.004	-18.206	-15.497	1.171 (0.484)*
	$10k to $20k	.551	.208	-.427	16.334	-.679	-17.551	-.378	-.098	-.035
	$20k to $30k	.091	-.483	.083	16.883	-1.572	-.201	-1.178	16.333	-.042
	$30k to $40k	-.046	-.702	1.373	17.050	-.919	-.104	.733	15.052	-.143
	$40k to $50k	-.203	-.627	-13.389	17.538	-16.044	.925	.615	15.530	-.543
	$50k to $60k	.007	-.554	1.395	17.744	.047	.637	.770	15.580	.037
	Over $60k	.353	-.095	-13.498	17.319	-.731	-.186	.668	14.724	-.294
Social assistance		-.677 (0.347)**	-1.536 (0.536)*	1.280	.221	1.245	.508	-.422	-.334	.268
Aboriginal		-1.318	-.211	2.025	.350	.699	1.209	-1.189	-15.605	.054
Disability		-.147	1.604 (0.411)*	1.237	.706	1.799 (0.957)**	1.219 (0.578)*	.548	.346	-.058
Minority		-.334	.365	.097	-17.041	.430	-.272	.267	.505	.359
Constant		-21.367	-20.804	-53.385	-38.716	-38.483	-4.925	-21.524	-33.856	-2.875

'Problem type' is the dependent variable for each model. Regression coefficients for the independent variables are reported in the table, standard errors in parentheses; *p ≤ 0.05; **p ≤ 0.10.

Appendix C

Mixed-Effects Regression Results: Predictors of Advice-Seeking Behaviour

Parameter	β	S.E.	Sig.
Intercept	1.8355*	0.7669	0.0167
Demographic and socio-economic characteristics			
No education	46.4007	0.0000	–
Elementary	−1.0054	0.9178	0.2733
High school	−1.1053	0.6274	0.0781
Postsecondary	−1.0878	0.6180	0.0784
Age (18–29)	−0.3932	0.6733	0.5593
Age (30–44)	−0.1934	0.6104	0.7514
Age (45–59)	−0.8363	0.5637	0.1379
Disability status	0.1353	0.4614	0.7693
Minority status	−0.9532	0.5544	0.0855
Received Social Security	−0.7757	0.4287	0.0704
Problem type			
Employment	0.1278	0.6960	0.8543
Money/debt	1.0371	0.9115	0.2552
Social assistance benefits	0.9756	1.5089	0.5179
Housing	0.6704	0.6210	0.2803
Immigration	1.9164	1.5756	0.2239
Discrimination	0.4901	1.4862	0.7416
Criminal	2.0609*	0.8387	0.0140
Family	1.8493*	0.5032	0.0002
Wills and estates	2.5968*	0.7381	0.0004
Personal injury	1.6049	0.8406	0.0562
Hospital claim	1.6923	1.9104	0.3757
Legal action	1.8185	1.1655	0.1187
Disability	31.0625	0.0000	–
Neighbour	−1.2525	1.3174	0.3417
Real estate	3.8660*	1.1048	0.0005
Small business	0.3825	1.3923	0.7835
Random effects			
Intercept	14.4003*	3.3676	0.0000

Dependent variable is 'decision to seek legal advice (versus not seeking advice)'; *p ≤ 0.05.

PART 3

'Front-End' Proactive Solutions

3 Front-End Strategies for Improving Consumer Access to Justice

ANTHONY DUGGAN AND IAIN RAMSAY

I. Introduction

Access to civil justice is not exclusively a poverty-related concern. In other words, the problem is not just that some people cannot afford to pay legal fees, but also that legal costs are often high relative to the amount in dispute so that it becomes uneconomical for the claimant to take her case to court regardless of how poor or wealthy she may be. The bottom line is that typically it makes no sense to litigate small to medium-sized claims in the traditional way.[1] The problem affects civil disputes across the board, but surveys in Ontario and elsewhere suggest that unmet legal needs are highest in the areas of family, employment, and consumer and debtor–creditor law.[2]

Ontario, in common with most other jurisdictions, has various measures in place to ameliorate the access to justice problem. In the consumer disputes area, perhaps the most prominent of these are the small claims court and the class action procedure.[3] However, neither of these

---

1 See Anthony Duggan, 'Consumer Access to Justice in Common Law Countries: A Survey of the Issues from a Law and Economics Perspective' in *International Perspectives on Consumers' Access to Justice*, ed. Charles E.F. Rickett and Thomas G.W. Telfer (Cambridge: Cambridge University Press, 2003), 46 at 48–50 and works there cited.

2 University of Toronto Faculty of Law, Middle Income Access to Civil Justice Initiative, *Background Paper*, 5, http://www.law.utoronto.ca/documents/conferences2/AccessToJustice_LiteratureReview.pdf [*Background Paper*].

3 This is not to overlook the numerous industry-specific alternative dispute resolution initiatives operating in Ontario, including ombudsman services and dedicated tribunals, or the dispute-handling function of government agencies such as the Ontario Ministry of Consumer Services' Consumer Protection Branch. For a short account of

initiatives is a 'silver bullet.'[4] The small claims court is used more by business creditors as a debt collection mechanism than it is by consumers as a cheaper form of justice. The complexity of small claims court forms and procedures makes it difficult for consumers to navigate the system themselves; but by the same token, in many cases it will not be worthwhile for the consumer to hire a lawyer.[5] Furthermore, certain types of consumer dispute, such as complaints about billing practices or disputes with credit reporting agencies, are not particularly amenable to small claims court adjudication.[6] The main problem with the class action procedure is that it caters to group or mass claims and is no use to the consumer with an individual complaint. Furthermore, there is a concern that the system tends to favour big cases, where either the class is numerous or class members' individual claims are substantial, because big cases are more profitable for law firms.[7]

Extrapolating from these observations, it can safely be said that, while there is considerable room for improvements on the dispute resolution front, there is no panacea.[8] With this unpalatable truth in mind, it makes sense to think about law reform strategies that might minimize the need for litigation by preventing disputes from arising in the first place. The idea is well captured by Richard Susskind's metaphor of a cliff located in a highly populated area, creating a danger of accidents. The local council is considering a combination of two measures: the first is implementing an ambulance response system at the bottom of the cliff for those who are injured and the second is building a fence at the top of the cliff to prevent accidents.[9] The ambulance response system is a back-end solution to the accident problem in the sense that

---

some of these measures, see *Policy Options with Respect to Consumer and Debtor/Creditor Law*, *infra* this volume, Parts II and IV ['Policy Options Paper'].

4 Jacob Ziegel, 'Canadian Consumer Law and Policies Forty Years Later: A Mixed Report Card' (2011) 50 Can. Bus. L.J. 259 at 292.

5 For a fuller account, see Shelley McGill, 'Small Claims Court Identity Crisis: A Review of Recent Reform Measures' (2010) 49 Can. Bus. L.J. 213; Ziegel, 'Canadian Consumer Law,' *supra* note 4.

6 For the reasons Shelley McGill explains in 'Challenges in Small Claims Court Design: Does One Size Fit All?' *infra* this volume, Part IV.C.

7 For a fuller account, see Jasminka Kalajdzic, 'Consumer (In)Justice: Reflections on Canadian Consumer Class Actions' (2011) 50 Can. Bus. L.J. 356.

8 For a survey of the pros and cons of the various reform options, see Duggan, 'Consumer Access to Justice,' *supra* note 1.

9 Richard Susskind, *The End of Lawyers? Rethinking the Nature of Legal Services* (Oxford: Oxford University Press, 2008) at 231.

it aims to pick up the pieces, so to speak, after the accident has happened. The cliff-top fence is a front-end solution in the sense that it takes effect before the accident happens. In the consumer access to justice context, small claims courts and the like are back-end strategies. Front-end strategies might include (1) consumer education initiatives to help people make better purchasing decisions, (2) statutory disclosure requirements to equip consumers with basic information to help them with transactions, (3) cooling-off periods to give consumers a period of reflection in the immediate aftermath of a transaction and the opportunity to change their minds, (4) behaviour-modifying initiatives to facilitate choices that are consistent with consumers' longer-term or unrevealed preferences, and (5) substantive interventions to protect consumers from potentially welfare-reducing decisions by restricting their range of choices. All these measures are analogous to the cliff-top fence because their aim is to steer consumers away from bad choices and so, in turn, from dissatisfaction and dispute.

In the following sections of this paper, we examine each of these five strategies in the context of consumer credit. In Part II, we consider federal and provincial consumer educational initiatives, with particular reference to the Financial Consumer Agency of Canada's consumer financial literacy program and to the Ontario Consumer Protection Branch. In Part III, we discuss measures requiring disclosure of borrowing cost details and other information in consumer credit contracts and elsewhere. In Part IV, we address the use of cooling-off periods as a mechanism for giving consumers breathing space to absorb truth-in-lending disclosures and to avoid borrowing and credit purchase decisions that turn out to have been unwise. In Part V, we examine the contributions of the behavioural economics literature to the debate over consumer credit regulation. In Part VI, we examine product and supplier regulation, the role of minimum standards, and licensing. We assess the application of better regulation to the implementation and enforcement of consumer law and two regulatory initiatives: the 'treating customers fairly' program in the United Kingdom implemented by the Financial Services Authority (FSA); and the new U.S. Consumer Financial Protection Bureau,[10] an initiative aimed in part at stamping out dangerous financial products in much the same way that the

---

10 See *Dodd-Frank Wall Street Reform and Consumer Protection Act*, Pub. L. No. 111–203, 124 Stat 1376 (2010) (U.S. Dodd–Frank Act).

Consumer Product Safety Commission polices unsafe goods.[11] Part VII concludes.

The paper's focus is consumer credit, but this is simply for illustrative purposes. Our hope is that the options we identify in this relatively narrow area will serve as a springboard for a wider discussion about front-end responses to access to justice concerns across the range of civil disputes where unmet legal needs are high.

II. Consumer Education

A. Introduction

Consumer education may aim to provide consumers with the information and skills they need to shop wisely, or to teach them how to complain effectively on a self-help basis. Consumer education programs may target schoolchildren, the population at large, or groups with special needs such as immigrants or the elderly. The range of delivery methods includes school programs (consumer education may be delivered as part of the regular school curriculum or in the form of special presentations by outside experts or volunteers), adult education courses, handbooks and other forms of literature, and online programs.

In the consumer credit context, consumer education has come to prominence over the past decade or so as a result of the burgeoning financial literacy movement.[12] A key objective of the movement is to

---

11   Elizabeth Warren was a leading proponent of the bureau and the analogy to consumer product safety is hers. Oren Bar-Gill and Elizabeth Warren, 'Making Credit Safer' (2008) 157 U. Pa. L.R. 1.

12   The OECD has been a major player in this development, with the launch in 2003 of its Financial Education Project and a slew of publications in the years since. The aim of the OECD project is to encourage governments to develop regulatory initiatives for the enhancement of financial literacy within their own countries. For a critical review and citations to the main OECD publications, see Toni Williams, 'Empowerment of Whom and For What? Financial Literacy Education and the New Regulation of Consumer Financial Services' (2007) 29 *Law and Policy* 226; see also Iain Ramsay and Toni Williams, 'The Crash That Launched a Thousand Fixes – Regulation of Consumer Credit after the Lending Revolution and the Credit Crunch' in *Law Reform and Financial Markets*, ed. K. Alexander and N. Moloney (Cheltenham: Edward Elgar, 2011) 222 at 234. The Canadian federal government recently released a major report detailing thirty recommendations for improving financial literacy in Canada: Task Force on Financial Literacy, *Canadians and Their Money: Building a Brighter Financial*

empower consumers through the provision of information, the development of financial skills, and the fostering in consumers of a sense of financial responsibility.[13] The claim is that financial literacy will improve consumers' capacity to protect themselves against the risk of poor decisions in the buying and selling of financial products, including both loans and investments. Furthermore, as consumers become better informed and more self-reliant, they will become more active in the market and, as a result, demand for financial products will increase. This latter prospect has prompted many of the larger financial institutions to actively support financial literacy initiatives by partnering with governments in the establishment of programs.

B. Consumer Education in Canada

(1) THE FINANCIAL CONSUMER AGENCY OF CANADA

The Financial Consumer Agency of Canada (FCAC) is at the forefront of the financial literacy movement in Canada.[14] The FCAC is a federal agency established in 2001 with a dual mandate:

Future (Ottawa: December, 2010), http://www.financialliteracyincanada.com. ['Task Force on Financial Literacy Report'].

13 See Williams, 'Empowerment of Whom and For What?', *supra* note 12.

14 *Cf.* 'Task Force on Financial Literacy Report,' *supra* note 12, which among other things recommends an overhaul of current arrangements, including the establishment of a national strategy for financial literacy, the appointment of a Financial Literacy Leader to oversee the national strategy, and the formation of an advisory council on financial literacy. Returning to matters as they presently stand, the FCAC is not the only federal agency with a consumer education mandate, but it is the most active. Other agencies include the Office of Consumer Affairs and the Competition Bureau. The Office of Consumer Affairs is a unit within Industry Canada whose mandate includes disseminating consumer information and awareness tools. It is responsible for the Canadian Consumer Information Gateway, an information clearing house that provides links to a wide range of consumer-related websites. The Competition Bureau is an independent agency within Industry Canada, responsible for dealing with unfair or deceptive business practices, including misleading advertising. It makes information available to consumers on its website. The Consumer Measures Committee has the function of coordinating federal and provincial consumer protection programs and includes representatives of the provincial and territorial consumer protection bodies, the federal Office of Consumer Affairs, and the Competition Bureau. The Consumer Measures Committee's projects include the *Canadian Consumer Handbook*, which is a guide to a wide range of consumer-related issues.

- to expand consumer education and financial literacy so that consumers have the information and skills they need to make informed financial decisions and participate actively in the financial sector; and
- to consolidate and strengthen oversight of consumer protection measures in the federally regulated financial sector.[15]

In response to the first of these mandates, the FCAC has developed two programs, the Consumer Education program and the Financial Literacy program. The Consumer Education program 'seeks to enhance consumers' knowledge of the financial products and services that affect them, as well as their understanding of financial institutions' obligations toward them under federal consumer provisions,' while the Financial Literacy program 'aims to build the skills and confidence they need to better manage their financial affairs, from saving to credit and debt management.'[16]

As part of its Consumer Education program, the FCAC employs a wide range of publications, interactive tools and resources – such as hotlines, mail, and the Internet – and proactive outreach as its main delivery methods.[17] Its publications include the *Credit Cards and You* information series and the booklet *Service Fees on Credit Card Transactions*. Web Tool subjects include credit card and bank account selection, savings accounts, choosing a mortgage, and general management skills. Whereas the Consumer Education program focuses on the provision of information, the Financial Literacy program is skills oriented. It has two main components. The first is a school curriculum called *The City: A Financial Life Skills Resource*, which was developed in partnership with the British Columbia Securities Commission. Subjects include income, expenses and budgets, credit and debt, savings and banking, and financial planning.[18] The second component is a Web portal called *The Money*

---

15 Financial Consumer Agency of Canada, *Annual Report 2009–2010* (Ottawa, 2010) [FCAC, *Annual Report 2009–2010*] at 6. The FCAC's governing statute is the *Financial Consumer Agency of Canada Act*, S.C. 2001, c.9.

16 *Ibid.* at 14.

17 Financial Consumer Agency of Canada, *Annual Report 2008–2009* (Ottawa, 2009), 16.

18 FCAC, *Annual Report 2009–2010 supra* note 15 at 20. *The City* is a Web- and paper-based resource. Students learn from the experiences of eight fictional reality show-type characters, each facing different financial circumstances. There are two components: a classroom resource for teachers and ten interactive, self-directed modules for students.

Belt, which provides access to a range of online resources. It features quizzes, quick tips, teacher tools, and *The City* resource, as well as links to other financial education programs developed by FCAC partners.[19] Other FCAC initiatives include a *Financial Basics* course aimed at post-secondary students with little or no financial training, an adult financial education resource, and, in partnership with the Canadian Bankers Association, the development of *YourMoney*, a free in-class seminar program for high school students delivered by volunteers.[20]

(2) GOVERNMENT CONSUMER AGENCY WEBSITES

Government consumer agencies at both the federal and the provincial level also have a consumer education mandate, which they fulfil in part through the provision of information and advice online and in hardcopy formats. An important initiative of this kind at the federal level is the *Canadian Consumer Handbook*, published by the Consumer Measures Committee.[21] According to the *Consumer Handbook* website, the aim is 'to help you become a better-informed and more confident consumer' and 'to help you build your buying skills.'[22] The *Consumer Handbook* provides plain-language information and advice ('consumer tips') on a wide range of topics, including online shopping, contracts, housing and home renovations, identity theft, and a range of financial matters. Financial topics include collection agencies, contracts, credit reporting, debit card fraud, debt, financial services, and payday lending. The *Handbook* also includes a directory of government and non-government contacts.

The Ontario Consumer Protection Branch (CPB), which is part of the Ministry of Consumer Services, is the agency mainly responsible for administering the province's *Consumer Protection Act*.[23] The CPB's website includes information and advice on a wide range of matters. It provides links to industry-specific regulatory bodies such as the Ontario Motor Vehicle Industry Council, the Real Estate Council, and the Travel Industry Council; information about the most frequent areas of consumer complaint; a 'Consumer Beware' list of firms that have failed to cooperate with the CPB's complaint resolution process; a Consumer

---

19 *Ibid.* at 17, 20.
20 *Ibid.* at 22.
21 On the Consumer Measures Committee, see *supra* note 14.
22 Consumer Measures Committee, *Canadian Consumer Handbook* (Ottawa: Industry Canada), http://www.consumerhandbook.ca/en/about.
23 S.O. 2002, c.30.

Protection Survival Guide, which contains a summary of consumers' rights under the *Consumer Protection Act*; information about how to lodge complaints with the CPB; and chapters on selected specific topics, including payday loans, collection agencies, and motor vehicle repairs.

The CPB also publishes brochures, both online and in print, on many topics, such as buying appliances, cancelling contracts, collection agencies, gift cards, and home renovations. All these publications are in plain English and French, while some are available in a variety of other languages including Italian, Chinese, Vietnamese, Punjabi, and Tamil. As with the *Canadian Consumer Handbook*, the information in these brochures and the Survival Guide is a mix of tips on how to shop wisely, basic information about legal rights on a range of matters, and information and advice on how to lodge complaints. There is some overlap in content between the Handbook and the CPB's publications, but the CPB's publications devote more space to smart shopping, and in this respect they arguably demonstrate a stronger commitment to the prevention philosophy. For example, the Survival Guide's chapter titled 'Smart Consumer Tips' goes beyond urging consumers to read their contracts; it also tells them, among other things, to obtain estimates, to protect their personal information, to avoid 'free' gifts, and to check the ministry's Consumer Beware List before dealing with a supplier. In the same connection, the 'Payday Loans' chapter contains a useful summary of the consumer's rights under the *Payday Loans Act*,[24] followed by some basic information about credit counselling and a link to the Ontario Association of Credit Counselling Services. The CPB's brochures supplement the Survival Guide by providing 'quick tips' on specific transactions, such as buying or repairing home appliances, buying big-ticket items, and car repairs.

C. Assessment

The FCAC operates on a much smaller budget than comparable agencies in other countries and this has forced it to proceed in a relatively 'low-key fashion.'[25] Nevertheless, the agency appears to have made the best of the limited resources available to it, using strategic partnerships, the media, and community outreach to maximize its visibility.[26] A more

---

24 S.O. 2008, c.9.
25 Williams, 'Empowerment of Whom and For What?', *supra* note 12 at 239.
26 FCAC, *Annual Report 2009–2010, supra* note 15 at 19.

fundamental concern – one that applies not just to the FCAC but to the financial literacy movement at large – is that, although 'financial literacy has become part of the discourse of policy makers and the helping professions,' the effectiveness of financial literacy programs remains largely untested.[27] As the World Bank has noted, 'improving financial literacy is a long term process for which little is clearly understood as to what works (and what does not) in improving financial behavior.'[28]

The financial literacy movement proceeds on the basis of the rational actor model in neoclassical economics – namely, that consumers make mistakes because of poor information and that a properly informed consumer will always act in her own best interests. The behavioural economics literature has thrown down a strong challenge to this assumption, suggesting that the problem consumers face is not lack of information, but behavioural biases, including inertia (or *status quo* bias), a tendency to discount longer-term costs and benefits, poor risk assessment capabilities, and inadequate self-control.[29] To the extent this is true, programs aimed predominantly at providing consumers with 'the information and skills they need to make informed financial decisions' may fail to have the desired impact.

In a recent review of evidence on the effectiveness of education in improving financial capability and outcomes in the context of retirement planning, Saul Schwartz found 'mixed results at best.'[30] According to Schwartz, there are two key questions: (1) Does financial education lead to improved financial capability? and (2) Do those with greater financial capability make better financial decisions? The answers are discouraging: financial education programs have not been shown to increase financial knowledge, while improved financial capability

---

27 Ramsay and Williams, 'The Crash That Launched a Thousand Fixes,' *supra* note 12 at 237.

28 World Bank, *Good Practices for Consumer Protection and Financial Literacy in Europe and Central Asia: A Diagnostic Tool* (2008) at 5, quoted in Ramsay and Williams, 'The Crash That Launched a Thousand Fixes' *supra* note 12 at 237. See also Omri-Ben Shahar and Carl E. Schneider, 'The Failure of Mandated Disclosure' (2010), University of Chicago Law School, John M. Olin Law and Economics Research Paper No. 516; and University of Michigan Law School Law and Economics, Empirical Legal Studies Center Paper No. 10-008 (SSRN) at 55, arguing that financial literacy education programs and the like are subject to the same flaws as statutory disclosure requirements (as to which, see Part 3.)

29 See Part V.

30 Saul Schwartz, 'Can Financial Education Improve Financial Literacy and Retirement Planning?', IRPP Study No. 12 (Montreal: Institute for Research on Public Policy, 2010) at 1.

has at best modest positive effects on outcomes. The problem is that, after students leave school, 'it becomes exceedingly difficult to deliver any form of intensive education' and 'it is therefore natural to recommend that financial capability be taught in elementary and secondary schools.' However, 'financial decisions such as saving for retirement or buying a house have little relevance for elementary and secondary school students. This lack of salience means that even if students can be taught about financial matters, they are unlikely to retain the information into their adult years.'[31]

The following conclusions might be drawn: (1) financial literacy programs by themselves are unlikely to substantially improve consumer decision making, so they should be seen as a complement to, not a substitute for, other methods of consumer protection (see further, below); (2) the designers of financial literacy programs should revisit their commitment to the economic rational actor model of consumer decision making and pay closer attention to the lessons from the behavioural economics literature about how people process information and make decisions in real life; and (3) in particular, program designers should address the salience issue by exploring ways of making digestible information and advice available to consumers at times when they are most likely to use it (e.g., at the point of purchase or when they are on the verge of default).[32] In Part III, which deals with contractual disclosures, we offer some more concrete suggestions in this regard.

The FCAC's Consumer Education program aims in part to provide consumers with information they may need in advance of a particular transaction, whereas the Financial Literacy program is more concerned with teaching life skills. Both the CMC's *Consumer Handbook* and the CPB's Survival Guide and other publications focus mainly on the first of these objectives. In this respect, they are subject to the same behavioural concerns as the FCAC's program, but there is also an accessibility issue. The problem is that, while a consumer protection agency may be a natural place to go once a dispute has materialized, it will not occur to many consumers that they should consult the agency or its website in *advance* of the transaction. There is a kind of Catch-22 here: the one smart shopping tip an agency cannot easily provide is to consult the agency's smart shopping tips before buying. Outreach and publicity initiatives may address the problem to some extent, but budg-

---

31 *Ibid.* at 9.
32 *Cf.* 'Task Force on Financial Literacy Report,' *supra* note 12 at 38 and Recommendation 7.

etary and human resource constraints typically limit agencies' efforts in this regard. In any event, many consumers lack access to high-speed Internet services. Slower Internet connections restrict the online content users may view, while consumers who have no Internet access at all must fall back on hardcopy alternatives, which may not be readily available.[33] Yet another concern is comprehensibility: some consumers may not have the necessary literacy or language skills to process the information the agency provides. The CPB, in particular, has worked hard on this front, as the account in Part II.B, above, indicates, but its materials are probably still beyond the comprehension of a significant subset of consumers.

To summarize, consumer education features prominently in federal and provincial government policy as a method for promoting more careful shopping and for avoiding disputes. However, while consumer education may be a useful preventive strategy, it is subject to a number of important limitations: (1) consumers may be disinclined, because of behavioural bias, either to access the educational resource at all or to heed the message if they do; (2) consumers may not be aware of the resource or able to access it easily; and (3) some consumers may be unable, because of learning or language difficulties, to understand the information provided. To date, governments have arguably not taken sufficient account of limitation (1), focusing instead on limitations (2) and (3), with varying degrees of success.[34] Measures to address limitations (2) and (3) include the development of school programs to supplement and reinforce information the agencies provide; publicity and outreach initiatives to increase the visibility of the agency and its programs; and the adoption of clear language principles in framing the message. However, budgetary and other resource constraints limit the amount that can be done on all these fronts.

III. Mandatory Information Disclosure

A. Introduction

Mandatory information disclosure is related to the educational initiatives discussed in Part II; in both cases the aim is to provide the

---

33 See 'Policy Options Paper,' *supra* note 3 at 5–6.
34 *Cf.* 'Task Force on Financial Literacy Report,' *supra* note 12 at 7 and 54, recognizing the 'importance of the environment or "architecture of choice"' and endorsing the adoption of 'nudging' interventions.

consumer with information so that she can make better choices. One difference is that in the one case, the information provider is a third party (a teacher, a financial expert, or a government agency), whereas in the other case, the information is provided by the other contracting party (the credit provider or the supplier, as the case may be). A second difference is that information a consumer may obtain from an education program is typically not transaction specific, whereas mandatory information disclosures are directly relevant to the contract in question. For both these reasons, mandatory information disclosure seems to offer more promise on the salience front. But for reasons we will touch on below, by and large the measure has not lived up to expectations.

Mandatory information disclosure is a prominent component of consumer credit regulation in many countries. The measure in its modern form originated with the U.S. *Consumer Credit Protection Act* enacted in 1968 (the 'Truth in Lending Act')[35] and was quickly imported by many other countries, including Canada.[36] 'Truth in lending' refers to the pre-contractual disclosure of the cost of borrowing stated as a cash figure and as a standardized annual percentage rate (APR). As originally envisaged, the purpose of providing this information was to stimulate comparison shopping for credit, induce competition, and reduce price dispersions in the market. A secondary function was to promote restraint in borrowing by alerting consumers to the true cost of credit.

B. The Timing Problem

The Federal Reserve Board oversees the U.S. truth in lending laws and has conducted periodic studies to test the impact of the legislation on consumers' borrowing habits and interest rate awareness. The results

---

35 *Consumer Credit Protection Act*, 15 U.S.C. §1601 (1968); *Truth in Lending Regulations* ('*Regulation Z*'), 12 C.F.R. §226 (2010).

36 In Canada, there are truth-in-lending laws at both federal and provincial levels. The federal provisions apply to financial institutions under federal government control, primarily banks, credit unions, and insurance companies; they are located in the *Cost of Borrowing Regulations* made pursuant to the statute that regulates the class of institution in question: see, for example, *Cost of Borrowing (Banks) Regulations* S.O.R./2001-101 [*Bank Act Regulations*] made pursuant to the *Bank Act* S.C. 1991, c.46. The Ontario provisions apply to financial institutions other than those under federal government control and are located in regulations made pursuant to the *Consumer Protection Act* S.O. 2002, c.30: O. Reg. 17/05, Part VII ('*CPA Regulation*').

are consistently not very encouraging. They suggest that the legislation has been only moderately successful in stimulating interest rate awareness and not particularly successful in promoting comparison shopping. Similar studies in other countries point to the same conclusions,[37] while the sub-prime mortgage crisis in the United States is a spectacular demonstration of the legislation's shortcomings. Various explanations have been offered for truth in lending's limited success. One is that because the contract document is the primary disclosure vehicle, at least for closed-end contracts (loans and credit sales, as opposed to credit cards and the like), the information reaches the consumer too late to be useful for shopping around; by the time the consumer gets the information, she will already be committed to the transaction, psychologically if not legally.[38] If this is really the problem, a possible response would be to require that the disclosures appear in a separate document. However, unless the legislation goes on to say that the lender may not conclude the contract until a prescribed time after the disclosure date, the initiative is unlikely to be effective.[39] A variation on the same theme might be to enact a cooling-off period following the making of the contract (as to which, see Part IV, below).

C. The Information Overload Problem

Information overload is another traditional explanation for the weak performance of truth in lending laws. Truth in lending disclosures are

---

37 Anthony Duggan and Elizabeth Lanyon, *Consumer Credit Law* (Sydney: Butterworths, 1999) at 86 and studies there cited. See also Ben-Shahar and Schneider, 'The Failure of Mandated Disclosure,' *supra* note 28 at 15; U.K., Financial Services Authority, *Mortgage Market Review* (London, 2009) at 72–77, http://www.fsa.gov.uk/pubs/discussion/dp09_03.pdf.

38 Jonathan M. Landers and Ralph J. Rohner, 'A Functional Analysis of Truth in Lending' (1979) 26 UCLA L. Rev. 711.

39 *Cf.* the *Bank Act Regulations*, *supra* note 36 at s.6(1), which provides that a disclosure statement may be a separate document or part of the credit agreement, and s.6(2.2), which provides that a separate disclosure statement may be provided before entering into the agreement or together with the agreement. Section 7(1) requires two clear days between the initial disclosure statement and the completion of the credit agreement, but this provision only applies if there is a real property mortgage or hypothec and the borrower may waive the benefit. In Ontario, the *Consumer Protection Act*, s.79, provides for delivery of the initial disclosure statement 'at or before the time the borrower enters into the agreement,' while s.70 of the *CPA* Regulation provides that a disclosure statement may be in a separate document or part of another document.

detailed and technical and require a considerable amount of effort on the consumer's part to absorb. In this respect, truth in lending laws resemble the prospectus disclosure requirements in securities legislation; both initiatives confront readers with the challenge of wading through a mass of detail and sorting the wheat from the chaff. Recently enacted amendments to the Canadian federal cost of borrowing regulations attempt to address this concern by providing for a summary box in credit contracts and application forms that prominently sets out key features, including the annual percentage rate and fees.[40] This is a promising development as far as it goes, but it encourages the reader to ignore the disclosures outside the box, which in turn raises a question about the continued utility of these additional items.

D. Consumer Irrationality

In common with the consumer education initiatives described in Part II, truth in lending laws presuppose a rational consumer and assume that lack of information is the only reason for poor credit choices. Again, the behavioural economics literature casts doubt on these assumptions and, at the same time, suggests a more fundamental reason for the failure of truth in lending. We elaborate on in this concern and possible responses to it in Part V.

E. Post-Contractual Disclosure

Truth in lending laws focus on the front end of the contract; the aim is to help the consumer find the best deal, or at least to avoid bad deals. However, consumer credit laws typically require disclosure at the back end of the contract as well when things go wrong and the consumer is in default. The traditional approach is to require the credit provider to give the consumer a notice before taking enforcement action and to provide the consumer with information about the state of the account at various stages of the enforcement process. However, in an interesting development, the U.K. *Consumer Credit Act* 1974 also provides that any arrears or default notice must be accompanied by an Information Sheet in the prescribed form. The Arrears Information Sheet urges the consumer to contact the credit provider, provides information about sources of financial advice with links and phone numbers, and includes

---

40 See, for example, *Bank Act Regulations, supra* note 36 at s.6 (2.1–2.4).

basic financial and legal advice. The Default Information Sheet urges the consumer to read the default notice carefully, advises the consumer to get help, and explains the consequences of failing to act. Like the Arrears Information Sheet, it also provides information about where the consumer can get free help and advice.

As discussed in Part II, the Ontario Consumer Protection Branch, in common with other consumer agencies across Canada, provides advice and information on its website about a wide range of consumer matters. This is a worthwhile initiative as far as it goes, but the challenge is to make consumers aware of the facility and to encourage them to use it. The U.K. measure suggests another, perhaps more promising initiative, at least for some types of consumer problems: the mandatory disclosure approach ensures that the consumer gets the information and it does not depend on the consumer's taking the initiative to go looking for it. Moreover, while consumers cannot be forced to act on the advice contained in the Information Sheet, the urgency of the document's language at least impresses on them the importance of doing so.

A similar technique might work for some front-end contractual problems as well. For example, in Canada there are currently only minimal cost of credit disclosure requirements for credit advertising: the APR and other basic information must be disclosed, but the requirement is only triggered if the advertisement makes some mention of the interest rate. Furthermore, if the credit provider offers different rates depending on the type of loan or the borrower's profile, it is sufficient to state a representative rate.[41] Advertising disclosure has the advantage of timeliness, but the credit provider can avoid the requirements by being careful not to make a triggering statement. Furthermore, a representative rate is not necessarily reliable information for comparison shopping purposes. A possible solution, building on the idea described above, might be to require the disclosure in consumer credit advertisements of contact details for free online or telephone advice about comparative credit costs, budgeting, and other matters relevant to the loan under consideration.[42] The same technique could perhaps be employed for

---

41 See for example, the *Bank Act Regulations, supra* note 36 at ss.19–21; and *CPA Regulations,* s.61.

42 The Task Force on Financial Literacy Report recommends the establishment of a single-source website for financial literacy: *supra* note 12 at Recommendation 18. If this initiative materializes, it could be used as the basis for the recommendation in the text.

some of the other matters the CPB addresses on its website. For example, payday lenders could be required to disclose, in advertising, store signs, and contracts, the link to the CPB website, as could auto mechanics, retailers of big-ticket items, and so on.

IV. Cooling-Off Periods

A. Introduction

A cooling-off period allows the consumer to terminate a contract within a prescribed time – usually a few days – after the agreement date, without having to provide a justification.[43] In Ontario, the *Consumer Protection Act*, Part IV, enacts a ten-day cooling-off period for direct sale agreements (door-to-door sales), time share agreements, personal development agreements, credit repair agreements, and loan broker agreements, while the *Payday Loans Act* gives borrowers a two-day cooling-off period.[44] Other jurisdictions go further: in New York, for example, there are cooling-off periods for automobile purchases, telephone sales, dating service agreements, and so on, while in California, examples include mobile telephone contracts, funeral contracts, dental service contracts, and dance studio subscriptions.[45]

B. The Costs and Benefits of Cooling-Off Periods

Rekaiti and Van den Bergh identify three kinds of inefficiency a cooling-off period may help to address: (1) irrational consumer behaviour, (2) situational monopoly, and (3) information asymmetry. High-pressure selling techniques, as employed by some door-to-door sellers, are one cause of consumer irrationality. A consumer who is pressured into making a purchase may regret her decision later. In most contractual settings, the consumer's intention at the date of contracting is the key factor, but pressure may distort the consumer's decision-making proc-

---

43 Pamaria Rekaiti and Roger Van den Bergh, 'Cooling-Off Periods in the Consumer Laws of the EC Member States: A Comparative Law and Economics Approach' (2000) 23 *Journal of Consumer Policy* 371. See also Horst Eidenmuller, 'Why Withdrawal Rights?' (17 August 2010) (SSRN).

44 *Payday Loans Act*, 2008, S.O. c.9, s.30.

45 Jan M. Smits, 'The Right to Change Your Mind? Rethinking the Usefulness of Mandatory Rights of Withdrawal in Consumer Contract Law' (Maastricht: European Private Law Institute Working Paper No. 2011/01) at 3.

ess so that her intention at the time of contracting does not accurately reflect her real preferences. Or, as Retaiki and Van den Bergh put it, 'the consumer is pushed out of a deliberative frame of mind,' her 'perception of risk diminishes,' and there 'is a strong chance that, in the end, the consumer will not be content with' her choices.[46] The cooling-off period gives the consumer an opportunity, away from the initial pressure, to reassess the purchase and decide whether she wants to go ahead. In the same connection, the cooling-off period potentially also serves a deterrence function because the consumer's right of cancellation reduces the effectiveness of resort to high-pressure selling techniques in the first place.

Situational monopoly is another potential by-product of high-pressure or deceptive selling techniques. For example, claims in direct market advertising that the product is not available from normal retail outlets may create the impression that the product is unique or that the seller is the sole source of supply. Door-to-door sellers may make similar statements. The effect is to discourage the consumer from shopping for a better deal and to insulate the seller from competition. Other marketing strategies, such as 'buy now and receive a free gift,' or 'special low price available only for limited time' may also entice consumers into paying supra-competitive prices.[47] A cooling-off period allows the consumer to back out of the deal if she discovers shortly afterwards that she has overpaid. Many jurisdictions have enacted cooling-off periods for distance sales where one of the concerns is that the consumer has no opportunity to inspect the goods before buying them. In other words, there is an informational asymmetry between buyer and seller. Lack of pre-purchase information prevents a consumer from differentiating between good and bad quality products and this, in turn, may trigger an adverse selection problem and the eventual unravelling of the market.[48] There are various market mechanisms available to mitigate the information problem, including reputational investments (intensive advertising campaigns and the like); signalling devices, such as the provision of warranty protection; and collective industry action, such as the establishment of trade association-run labelling schemes and seal of approval programs. A statutory

---

46 Rekaiti and Van den Bergh, 'Cooling-Off Periods,' *supra* note 43 at 377.
47 *Ibid.* at 378.
48 *Ibid.* at 379–81; George Akerlof, 'The Market for Lemons: Qualitative Uncertainty and the Market Mechanism' (1970) 84 *Quarterly Journal of Economics* 487.

cooling-off period may complement these measures by creating an incentive for sellers to disclose, through the price mechanism, information about the quality of their products.[49]

The costs of cooling-off periods include moral hazard, transactions costs, and potential counterproductive effects. There is a moral hazard problem because a cooling-off period may allow the consumer to obtain free short-term use of a product with no intention of keeping it. A possible solution might be a requirement for some sort of rental payment, but a rental payment may not cover the whole cost of the consumer's use. The transaction costs of cooling-off periods include uncertainty and delay; the seller cannot be sure until the end of the cooling-off period whether the sale is firm. If the consumer elects to cancel the deal, the seller will incur the additional costs of taking the goods back together with the sunk costs of negotiating the transaction and delivering the goods in the first place. Even if the consumer elects not to cancel, the seller will still bear the cost of delayed payment or, if the consumer pays upfront, the cost of being unable to use the funds until the end of the cooling-off period. The seller is likely to pass on these costs to consumers in the form of higher prices. A statutory intervention may have counterproductive effects if it ends up harming the class of individual it was intended to protect. One concern with cooling-off periods in this connection is that sellers may respond by withholding delivery of the product until the period has expired; this delay may harm consumers who need the product immediately.[50] To justify a cooling-off period, the benefits must exceed the costs. However, this is a difficult assessment to make, not least because the benefits are in part a function of the predicted take-up rate – 'cooling-off periods will be ineffective when the cancellation right is exercised only occasionally'[51] – and there is a lack of empirical data on this front.[52]

---

49 Retaiki and Van Den Bergh, *supra* note 43 at 380–1. *Cf.* Eidenmuller, 'Why Withdrawal Rights?', *supra* note 43 at 7–11, arguing for an opt-in approach in the distance selling context (sellers would be required to offer consumers the option of a contract with a cooling-off period attached).

50 Retaiki and Van Den Bergh, 'Cooling-Off Periods,' *supra* note 43 at 381–4.

51 *Ibid.* at 393.

52 The modest empirical evidence suggests that cooling-off periods are rarely exercised in door-to-door sales but may be exercised more often in distance sales: Eidenmuller, 'Why Withdrawal Rights?', *supra* note 43 at 15–16 (1–5 per cent in doorstep selling transactions and 25–35 per cent in distance sales).

C. Cooling-Off Periods for Consumer Credit Contracts

As discussed in Part III, the primary objectives of truth in lending laws are to increase consumer awareness of interest rates, promote comparison credit shopping, and stimulate competition in the consumer credit market. Empirical studies indicate that the legislation has been at best marginally successful. A common explanation for this points to the timing of the disclosures: the information typically appears in the contract document, which the consumer does not get until the deal is already effectively done. A possible solution would be to legislate for a delay between the handing over of the disclosure statement and the completion of the agreement; and, as it happens, the Canadian federal truth in lending laws have taken this step, but only for mortgages (home loans).[53] An alternative approach would be to enact a cooling-off period allowing the consumer to cancel the contract within a prescribed time after its completion.[54] Both approaches come to much the same thing: in each case, the aim is to give the consumer time to absorb the truth in lending disclosures before the contract is finalized. In other words, both approaches are informational asymmetry measures.

Truth in lending's broader goals include the facilitation of comparison shopping for credit and the stimulation of price competition in the consumer credit market. For the cooling-off period to be effective on these fronts, it would be necessary for consumers in reasonably substantial numbers not just to read the disclosures, but also to seek out information about the terms offered by one or more competing lenders, compare this with the disclosures, and take whatever action the comparison indicates. The truth in lending laws have been unsuccessful over the years in influencing consumer behaviour to this extent, and it is hard to believe that the introduction of a few days' further reflection will make a difference. However, this is not to dismiss the cooling-off period out of hand. Another, more modest truth in lending goal is to increase consumer sensitivity to interest rates and charges. In this connection, the disclosures may help draw the consumer's attention to an unusually bad deal and also, perhaps, to the additional cost of buying

---

53 See the *Bank Act Regulations, supra* note 39.

54 See, for example, Article 14 of EC, *Directive 2008/48/EC of the European Parliament and of the Council of April 23 2008 on Credit Agreements for Consumers and Repealing Council Directive 87/102/EEC,* [2008] O.J. L 133/66 at 79, which gives the consumer fourteen days to withdraw from a credit agreement without having to show cause.

on credit relative to paying cash.[55] The extra time a cooling-off period provides may facilitate the 'alert function' of truth in lending laws so that more consumers avoid bad deals. Against this benefit there must be weighed the costs of cooling-off periods identified above, including moral hazard, transaction costs, and counterproductive effects (including the possibility that lenders may refuse to advance the funds until the cooling-off period has expired). A possible cause for concern is that, at least in the case of a closed-end transaction, the consumer may already be psychologically committed to the deal and, in this frame of mind, she will tend to discount any information that is adverse to it.[56] This speculation is consistent with limited evidence suggesting that cooling-off periods are rarely exercised.[57]

V. The Behavioural Economics Approach

A. Introduction

Traditionally, there have been two main approaches to consumer credit regulation: disclosure *via* truth in lending laws (see Parts III and IV) and substantive interventions – for example, licensing requirements,

---

55 See Landers and Rohner, 'A Functional Analysis,' *supra* note 38 at 737: 'This "alert function" might work as follows. A consumer making a credit purchase of a new car brings an awareness that the APR should be in the twelve to eighteen percent range. A consumer quoted an APR of seventeen to eighteen percent does not shop elsewhere because this is consistent with his expectations ... But a consumer who receives a TIL statement with an APR of thirty percent will be alerted, at least, to question the reason for such a rate, and perhaps, to take his business elsewhere.' See also Omri Ben-Shahar and Eric Posner, 'The Right to Withdraw in Contract Law' (March, 2010) (SSRN), advocating a right of withdrawal, among other things, for transactions involving complex contracts.

56 This is the phenomenon that psychologists refer to as 'cognitive dissonance': see Iain Ramsay, 'Consumer Redress and Access to Justice' in *International Perspectives on Consumers' Access to Justice*, ed. Charles E.F. Rickett and Thomas G.W. Telfer (Cambridge: Cambridge University Press, 2003), at 29. More generally, Ben-Shahar and Schneider argue that mandatory disclosure is fundamentally flawed and, if this is right, the addition of a cooling-off period will make no difference: see 'The Failure of Mandated Disclosure,' *supra* note 28.

57 *Ibid.* Eidenmuller suggests that the effectiveness of cooling-off periods might be enhanced by lowering the costs of withdrawal (e.g., allowing withdrawal by e-mail) and standardizing the instructions on the exercise of withdrawal rights: 'Why Withdrawal Rights?', *supra* note 43 at 15–18.

usury laws, and product restrictions (see Part VI).[58] From a behavioural economics perspective, truth in lending laws as currently drafted are flawed because they are based on the rational actor model of consumer behaviour and because they assume that so long as the consumer is given the right information in a timely fashion, she will make intelligent choices. This model overlooks mounting evidence that consumer decision making is subject to a range of systematic biases, including poor risk assessment and a tendency to overestimate the short-term benefits of a transaction relative to its longer-term costs.[59] Consequently, consumers do not respond to truth in lending disclosures in the manner that classical economic theory would predict: 'the availability of data does not necessarily lead to communication and knowledge; understanding and intention do not necessarily lead to action; and contextual nuances can lead to poor choices.'[60]

At the other end of the scale from truth in lending laws, substantive regulation assumes that consumers are poor decision makers and that the best way of protecting them is to take away or restrict their choices. The downside of this approach is that it may limit access to credit or reduce innovation in financial products.[61] The behavioural economics approach steers a middle course between disclosure and prohibition: building on what we know about how people make decisions in real life, the aim is to develop creative strategies for influencing consumer choice. Weapons in the behavioural economics armoury include the framing of information to increase its salience; the setting of default or opt-out rules, which channel consumer choices in the direction of welfare-enhancing contractual outcomes; and the establishment of voluntary exclusion regimes that would allow a consumer to make a decision at Point A limiting her choices at Point B.[62]

B. Improving Disclosures

Disclosures could be more effective if lawmakers paid better atten-

---

58 Michael S. Barr, Sendhil Mullainathan, and Eldar Shafir, *Behaviorally Informed Financial Services Regulation* (Washington: New America Foundation, 2008) at 1.

59 See Richard H. Thaler and Cass R. Sunstein, *Nudge: Improving Decisions about Health, Wealth, and Happiness* (New York: Penguin Books, 2009), Part 1, identifying and explaining the various manifestations of irrational decision making.

60 Barr *et al.*, *Behaviorally Informed Financial Services Regulation*, *supra* note 58 at 1.

61 *Ibid.*

62 *Ibid.* at 2. See also Thaler and Sunstein, *Nudge*, *supra* note 59.

tion to the notion of salience, which in turn is a function of both timing and content. As mentioned above, one of truth in lending's goals is to increase consumer awareness of borrowing costs with a view to preventing overuse of credit. Information about borrowing costs is most likely to be effective if it is disclosed at the point of borrowing and if it is tailored specifically to the individual consumer's case. In the credit card context, the point of borrowing arrives when the consumer has to decide whether to pay her monthly account balance in full or to make only a part payment and incur interest charges. Truth in lending laws do require disclosures in the monthly statement of account, but as Ronald Mann points out, at least until recently, the requirements did not go beyond mechanical information relevant to the status of the account.[63] Mann suggests a requirement that each account statement also include the date by which the consumer would pay her balance in full if she made no further purchases and continued to make equal monthly payments in an amount equal to the last monthly payment.[64] Recently enacted credit card regulations in the United States and Canada include a measure along these lines.[65]

These reforms may make a difference, provided consumers pay attention to the information. The trouble is that, at least in the Canadian version, there is not enough to catch the consumer's attention in the first place. The U.S. version is a little better because it also requires the inclusion of a 'minimum payment warning,' to the effect that making only the minimum payment will increase the interest payable and the time necessary to pay off the balance. However, the wording is bland and may not be sufficiently eye-catching.[66] By way of contrast, Bar-Gill, inspired by the success of mandatory warning labels on cigarette packaging, has suggested a statement such as: 'Debt Increasing – At current repayment rate, it will take you 34 years to repay your debt and you will end up paying 300% of the principal.'[67] Shock tactics along these lines might be more effective than the standard form of statutory disclosure requirement.

---

63 Ronald Mann, *Charging Ahead: The Growth and Regulation of Payment Card Markets* (Cambridge: Cambridge University Press, 2006) at 160.
64 *Ibid.* at 160–1.
65 U.S.: *Truth in Lending Act*, 15 U.S.C. §1601 at §1637(b)(11) as am. by *Credit Card Accountability, Responsibility and Disclosure Act of 2009*, Pub.L. No. 111–24, 123 Stat. 1734 at §201(a); Canada: *Bank Act* Regulation, *supra* note 36 at s.12(5)(d) and (e).
66 In apparent recognition of this point, the legislation authorizes the Federal Reserve Board to substitute a different form of warning based on consumer testing.
67 Oren Bar-Gill, 'Seduction by Plastic' (2004) 98 Nw. U. L. Rev. 1373 at 1419.

Similar thinking underlies the requirement in some jurisdictions for payday lenders to place prominent signs on their premises warning that payday lending is a high-cost form of credit and that consumers should only use the service for short-term cash needs.[68] Likewise, U.K. legislation provides that advertisements for home mortgages must contain the following warning: 'YOUR HOME MAY BE REPOSSESSED IF YOU DO NOT KEEP UP REPAYMENTS ON A MORTGAGE OR ANY OTHER DEBT SECURED ON IT.'[69] Barr *et al.*, addressing the wide range of home loan products available to consumers and the challenges of choosing wisely among them, suggest that information about the failure rate of particular products might help: '2 out of 10 borrowers who take this kind of loan default.'[70] They also propose requiring the lender, at the time it offers a mortgage loan, to disclose information the lender knows about the borrower that the borrower does not necessarily know about herself and that may help shape the borrower's choice: for example, the borrower's credit score and her qualifications for all the lender's mortgage products.[71]

C. Opt-Out Default Rules

Barr *et al.*'s proposals for the regulation of home loans in the wake of the sub-prime mortgage crisis provide a good illustration of the opt-out default rule approach. Starting from the premises that (1) many borrowers took out loans they did not understand and could not afford, and (2) improved disclosures might not be enough to counteract market pressures and consumer confusion, they argue for 'an opt-out strategy to make it easier for borrowers to choose a standard product and harder for borrowers to choose a product that they are less likely to understand.'[72] As the default position, lenders would be required to offer borrowers a 'plain vanilla' standard mortgage agreement. They would remain free to offer whatever loan products they wanted outside the standard package, but borrowers would get the standard package unless they consciously opted out in favour of some other alternative.

---

68 For details, see Ronald J. Mann and Jim Hawkins, 'Just Until Payday' (2007) 54 UCLA L. Rev. 855 at 876.
69 *Consumer Credit (Advertisements) Regulations 2004*, S.I. 2004/1484, s.7.
70 Barr *et al.*, *Behaviorally Informed Financial Services Regulation, supra* note 58 at 6.
71 *Ibid.*
72 *Ibid.* at 9.

A borrower's decision to opt out would depend on truthful and comprehensible disclosures from the lender about the terms and risks of the alternative transaction.

As a means of enforcing the disclosure requirement and to make the default more 'sticky,' if an opt-out borrower defaults on the non-standard mortgage, she would be allowed to argue the inadequacy of the lender's disclosures as a defence to bankruptcy or foreclosure proceedings. Alternatively, the relevant supervisory agency might be given authority to police disclosures and to impose a fine or some other appropriate penalty on lenders whose disclosures are inadequate. In terms of stringency, these measures go beyond a simple disclosure requirement, because they involve an element of compulsion on both the borrower and the lender sides, but they fall short of product regulation because they do not restrict the range of products lenders may offer or borrowers' freedom to purchase them. In summary, the aim of an opt-out mortgage system is to increase the chances of borrowers getting 'straightforward loans they [can] understand.'[73]

The same authors also propose an opt-out payment plan for credit cards, to address concerns that many consumers do not fully appreciate the costs of an outstanding credit card balance over the longer term.[74] As indicated in Part V.B, above, improved disclosures in the monthly statement of account are one response to the problem and governments have already started going down this track. However, more aggressive intervention might be warranted if these recently enacted measures turn out not to have the desired effect. The default rule under the opt-out payment plan proposal would require the card issuer to offer a standard set of contract terms under which the borrower agrees to pay off her existing balance within a prescribed, relatively short period. As in the home loan context, lenders would be free to offer alternative contracts providing for longer repayment periods, but first the consumer would have to affirmatively opt out of the standard version. The assumption is that the majority of consumers will not opt out, some because they actively prefer the standard version, and others because of inertia. Either way, the anticipated result is a reduction in the amount of interest consumers pay and a lower incidence of financial failure. In this last connection, it is worth noting that credit card debt is one of the

---

73 *Ibid.*
74 *Ibid.* at 13–14.

most commonly listed causes of consumer bankruptcy in the United States, Canada, and elsewhere.[75]

D. Voluntary Self-Exclusion

One of the most basic propositions in the behavioural economics literature is that, contrary to neoclassical economic theory, individual preferences are not stable over time: a person might make a choice at Point A that she would not make at Point B. For example, a decision maker at Point B may regret a choice made at Point A. Or alternatively, a decision maker may have enough self-control to avoid a bad choice at Point A, but not at Point B. In the second case, the decision maker may anticipate at Point A her loss of self-control at Point B and take steps to prevent it. The story of Ulysses and the Sirens is a case in point: Ulysses, knowing that he will be unable to resist the Sirens' song once he is within hearing range, instructs his crew to tie him to the mast so that he will not steer the ship towards them. Ulysses' action was a form of voluntary self-exclusion: his choice at Point A, where he had self-control, restricted his choices at Point B where, as he anticipated, his self-control would desert him.[76] There are many real-life examples of variations on the same theme. A commonly cited case is the gambling exclusion laws. In some parts of the United States, and in other countries as well, gamblers can request to be excluded from casinos. If a gambler makes this request, his name is put on a list that is circulated to the casinos. A listed gambler caught in a casino is subject to a range of state-imposed penalties, including ejection from the casino, confiscation of winnings, and imprisonment.[77]

Related measures have been proposed in a variety of consumer credit contexts. For example, Bar-Gill canvasses the possibility of unbundling the payment and credit functions of credit cards by requiring issuers to

---

75 See, for example, Anthony Duggan, 'Consumer Bankruptcy in Canada and Australia: A Comparative Overview' in *Annual Review of Insolvency Law 2006*, ed. Janis Sarra (Toronto: Carswell, 2007) at 857.

76 See Thaler and Sunstein, *Nudge, supra* note 59, chapter 2.

77 *Ibid.* at 235. See also Kurt Eggert, 'Lashed to the Mast and Crying for Help: How Self-Limitation of Autonomy Can Protect Elders from Predatory Lending' (2003) 36 Loy. LA. L. Rev. 693 at 748, cited in Canadian Centre for Elder Law, *Study Paper on Predatory Lending Issues in Canada* CCEL Report No. 4; BCLI Study Paper No. 3 (February 2008) at 23–4.

allow automatic payment of balances from the consumer's chequing account.[78] The concern this proposal addresses is that at Point A, the time she obtains the card, the consumer may be resolved not to chalk up debt on it, but by the time she gets to Point B, when she receives her monthly statement of account showing an outstanding credit balance, she may be unable to resist making only the minimum payment. By subscribing to the automatic payment plan at Point A, she prevents herself from succumbing to temptation at Point B.

A similar measure has been suggested as a solution to the problem of predatory lending to elderly borrowers. The idea is for the development of a formal document, called an 'Elder Home Equity Loan Instrument,' to be signed by seniors wanting protection against the risk of being duped down the track. The instrument would limit the terms of any future loan they might take out on the security of their principal residence and would allow seniors to exclude themselves from any transaction with potentially confusing or harsh terms. Seniors could cancel their subscription and obtain a loan with barred terms, but first they would need a certificate from an independent financial counsellor stating either that the loan is appropriate or that the counsellor has discussed its benefits and detriments with the borrowers.[79]

E. Conclusion

As with all regulatory interventions, behavioural economics measures are not cost-free and at least some of the measures discussed above may turn out to be not cost-justified. Space constraints preclude us from exploring this possibility or closely debating the merits of the various proposals. It follows that we are not necessarily endorsing the specific approaches we have identified in this section of the paper. Our purpose is simply to convey the flavour of the behavioural economics approach and to emphasize the importance of thinking more creatively about regulatory alternatives than lawmakers and commentators have been accustomed to do. Current consumer credit laws rest heavily on the twin pillars of mandatory disclosure and prohibition. As Shahar and Schneider suggest, regulators should avoid falling back on stock

---

78 Bar-Gill, 'Seduction by Plastic' *supra* note 67 at 1422. See also Thaler and Sunstein, *Nudge, supra* note 59 at 144–64.
79 See sources cited in *supra* note 77.

measures, such as these, without regard to their effectiveness, and they should begin 'the burdensome and politically painful work of tailoring solutions to problems.'[80] Tailoring solutions to problems is precisely what behavioural economics tries to do.

VI. Substantive Regulation

A. Introduction

Given the limits of demand-side regulation through disclosures, cooling-off periods, or altering the 'choice architecture' of consumers, product and supplier regulation may be justified. If credit is a potentially dangerous product[81] – a perception that would seem to be confirmed by the sub-prime mortgage debacle – then governments may be justified in taking action *ex ante* to prevent the circulation of dangerous credit products.[82] These measures might include product or supplier licensing, minimum standards, bans, and price caps. Distributional concerns may also favour *ex ante* protections on the basis that this is more effective in protecting vulnerable consumers than reliance on *ex post* individual litigation. This was one justification for the licensing of credit suppliers in the United Kingdom.

The definition of a safe credit product is, of course, not free from controversy. Safety could mean free from risk, a cost–benefit assessment of risk, or a socially acceptable risk. Any cost–benefit calculation must assess the costs of restricting consumer choice and innovation. However, it is possible that the benefits to a majority of consumers from restrictions on the provision of a complex product may outweigh the costs to the minority who are denied access. The issue of the optimal level of safety is therefore not always obvious and will require both technical expertise and political judgments. The U.S. Consumer Financial Protection Bureau adopts a cost–benefit approach to safety in rule making that includes assessing the impact of standards on financial access and vulnerable groups.

---

80 Shahar and Schneider, 'The Failure of Mandated Disclosure,' *supra* note 28 at 4.
81 Oren Bar-Gill and Elizabeth Warren, 'Making Credit Safer,' *supra* note 11 at 1.
82 Warren's argument was the inspiration for the creation of the Consumer Financial Protection Bureau in the U.S. *Dodd-Frank Act*, which confers supervision, rule-making, and enforcement powers on the new agency.

B. *The Application of Better Regulation Principles*

Better strategies for the implementation and enforcement of consumer protection are key to the success of public regulation. The success of *ex ante* regulation is the ability to obtain systematic information on existing and potential problems, identify the most significant risks, and make timely interventions. Such an approach requires systematic gathering and analysis of data on market performance. An example is the European Union Consumer Market Watch, which screens markets in the EU against five indicators – prices, complaints, switching rates, satisfaction, and safety. This identifies specific markets for investigation and potential corrective action and is based on the assumption that 'reliable and up-to-date information (quantitative and qualitative) is essential for better policy making.'[83] The FSA has developed indicators of potentially problematic product features such as cross-subsidization, bundling, and teaser rates.

The development of evidence-based policy through impact analysis is intended to ensure better regulation by avoiding regulation by headlines – where agencies overreact to media coverage of events with unnecessary front-end prevention, or do not adequately consider all potential regulatory alternatives. The OECD has recently outlined the importance of strengthening evidence-based impact assessment to support policy coherence – to pay more attention to the voice of users (consumers), who need to be part of the regulatory development process – as well as the increased importance of measuring the distributional (equitable) impact of regulation.[84]

At the level of implementation and enforcement, it is possible to measure certain regulatory inputs (e.g., staffing levels) and outputs (enforcement actions and sanctions). However, while this exercise may be useful for broad-brush comparisons, it does not necessarily have a close relationship to regulatory outcomes.[85] A key aspect of policy is

---

83 EC, European Commission Directorate General for Health and Consumers, Consumer Affairs, *Consumer Markets Scorecard*, http://ec.europa.eu/consumers/strategy/facts_en.htm#background. The Canadian Federal Office of Consumer Affairs has also recently published an approach to consumer impact assessment: Office of Consumer Affairs, *Consumer Impact Assessment: Assessing How Proposed Policies May Impact Consumers* (Ottawa: Industry Canada, 2010).

84 OECD, *Regulatory Policy and the Road to Sustainable Growth*, Draft Report (2010).

85 For the problems of attempting to do this in securities regulation, see Howell Jack-

measuring regulatory outcomes rather than regulatory outputs. For example, the number of prosecutions or charges laid is a useful but not sufficient measure of an agency's performance. Reductions in complaints are one measure, albeit a crude and ambiguous one, since more complaints may be stimulated by high-profile enforcement. Estimating the financial impact of consumer protection enforcement is a relatively new process and very much a work in progress.[86] In Ontario, the development of outcome measures for consumer protection is a continuing challenge; the use of benchmarking between provinces is relatively modest.[87] User input is also problematic given the relatively weak consumer movement in Canada. In the United Kingdom, the Office of Fair Trading has agreed with the Treasury to provide direct financial benefits to consumers of at least five times its cost to the taxpayer. This target is monitored by the requirement of positive impact estimates. However, it is difficult to measure the benefits of consumer policies, which may include intangibles such as consumer confidence.[88] It is much easier to measure costs. Impact analysis must also consider issues of equity. There are several approaches here, such as putting a higher valuation on benefits to vulnerable groups.[89]

Agencies must often rely on industry and consumer input as well as

son, 'The Impact of Enforcement: A Reflection' (2007) 156 U. Pa. L. Rev. 400 responding to John Coffee, 'Law and the Market: The Impact of Enforcement' (2007) 156 U. Pa. L. Rev. 229.

86 See U.K., Office of Fair Trading, *Positive Impact 09/10: Consumer Benefits to the OFT's Work* (OFT 1251) (July, 2010) at 19; U.K., Office of Fair Trading, *A Guide to OFT's Impact Estimation Methods* (OFT 1250) (July 2010); and U.K., Office of Fair Trading, *A Review of OFT's Impact Estimation Methods* (OFT 1164) by Stephen Davies (January 2010).

87 The review of the Delegated Authorities in Ontario notes that 'OMVIC does not have a single metric that reflects consumer protection. The organization has attempted to define outcome measures, but finds it difficult to define measures that truly reflect the outcome of consumer protection. An increase in the number of curbsiders (unregistered salespersons) and more complaints could indicate more unregulated activity or it could actually indicate better awareness.' Todres and Associates, *Delegated Administrative Authority Model Review* (2009) at 190.

88 See OECD, *Regulatory Policy, supra* note 84 at 42.

89 Richard Vaughan, *Distributional Issues in Welfare Assessment and Consumer Affairs Policy* (London: OFT, 1998). See also Matthew Adler and Eric Posner, *New Foundations of Cost–Benefit Analysis* (Cambridge, MA: Harvard University Press, 2006); and Amy Sinden, Douglas A. Kysar, and David M. Driesen, 'Cost–Benefit Analysis: New Foundations on Shifting Sand' *Regulation and Governance* 3 (2009): 48–71.

their own studies. Studies note that regulatory regimes often combine governmental and non-governmental actors, none of whom have comprehensive knowledge about how to solve a particular problem. Such a characterization undermines sharp distinctions between the public and the private realm, going beyond simple 'public interest' or the amorphous capture theory; regulation may be a cooperative endeavour and not merely an issue of securing compliance from unwilling firms.[90] Variations on self-regulation have developed. The delegated administrative authorities in Ontario, where industry administers regulations but is accountable to government, are one example. Legislation often builds in third-party monitors to reduce the likelihood of capture. These may include conferring powers on public interest groups to put items on the regulatory agenda – for example, the U.K.'s super-complaint procedure[91] – or ensuring effective consumer representation in the agency.

C. Minimum Standards

Minimum standards may be general or specific and relate to the performance or design aspects of a product. Regulatory issues relate to optimal precision (rules vs standards), an effective and democratic development process, and ensuring that regulations do not limit innovation. An increasingly common technique in many jurisdictions is the combination of general standards such as 'safe' or 'fair' with more specific rules. This combination is intended to reduce both future rule-making costs (through future-proofing) and consumers' search costs, by providing a signal that consumers can reasonably expect 'fair' outcomes, while addressing the problem of the 'amoral calculator' who will exploit any loophole in more detailed rules. The addition of spe-

---

90 See Tony Prosser, *The Regulatory Enterprise: Government Regulation and Legitimacy* (Oxford: Oxford University Press, 2010); Julia Black, 'Decentring Regulation: Understanding the Role of Regulation and Self-Regulation in a "Post-Regulatory" World' 54 *Current Legal Problems* 103. See, generally, Bronwen Morgan and Karen Yeung, *Regulation* (Cambridge: Cambridge University Press, 2008).
91 This is a procedure under s.11 of the *Enterprise Act 2002*, c.40, which permits designated consumer bodies to present evidence through a complaint to the OFT that features of a market appear to be significantly harming consumers' interests. The OFT must respond within ninety days indicating how it proposes to deal with the complaint. This technique was used in relation to concerns about payment protection insurance.

cific rules may reduce monitoring, compliance, and enforcement costs. Self-enforcing rules that do not require the intervention of a third party are attractive in consumer protection, where many disputes are settled at the two-party level. Examples include fixed periods for rejecting defective goods (e.g., 60 days) or the application of a default rule of 'satisfaction guaranteed or money refunded.'[92]

A general fairness signal may be more effective than detailed rules in stimulating consumers to take action in response to perceived unfairness. The transparency of the fairness signal for consumers depends on a congruence between lay and legal conceptions of fairness, suggesting that the interpretation of such a norm be entrusted to a body that will be sensitive to lay conceptions of fairness. Neoclassical economics has little to say about fairness. Behavioural economics, however, indicates that consumers do have intuitive ideas of unfairness that override rational economic calculation. [93]

A variety of institutional approaches might be adopted for developing a regime of rules and standards. The general standard might be fleshed out by more specific standards that are drawn up with both consumer and industry input: conformity with the specific standard would presume congruence with the general standard.[94] The detailed development of the standard might be delegated to an agency that acts as a bargaining agent for consumers. A further variation is to require firms to develop self-regulatory systems which will achieve the desired outcomes (fairness) and to hold them to account for systems that create an undue risk of unfairness.[95]

Comparative analysis of unfair terms regulation provides an example of the merits of *ex post* versus *ex ante* regulation through minimum standards.[96] The European Directive on Unfair Terms in Consumer Con-

---

92 See Iain Ramsay, 'Consumer Redress Mechanisms for Defective and Poor Quality Products' (1981) 21 U.T.L.J. 117. See also Ben-Shahar and Posner, 'The Right to Withdraw in Contract Law,' *supra* note 55.

93 See the studies cited in chapter 2 of George Akerlof and Robert Shiller, *Animal Spirits: How Human Psychology Drives the Economy, and Why It Matters for Global Capitalism* (Princeton: Princeton University Press, 2009).

94 For example, the European Consumer Product Safety system.

95 See discussion of FSA below. For discussion of different approaches in this area, see Sharon Gilad, 'Institutionalizing Fairness in Financial Markets: Mission Impossible?' (2011) 5 *Regulation & Governance* 309.

96 See Fabrizio Cafaggi and Hans-W. Micklitz, eds., *New Frontiers of Consumer Protec-*

tracts envisages the possibility of public agencies taking action to prevent the use of unfair terms.[97] There is more *ex ante* public regulation of unfair consumer terms in Europe than there is in Canada. An example is the U.K. Office of Fair Trading (OFT), which has an injunctive power to prevent the continued use of unfair terms, but which also reviews and provides guidance on unfair terms, though there is no requirement of pre-approval. Through these processes, many terms in standard-form consumer contracts have been removed or clarified. The assessments of the OFT's performance are generally favourable in terms of financial savings to consumers from the removal of unfair terms, the ability to engage in wholesale industry changes in terms through negotiations with trade bodies (rather than case-by-case 'sniping'), and greater clarity in contract terms.[98] This work highlights the limitations of *ex post* private enforcement in changing contracting practices. On the cost side there are the costs of the process, including – in some cases – the relatively long period required to negotiate changes. Because individual terms are considered in the abstract, it may be difficult to assess fully how a term functions in practice. An administrative bargaining agent may have difficulties reflecting the heterogeneity of consumer preferences so that some consumers might be 'worse off receiving protection from a clause that affected them little or not at all in exchange for a higher price.'[99] The issues here may be difficult to weigh – for example, where a supplier reduces the price through the use of a limiting clause (e.g., on consequential damages), which places the possibility of a very large loss on a small number of consumers.

Oren Bar-Gill and Kevin Davis discuss these issues in the context of the problem of contractual modifications, where suppliers' contracts often have broad discretionary powers – for example, to change the

---

tion: The Interplay between Private and Public Enforcement (Belgium: Intersentia, Mortsel: 2009); and Giandomenico Majone, *Regulating Europe* (London: Routledge: 1996).

97 EC, *Council Directive 93/13/EEC of 5 April 1993 on Unfair Terms in Consumer Contracts* [1993] O.J. L 95/29. Unfairness is defined in the form of an open-textured standard supplemented by a 'grey list' of terms indicative of unfairness and a requirement that terms be drafted in plain and intelligible language.

98 See, for example, U.K., National Audit Office, *Report by the Comptroller and Auditor General, The Office of Fair Trading: Protecting the Consumer from Unfair Trading Practices* (HC 57 1999) and other material in Iain Ramsay, *Consumer Law and Policy: Text and Materials on Regulating Consumer Markets* (Oxford: Hart Publications, 2007) at 208–13.

99 V. Goldberg, 'Institutional Change and the Quasi-Invisible Hand' (1974) 17 *Journal of Law and Economics* 461.

interest rate on credit terms.[100] They suggest a *via media* between abstract *ex ante* government approval and *ex post* individual litigation. To ensure mutually beneficial modifications, consumers should have the right to nominate a bargaining agent – an expert Change Approval Board (CAB) funded by sellers – which consumers could pay for if they wished this protection. They assume that there could be a private market for CABs that would have a range of criteria for approving modifications. The price paid by the consumer would be related to the strictness of the change criteria. This approach would address the rigidity of *ex ante* administrative regulation and the delays and costs of *ex post* individual litigation. They argue that the new U.S. Consumer Financial Protection Bureau could stimulate the creation of this market by subsidizing the initial CABs and that their proposals could be applied to employment contracts. This plan as proposed would raise consumer information costs and, given consumers' cognitive limitations, may misestimate the value of buying into a CAB. There is also the possibility of CABs becoming more aligned with seller interests.

If there are identifiable differences between consumer preferences and competencies in contracting, then individuals might, under certain conditions, be permitted to contract out of regulatory protections. This is recognized in the U.K.'s *Consumer Credit Act,* where individuals may be classified by a third party as of 'high net worth' and contract out of protections in order to receive a lower price.[101] A further variation is to create an option for consumers to opt in to protection – for example, if a cooling-off period was thought to be overinclusive, then consumers might opt in. These examples suggest that future standard setting for consumer protection should attempt to recognize different consumer preferences. The greater complexity of such regimes must be balanced against the easy administrability of general, albeit overinclusive, rules.

Many jurisdictions prohibit specific terms in consumer credit contracts. These primarily relate to situations where individuals may not correctly weigh risks or the adverse consequences associated with a term (e.g., broad security interests over present and future goods).[102] These are generally subsidiary terms (e.g., relating to default) where

---

100 See O. Bar-Gill and K. Davis, 'Empty Promises' (2010) 84 S. Cal. L. Rev. 1.
101 *Consumer Credit Act 1974* (U.K.), 1974, c.39, s.16A.
102 See discussion in Iain Ramsay, 'Regulation of Consumer Credit' in *Handbook of Research on International Consumer Law,* ed. Geraint Howells, Iain Ramsay, and Thomas Wilhelmsson (Cheltenham: Edward Elgar, 2010) at 370–3.

justifications may include behavioural biases, paternalism, and externalities from credit default.

D. Performance Standards: The Responsible Lending Example

There is much interest in harnessing responsible supplier conduct in regulation. In consumer credit, responsible lending is a nascent principle of international consumer credit law. Although its scope and application differ between countries, it generally requires that lenders assess whether individuals are likely to be able to repay (and not merely whether lenders will recover their money) and that lenders treat borrowers fairly and consider their interests throughout the credit relationship.[103] A responsible lending duty may be justified economically by the existence of superior creditor information and ability to assess risk. Given the existence of behavioural biases in consumers, it may protect an individual's future self against the myopia of her present self. More positively, it may ensure that a product is not unsuitable for an individual's needs. A responsible lending provision may also represent a collective 'hands-tying' by creditors against engaging in the 'irrational exuberance' associated with market cycles. It may reduce pressure on firms to follow practices that are unfair or that exploit consumers' behavioural biases because firms fear losing a competitive edge. It can

---

103 The U.S. Dodd-Frank Act does not use the term responsible lending but does require mortgage lenders to make a reasonable and good-faith determination based on verified and documented information that, 'at the time the loan is consummated, the consumer has a reasonable ability to repay the loan according to its terms.' This determination shall include 'consideration of the consumer's credit history, current income, expected income the consumer is reasonably assured of receiving, current obligations, debt-to-income ratio or the residual income the consumer will have after paying non-mortgage debt and mortgage-related obligations, employment status, and other financial resources other than the consumer's equity in the dwelling or real property that secures repayment of the loan. A creditor shall determine the ability of the consumer to repay using a payment schedule that fully amortizes the loan over the term of the loan.' The European Directive on Consumer Credit requires lenders to provide 'adequate explanations' about the characteristics of the credit product and to check the creditworthiness of borrowers, where appropriate, by reference to credit databases. Australia requires lenders to conduct an assessment that a credit contract is 'not unsuitable' for a consumer. The UK Office of Fair Trading has developed guidance on 'irresponsible lending' that requires creditors to assess a borrower's ability to undertake a specific credit commitment 'in a sustainable manner, without the borrower incurring (further) financial difficulties and/or experiencing adverse consequences.'

reinforce prudential regulation and may affect the general culture of lending.

The perceived disadvantages of broad responsible lending requirements are that they will raise compliance costs, make creditors more risk averse, and result in a denial of access to credit for some consumers. Denial of access for some consumers may of course be the objective of a responsible lending requirement. Responses to the costs arguments might include the provision of safe harbours for products that meet certain standards[104] or giving an agency responsibility for providing guidance to lenders.

Canada has not adopted a general norm of responsible lending. However, specific rules on mortgage lending require homebuyers to purchase insurance for mortgages above a certain loan-to-value ratio and impose minimum down payments. Lenders providing government-backed high-ratio mortgages must make reasonable efforts to verify that the borrower can afford the loan payment, check the borrower's source of income, and ensure that the property valuation has a reasonable basis.[105] The specificity of the Canadian rules reduces monitoring and enforcement costs, particularly given Canada's relatively concentrated financial sector. The disadvantage of specific rules is that they are both under- and over-inclusive and may invite the exploitation of loopholes. Based on a static model of compliance, they also provide little incentive for firms to engage in continuous improvement of their practices.

---

104 For example, §1412 of the U.S. Dodd-Frank Act provides a safe harbour by virtue of a presumption of the ability to repay where a residential loan includes certain characteristics such as no increase in the principal balance, no balloon payments (more than 2x regular payment), where total points and fees do not exceed 3 per cent of the total amount and the term does not exceed thirty years. If a loan complies with the safe harbour requirements, a consumer may not raise the defence of no reasonable ability to repay against a mortgage foreclosure. Such a mortgage is more likely to be purchased on the secondary market. The safe harbour technique might be analogized to the approach adopted by the EU to unsafe products where conformity to a voluntary EU standard creates a strong presumption of conformity with the general safety obligation.

105 See *National Housing Act*, R.S.C. 1985, c. C-11, ss.5–6; *Canada Housing and Mortgage Corporation Act* R.S.C. 1985, c. C-7, s.5, and Ministerial direction made thereunder; see, for example, Department of Finance Canada, News Release, 2011–003, 'The Harper Government Takes Prudent Action to Support the Long-Term Stability of Canada's Housing Market' (17 January 2011), http://www.fin.gc.ca/n11/11-003-eng.asp.

E. Ex Ante *Regulation: Licensing*

Licensing is generally justified because of high information asymmetries, externalities, and paternalism. The high costs of consumer error – a mistaken diagnosis or purchase of a dangerous product – identify those markets where licensing is a most compelling form of regulation. Licensing may be of suppliers or products. The former is more common in consumer protection, with product licensing traditionally limited to products that pose physical dangers.[106]

Ex ante protection of consumers through licensing of suppliers for integrity and financial probity is a common form of consumer protection in Ontario and other Canadian provinces. Examples include motor vehicle dealers, moneylenders, credit reporting agencies, loan brokers, collection agents, and payday lenders.[107] In response to increased concerns about credit standards, licensing standards in the United Kingdom and Australia now include greater potential for the scrutiny of a company's business models and the competence of suppliers; this links supplier and product regulation.

There are several benefits from licensing. First, licensing compensates for potentially high information, monitoring, and enforcement costs that individual consumers might face in a particular market. It can pool information about the market, which can then be used to monitor and screen out irresponsible traders or unfair terms. It provides an information basis for rule making and for identifying high-risk areas. Licensing can ensure that there is less dissonance between the existence of a broad unfairness standard and consumers' reasonable expectations of suppliers. Second, licensing may have a progressive distributional impact by benefiting those consumers least knowledgeable or able to assert their rights and those most vulnerable to unscrupulous operators. Third, licensing may create or stimulate consumer confidence in a market, though it is difficult to measure the intangible value of this consumer confidence. Finally, licensing can reduce externalities associated with a product supply, such as third-party costs associated with overindebtedness.

There are some potential disadvantages with licensing regimes. First, there are significant administrative and information costs associated

---

106 Although there is the older tradition of 'merit regulation' of securities.
107 For a recent example, see *Payday Lending Act*, S.O. 2008, c.9, s.10; *Collection Agencies Act*, R.S.O. 1990, c.14, s.6.

with a licensing regime, particularly in a market with large numbers of suppliers. Also, the costs of licensing the whole market may draw resources away from a more finely tuned enforcement against unfair practices. Second, the costs and procedural constraints (requirements of administrative law) on assembling a licensing regime may reduce its effectiveness as a deterrent to the fly-by-night trader, particularly in markets where there are low entry and exit costs. Without additional sanctions, licensing may turn out to be a reactive, rather than proactive, form of regulation. Third, licensing regimes may give a misleading signal of quality or reduce a consumer's defences if suppliers are permitted to exploit the signal 'government licensed.' Fourth, the broad standards in licensing regimes may be valuable in screening out those who are obviously unfit to trade but may be less accurate in screening those who might potentially engage in unfair trading. Fifth, the licensing authority may be 'captured' by the industry or segments of it so that the licensing regime becomes a method of furthering industry rather than consumer interests. Finally, licensing might restrict innovation in credit markets either through excessive regulation or the influence of incumbents.

These considerations suggest that an optimal licensing regime should be well funded, have a range of sanctions, be able to obtain information at a low cost on emerging market practices, assess accurately those practices creating the greatest risks for consumers, be able to move quickly to regulate emerging problems, and be structured to avoid the dangers of capture. Experience of financial services licensing in the United Kingdom supports these propositions: the Financial Services Authority, exercising a broad range of supervisory and rule-making powers, has been more successful than the more reactive Office of Fair Trading, which relied on narrow licensing powers.[108]

A common approach to funding is through an industry levy: this is the approach adopted by Canada's FCAC and the Financial Services Authority and the Office of Fair Trading in the United Kingdom. By contrast, the U.S. Consumer Financial Protection Bureau is funded through the Federal Reserve System.[109] Information may be obtained from several

---

108 The FSA provided a model for the 2006 extension of the OFT licensing powers.
109 The bureau is financed through the Federal Reserve system with a funding cap of 10 per cent of the Federal Reserve System finances in 2011 (equivalent to about $440 million): U.S. Dodd-Frank Act, §1017(2). The SEC had a budget of approximately $900 million in 2009. The U.K. FSA has a budget of approximately £450 million funded by the financial industry. The FSA includes aspects of the role of the SEC in addition to those of the bureau.

sources: examination visits, research, and third parties such as consumer groups and consumer complainants. Given the potential complexity of financial products, agencies should be able to draw on individuals with expertise in these areas. Ideally, credit regulation should be carried out by a dedicated financial consumer protection agency that can oversee the whole market. This is recommended by the World Bank in its best practices on consumer protection and financial services.[110]

There is some fragmentation of consumer credit regulation within Canada. While this may stimulate regulatory competition and ensure that regulation is responsive to local needs, there may be possibilities for greater coordination. Some steps have been taken through the Consumer Measures Committee. However, provincial licensing of specific areas of credit (payday lending, collection agents, loan brokers) may result in more opaque and possibly underinclusive regulation, and such an approach is more prone to industry capture or the possibilities of rent seeking by industry than a more generalized credit licensing regime.

It is difficult to measure empirically the outcomes of a licensing regime compared to one without licensing. Formal measures such as licence revocations do not provide an unambiguous guide to a reduction in unfair trading. In its impact analysis of the possible removal of credit licensing, the U.K. government highlighted unquantified increases in consumer detriment, increased burdens on individual dispute settlement mechanisms, loss of consumer confidence in the market, and an absence of information about traders. The requirement that all credit providers and brokers in the United Kingdom be licensed may have reduced the extent of sub-prime mortgage problems in the United Kingdom compared with the United States.

F. Meta-Regulation

A characteristic of contemporary regulation is the extent to which it harnesses private actors to achieve public goals. Christine Parker describes this approach as 'meta-regulation,' where law uses 'various mechanisms to enforce businesses to put in place internal governance structures, management systems and corporate cultures aimed at achieving responsible outcomes. Law attempts to constitute corporate

---

110 See Susan Rutledge, 'Good Practices for Consumer Protection and Financial Literacy in Europe and Central Asia: A Diagnostic Tool' (Washington: World Bank, 2010).

consciences.'[111] There has been limited empirical analysis of the success of this form of regulation.

The Financial Services Authority[112] in the United Kingdom has developed a 'treating customers fairly' initiative. The FSA regulates retail financial services through conduct-of-business rules, but in the early 2000s it developed the concept of 'principles based regulation,' based on the perceived limits of detailed regulation – which often elicited either resistance or merely formal compliance, through a 'tick the box' mentality – and the objective of ultimately reducing the need for external regulation if firms internalized norms of fair treatment.

The FSA requires financial firms to embed general principles such as 'treating customers fairly' (TCF) within their business models and organizational culture. Although this may be described as process-based regulation, it requires the achievement of a number of 'consumer outcomes': 'consumers can be confident that they are dealing with firms where the fair treatment of customers is central to corporate culture and is automatically taken into account in all relevant business decisions'; 'products and services marketed and sold in the retail market are designed to meet the needs of identified consumer groups and are targeted accordingly'; and 'consumers are provided with products that perform as firms have led them to expect and the associated service is both of an acceptable standard and as they have been led to expect.'[113]

Senior management must have adequate information to monitor TCF and must actively take responsibility for treating customers fairly and communicate this to their employees. Firms must not rely solely on consumer satisfaction studies to determine whether there is fair treatment of consumers since consumers may be satisfied with an unsuitable product and dissatisfied with a fair product.

The FSA's approach is intended to embed attentiveness to consumer welfare throughout the product life cycle – that is, financial product

---

111 Christine Parker, 'Meta Regulation: Legal Accountability for Corporate Social Responsibility' in *The New Corporate Accountability: Corporate Social Responsibility and the Law*, ed. Doreen McBarnet, Aurora Voiculescu, and Tom Campbell (Cambridge: Cambridge University Press, 2007).

112 See *Financial Services and Markets Act 2000* (U.K.), 2000, c.8. Since 2004, the FSA has regulated primary mortgage lending and insurance, which includes credit insurance. The OFT regulates unsecured credit and secondary mortgage lending. It is proposed to confer on the FSA jurisdiction over all mortgage regulation.

113 Financial Services Authority, *Treating Customers Fairly – Towards Fair Outcomes for Consumers* (July 2006) at 3, http://www.fsa.gov.uk/pubs/other/tcf_towards.pdf.

design, development and marketing and financial contract formation, performance, and complaint handling and redress. While this approach ultimately harnesses self-regulation, the FSA has required financial firms to identify progress in implementing TCF, monitored firms for TCF compliance during routine supervision, and taken enforcement action, including the levying of substantial fines where it has identified significant violations of the principles. In the wake of the financial crash, the FSA has developed an 'Intensive Supervision' model that, building on the fairness initiative, emphasizes 'outcomes testing' to a much greater extent than before. This may include more extensive analysis of a firm's business model and acting 'proactively' to influence outcomes.[114] The model will be carried forward into the proposed stand-alone agency that will regulate consumer financial services.

Experience of the FSA initiative suggests that firms – particularly smaller firms – had difficulty in transforming the FSA requirements into concrete changes. In addition, many firms could not see the need for change since they viewed themselves as successful firms which treated customers fairly, notwithstanding the prevalence of widespread mis-selling practices that seemed to be embedded in existing corporate organizational structures of selling.[115] The fairness initiative conflicted with their organizational identity. Other studies have identified barriers to internalization of norms, including the conflict between regulation and profitability, and mistrust between employers and employees.[116] Meta-regulation may be a complex task, one that requires organizations to translate and reframe regulatory objectives to fit their corporate goals.[117]

Studies also indicate, however, the limits of coercive external regulation in bringing about internal corporate change through traditional approaches such as punitive fines.[118] More complex approaches to enforcement require substantial expertise from regulators. If there are

---

114   See the FSA's discussion of this approach in U.K., Financial Services Authority, *Product Intervention* (Discussion Paper 11/01) (London: January, 2011).
115   Useful examples are found in the cases brought by the FSA in relation to the marketing of payment protection insurance. See, for example, Financial Services Authority, Press Release, 'FSA Fines HFC Bank £1.085 Million for PPI Failings' (16 January 2008), http://www.fsa.gov.uk/pages/Library/Communication/PR/2008/004.shtml.
116   See Neil Gunningham and Darren Sinclair, 'On The Limits of Management Based Regulation' (2009) 43 *Law and Society Review* 865.
117   See Gilad, 'Institutionalizing Fairness,' *supra* note 95.
118   See Robert Baldwin, 'The New Punitive Regulation' (2004) 67 Mod. L. Rev. 351.

limits on public resources, then this may be an argument for simple, straightforward rules and remedies that are easily administrable.

G. The U.S. Consumer Financial Protection Bureau

The 2010 Dodd-Frank Act has created the U.S. Consumer Financial Protection Bureau as an independent agency within the Federal Reserve with rule-making, supervisory, and enforcement powers. The objectives of the bureau include these: ensuring the provision of timely and understandable information so that consumers can make responsible decisions; protecting consumers from unfair,[119] deceptive, and abusive[120] acts or practices; identifying and addressing outdated, unnecessary, or unduly burdensome regulations; and ensuring that markets for consumer financial products and services operate transparently and efficiently to facilitate access and innovation.[121]

Key aspects of the legislation include these: (1) the bureau is able to monitor credit market developments through a variety of means, including supervisory examinations of regulated entities; (2) rule-making powers are subject to a cost–benefit analysis, taking into account the impact of a rule on financial exclusion; and (3) there is a requirement for empirical testing of mandatory disclosures. The bureau's enforcement powers include the ability to impose cease-and-desist orders and civil penalties, obtain compensation, require public notification by the business of a violation, and impose controls on the activities of a business. Elizabeth Warren, who was until recently the interim head of the bureau, emphasized the importance of the supervisory power as enabling swift intervention before problems become national issues.[122]

---

119 Unfairness is defined in the same manner as the existing definition of unfairness by the Federal Trade Commission, namely that the practice is likely to cause a substantial injury to consumers which is not reasonably avoidable by consumers and is not outweighed by countervailing benefits to consumers or competition. U.S. Dodd-Frank Act, §1031(c).

120 An abusive practice materially interferes with the ability of a consumer to understand the terms or conditions of a consumer financial product or service or takes unreasonable advantage of a lack of understanding of consumers as to material risks, inability of the consumer to protect herself, or reasonable reliance by the consumer on a regulated business to act in the interests of the consumer.

121 *Consumer Financial Protection Act 2010*, Pub. L. 111–203, 124 Stat. 1981, §1021(b)(1–5).

122 See Elizabeth Warren, Media Release, 'Standing Up the Consumer Financial Protection Bureau' (28 October 2010), White House Blog, http://www.whitehouse.gov/blog/2010/10/28/standing-consumer-financial-protection-bureau.

Discussion of the Dodd-Frank Act has focused on the extent to which it provides protection without limiting innovation and consumer choice. Several provisions require the bureau to consider the impact of its decisions on consumer choice. The legislation does not impose mandatory product standards, such as a requirement that mortgage providers offer a 'plain vanilla' mortgage, but it does provide a safe harbour against consumer claims where mortgages meet certain standards.

The bureau has also been designed to prevent the diffuse interests of consumers from being outweighed by the interests of financial industries. Relevant features include these: secure funding; linkages to state enforcement that permit states to 'take up the slack' caused by failures in the federal agency; the requirement of a consumer advisory board; and timely responses on actions taken in response to complaints. The bureau's jurisdiction over credit providers, intermediaries, and enforcers is broad,[123] so initial administrative costs may be high and establishing priorities may pose a challenge.

It is not clear to what extent the bureau will, like the FSA, focus on *ex ante* issues of product design and business plans that create an unacceptable risk to consumers. Its focus on whether a practice is unfair or abusive requires weighing the costs and benefits of the practice for consumers and the limits on consumer choice resulting from regulation.

Limitations on consumer choice should be examined carefully. However, unless we assume that all limits on choice are problematic – undoubtedly a view held by some libertarians – some valuation of the consumer choices forgone should be made. This is not always a simple task and may depend on political judgments about the relative values of consumer protection and consumer choice. The differences between the common law provinces and Quebec on interest rate controls underline this point: Quebec effectively prohibits payday lenders since it will not license lenders whose annual interest rates exceed 35 per cent. Assessment of costs and benefits may also depend on existing laws – that is, consumers may value an existing right more highly than potential new protections, and the benefits of consumer protection regulation are often harder to measure than the immediate costs. Existing protections may be more difficult to remove even if they are ineffectual. Also, assessing 'innovation' in credit products is not simple partly because there is no clear definition of what constitutes innova-

---

123 Although there are some special interest exemptions, such as automobile dealers, which are often credit intermediaries and which must be licensed under the U.K. credit regime.

tion. New credit products can hardly be analogized to pharmaceutical drugs and the introduction of a new credit product may initially create significant risks for vulnerable groups. Payday loans and endowment mortgages are two examples. One possible approach would be to adopt a 'precautionary principle' in relation to novel products or – given the uncertainty of different approaches to regulation – to ensure that there is an institutional opportunity for swift dialogue between different stakeholders that could inform a response.

Regulation in the United States goes through cycles, with some agencies more successful than others. The Consumer Product Safety Commission, for example, though a pioneer in approaches to consumer safety in the 1960s and 1970s, was eclipsed in the early 1980s after becoming immersed in complex rule-making procedures. The U.S. Food and Drug Administration, in contrast, has retained international respect as 'the gold standard' in pharmaceutical control.[124]

H. Enlisting Private Gatekeepers

Imposing liability on a party who has power to control access to a market may be superior to private enforcement or government enforcement. Third-party gatekeepers may be in a better position than consumers or governments to collect information and monitor and control access to a market. Gatekeeper liability is 'imposed on private parties who are able to disrupt misconduct by withholding their cooperation from wrongdoers.'[125] Gatekeepers might include Internet service providers, auditors, employers of undocumented immigrants, or bar owners. Kraakman argues that the comparative effectiveness of gatekeeping to other strategies requires an assessment of the adequacy of existing penalties and the identification of reliable gatekeepers who can effectively detect misconduct at a reasonable cost if legal liability is imposed upon them. The actual application of gatekeeper liability depends on empirical analysis of these criteria.

Much research on gatekeepers has concerned their role in preventing corporate malfeasance in securities regulation.[126] Gatekeeping liability,

---

124 See Daniel Carpenter, *Reputation and Power: Organizational Image and Pharmaceutical Regulation at the FDA* (Princeton: Princeton University Press, 2010).

125 Reinier Kraakman, 'Gatekeepers: The Anatomy of a Third-Party Enforcement Strategy' (1986) 2 J. L. Econ. & Org. 53.

126 For a Canadian example, see Stephanie Ben-Ishai, 'Corporate Gatekeeper Liability in Canada' (2007) 42 Texas Int'l L. J. 441.

however, also plays a role in consumer credit. Payment intermediaries such as credit card providers are important gatekeepers, and several jurisdictions impose liability on payment intermediaries for problems in connected supply contracts – for example, defective goods or services. Financiers may often be in a better position than consumers to monitor and prevent transactions (e.g., use of credit cards for online gambling) and access to markets by suppliers associated with fraudulent or deceptive practices. Payment intermediaries already have incentives to stimulate consumer confidence in making purchases online or in unfamiliar locations. Imposing liability may increase incentives to monitor.[127] A connected financier may be the least-cost loss avoider and risk spreader, particularly for distance contracts or situations where an individual has made a purchase outside her jurisdiction. The scope of connected lender liability differs between countries. Canada, for example, imposes no general connected lender liability on credit card companies, whereas the United Kingdom imposes joint and several liability. The costs of this insurance will be passed on to the consumer so that individuals might be offered the choice of paying a premium for this protection as an alternative to debit card payment where there is no protection.

Lawyers can perform gatekeeper functions in drafting standard form contracts for businesses. Consumers have little input into these forms and many lawyers probably follow Llewellyn's observation that 'business lawyers tend to draft to the edge of the possible.'[128] In consumer transactions a case may be made for lawyers to ensure both that contracts are drafted in plain and intelligible language and are not drafted according to the Llewellyn aphorism. Indeed, this approach is argued to be a consequence of the European directive on unfair terms in that it turns 'on its head the general duty of lawyers to draft wholly and exclusively in the interests of their client, in whatever language is best adapted to preserve and enhance the clients' legal position.'[129]

---

127 For the use of intermediaries in credit markets, see Mann, *Charging Ahead, supra* note 63.

128 Statement of Professor Karl Llewellyn in U.S., Report of New York State Law Revision Commission, *Report of the Law Revision Commission for 1954 and Record of Hearings on the Uniform Commerical Code* (L. Doc. No. 65) (1954) at 113–14, cited in William Vukowich, *Consumer Protection in the Twenty-First Century: A Global Perspective* (Ardsley: Transnational Publishers, 2002) at 506.

129 See Office of Fair Trading, 'Unfair Contract Terms Bulletin 4' (December 1997); and William Vukowich, 'Lawyers and the Standard Form Contract System: A Model Rule That Should Have Been' (1993) 6 Geo. J. Legal Ethics 799.

I. *Safety Nets*

Regulation might also be combined with better use of safety nets (which catch you if you fall off the cliff). Credit insurance provides a safety net, though unfortunately it is associated with significant abuses in relation to unsecured credit. However, innovative approaches to finance mortgage insurance to cover payments for a period of unemployment, accidents, and sickness might be developed.[130] Bankruptcy, as a form of insurance, also provides a safety net, and Canada has the ambiguous distinction of having the highest rate of personal bankruptcy in the world. However, bankruptcy also involves a significant price in terms of financial and personal costs.

J. *Changing the Institutional Structure of Credit Provision*

A logical development to participation by users in regulation is changing the ownership structure of credit provision so that users are also owners. Mutuals and credit unions provide this alternative in credit by offering greater opportunity for user control and direction. Governments can facilitate institutional changes through tax and subsidy policies. Participation is an important value generally in regulation since individuals are more likely to perceive rules as fair if they have had an opportunity to participate in framing the rules.

VII. Conclusion

By way of conclusion, we offer the following specific suggestions, drawn from the foregoing discussion, for improving the consumer credit laws with the aim of heading off disputes that might otherwise lead to costly litigation. Our suggestions relate specifically to consumer credit, but we hope they may provide some inspiration for reforms in other areas of law where the unmet need for legal services is high.

1 Lawmakers must work harder at 'tailoring solutions to problems.' This will involve a greater commitment to evidence-based policy analysis, regulation design, and empirical testing of regulation outcomes.

---

130 See, for example, Mark Stephens, Mike Dailly, and Steve Wilcox, *Developing Safety Nets for Home-Owners* (University of York: Joseph Rowntree Foundation, 2008).

2 Consumer education programs may need some reconsideration to take account of the lessons from the behavioural economics literature about how people process information and make decisions in real life. One important issue is the usefulness of school programs and the like as against the provision of information and advice at times when consumers are most likely to use it.

3 In the consumer credit context, consumers are most likely to need information at the point of entering into a transaction and at the point of default. One possibility at the point of entry might be to require credit providers to include in their advertising contact details for free online or telephone advice about comparative credit costs, budgeting, and related matters. A possibility at the point of default might be to require credit providers to include information in default notices about sources of financial advice, with links and phone numbers (as is required in the United Kingdom).

4 The policy objectives of the truth-in-lending laws require reappraisal and clarification with the following questions in mind: (a) Is the objective to help consumers find the best credit deal, or is it to help them avoid especially bad deals? (b) Are the current laws ap-propriately designed to achieve whichever of these objectives is the operative one, having regard in particular to the timing and content of the disclosures? (c) Apart from the matters of timing and content, are there ways of framing the message to increase its salience?

5 Lawmakers should reassess the viability of cooling-off periods, having regard to the apparently low take-up rates, particularly for door-to-door sales. One possible improvement might be to make it easier for consumers to exercise their cancellation rights, for example, by allowing e-mail cancellations. Consideration should also be given to more effective ways of alerting consumers to their cancellation rights. In the consumer credit context, a cooling-off period may be a useful supplement to the truth-in-lending laws, as a means of addressing the disclosure timing problem.

6 Lawmakers should be encouraged to think more creatively about regulatory responses to consumer problems. The behavioural economics movement suggests a third way, between disclosure laws on the one hand and outright prohibitions on the other, which opens up some interesting new possibilities, including disclosures with a nudge element, opt-out default rules, and voluntary self-exclusion initiatives.

7 Given the limits of demand-side measures such as disclosures, cooling-off periods, or altering consumers' choice architectures, there is an important role for *ex ante* regulation through licensing and minimum standards. These may also have a more distributionally progressive outcome than reliance on individual *ex post* redress mechanisms.

8 Licensing regimes should be well funded, have a range of sanctions, have power to obtain information at low cost on emerging market practices, be able to move quickly to regulate emerging problems, and be structured to avoid the dangers of capture. Further work should be undertaken on measuring the outcomes rather than outputs of licensing regimes.

9 Experimentation with embedding corporate responsibility norms within corporate decision-making structures should continue. The experience of the U.K. Financial Services Authority's 'treating customers fairly' initiative in financial services suggests, however, that this may require substantial regulatory resources to ensure its effectiveness.

10 There are trade-offs in designing minimum standards to achieve optimal precision and ensuring that they do not limit beneficial innovation in credit products. Given the changing nature of credit markets, a regulator should have the power to modify or discard outdated standards.

11 Enlisting intermediaries as private gatekeepers (payment intermediaries, Internet service providers, employers) can be a useful regulatory strategy in cases where the intermediary is better placed than the consumer, or government, to monitor the supplier and to discipline misconduct by withdrawing cooperation or support.

12 Changing the institutional structure of market provision (for example, the development of credit unions) may provide greater opportunity for users to influence the outputs of an industry.

PART 4

Non-Lawyer Forms of Assistance

4 Opportunities and Challenges: Non-Lawyer Forms of Assistance in Providing Access to Justice for Middle-Income Earners

RUSSELL ENGLER

I. Introduction

In this paper, I address the issue of non-lawyer forms of assistance and middle-income access to justice as part of a comprehensive strategy to promote meaningful access to justice. I do so by presenting the ideas of 'non-lawyer' and 'middle income' as variables in, or components of, the larger Access to Justice question. As the Background Paper to the Colloquium cautions, we should be 'attentive to the fact that a focus on solving access to justice problems of the middle class may have an impact on low-income individuals and communities.'[1] How can we be sure whether the steps we propose to assist middle-income earners are not achieved at the expense of low-income individuals and communities? How would we measure the trade-offs?

The danger of pitting middle-income earners against low-income ones is only one reason to address the problem as a component of a coherent approach to access to justice. Since the challenges that call for the provision of increased access to justice flow from the shortage of affordable lawyers in relation to the needs of those who cannot afford lawyers, responses involve a range of solutions short of providing lawyers for all low- and middle-income earners for all their legal needs. Viewed one way, this is an inevitable and appropriate response to a

---

1 University of Toronto Middle-income Access to Civil Justice (MIACJ) Initiative Steering Committee, *University of Toronto Faculty of Law MIACJ Initiative: Background Paper,* background paper for the MIACJ Colloquium, University of Toronto Faculty of Law, 10 and 11 February 2011 [unpublished] at 5 [MIACJ, *Background Paper*], http://www.law.utoronto.ca/documents/conferences2/AccessToJustice_LiteratureReview.pdf.

shortage of resources. Viewed another way, we are resorting to the provision of legal services on the cheap. How will we know whether our responses are appropriate and effective, as opposed to taking us down the path of second-class justice? To what extent is the access we are providing *mere* access as opposed to *meaningful* access to justice?

Part II provides the backdrop to the conversation, including unmet legal needs, the legal services delivery system, the flood of unrepresented litigants in the courts, the available data on the impact of counsel on case outcomes, and the Access to Justice and Civil Right to Counsel Movements. The balance of Part II discusses self-help and limited assistance programs, including the use of non-lawyers, which occurs against the backdrop of these trends. The varying forms that the programs can take and the limited data available as to the effectiveness of assistance programs have profound implications for an access to justice agenda that seeks to provide meaningful access, rather than second-class justice, to those who cannot afford full representation by counsel.

Part III urges a three-pronged approach to a coordinated, overarching access to justice strategy. It includes the following: (1) revising the roles of the key players in the court system; (2) the increased use of assistance programs short of full representation, but paired with evaluation measures to prioritize the programs that impact case outcomes; and (3) where lesser steps are insufficient and basic human needs are at stake, the provision of counsel. While the three-pronged approach focuses on the court system, its analysis applies not only to administrative agencies as well, but also to front-end initiatives aimed at prevention. Part IV returns to the variables, discussing first the implications that flow from a focus on middle-income, as opposed to low-income, individuals and communities and concluding with the question of where the opportunities for non-lawyer assistance might lie.

II. The Context of the Conversation

The exploration of the opportunities and challenges in utilizing non-lawyer forms of assistance occurs in the context of trends that shape the larger access to justice challenges. Assistance programs developed against this backdrop vary in structure, goals, and services they offer. Conversations involving programs must distinguish between the forms of assistance under consideration. A brief discussion of issues of ethics and evaluation that arise with assistance programs concludes the background conversation.

A. Six Key Trends

(1) *Unmet legal needs.* One premise of the colloquium is the vast extent of unmet legal needs for middle-income earners. 'Broadly speaking, our goal is to identify the most acute unmet civil legal needs in the province for middle-income Ontarians across different key areas of law, and to explore a range of existing and possible solutions to these problems.'[2] The Background Paper surveys the literature on 'unmet legal needs,' also discussed as 'Justiciable Problems.'[3] The colloquium's First Plenary Session and the accompanying papers were dedicated to the topic as well.[4] The break-out sessions on Day 2 focused on unmet legal needs in the key areas of consumer, employment, and family law.[5] In the United States, legal needs studies consistently show that 70 to 90 per cent of the legal needs of the poor go unaddressed.[6] Many unmet legal needs involve housing, family, and consumer issues.[7] As Chief Justice Beverley McLachlin noted in her keynote address:

> Do we have adequate access to justice? I think the answer is no. Among those hardest hit are the middle class and the poor. We have wonderful justice for the corporations, and for the wealthy.[8]

(2) *The shortage of affordable legal services.* The related premise is the shortage of available and affordable legal services. The funding for legal aid in Canada 'is limited and the income threshold for legal aid certificates

---

2 MIACJ, *Background Paper, supra* note 1 at 4.

3 *Ibid.* at 22–8.

4 See Pascoe Pleasence and Nigel J. Balmer, *Caught in the Middle: Income, Justiciable Problems, and the Use of Lawyers, supra* this volume.

5 *Id.*

6 Legal Services Corporation, *Documenting the Justice Gap in America: The Current Unmet Civil Legal Needs of Low-Income Americans,* 2nd ed. (Washington: Legal Services Corporation, 2007), http://www.lsc.gov/justicegap.pdf [LSC, *Documenting the Justice Gap*]. Virtually 'all of the recent state studies found a level of need substantially *higher* than the level' found in a 1994 American Bar Association study (emphasis in original); *ibid.* at 13.

7 *Ibid.*

8 Michael McKiernan, 'Lawyers Integral in Making Justice Accessible: McLachlin,' *Law Times,* 21 February 2011, http://www.lawtimesnews.com/201102218262/Headline-News/Lawyers-integral-in-making-justice-accessible-McLachlin [McKiernan, 'Making Justice Accessible'].

or for clinic services is very low.'[9] While making too much money to qualify for legal aid, middle-income earners, as Chief Justice McLachlin observed, cannot hope to pay legal fees that average $338 per hour, leaving them little option but to represent themselves in court or go away empty-handed.[10] Even for low-income Canadians, legal aid does not cover many areas of civil law in which low-income clients need assistance.[11] In the United States, legal services offices represent only a fraction of eligible clients seeking assistance.[12] The worst recession since the Great Depression has dramatically increased the numbers of Americans whose basic human needs are at issue in legal proceedings and who need counsel.[13] Yet the same funding crisis that has expanded the numbers of those needing help has decimated the ability of legal services offices to provide assistance.[14]

(3) *The flood of unrepresented litigants in courts.* In the face of unmet legal needs and the shortage of lawyers, courts are flooded with unrepresented litigants. 'In Ontario, as elsewhere, unrepresented litigants have become a regular feature of the courts.'[15] 'For the most part, the increasing number of unrepresented litigants is a result of rising costs of legal

---

9 MIACJ, *Background Paper, supra* note 1 at 9.

10 McKiernan, 'Making Justice Accessible,' *supra* note 8.

11 *Ibid.*

12 See Alan W. Houseman, 'The Future of Legal Aid: A National Perspective' (2007) 10 U.D.C. L. Rev. 35, 43–46.

13 'The current economic crisis, with its attendant problems of high unemployment, home foreclosures and family stress, has resulted in legal problems relating to consumer credit, housing, employment, bankruptcies, domestic violence and child support, and has pushed many families into poverty for the first time.' LSC, *Documenting the Justice Gap, supra* note 6 at 5, http://www.lsc.gov/pdfs/documenting_the_justice_gap_in_america_2009.pdf.

14 See *ibid.,* at 6. Offices relying on money from Interest on Lawyers Trust Accounts (IOLTA) have faced devastating cutbacks, with plummeting interest rates and the collapse of the real estate market, while offices dependent on aid from state and local governments have faced cutbacks as a result of the fiscal crises facing governments. 'While a long-term trend of increased state funding for civil legal aid has continued, budget crises have put this funding at risk in some states. Revenues from state Interest on Lawyers' Trust Accounts (IOLTA) programs rose in some states with new revenue enhancement techniques, but have recently fallen precipitously in many states as a result of low interest rates and the declining economy, reducing trust account deposits.' In November 2011, Congress approved a spending package for FY2012 that will result in a 14.8 per cent cut to local legal aid programs that receive funding from the Legal Services Corporation. See, Robert Echols, *Access to Justice Headlines,* 1 December 2011, http://www.ATJsupport.org.

15 MIACJ, *Background Paper, supra* note 1 at 9.

services.'[16] While studies of unrepresented litigants in Ontario have not been published by the court system, available evidence indicates that unrepresented litigants are a regular feature in many courts, and are particularly prevalent in family courts.[17] Some statistics from across Canada indicate that the number of unrepresented litigants has been rising in the past fifteen years.[18] In the United States, most family law cases involve at least one party without counsel, and often two.[19] Most tenants, many landlords, and most debtors appear in court without counsel.[20] Unrepresented litigants disproportionately are minorities and typically are poor.[21] They often identify an inability to pay for a lawyer as the primary reason for appearing without counsel.[22]

---

16 *Ibid.*

17 See, for example, Anne-Marie Langan, 'Threatening the Balance of the Scales of Justice: Unrepresented Litigants in the Family Court of Ontario' (2004–5) 30 Queens L.J. 825 [Langan, 'Scales of Justice'].

18 Alberta Rules of Court Project, *Self-Represented Litigants: Consultation Memorandum 12.18* (2005).

19 Russell Engler, 'And Justice for All – Including the Unrepresented Poor: Revisiting the Role of Judges, Mediators, and Clerks' (1999) 67 *Fordham Law Review* 1987 at 2047–52 [Engler, 'And Justice for All']. John M. Greacen, *Self-Represented Litigants and Court and Legal Services Responses to Their Needs: What We Know* (2002) at 3–6, http://www.courtinfo.ca.gov/programs/cfcc/pdffiles/SRLwhatweknow.pdf, accessed 14 July 2010. For an edited version of the article, see John M. Greacen, 'An Administrator's Perspective: The Impact of Self-Represented Litigants on Trial Courts – Testing Stereotypes against Real Data' (2002) 41 *Judges Journal* 32 [Greacen, 'An Administrator's Perspective']. Surveys of litigants in New York City found that 75 per cent of the litigants in the New York City Family Court and 90 per cent of the tenants in Housing Court appeared without counsel: New York, Office of the Deputy Chief Administrative Judge for Justice Initiatives, *Self-Represented Litigants: Characteristics, Needs, Services: The Results of Two Surveys*, Office of the Deputy Chief Administrative Judge for Justice Initiatives (November 2005) [Justice Initiatives, *Two Surveys*].

20 See, for example, Russell Engler, 'Connecting Self-Representation to Civil Gideon: What Existing Data Reveal about When Counsel Is Most Needed' (2010) 37 Fordham Urb. L.J. 37 [Engler, 'Connecting Self-Representation to Civil Gideon'].

21 See, for example, Engler, 'And Justice for All,' *supra* note 19; Greacen, 'An Administrator's Perspective,' *supra* note 19. Surveys from 2005 in New York City found that 79 per cent of the self-represented litigants in Family and Housing Court were African-American or Hispanic. Justice Initiatives, *Two Surveys, supra* note 19 at 3. Regarding income, 21 per cent had incomes below $10,000, an additional 36 per cent had incomes between $10,000 and $20,000, and another 26 per cent had incomes between $21,000 and $30,000; thus 83 per cent of the self-represented litigants had incomes below $30,000. *Id.* at 4. Spanish-speaking litigants had less formal education than English-speaking litigants: *ibid.*

22 'According to most studies, litigants are usually unrepresented because they are unable to afford a lawyer or have been turned away from legal aid': MIACJ, *Background*

(4) *The impact of the absence of counsel.* The consequences of appearing without counsel are devastating, since unrepresented litigants often fare poorly in the courts.

> [I]n housing courts, representation has a large impact on tenants' outcomes, but typically little impact on landlord outcomes. Similar conclusions apply in family law cases (with some caveats), debt cases, and the administrative context, including social security disability appeals and unemployment and immigration cases. Further, representation of only one party may impede the settlement process, for example, by reducing the likelihood of productive negotiations.[23]

Studies from Canada found that (1) representation positively influences outcomes in contested hearings before the Ontario Rental Housing Tribunal;[24] (2) a lack of representation in the Tax Court of Canada may prevent the litigants from obtaining fair outcomes;[25] and (3) 87.5 per cent of judges in a Nova Scotia study thought that unrepresented litigants were generally disadvantaged by a lack of representation.[26] '[U]nrepresented litigants struggle with the process and tend to raise concerns in the courtroom that are irrelevant to the legal issues in question thereby causing frustration for judges.'[27]

(5) *The access to justice movement.* Concern about the fate awaiting un-represented litigants in the courts gave rise to a renewed com-

---

Paper, supra note 1 at 15. See also Engler, 'Connecting Self-Representation to Civil Gideon,' *supra* note 20 at 41.

23 MIACJ, *Background Paper, supra* note 1 at 21 (citations omitted), relying on my meta-study from the United States, Engler, 'Connecting Self-Representation to Civil Gideon,' *supra* note 20 (discussing and analysing many of the studies showing the impact of counsel on case outcomes). But see D. James Greiner and Cassandra Wolos Pattanayak, 'Randomized Evaluation of Legal Assistance Programs: What Difference Does Representation (Offer and Actual Use) Make?' (2012) 112 Yale L.J. [forthcoming] (finding no statistical difference between outcomes between the control and study group for offers of representation by a law school clinic in unemployment appeals).

24 Tenant Duty Counsel Program, *Toronto East Representation Pilot Project Report* (Ontario: Advocacy Centre for Tenants, 2006) [Tenant Duty Counsel Program, *Toronto East Pilot Project Report*].

25 Andre Galant, 'The Tax Court's Informal Procedure and Self-Represented Litigants: Problems and Solutions' (2005) 53 Canadian Tax J. 333.

26 Nova Scotia Department of Justice, *Self-Represented Litigants in Nova Scotia: Needs Assessment Study* (2004).

27 Langan, 'Scales of Justice,' *supra* note 17 at 839–41.

mitment to access to justice. This colloquium uses the ongoing initiatives in Canada and abroad, largely involving access to justice for the poor and working poor, and seeks to focus the conversation on middle-income earners.[28] In the United States, Conferences of Judges and State Court Administrators have adopted resolutions calling for the courts to provide meaningful access to justice.[29] Over the past fifteen years, access to justice initiatives intensified across the United States, spurred by conferences dedicated to the topic.[30] The number of State Access to Justice Commissions increased rapidly; sixteen states created commissions between 2003 and 2008.[31] The commissions, created by order of state supreme courts, are comprised of members from an array of stakeholders in the legal system.[32] The Commissions

---

28 See Michael Trebilcock, Anthony Duggan, and Lorne Sossin, 'Introduction,' *supra* this volume.

29 In 2000 the National Conference of State Court Administrators called on the courts to provide access to justice for those without counsel: *Position Paper on Self-Represented Litigation* (Arlington: Government Relations Office, 2000), http//costa.ncsc.dni.us/WhitePapers/selfrepresentation.pdf.
    The following year, the Conference of Chief Justices promulgated Resolution 23, titled 'Leadership to Promote Equal Justice,' resolving in part to '[r]emove impediments to access to the justice system, including physical, economic, psychological and language barriers': Resolution 23 (adopted 25 January 2001), http://ccj.ncsc.dni.us/AccessToJusticeResolutions/resol23Leadership.html. In 2002 the two conferences jointly issued Resolution 31, resolving that 'courts have an affirmative obligation to ensure that all litigants have meaningful access to the courts, regardless of representation status.' See, for example, Resolution 31 (adopted 1 August 2002), National Center for State Courts, http://www.ncsconline.org/WC/Publications/Res_ProSe_CCJCOSCAResolution31Pub.pdf.

30 For example, Eastern Regional Conference on Access to Justice for the Self-Represented Litigant (White Plains, 2006); the New York State Unified Court System Access to Justice Conference (Albany, 2001).

31 Karla M. Gray and Robert Echols, 'Mobilizing Lawyers, Judges, and Communities: State Access to Justice Commissions' (2008) 17 *Judges Journal* 33 at 35–6. Although only five states had Access to Justice Commissions in 1999, the number had increased to twenty-three by June 2006. More than a dozen additional states had an active committee of the state bar or bar association charged with the broad access to justice function. See Access to Justice Support Project, *Access to Justice Partnerships, State by State* (2005) at 1, http://www.nlada.org/Civil/Civil_SPAN/SPAN_Report, accessed 29 June 2010. Kentucky, by order of its Supreme Court in October 2010, became the most recent state to create an Access to Justice Commission: Robert Echols, *Access to Justice Headlines*, 2 February 2011, on file with author; see also Resource Center for Access to Justice Initiatives, http://www.ATJsupport.org.

32 Robert Echols, 'The Rapid Expansion of State Access to Justice Commissions' (2005) *Management Information Exchange Journal* 41. The stakeholders typically include the courts, organized bar, civil legal aid providers, and law schools: *ibid*.

have a broad charge to engage in an ongoing assessment of the civil legal needs of the poor and to develop initiatives to respond to those needs.[33]

(6) *The revitalized civil right to counsel movement.* In the United States the years after 2003, the fortieth anniversary of *Gideon v. Wainwright*,[34] saw a sharp increase in activity supporting a civil right to counsel. Articles,[35] conferences,[36] and speeches[37] addressed the issue, while membership surged in the newly formed National Coalition for a Civil Right to Counsel.[38] Some advocates pursued test case strategies attempting to establish the right to counsel by court decision,[39] while others pursued a legislative strategy.[40] In 2006, the American Bar

---

33 *Ibid.*

34 372 U.S. 335 (1963).

35 See, for example, 'Special Issue: A Right to a Lawyer? Momentum Grows' (2006) 40 *Clearinghouse Review* 163–293 ['Momentum Grows']; '2006 Edward V. Sparer Symposium, Civil Gideon: Creating a Constitutional Right to Counsel in the Civil Context' (2006) 15 Temple Political & Civ. Rights L. Rev. 697–800.

36 Conferences across the country included panels on Civil Gideon as part of the broader discussion of access to justice in civil cases. For example, the symposium 'Legal Representation and Access to Justice: Breaking Point or Opportunity to Change,' jointly sponsored by the Korematsu Center for Justice and the Seattle University School of Law, was held on 19 February 2010. The Sparer Symposium, held on 28 March 2006 and titled 'Civil Gideon: Making the Case,' was co-sponsored by Rutgers, Penn, Villanova, and Widener Law Schools: http://www.law.upenn.edu/pic/students/Sparer06Program.pdf. Washington State's Access to Justice Conference in 2002 included a panel dedicated to the topic. See Paul Marvy, 'To Promote Jurisprudential Understanding of the Law: The Civil Right to Counsel in Washington State' (2006) 40 *Clearinghouse Review* 180.

37 Justice Johnson's speech, delivered at the Pathways to Justice Conference in Los Angeles, 7 June 2008, was published in *Clearinghouse Review:* 'Three Phases of Justice for the Poor: From Charity to Discretion to Right' (2009) 43 *Clearinghouse Review* 486. See also Robert J. Derocher, 'Access to Justice: Is Civil Gideon a Piece of the Puzzle?' (2008) *ABA Bar Leader* 11 at 11.

38 See, for example, Paul Marvy and Debra Gardner, 'A Civil Right to Counsel for the Poor' (2005) 32 *Human Rights* 8 at 9.

39 See, for example, *Frase v. Barnhart*, 840 2d 144, 379 Md. 100 (2003); *Kelly v. Warpinski*, No. 04-2999-0A (Wisc. Sup. Ct., filed 17 November 2004); *King v. King*, 162 Wash. 2d 378, 174 P. 3d 659 (2007).

40 See, for example, Texas H.B. No. 2124, 79th Leg., Reg. Sess. (Tex. 2005), relating to appointment of counsel in appeals of certain eviction suits. A model statute from California became the basis for a more recent *Model Access Act* adopted by the American Bar Association. See Clare Pastore, 'The California Model Statute Task Force' (2006) 40 *Clearinghouse Review* 176 [Pastore, 'California Model Statute Task Force']; the ABA Model Act, and accompanying Basic Principles, are available at http://www.abanet.

Association unanimously adopted Resolution 112A, urging the provision of

> legal counsel as a matter of right at public expense to low income persons in those categories of adversarial proceedings where basic human needs are at stake, such as those involving shelter, sustenance, safety, health or child custody, as determined by each jurisdiction.[41]

The adoption of ABA Resolution 112A spurred a flurry of activity often coordinated with, and bolstered by, the work of state Access to Justice Commissions. In Massachusetts, the Boston Bar Association (BBA) created its Task Force on Expanding the Civil Right to Counsel, which included members from key statewide stakeholders; the task force identified nine pilot projects in four substantive areas in an effort to explore starting points for expansion of the right to counsel.[42] In California, advocates drafted two model statutes providing for an expanded civil right to counsel,[43] before the state enacted, in the fall of 2009, legislation to provide funding for civil right to counsel pilot projects.[44] In

---

org/legalservices/sclaid/downloads. Advocates in New York expanded the reach of the statutory right to counsel in divorce cases to the Supreme Court and drafted and arranged for the filing of legislation initiatives covering the elderly in eviction and foreclosure cases. See N.Y. Judiciary Law, Section 35 (8) (amended September 2006); Manny Fernandez, 'Free Legal Aid Sought for Elderly Tenants,' *New York Times,* 16 November 2007, http://www.nytimes.com/2007/11/16/nyregion/16housing.html?_r=1&oref=slogin, accessed 14 July 2010.

41 The ABA House of Delegates adopted the resolution on 7 August 2006 at its Annual Meeting. For the resolution and the report of the ABA Task Force on Access to Civil Justice, see *Report to the House of Delegates* (7 August 2006), http://www.americanbar.org/content/dam/aba/migrated/legalservices/sclaid/downloads/06A112A.authcheckdam.pdf.

42 *Gideon's New Trumpet: Expanding the Civil Right to Counsel in Massachusetts,* Report of the Boston Bar Association Task Force on Expanding the Civil Right to Counsel in Massachusetts (September 2008), http://www.bostonbar.org/prs/reports/GideonsNewTrumpet.pdf [*Gideon's New Trumpet*]. The Boston Bar Association (BBA) and Massachusetts Bar Association held a joint conference to begin implementing the resolution. For a description of the Joint MBA/BBA Civil Gideon Symposium, held in October 2007, see Kelsey Sadoff, 'Civil Gideon Symposium Mobilizes Legal Community Behind Equal Justice in Law,' http://www.massbar.org/for-attorneys/publications/lawyers-journal/2007/november/civil-gideon-symposium-mobilizes-legal-community-behind-equal-justice-in-law.

43 See Pastore, 'California Model Statute Task Force,' *supra* note 40.

44 See Carol J. Williams, 'California Gives the Poor a New Legal Right,' *Los Angeles Times,* 17 October 2009, http://www.latimes.com/news/local/la-me-civil-gideon17-2009oct17,0,7682738.story, accessed 14 July 2010. Assembly Bill 590, creating the

New York, Chief Judge Lippmann called for implementation of a civil right to counsel and appointed a Task Force to Expand Access to Legal Services.[45] In 2011, the Maryland Access to Justice Commission released its report, 'Implementing a Civil Right to Counsel in Maryland.'[46] In Canada, the Supreme Court has thus far declined to recognize a broad right to counsel in civil settings.[47] Nor has the Court recognized access to justice as a constitutional basis for requiring state-funded civil legal services.[48]

---

pilot projects, was signed into law by Governor Schwarzenegger on 11 October 2009: http://www.leginfo.ca.gov/pub/09-10/bill/asm/ab_0551-0600/ab_590_bill_20091011_chaptered.pdf, accessed 14 July 2010. See also 'Note: California Establishes Pilot Program to Expand Access to Counsel for Low-Income Parties' (2010) 123 Harv. L. Rev. 1532.

45 Chief Judge Lippmann issued one call for an expanded civil right to counsel in a speech to the Central Synagogue of New York on 5 February 2010, titled '"Justice, Justice Shall You Pursue": The Chief Judge's Perspective on Justice and Jewish Values' (speech on file with author). 'The time has come for New York State to make good on its promise of Gideon and ensure that there is a right to counsel at public expense in at least those cases where basic human needs are at stake, like shelter, sustenance, safety, health and children': *ibid.* at 13–14. Regarding the creation of the task force, see Daniel Wise, 'Lippman Names 28 to Task Force to Expand Access to Legal Services,' *New York Law Journal* (10 June 2010), http://www.law.com/jsp/nylj/PubArticleNY.jsp?id=1202462459386&Lippman_Names__to_Task_Force_to_Expand_Access_to_Legal_Services&slreturn=1&hbxlogin=1, accessed 22 June 2010. New York advocates also convened a day-long symposium in March 2008, designed to create a blueprint for a Civil Right to Counsel in their state. The proceedings, and related articles, are published in the symposium volume 'An Obvious Truth: Creating an Action Blueprint for a Civil Right to Counsel in New York State' (2009) 25 Touro L. Rev. 1–539.

46 The report is available at http://www.mdcourts.gov/mdatjc/pdfs/implementing acivilrighttocounselinmd2011.pdf. Advocates in Maryland held a conference dedicated to the topic in 2007. See Stephen H. Sachs, 'Keynote Address: Seeking a Right to Counsel in Appointed Civil Cases in Maryland' (2007) 37 U. Balt. L. Rev. 5.

47 While a general right to counsel in criminal justice contexts is set out in s.10(b) of the Canadian *Charter of Rights and Freedoms*, the right to counsel in civil contexts is assessed on a case-by-case basis. As the Court stated in a *per curiam* judgment in *British Columbia (A.G.) v. Christie* 2007 SCC 21 at para. 25: 'Section 7 of the *Charter*, for example, has been held to imply a right to counsel as an aspect of procedural fairness where life, liberty, and security of the person are affected: see *Dehghani v. Canada (Minister of Employment and Immigration)*, [1993] 1 S.C.R. 1053, at p. 1077; *New Brunswick (Minister of Health and Community Services) v. G. (J.)*, [1999] 3 S.C.R. 46. But this does not support a general right to legal assistance whenever a matter of rights and obligations is before a court or tribunal. Thus in *New Brunswick*, the Court was at pains to state that the right to counsel outside of the s. 10(*b*) context is a case-specific multi-factored enquiry (see para. 86).'

48 The Court affirmed in *Christie, ibid.,* that 'the text of the Constitution, the jurispru-

B. The Evolution of Self-Help Programs and Assistance Programs

While many of the trends discussed in the previous section have accelerated in recent years, the problems of unmet legal needs and the shortage of affordable counsel are not new. The past ten to fifteen years have seen an explosion of forms of assistance short of full representation by counsel, as various players have struggled to assist bewildered and often desperate low-, moderate-, and middle-income families. The programs include hotlines, technological assistance, clinics, *pro se* clerks' offices, Lawyer-of-the-Day programs, and self-help centres, developed to provide assistance to litigants who otherwise would receive no help at all.[49] Programs that comprise the 'legal services spectrum' short of full representation and holistic services include the following: self-help services; public legal education and information; advice from non-lawyers and non-paralegals; paralegals; summary advice; brief services; and referrals and duty counsel.[50]

In a world of scarce resources, it will be an essential component of an effective access to justice strategy to understand which types of assistance programs are most effective in dealing with which types of legal problems and clients. We must target scarce resources to scenarios in which they will truly assist, and avoid squandering resources where they are likely to be ineffective. The next sections use familiar variables to understand the range of possible programs; flag ethical concerns that might limit the applicability of some programs in some scenarios; and explore what we know from efforts at evaluating the programs.

(1) THE VARIETY OF POTENTIAL ASSISTANCE PROGRAMS

As extensive as the list of forms of assistance program may be, it takes little imagination to realize that programs will continue to emerge, each a bit different from programs known in other contexts. Thus, the familiar categories of Who, What, When, Where, Why, and How, although in a different order, illustrate the potential for creativity in the construction of assistance programs in a given context.

---

dence and the historical understanding of the rule of law do not foreclose the possibility that a right to counsel may be recognized in specific and varied situations. But at the same time, they do not support the conclusion that there is a general constitutional right to counsel in proceedings before courts and tribunals dealing with rights and obligations' (at para. 23).

49 Houseman, *supra* note 12, at 40–3; Engler, 'And Justice for All,' *supra* note 19 at 2003–6.

50 MIACJ, *Background Paper, supra* note 1 at 30–49.

What may involve the type of program employed. The range suggested by the legal services spectrum, such as hotlines, self-help centres, and duty lawyers, illustrates the types of programs available. 'What' may refer as well to the services provided. Does the program provide only information or advice as well? Do those utilizing the service receive assistance in filling out court documents? Or does the program provide general information with referral numbers?

Who can involve lawyers and non-lawyers, alone or in combination. Where lawyers are involved, are they funded publicly or privately? Do the lawyers volunteer, or are they compensated for their work? Are court personnel involved, and if so, are they clerks, court-connected mediators, judges, or someone else? Where lay advocates are involved, they may be court personnel, paralegals, volunteers, law students, social services agencies, members of government offices, or law and public librarians, among the many possibilities.

The categories of *how*, *where*, and *when* can overlap, depending on the type of program. Is the assistance being provided in person, over the phone, via e-mail, or through a website? Is the office providing assistance inside or outside the courthouse? In terms of timing, is the assistance provided in advance of court or an administrative hearing, during the day of the hearing, after the hearing has been completed, or as some form of front-end prevention designed to avert the court date or hearing in the first place?

Ultimately, the category of *why* may be the most salient question, since forms of assistance should be designed to address certain identified needs. *Why* should then be thought of in terms of goals: What is the program attempting to accomplish, and why is a particular format, using certain personnel, the best design for addressing the goals?

(2) ETHICAL ISSUES FLOWING FROM VARYING STRUCTURES

The realization that there are innumerable formulations for potential assistance programs makes the development and prioritization of goals a key component of program design and analysis. Some structures may be more likely to achieve articulated goals in a particular setting. Ethical issues surrounding the development and operation of assistance programs may also impact the choices. Although a detailed exploration of ethical issues is beyond the scope of this paper,[51] the

---

51 For an analysis in the context of the United States, see Russell Engler, 'Approaching Ethical Issues Involving Unrepresented Litigants' (2009) 43 *Clearinghouse Review* 377 [Engler, 'Approaching Ethical Issues'].

variables identified in the preceding section suggest related ethical issues.

Where responses to access to justice issues involve the roles of judges, court-connected mediators, clerks, and other personnel, the issues surrounding the provision of assistance while remaining impartial and without providing legal advice are the subject of much analysis.[52] Where lawyers provide assistance short of full representation, the ethical issues involving unbundled legal services and ghostwriting have captured the lion's share of the attention.[53] A closer analysis reveals that those issues entail the application, to unfamiliar scenarios, of the familiar ethical issues, including the scope of representation, the measure of competent representation, the establishment of the lawyer–client relationship, the application of the conflict of interest rules, and the duty of candor.[54] Where the programs utilize non-lawyers, including law students, the issues relate to the unauthorized practice of law, most notably the challenges of parsing the distinction between the giving of legal advice and the provision of legal information.[55]

(3) WHAT WE KNOW AND WHAT THE KNOWLEDGE IMPLIES

While the assessment of goals and analysis of ethical issues should be key components in designing assistance programs that provide meaningful access to justice, the effectiveness of particular programs in certain settings should be key as well. Yet '[w]ith programs facilitating self-representation, litigants and court personnel report high levels of satisfaction with the programs; the programs' impact on case outcomes is less clear.'[56] The importance of including the study of case outcomes in evaluating assistance programs is illustrated by a 2003 evaluation of a self-help centre in California: in rent disputes, Center-assisted litigants consistently agreed to pay landlords *higher* amounts of back rent than unassisted litigants.[57] Whatever the challenges of measuring improved

---

52 See, for example, Russell Engler, 'Ethics in Transition: Unrepresented Litigants and the Changing Judicial Role' (2008) 22 Notre Dame J.L. Eth. & Pub. Pol'y 67 [Engler, 'Ethics in Transition']; Engler, 'And Justice for All,' *supra* note 19.

53 See, for example, Engler, 'Approaching Ethical Issues,' *supra* note 51 at 378–81. Plenary Session 4 of the Colloquium, dedicated to Access to Lawyers, included a paper presentation and discussion of the issues surrounding unbundling: Samreen Beg and Lorne Sossin, 'Should Legal Services Be Unbundled?', *infra* this volume.

54 See, for example, Engler, 'Approaching Ethical Issue,' *supra* note 51 at 381–2.

55 See, for example, *ibid.* at 382.

56 Engler, 'Connecting Self-Representation to Civil Gideon,' *supra* note 20 at 3.

57 *Ibid.* at 88–9, discussing the Empirical Research Group, UCLA Law School, 'Evaluation of the Van Nuys Legal Self-Help Center, Final Report' (2003) at 1, 11. Professor

access to justice, an assistance program that leaves less money in the pockets of those who seek assistance than they would have had they bypassed the assistance cautions against the breezy assumption that any help will always make things better, not worse.

If the evaluations of assistance programs provide little guidance for measuring case outcomes, the reports of the impact of full representation indicate the types of data points that could be studied. For example, eviction cases from the United States have used possession, rent abatements, repairs, and time between the court date and an eventual move-out as data points for evaluation.[58] Studies of family law issues have assessed the awards of custody, alimony, and child support and restraining orders;[59] while debt collection cases explore the default rate, who wins the judgment, and the amount of any judgment awarded against a defendant.[60] The outcomes of administrative hearings involving government benefits typically involve fewer variables, focusing on the award or denial of benefits.[61]

The dearth of reliable studies of assistance programs and case outcomes suggests the need for further research; nonetheless, the reports provide important clues for our responses to the problems of unmet legal needs and the shortage of affordable lawyers. The data from the reports that attempt to measure the impact of counsel show that the greater the imbalance of power between the parties, the more likely it will be that extensive assistance will be necessary to impact the case outcome. The power or powerlessness can derive from the substantive or procedural law, the judge, and the operation of the forum; those features in turn may be considered other variables, beyond representation, that impact case outcomes. Disparities in economic resources, barriers (such as those due to race, ethnicity, disability, language, and education), and the presence of counsel for only one side can affect the calculus as well. The greater the imbalance of power, the greater is the need for a skilled advocate with expertise in the forum to provide the needed help.[62]

Gary Blasi, involved in the first Van Nuys evaluation, theorizes that the centre acted as a 'dispenser of norms,' raising expectations by explaining how the legal system should work, as opposed to how it likely would work: *ibid.* at 88.

58 See Engler, 'Connecting Self-Representation to Civil Gideon,' *supra* note 20 at 46–51.

59 *Ibid.* at 51–5.

60 *Ibid.* at 55–8.

61 *Ibid.* at 58–66.

62 For a more detailed exploration of these issues, see *ibid.* at 73–85.

III. An Overarching Access to Justice Strategy

The preceding sections underscore the need for an overarching, coordinated access to justice strategy. The extent of unmet legal needs and the devastating consequences of the lack of appropriate assistance require that we identify ways to provide meaningful access. Not only must every tool in the legal services delivery spectrum play a role in the strategy, but the strategy must look beyond the delivery system for approaches to removing barriers and increasing access. At the same time, however, the danger that solutions to one part of the access to justice problem might exacerbate problems elsewhere serves as a reminder that the strategies must not only be coordinated and comprehensive, but also include evaluation components to ensure that the responses we craft are truly solutions. This section outlines a broad strategy, initially focused on the court system, before expanding the vision beyond the courts.

A. A Framework for Decision Making

I articulate elsewhere an overarching, coordinated access to justice strategy that includes three prongs:

1 the expansion of the roles of the court system's key players, such as judges, court-connected mediators, and clerks, to require them to assist unrepresented litigants as necessary to prevent a forfeiture of important rights;
2 the use of assistance programs, rigorously evaluated to identify which most effectively protect litigants from the forfeiture of rights; and
3 the adoption of a civil right to counsel where the expansion of the roles of the key players and the assistance programs do not provide the necessary help to vulnerable litigants.[63]

---

63 See, for example, Russell Engler, 'Towards a Context-Based Civil Gideon through Access to Justice Initiatives' (2006) 40 *Clearinghouse Review* 196. For a discussion of the importance of understanding the civil Gideon initiative as an exercise in effectuating social change rather than framing legal claims, see Engler, 'Shaping a Context-Based Civil Gideon from the Dynamics of Social Change' (2006) 15 Temple Political and Civ. Rights Law Rev. 697.

With Prong 1, the need and justification for a revision of the roles of the key players flows from fundamental principles of justice that are the hallmark of our adversarial system. The rules that implicate the analysis are general, and the standard application of the rules governing judges, mediators, and clerks to fact patterns that confront court personnel daily depends on the customs established in courts, not the text of the rules.[64] While judges and clerks historically viewed their roles towards unrepresented litigants passively, the past decade has seen a shift in attitudes.[65]

The need to revise the roles of key players flows from needs of the litigants – the courts' 'consumers' – who are appearing without counsel in vast numbers.[66] The underlying goal of our justice system is to be fair and just. The ethical rules shaping the roles of the players in the adversary system imply that unrepresented litigants are the exception. Given the realities of many of our courts, our traditional understanding of the roles frustrates rather than furthers the goal of fairness and justice. As between abandoning the goal and changing the roles, we should change the roles.

The focus on fairness and justice, in substance and not simply appearance, requires shifting the approach to cases involving unrepresented litigants. We must revise our understanding of what it means to be impartial, rejecting the idea that impartiality equals passivity.[67] A system favouring those with lawyers, without regard to the law and facts, is a partial, not impartial, system. Judges, court-connected mediators, and clerks must play an active role to maintain the system's impartiality and ensure that unrepresented litigants do not forfeit rights due to the absence of counsel.[68]

Prong 2 covers assistance programs beyond the work of court personnel and short of full representation by counsel. Part II above explores the range of programs and suggests the innumerable possible formulations of such programs.[69] Innovative programs are an important component in the strategy to increase access to justice. Yet a comprehensive access

---

64 See, for example, Engler, 'And Justice for All,' *supra* note 19.
65 See Engler, 'Ethics in Transition,' *supra* note 52.
66 See Part II.A.iii, *supra*.
67 See, for example, Engler, 'And Justice for All,' *supra* note 19 at 2023–4; Jona Goldschmidt, 'The Pro Se Litigant's Struggle for Access to Justice: Meeting the Challenge of Bench and Bar Resistance' (2002) 40 *Family Court Review* 36.
68 Engler, 'And Justice for All,' *supra* note 19 at 1992–8, 2007–40.
69 See Part II.B.1, *supra*.

to justice strategy requires that we evaluate the programs carefully. Evaluation tools must identify which programs help stem the forfeiture of rights and which only help the courts run more smoothly, without affecting case outcomes.[70] Programs not affecting case outcomes may be worthwhile, but are not a solution to the problem of the forfeiture of rights due to the absence of counsel.

When revising the roles of judges, mediators, and clerks and using assistance programs short of full representation are insufficient, we can no longer accept the denial of access and routine forfeiture of rights as acceptable outcomes. In those instances, we must recognize and establish a right to counsel in civil cases. The 2006 ABA Resolution,[71] with its focus on basic human needs, is an important starting point. However difficult it may be to envision starting points for an expanded civil right to counsel, particularly in the face of legal aid cutbacks, the desperate times compel us to press ahead.[72]

B. The Pieces Are Already in Place

If the challenges facing the implementation of an overarching strategy seem overwhelming, the reality that steady progress has been achieved on each prong should provide some measure of solace. Regarding Prong 1, the attitudes towards the roles of judges, court-connected mediators, and clerks have undergone a sea change over the past fifteen years.[73] Conferences, trainings, Access to Justice Resolutions, and the work of state Access to Justice Commissions have accelerated the trends.[74] Regarding Prong 2, the ongoing development of assistance programs ensures that energetic and innovative advocates will continue to try to identify ways to provide assistance, despite the shortage of resources.[75]

---

70 See Part II.B.3, *supra*.

71 See Part II.A.6, *supra*.

72 For an exploration of these ideas, and a proposed seven-step approach for identifying starting points for a civil right to counsel, see Russell Engler, 'Pursuing Access to Justice and Civil Right to Counsel in a Time of Economic Crisis' (2010) 15 Roger Williams Law Rev. 472.

73 See, for example, Engler, 'Ethics in Transition,' *supra* note 52. The recent Supreme Court decision in *Turner v. Rogers*, No. 10-10, 564 U.S. (20 June 2011). For a discussion of *Turner*, see Richard Zorza, 'A New Day for Judges and the Self-Represented: The Implications of *Turner v. Rogers* (2011) 50 Judges' Journal 16.

74 *Ibid.*

75 See Part II.B., *supra*.

The careful articulation of goals, the commitment to match needs with structures of assistance programs likely to effectuate the goals, and the use of evaluative tools to ensure that the programs are delivering as anticipated are essential tools for the Prong 2 strategy. While sceptics might question the extent of progress achieved by the civil right to counsel movement, the strategies employed over the past decade suggest that the issue will not go away and that the ultimate success of the initiatives might be as components of, rather than substitutes for, larger access to justice strategies.[76]

C. Beyond the Court-Based Focus on the Key Prongs

That the three-pronged strategy is focused on the courts derives from the reality that unrepresented litigants are flooding the courts in unprecedented numbers, causing challenges for the courts and opposing counsel, while resulting in the forfeiture of important rights by the unrepresented litigants due to the absence of counsel. While the courts may present the most immediate challenges, the effectiveness of the overarching strategy requires broadening its reach in two respects. First, the scope of Prong 1 should expand beyond the courts to administrative agencies and tribunals. Issues important to many lower and middle-income earners are resolved in the administrative agencies, rather than the courts. The lack of representation affects court and *tribunal* processes and fairness of outcomes, as the example of the Ontario Rental Housing Tribunal illustrates.[77] Studies from the United States regarding the impact of representation reveal problems facing unrepresented claimants in administrative agency proceedings.[78]

Second, to the extent that the focus on courts and tribunals involves back-end solutions, access to justice strategies must include front-end solutions as well. In one sense, the focus on administrative tribunals is both a back-end issue and a front-end approach, at least where judicial review follows the tribunal decision. Improvements to the tribunal and agency processes might result both in an increase in meaningful access and in a decrease in the resulting court challenges. Yet the front-end

---

76 See Part II.A.6, *supra*. For one recent articulation of an 'emerging consensus' that includes the pieces in the Access to Justice strategy proposed here, see Richard Zorza, 'Access to Justice: The Emerging Consensus and Some Questions and Implications' (2011) 94 *Judicature* 156.

77 Tenant Duty Counsel Program, *Toronto East Pilot Project Report, supra* note 24, discussed in *Background Paper, supra* note 1 at 21 (emphasis in original).

78 See Engler, 'Connecting Self-Representation to Civil Gideon,' *supra* note 20 at 58–66.

strategies are far broader than efforts to improve the operations of tribunals and agencies. Plenary 2 of the colloquium focused on 'Front-End' Proactive Solutions, with the accompanying paper by Professors Duggan and Ramsay using the context of consumer cases to illustrate the range of tools that comprise the arsenal for front-end solutions.[79] Education programs, licensing and certification regimes, and regulatory frameworks are 'a very small sample of the myriad opportunities we have to develop programs, resources, and systems that will minimize or eliminate the need to resort to the legal system in order to resolve some disputes for specific individuals.'[80]

D. Illustrating the Point

Key to the overall strategy not only is the utilization of all three prongs with the front-end strategies, but also the coordination of the various strategies. Even assuming that an expanded right to counsel will be a key component of an overall strategy, how can we understand the scope of the right, and where might lesser steps suffice? The scope of the right to counsel is directly dependent on the effectiveness of the first two prongs in the access to justice strategy. Where steps short of full representation succeed in protecting litigants from the devastating outcomes that might occur where their basic human needs are at stake, appointment of counsel might not be needed. As a result, the more that judges, mediators, clerks, and assistance programs are effective in stemming the forfeiture of rights due to the absence of counsel, the smaller will be the pool of cases in which counsel is needed. Where nothing short of full representation can provide the needed assessment, the right to counsel must attach.

An example from the efforts to assist tenants in Massachusetts illustrates the importance of utilizing a comprehensive strategy. In Massachusetts, as elsewhere in the United States, eviction cases typically proceed in court, with virtually all tenants appearing without counsel, while in many settings landlords are represented by counsel; available reports indicate that tenants are steamrolled by the process, losing swiftly and dramatically in comparison to represented tenants.[81]

A 2008 study of evictions in the District Court in Cambridge, Mass-

---

79 See Anthony Duggan and Iain Ramsay, 'Front-End Strategies for Improving Consumer Access to Justice,' *supra* this volume.

80 *Background Paper, supra* note 1 at 30.

81 For a more detailed discussion of the reports of the impact of counsel in housing cases, see Engler, 'Connecting Self-Representation to Civil Gideon,' *supra* note 20 at 46–51.

achusetts, revealed that a high percentage of evictions are brought by the Cambridge Housing Authority, often for non-payment of rent of amounts totalling less than $1,000.[82] One response to this problem is to provide counsel for all tenants. A solution focused entirely on a civil right to counsel would need to calculate the number of cases per year, estimate the number of hours per case, settle on an hourly rate for the work, and propose the resulting, presumably large, price tag as the cost needed to respond to the problem. Alternatively, courts could modify their procedures, or a program might be designed to provide some assistance to tenants.

The comprehensive strategy suggests use of a fuller range of responses in coordination. At Prong 1, the roles of the judges, court-connected mediators, clerks, and other court personnel should be re-examined to ensure that the players are part of the solution, rather than the problem. Each aspect of the court's process is ripe for reform to ensure that procedures, forms, and materials enhance rather than frustrate meaningful access. The tools available as part of front-end strategies will be particularly valuable with the realization that the Housing Authority is an independent government agency; its practices could be modified to place the emphasis on keeping tenants in their homes and reducing the use of eviction proceedings. Where the authorities receive federal funding, oversight and regulation from the federal government can impact the calculus; the role of state governments is similarly implicated for state-funded authorities.

At Prong 2, the full menu of assistance programs may be utilized, but paired with evaluation, to identify which programs actually impact case outcomes.[83] Prong 2 also envisions non-legal forms of assistance. In Massachusetts, for example, the Tenancy Preservation Program connects vulnerable tenants to social services agencies, as an attempt to address underlying issues in households that may be the deeper causes of the problems that manifest themselves in court as non-payment of rent issues.[84] Finally, the use of counsel at Prong 3 remains an essential

---

82 Jennifer Greenwood et al., Tenancy at Risk: Leveling the Playing Field, Northeastern University School of Law Legal Skills in Social Context Community Lawyering Program (May 2008) (unpublished report on file with author).

83 The lessons of the Massachusetts legal services pro se clinics suggest that the minimal assistance alone might be ineffective, but the effect increases when used in conjunction with greater levels of assistance. See Engler, 'Connecting Self-Representation to Civil Gideon,' supra note 20 at 67–8.

84 For a description and account of the effectiveness of the program, see Massachu-

component of the response. Its use as part of a larger strategy, however, suggests the potential for a far smaller price tag, in keeping with the idea that counsel is needed where something important is at stake (the roof over a family's head must be at or near the top of any such list) and nothing short of full representation will suffice to provide meaningful access to justice.

IV. The Variables of Middle-Income and 'Non-Lawyers'

Using the three-pronged access to justice strategy as a framework, it becomes easier to focus on the variables of middle-income and non-lawyers. The framework not only suggests opportunities but also provides cautionary concerns to help assess where the responses are likely to be part of the solution as opposed to part of the problem. As the next section reveals, not only will virtually every tool in the access to justice arsenal apply with full force to the problems of middle-income earners, but the tools short of full representation might actually be more effective for middle-income earners than low-income earners. The framework also suggests the range of opportunities for non-lawyer forms of assistance, as the final section explores.

A. The Question of Middle-Income versus Low-Income Earners

Using the three prongs as a starting point, each initiative involving access to justice with low-income earners should apply with full force to middle-income earners for the simple reason that the initiatives are not means-tested in their application. Regarding the players in the court system at Prong 1, to the extent we revise the roles of judges, court-connected mediators, and clerks, every unrepresented court user would benefit, whether low or middle income. The Background Paper ends by discussing Adjudicative Processes and Alternatives; the ideas include Informal Complaint Systems, Mediation, and – under the category of Court Reform – Proportionality, Diversion and Streaming, Simplifica-

---

setts Housing Finance Agency Press Release, 'UMass Study Finds Mass Housing Tenancy Preservation Program Highly Effective in Preventing Homelessness among Tenants with Disabilities' (25 March 2010), https://www.masshousing.com/portal/server.pt/gateway/PTARGS_0_2_8580_0_0_18/2010-03-25-TPP.pdf. The full report is available at https://www.masshousing.com/portal/server.pt/gateway/PTARGS_0_2_8582_0_0_18/TPP_Presentation_Final.pdf.

tion, and Case Management and Technology.[85] Each of these structural changes applies to all court users, including middle-income earners.

Proposals from Massachusetts illustrate the point. The Massachusetts Supreme Judicial Court responded to the flood of unrepresented litigants in the courts by creating a Steering Committee on Self-Represented Litigants. The Steering Committee's work, which relates directly to the Prong 1 analysis, included a focus on judicial guidelines and training, guidelines and training for court staff, and user-friendly courts among its six major areas of inquiry.[86] The Steering Committee's final recommendations included the following:

(2) further guidance to judges on ethical conduct and useful courtroom techniques in cases involving self-represented litigants;

(3) additional simplified forms and self-help materials for self-represented litigants;

(4) educational programs for court staff;

(5) expanded use of technology;

(6) experimentation with court service centers in courthouses, particularly in those that have multiple court departments; … and

(8) establishment of a senior-level position with the Administrative Office of the Trial Court to direct court-based policy and programs relating to Access to Justice or, alternatively, an appointment of a judge in each Trial Court Department to serve as the coordinator of services for self-represented litigants.[87]

Each of the recommendations attacks the problem of the lack of access for both low and middle-income earners.

At Prong 2, there is no inherent reason why the assistance programs

---

85 *Background Paper, supra* note 1 at 79–121.

86 Massachusetts Supreme Judicial Court Press Release, 'Supreme Judicial Court Steering Committee on Self-Represented Litigants Presents Final Report and Recommendations to Justices' (21 January 2009), http://www.bostonbar.org/pub/bw/0809/011209/sjc1.pdf. The other three major areas were expanding access to legal representation through limited assistance representation (sometimes referred to as 'unbundling' of legal services); a resource and referral guide for self-represented litigants; and technology initiatives: *ibid.* The full report of the Massachusetts Supreme Judicial Court's Steering Committee on Self-Represented Litigants, titled 'Addressing the Needs of Self-Represented Litigants in Our Courts: Final Report and Recommendations' (21 November 2008) ['Addressing the Needs'] is available at http://www.mass.gov/courts/sjc/docs/self-rep-final-report.pdf.

87 *Ibid.*

would be inapplicable to middle-income users. Hotlines, self-help centres, technology-based initiatives, *pro se* clinics – each of these could serve middle-income earners or low-income earners, with the restrictions flowing only from means-testing imposed by funders, as opposed to the particular features of one of the tools. The legal needs studies typically show 'that unrepresented litigants tend to have low-to-middle incomes.'[88] The evaluation of the B.C. Supreme Court Self-Help Information Centre found that, of the clients for whom data were available, '30 percent reported incomes less than $12,000, 60 percent reported incomes less than $24,000, and 80 percent reported incomes less than $36,000.'[89] As long as middle-income users are priced out of the market for hiring lawyers for full representation, they will be frequent users of the remaining forms of assistance at their disposal.

While Prong 3, involving representation by counsel, is largely beyond the scope of an article focused on non-lawyer forms of assistance, the question of middle versus low income provides for interesting analysis. On the one hand, since an expanded civil right to counsel would likely target indigent litigants, the prong might seem less useful in a discussion of access to justice for middle-income earners. On the other hand, the remaining tools for expanding the availability of counsel might prove more useful to middle-income earners than low-income ones. Plenary Session 4 at the colloquium covered unbundled legal services.[90] If the logic behind unbundled legal services includes the idea that some clients might be able to afford some aspects of a lawyer's assistance, but not the price tag for full representation, then the greater the income of the client, the greater the chances that she or he will be able to afford even unbundled services. With fee-shifting statutes, both low and middle-income litigants might benefit from modifications in practice and procedure. In the United States, greater use of fee-shifting statutes would allow private lawyers to represent clients regardless of their ability to pay. At least with respect to small claims court in Canada, Deputy Judge Shelley McGill's reforms proposed at Plenary Session 5 include protection from extensive 'loser pays' rules with the goal of increasing access to middle-income litigants.[91]

88 *Background Paper, supra* note 1 at 17.
89 *Ibid.*
90 Samreen Beg and Lorne Sossin, 'Should Legal Services Be Unbundled?', *infra* this
    volume.
91 Shelley McGill, 'Challenges in Small Claims Court System Design: Does One Size Fit

While the tools at each prong available for middle-income earners might be substantially the same as those available for low-income earners, the data and evaluation suggest that many of those tools might be more effective for middle-income earners than for many low-income earners. The Background Paper cautions that we 'remain attentive to differences of education, literacy, language, geography, culture, mental health and other systemic barriers that affect the availability of legal resources for middle-income individuals, as well as the range of appropriate responses to the problem.'[92] While focused on distinctions among middle-income earners, the idea applies across the spectrum of low- and middle-income earners. The studies of Law Help Ontario's project and the B.C. Self-Help Centre found that users were likely to be among the more educated in their income level;[93] the acknowledgment that 'there is a self-selection bias in their clientele' illustrates the point.[94] A study of the effectiveness of hotlines in the United States found that clients who rated their outcomes most favourably 'were significantly more likely to be white, English-speaking, [and] educated at least to the eighth grade.'[95]

These findings fit neatly into the analysis in Part II, suggesting that the greater the extent of power imbalances, the greater the need for more extensive intervention if assistance is to be effective.[96] Where middle-income earners face fewer barriers in terms of language, education, employment, and the absence of disabilities, they stand a better chance of utilizing more effectively the forms of limited assistance. As the barriers increase, with litigants increasingly without power and without options, forms of self-help are likely to be less and less effective. The findings likely will hold true whether we are exploring back-end or front-end solutions. While not all middle-income earners are free of barriers, and not all low-income earners are unable to overcome barriers, as a general proposition, the distinction posed by the variable of income is less the menu of options available, but rather the likelihood of their effectiveness.

All?, *infra* this volume. ('The small claims court was never contemplated as a high stakes game where litigants are punished for having their day in court. A loss should mean the loser must pay what is owed, not with an added penalty for trying to defend': *ibid.*)

92 *Background Paper, supra* note 1 at 6.
93 *Ibid.* at 17–18.
94 *Ibid.* at 18.
95 Engler, 'Connecting Self-Representation to Civil Gideon,' *supra* note 20 at 71.
96 See II.B.3, *supra.*

B. The Use of Non-Lawyers

The three-pronged strategy provides the framework for analysis of the final variable: the use of non-lawyers as opposed to lawyers. Virtually every initiative at Prongs 1 and 2 creates the opportunity for utilization of non-lawyers. The call for evaluation serves as a constant reminder that the question of where they may be used is only part of the calculation; where non-lawyers may most effectively be used will depend on how successfully we frame and measure that inquiry. The inclusion of Prong 3 suggests that non-lawyers may be utilized alone, or in conjunction with lawyers. Even where lawyers are necessary under the rules of court and ethics, their work can be enhanced by their association with trained and effective non-lawyers.

At Prong 1, the opportunities for non-lawyers flow from the recitation of initiatives. Non-lawyers can play key roles in clerks' offices, self-help centres, and court information centres. Some court-connected mediators will be lawyers, but some will not. While the work of non-lawyers will be limited by work that does not constitute legal advice and the practice of law, our evolving understanding of those concepts results in the recognition that more of the help that litigants need, particularly when offered under the auspices of programs authorized by the court, is unlikely to run afoul of rules prohibiting the unauthorized practice of law.[97] The increased use of technology provides twin opportunities for the use of non-lawyers. Those with the technological skills to design, implement, and maintain the systems may or may not be lawyers. At the same time, as technology lowers the barriers to access, the level of accompanying assistance that is still needed might require less legal training than would be needed in the absence of the technology. With a

---

97 Responding to a complaint filed against a Family Court Manager in the Vermont Courts based on the claim that her work constituted the unauthorized practice of law, the Attorney General's Office dismissed the complaint with the following explanation: 'It is my opinion ... that the activities of a case manager in conformance with the job description does not constitute the practice of law. Even if they did, since the activities are authorized by the Court and performed on its behalf, the Attorney General would be hard pressed to argue that they are unauthorized (albeit unlicensed) ... There may be a policy argument against allowing court personnel to help litigants complete forms and understand their right [sic] and the legal process, but I do not know what that argument might be'; Engler, 'And Justice for All,' supra note 19 at 2041, n241, quoting Letter from William Griffin, Chief Assistant Attorney General, State of Vermont Office of the Attorney General, to Jan Rickless Paul, Esq., Paul & Paul (8 August 1994) at 2.

vision of Prong 1 expanded to include agencies and tribunals, as well as front-end work, the information and assistance provided at every turn may be provided by non-lawyers. Support, oversight, and training are key ingredients to ensure that the assistance is competent and effective.

A similar analysis applies at Prong 2. Each stage in the delivery spectrum provides opportunities for the use of non-lawyers, subject to the twin restrictions of ethics and effectiveness. The analysis in Part II above, designed to expand our ideas of potential assistance programs with shifting combinations of the variables of who, what, when, where, how, and why, reveals similar opportunities with each formulation. Hotlines, *pro se* clinics, form preparation, websites – each of these vehicles may be staffed either entirely by non-lawyers, or by non-lawyers under the supervision of lawyers where the assistance falls clearly within the ambit of legal advice.

Since Prong 3 typically focuses on representation by counsel, the opportunities for non-lawyers might seem limited. However, many if not most lawyers and legal aid offices utilize non-lawyers, including paralegals, as part of the delivery model. Moreover, not all scenarios limit representation to lawyers. Ontario began regulating paralegals following the enactment of the *Access to Justice Act, 2006*. [98] 'Under this regime, licensed paralegals can provide advice, draft documents, conduct negotiations and represent clients in small claims court, before administrative tribunals, and before the Ontario Court of Justice for summary conviction offences, hybrid offences where the Crown elects to proceed summarily, and matters falling under the *Provincial Offences Act*.'[99] Deputy Judge McGill discussed the use of paralegals in Small Claims Court.[100] In March 2009, the Law Society of Upper Canada stated that today's licensed and insured paralegals are 'providing consumers throughout the province with more choice, protection and improved access to justice.'[101] Lay advocates may represent claimants before most adminis-

---

98 S.O. 2006, c.21. See *Background Paper, supra* note 1.
99 *Ibid.*
100 McGill, 'Challenges in Small Claims Court System Design,' *infra* this volume. 'Externally, the regulation of paralegals, although part of a wider access to justice and quality control measure, directly impacts the small claims courts. There are now over 2700 paralegals in Ontario offering litigants a wide choice of representation, at least theoretically, at different price points' (citations omitted).
101 Law Society of Upper Canada, Media release, 'Paralegal Regulation Sets Precedent for Consumer Protection,' 30 March 2009, http://www.lsuc.on.ca/WorkArea/DownloadAsset,aspx?id=8872.

trative agencies in the United States, and some studies from the United States and the United Kingdom suggest that lay advocates can be as effective, and at times more effective, than lawyers in certain settings.[102]

As the three-pronged analysis reveals, the opportunities abound for non-lawyers to play crucial roles in providing access to justice for middle-income earners. That reality returns the analysis to the question of 'who' and the concerns of effectiveness and evaluation. The rubric of non-lawyers includes court personnel, paralegals, volunteers (such as senior citizens and university students), law students, staff of social service agencies, government officials, and public and law librarians. Many of those people would embrace the role of comprising a portion of the access to justice delivery system. Others might recoil, believing that their jobs necessitate their interaction with members of the public, but not in the sense of providing legal assistance. For those committed to tackling the problem of providing increased access, the mindset of the particular non-lawyers should be considered and understood, but their ability to provide meaningful assistance and support to those they encounter should be nurtured and supported regardless of their understanding of their roles.

As long as the problem of unmet legal needs remains a problem to be solved by those with legal training, we lose the opportunity to increase dramatically the resources potentially at our disposal. We need to analyse carefully how people with legal needs or justiciable problems respond to those scenarios, and design our responses in ways that reach those who need help, respond appropriately to their needs, and ensure that the responses are effective in resolving the problems. A full array of non-lawyers is essential to that challenge, and careful and continuous evaluation will help match the available non-lawyers with the scenarios in which they are most effective.

V. Conclusion

As this paper demonstrates, a range of options exists for using non-

---

102 See, for example, Engler, 'Connecting Self-Representation to Civil Gideon,' *supra* note 20 at 82 ('With lay advocates, [Herbert] Kritzer's data indicates that the success rate of skilled lay advocates can rival that of skilled attorneys in certain settings … Authors of one study from England conclude that "specialization, rather than professional status, seems to be the best guarantee of such protection,"' citing Richard Moorhead, Avrom Sherr, and Alan Paterson, 'Contesting Professionalism: Legal Aid and Non-Lawyers in England and Wales' (2003) 37 Law and Soc. Rev. 765).

lawyers in an effort to increase access to justice for middle-income earners. The solutions we identify, however, will inevitably be shaped by the questions we ask and the ways in which we define the problems we are trying to solve. With access to justice, the flood of unrepresented litigants and the prevalence of unmet legal needs cause problems for all involved, including judges, court personnel, and opposing counsel. Yet the most important problem to solve is the reality that on a daily basis, in Canada, the United States, and elsewhere, vulnerable litigants – and those who never reach the formal legal system – forfeit important rights and jeopardize basic human needs not because the law and facts are against them, but because they lack legal representation. Our solutions must be driven by the determination to make a reality of the image of the balanced scales of justice, and stem the routine forfeiture of rights by those without the power to protect their rights or to hire lawyers to do so for them. Anything less suggests that by access to justice, we mean mere access, rather than meaningful access.

5 Middle Income Access to Civil Justice: Implication of *Proposals for the Reform of Legal Aid in England and Wales*

ROGER SMITH

I. Introduction

This paper addresses the content and implications of a consultation paper, titled *Proposals for the Reform of Legal Aid in England and Wales,* which was published on 15 November 2010.[1] The proposals themselves cover both criminal and civil cases. However, this paper is concerned only with those that relate to civil matters and, in particular, legal advice or, as it is now known technically, 'legal help.' English experience might be relevant to Canada in three ways:

- The government's proposals indicate those areas of law that the current U.K. government considers are sufficiently grave in their effects on potential clients that public funding should remain, even in the current parlous state of the government's finances.
- It is possible that there are lessons for Canada in looking at how the overall provision of advice and legal services has developed within the U.K.
- There is support from our experience for more experiment with the use of the Internet and telephone call centre – though the breakthrough point may not yet have arrived.

A certain amount of background is necessary before the current proposals can be understood in their context. Canada and the U.K. are two

---

1 U.K., Ministry of Justice, *Proposals for the Reform of Legal Aid in England and Wales* (Consultation Paper CP 12/10), Cm 7967 (London: HMSO, 2010) [Consultation Paper].

very different countries and the differences need to be marked to avoid overhasty comparison.

There are some initial issues of terminology. The United Kingdom is not quite as unitary as its name suggests. Indeed, it is, in some ways, increasingly disunited, or at least, powers are increasingly being devolved. The U.K. has a national government that makes policy and passes legislation relating both to the U.K. as a whole – for example, defence policy – and England – for example, education. The U.K. contains three legal jurisdictions; Scotland, Northern Ireland, and England and Wales. It has, however, four Parliaments or Assemblies: for Scotland, Northern Ireland, and Wales, and in Westminster, for the U.K. (and England). Thus, the legal aid proposals being considered here relate only to England and Wales. It is not yet clear whether equivalent proposals will be forthcoming for Scotland and Northern Ireland: the form of legal aid has, however, increasingly diverged. The U.K. would not yet, as would Canada, see itself as a federal entity, and there remain what might appear to be incoherencies. Thus, these proposals emanate from the national U.K. government but relate only to England and Wales.

The proposals cover the whole of legal aid. They are designed, overall, to save somewhere around £370 million annually by 2014–15 from the current legal aid budget of around £2 billion (the government estimates the range of savings as between £310 and £430 million, with £370 million as the best estimate). Of these cuts, somewhere between £251 and £286 million will come from reduction in scope, leading to an estimate of around 500,000 people losing entitlement. A further £114 to £154 million will be saved by cuts to the remuneration of lawyers, who will be expected to act as now but be paid less. In relation to civil legal aid, for example, all rates are cut by a straight 10 per cent: a more complex set of cuts is in store for criminal practitioners. This paper relates only to the cuts to civil legal aid and legal help.

Two reasons are given in the consultation paper for the proposed cuts. The Secretary of State, Ken Clarke, in a foreword, says:

> I want to discourage people from resorting to lawyers whenever they face a problem, and instead, encourage them, wherever it is sensible to do so, to consider alternative methods of dispute resolution which may be more effective and suitable.[2]

---

2 *Ibid.* at 3.

However, this justification is somewhat half-hearted. The more comprehensible reason is that:

> Legal aid must also play its part in fulfilling the Government's commitment to reducing the fiscal deficit ...[3]

Indeed, cuts of 23 per cent were announced to the Ministry of Justice budget by the Chancellor of the Exchequer in his statement on the spending review of 20 October 2010. The review itself promised:

> The Government will consult on major reforms to the legal aid system to deliver access to justice at lower cost to the taxpayer. This will involve taking tough choices about the types of case that should receive public funding, and focusing support on those who need it most. The reforms will also increase competition in the market and reform remuneration for providers to ensure the legal aid system is effective and affordable.[4]

II. Legal Aid in England and Wales

The legal aid scheme for England and Wales was established as a result of the Rushcliffe Report published in 1945. It was originally limited largely to family matters, but the express intention was to create a scheme with high eligibility. The goal was that the scheme should not be limited to those 'normally classed as poor' and should be extended to those of 'small and moderate means.'[5] This has had an abiding effect on developments, encouraging relatively high financial eligibility until recently and, thereby, inhibiting the development of alternative sources of assistance. As a consequence of wide scope, high eligibility, and relatively high remuneration levels, legal aid in England and Wales is expensive. In particular, costs rocketed during the 1980s and 1990s. In its turn, this triggered a concern by government to hold them down. Total costs (in real terms, that is, adjusted to 2008–9 rates) reached £1 billion for the first time in 1990–1, and they had doubled by 1998–9. Since then, they have been held at roughly around £2 billion. The cuts

---

3 *Ibid.*

4 U.K., HM Treasury, *Spending Review 2010*, Cm 7942 (London: HMSO, 2010) at para. 273.

5 U.K., *Report of the Committee on Legal Aid and Advice in England and Wales*, Cmd. 6641 (London: HMSO, 1945).

are designed to reduce this further. Until now, civil costs have been sacrificed to crime in order to hold the budget steady. In 2008–9, civil and family representation cost £650 million and civil and family legal help (i.e., advice) was £263 million. The severity of previous cuts to civil advice can be seen in the fact that in 2003–4 (on adjusted 2008–9 rates), civil legal help alone cost £436m.[6]

The relatively high cost of legal aid in England and Wales has been a political issue for some time. In 2009, the Ministry of Justice published comparative research as to why expenditures in England and Wales seemed so high.[7] This is worth quoting at some length because its points are well made and also because the researchers included comparison with Canada:

> The legal aid scheme in E&W (England and Wales) was well-known to involve a high volume of support, comparatively high spending levels per case and thus high spending per head.

> Reform of the scope of the scheme, eligibility criteria and procurement arrangements had together stemmed the rapid rate of increase in spending that had continued over an extended period. Changes to the eligibility rules for civil legal aid had resulted in a sharp drop over later years in the proportion of the population eligible for civil representation. The proportion fell … from 52% in 1998 to 46% in 2001 and then to 29% in 2007.

> The scheme had traditionally been intended to cover middle income groups as well as low income groups and had not encouraged the development of self-representation or highly selective coverage found in countries such as the US.

> High divorce rates … [were] a potent source of upward pressure on demand. There was evidence that the high costs of legal aid were offset to some degree by costs elsewhere in the justice system … There has been criticism that lawyers working on family law legal aid cases had been reluctant to encourage clients to consider alternatives to court or solicitor-negotiation approaches such as mediation.

---

6 Consultation Paper, *supra* note 1 at 198, Annex K, Table B ('Legal aid spending (real terms) 1988-89 to 2008-09').

7 Roger Bowles and Amanda Perry, *International Comparison of Publicly Funded Legal Services and Justice Systems* (Ministry of Justice Research Series 14/09) (2009).

There were signs of innovation in some areas such as the development of Community Legal Advice Centres and Networks and the web-based Community Legal Service Direct information and advice service … There was a small *pro bono* sector supported by some of the large firms but it was marginal.

So, what did the same researchers make of Canada?

The average costs per case were lower for both criminal and civil cases compared with E&W. The rate of cases supported was much lower than in E&W, partly at least because of the much lower ceiling on income levels at which individuals were eligible for legal aid … There were also quite complex limits on the value of household assets … There was more of a tradition in the provision of services, including the provision of on-line information (for example the Family Law in British Columbia site), the use of call centres and the provision of advice and representation through independent Community Legal Clinics. In Manitoba, lawyers offered 'collaborative law' as an alternative to the courts. Nova Scotia had a legal information line, a Lawyer Referral Service, a speaker's bureau, pamphlets and booklets, Dial-a-law and a community outreach programme.

There are some quibbles to make about these judgments. For example, collaborative law is becoming popular in England and Wales as well as Canada. However, the basic judgment is probably correct. We have basically relied on state funding for advice and representation for 'middle income' people in a way that has buttressed traditional forms of provision (a few law centres and the recent growth of not-for-profit providers notwithstanding). On the other hand, in Canada and the United States, less traditional ways of filling the gap have been found. This may mean that England and Wales has a relatively straightforward – but politically unpopular – message. Legal aid should be publicly available for all those who cannot afford to get it privately.

III. Advice

The overall picture of legal advice giving in England and Wales is complex. This is because the U.K. has no equivalent of U.S. provisions against the giving of legal advice by non-lawyers. Thus, anyone can give advice. Membership in the regulatory bodies of the legal profession is required only in relation to 'reserved work' such as court advocacy and conveyancing. Anyone can currently advise, for example, on a will – although regulation is now being considered. Anyone can advise on a matter relating to employment law. The major provider of legal advice outside of the legal profession is the Citizens Advice Bureaux movement. This has its origins in volunteers who advised on regulations during the Second World War. Immediately afterward, the bureaux came close to extinction, but were revived in the late 1960s onwards. In addition, there is Advice UK, a loose network of other agencies funded by local authorities. There is less centrally published information about these agencies because they are generally smaller and more individual, but Advice UK estimates that around seventy of its members, some of which are law centres (of which there are currently fifty-six), are sufficiently substantial providers of legal advice to be contracted to provide it under the legal aid scheme.

Citizens Advice Bureaux are, essentially, a franchised national network of advice agencies that work under a common brand and with the assistance of a central organization, Citizens Advice, which provides information systems, support for individual bureaux, and national representation. CABs have a spine of permanent staff, some specialists, and many volunteers who carry on the tradition of voluntary assistance with which the bureaux began. In addition, some CABs have developed specifically legal units and are contracted to the Legal Services Commission (LSC) to provide advice. The CAB service employs more than three hundred CAB specialist advisers, who in 2009–10 dealt with 43,234 welfare benefit problems, 56,990 debt problems, 9,129 housing problems, and 2,954 employment problems under contract with the LSC. The full statistics of its advice giving for that period are set out below:[8]

There is no information on the financial position of those consulting the CABs, which operate no means tests except where those are required under LSC contract. Nor is there any information on the level of work that CABs undertake. We do know figures for some elements of quantity if not quality. Approximately 90 per cent of the bureaux are involved in providing advice and representation for tribunal hearings for up to 150,000 clients per year. We do know that fifty-six bureaux provide advice/duty desks in county courts and that fifty-seven provide them in prisons (that is about 40 per cent of the total). In addi-

---

8 Citizens Advice Annual Advice Statistics 2009–10, http://www.citizensadvice.org. uk.

Table 5.1. Advice Statistics: Citizens Advice Bureau 2009–10

	2009–10	Percentage increase on previous year
Total inquiries	7,097,923	18%
Debt	2,374,273	23%
Benefits & tax credits	2,074,208	21%
Employment	586,185	6%
Education	29,772	29%
Financial products & services	140,574	19%
Housing	467,854	14%
Immigration, asylum, and nationality	94,480	17%
Tax	53,493	10%
Utilities & communications	103,813	5%
Travel, transport, & holidays	47,846	13%
Legal	298,226	13%
Consumer goods and services	139,107	13%
Relationships & family	330,312	14%
Health & community care	77,520	12%
Discrimination (within above categories)	28,104	11%

tion, the Royal Courts of Justice CAB, a specialist bureau that attracts considerable assistance from the legal profession, has supported clients in seventy different prisons through its work to support victims of miscarriages of justice. Fourteen bureaux operate in twenty regular and fourteen irregular probation offices.

Nationally, the CABs are quite a force. Bureaux employ 7,000 staff and use 21,500 volunteers. Over the country, there are 394 full bureaux, with some having more than one office. In 2009–10, 2.1 million clients were advised on 7.1 million problems, a creditable result. Individual bureaux are funded generally by local authorities, but the central Citizens Advice organization gets a main grant from the government of £21 million – its total income was £62 million. There is some indication that this might not be cut too dramatically, which will enhance the importance of the CABs. The total income of the bureaux was £179 million in 2009–10 – £27 million (15 per cent) came from the LSC. In addition to face-to-face services, which can become overwhelmed by numbers particularly in inner-city areas, Citizens Advice operates telephone, e-mail and online assistance via the website www.adviceguide.org.uk. The website received 10.6 million visits in 2009–10.[9]

9 *Ibid.*

The existence of the CABs is probably one of the reasons why law centres did not take off in England and Wales in the way that community legal clinics did in Ontario. The CABs provided a basic level of advice to all comers, which blunted the impact of the need for legal assistance. The simultaneous existence of a broad legal advice scheme with relatively high eligibility criteria also directed people towards private practitioners, who began to invite referrals. The case for law centres got caught between the two.

During the 1990s, law centres began increasingly to depend on contracts with the LSC to deliver advice in what North Americans would call poverty law – those areas of law that are disproportionately relevant to poor people. Advice agencies, both within the CAB movement and outside, sought similar contracts. The result is that both constituencies are particularly vulnerable to the cuts to advice proposed by the government. Estimates are that the £78 million paid by the LSC in 2008–9 to not-for-profit agencies, both advice agencies and law centres, will be reduced by £60 million, a cut of 77 per cent. By contrast, solicitors in private practice will suffer a cut of 28 per cent.

IV. Online Information and Call Centres

There are two national sources of online legal information – Citizens Advice www.adviceguide.org.uk and www.communitylegaladvice.org.uk, which is run by the Legal Services Commission. These are, thus, potentially providing legal advice to middle income people. Predictably perhaps, the legal aid consultation paper foresees a greater use of community legal advice – which includes a telephone helpline. The community advice site is more of a compendium of links to information on other sites than a source of original advice. For example, anyone seeking advice on 'marriage, civil partnership and cohabitation' is referred to one other government website, two parts of the Citizens Advice website, and three other non-government agencies. A searcher consulting the website under the heading 'family' will find links under twenty-six topics literally running from birth to death or from registering to ending a civil partnership. Legal advice on particular areas of law is available from the websites of other specialist organizations – for example, from the Child Poverty Action Group regarding welfare benefits.[10]

---

10 http://www.cpag.org.uk.

Table 5.2. Legal Services Commission: Advice Cases 2005–6 to 2009–10

	2005–6	2006–7	2007–8	2008–9	2009–10
Solicitors	449,890	446,794	419,230	452,002	465,108
NfPs	163,140	201,875	214,090	239,026	243,749
Others	21,855	36,575	34,747	38,419	36,980
CLACs				6,950	9,538
Total face-to-face	634,885	685,244	668,067	736,397	755,375
CLA specialists	73,625	111,319	84,575	100,851	126,866
Total specialist	708,510	796,563	752,642	837,248	882,241
CLA triage				235,947	290,574
Total				1,073,195	1,172,815

The Community Legal Advice (CLA) phone line is available on weekdays from 9 a.m. to 8 p.m. and on Saturday mornings. Calls cost 4 pence a minute on a landline or more on a mobile, though a caller can ask to be called back. The usual financial eligibility test for legal advice applies. CLA undertakes 'triage,' with choices between referral to a face-to-face service, ending the call, or referral to a telephone CLA 'specialist.' It gives advice in six areas:

- Debt
- Welfare benefits and tax credits
- Housing
- Employment
- Education
- Family

The expansion of telephone advice can be seen from Table 5.2, published by the Advice Services Alliance, which indicates the type of advice funded by the LCS over the past four years.[11]

The use of telephone advice on this scale has yet to be properly researched. The only testing to date has been by a journalist, who found a somewhat mixed result when he tried a 'mystery shopper' test and encountered shrewd comment:

For our admittedly rough and ready test, we had a panel of experts reviewing advice given in 10 scenarios. At the time Lambeth county court was routinely stamping all envelopes containing claims forms for tenants in

---

11 See the ASA website: http://www.asauk.org.uk.

possession cases with CLS Direct's 0845 number. Out of those 10 calls, six prompted detailed responses and, in four of those cases, further advice was needed. The results were largely very positive (scoring at least seven out of 10), however, in two cases callers were actually prevented from taking appropriate legal action (both scoring two out of 10). One scenario related to a tenant whose flat (on the Woodberry Down estate in Hackney, east London) was infested by ants. The facts were based on a real case that settled for £5,000. No legal remedy was suggested by the adviser. Our judge (a member of the Law Society's access to justice committee) described the advice as 'simply wrong.' 'On this snapshot, the advice seems somewhat variable,' commented Roger Smith, the director of Justice and one of the judges. He expressed concern that advisers seemed reluctant to refer callers on for face-to-face help. 'The LSC has to make sure that CLS Direct isn't just a mechanism for deterring demand,' Smith said.[12]

The difficulty of evaluating advice provision, whether on the telephone or not, is immense. The legal aid scheme is paying for advice in just over a million cases and the CAB alone is providing advice to 2 million people with 7 million problems. We just do not know the relative difficulty of the cases presented or the relative sophistication of the advice given.

V. Consultation Proposal for a Call Centre

The consultation paper enthusiastically backs an extension of the Community Legal Advice call centre in a proposal that may be worth setting out at length because of its relevance to the provision of legal assistance to those with middle incomes:

> We propose that, in future, we will provide a simple straightforward telephone service, based on the current Community Legal Advice (CLA) helpline (first established nationally in 2004). This advice service will be able to refer clients to the source of advice most appropriate to them, and will act as a reliable one-stop shop for clients looking for legal advice. The CLA helpline will be established as the single gateway to civil legal aid services. All clients will be able to access the first tier of the service (the Operator Service) while the second tier will offer specialist advice to eligible clients in

---

12 Jon Robins, 'The Legal Aid Helpline Should Not Be Another Hurdle for the Vulnerable,' *The Guardian* (13 December 2010), http://www.guardian.co.uk/law/2010/dec/13/legal-aid-helpline.

all categories of law within the scope of civil legal aid. In the vast majority of cases this will mean that clients will make their initial contact to access civil legal aid services through the Operator Service, rather than through a face to face provider. However the services will be designed to minimise the risk that clients with emergency cases experience delay in accessing the help they need.

Clients calling the helpline will, as at present, initially speak to an operator who will diagnose their problems, and determine their eligibility for legal aid services. The operator will discuss with clients the range of options available to them and route them to the service most suited to their circumstances, including legal aid specialists, a paid for service, or alternative sources of help.

In cases where the diagnosis at the Operator Service stage is that more detailed advice is the most suitable route, clients will be able to access specialist services if their case is within the scope of legal aid and they meet the relevant financial eligibility criteria. In the majority of these cases, CLA operators will transfer the call to the CLA specialist telephone advice service. This service will be available in all categories of law within the proposed scope of civil legal aid.

Clients will be assessed to identify whether they have particular needs (for example, specific language requirements) and the CLA helpline service will seek to accommodate them. Face to face advice provision will be available where cases are too complex to be dealt with appropriately by telephone or where the client's specific needs would not be met (for example, due to mental impairment). This will be assessed on a case-by-case basis and, where appropriate, clients will be referred to face to face advice services.

The number of cases that are likely to be dealt with by face to face specialist advice services will vary between categories of law depending on the nature of the case in that category and the needs of the client groups who most typically experience these problems.

We also propose to expand the CLA service to include the option for paid-for advice services for clients who are ineligible for legal aid.

Under this proposal, in addition to providing advice services to legally aided clients, CLA operators would be able to refer clients who are ineligible for legal aid to a paid-for service. The Operator Service would discuss with the client the options available to them, explain the charges associated with the paid for service, and make the relevant referral.

The LSC would set out in the relevant tender the requirements in respect of quality standards, maximum rates to be charged, assurances about standards of service for both eligible and non-eligible clients, and so on. This pro-

posal would enable CLA operators to route non-eligible clients to quality
assured paid services seamlessly.

   This approach will ensure that those who are not eligible for legal aid will
still be helped to find a source of advice. It could also lead to legal aid fund
savings.[13]

This is an interesting proposal because it combines:

- a national, non-means-tested telephone diagnostic advice service;
- an initial test of eligibility and scope by telephone;
- referral, where appropriate, to a legal aid practitioner; and
- referral to paid-for services that may be run by the advice provider
  and, thus, assist in offsetting the cost.

In some ways, this would be an innovative addition to the existing pattern of provision in England and Wales. It has been welcomed by some
commentators – including a spokesperson for Citizens Advice, which
may well have some hopes of obtaining the contract. The danger, of
course, is that the proposed gateway will become a closed gate because
of the low skills, high inclination, and corporate financial interest of
gatekeeping staff, who will be rewarded for referrals to paid-for services. In addition, there is the question of the extent to which some of the
hardest-to-find clients will feel confident in talking about their problems on the telephone. As a result, it would seem important that the
expanded CLA program run alongside a continuing ability for clients
to reach lawyers face to face, at least for sufficient time for the process
to be evaluated properly.

VI. Cuts to Scope in Civil Justice

The scope of the services for which legally aided clients will be eligible
is planned to be significantly curtailed. The original legal advice scheme
introduced in 1973 was for two hours of advice on any topic of English
law. Extension was possible in exceptional cases. The problem became
that the scheme was effectively a blank cheque for solicitors to take on
work. On the other hand, it was certainly also an incentive for solicitors
in private practice to diversify their practices into areas in which they
had previously been uninterested. Eventually, measures were taken to
control usage. Practitioners were required to have a contract with the

---

13 Consultation Paper, *supra* note 1 at paras. 4.272–80.

Legal Services Commission for a specified number of 'matter starts.' This significantly limited the number of providers. By 2008–9, there were firms with 5,650 civil contracts for different areas of work. The main area was family law, with 2,677 contracts. Not-for-profit providers – law centres and advice agencies – held 934 contracts, with their three largest areas being welfare benefits (298), debt (265), and housing (170). The subject matter of civil advice was as follows in 2008–9:[14]

Family	**255,120**
Welfare benefits	135,074
Housing	133,613
Debt	125,928
Mental health	35,322
Employment	24,618
Community care	6,045
Miscellaneous	5,138
Actions against the police etc.	4,182
Clinical negligence	3,583
Consumer	3,196
Education	6,547
Personal injury	2,001
Public law	1,773
Total non-family/immigration	**487,020**
Immigration: asylum	157,539
Immigration: nationality and visit visas	145,253
Total Immigration	**102,792**
Total non-family	**589,812**
Total	**844,932**

For a Canadian audience interested in middle income access to justice, the most relevant element of the government's proposals may be the areas of law where it is not proposing any alteration to the existing form of legal provision. The government sets out its rationale for these decisions:

> In reaching our view about which types of issue and proceeding should continue to justify legal aid, we have taken into account the importance of the issue, the litigant's ability to present their own case (including the venue before which the case is heard, the likely vulnerability of the litigant

---

14 Legal Services Commission, *Statistical Information 2008/09* (London, 2009) at Table CLS4.

and the complexity of the law), the availability of alternative sources of funding and the availability of alternative routes to resolving the issue. We have also taken into account our domestic, European and international legal obligations. Each of these factors is explained in more detail below.[15]

It is clear from the paper that the government has, sensibly enough, put particular weight on the provisions of the European Convention on Human Rights that apply directly in English law through the *Human Rights Act* (1998). The European Court of Human Rights has emphasized the need for legal representation in the civil issues covered by the Convention in cases where it is required for the 'effective participation' of the parties.[16] The Convention does not cover all civil cases but does guarantee a fair trial for those cases involving 'the determination of … civil rights and obligations.'[17] So concerned is the government not to break this requirement that it proposes that legal aid will be available for cases that would otherwise be excluded,

> where the Government is satisfied that the provision of some level of legal aid is necessary for the United Kingdom to meet its domestic and international legal obligations, including those under the European Convention on Human Rights (ECHR, in particular article 2 and article 6), or where there is a significant wider public interest in funding legal representation for inquest cases (see paragraphs 4.255). It is not intended that exceptional funding will generally be available except where it can be demonstrated that it is necessary to discharge those legal obligations, or where we are satisfied that the relevant test for legal representation has been met in inquest cases.[18]

The main retentions are set out below:

Area	*Reason*
Asylum	Importance of issue; International obligations

---

15 Consultation Paper, *supra* note 1 at para. 4.12.

16 See, for example, *Airey v. Ireland* (1979), 32 E.C.H.R. (Ser. A), 2 E.H.R.R. 305; *Steel and Morris v. The United Kingdom*, no. 68416/01, [2005] E.C.H.R. 103, [2005] E.M.L.R. 314.

17 *Convention for the Protection of Human Rights and Fundamental Freedoms*, 4 November 1950, 213 U.N.T.S. 221 at 223, Eur. T.S. 5 at art. 6.

18 Consulation Paper, *supra* note 1 at para. 4.34.

Claims against public authorities where abuse of position of power; and/or significant breach of human rights; and/or negligent acts/omissions falling very far below required standard of care	Inability to self-represent; Importance of issue
Claims for abuse and sexual assault	Importance of issue; Inability to self-represent
Community care	Importance of issue; Inability to self-represent
Debt but only where home at immediate risk	Importance of issue; Inability to self-represent
Discrimination proceedings	Importance of issue; Inability to self-represent
Environmental matters	Importance of issue; International obligations; Few sources of funding
European Union cross-border cases	Importance of issue; International obligations; EU obligations; Inability to self-represent; Few sources of funding or assistance
Family/ancillary relief/children where domestic violence or forced marriage related issue	Importance of issues; Risk of harm; Inability to self-represent; No alternative sources of funding or assistance
International child abduction	Importance of issue; International and EU obligations; Inability to self-represent; No alternatives

| **International family maintenance** | Importance of issue; International and EU obligations; Inability to self-represent; No alternatives |

Housing where:
(a) **action for possession;**
(b) **disrepair counterclaim in possession proceedings;**
(c) **homelessness appeals;**
(d) **mobile home eviction appeals;**
(e) **disrepair claim for specific performance;**
(f) **related anti-social behaviour order**

Importance of issue

| **Immigration detention** | Importance of issue; No alternatives; |

| **Mental health** | Importance of issue; Inability to self-represent; No alternatives |

| **Miscellaneous** **Confiscation proceedings** | Importance of issue; Inability to self-represent; No alternatives |

| **Injunctions for gang-related violence** | Importance of issue; Inability to self-represent; No alternatives |

| **Independent Safeguarding Authority appeals** | Importance of issue; No alternatives |

| **Inquests – advice and, with restrictions, representation** | Importance of issue; No alternatives |

| **Protection from Harassment Act** | Importance of issue; Inability to self-represent; No alternatives |

'Quasi criminal' cases (e.g., civil penalties)	Importance of issue; Inability to self-represent; No alternatives
Public law	Importance of issue; Inability to self-represent; No alternatives
Public law (children)	Importance of issue; Inability to self-represent; No alternatives
Registration and enforcement EU judgments	Importance of issue; International obligations

This is the list of the saved. The list of those areas cut is longer. The majority of the money is being saved by cutting advice and assistance in ancillary relief family cases and clinical negligence.

VII. Lessons

For a Canadian audience, the importance of events across the Atlantic in England and Wales is whether there are any lessons that can be taken from them. As a long-term observer of the two jurisdictions, I counsel care at this point. Jurisdictions can be very different, especially where they are divided by a common language that suggests greater compatibility than in reality exists. For example, the responsiveness of clients to telephone or online advice may well differ. In at least some areas of Canada, there may be a stronger tradition of working collectively to rectify problems than remains in England and Wales. With these provisos, I would tentatively advance four lessons where it seems to me that there might be a useful discussion prompted by current English experience.

First, there is real value in a national advice facility that provides at least initial advice for all. That is what England and Wales has in its Citizens Advice Bureaux and other local advice agencies networks and in the Community Legal Advice website and call centre. The equivalent in Ontario is presumably the network of clinics, which have the advantage over the CABs of comprehensively integrating lawyers within their staffs and maintaining an overtly community orientation.

Second, it is an interesting exercise and useful to do what our Ministry of Justice has, in effect, done – that is, compile a list of the types of cases that government should fund because otherwise substantial injustice will result. To what extent does this transfer to Ontario specifically and to Canada generally? Would Canada prioritize the same issues for the same reasons? And does Canada have adequate provision to meet need?

Third, there is an interesting silence in the consultation paper. It makes no mention of *pro bono* legal services, to the advantages of which governments that face expenditure limitations are usually drawn. I would argue that, at least for England and Wales, this is correct. *Pro bono* legal service is invaluable: my own organization depends upon it. But, though *pro bono* can be really valuable in maintaining and succouring provision of a particular and targeted type, at least with England and Wales, it cannot be looked for to supply mainstream services. That is not to denigrate *pro bono* work; it is to be realistic about what its providers can – or would want – to deliver.

Fourth, we must find a way to tap the potential of the Internet and the phone. Intuitively, it must be right that new means of communication with which increasing numbers of the population have experience will change part of the delivery of legal services just as they are beginning to transform part of the delivery of groceries. But how? And for whom? Poor people still tend to use the expensive corner shop rather than the distant supermarket or the online grocery store. How can we integrate new ways of offering services? And what categories of people will require face-to-face contact for the foreseeable future? My own view is that a massive leap forward will be possible when the phone, the television, and the computer merge so that a person can consult the 'net through their TV and move seamlessly into phone conversations. However, it seems to me that our government will make a massive error if it implements an exclusive or virtually exclusive call centre filtering operation for those seeking help in civil cases – as it proposes. Our proposed cuts will deepen dependence of the most vulnerable people on the universal source of advice – our CABs and independent advice agencies – as a source of free, generalist advice. A national phone service will provide a real boon to the well educated but will not work for those who, for whatever reason, lack communication skills.

PART 5

Access to Lawyers

6 Should Legal Services Be Unbundled?

SAMREEN BEG AND LORNE SOSSIN

I. Introduction

The purpose of this paper is examine and evaluate the phenomenon of unbundling legal services as a means of enhancing access to justice, particularly for the middle class.[1] We argue that unbundling has significant potential to enhance the efficiency and effectiveness of delivering legal services, but in order to achieve these outcomes, unbundling will require changes both in the regulatory culture and in the business model of the legal profession.

As Michael Trebilcock asserted in the *Report of the Legal Aid Review 2008*, 'if the rule of law is considered to be based on laws that are knowable and consistently enforced such that individuals are able to avail themselves of the law, then individuals must have the tools to access the systems that administer those laws.'[2] Access to justice should not be confused with access to lawyers.[3] There are a wide variety of mecha-

---

1 This paper is based on research conducted for an independent research course at the Faculty of Law, University of Toronto, titled 'Access to Justice for Middle-Income Canadians.' The authors are grateful to the faculty and students participating in that course. We are also grateful to the participants in the Middle Income Access to Justice Colloquium, University of Toronto, 10–11 February 2011, to Stephen Ginsberg for his insightful comments at the presentation of this paper at the colloquium, and to Michael Trebilcock for his constructive suggestions.
2 Michael Trebilcock, *Report of the Legal Aid Review 2008*, http://www.attorneygeneral.jus.gov.on.ca/english/about/pubs/olar.
3 See Roderick A. Macdonald, 'Access to Justice in 2003 – Scope, Scale, Ambitions' in J. Bass, W.A. Bogart, and F. Zemans, *Access to Justice for a New Century: The Way Forward* (Toronto: Law Society of Upper Canada / Irwin Law, 2005) at 19.

nisms for delivering legal information, legal advice, and legal services that do not involve the conventional solicitor–client relationship (multilingual legal brochures, online public legal information, telephone summary advice, paralegals and community workers, duty counsel, etc.). That said, legal representation remains vital to the successful functioning of the civil justice system.[4]

The reality is that many litigants cannot access the legal services they need and are thus forced to navigate the complex justice system on their own. The number of unrepresented litigants in Ontario and elsewhere in Canada is on the rise. According to Pro Bono Law Ontario (PBLO), 10 to 15 per cent of the 49,900 civil litigants who entered the Superior Court in Toronto in 2008 were unrepresented.[5] Anecdotal evidence suggests that the number is likely much higher in the family law context, with one judge estimating that the number is probably around 80 per cent.[6]

Unrepresented litigants and unrepresented people with legal problems now pose one of the greatest challenges to the Ontario justice system.[7] The effects of unmet legal needs are wide ranging, and include personal and social harms for those people whose rights are infringed, and additional cost and delay in the court system.

The problem is likely broadest outside of formal litigation processes, but it is most acutely experienced within the court system. The challenge of unrepresented litigants has proven so vexing to judges that in 2006 the Canadian Judicial Council issued guidelines to judges for how best to handle proceedings with unrepresented litigants. The first principle animating these guidelines is set out in the following terms: 'Judges, the courts and other participants in the justice system have a responsibility to promote opportunities for all persons to understand

---

4 Legal representation remains vital to the successful functioning of the criminal justice system as well. However, given the constitutional implications of legal representation in criminal proceedings, and the significant presence of legal aid for those unable to afford legal representation, our study will focus on the civil justice system. We define civil justice broadly, to encompass any legal problem that does not engage the criminal justice system.

5 Pro Bono Law Ontario, *Evaluation of Law Help Ontario as a Model for Assisting Self-Represented Litigants in the Ontario Superior Court of Justice at 393 University Avenue in Toronto* by Ken Smith (2009), http://www.pblo.org/library/item.282062-Evaluation_of_Law_Help_Ontario [PBLO, *Evaluation of Law Help Ontario*].

6 Furthermore, an older statistic from Ontario's Unified Family Court shows an increase of 500 per cent in unrepresented litigants between 1995 and 1999: Canadian Bar Association, *The Future of the Legal Profession: The Challenge of Change* (2000), http://www.cba.org/CBA/EPIIgram/pdf/future.pdf [CBA, *The Future of the Legal Profession*].

7 We will use 'justice system' and 'legal system' interchangeably throughout the paper.

and meaningfully present their case, regardless of representation.'[8] More than the fairness of proceedings is at stake. Unrepresented litigants can slow down proceedings and create challenges for opposing counsel, who may be confused about the nature of an unrepresented litigant's claim and how to effectively respond.

There has been much discussion on how to 'solve' the problem of unrepresented litigants. Some of the suggestions revolve around making the legal system more user friendly through streamlined proceedings, increased information, and simplified procedures.[9] Even with the simplification of legal processes, however, situations may arise where an unrepresented litigant finds it extremely difficult to undertake part of a legal proceeding on his or her own. In these situations, retaining a lawyer may still be of great benefit to an unrepresented litigant, and in more complex contexts, a lawyer may still represent the difference between a just and an unjust result for the parties involved.

In some parts of the United States and most recently in British Columbia, 'unbundled' or 'limited scope' legal services have been recognized as a significant measure to address this concern. An unbundled legal service is a service of limited scope for which a lawyer, paralegal, or legal service provider is retained. For example, a client might retain a lawyer to provide general advice on a series of legal options, which the client might then pursue on her or his own. Alternatively, a client might retain a lawyer to draft an agreement following a negotiation that the client has conducted. A lawyer may be hired to draft a factum, conduct discoveries, or argue a motion in court. In each of these settings, the lawyer is performing familiar legal services, but in the often unfamiliar position of doing so as part of a limited representation, and without the general expectation that the lawyer represent the client generally or be the solicitor of record for the client.

Endorsement of unbundled legal services in Canada appears to be on the rise. The Civil Justice Needs Project, for example, identified unbundling as something that may make legal services more economically

---

8 See Canadian Judicial Council, 'Statement of Principles on Self-Represented Litigants and Accused Persons,' http://www.cjc-ccm.gc.ca/cmslib/general/news_pub_other_PrinciplesStatement_2006_en.pdf. See also D.A.R.R. Thompson, 'The Judge as Counsel,' *Canadian News and Views on Civil Justice Reform* (Canadian Forum on Civil Justice), Issue 8 (2005).

9 See Coulter Osborne, Civil Justice Reform Project (2007), http://www.attorneygeneral.jus.gov.on.ca/english/about/pubs/cjrp/CJRP-Report_EN.pdf. See also Janet Walker and Lorne Sossin, *Civil Litigation* (Toronto: Irwin, 2010), ch. 10, 'Civil Justice Reforms' [Walker and Sossin, *Civil Litigation*].

accessible for some litigants. In 2009, as a response to the challenges of duty counsel projects offering *pro bono* limited representation to those unable to afford a lawyer, the Law Society of Upper Canada (Law Society or LSUC) enacted a rule to relieve lawyers who undertake limited representation in *pro bono* settings from some types of conflict of interest. In 2010 the Law Society struck a working group that includes representatives from the Professional Regulation, Paralegal Standing, and Access to Justice Committees. The focus of the working group is 'ethical guidance' in relation to unbundling.[10] The issues addressed by the working group touch on clarity of the agreement between the lawyer or paralegal and the client for limited legal representation, communications between counsel for another party, and the client receiving unbundled services and disclosure of the assistance of counsel. The working group also has been tasked with initiating a 'dialogue with legal organizations and institutions to identify the key procedural issues associated with limited scope services in litigation and changes that may be appropriate to better facilitate them.'[11]

In light of the newfound interest in and enthusiasm for unbundling legal services, in this paper we explore whether unbundled legal services can facilitate a more accessible civil justice system, and, more specifically, alleviate some of the challenges faced by unrepresented litigants in accessing the justice system.

The paper proceeds as follows. Part II describes the movement towards unbundling legal services and the economic, professional, and regulatory contexts relevant to unbundling. Part III sets out three potential service delivery models for unbundling and how they could assist unrepresented litigants during a litigation proceeding. Part IV considers potential problems with unbundling and how these problems may be mitigated. Part V discusses how unbundling could be further facilitated. Part VI touches on some remaining areas of uncertainty, and Part VII concludes.

II. The Contexts for Unbundling in Ontario

Unbundling legal services should be seen against a particular economic, professional, and regulatory backdrop. Unbundling is not new.

---

10 See 'Unbundling of Legal Services and Limited Representation Working Group' at http://www.lsuc.on.ca/unbundling.
11 *Ibid.*

Many would argue that it simply is a new label for situations in which a lawyer provides limited representation to a client. For example, where lawyers provide a client with independent legal advice (ILA), the lawyer doing so usually is not the client's lawyer of record, but is performing a discrete legal service, usually for a set fee. Similarly, duty counsel is a long-standing feature of Ontario's legal aid scheme and similarly represents a form of unbundled legal services.

The main impetus for unbundling is its potential to lower the cost of obtaining legal services. Unbundling creates an important halfway house between the unrepresented and the represented. While unbundled services may be offered on a *pro bono* basis or an hourly basis, these services are often associated with fixed fees. As is discussed elsewhere in this volume, the high cost of accessing justice through a lawyer is one of the major reasons litigants choose to represent themselves. As Chief Justice Beverley McLachlin has noted, those middle class Canadians who are not willing to mortgage their homes or exhaust their life savings to pay for a lawyer face the choice of representing themselves or giving up on pursuing their claim.[12]

There has been a lot of focus on lawyer fees and hourly billable rates as an explanation for why unrepresented litigants have not been able to access legal services. It is important to note, however, that 'the relationship between lawyers' fees and the client's capacity to pay requires more thought than merely looking at fees alone.'[13] For example, court processes consume more time and resources than they did in the past.[14] The high cost of litigation is the product of factors including lawyer fees, protracted litigation proceedings, the low take-up of legal expense insurance, and the inability of the average person to save for the unexpected costs of significant litigation.

According to former Ontario Court of Appeal Justice Coulter Osborne's 2007 *Civil Justice Reform Project*, 'the civil justice system must exist to serve members of the public – whether represented or not.' Further, he added, 'a reasonable modicum of resources and assistance ought to be made available … to permit them [unrepresented litigants]

---

12 Beverley McLachlin, 'The Challenges We Face,' remarks to the Empire Club of Canada, 8 March 8, 2007, http://www.scc-csc.gc.ca/court-cour/ju/spe-dis/bm07-03-08-eng.asp.

13 See Draft Final Report of the B.C. Law Society Unbundling Task Force, 3–4, http://www.lawsociety.bc.ca/publications_forms/report-committees/docs/LimitedRetainers_2008.pdf at 17 [B.C. Law Society Unbundling Task Force].

14 *Ibid.* at 17.

to more easily represent themselves in a system that can be foreign and complex to those without formal legal training.'[15] The growing influx of unrepresented litigants has led some to suggest that procedures need to be relaxed and court rules adjusted, rather than relying on 'ad hoc' adjustments by judges.[16] Several jurisdictions have moved to expand informal or streamlined pathways within the court system; an example is Ontario's recent expansion of the scope of its Small Claims Court and simplified procedure.[17] While such measures may ameliorate the impact of a lack of representation in individual cases, the inaccessibility of legal services remains a significant barrier to a fair and efficient justice system. Until and unless that changes, unbundling represents a potentially significant and positive impact.

In considering the case for unbundling (below), we draw on normative and empirical perspectives. While unbundling has some appeal on principle (i.e., consumers ought to be able to determine the precise nature of the legal services they need and obtain them for the precise value of their worth), the primary rationale for developing unbundling is the empirical claim that it will enhance accessibility, especially for middle income litigants. While more evidence is needed to sustain this empirical claim, it continues to animate the case for unbundling, as discussed below.

A. The Case for Unbundling

Legal representation continues to matter in our justice system. For example, in an experimental evaluation of legal assistance programs for low income tenants in New York City's Housing Court, only 22 per cent of represented tenants had final judgments rendered against them, as opposed to 51 per cent of unrepresented tenants.[18] In another study, the American Bar Association found that unrepresented litigants fared

---

15 Coulter A. Osborne, Ministry of the Attorney General, *Civil Justice Reform Project: Summary of Findings and Recommendations* (November, 2007) at 44, http://www.civil-justicereform.jus.gov.on.ca/english/default.asp.

16 Thompson, 'The Judge as Counsel,' *supra* note 8.

17 See Shelley McGill, 'Challenges in Small Claims Court System Design: Does One Size Fit All?', *infra* this volume.

18 Caroll Seron, Martin Frankel, and Gregg Van Ryzin, 'The Impact of Legal Counsel on Outcomes for Poor Tenants in New York City's Housing Court: Results of Randomized Experiments' (2001) 35 Law & Soc'y Rev. 419.

significantly worse in divorce proceedings – they received lower maintenance orders and did not use temporary orders as frequently.[19]

The traditional legal service delivery model of full representation relies on a lawyer taking on all aspects of a client's legal issue. The client pays the lawyer and agrees to continue paying until services are completed.[20] The lawyer's fees are usually calculated on an hourly basis, which may make it difficult to anticipate what the total cost of the services will be from beginning to end. A litigant may know at the outset that he or she cannot afford to hire a lawyer, or may realize this fact when he or she can no longer afford to continue paying for the service. Accessing legal services is thus an 'all or nothing' system where a litigant relies on a lawyer for all aspects of a litigation proceeding or none at all. Further, legal representation is a cost difficult to calculate. The same dispute might cost one litigant $30,000 and another $60,000. Two people with the same legal problem may end up paying significantly different amounts. In this sense, legal expenses tend also to be unexpected. While anyone who owns a house knows that the roof will have to be replaced every ten to fifteen years, and while most people know they will eventually go through sickness, litigation is not an expense that is planned for (or, presently, insured for).[21]

Unbundled services would soften the harshness of the 'all or nothing approach' by being a midway point between full representation and no representation. This model would also allow the informed litigant to 'play to her strengths' – purchasing representation to assist with the identification of arguments or the preparation of materials or the oral advocacy, but not necessarily all three. These assumptions, however, will not always hold true. For the person who is not well informed, or who has little or no basis to prefer assistance in one aspect of litigation or another, some obvious hazards become apparent. Some guidelines for lawyers who enter into limited purpose retainers, and some guidelines for regulators who must supervise the rules of professional conduct in the unbundled context, will be needed

---

19 CBA, *The Future of the Legal Profession, supra* note 6 at 75.
20 Jeanette Fedorak, 'Unbundling Legal Services: Is the Time Now?', *Canadian News and Views on Civil Justice Reform* (Canadian Forum on Civil Justice), Issue 12 (2009) [Fedorak, 'Unbundling Legal Services'].
21 See Sujit Choudhry, Michael Trebilcock, and James Wilson, 'Growing Ontario Legal Aid into the Middle Class: A Proposal for Public Legal Expenses Insurance,' *infra* this volume.

to ensure that coherent, ethical, and predictable standards accompany the move to unbundling.

Unbundled legal services could also provide benefits unrelated to access *per se*. The first of these benefits relates to the efficiency of the court system. Courts may find that partial representation makes it easier to determine the relevant points in a litigant's case, which in turn could accelerate litigation proceedings. The second benefit is connected to the expansion of the legal market. For parties who can afford, say $5,000 towards litigation but no more, the only real option now is to forge ahead unrepresented. In an unbundled market for legal services, $5,000 may well be enough to afford a set of discrete legal services. Is this likely to leave the party in a comparable position to the one she would be in if she had a lawyer provided by legal aid, or even acting on a *pro bono* basis? The answer is probably not. However, in our view, unbundling must be assessed against the alternative of being self-represented, and the market for lawyers willing to cater to clients who request unbundled services is a market presently untapped. Unbundling, in other words, is a way of ensuring that the perfect does not become the enemy of the good. Or, as Tracey Tyler succinctly put it, 'lawyers could be cheaper *à la carte.*'[22]

Because the downsides of unrepresented litigants are partially mitigated by unbundling, unbundling holds the promise for more efficient and effective legal proceedings. Unbundling may also enhance efficiency by providing clients with better information and greater market power. While it is difficult to predict the cost of a contested divorce proceeding, it is less difficult to predict the cost of drafting a statement of claim or a separation agreement, or of providing advice on a specific and discrete aspect of a proceeding. It is also easier for clients to compare lawyers' rates with respect to such limited retainers, allowing clients to be more effective consumers of legal services.

In addition to efficiency benefits, unbundling may also enhance the quality and effectiveness of litigants' submissions. Those litigants who would previously have been unrepresented, and who may have been unable to navigate the complexities of a legal problem, with unbundling would be in a better position to resolve their legal problem.

Besides efficiency and effectiveness, a measure of empowerment

---

22 T. Tyler, 'Lawyers Could Be Cheaper a la Carte,' *Toronto Star,* 18 September 2008, http://www.pblo.org/news/article.211190-Lawyers_could_be_cheaper_%C3%A0_la_carte.

may flow from unbundling as well. As the 2008 British Columbia Law Society Report on Unbundling observed, unbundling reflects a growing desire among many to play a greater role in the legal process.

> [P]art of the rise in self-representation reflects a cultural shift that is taking place in the information age. The Internet and related technologies are transforming the way information is collected, disseminated, and used. Legal information is now easily available to those with access to the Internet ... Many of these litigants will not see the value in hiring a lawyer to collect and process information they might easily collect themselves. Some will feel they need little or no help from a lawyer when it comes time to advance their case in court. Limited scope legal services provide an opportunity for lawyers to assist this growing demographic in synthesizing information and refining legal arguments. In short, the regulation of limited scope legal services demonstrates the adaptation of the legal profession to an evolving marketplace.[23]

In this sense, unbundling could give lawyers new opportunities and the ability to develop specialized practice areas that focus on providing limited scope services. In their comment on 'A Nation of Do-It-Yourself Lawyers,' John Broderick (Chief Justice of New Hampshire) and Ronald George (Chief Justice of California) sum up the argument for unbundling in the following terms:

> Litigants who can afford the services of a lawyer will continue to use one until a case or problem is resolved. Lawyers make a difference and clients know that. But for those whose only option is to go it alone, at least some limited, affordable time with a lawyer is a valuable option we should all encourage.[24]

While these broader benefits are worthy of consideration, the focus of this study is on whether unbundling can contribute to access to justice for middle income parties to disputes. To assess this potential, it is important to examine not just the rationale for unbundling but also the

---

23 See Draft Final Report of the B.C. Law Society Unbundling Task Force at 3–4, http://www.lawsociety.bc.ca/publications_forms/report-committees/docs/LimitedRetainers_2008.pdf.

24 J. Broderick and R. George, 'A Nation of Do-It-Yourself Lawyers,' *New York Times*, 1 January 2010, http://www.nytimes.com/2010/01/02/opinion/02broderick.html?_r=1.

experience of other jurisdictions with unbundling. It is to that task that we now turn.

B. *Lessons Learned from Unbundling in the United States*

In the United States, unbundled legal services have been developed over the past ten to fifteen years. Some lawyers now have built their practices around it.[25] The movement towards unbundled legal services began in the 1990s and gained momentum after a national conference on unbundling was held in Baltimore, Maryland, in 2000.[26] The conference resulted in the creation of the website www.unbundledlaw.org and the development of a range of recommendations to courts, legal services, and the bar.[27] In that same year, the American Bar Association (ABA) released a White Paper titled 'An Analysis Of Rules That Enable Lawyers To Serve Pro Se Litigants,' highlighting rules changes in various states intended to coordinate lawyers' ethical and procedural responsibilities so as to facilitate access, including unbundling.

In 2002, the ABA adopted amendments to its Model Rules of Professional Conduct. The Model Rule sanctions the limited representation of individual clients, affording both lawyer and client 'substantial latitude to limit the representation,' according to Comment 7. The comment elaborates that the scope of a lawyer's services may be limited by agreement or by the terms under which the services are made available. The Model Rule, as subsequently revised, specifically addresses the issue of access by providing that the representation 'may exclude specific means' to accomplish the client's objectives – such as actions the client 'thinks are too costly.' The Model Rule was intended in part to provide a framework for expanding access to legal assistance.

The ABA Model Rule was first adopted by Washington State in its rules of professional conduct. The amendment to the Washington rule states: 'A lawyer may limit the scope of the representation if the limitation is reasonable under the circumstances and the client gives informed consent.'[28] Washington also adopted another rule applying

---

25 CBA, *The Future of the Legal Profession, supra* note 6 at 75; Fedorak, 'Unbundling Legal Services,' *supra* note 20.

26 Madelynn M. Herman, National Centre for State Courts, *Pro Se: Self-Represented Litigant Trends in 2003: Limited Scope Legal Assistance: An Emerging Option for Pro Se Litigants* (2003) at 2.

27 *Ibid.*

28 Washington State Court, *Rules of Professional Conduct* , Rule 1.2(c), http://www.courts.wa.gov/court_rules/?fa=court_rules.list&group=ga&set=rpc.

to unbundled services provided *without a fee*, which exempts from the general rule on conflict of interest

> [a] lawyer who, under the auspices of a program sponsored by a nonprofit organization or court, provides short-term limited legal services to a client without expectation by either the lawyer or the client that the lawyer will provide continuing representation in the matter and without expectation that the lawyer will receive a fee from the client for the services provided.[29]

Other states, including California and Florida, also adopted rules to better facilitate the provision of unbundled legal services (e.g., through less onerous rules regarding conflicts of interest).[30] Writing in 2004, Thomas Yerbich observed, '[A]cceptance of limited representation in litigation is gaining momentum across the country.'[31] As of 2010, forty states have adopted rules that substantially follow the ABA Model Rule 1.2(c).[32] All of these initiatives together have officially opened the door to unbundling in the United States. The result has been that, according to Fedorak, 'Previously fearful lawyers, concerned about being sued or having the courts expand their limited retainer, have instead found satisfied clients and grateful courts.'[33] The picture is not entirely rosy. Important questions remain as to the ethical obligations of counsel providing unbundled services. Eaton and Holtermann raise just some of the concerns to which lawyers providing limited representation to clients can give rise:

> This raises some obvious questions for lawyers who consider providing limited representation in court. For example, can I represent a client in only one hearing in a case? How do I inform the court that I am appearing on a limited basis? Can I draft a pleading for a pro se litigant? Do I need to tell the court if I do?[34]

---

29 *Ibid.*, Rule 6.5(a).
30 Herman, *Pro Se, supra* note 26 at 3.
31 Thomas J. Yerbich, 'Testing the Limits on Unbundled, Limited Representation,' 2004 *American Bankruptcy Institute Journal* 1 at 8.
32 See J.T. Eaton and D. Holtermann, 'Limited Scope Representation Is Here' (2010), http://www.abanet.org/legalservices/delivery/downloads/feature_eaton.pdf [Eaton and Holterman, 'Limited Scope Representation'].
33 Fedorak, 'Unbundling Legal Services,' *supra* note 20.
34 Eaton and Holterman, 'Limited Scope Representation,' *supra* note 32. See also Alicia M. Farley, 'An Important Piece of the Bundle: How Limited Appearances Can Provide an Ethically Sound Way to Increase Access to Justice for Pro Se Litigants' (2007) 20 *Georgetown Journal of Legal Ethics*.

In addition to the ethical ambiguities, uncertainty remains as to the impact of unbundling. While rigorous social science assessments remain to be undertaken, the anecdotal evidence suggests significant benefits for lawyers, clients, and judges. For example, a Massachusetts pilot initiative has led to testimonials from a range of those involved. Chief Justice Paula M. Carey of the Massachusetts Probate and Family Court stated,

> The benefit to the court is significant. People are more informed, pleadings are better prepared, even if we have a temporary order stayed, that sets the stage for things to settle. I would rather have someone [represented] from start to finish, but this is an opportunity for those who wouldn't have any [representation].[35]

One of the lawyers involved notes that unbundling has enhanced lawyers' ability to provide legal representation, on both a *pro bono* and a fee-for-service basis, and is now part of their marketing strategies.

C. *Unbundling in Canada*

Unbundling initiatives have been less common in Canada, though there are signs that things have started to change. The B.C. Law Society created the 'Unbundling Legal Services Task Force,' which endorsed a model for unbundled legal services through its report of 4 April 2008. B.C., like Washington State, also made rule changes to its conflict of interest rules in order to facilitate the provision of free unbundled legal services through not-for-profit organizations.[36]

In late 2007, Pro Bono Law Ontario's free court-based 'brief service' program came to include Law Help Ontario (LHO). LHO was established as a walk-in self-help centre on the ground floor of the Superior Court in Toronto. The program, at no cost to the litigant, includes summary legal advice from *pro bono* lawyers and in some cases representation. The initial stage of the project has been considered a success: on the whole, liti-

---

35 C. O'Neill, 'Law a la Carte,' *Massachusetts Bar Journal* (2010), http://www.massbar.org/publications/lawyers-journal/2010/july/law-à-la-carte-limited-assistance-representation's-impact-on-the-court-system-and-lawyers.

36 Law Society of British Columbia, *Annotated Professional Conduct Handbook*, Rules 7.01-7.04, http://www.lawsociety.bc.ca/page.cfm?cid=383&t=Professional-Conduct-Manual.

gants have been helped, especially since they now have the opportunity to consult with a lawyer before or during court proceedings.[37]

Ontario has now adopted a variation of B.C.'s new conflict of interest rules to permit lawyers participating in Pro Bono Law Ontario's free court-based brief service programs to provide services to a client within the program without a conflict check unless the lawyer knows of a conflict of interest.[38] In January 2010, the Law Society of Upper Canada passed an amendment to Rule 2.04 of the Rules of Professional Conduct respecting Pro Bono Short Term Limited Legal Services.[39] This modest rule change was intended to address the particular challenge of *pro bono* unbundled services, such as Small Claims and Superior Court duty counsel. The rule change provided for safeguards against lawyers acting in the face of actual, known conflicts, but even where such a conflict existed, it would not be imputed to other members of that lawyer's firm. In discussing the rationale for the rule change, the Law Society committee noted that the sub-rule would apply in circumstances in which the limited nature of the legal services being provided significantly reduced the risk of conflicts of interest with other matters being handled by the lawyer's firm.

In the fall of 2010, the LSUC decided to explore broader reforms designed to facilitate unbundling. The Background Report to the unbundling initiative issued in November 2010 proposed farther-reaching rule reforms to facilitate unbundled services.[40] These reforms relate to three general areas: (1) defining the scope of representation; (2) clarifying communications between counsel and parties (e.g., how to apply the professional conduct rules where the lawyer/paralegal providing limited legal services may not be counsel of record or may not consider himself or herself retained for the purposes of the rule); and (3) the lawyer's or paralegal's role in document preparation, including disclosure of such assistance (and, specifically, whether the court must be advised that the client has counsel for a particular part of the case). The report further clarified that the guiding principle behind adapting

---

37 PBLO, *Evaluation of Law Help Ontario, supra* note 5.
38 Law Society of Upper Canada, *Report to Convocation January 28, 2010* at 14, htttp://www.lsuc.on.ca/media/conjan10_PRC.pdf. [LSUC, *Report*] Alberta is also exploring options for unbundling.
39 See http://www.lsuc.on.ca/media/convapril10_prc.pdf.
40 Law Society of Upper Canada, 'Unbundling of Legal Services and Limited Legal Representation,' http://www.lsuc.on.ca/WorkArea/DownloadAsset.aspx?id=2147483764.

the Rules of Professional Conduct to the context of unbundling would be that any new measures not create a lesser standard of professional conduct than is otherwise expected of a lawyer or paralegal. The report emphasized that 'any amendments would not create new standards but confirm existing standards with awareness around how they apply in the unbundled context.' In September 2011, in response to the recommendations of the Unbundling of Legal Services Task Force, the Law Society of Upper Canada approved amendments to the Rules of Professional Conduct that define limited scope retainers and clarify the circumstances under which they are permitted in Ontario.[41]

Ontario and B.C. are not the only jurisdictions seeking to encourage unbundling through rule changes. Alberta's Code of Professional Conduct now contemplates unbundled services as well. Rule 2 of Chapter 9 of the Code, dealing with the lawyer as adviser, states that '[e]xcept where the client directs otherwise, a lawyer must ascertain all of the facts and law relevant to the lawyer's advice.'[42] Commentary under this rule discusses a lawyer's obligation to be economical and to balance this obligation with the obligation to ascertain all of the facts and law necessary to provide meaningful advice. It suggests that a lawyer should consult with the client regarding the scope of investigations and provide an estimate of costs. The Commentary also states:

> Occasionally, a client will specifically request that a lawyer provide an opinion or advice based only on limited facts or assumptions or without the benefit of legal research. While it may be proper in some cases to agree, the lawyer must ensure that the client understands the limitations of such advice. Not infrequently, a legal opinion based on limited facts or assumptions will be so restricted and qualified as to be practically worthless. Similarly, advice given without research in an area in which a lawyer lacks knowledge or experience is likely to be unreliable.

The Nova Scotia Barristers' Society's Legal Ethics Handbook provides commentary that deals expressly with this concept.[43] The Nova

---

41 See http://www.lsuc.on.ca/unbundling. See also M. McKiernan, 'LSUC Sets Out Rules for Unbundled Services,' *Law Times*, 30 September 2011, http://www.law-timesnews.com/201109308692/Headline-News/LSUC-sets-out-rules-for-unbundled-services.

42 Law Society of Alberta, *Rules of Professional Conduct*, http://www.lawsociety.ab.ca/files/regulations/Code.pdf.

43 See http://www.nsbs.org/legalethics/toc.htm.

Scotia commentary (in the numbered 'Application of the Rule' and 'Notes') under Rule 3 (Quality of Service) addresses 'Limited Retainers.' Application 3.12 states as follows:

> A lawyer may accept a limited retainer, but in doing so, the lawyer must be honest and candid with the client about the nature, extent, and scope of the work which the lawyer can provide within the means provided by the client. In such circumstances where a lawyer can only provide limited service, the lawyer should ensure that the client fully understands the limitations of the service to be provided and the risks of the retainer. Discussions with the client concerning limited service should be confirmed in writing. Where a lawyer is providing limited service, the lawyer should be careful to avoid placing him or herself in a position where it appears that the lawyer is providing full service to the client.[44]

The notes to this rule provide that '[a] lawyer must therefore carefully assess in each case in which a client desires abbreviated or partial services whether, under the circumstances, it is possible to render those services in a competent manner ... As long as the client is genuinely fully informed about the nature of the arrangement and understands clearly what is given up, it should be possible to provide such services effectively and ethically.'[45]

Based on the premise underlying unbundling and the growing experience with unbundling in Canada and the United States, we believe that the case for facilitating unbundling is strong. The main arguments against unbundling are that consumers may lack sufficient information to make sound decisions on which legal services to obtain, and that lawyers will be likelier to engage in unethical practices because many of the professional duties – such as those relating to conflicts of interest – are applied in less rigorous ways in an unbundling context. These concerns, while significant, strike us not as reasons to oppose unbundling, but rather as reasons to ensure that unbundling is facilitated in a way that promotes consumer information and that regulates effectively the ethical conduct of lawyers. It is to how unbundling could work – and why, in our view, unbundling *should* work – that our analysis now turns.

---

44 *Ibid.*
45 *Ibid.*

III. Why and How Unbundling Could Work

In our view, as discussed above, the benefits of unbundling are likely to exceed the risks. Further, the benefits can be achieved while mitigating the most egregious of the risks. This section discusses the possible ways that unbundled legal services could be provided in practice. The discussion will be organized around three service delivery models: (1) general counselling and legal advice; (2) limited court appearances; and (3) assistance in preparing documents.[46] The idea is that the service delivery models would interact with one another to provide a spectrum of services available to litigants. One person might wish legal services for purposes of advice and preparation of a document, while another might seek assistance only for a court appearance. If unbundling is to fulfil its promise, it will be necessary for parties to understand the scope and value of each service, how they may be combined and disaggregated, and what a fair price for the service should be.

A. General Counselling and Legal Advice

General counselling and legal advice is one way that unrepresented litigants could access unbundled legal services. This form of service is already available to the extent that individuals might decide to approach a lawyer before beginning to pursue their claim – indeed, many jurisdictions offer referral services involving a first hour of 'free' advice from a lawyer. Other jurisdictions have explored the provision of 'summary advice,' whether in person or over the phone, often through legal aid clinics or other public interest or community bodies.

Lawyers contacted for general counselling and advice in turn may provide an assessment of the legal issues and give an opinion on the merits of the claim. Currently, an unrepresented litigant could also consult with a lawyer after the claim has been initiated. But the assumption with this form of consultation as well as consultations prior to a claim is that the litigant would then make a decision about whether he or she wanted to retain the lawyer for the duration of the proceeding or be unrepresented. Once retained under the conventional model, the lawyer becomes the solicitor of record, and in that capacity is subject to a range of professional duties, legal obligations, and civil liabilities.[47]

---

46 *Ibid.*; B.C. Law Society Unbundling Task Force, *supra* note 13 at 19.
47 For discussion of the implications of a solicitor–client relationship, see *R. v. Neil* 2002 SCC 70.

Unbundling, on the other hand, would give unrepresented litigants the flexibility to consult with a lawyer throughout their proceedings without being obliged to retain the lawyer for all aspects of their case, or even beyond a single consultation. By the same token, the lawyer would be insulated from many of the duties, obligations, and liabilities that flow from the solicitor–client relationship, though the actual service or representation provided in an unbundled context would remain subject to professional and legal oversight and consumer protection regulation.

A lawyer consulted for advice would be well positioned to assess an unrepresented litigant's 'self-diagnosis' of the case and could act as a buffer between the legal system and the litigant. A lawyer would inform an unrepresented litigant of his or her legal rights arising out of a claim[48] and could advise the litigant about taking steps to protect these rights. Counselling and advice in the unbundled context might result from reviewing correspondence, court documents, and any other information that is pertinent to the litigant's case. Counselling and advice could also encompass a wide range of other possible services. These include providing an unrepresented litigant with 'an adequate knowledge base upon which to understand the litigation process'[49] through basic information about legal processes and stages in a litigation proceeding. A lawyer could advise on what documents need to be prepared and how to file and serve documents. A lawyer could also advise a litigant about the availability of alternative dispute resolution mechanisms that the litigant might not have been aware of, such as mediation and arbitration.

In the United States, counselling and advice has also come to include 'coaching' litigants on how to conduct court proceedings or negotiations on their own.[50] In a trial situation, a litigant might be advised about the types of questions to ask in cross-examination or the types of legal arguments that might be relevant to a judge's decision.[51] Some lawyers might also offer this service with respect to mediation by helping the unrepresented litigant devise a plan that he or she could take into mediation. The lawyer could also advise on whom to select as a mediator as well as any form of settlement agreement after mediation has occurred.[52]

---

48 Forrest Mosten and Lee Borden, 'Unbundled Legal Services,' http://www.zorza. net/resources/Ethics/mosten-borden.htm [Mosten and Borden, 'Unbundled Legal Services'].
49 B.C. Law Society Unbundling Task Force, *supra* note 13 at 17.
50 CBA, *The Future of the Legal Profession, supra* note 6 at 75.
51 *Ibid.* at 76.
52 *Ibid.*

Coaching might also include how to conduct negotiations more generally. For example, in the family law setting a lawyer may be able to help an unrepresented litigant develop a negotiating style that would prevent emotions from interfering with the negotiations. A lawyer could also 'role-play' with the litigant and remain 'on-call' during the actual negotiation if the litigant wishes to consult the lawyer.[53]

B. Limited Court Appearances

For unbundled services that provide counselling and legal advice, the assumption is that the litigant will remain unrepresented and that the lawyer will provide 'behind the scenes' guidance and advice for a particular aspect of the litigant's case. Services consisting of unbundled or limited court appearances operate differently in that a lawyer will actually represent a litigant in court if hired to do so. Limited court appearances are already offered in Ontario to a certain extent through Pro Bono Law Ontario's duty counsel program at the Small Claims Court and on a more limited basis through Law Help Ontario at the Superior Court. However, when limited court appearance services are offered for a fee, there will likely be an increase in the number of unrepresented litigants who receive partial representation. Also, litigants will have more choice over the lawyer they wish to retain (as opposed to being assigned one).

Unrepresented litigants might decide to hire a lawyer to represent them for those areas of a proceeding that are complex or where a litigant feels more comfortable having a trained advocate act on his or her behalf. A lawyer could appear in court on behalf of a litigant for a single application, multiple motions, or even a trial. When appearing on behalf of a litigant on a limited basis, should lawyers inform the court that the scope of their retainer is limited? While there is some controversy surrounding whether such disclosure ought to be mandated, it seems clear to us that it is appropriate for the Court to be aware of the context of the lawyer's services.

C. Preparing Documents

Unrepresented litigants could also access unbundled legal services by retaining a lawyer for the purpose of preparing and drafting docu-

---

53 *Ibid.*

ments. These documents might include pleadings, affidavit materials, or any other documents that may be required during the course of a proceeding.[54] The scope of these services may consist of a lawyer simply reviewing an unrepresented litigant's document. In other cases a lawyer could assist the litigant in drafting the document or draft the document in its entirety.[55]

A properly drafted document would assist the court in processing an unrepresented litigant's argument since the quality of the documents placed before the court would likely be improved.[56] Retaining a lawyer would hopefully result in documents being written in clear, plain language. The document would be informed by a lawyer's knowledge of substantive and procedural issues as well as methods of research and analysis that the unrepresented litigant may not have the capacity to undertake. The idea behind offering these types of services is that the documents drafted or assisted by a lawyer are typically easier to understand than documents written by unrepresented litigants.[57] In this context, unbundling may involve paralegals and law clerks as well.

After the documents have been written they need to be explained by the lawyer to the litigant so that the litigant has the ability to speak to the document before the court if required to do so.[58] The lawyer needs to ensure that the document is understood by the litigant and that the litigant understands the relevance of the document and any consequences that might arise out of it.[59] As the B.C. Law Society recommendations emphasize, in the context of unbundled services, the lawyer cannot take a 'passive' approach to drafting by mechanically producing the document that she or he has been hired to prepare. The lawyer must thoroughly consider the litigant's representation of the facts and always be 'alert to fraud, and remain mindful of his or her obligation to the courts.'[60]

In the United States, unbundled drafting services are sometimes referred to as 'ghostwriting.'[61] There has been disagreement in the

---

54 B.C. Law Society Unbundling Task Force, *supra* note 13 at 37.
55 *Ibid.*
56 *Ibid.* at 20.
57 *Ibid.* at 38.
58 *Ibid.* at 21.
59 *Ibid.*
60 *Ibid.*
61 Mosten and Borden, 'Unbundled Legal Services,' *supra* note 47. See also John Rothermuch, 'Ethical and Procedural Implications of "Ghostwriting" for Pro Se Litigants' (1999) 67 Fordham L. Rev. 2687; Ira Robbins, 'Ghostwriting: Filling in the Gaps for

United States regarding whether or not the name of the lawyer providing the 'ghostwriting' services needs to be disclosed. Three primary
approaches exist in the United States. The first is that the face of the
document must disclose the lawyer's name. The second approach is
that the face of the document must disclose that the document has been
prepared by a lawyer or with the assistance of a lawyer, though the
name of the lawyer is not required to be disclosed. The third approach
is that there is no requirement to disclose the lawyer's involvement if
the lawyer is not appearing on the record.[62]

Some of the talk in the United States touches upon whether ghostwriting should constitute an entry of appearance by the lawyer. In the
event that it did constitute an entry of appearance, the lawyer providing drafting assistance might be required to make a court appearance as the litigant's representative. However, the B.C. Law Society
Task Force Report states that even in American jurisdictions where the
name of the lawyer providing drafting assistance must be disclosed
on the face of the document, the lawyer is not required to appear 'on
the record' as a litigant's representative.[63] The B.C. report endorsed
the view that there should be no requirement to disclose a lawyer's
involvement in drafting documents as part of a limited scope retainer.[64] The Task Force also endorsed the view that in the event that a
lawyer's involvement in drafting the documents *was* disclosed, it
should not constitute an entry of appearance by the lawyer as the litigant's representative.[65]

D. Interaction between the Models

None of the models described above are meant to be mutually exclusive from one another. An unrepresented litigant may decide to retain
a lawyer for advice on one occasion while another litigant may retain
a lawyer for multiple aspects of the case, from initial advice to drafting
a statement of claim to a court appearance on a motion. A litigant and

---

Pro Se Prisoners' Access to the Courts' (2010) 23 Georgetown J. of Legal Ethics 271;
and 'CURRENT DEVELOPMENT 2007–2008: The Ethics of Ghostwriting: The American Bar Association's Formal Opinion 07-446 and Its Effect on Ghostwriting Practices in the American Legal Community' (2008) 21 Georgetown J. of Legal Ethics 765.

62 B.C. Law Society Unbundling Task Force, *supra* note 13 at 39–40.
63 *Ibid.*
64 *Ibid.* at 40.
65 *Ibid.* at 41.

counsel might even devise a plan beforehand that details the tasks a lawyer will take on and the tasks a litigant will perform.

For example, an unrepresented litigant may meet with a lawyer to discuss his or her legal issues and the limited scope options. The litigant may decide that there are aspects of the case that he or she is capable of conducting while there are other aspects of the case that the lawyer is better equipped to deal with. As a result, the litigant and the lawyer may apportion tasks between themselves. The lawyer will undertake tasks that may or may not include court appearances and drafting documents, while the litigant may also undertake tasks that may or may not include court appearances and drafting documents. The result is that the unrepresented litigant can choose how and when he or she wants to be represented, resulting in a flexibility of services and reduced costs.

E. Engagement Letters and Acknowledgment Forms

It is essential that a lawyer offering unbundled legal services ensure that the litigant understands the limited scope of the services. One way of making certain that the litigant is aware of the exact nature of the services being provided is through an engagement letter setting out the terms of the services provided. Another option is to design a 'limited scope engagement agreement' that outlines all of the potential services available from the lawyer on a limited basis.[66] The recent amendments to the Rules of Professional Conduct in Ontario require that limited scope retainers are provided in writing to the client.[67] The specific services provided by the lawyer would be checked off, while those not checked off would indicate that the litigant must undertake those tasks. The advantage of such a form is that the lawyer's role would be defined; in addition, the client would be aware of the steps needing to be performed in general.[68] This safeguard depends, however, on a well-informed client, and it may fall to the Law Society or to NGOs such as the PBLO to engage in activities to raise client awareness respecting unbundled services.

Clearly, a face-to-face conversation about the legal services to be pro-

---

66 CBA, *The Future of the Legal Profession, supra* note 6 at 80.
67 See Rule 2.02 (6.1) and (6.2) at http://www.lsuc.on.ca/WorkArea/DownloadAsset. aspx?id=2147486159.
68 *Ibid.*

vided is preferable to a letter alone. It would therefore be advisable that a lawyer offering unbundled legal services explain the scope of the services orally in addition to providing the litigant with a limited scope engagement agreement. That said, at the other end of the spectrum, it is also possible for unbundled services to be offered entirely through virtual means. Indeed, the rise of virtual law firms appears to be premised on the capacity of such firms to handle unbundled or outsourced work.[69] As an additional precaution, it might also be useful to design an express acknowledgment form that explicitly states that the lawyer will not be providing services beyond the services agreed to. This form would be explained to and signed by the litigant. In the United States, 'Notice of Withdrawal' forms have also been designed. Lawyers can serve these to a litigant when they have completed the tasks they were retained for.[70]

IV. Mitigating the Risks of Unbundling

Unbundled legal services may provide litigants with more choice, flexibility, and the ability to 'pay as they go.' By the same token, however, unbundling disrupts the norm of a comprehensive solicitor–client relationship formed when a client retains a lawyer to act on her or his behalf. This different approach to solicitor–client relationships gives rise to a number of principled and practical challenges, which we explore below.

The first practical concern of unbundling stems from the general issue of continuity. Although unbundling would allow unrepresented litigants to choose when and by whom they want to be represented, the 'on-again, off-again' nature of the representation may result in inconsistencies within the litigant's file. This may especially be the case where more than one lawyer is retained at different points by a litigant, resulting in conflicting strategies and approaches to the legal problem.

Furthermore, there is no neat division between different stages of a proceeding. Every stage of litigation is connected to another part of the

---

69 See Carolyn Elefant, 'Virtual Law Firms Go Viral' (26 June 2009), http://legalblog-watch.typepad.com/legal_blog_watch/2009/06/virtual-firms-are-virtually-every-where.html.

70 Sample Retainer agreements from http://www.unbundledlaw.org/retainer_agree-ments/CA%20Rules%20&%20Agreement.pdf.

litigation, which may make it difficult for a lawyer to suddenly step in and represent a litigant's best interests. For example,

> [a] lawyer might ... assist a client in preparing an affidavit for a custody hearing. The lawyer might do a perfectly good job of taking the client's instructions and preparing the document, but not know enough about the background to realize that the approach being taken by the client will harm, rather than help, the cause ... Similarly, what if a client only wants assistance in drawing up a document reflecting the settlement that has been agreed to ... Shouldn't the lawyer first be satisfied that the settlement is a reasonable one, and that the client understands what he or she is giving up?[71]

Unbundling may result in increased access to legal services for a litigant, but decreased consideration of a legal problem as a whole.

Another practical problem related to continuity is that it might be difficult for a lawyer retained on a limited basis to get 'up to speed' on a file in a timely fashion. For example, a lawyer who has been hired by a litigant for limited representation at a discovery would have to extensively prepare for the discovery without having the advantage of earlier knowledge or direct access to all matters in the file. Complicating matters is the fact that the legal system is still largely a paper-based system. With no centralized system to keep track of documents, it might be difficult for a lawyer to access pertinent documents in the first place. The interconnectedness of litigation might make it difficult for a lawyer to perform his or her task in total isolation from other parts of the litigation.

The lack of continuity may result in deadlines or limitation periods being missed or required elements of a litigation being overlooked. The lack of continuity also raises a concern with respect to the potential for exploitation or abuse by lawyers of unsuspecting clients, who may not know when a particular legal task begins or ends, and who bear in such circumstances the liability should they wish to seek recourse for losses flowing from inadequate representation in an unbundled setting. This can be mitigated through clearly worded rules and commentaries.

The LSUC 2010 Unbundling Working Group recommendations, for example, address this issue. The Working Group recommends that

---

71 CBA, *The Future of the Legal Profession, supra* note 6 at 78.

the lawyer ensure that the client understands the limited scope of the retainer, as well as the limits and risks associated with such services, and confirm this understanding, where reasonably possible, in writing. Another recommendation would oblige the lawyer who acts for a client only in a limited capacity to promptly disclose the limited retainer to the court and to any other interested person in the proceeding, if failure to disclose would mislead the court or that other person. Unless otherwise required by law or a court, the discretion to divulge the identity of the lawyer who provided drafting assistance should lie, according to the Working Group, with the client. Finally, save for the earlier rule enacted to relieve *pro bono* duty counsel of the full conflicts regime, the regular rules governing conflicts of interest and duty of loyalty should apply to limited scope legal service retainers.

The starting point for mitigating these difficulties is recognizing that unbundled legal services can *alleviate* some of the access problems unrepresented litigants face, but will not *solve* the problems of unrepresented litigants.

In response to the continuity concerns, the quality of legal services should always be high and lawyers should undertake their services with the intention of promoting their clients' best interests. This should be done to the best of the lawyers' knowledge. If a lawyer feels uncomfortable providing the services – for example, where documents that will shed more light on a relevant situation are missing, or the lawyer is not satisfied with the factual elements of the litigant's case – the lawyer can and should decline to provide the service. If a lawyer provides unbundled services, however, it is likely that she will need to adopt protocols or practices to address these kinds of situations, which may recur.

With respect to costs, unbundled legal services may still be out of the price range of some unrepresented litigants. The reality of providing services is that the more extensive the service is, the more costly it will be. However, the *degree* to which unbundled services may be out of a litigant's price range is a marked improvement on the degree to which full representation is currently out of a litigant's price range. Simply giving unrepresented litigants the option to access a range of services on a limited basis for less money than full representation could still alleviate some of the access issues that unrepresented litigants face today.

V. Unbundling: Next Steps

The following section outlines three main steps that need to be taken in order to open up the market to unbundled legal services. The first step is to address any necessary rule changes to remove barriers to unbundled legal services. The second is to facilitate the development of unbundled legal services as a viable business model for lawyers. The third is to devise a regulatory framework that protects consumers. These steps are not intended to be sequential. In other words, it may be that the establishment of consumer protection frameworks for clients of unbundled services ought to be the first step, for it would make possible the development of a more robust market for such services.

A. Rule Changes

While unbundling may not be inconsistent with existing rules in most jurisdictions, Ontario is one of several provinces that, as indicated above, is implementing and/or examining rule changes to facilitate unbundling. Three areas of rules in particular are implicated: limited court appearances by a lawyer, conflicts of interest, and ethical standards pertaining to limited representation.

(1) *Limited appearances by a lawyer in court.* Lawyers making limited appearances in court on behalf of a litigant will need to have assurances that they will not be 'on the record' as a litigant's full representative – responsible for all aspects of the litigant's case – once their role in a proceeding is complete. This assurance is particularly important in light of expansive Supreme Court jurisprudence on the nature and scope of a lawyer's obligations to a client who has retained her.[72]

The B.C. Task Force asserted in its report that if a lawyer makes a court appearance in a limited capacity, that lawyer should appear on the record only for the portion of the proceeding for which he or she was acting for a litigant. The Task Force held that there needed to be 'simplified rules and procedures for getting on and off the record'[73] so that the lawyer would not remain on the record after appearing in court. The Task Force recommended that courts provide both the lawyer and the client a form to sign that would set out the scope of the lawyer's appearance before the court.[74]

Rules for informing opposing counsel and/or the court about a law-

---

72 See *Neil, supra* note 46.
73 B.C. Law Society Unbundling Task Force, *supra* note 13 at 25.
74 *Ibid.*

yer's limited scope should also be developed. The B.C. Task Force recommended that 'the onus should lie with the lawyer who is providing limited scope legal services to notify opposing counsel of the existence and scope of the limited retainer.'[75]

The rules also need to reflect how communication between opposing counsel and partially represented litigants is to be handled. The Ontario Working Group and the B.C. Task Force recommend rule changes that would allow opposing counsel to directly communicate with a litigant who has retained a limited scope lawyer except where: the lawyer has been notified of the limited scope lawyer's involvement; the communication concerns an issue within the scope of a limited scope lawyer's involvement; and the limited scope lawyer and his or her client have asked the lawyer to communicate with the limited scope lawyer about the issue in question.[76] Rules of this nature would clearly delineate the parameters of communication between opposing counsel, a limited scope lawyer, and a litigant.

(2) *Conflicts of interest.* Ontario recently changed its conflict rules to permit lawyers participating in Pro Bono Law Ontario's court-based brief service programs to provide free unbundled services to a client within the program *unless* the lawyer knows of a conflict of interest.[77] The Ontario Working Group recommends that these conflict rules not be extended to fee-based unbundled services. A lawyer providing unbundled legal services for a fee should already have an internal conflict system in place, making conflict checks less time consuming.

(3) *Ethical issues.* Currently a lawyer providing full representation can serve his or her client's best interest based on knowledge of what occurred earlier in a litigation proceeding. However, a lawyer providing unbundled services may not have the same type of knowledge base and thus will not be able to represent a client's best interests at the same level as a lawyer providing full representation. Although the quality of legal services must always be high and a lawyer should always promote a client's best interests, this should be done to the best of a lawyer's knowledge. It might be helpful to develop a rule that specifically addresses the ethical obligations of lawyers providing unbundled legal services. This rule should take into account the very different starting

---

75 *Ibid.*
76 *Ibid.* at 22.
77 LSUC, *Report, supra* note 38.

point a limited scope lawyer has compared to that of a lawyer providing full representation.

B. Creating a Supportive Environment

The second step that needs to be taken in order to open up the market to unbundled legal services is to create an environment within the legal community that facilitates unbundling as a legitimate option for the delivery of legal services. This could begin with an endorsement of unbundled legal services from legal regulators.

It is important to also garner the support of the local bar and the bench. One way to do this is to first educate lawyers about unbundling and provide educational initiatives through the bar associations and other legal organizations. Educational initiatives should also extend to members of the bench. In California, one of the models for unbundling consisted of a partnership between members of the bar and the bench: many lawyers wanted reassurance that the judges would honour the limitation on scope and let them withdraw from a case at the conclusion of their duties. In exchange, the bar committed to providing training to its members so that quality services would be provided.[78] Although this form of partnership is not necessary, it is important to emphasize and demonstrate to judges the positive benefits of unbundling in the day-to-day operations of the court. For example, a judge could be shown how pleadings would likely contain more relevant and reliable information and how unrepresented litigants might take less of a judge's time during a proceeding.[79]

The main goal of creating a supportive environment should be to make lawyers more comfortable with the idea of providing unbundled legal services. Lawyers should not have to worry that the scope of their duties will automatically be expanded or that unbundling will lead to circumstances where they will inevitably be sued or disciplined. Arguably, the more comfortable lawyers are with the idea of unbundling as a service delivery model, the more likely it is that the service will be made available to otherwise unrepresented plaintiffs.

C. Consumer Protection

The regulatory framework governing unbundled legal services should

---

78 Sue Talia, 'Roadmap for Implementing a Successful Unbundling Program' (2005) at 4.
79 *Ibid.* at 4.

ensure that litigants who want to access these services are not taken advantage of because they lack knowledge of the law or the legal system. For example, as Michael Trebilcock has observed, in professional services that are not effectively regulated, consumers generally

> may be ill-equipped to diagnose or identify the precise nature of the problem or need they are confronting ... [E]ven if they can identify the problem or need, they may be ill-equipped to choose an appropriate service provider, to exercise meaningful judgment over the appropriate service provider, and to monitor effectively performance by the service provider of the relevant procedure thereafter and the time and costs associated therewith.[80]

The concern is that some individuals providing professional services might prey upon ill-equipped consumers and supply defective services at either an affordable cost or a high one. In order to protect against such situations, the Law Society of Upper Canada has closely regulated unbundled legal services by setting special standards of practice.[81] The recent reforms to the Rules of Professional Conduct in Ontario and elsewhere represent important steps on the journey to reform, but are not in and of themselves a destination. Law Societies across the country should also promote competence as a major objective of its regulatory framework and pursue 'a variety of strategies designed to identify and eradicate cases of incompetence.'[82]

One approach would be for those lawyers providing unbundled legal services to be registered as unbundled or limited scope service providers and to be subject to additional monitoring for a period of time. Those registered could also be required to participate in mandatory continuing legal education programs that address systemic practice deficiencies in unbundling.[83] Pilot initiatives could be conducted within specific subject areas (unbundling in family law settings, for example), with the collaboration of the bench and bar in order to assess the impact, benefits, and risks of unbundling. Whatever form unbundling takes, educating clients and legal service providers will be essential to

---

80 Michael Trebilcock, 'Regulating the Market for Legal Services' (2008) 45 Alta. L. 215–32.
81 *Supra* note 41.
82 *Ibid.*
83 *Ibid.*

ensure that unbundling increases the fairness and transparency of the market for legal services.

VI. Remaining Uncertainty

While the analysis above mostly concerns what we know or think we know about unbundling, what we do not know about unbundling is just as important, if not more so. For example, how should courts in Canada approach the issue of costs when a party may have used a lawyer as a ghostwriter or simply to handle oral argument? In what circumstances could lawyers providing unbundled services be found liable for negligence to a client? Do the answers to these questions differ where unbundled services are provided on a *pro bono* basis as opposed to a fee-paying basis? Could a lawyer providing unbundled services enter into a contingency fee retainer with a client? These kinds of questions merely scratch the surface of the variety of areas where we have an insufficient or uncertain grasp of the full implications of unbundling.

VII. Conclusion

Our aim in this brief analysis has been to examine the potential of unbundling to enhance access to justice, particularly for the middle class, who may be able to afford modest fees for some legal services but for whom full legal representation on the conventional solicitor–client model is simply out of reach. While unbundling is not without risks both to litigants and to lawyers, and while further data will be needed before any empirical conclusions become possible, our view is that, at this stage, the potential benefits outweigh the potential downsides.

We have examined the experience of jurisdictions where unbundling has been in place, and considered the recommendations of various Working Groups and Task Forces that have advocated unbundling. It is worth noting that these Working Groups and Task Forces invariably have recommended moving to one form or another of unbundling (though it may be that such initiatives are only struck when a political decision already has been made to pursue reform of this kind). Finally, we have explored the steps necessary to implement unbundling in a manner that mitigates risk. While only one piece of a massive puzzle, unbundling, in our view, represents a significant and positive step toward a more accessible civil justice system.

7 Money Isn't Everything: Understanding Moderate Income Households' Use of Lawyers' Services[1]

REBECCA L. SANDEFUR

I. Introduction

We know surprisingly little about the use of lawyers by moderate income people. What we do know includes some unexpected elements. Despite a widely shared perception that lawyers' services are prohibitively expensive, a survey of Americans who have used lawyers' services finds that Americans are often satisfied with the fees they paid, while surveys of Americans who considered and decided not to use lawyers have found that this decision is motivated by cost in only a minority of instances.

Drawing on fundamental insights from sociology, I propose two additional factors that may shape middle income Americans' use of lawyers: the social construction of legality and social searching. The legal nature of any given civil justice problem is socially constructed. In many instances, people do not think of their civil justice problems in legal terms and so do not consider legal staff, such as lawyers, as an appropriate source of assistance. Social searching reflects a common way that people respond to the challenges attendant on finding service providers in markets: people rely on people whom they already know as sources of referrals to specific attorneys or as providers of legal services. The costs of lawyers' services are a part of what is shaping moderate income families' behaviour, but they are not the only factor. The findings have implications for access to justice policy.

---

1 I am grateful to Stephen Ginsberg, Michael Trebilcock, and other participants at the colloquium for comments, questions, and suggestions.

II. Public Experience with Civil Justice Problems in the United States

In contemporary market democracies, law reaches deeply into many aspects of daily life. Civil justice problems are common and widespread.[2] Though such problems come in many different forms that affect different aspects of people's lives and concern different kinds of relationships, they share a certain important quality: they are problems that have civil legal aspects, raise civil legal issues, and have consequences shaped by civil law, even though the people who experience them may never think of them as 'legal' and may never attempt to use law to try to resolve them.[3]

For many people living in market democracies, such troubles emerge 'at the intersection of civil law and everyday adversity.'[4] For example, conservative estimates suggest that more than 100 million Americans are currently living in households that are experiencing at least one civil justice problem involving key areas of contemporary life such as livelihood, shelter, employment, health care, the intergenerational conservation of property, intimate relationships, and the care and support of dependent children and adults.[5] Recent justice surveys conducted in Canada similarly find high rates of contact with civil justice problems.[6]

---

2 Albert W. Currie, 'The Legal Problems of Everyday Life' in *Access to Justice*, ed. Rebecca L. Sandefur (Bingley: Emerald, 2009) at 1 [Currie, 'The Legal Problems of Everyday Life']; Hazel Genn, *Paths to Justice: What People Do and Think about Going to Law* (Portland: Hart Publishing 2009) [Genn, *Paths to Justice*]; Gillian K. Hadfield, 'Higher Demand, Lower Supply? A Comparative Assessment of the Legal Resource Landscape for Ordinary Americans' (2010) 37 *Fordham Urban Law Journal* 129 [Hadfield, 'Higher Demand']; Pascoe Pleasence, Nigel J. Balmer, and Alexy Buck, *Causes of Action: Civil Law and Social Justice*, 2nd ed. (London: TSO 2006); Rebecca L. Sandefur, 'Access to Civil Justice and Race, Class, and Gender Inequality' (2008) 34 *Annual Review of Sociology* 339.

3 Genn, *Paths to Justice, supra* note 2.

4 Rebecca L. Sandefur, 'The Importance of Doing Nothing: Everyday Problems and Responses of Inaction' in *Transforming Lives: Law and Social Process*, ed. Pascoe Pleasence, Alexy Buck, and Nigel Balmer (London: TSO 2007) at 113 [Sandefur, 'The Importance of Doing Nothing'].

5 Rebecca L. Sandefur, 'The Impact of Counsel: An Analysis of Empirical Evidence' (2010) 9 *Seattle Journal for Social Justice* 56 [Sandefur, 'The Impact of Counsel']; idem, 'The Fulcrum Point of Equal Access to Justice: Legal and Non-legal Institutions of Remedy' (2009) 42 *Loyola of Los Angeles Law Review* 949 [Sandefur, 'The Fulcrum Point'].

6 Currie, 'The Legal Problems of Everyday Life,' *supra* note 2.

More accurate data collection would likely produce substantially higher estimates of public contact with civil justice problems.[7] In both Canada and the United States, most of these justice problems never make it to law: they are not taken to lawyers for advice or representation, nor do people pursue them in court.[8]

The United States' more than 300 million people experience many problems that have civil legal aspects and raise civil legal issues. Here, and in other Western market democracies, these problems are so common as to be 'nearly normal features of everyday life.'[9] The best estimates available for the scope of the American public's experience with civil justice problems are based on information that was collected long before the recent recession. The most recent civil justice survey of the population comes from 1992 and provides information representing the experiences of only a portion of the American public. This survey, funded by the American Bar Association (ABA), excluded the highest-earning 20 per cent of households.[10] The last truly comprehensive surveys of public experience with civil justice problems are more than three decades out of date, conducted in the 1970s.[11]

Like most contemporary civil justice surveys, the 1992 ABA survey presented respondents with lists of specific problems, each carefully selected to raise issues in civil law, and then asked whether respondents had experienced each during a specified period of time before the survey – in this case, one year. General categories queried included those involving family, work, benefits, housing, debt, credit, and neigh-

---

7 Jon Johnsen, 'Studies of Legal Needs and Legal Aid in a Market Context' in *The Transformation of Legal Aid: Comparative and Historical Studies*, ed. Francis Regan, Alan Paterson, Tamara Goriely, and Don Fleming (Oxford: Oxford University Press, 1999) at 205 [Johnson, 'Studies of Legal Needs and Legal Aid']; Pascoe Pleasence, Nigel J. Balmer, and Tania Tam, 'Failure to Recall: Indications from the England and Welsh Civil and Social Justice Survey of the Relative Severity and Incidence of Civil Justice Problems' in *Access to Justice,* ed. Rebecca L. Sandefur (Bingley: Emerald, 2009) at 43 [Pleasence, 'Failure to Recall'].

8 Currie, 'The Legal Problems of Everyday Life,' *supra* note 2. See, generally, Sandefur, 'The Impact of Counsel,' *supra* note 5.

9 Currie, 'The Legal Problems of Everyday Life,' *supra* note 2 at 5.

10 Consortium on Legal Services and the Public, *Report on the Legal Needs of the Low- and Moderate-Income Public* (Chicago: American Bar Association 1994), 3 [Consortium, *Report*].

11 Barbara A. Curran, *The Legal Needs of the Public: The Final Report of a National Survey* (Chicago: American Bar Association 1977); David M. Trubek, Joel B. Grossman, William L.F. Felstiner, Herbert M. Kritzer, and Austin Sarat, *Civil Litigation Research Project: Final Report* (Madison: University of Wisconsin Law School, 1983).

bourhood problems. Specific problems included events like 'not having money to pay bills,' 'serious dispute with tax people,' 'had difficulty collecting pay,' and 'separation, divorce, or annulment.' The survey revealed that about half of surveyed households had been experiencing at least one serious civil justice problem in the twelve months prior to the survey.[12] If one projects forward that rate of problems experience to today, this implies that more than 44 million households, in which live more than 100 million people, are experiencing at least one non-trivial civil justice problem.[13]

One hundred million people affected is actually a conservative estimate for the scope of the American public's experience with civil justice problems in at least three respects. First, the estimate reflects only the experiences of those in households with incomes of less than $90,000 a year, and thus excludes the justice problems experienced by the rest of the population, the additional 90.9 million people who live in households with incomes of $90,000 per year or more.[14] Second, the present moment is one of great economic turbulence, unprecedented since the early part of the twentieth century. The recent recession will likely have increased the number of people experiencing hardships like foreclosure, job loss, trouble paying medical bills, difficulties with consumer debt, and eviction – all of which can produce civil justice problems or be civil justice problems in and of themselves.[15] Third, the survey techniques used in the 1992 national study may lead to underestimates of how often people experience different kinds of justice problems. Traditional surveys typically use the past twelve months to five years as their frame of reference when asking people to report on their justice problems.[16] Some scholars argue that the retrospective focus of such studies leads to underreporting because people fail to remember or report all the problems that they have experienced in the past.[17] A recent study estimates that these kinds of surveys may understate the incidence of civil justice problems by as much as two-thirds.[18]

While the myth of Americans' litigiousness persists, most Americans' civil justice problems are in fact handled in ways that involve no

---

12 Consortium, *Report, supra* note 10 at 5.
13 Sandefur, 'The Impact of Counsel,' *supra* note 5 at 56.
14 *Ibid.* at 57.
15 *Ibid.*
16 Currie, 'The Legal Problems of Everyday Life,' *supra* note 2, Table 1.
17 Johnsen, 'Studies of Legal Needs and Legal Aid,' *supra* note 7 at 217–18.
18 Pleasence, 'Failure to Recall,' *supra* note 7 at 60.

direct contact with the staff of the civil justice system.[19] Only a minority of the American public's civil justice problems are ever taken to lawyers in the hope of securing advice or representation: 24 per cent according to the 1992 survey.[20] Similarly, most civil justice problems do not involve contact with courts or tribunals. The same survey found that 37 per cent of family and domestic problems involved a court or tribunal, while 12 per cent of employment-related problems and 11 per cent of civil justice problems involving personal finances involved courts or tribunals. Overall, 14 per cent of civil justice problems came to the attention of some kind of court or tribunal.[21] When ordinary Americans face civil justice problems, turning to law is a relatively uncommon response.

A predominant account of why Americans do not take their problems to law features cost[22] – not the cost of the civil justice system itself, which Americans have in a sense already paid for with their taxes, but the direct costs of using the system, particularly the cost of lawyers' services.

III. The Cost of Lawyers' Services

A quick glance at the disparity between the average lawyers' earnings and the average American's earnings reveals some of the basis for the perception that lawyers' services are priced out of the reach of many ordinary people. In 2009, the median annual earnings of American lawyers were $113,240.[23] Compare that with the median income for an American household in the same year, $49,777,[24] and one sees that a

---

19 R.E. Miller and A. Sarat, 'Grievances, Claims, and Disputes: Assessing the Adversary Culture' (1980–1) 15 *Law and Society Review* 525; Sandefur, 'The Impact of Counsel,' *supra* note 5 at 59–60.

20 Computed from Consortium, *Report, supra* note 10, Table 4–7. See also Herbert M. Kritzer, 'To Lawyer or Not to Lawyer: *Is* That the Question?' (2008) 5 *Journal of Empirical Legal Studies* 875 [Kritzer, 'To Lawyer or Not to Lawyer'].

21 Computed from Consortium, *Report, supra* note 10, Table 4–10.

22 Hadfield, 'Higher Demand,' *supra* note 2; Gillian K. Hadfield, 'The Price of Law: How the Market for Lawyers Distorts the Justice System' (2010) 98 Michigan Law Review 953 [Hadfield, 'The Price of Law']; Kritzer, 'To Lawyer or Not to Lawyer,' *supra* note 20; Leon Mayhew and Albert J. Reiss, Jr, 'The Social Organization of Legal Contacts' (1969) 34 *American Sociological Review* 309.

23 Bureau of Labor Statistics, 'Occupational Employment and Wages, 2009: Lawyers' (2010), http://www.bls.gov/oes/current/oes231011.htm, accessed 10 December 2010.

24 U.S. Census Bureau, Table H–6: 'All Races by Median and Mean Income: 1975–2009'

single lawyer, on average, earns more than twice as much in a year as an entire American household, many of which include more than one earner.[25] Lawyers do make a lot of money, at least on average and in relative terms.

However, when we examine not lawyers' earnings but what people pay lawyers, we learn quickly that we do not know a great deal about the costs of personal legal services – the kind that might be purchased by middle income folks when they face a divorce, or need to settle an estate, or have a problem with their employer, or experience identity theft, for example. No major contemporary survey asks Americans how much they paid for lawyers' services to handle a specific justice problem; nor do any of the recent social scientific surveys of lawyers ask attorneys or firms how much they charged for a case or consultation or body of work.[26]

The information that does exist about what lawyers charge and what people pay for common legal services is thin, but it suggests that the costs of legal services vary greatly, from sums that would be affordable out of pocket for many moderate income households to sums that are potentially ruinous. A small body of work examines lawyers who work on contingent fee arrangements in tort cases, such as medical malpractice and auto accidents.[27] Much of this work explores how lawyers secure clients, select cases, and allocate their work effort. When it explores lawyers' fees, the typical finding is that the effective hourly rates charged by contingent fee attorneys are, on average, modest: the

(2010), http://www.census.gov/hhes/www/income/data/historical/household/index.html, accessed 10 December 2010.

25 Carmen DeNavas-Walt and Robert W. Cleveland, 'Money Income in the United States: 2001' (Washington: U.S. Census Bureau, 2002), http://www.census.gov/prod/2002pubs/p60-218.pdf, accessed 27 January 2010.

26 See, for example, Ronit Dinovitzer *et al.*, *After the JD: Second Results from a National Study of Legal Careers* (Chicago and Dallas: American Bar Foundation and NALP Foundation for Law Career Research and Education 2009); John P. Heinz, Robert L. Nelson, Rebecca L. Sandefur, and Edward O. Laumann, *Urban Lawyers: The New Social Structure of the Bar* (Chicago: University of Chicago Press, 2005).

27 See, for example, Stephen Daniels and Joanne Martin, 'It Was the Best of Times, It Was the Worst of Times: The Precarious Nature of Plaintiffs' Practice in Texas' (2002) 80 *Texas Law Review* 1781; Herbert M. Kritzer, *Risks, Reputations, and Rewards: Contingency Fee Legal Practice in the United States* (Stanford: Stanford University Press, 2004) [Kritzer, *Risks, Reputations, and Rewards*]; Mary Nell Trautner, 'Personal Responsibility v. Corporate Liability: How Personal Injury Lawyers Screen Cases in an Era of Tort Reform' in *Access to Justice*, ed. Rebecca L. Sandefur (Bingley: Emerald 2009) at 203.

mean effective hourly rate that lawyers received for contingent fee service circa 1980 was $47 per hour.[28] These studies are informative, but they tend to focus more on lawyers than on consumers. They also provide information about only one group of justice problems. Some common justice problems, such as divorce and child support, may not be served through contingent fee arrangements.[29] Other justice problems involve stakes that are too small to support contingent fee legal services, or appear to attorneys to have too low a likelihood of success to justify the costs of pursuing a case. In general, contingent fees are not practical for contractual work in which no money changes hands, such as writing a will or renegotiating the terms of a lease, or for preventative legal advice.

Information more to the point comes from a smattering of sources that survey lawyers about what they charge for specific services or ask consumers about what they actually paid. Tables 7.1 and 7.2 present information about the costs of lawyers' services in the United States. Table 7.1 presents estimated costs for five different kinds of legal work, based on two distinct data sources. The first is a survey, conducted in 1987 and 1988, that inquired into lawyers' typical charges for specific legal services as part of their applications to participate in a group legal services plan. The quantities reported are the average full retail cost that lawyers reported in the survey, which I am terming a 'rack rate' in recognition of the fact that many clients will pay less.[30] The price estimates are adjusted to current dollar figures through two different means. Rack Rate I uses the overall Consumer Price Index (CPI) to make the adjustment.[31] Rack Rate II uses the legal services component of the CPI, which results in higher current dollar costs, as the price of legal services has increased faster than overall prices since the 1980s.[32]

The second source of cost information, which I am terming the Anec-

---

28 Kritzer, *Risks, Reputations, and Rewards, supra* note 27, Table 6.1.
29 American Bar Association, *Model Rules of Professional Conduct*, Rule 1.5[d].
30 William A. Bolger, Jeffrey K. Anderson, and Thomas P. Chiancone, *The Cost of Personal Legal Services: A National Study* (Washington: National Resource Center for Consumers of Legal Services, 1988) at 8.
31 Calculators abound. I used one provided by the Bureau of Labor Statistics, http://www.bls.gov/data/inflation_calculator.htm, accessed 8 April 2011.
32 For Rack Rate II calculations, I used the Legal Services CPI reported by Economagic. com, http://www.economagic.com/em-cgi/data.exe/blscu/CUUR0000SEGD01, accessed 8 April 2011.

Table 7.1. Potential costs of lawyers' services for selected civil justice problems

	Rack rate (I)	Rack rate (II)	Anecdata Cost
Simple will	$139	$201	$150–600+
Contested divorce			$5,000–25,000+
Uncontested divorce	$848	$1,225	$1,000–10,000
Real estate settlement	$731	$1,056	$500–1,500
Reviewing rental contract or lease			$150–250

Notes: Rack rates come from a 1987–88 survey of attorney applicants to participate in a group legal services plan (Bolger *et al.* 1988: 2). Rack Rate I employs the Consumer Price Index (CPI) to inflate prices from 1988 to 2010. Rack Rate II employs the legal services component of CPI to calculate the inflation. Anecdata Costs come from Cost Helper, a website that collects cost quotes from the public and providers.

data Cost, comes from a website, CostHelper, that receives cost estimates for selected services from consumers and providers who visit the site.[33] This information is 'anecdata' because it is a sample of convenience, reflecting the reports of people who happened to post to the website. Anecdata give us a glimpse of some people's experiences, but give us no information about how representative those experiences are. Nevertheless, CostHelper is a contemporary source and produces estimates that are on par with the inflation-adjusted estimates based on the 1987–88 survey of attorneys.

As Table 7.1 reports, some kinds of basic, transactional legal services appear to be relatively affordable. Based on the attorney survey, real estate settlements cost in at a Rack Rate of around $1,000, depending on one's assumptions about inflation. Anecdata suggest that residential contract review may cost a couple of hundred dollars. A simple will has an average Rack Rate cost of $139 to $201, depending on assumptions about inflation, and an Anecdata Cost range of $150 to $600 or more. To put these amounts in perspective, in 2009 American households spent an average of about $2,600 on eating out in restaurants, and an additional about $2,700 on various forms of entertainment.[34] Given these expenditures, we can surmise that many households probably could have afforded the costs of, for example, a simple will.[35] On the other

33 http://www.costhelper.com, accessed 8 April 2011.
34 Bureau of Labor Statistics, 'Consumer Expenditures – 2009,' http://www.bls.gov/news.release/cesan.nr0.htm, accessed 27 January 2010.
35 Available evidence suggests that most Americans do not have wills. A recent survey

Table 7.2. The costs of ordinary litigation: Total legal fees for litigated civil cases

Total legal fees I	Total legal fees II	All cases	Federal	State
$0–3,340	$0–4,920	46%	34%	59%
$3,343–8,350	$4,925–12,300	24	23	25
$8,353–16,700	$12,305–24,600	14	18	10
$16,703–33,400	$24,605–49,200	8	12	4
$33,400+	$49,200+	8	13	2

Notes: Total legal fees come from the Civil Litigation Research Project (Trubek, Sarat *et al.* 1983). Total legal fees I employs the Consumer Price Index to inflate prices to 2010. Total legal fees II employs the legal services component of the CPI to calculate the inflation. See note 40 for details.

hand, some kinds of personal legal services are more expensive. The notable example is divorce. Especially when substantial litigation is involved, as in the case of contested divorces, legal services can be quite costly, running into the tens of thousands of dollars. To put the costs of contested divorce into perspective, consider that, for what an American might pay in legal fees for a contested divorce, he or she could alternatively buy a new car.[36]

Table 7.2 reports additional information about lawyers' fees in lawsuits, including contested divorces. These findings come from the Civil Litigation Research Project (CLRP), a landmark study of public civil disputing behaviour.[37] Among its data sources, CLRP included a sample of lawsuits and lawyers involved in what project authors termed 'ordinary litigation': civil disputes in state and federal courts that were not part of a small group of about three dozen 'megacases' but that had amounts at stake of at least $1,000.[38] Unlike the first table, this one includes legal

---

funded by Lawyers.com found that most Americans (65 per cent) reported that they do not have a will. Just over half (51 per cent) reported having some kind of estate planning document. See Lawyers.com, 'Survey Reveals Drop in Estate Planning,' http://press-room.lawyers.com/2010-Will-Survey-Press-Release.html, accessed 27 January 2010.

36 For example, according to the Kelly Blue Book, the fair purchase price of one version of the 2010 Dodge Ram 1500 pickup is around $20,000; see http://www.kbb.com, accessed 8 April 2011.

37 David M. Trubek, Austin Sarat, William L.F. Felstiner, Herbert M. Kritzer, and Joel B. Grossman, 'The Costs of Ordinary Litigation' (1983) 31 *UCLA Law Review* 71, Table 4 [Trubek, 'The Costs of Ordinary Litigation'].

38 *Ibid.* at 80–1.

services purchased by businesses as well as individuals; and, also unlike the first table, this one focuses on that rarified subset of justice problems that become cases filed with courts. We might expect that justice problems that become lawsuits are among the most complex, protracted, and costly in terms of the consumption of lawyers' services.

To use the language of the authors of the CLRP report, 'legal fees … are modest' for justice problems that do involve filing a lawsuit.[39] The CLRP sample represents the landscape of ordinary litigation in 1978. As above, two different inflation calculators are used to transform the 1978 figures to current dollars. Total Legal Fees I employs the general rate of inflation; Total Legal Fees II uses the legal services component of inflation.[40] In the United States, most civil litigation occurs in state courts. In a majority of these cases (59 per cent), depending upon assumptions about inflation, total lawyers' fees were less than $3,500 to $5,000 in current dollars, while a small number of cases were quite costly, leading to tens of thousands of dollars in lawyers' fees. It is possible that law has become more complex, such that any given type of case now requires more legal work than it did thirty years ago.[41] It is not clear just how much that greater complexity would lead contemporary ordinary litigation to cost.

Taken together, the available data reveal that some legal services, in particular contested divorces, may cost tens of thousands of dollars. Other legal work, such as writing a simple will or settling the sale of a house, may cost as little as a few hundred dollars. The central fact, though, is that we know little about how much individuals who buy lawyers' services today typically pay for them.

Americans' assessments of lawyers' fees depend strongly on what questions they are asked. When asked to reflect on lawyers in the abstract, Americans often accuse them of an excessive love of money, if

---

39 *Ibid.* at 92.
40 I was able to find the CPI for legal services only for years from 1986 forward. To construct an index that would permit me to construct the 'II' rate for dollars from 1978, I did the following rough calculation. Between December 1986 and December 2010, the cost of legal services increased by 293 per cent, according to the figures published by Economagic.com. According to the U.S. Bureau of Labor Statistics, overall prices increased by 199 per cent over that same period. So the inflation factor for legal services is 1.47 (= 293/199) times the inflation factor for overall prices when comparing 1986 to 2010. To calculate the 'II' rate in 2010 dollars from 1978 figures, I multiplied the overall CPI by 1.47.
41 Hadfield, 'The Price of Law,' *supra* note 22.

not outright greed. Over two-thirds (69 per cent) of respondents to a 2001 telephone poll of Americans agreed with the statement that '[l]awyers are more interested in making money than in serving their clients.'[42] However, when Americans reflect on their own experiences with purchasing legal services from attorneys, the picture changes. The same survey also found that, among those who had used an attorney's services in the five years prior to the study, more than three-fifths (62 per cent) were 'very satisfied' with 'the fees the lawyer actually charged' them.[43]

The little we know about the costs of legal services to ordinary Americans suggests that these costs vary from affordable to expensive. What we know about consumer satisfaction with legal fees suggests that when Americans purchase lawyers' services, they are often content with what they had to pay. Taken together, these two findings suggest that other factors besides money must be at play when people who are facing justice problems consider what to do about them. Indeed, when we turn to people's own accounts of why they do not turn to lawyers for their justice problems, cost plays a role, but it is not the predominant reason that people report for not taking their civil justice problems to lawyers.

IV. The Social Construction of Legality

Among the most important reasons that people do not take their problems to lawyers is that they do not think of those problems as legal. The legal nature of any given civil justice problem is not a self-evident fact; rather, it but is socially constructed.[44] When confronted with a specific situation, the characterization of that situation as a legal problem reflects both how people think about and what people do about their own troubles, as well as the interactions they have with the friends, neighbours, family members, and service providers to whom they may bring their troubles.

When Americans are asked not about their use of law, but simply about

---

42 Leo A. Shapiro and Associates, *Public Perceptions of Lawyers: Consumer Research Findings,* report prepared for Section on Litigation (Chicago: American Bar Association 2002) at 7.

43 *Ibid.* at 20.

44 Patricia Ewick and Susan S. Silbey, *The Common Place of Law: Stories from Everyday Life* (Chicago: University of Chicago Press, 1998) [Ewick and Silbey, *The Common Place of Law*]; William Felstiner, Richard Abel, and Austin Sarat, 'The Emergence and Transformation of Disputes: Naming, Blaming, Claiming ...,' (1980–1) 15 *Law and Society Review* 631; Susan S. Silbey, 'After Legal Consciousness' (2005) *Annual Review of Law and Social Science* 323 [Silbey, 'After Legal Consciousness'].

Figure 7.1. Show Card for Focus Groups Discussing 'Challenges Facing American Families Today'

Food: not having enough to eat

Government or Non-profit Programs: benefits or access denied

Health/Disability: Medicaid, no health insurance, prescriptions

Employment: unemployment, discrimination, harassment

Family: divorce, custody, child support

Housing: evictions, repairs, foreclosures, homelessness, utilities cut off

Money: debt, credit problems, bankruptcy, collections, identity theft

their experiences with justice problems, it becomes quickly evident that they often do not think of their justice problems in legal terms. In some of my own recent work, I invited randomly selected low and moderate income Americans living in two middle-sized cities in the U.S. Midwest to attend focus group meetings where they could discuss their experiences with 'challenges facing American families today.' The group meetings lasted one-and-a-half to two hours and took place on weekday evenings in locations that were easily accessible by either car or public transportation, such as community centres and libraries. The groups were income stratified, so that people discussed these challenges in a context where other participants had faced similar general economic circumstances and were eligible for similar kinds of charitable and public services.

People face many different kinds of problems and challenges; my interest was in those that might have civil legal aspects. Therefore, to help focus the participants' thinking on common justice problems, they were handed a card that listed some common kinds of challenges, all of which can involve civil justice problems. Figure 7.1 reproduces this card, which was developed after pre-testing interviews that sought to uncover the language that ordinary people might use to talk about these sorts of troubles. In the meetings, the first exercise was to go around the room and invite each participant to tell a story about his or her own experiences with a problem like the kinds listed on the card. If participants had no personal experience with any such problems, they were invited to tell a story about the experiences of a friend or relative. Almost everyone talked about his or her own experiences. And almost all of the problems they described were civil justice problems in the sense that they had justiciable, or legally actionable, aspects.

One quality common to many participants' accounts of their experiences with civil justice problems was alegality: people described their experiences with problems that had clear legal aspects, raised obvious legal issues, and often had routes to remedy provided by formal law, but they did so in terms that made no reference to law, lawyers, or courts. For example, one woman in a moderate income focus group told the following story when asked to recount her experiences with a problem:

> When I was pregnant with my oldest one, her natural father passed away. And when I went to social security and other agencies, social security told me I could not receive [death] benefits because it was not common knowledge that he was the father of my child, because he did not tell anybody … I was denied benefits. I don't know what they call it, you know, like where you get money from the government to help live on and stuff like that … I was denied public aid because I did have a full-time job and my numbers with my gross was less than $100 above … So my daughter is growing up without knowing that I had help – I had no help from his family, either, because the day he passed away he – his sister asked me to contact her, and whenever I tried she was never available. So I just pretty much let it go and I had people telling me, 'Well, why don't you go get a blood test?' Well, I can't, because he was cremated. 'Well, why don't you go to his parents?' I can't, because he was adopted. So I was a single mother with no help with a $8 an hour full-time job. And that's what I went through.

There are clear legal aspects in the situation this person described. For example, she wanted to make a claim for the death benefits to which her child would be entitled under the federal Social Security program, a publicly subsidized life insurance program that pays survivors' benefits to the minor children of decedents who had been employed in eligible occupations and who had made tax contributions into the system before death.[45] In order to secure these benefits, petitioners must go through a

---

45 Social Security Administration, 'Survivors' Benefits,' SSA Publication No. 05-10084, August 2009, ICN 468540, http://www.socialsecurity.gov/pubs/10084.html, accessed 29 January 2011.

Figure 7.2. How People Describe Their Own Justice Problems: Word Cloud Analysis of Difficulty Receiving Social Security Death Benefits and Other Public Aid, USA, 2007

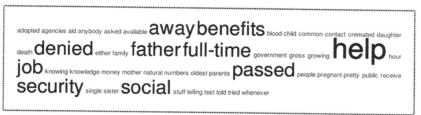

formal process that requires properly filling out specific forms and submitting documents in support of the application. In this case, a successful application would have required providing evidence establishing the paternity of the child. It appears that this person's initial application was denied, which means that, in order to pursue her claim, she would have had to file a formal appeal asking for a reconsideration of her file, leading perhaps eventually to an administrative hearing.

But despite law being 'all over' her situation, she never mentions law, lawyers, or attorneys in her account.[46] On the other hand, among the most common words in her account is 'help.' One way to see this is to examine the word cloud analysis of Figure 7.2. A word cloud represents with relative font size the frequency with which specific words appear in a text.[47] This focus on help, but not specifically legal help, was a common quality of people's stories about their experiences with their civil justice problems. People wanted help with their problems, but it was often not legal help that they described wishing for or turning to.

The pattern of alegality that I found in my study of public experience with civil justice problems is consistent with findings from studies of rights consciousness. This work seeks evidence of how people understand their legal rights when confronted with different kinds of situations that are formally governed by those rights. What I am terming alegality,

---

46 Austin Sarat, '"The Law Is All Over…": Power, Resistance, and the Legal Consciousness of the Welfare Poor' (1990) 2 *Yale Journal of Law and the Humanities* 343.

47 This word cloud was produced with Tag Crowd. The analysis excludes certain common words, such as pronouns like 'I,' as well as verb contractions. If the latter were included, 'can't' would also be revealed as a very frequent word in this account of experience with civil justice problems.

the absence of thinking in terms of law or rights, turns out to appear in people's experiences with a wide variety of justice problems, including those involving family relationships, personal injury, invasions of privacy, street harassment, and employment and working conditions.[48]

How people conceptualize their own justice problems appears to play a large role in how they respond to them. A recent study in Britain found that a significant factor predicting whether people would take a hypothetical civil justice problem to a legal adviser was whether or not they understood the justice problem as a 'legal' problem – rather than, for example, a social problem, a moral problem, a private problem, or bad luck. Controlling for other factors, such as how severe people thought a problem was, when they thought of a problem as a 'legal' problem, they were six to seven times more likely to think of seeking legal advice for that problem than when they did not think of the problem as legal.[49]

A pattern of pervasive alegality is consistent with the behaviours people report in response to their justice problems in U.S. surveys that inquire about problem experience and lawyer use. Among moderate income households in the 1992 ABA survey, law 'was not considered at all' for the majority – 60 per cent – of civil justice problems experienced.[50] Figure 7.3 reports on the various ways in which moderate

---

48 For illustrations, see, for example, Robert C. Ellickson, *Order Without Law: How Neighbors Settle Disputes* (Cambridge, MA: Harvard University Press, 1991) [Ellickson, *Order Without Law*]; David M. Engel, 'The Oven Bird's Song: Insiders, Outsiders, and Personal Injuries in an American Community' (1988) 18 *Law and Society Review* 551 [Engel, 'The Oven Bird's Song']; John Gilliom, *Overseers of the Poor: Surveillance, Resistance, and the Limits of Privacy* (Chicago: University of Chicago Press, 2001); Carol J. Greenhouse, *Praying for Justice: Faith, Order, and Community in an American Town* (Ithaca: Cornell University Press, 1986) [Greenhouse, *Praying for Justice*]; Anna-Maria Marshall, 'Idle Rights: Employees' Rights Consciousness and the Construction of Sexual Harassment Policies' (2005) 39 *Law and Society Review* 89; and Laura Beth Nielsen, *License to Harass: Law, Hierarchy, and Offensive Public Speech* (Princeton: Princeton University Press, 2004). See Silbey, 'After Legal Consciousness,' *supra* note 42, for a thoughtful riposte.

49 Pascoe Pleasence, Nigel Balmer, and Stian Reimers, 'What Really Drives Advice Seeking Behaviour? Looking Beyond the Subject of Legal Disputes' (under review, 2010), 12 [Pleasence, 'What Really Drives Advice-Seeking Behaviour?'].

50 Calculated from Consortium, *Report, supra* note 10 at 25. For the purposes of the study, the ABA defined a moderate-income household as one in which household earnings were too high to meet the means test for Legal Services Corporation–funded civil legal assistance (above 125 per cent of poverty) and less than the 80th percentile of the household income distribution, or $60,000 in 1992.

income Americans reported handling their justice problems. As the figure depicts, moderate income households took 28 per cent of their justice problems to attorneys. Most of the time (89 per cent = .25/.28), an attorney took the case and provided some kind of advice or representation; but in a minority of cases (11 per cent = .03/.28), attorneys declined.

For the almost three-quarters of justice problems that were not taken to attorneys, the survey asked respondents why they did not seek legal help. People gave a variety of responses, which are revealing about how Americans may think about their justice problems. The most common responses reflected resignation to the problem (27 per cent of total problems): people did not think law would help, or they believed that the problem was 'not really a problem,' or they 'never got around to it.' Another common reason people reported for not turning to law was that they had handled the problem in some other way, taking action either on their own or with the help of some non-lawyer third party; 13 per cent of all civil justice problems were handled in this way. Other reasons for not turning to law with justice problems included fear, or not 'want[ing] to make trouble'; 4 per cent of justice problems received this characterization. For only 6 per cent of all civil justice problems did moderate income households report not turning to law because they were concerned about the costs of doing so.

If we take people's behaviour as indicative of what is shaping their thinking, we can infer an important factor that shapes the social construction of legality: the institutions of remedy that are available to people facing civil justice problems. Institutions of remedy provide ways of understanding civil justice problems, tools for handling them, and established, regularized routes to their resolution.[51] Law is one such institution of remedy, but people regularly handle their problems in other ways – for instance, by turning to other kinds of third parties for assistance, as Figure 7.3 shows. For some civil justice problems in the U.S. context, however, there are few alternative routes to resolution besides law. Divorce is a prime example of this. While one can quit a job without going to court, it is not possible to formally dissolve a marriage or authoritatively assign custody of dependent children without

---

51 See Sandefur, 'The Fulcrum Point of Equal Access to Justice,' *supra* note 5. See also Ewick and Silbey, *The Common Place of Law*, *supra* note 42; and Leon Mayhew, 'Institutions of Representation: Civil Justice and the Public' (1974–5) 9 *Law and Society Review* 401.

Figure 7.3. How Moderate Income Households Handle Their Civil Justice
Problems, USA, 1992

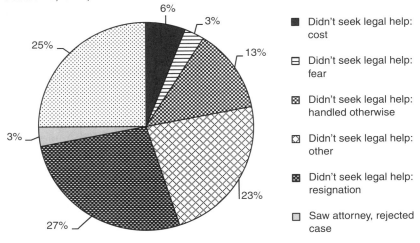

Didn't seek legal help:
cost

Didn't seek legal help:
fear

Didn't seek legal help:
handled otherwise

Didn't seek legal help:
other

Didn't seek legal help:
resignation

Saw attorney, rejected
case

Source: Author's calculations from Consortium on Legal Services and the
Public (1994).

a legal process. It is not surprising, therefore, that the category of civil
justice problem most likely to involve lawyers is 'family and domestic' matters. In the 1992 ABA survey of moderate income households,
63 per cent of justice problems involving family and domestic matters
involved consultation with a lawyer, by comparison with 28 per cent of
civil justice problems overall.[52]

Since law is the principal institutionalized route to divorce, we might
suspect that people tend to think of divorce as a legal problem more
often than other kinds of problems for which there may be clearer alternatives to law. This is, in fact, exactly what Pleasence and colleagues
have found in their study of problem characterization in England and
Wales. When presented with hypothetical justice problems and asked
to characterize them as 'moral,' 'social,' 'criminal,' 'legal,' 'bad luck,'
'private,' or 'none of these,' respondents to the survey characterized
about 75 per cent of problems related to divorce as legal. By compari-

---

52 Consortium, *Report, supra* note 10, Table 5-8.

son, only about half of benefits and pensions problems were characterized as legal, and only about one-third of problems with children's education.[53]

A second factor that seems to shape the social construction of legality is one's associates. Communities develop norms regarding which kinds of civil justice problems are appropriate objects of legal action, and which are not.[54] People's personal networks also play a role in shaping how they decide to handle their justice problems. In particular, knowing someone who has used law for a similar problem has been shown to be correlated with turning to law oneself. For example, in a classic study of bankruptcy, Herbert Jacob found that 'debtors who knew others who had gone through bankruptcy were much more likely to avail themselves of personal bankruptcy than similarly burdened debtors without such social links.'[55] These personal networks play a role not only in how people may conceptualize and respond to their civil justice problems, but also in how they choose which specific sources of assistance or advice to visit.

V. How Americans Find Lawyers

Purchasing a lawyer's services is an uncertain business. Law is both what economists term a credence good and what they term an experience good. The signal quality of a credence good is that consumers cannot evaluate providers' performance: producers of credence goods identify and treat problems that their clients do not know how to solve and may not even recognize that they confront.[56] An experience good is one for which consumers cannot 'evaluate [its] quality ... prior to purchase, but [for which] they may be able to assess quality ... after purchase.'[57] While a consumer of legal services may not be able to assess whether a lawyer's work was legally correct after the fact, she can certainly assess some of the customer service aspects of lawyers'

---

53 Pleasence, 'What Really Drives Advice Seeking Behaviour?', *supra* note 49, Figure 3.

54 See, for example, M.P. Baumgartner, *The Moral Order of a Suburb* (New York: Oxford University Press, 1988); Ellickson, *Order Without Law, supra* note 48; Engel, 'The Oven Bird's Song,' *supra* note 48; and Greenhouse, *Praying for Justice, supra* note 48.

55 Herbert Jacob, 'The Elusive Shadow of the Law' (1992) 26 *Law and Society Review* 571.

56 Michael R. Darbi and Edi Karni, 'Free Competition and the Optimal Amount of Fraud' (1973) 16 *Journal of Law and Economics* 67.

57 David Dranove and Ginger Zhe Jin, 'Quality Disclosure and Certification: Theory and Practice' (2010) 48 *Journal of Economic Literature* 937.

work – whether the lawyer returned her calls, explained things clearly, seemed sympathetic, and so forth. Research in the field of economic sociology has found that uncertainty leads people looking for service providers to use strategies that I term social searching: they turn to people they already know either to provide the services or to give advice about whom to choose as a provider.[58]

The most recent available information about how Americans find attorneys comes from a supplement to the 1996 General Social Survey (GSS), a biennial omnibus survey of the U.S. population that collects a variety of information from a representative sample of about 1,500 people. The 1996 GSS included a special questionnaire, distributed to a subset of those interviewed, that inquired into how people found different kinds of service providers, including real estate agents, home repair services, and lawyers. Respondents to this questionnaire were first asked if they had 'hired a lawyer for any legal work in the past ten years.' If they said yes, they were asked questions about 'the most recent time [they] hired a lawyer,' 'what made [them] choose this law firm or attorney,' and the nature of their 'relationship ... to the attorney who provided the services or to another attorney in the firm.'

The 1996 GSS reveals that Americans often turn to people they already know to provide their legal services. Figure 7.4 reports, for people in each quintile of the household income distribution, the percentage reporting four different kinds of relationships they might have had with the attorney or firm who provided their most recent legal services: an attorney was a friend or relative; an attorney was a friend of a friend; an attorney was a previous business contact; or there was no relationship between the consumer and any of the attorneys at the firm where the consumer most recently hired a lawyer. Across the income distribution, most people do not have a personal relationship with the attorney or firm they most recently hired: for each income group, 52 to 71 per cent of respondents report no pre-existing relationship with the attorney they hired for their most recent use of legal services. But a substantial plurality of each income group does report some kind of personal relationship, and closer personal relationships are more common than more distant ones. For each income group, buying legal services from relatives, friends, or people with whom one has had a previous busi-

---

58 Paul DiMaggio and Hugh Louch, 'Socially Embedded Consumer Transactions: For What Kinds of Purchases Do People Most Often Use Networks?' (1998) 63 *American Sociological Review* 619.

Figure 7.4. Americans' Relationship to the Attorney They Most Recently Hired, by Quintile of Household Income, 1996

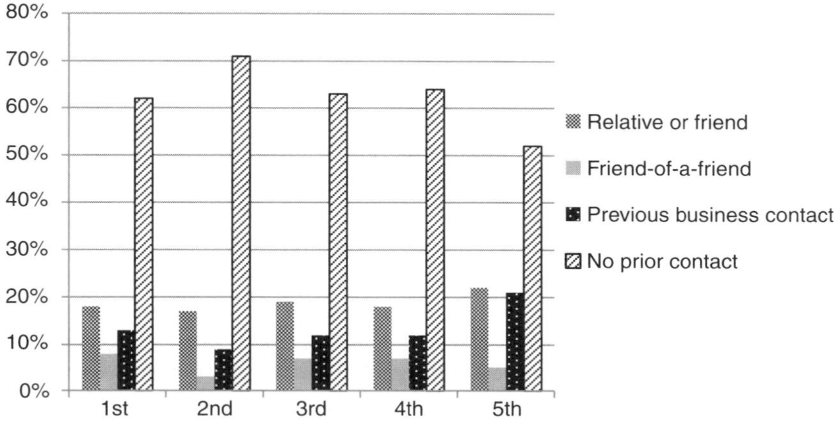

Source: Author's calculations from the General Social Survey.

ness contact is more common than buying legal services from second-order acquaintances such as friends of friends. People in the highest quartile of household income are most likely to have bought legal services from close personal associates or previous providers.

The survey also reveals that people seeking attorneys often turn to their intimate personal networks for information about which attorney to choose. This pattern appears to be particularly true for middle income people, as Figure 7.5 reveals. The figure reports the 'most important reason' that the respondent chose the specific attorney or firm she most recently hired, again by quintile of the household income distribution. Consistent with the discussion of the role of cost above, few respondents in any income group reported that searching for the best price was the most important factor in their selection of an attorney. Even fewer respondents relied on advertising to select a specific attorney. Rather, respondents in the highest income group relied on their own previous knowledge of specific firms and attorneys. For 44 per cent of high income respondents, this was the most important reason for choosing the attorney, in comparison with about one-quarter of respondents in the 3rd and 4th quartiles of household income and 15 to 18 per cent of respondents in the bottom two quartiles of the household income distribution. Low and moderate income people relied on others in their intimate personal networks to guide them to attorneys: these network contacts were the most important reason they selected the attorney or firm for 46 to 49 per cent of respondents across the bottom four income categories. Finally, notable groups in each income category relied on the attorney's or firm's 'general reputation in the community' as the most important means of selecting a specific provider. This search strategy was more common among lower income respondents – it was used by 27 and 24 per cent of 1st and 2nd quintile respondents respectively. Third, 4th, and 5th quintile respondents were less likely to highlight general reputation as most important, with 17, 21, and 15 per cent doing so, respectively.

In addition to the fixed categories offered in the questionnaire, respondents were allowed to suggest other important reasons for choosing their attorney. It is instructive that lawyer referral services (LRSs) were not mentioned frequently enough to justify creating an additional category of response. LRSs are listing services, often maintained by bar associations, which members of the public may call for referral to a local attorney who may be able to assist them with a specific justice problem. The referral typically includes a fixed period of consultation, such as half an hour, in return for a modest fixed fee.[59] Though LRSs have existed in many communities for a number of years, existing survey data indicate little use of these services. Consistent with the findings of the 1996 GSS, the 1992 ABA survey found that 4 per cent of lawyer contacts reported by moderate income households were found through a lawyer referral service.[60] These findings suggest that, when Americans look for specific attorneys, they engage in a social search, typically relying on their existing networks of relationships to find those attorneys, either by hiring attorneys whom they already know, or by asking people they know for recommendations and advice.

While there are reasons to believe that Americans' strategies for selecting attorneys have changed since 1996, there are also reasons to believe that patterns of social search persist. An important possible new mechanism for search is of course the Internet. Access to the Internet has expanded dramatically since the 1990s, and Web-based services have been developed that seek to assist people in finding and selecting

---

59 Katherine Huenke and Nathan Mintz, 'Lawyer Referral Services and the Model Rules: Balancing Legal Accessibility with Professional Independence' (2001) 15 *Georgetown Journal of Legal Ethics* 828.

60 Consortium, Report, *supra* note 10, Table 5–11.

Figure 7.5. How Americans Selected the Attorney They Most Recently Hired, by Quintile of Household Income, 1996

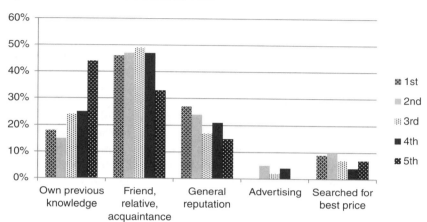

Source: Author's calculations from the General Social Survey.

many kinds of service providers, including lawyers. Websites like Find-Law, for example, allow people to search for attorneys who provide services in their geographic area and who purport to work on specific kinds of legal problems. However, it is not clear that these kinds of listing services would radically simplify the process of choosing an attorney. Selecting a specific lawyer is not made any less uncertain simply because one now has access to lots of information about many attorneys, instead of – as was the case twenty years ago – access to less information about the few who happened to buy listings in the advertising section of the telephone directory. Locating a pool of potential attorneys is likely simpler now than before the advent of the Internet, but selecting a specific one to work with still holds many uncertainties that a personal recommendation from a friend or relative may help resolve. Indeed, a recent survey commissioned by the ABA found that patterns of social searching persist today: 46 per cent of Americans surveyed reported that 'ask[ing] a friend, family member, or colleague' would be their primary way of finding a lawyer for a personal legal matter. Another 34 per cent reported that they would find such an attorney by 'contact[ing] a lawyer [they] know or have used in the past.' Only 7 per cent reported that they would search the Internet for an attorney to help them if they had a legal problem.[61]

VI. Conclusion

Like the middle income residents of Canada, many middle income Americans experience civil justice problems, and most do not take these problems to lawyers or pursue them in courts.[62] A prominent explanation for this pattern is that lawyers' services are simply too costly for middle income families to afford. A review of available evidence suggests that this conclusion is premature. We actually know surprisingly little about middle income Americans' use of lawyers' services in the contemporary period – including under what circumstances middle income Americans use attorneys, why they choose legal rather than other routes to resolving their problems, how they find attorneys, and how much they pay for them. What evidence we do have suggests that the cost of lawyers' services may play some role in explaining why justice problems are seldom taken to attorneys, but that other important factors are also at play. If increasing middle income people's use of lawyers' services is a policy goal, the present analysis suggests that potential market innovations or public policies that focus solely on lowering prices or subsidizing purchase may not be as effective as desired.

One important reason that middle income people handle their civil justice problems without law is that they apparently do not think of those justice problems as legal, nor do they think of courts or of attorneys as appropriate providers of remedy. This pattern holds not only in the United States, but also in other studied similar societies, such as the United Kingdom, and we can reasonably suspect that it characterizes Canada as well. In contexts where this pattern holds, simply making legal services cheaper is unlikely to change this, because how people understand their justice problems is a function of more than those services' cost. In part, how people think about their justice problems reflects how different kinds of problems have become institutionalized

---

61 Standing Committee on the Delivery of Legal Services, American Bar Association, *Perspectives on Finding Personal Legal Services: The Results of a Public Opinion Poll* (Chicago: American Bar Association 2011), 8.

62 Currie, 'The Legal Problems of Everyday Life,' *supra* note 2; Herbert M. Kritzer, Neil Vidmar, and W.A. Bogart, 'The Aftermath of Injury: Cultural Factors in Compensation Seeking in Canada and the United States' (1991) 25 Law & Soc. Rev. 499.

as remediable through different means, or as not remediable at all.[63] One way to try to change how people think about their justice problems would be through campaigns of public legal education, in an effort to encourage people to think of certain kinds of problems as legal problems and to go to attorneys for advice about them. An alternative or complementary strategy might be to ask people about the kinds of help they would like with their own justice problems and then develop services that meet people's own perceived needs – even if those services turn out not to be traditional legal services.[64] In the U.S. context, it is likely that providing some of the kinds of services that the public might envision as helpful would require changes in the regulation of lawyers' monopoly.[65]

Policies that would address only the costs of legal services also do nothing to assist middle income people with another problem they face when they want to use lawyers – the problem of selecting a specific provider. Even in a context like the United States, where lawyer advertising has long been permitted and where bar-sponsored lawyer referral services have existed in many communities, members of the public seeking attorneys appear to eschew these impersonal sources in favour of information that comes with a personal warrant, whether from their own experience or from the recommendation of someone they know. Expanding access to matching institutions that provide some kind of warrant of quality for providers, such as group legal services plans with performance assessments of serving attorneys, might be one mechanism for assisting people in selecting attorneys.

---

63 See Sandefur, 'The Importance of Doing Nothing,' *supra* note 4; and 'The Fulcrum Point', *supra* note 5.
64 Jeanne Charn, 'Legal Services for All: Is the Profession Ready?' (2009) 42 *Loyola of Los Angeles Law Review* 1021; Sandefur, 'The Fulcrum Point,' *supra* note 5.
65 Hadfield, 'Higher Demand, Lower Supply?', *supra* note 2.

8 Legal Services Plans: Crucial-Time Access to Lawyers and the Case for a Public–Private Partnership

PAUL A. VAYDA AND STEPHEN B. GINSBERG

I. Introduction

A fair legal system aspires to provide justice to all. This requires that all people have access to appropriate legal services as soon as they are needed. The crucial time is often well before the legal crisis occurs; it is when the seeds of the future dispute are sown. If crucial-time legal services are not obtained, poor decisions are made and an easily resolved problem will grow into one that only litigation can solve. When legal services are provided at an earlier, crucial time, overall cost is substantially reduced. The general public may not believe that private legal disputes should be subsidized by public funds,[1] but unmet crucial-time legal needs may be just as financially catastrophic to lower and middle income people, and just as much a burden to taxpayers, as unmet crucial-time medical needs.

Consider a concrete example. Rex has proudly avoided lawyers whenever possible. He is a fifty-eight-year-old widower with three grown children who are always feuding and a girlfriend who has been living with him and taking care of him, on and off, for the past three years. Rex arrives at hospital with a progressively debilitating disease. His condition is worsening quickly. He thinks he may have 'written out' a will years ago, before his wife passed away, but he cannot recall where he put it. He has never signed a power of attorney. He has no cohabitation agreement. He does not want any unusual medical intervention and only trusts his eldest child, who lives in Germany, to do

---

1 Kent Roach and Lorne Sossin, 'Access to Justice and Beyond' (2010) 60 UTLJ 373 at 390 [Roach and Sossin, 'Access to Justice'].

the right thing. His financial and personal affairs are in disarray. Rex needs immediate legal advice and services. This is his 'crucial time.' In our present system, if his legal needs are not met, significant private and public funds will be used to address the mess that Rex leaves behind.

II. Access to Lawyers: Overview

A. Need for Legal Services Is Greater Than Perceived Demand

Rex did not perceive that he needed a lawyer, on many occasions, and he is not alone. Market research conducted by the Pollara Group for a private Canadian company (Law Protector International Inc.) found that one-third of Canadian families experience a legal need each year and that many do not seek the assistance of a lawyer.[2] A 2006 study of the Canadian Department of Justice presented at the Legal Aid Ontario / Osgoode Hall Law School Symposium, 'Rethinking Civil Legal Needs,' suggests a similar situation.[3] Data from the United Kingdom also suggest a disconnect between the public's legal needs and its demand for legal services. For example, over one-third of those surveyed in 2004 had experienced a legal problem in the past year, yet only 13 per cent of them received any advice from a lawyer.[4] In the United States the findings are similar. A 1994 study by the Institute for Survey Research at Temple University found that about one-half of low and moderate income American households faced one or more situations that could be addressed by the system of civil justice, but only one-third of these situations found their way into the justice system.[5] Respondents' most common course of action was to handle the situation on their own, yet

---

2 Stephen Ginsberg, 'Legal Services Plans in the Year 2020' in Canadian Bar Association, *Access to Affordable and Appropriate Law Related Services in 2020* (1999) at 55 [Ginsberg, 'Legal Services Plans'].
3 Ab Currie, 'Justiciable Problems and Access to Justice in Canada,' paper presented at the Osgoode Hall Law School Legal Aid Roundtable and Legal Aid Ontario Strategic Research, 5 November 2007.
4 Pascoe Pleasance *et al.*, 'Causes of Action: Civil Law and Social Justice' (Norwich: TSO, 2006) at 81.
5 Ginsberg, 'Legal Services Plans,' *supra* note 2 at 55. For discussion of why people who encounter legal problems commonly do not seek legal assistance, see Rebecca Sandefur, 'Money Isn't Everything: Understanding Moderate Income Households' Use of Lawyers' Services,' *supra* this volume.

they were more likely to be satisfied with the ultimate resolution of the matter if it was brought into the justice system than if it was not.

The recently completed Ontario Civil Needs Project, 'Listening to Ontarians,' revealed that one-quarter of the low and middle income Ontarians surveyed had experienced a civil legal problem or issue in the past three years for which they had sought legal assistance, but 14 per cent of the respondents said that they had a legal problem or issue in the past three years for which they had not sought legal assistance, even though it would have been helpful.[6] The same survey reported that one-third of all the respondents said they would prefer to resolve their legal needs with legal advice, but not necessarily with the assistance of a legal professional.[7] It is arguable these findings reveal that access to justice for low to middle income people requires only accurate legal information, and that this creates empowerment for proper action. It is more likely that these statistics reveal the public fear of ballooning legal fees.[8]

B. Public Legal Aid Falls Short

Notwithstanding this need, there appears to be little political will in Canada to expand the existing legal aid system to a point where it resembles the commitment to a public health insurance system.[9] The Canadian Bar Association has argued unsuccessfully in the British Columbia Supreme Court that it is unconstitutional to deny civil litigants legal aid.[10] Only low income people presenting at legal aid offices requesting the 'right' kind of legal services have been able to get legal aid certificates. Individuals are refused legal aid when they have

---

6 Ontario Civil Needs Project Steering Committee, *Listening to Ontarians: Report of the Ontario Civil Needs Project* (Toronto, May 2010), http://www.lsuc.on.ca/media/may3110_oclnreport_final.pdf at 21 [Ontario Civil Needs Project]. For discussion and analysis of the Ontario Civil Needs Project, see Jamie Baxter, Michael Trebilcock, and Albert Yoon, 'The Ontario Civil Needs Project: A Comparative Analysis of the 2009 Survey Data,' *supra* this volume.

7 *Ibid.* at 4.

8 But see Rebecca Sandefur, 'Money Isn't Everything: Understanding Moderate Income Households' Use of Lawyers' Services,' *supra* this volume, arguing that costs are not the only consideration.

9 For a detailed proposal along these lines, see Sujit Choudhry, Michael Trebilcock, and James Wilson, 'Growing Ontario Legal Aid into the Middle Class: A Proposal for Public Legal Expenses Insurance,' *infra* this volume.

10 *The Canadian Bar Association v. HMTQ et. al.* (2006), 59 B.C.L.R. (4th) 38 (SC).

incomes that exceed the maximum threshold or when they request services that are not covered; their only options are a legal aid clinic and the duty counsel system, and they often represent themselves after receiving cursory advice.[11]

In Ontario, universality has never been the goal of legal aid. Operating within a low income threshold and means-driven system, the direction for legal aid in Ontario has been to provide limited, covered legal services (mostly criminal), initial advice delivered by revolving duty counsel, and legal education through government information services. Certainly the new legal information sources identified by the Ontario Civil Needs Project, such as Law Help Ontario and CLEO.net,[12] are useful in much the same way that medical sites help lay people understand a particular disease. But raw information is an inadequate substitute for advice and ongoing guidance from a legally trained person.

It is interesting to note that the European legal aid model, although based on means testing, has remained much more comprehensive and entrenched than the present North American model, especially in Sweden and the Netherlands.[13] As a further indication that fully socialized legal aid can act as an effective delivery model at a cost that can be borne by society as a whole, one needs only to view the Finnish system, which is both accessible and wide ranging and has been enhanced rather than constrained in recent years.[14] In their study of the Finnish legal aid system, Regan and Johnsen used a 'best practices model' to analyse the efficacy of a legal aid system, concluding that the Finnish system came closest to that goal with its highly comprehensive and highly universal plan, in which three-quarters of the Finnish population fitted under the means cap.[15] Along with the means test, the Finns apply a merit test. Regarding merit, '[t]he main criterion is that the applicant is in need of a lawyer to handle the issue competently. Coverage relates to seriousness, not the legal nature of the problem.'[16] The Finnish system provides publicly funded, salaried lawyers who deliver a wide array

---

11 Ontario Legal Aid, 'Getting Legal Help,' http://www.legalaid.on.ca/en/getting.
12 Ontario Civil Needs Project, *supra* note 6 at 5.
13 David Luban, *Lawyers and Justice: An Ethical Study* (Princeton: Princeton University Press, 1988) at 242.
14 Francis Regan and Jon Johnsen, 'Are Finland's Recent Legal Services Policy Reforms Swimming Against the Tide of International Reforms?' (2007) 26 *Civil Justice Quarterly* 341.
15 *Ibid.*
16 *Ibid.* at 350.

of legal services, including legal advice, litigation, and 'non-litigation aid.' The private bar also provides litigation representation, paid for by public funds.

C. Supplementing Public Legal Aid: Organizing More Access to Lawyers

The term 'access to justice' has been analysed from many perspectives. Some writers have concentrated on the 'justice' side of the phrase, arguing that the end product of the system must seek to achieve justice irrespective of the ability of all citizens to access that justice. MacDonald asks: 'How do we give as much emphasis to the "justice" component of the phrase "access to justice" as we do to the "access" component so that citizens will actually want to pursue justice in courts?'[17] Writers such as Bhabha,[18] understanding the need to emphasize the access and procedural side of the phrase, argue that a just result without universality of access is not true justice for all. Surely access to the system is a prerequisite to achieving a truly just system. Universal accessibility cannot be overlooked. *Ubi jus, ibi remedium* – there is no right without a remedy.

Bachman argues that for low and moderate income people,

> access to justice is less a function of access to the courts than it is access to organization because justice tends to go to those who are organized … [L]ow and moderate income people need lawyers less than they need organization … [L]ow and moderate income people should focus more on self-organizing efforts, and less on what they can get from courts.[19]

Bachman emphasizes the advantage of focusing less on connecting individuals in need to lawyers and more on connecting them to helpful organizations that address the structural reasons for poverty-related legal issues. But these two connections are not mutually exclusive. If individuals could obtain legal advice or services when they needed them, their need for collective organization might lessen. There are

---

17 Roderick A. MacDonald, 'Access to Justice and Law Reform' (1990) *Windsor Yearbook of Access to Justice* 317 at 320.

18 Faisal Bhabha, 'Institutionalizing Access-to-Justice: Judicial, Legislative, and Grassroots Dimensions' (2007) 33 Queen's L.J. 139.

19 S. Bachman, 'Access to Justice as Access to Organizing' (2002) 4 Jnl. Law and Social Challenges 1.

many helpful, law-related 'organizations' that address access to justice needs. Public legal aid plans are the most common example of helpful, lawyer-centred organizations, but as discussed above, this is not enough. Fortunately, there are other options.

(1) *Pro bono*. Initiatives recognizing lawyers' ethical duty to the community in providing mandatory *pro bono*, as a social contract, eloquently espoused by Professors Richard Devlin[20] and Lorne Sossin,[21] create a framework for lawyer participation in alleviating financial access disparities. But the good will of the legal profession is limited, and it should not be expected to provide more than one piece to the solution of the access puzzle.

(2) *Class actions and contingency fees*. Class action lawsuits are an extremely useful access to justice innovation, allowing an individual to obtain an otherwise financially unobtainable remedy through group organization. In class actions, the law firm is the organizing force or helpful organization. Similarly, contingency fees allow lawyers to take on cases that otherwise would be abandoned, and have encouraged lower and middle class access to justice for clearly meritorious cases.[22] But like *pro bono* initiatives, contingency fees and class actions cannot help all people who are in need of crucial-time legal services. They cannot help Rex.

(3) *Private legal services plans*. Private legal services plans can help Rex, and many others. They are arguably the most commonly used vehicle for access to lawyers in Canada. Stephen Ginsberg, in an unpublished study conducted for the American Prepaid Legal Services Institute in 2006, found that well over 5 million Canadians are members of a private legal services plan. Most members of such plans are in access plans that are an add-on benefit to an Employee Assistance Plan (EAP). Unfortunately, most EAP members probably do not know they have this crucial-time legal services coverage, as it is not well publicized.

---

20 'Breach of Contract?: The New Economy, Access to Justice, and the Ethical Responsibilities of the Legal Profession' (2002) 25 Dalhousie L.J. 335.
21 'The Public Interest, Professionalism, and Pro Bono Publico' (2008) 46 Osgoode Hall L.J. 131.
22 Herbert M. Kritzer, 'Fee Regimes and the Cost of Civil Justice' (2009) 28 *Civil Justice Quarterly* 344.

The organization behind these legal services plans is sometimes a labour union negotiating the benefit in a collective agreement, but more often it is a lawyer-entrepreneur who has created a commercial access plan (described in more detail below) and sold it to an Employee Assistance Plan (EAP) as an add-on benefit to the more commonly known EAP benefits such as psychological counselling.

Public and private legal services plans and the other access solutions mentioned above are indeed 'helpful organizations' that connect individuals to lawyers. If individuals obtain legal advice or services when they need them, delivered at the crucial time, their need for helpful community organizations may decrease.

D. Supplementing Access to Lawyers

(1) *Self-help.* The proposals offered by the Ontario Civil Needs Project, 'Listening to Ontarians,' stressed innovation and a move away from one-size-fits-all solutions, and reminded Ontarians of a number of initiatives that are presently ongoing, such as walk-in centres sponsored by Law Help Ontario, the lawyer referral service sponsored by the Law Society of Upper Canada (LSUC), and an Internet-based information service sponsored by Canadian Legal Education Ontario (CLEO.net). It suggested a combination of non-lawyer-based legal education, unbundling of legal services, and the traditional lawyer–client model when required.[23]

(2) *Delegation to other professionals.* There are simply not enough lawyers to meet the ongoing spectrum of middle income needs. This is, arguably, one of the reasons why the Province of Ontario licensed paralegals. The delivery of legal services by professionals who are not legally trained was observed in the aforementioned study as an important source of legal information and assistance.[24]

In a 1988 California study, Lash, Gee, and Zelon described the present incapability of the justice system to meet the basic human needs of every resident of that state. For instance, the justice system was consistently failing to provide the legal assistance necessary for 75 per cent of poor Californians to acquire health care, food, and shelter. *Pro bono* services, self-representation, and 'the bar and bench alone cannot achieve access

---

23 Ontario Civil Needs Project, *supra* note 6 at 5–6.
24 *Ibid.* at 24.

to justice for all. [W]e must broaden responsibility and accountability for equal access to civil justice beyond the legal profession to involve the entire community.'[25]

Licensing paralegals is an excellent first step towards meeting the needs of people requiring relatively basic legal services that can be provided by professionals without law school degrees. There are other roles for non-lawyers that could enhance crucial-time access to justice, but these roles have yet to be defined. For example, there is a union-based legal services plan in the United States that has full-time social workers on staff.

III. Legal Services Plans

There are many different types of legal services plans, with many different combinations of benefits and many different coverage permutations. In Part IV below, we provide an overview of the legal services plan industry and related issues. The chart at the end of Part IV shows the legal services industry as it exists today in Canada and the United States. Government legal aid plans are included in the chart because they are, in effect, legal services plans.

With over 5 million Canadians covered privately, and hundreds of thousands of Canadians receiving public legal aid every year, public–private legal services plan partnerships should be a very important part of the access-to-lawyer solution, especially for crucial-time legal services. To address the need for crucial-time legal services, two new policy directions are required:

- more research into legal services plans
- expansion of legal services plans, both private and public

A. More Research Required

It would appear that more research may lead to a paradigm shift. As mentioned earlier, most people covered by access plans probably do not even know it, and there is a dearth of academic attention to private legal services plans and the middle class. For example, the Ontario

---

25 Karen A. Lash, Pauline Gee, and Laurie Zelon, 'Equal Access to Civil Justice: Pursuing Solutions Beyond the Legal Profession' (1998) 17 *Yale Law and Policy Review* 489 at 494.

Civil Needs Project, 'Listening to Ontarians,' conducted 2,200 interviews of Ontarians in June 2009 and also used focus groups, but did not mention private legal services plans, either in the collection of data or in the proposed solutions.

The only mention of legal insurance in the report was in response to a question asking whether a participant would consider purchasing legal expense insurance if it was available. This may not lead to accurate predictions of true consumer interest in a comprehensive legal plan. The question used the value-laden word 'insurance' and did not describe what the legal insurance might cover. Even using these negative-sounding words, the researchers found that one-third of respondents would be interested in obtaining legal insurance. But they focused on the other two-thirds who indicated a lack of interest. One-half of those individuals said they did not believe they would need it (56 per cent), and nearly one-third of respondents thought it would be too expensive. From a policy point of view, the answers to these questions once again reinforced the perceived lack of need for a lawyer and the perceived high cost of legal services (perhaps in this case, the high cost of insurance as well). From a marketing point of view, finding that almost one-third were interested was very significant, but the reasons why these people were interested were never pursued. Notwithstanding the interpretation of these results as showing a negative response, the report suggested:

> Given the success of legal expense insurance in other jurisdictions and the entrée of new legal expense insurance providers into the Ontario market, this product has potential to enable low and middle-income Ontarians to gain enhanced access to legal services in the future.[26]

A 1988 study of the CAW Legal Services Plan concluded that prepaid legal plans were an effective tool for middle class earners to access the justice system. It showed high satisfaction levels for both clients and the lawyers delivering the benefit. The study concluded:

> [T]he positive features recommend prepaid plans as legitimate, alternative methods of legal service delivery that do not compromise professional values. We recommend that governments, lawyers' groups, plan sponsors and consumers work together for the growth and development

---

26 Ontario Civil Needs Project, *supra* note 6 at 39.

of legal services plans ... The CAW Legal Services Plan has been shown to deliver legal services to its clients in an efficient and professional manner.[27]

According to Hein online, a legal database that provides 'comprehensive coverage from inception of more than 1,400 law and law-related periodicals,'[28] this case study has *never been cited*. Arguably, there has been little academic interest in the data collected in that study.

There is a need for more research into legal services plans so that their already prominent role in the promotion of middle class access to justice can be expanded. This sentiment is supported by Roach and Sossin:

> [S]ome influenced by public choice analysis have argued that unorganized groups such as consumers and the middle class may actually suffer more disdvantages than minorities who are organized. Leaving aside this controversial claim, in our view, it should be uncontroversial that access to justice studies should include the middle class and their problems. Such an approach would allow scholars to revisit practical problems concerning consumer goods and financial services that are experienced by the middle class as well as the poor and disadvantaged groups.[29]

B. Expansion of Legal Services Plans: Public–Private Partnerships

Reference was made earlier to the European legal aid system, most notably the Finnish system, whose high means threshold allows many more who are affected by the legal system to obtain broad coverage. But in Canada, there is not enough public will and/or public financial resources to move in that direction. According to Roach and Sossin,

> [t]hose who have focused on solutions to the question of access to legal services have tended to emphasize the recognition of a 'right' to legal services. Such a right has been recognized in some criminal law contexts, and in some family law and administrative law settings. A number of scholars

---

27 Christopher J. Wydrzynski, Kai Hildebrandt, and Dolores J. Blonde, 'The CAW Prepaid Legal Services Plan: A Case Study of an Alternative Funding and Delivery Method for Legal Services' (1990) 10 Windsor Y.B. Access Just. 22 at 72.

28 http://home.heinonline.org/about/what-is-hein-online.

29 Kent Roach and Lorne Sossin, 'Access to Justice and Beyond,' http://www.law. utoronto.ca/documents/conferences 2/Trebilcock09_Roach-Sossin.pdf at 19 [Roach and Sossin, 'Access to Justice Conference Paper'].

and advocates have argued that a similar logic applies in a variety of areas of civil justice – such as consumer protection ... which feature litigants who cannot afford legal services. The Canadian Bar Association has gone so far as to launch a Charter challenge in British Columbia asserting the right to legal aid in civil litigation settings.

Behind every claim to a right, however, is a claim on resources. This is especially true in the context of access to justice and the delivery of legal services ... [T]he notion 'that any claim, no matter how small, warrants Ritz Hotel style justice' must go.[30]

Universality is a hallmark of the Canadian health care system. And although Canadians would not welcome a 'Ritz Hotel style' expansion to public legal services plans, Canadians may arguably welcome low cost, universal legal services initiatives provided by a public–private partnership. As Roach and Sossin argue,

> [w]hile publicly funded representation for all civil justice litigants in need may be unrealistic, a solution, ... is for [Legal Aid Ontario] to address access to justice needs for the middle class – to evolve, in other words, from a needs-based social benefit to a universal program of accessible justice.
>
> Providing universal legal representation for the middle-class individual's civil litigation needs is neither tenable nor desirable (why should the public subsidize the decision of a particular individual to seek damages from a business partner or neighbor on grounds which may or may not be meritorious?). [There is an argument] instead for deploying legal aid clinics to provide public legal information, summary advice and other limited legal services ... [T]here should be a 'more integrated system for providing low cost information and summary advice services to a broader range of citizens than is currently available.'[31]

Legal services plans, particularly access plans, fit well into this niche. Legal Aid Ontario already has a partnership with a private legal services plan for jailhouse calls.[32] Research is required to see wheth-

---

30 Roach and Sossin, 'Access to Justice,' *supra* note 1 at 382–3, quoting M.J. Trebilcock, 'Protecting Consumers Against Purchases of Defective Merchandise' (1971) 4 Adelaide L. Rev. 12 at 41.
31 *Ibid.* at 390, quoting Michael J. Trebilcock, *Legal Aid Review* (Toronto: Ministry of the Attorney General, 2008) at 88.
32 See also Kenneth Jull, '*Clarkson v. The Queen* – Do We Need a Legal Emergency Department?' (1987) 32 McGill L. J. 359.

er other public–private partnerships, on the civil side, could raise the threshold for publicly funded middle class access plans. The answer lies not in universal access that would cover the expense for a lawyer's services whatever the cost or circumstances; it lies in making crucial-time legal services universally available at an affordable price. There would be several layers of coverage.

The first layer of coverage would be a publicly funded and publicly and privately delivered telephone access plan. The client would initiate the legal service by telephoning for advice; that call would be answered, no matter when made, by a paralegal who has been trained to perform legal triage. Simple questions could be answered by the paralegal directly; more difficult inquiries would necessitate a call back from a lawyer the next business day. Emergencies would be handled by an on-call lawyer. More important, such crucial-time advice would likely stop the caller from inappropriate action or inaction, at less cost to both the caller and the general public. The call centre would employ the paralegals and lawyers either on staff or on contract, and this service would be fully paid for by public funds. Other administrative issues require further, detailed research beyond the scope of this essay.

The second layer of coverage would be a referral to a lawyer. There may not be any public finances available for this layer, except, perhaps, for its public administration, preferably by a Crown corporation. Coverage for layer two would not be universal but hopefully would be easily accessible. Whatever is not covered by public funding would be paid for by the private sector. There should be no coverage for lawsuits below a certain monetary threshold where it is reasonable for the litigant to self-represent and where the financial gains or losses would be minimal. For example, the CAW Legal Services Plan presently uses $3,000 as its monetary threshold, with the participant having four hours of legal services for claims below that threshold, and 30 hours of legal services for claims above that threshold. There should be no compensation allowed for adverse costs awarded against the plan member. Our experience at the CAW Legal Services Plan has revealed that the risk of an adverse cost award is a necessary constraint on launching questionable litigation or mounting a poor defence. Further, only first-party personal injury claims should be covered, not the tort claim, as the contingency fee system adequately addresses the access issue for those sorts of claims in Ontario.

Individual and/or employer-paid premiums would be at different rates, for different benefit schedules containing different co-pays and maximums. If employers pay the premium, it should be a non-taxable benefit to its employees (see Part IV, below). Employers could be encouraged to pay for such a plan with some tax incentives as well. Once again, administrative details such as lawyer delivery systems and lawyer payments are beyond the scope of this paper. But larger groups might set up their own staff offices much like the CAW Legal Services Plan, and may consider paying for disbursements such as filing fees, expert witnesses, and mediation services.[33]

One fear always raised in connection with subsidized legal expenses is that they will lead to increased litigation. As discussed below, litigation in Germany is heavily subsidized by both legal insurance and legal aid, and monopolized by lawyers. Yet studies in Germany have found that

> Germans who hold a legal cost insurance [*sic*] do not litigate significantly riskier cases, nor do they appeal more often, nor do they settle less out of court than do non-insured parties. Even though lawyer surveys indicate that attorneys believe they are more likely to litigate cases of clients under insurance coverage than those of non-insured clients, a control group comparison of their case files does not generally affirm such subjective self-estimates.
>
> Thus, the moral dilemma which legal economists are warning about, of legal cost insurance producing the very behaviour that it is insuring against, is refuted by the empirical data. The 'litigation-proneness' of private households turns out to be much more inelastic to price decreases than had been expected. Only repeat players with many legal risks (such as, *e.g.*, taxi companies) can calculate their legal costs rationally.'[34]

Keeping in mind Trebilcock's 'do no harm principle,'[35] what would these reforms do?

- Access to justice would be enhanced.
- People would feel empowered and enfranchised, increasing a sense of social justice.

---

33 Compare the proposal for a public legal expenses insurance program in Sujit Choudhry, Michael Trebilcock, and James Wilson, 'Growing Ontario Legal Aid into the Middle Class,' *infra* this volume.

34 Erhard Blankenberg, 'Private Insurance and the Historical "Waves" of Legal Aid' (1993) 13 Wind. Yearbook Access to Justice 185, at 198 [Blankenberg, 'Private Insurance'].

35 Roach and Sossin, 'Access to Justice Conference Paper,' *supra* note 29 at 21–2.

- The rule of law would be enhanced as more middle class disputes would be resolved within the legal system.
- Participants would have full freedom of choice of lawyer.
- Lawyers could choose not to participate.
- Traditional lawyer–client relationships would be supported, with no steering or loss of control.
- Tort claims and the positive effects of contingency fees would be supported.
- Mediation initiatives could be supported.
- There would be no effect on business-related legal services.
- Larger groups could create their own plans with staff lawyers.

A public–private legal services plan partnership is neither a frill nor a Band-Aid solution to the problem of middle class access to justice. Properly administered and promoted, it could be the central solution.

IV. Legal Services Plans: Industry Overview

A. Types of Plans

There are two main types of legal services plans: access plans and comprehensive plans. Access plans are basic plans that usually offer unlimited telephone advice, brief in-office consultation, document review, short letters or phone calls to adverse parties, a simple will, and discounted fees for additional services. The fact that a person can easily pick up the phone and talk to a lawyer is an indispensable step forward for the notion of crucial-time access to justice. As Ginsberg notes: 'One in 10 people accessed legal assistance through a telephone advice line in the last three years, and approximately 7 in 10 expressed satisfaction with the service they received.'[36]

Comprehensive plans encompass a wide circle of benefits and are designed to take care of 80 to 90 per cent of the average person's legal needs.[37] They are conceptually similar to extended health benefits. There are often deductibles, co-payments, and fee caps, depending on the particular legal problem.

---

36 Ontario Civil Needs Project, *supra* note 6 at 37.
37 Ginsberg, 'Legal Services Plans,' *supra* note 2 at 58.

B. Delivery Methods

A legal services plan may employ either unaffiliated lawyers or affiliated lawyers. Where services are provided by an unaffiliated lawyer, the subscriber submits the lawyer's bill to a plan for reimbursement in accordance with the plan's fee schedule. There are various ways that lawyers may be affiliated with a plan. Panel lawyers contract with a plan to provide services at specified, discounted rates. Some services are billed directly to the plan (i.e., 'prepaid' benefits); other services are billed to the client. Staff lawyers are employed by a plan, work in offices owned by the plan, and provide services to plan members. All or some of the services are free ('prepaid' benefits); other services are billed to the client at specified, discounted rates. Access/referral law firms, or 'intake firms,' contract with a plan to provide access benefits only. If the matter is more complex, the plan member will be referred to a panel lawyer at a different law firm (some plans allow the same law firm to continue the case). Intake firms are paid a per capita fee based on the number of plan members in the service area and/or a flat fee per call received.

C. Legal Expense Insurance Plans

There is a functional distinction between legal expense insurance plans and other kinds of legal services plans. Insurance, as it is commonly defined, is an arrangement that assists for unforeseen events (discussed below). Legal plans, or more commonly prepaid legal plans and access plans, on the other hand, include foreseen events such as a real estate transaction or a will. Legal expense insurance generally reimburses for legal services in connection with an unforeseen event, such as an automobile accident, a traffic ticket, or a lawsuit defence. Legal defence insurance covering the cost of defending a lawsuit arising out of a motor vehicle accident is typically included in automobile policies and is now mandatory in Ontario. More recently, stand-alone legal expense insurance plans have become available to individuals, increasing the scope of this basic coverage.

Until 2010, legal expense insurance in Ontario was usually marketed only to specific groups rather than to individuals. For example, Sterlon Underwriting Managers Ltd. offered groups of professionals and commercial entities legal insurance relating to their particular profession or business, to cover typical litigation such as wrongful dismissal. This insurance was sold through brokers.[38] The main product available to individuals was the access plan, offered by companies such as Pre-Paid Legal Services, Inc. However, in 2010 DAS Canada, the Canadian subsidiary of a German insurance company, began offering a new legal expense insurance product to individuals. The product is sold through independent brokers.[39] DAS offers three different policies to meet the unique needs of consumers and business owners:

- DAS*drive:* designed to provide support when legal conflicts arise from the use or ownership of an automobile: premiums – $80 for first vehicle + $60 each additional vehicle (up to 5 in total);
- DAS*living:* providing legal advice, assistance, and cost coverage for individuals and families facing many of society's common legal problems: premiums $360 for primary residence + $100 each additional residence (up to 3 in total); and,
- DAS*business:* to protect businesses against the cost of potential legal disputes.[40]

According to the DAS website, coverage includes (among other things):

- Legal advice;
- Contract disputes;
- Employment disputes;
- Property protection;
- Tax protection; and,
- Legal defence.[41]

Coverage in some of the policies includes not only the participant's legal costs, but also the legal costs of the opposing party if ordered against the policyholder, and some disbursements as well, such as experts' reports. As DAS states in its promotional material sent to interested brokers:

Disputes Arising from Nine of the Top 10 Consumer Complaints in Ontario now Covered by DAS Canada's Legal Expense Insurance. Accord-

---

38 Sterlon Underwriting Managers Limited, http://www.sterlon.com/index.html.
39 DAS Canada, http://www.das.ca.
40 *Ibid.,* http://www.das.ca/html/products.
41 *Ibid.,* http://www.das.ca/html/products.

ing to the Government of Ontario website, the top consumer complaints in the province for 2009 included disputes regarding debt collection, home repairs, and vehicle and appliance purchases or sales. In many cases, successful resolutions involve hiring a lawyer and paying their fees.[42]

The DAS plan has limited or advice-only coverage for a number of dispute categories that have been identified by many legal needs studies as high need for middle income earners, such as family law, debtor/creditor, and housing issues (including residential tenancies and disputes over contracts of sale).[43] These omissions reveal a serious gap in necessary coverage. In contrast, the CAW Legal Services Plan allows twelve hours of legal services for family law issues and thirty hours of legal services for litigation concerning debt matters, tenancy issues, or agreements of purchase and sale of land. It should be noted that in the area of family disputes, there are legitimate underwriting concerns about spiralling costs. There have also been fairness concerns where one party in a family dispute has a significant advantage because of a greater capacity to pay legal fees. Reasonably capped coverage in these high-need areas would result in broader coverage without significantly increasing premium costs.

D. International Comparisons

Germany is similar to Ontario in its approach to legal access. In Germany, giving legal advice is restricted to lawyers, and Germany has a means-driven legal aid system that has seen substantial cutbacks in funding. Private legal expense insurance has thrived, with insurance company payments to lawyers far exceeding payments from the public legal aid system.[44] However,

> legal aid (assistance under the Legal Advice Scheme and assistance with court costs) is given when the applicant's personal and economic circumstances are such that he cannot raise the necessary funds and has no other reasonable possibility of obtaining assistance (e.g. legal protection insurance, advice from a tenants' association or trade union). The intended

---

42 From a marketing sheet given to prospective brokers by DAS Legal Protection Insurance Company Ltd.

43 Ontario Civil Needs Project, *supra* note 6.

44 Blankenburg, 'Private Insurance,' *supra* note 34 at 198.

exercise of rights must be neither wilful nor malicious. For assistance with court costs to be given, the planned prosecution or defence must also have a reasonable chance of success. The court that rules on the application for assistance with court costs must consider, on the basis of the applicant's representation of the facts and the available documentation, that the legal viewpoint is correct or at least justifiable and be convinced that it is possible to present a case. Where these conditions are satisfied, the applicant is entitled to assistance under the Legal Advice Scheme and assistance with court costs.[45]

Private legal insurance has arguably thrived in Germany because Germany's fixed legal cost system (in contrast to the open-ended legal costs found in Ontario) makes for more predictable underwriting. Good legal insurance policies in Germany cover disputes with landlords or neighbours, road traffic issues, tax issues, and personal injury, with limited coverage of inheritance and family law.[46] As noted above, legal insurance is primary, with legal aid only a secondary system for those who do not have such insurance. Consequently, in Germany the public legal aid system has remade itself, covering only those who cannot afford legal insurance or who do not have legal insurance as an employee benefit. Many people may still fall within the gap between the legal aid means test and affordable legal insurance, and much like the DAS Canada policy, the typical German policy is not comprehensive.

Similarly, in Sweden legal aid is the secondary insurer, but private legal insurance is almost always part of a typical residence and automobile policy, rather than a stand-alone policy as in Ontario and Germany. Legal aid coverage is means driven, with a means threshold of approximately C$40,000, but overall coverage of both legal insurance and legal aid is more comprehensive. Importantly, one hour of crucial-time advice is included, and there is fully comprehensive coverage for any legal dispute over a base monetary threshold. However, only unforeseen events are covered, and routine legal services such as a will or property transfer are excluded.[47]

The DAS policy in Canada (and, ultimately, direct competitors' poli-

---

45 European Commission – European Judicial Network, http://ec.europa.eu/civiljustice/legal_aid/legal_aid_ger_en.htm.
46 How To Germany, http://www.howtogermany.com/pages/insurance.html.
47 Swedish National Courts Administration, 'Legal Aid in Sweden,' http://www.domstol.se/Publikationer/Informationsmaterial/Legal_aid_in_Sweden.pdf.

cies soon to come on the market) may represent a big step forward for those who can afford it. However, it is much too early to declare the middle class access to justice problem solved by DAS and its spin-off products. One needs to analyse the policy terms closely, and it is important to do so, because any new insurance products may mimic the first one. For example, a study comparing Ontario title insurance policies shows that the three leading policies are almost identical, despite the insurance companies' entering this new market at different times, and despite their being in direct competition with one another.[48] Further, the typical German policy covers much the same disputes as the DAS Canada policy.[49]

E. Regulatory and Tax Issues

Although legal services plans are largely a phenomenon of the past thirty years, consumer need for them is considerably older. In 1899, in the United States, the Physicians' Defense Company provided its subscribers with prepaid coverage for the legal defence of medical malpractice suits. Neither the legal profession nor government regulatory agencies were prepared for this novel approach to securing legal representation. This early group dissolved eleven years later, leaving in its wake a trail of conflicting opinions as to its legality, propriety, and regulation. In 1984, in Canada, the first major prepaid legal services plan was established through collective bargaining between the then Canadian branch of the UAW (now CAW) and the then Big Three (now Detroit Three) automobile companies. There were lawsuits and Law Society threats even before the plan became operational on 5 November 1985. The atmosphere is much calmer now, but the development of legal services plans in both countries is still hampered to some extent by unresolved regulatory issues, law society rules, and the income tax treatment of employer-paid legal services benefits.[50]

The definition of 'insurance' is almost identical in each province and is along the following lines:

---

48 Paul Vayda, 'Four Things Every Real Estate Lawyer Needs to Know About Title Insurance Coverage' (November 2002), LSUC Six-Minute Real Estate Lawyer Conference materials; see also 'Title Insurance Rightly Understood' (November 2006), Hamilton Law Association Real Estate Conference materials.

49 Blankenburg, 'Private Insurance,' *supra* note 34.

50 Ginsberg, 'Legal Services Plans,' *supra* note 2 at 59.

'Insurance' means the undertaking by one person to indemnify another person against loss or liability for loss in respect of a certain risk or peril to which the object of the insurance may be exposed, or pay a sum of money or other thing of value on the happening of a certain event.'[51]

A province might characterize a telephone access plan as 'insurance,' which would make it cost-prohibitive for new, non-insurance company start-ups. This problem was noted in the May 1991 Report of the Insurance Legislation Review Project to the Ontario Insurance Commission, in which the following recommendation was made, though never acted upon: 'Prepaid legal service arrangements in the nature of "access plans" should be excepted from the definition of "insurance" in the Insurance Act.'[52]

A similar recommendation was made, but never acted upon, with respect to union–employer plans: 'Any prepaid legal service plan for employees, retirees and their dependents arrived at as a result of the collective bargaining process should be excepted from the definition of "insurance" in the Insurance Act.'[53]

In the interests of access to affordable legal services, all provincial insurance legislation should be amended to clarify these issues, to provide ease of entry for access plans and union-based prepaid plans. Access to affordable legal services would be further enhanced if employer-paid legal services plans were not a taxable benefit to the employee. They should be on the same footing as employer-paid health benefits (e.g., drugs, dental, vision), which are non-taxable.

V. Conclusion

At the beginning of this paper, Rex arrived at the hospital with a progressively debilitating disease and a very messy set of financial and personal affairs – three children feuding with his fairly recent 'spouse,' no cohabitation agreement, no powers of attorney, probably no will, and no one to trust except his eldest child, who lives in Germany.

If Rex had a typical access plan, he likely would have tested it out

---

51 *Ibid.*
52 Ontario Ministry of Financial Institutions, *Insuring for the Future: Modern Insurance Legislation for Ontario: Report of the Insurance Legislation Review Project to the Ontario Insurance Commission* (May 1991) at 13.
53 *Ibid.* at 11.

Figure 8.1. The Legal Services Plan Universe

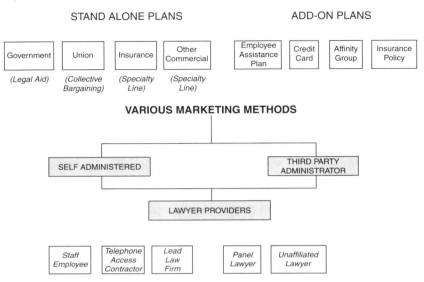

and made a simple will while his wife was still alive. He would have been comfortable calling for some advice when his first wife passed away. Rex would have signed a new will, as well as powers of attorney for property and personal care, and at the same time would have been advised about who to appoint as Estate Trustee and whether to choose a European resident to be his attorney. Later, upon the introduction of his girlfriend, a lawyer would have counselled Rex to protect his property and enter into a cohabitation agreement.

If Rex had a more comprehensive legal services plan, most or all of these services would have been delivered at a discount to prevailing market rates, and his fear of ballooning legal fees would have been assuaged. At each crucial time, Rex's legal needs would have been met, not only with advice, but also with appropriate documentation. Then, at the hospital, a telephone call would have confirmed that all his legal affairs were in order.

Even if he had done nothing until he reached the hospital, Rex would still have had time to resolve many of his issues. A telephone call from the hospital would have put Rex in touch with a lawyer, who would have immediately advised him, prepared a will and powers of attorney, and made a hospital visit to complete the attestation. In either case, expensive litigation and the use of significant private and public funds would likely have been avoided, and family conflict lessened.

Legal services plans are a way forward: accessible, appropriate, affordable, and attainable. The CAW Legal Services Plan has been operating successfully for over twenty-five years, attesting to the potential efficacy of the group legal plan model in Canada. All Canadians should have access to affordable and appropriate legal services at the crucial time – as soon as required. But needless and uncertain insurance regulation and the taxation of employer-paid legal services benefits are significant impediments. More research and more advocacy are required.

PART 6

Reforming the Dispute Resolution Process

9 Reforming Family Dispute Resolution in Ontario: Systemic Changes and Cultural Shifts

NICHOLAS BALA*

I. Introduction

A. A 'Fresh Conceptual Approach' and the Four Pillars of Reform

Ontario residents are more likely to have a dispute concerning a familial relationship than any other type of serious legal problem.[1] The family dispute resolution process has evolved considerably over the past few decades, but the pace of change has been frustratingly slow, with many sound reports and recommendations for reform ignored, resulting in continuing unaddressed concerns about the family justice system. Many of those embroiled in these often traumatic, life-altering disputes have difficulties gaining access to the justice system and must proceed without adequate legal advice and assistance. The 2010 Law Commission of Ontario Report on the 'broken' family justice system documented some of the problems.[2] Ontario's Chief Justice Warren K. Winkler recently declared that 'family law is in a state of crisis' and

* The author would like to thank the following for their generous comments on drafts of this paper: Dr Rachel Birnbaum, Justice George Czutrin, Dr Barbara-Jo Fidler, Dr Barbara Landau, Jane Long, Anne-Marie Predko, Tony Duggan, Carol Rogerson, and Noel Semple. The author would also like to thank Christine Ashbourne (Queen's JD, 2011) for her helpful research and editorial assistance.

1 *Listening to Ontarians: Report of the Ontario Civil Legal Needs Project* (Toronto: Ontario Civil Legal Needs Project Steering Committee, 2010), at Law Society of Upper Canada, http://www.lsuc.on.ca/media/may3110_oclnreport_final.pdf.
2 Law Commission of Ontario, *Voices from a Broken Family Justice System: Sharing Consultations Results* (Law Commission of Ontario, 2010), http://www.lco-cdo.org/family-law/family-law-process-consultation-results-highlights.pdf [LCO, *Voices*].

called for a 'fresh conceptual approach' with 'dramatic and pragmatic' changes,[3] suggesting there is an appetite for significant reform.

Over the past couple of years, members of the judiciary, government officials, and professional organizations have been engaged in extensive discussion about the family justice process, and there is significant consensus about the directions for reform. There is now cause for cautious optimism about the prospects for change, and the Ontario government has recently implemented the first stages of its 'Four Pillars' of Family Justice Reform. The Four Pillars reforms call for:

1 better access to information, including mandatory attendance at information sessions on the emotional and legal implications of separation;
2 an improved intake process ('triage'), with identification of high-conflict cases that require fast-tracking into courts, and steering of other cases to non-court services;
3 improved access to legal advice and early access to alternatives to litigation; and
4 streamlining of the court process, so that litigated cases will receive faster, more focused attention from the courts.

The broad support for the Four Pillars may in part reflect the fact that there has never been complete agreement about some important details of the plan, which has allowed different supporters to each cite their own preferred version.[4] Further, while the government has been supportive of the 'Four Pillars,'[5] and Ministry of the Attorney General

---

3 Chief Justice Warren K. Winkler, address delivered at the Carleton County Law Association Continuing Legal Education Program, 19 November 2010; Tracey Tyler, 'Chief Justice Seeks Compulsory Mediation in Family Cases,' *Toronto* Star, 15 September 2010.

4 The fullest articulation of the 'Four Pillars' plan is by Barbara Landau *et al., Home Court Advantage; Creating a Family Law Process That Works* (2009), at Ontario Bar Association, http://www.oba.org/en/pdf/011-0022_Family%20Law%20Process%20 Reform%20Report_final_web.pdf [Landau, *Home Court Advantage*]. This document was endorsed by three important professional organizations: the Ontario Bar Association (OBA), the ADR Institute of Ontario (ADRIO), and the Ontario Association for Family Mediation (OAFM). A somewhat different version of the Four Pillars was prepared by Nick Bala and Phil Epstein: 'Appendix 4: Summary Report by Professor Nick Bala and Phil Epstein' in Landau *et al., Home Court Advantage.*

5 The previous Attorney General, Chris Bentley, endorsed the 'Four Pillars,' although with somewhat less specificity than some of the other proponents of reform. See, for

expenditures on family justice support services have more than doubled over the past few years, there are no immediate plans to implement some of the more expensive parts of the reform scheme.[6]

This paper identifies the major problems with the present family justice process in Ontario and discusses ideas for reform,[7] with a particular focus on the Four Pillars and on improving access to family justice for middle income individuals. I argue that there is a need for both institutional reforms and changes in the 'culture' of family justice professionals.

One theme of this paper is that it is important to be realistic about family disputes and to recognize the strengths of the present system as well as the limitations of any social or legal interventions for dealing with high-conflict situations. It is also important to be realistic about improvements that will require additional resources and to identify changes that can be undertaken without corresponding increases in spending. Very strong arguments can be made that it is in society's long-term social and economic interests to provide more public resources to help parents resolve family disputes, in particular those involving children. However, in the present fiscal environment, it seems unlikely that there will be any commitment of significant additional government resources for the family justice system in the near future beyond those already announced.

Before turning to a discussion of the problems inherent in the present system and some of the possible reforms, it is important to understand what makes family relationship disputes different from other legal problems. Only if the unique nature of family disputes is recognized can the necessary changes be undertaken to make the family justice process *more effective* in terms of outcomes for children and their par-

---

example, Chris Bentley, 'Access to Justice for Ontarians' (29 September 2010) (podcast), at Ontario Ministry of the Attorney General, http://www.attorneygeneral.jus.gov. on.ca/english/AG_podcasts/Transcripts/20100929_access_justice_transcript.asp.

6 See Ontario Ministry of the Attorney General, News Release, 'Family Law Reform in Ontario' (9 December 2010), http://news.ontario.ca/mag/en/2010/12/family-law-reform-in-ontario.html. Expenditures on family justice services provided at the seventeen Unified Family Court sites were about $2.6 million per year.

7 The focus in this paper is on procedural reforms, although the substantive law is also important. Increasing legal certainty, as with the *Child Support Guidelines* in 1997 and the *Spousal Support Advisory Guidelines* in 2005, facilitates settlement and reduces conflict. Clearly more could be done in this regard, for example, by making common law spouses subject to the *Family Law Act* property regime or by providing more legislative guidance for dealing with parental relocation.

ents and *more efficient* in the use of public and private resources. The Four Pillars plan and the announced increases in government funding and services are most welcome and should result in more cases being settled in a non-litigious fashion. They should also facilitate the identification of those cases that need judicial intervention, resulting in cases moving more quickly through to a judicial resolution, and hence improving access to justice. However, more needs to be done; in particular, Unified Family Courts and family case management need to be extended across the province. These two further reforms can only occur if there is strong political and judicial leadership, but they will not require significant additional resources, and their implementation should actually result in savings.

As important as changes in the structure and services of the family justice system are, there must also be a 'cultural shift' among justice system professionals. While there have already been significant changes in professional attitudes and practices, family lawyers need to have as a primary objective helping parents achieve a child-focused, non-adversarial restructuring of their relationship. Those working in the family justice system must recognize their responsibilities not only to the adults who are in their offices and the courts, but also to the children who are absent but who are profoundly affected by the process.

A final theme of this paper is that there is a clear need for more data and better research about family justice. There is a paucity of basic statistical information about family justice in Ontario. For example, it is not even known what portion of family litigants appear in court without legal representation. There is little sound empirical research from anywhere in the world about the effects of some of the reforms of the sort that are being undertaken in Ontario, even though they have been implemented in a number of jurisdictions. There have been almost no solid cost–benefit analyses of possible reforms, research that governments would find especially persuasive.

B. What Makes Family Disputes Different

While familial problems such as marital unhappiness, infidelity, abuse, and desertion have been part of family life since the beginnings of recorded history, until relatively recently they were not regarded as legal problems. Historically, the justice system and the law developed with little concern about resolving family disputes. In England, until the middle of the nineteenth century, what today would be considered family law was dealt with not in the civil courts but rather in the ecclesiastical courts.[8] Over the past century and a half, enormous technological, cultural, demographic, social, economic, and legal changes have made family breakdown and divorce much more prevalent. Family law is now one of the largest areas of civil litigation. Yet only in the past few decades has family law become a distinct area of legal practice and scholarly study. The family justice system in Ontario still reflects the fact that it has been grafted onto a justice system that originally dealt with very different types of problems.

Historically the Canadian justice system dealt primarily with state prosecutions of alleged criminals and with disputes between individuals or institutions over economic or property matters. These cases usually involved no expectations of future dealings between the parties. The interest of the state in such cases was the peaceful settlement of disputes and the maintenance of public order, with judges expected to act as neutral arbiters, and with the parties having the responsibility of marshalling evidence and shaping the legal dispute. Most types of court cases are retrospective, with a judicial focus on ending a relationship on just terms. However, family cases, especially those involving children, are largely prospective. The key issue is what arrangements *will be* best for the children and provide most appropriately for the future economic well-being of the spouses. Although the family justice process will end the spousal relationship, if the parties have children their interrelationship will continue.

It is the restructuring of familial relationships rather than their termination that is the central objective of the family justice process[9]: changing parental attitudes and behaviour is often essential if good outcomes are to be achieved for children.[10] Variation, review, and enforcement

---

8 See, for example, Elizabeth Abbott, *A History of Marriage* (Toronto: Penguin Canada, 2010); and Nicholas Bala, 'The History and Future of Marriage in Canada' (2007) 4 JL & Equality 20.

9 For many of the same reasons, criminal prosecutions arising from violence in familial relationships are also different from other types of criminal cases, and it is for this reason that Ontario has established special Domestic Violence Courts. There are advantages to having both the criminal and family aspects of cases involving domestic violence dealt with by one judge, although there are also potential problems. A pilot Integrated Domestic Violence Court program is now being established at the Ontario Court of Justice in Toronto. This is an important initiative that needs to be studied, and if successful, replicated. See Liberty Aldrich and Judge Judy Harris Kluger, 'New York's One Judge–One Family Response to Family Violence' (2010) 61 Juv & Fam Ct J 77.

10 The concept of 'therapeutic jurisprudence' may be viewed as central to many family

proceedings are major issues for the family justice process. While the emotional relationships of witnesses and litigants are a significant factor in many types of litigation, they are often *the* central issue in family cases; further, only in these cases are decisions about the future of non-parties – the children – the focus of the legal process. The state's interest in family cases goes beyond dispute resolution: adoptions, custody orders, and divorces cannot simply be granted 'on consent,' as there is a judicial duty to ensure that a child's interests are protected.[11]

Another feature of family justice (outside the child welfare context) is the absence of institutional or repeat litigants who have a stake in the justice system. In every criminal case the Crown is a party, with responsibility for moving the case forward in the justice system and with a substantial commitment to the administration of justice. In many ordinary civil cases, there are insurance companies, financial institutions, or agencies involved that are likely to be 'repeat players' with at least some concern about their reputation in the justice system. The lack of institutional litigants in domestic cases means there is less commitment by the parties – especially those who are unrepresented – to the integrity of the justice system. In domestic cases, the parties almost always begin the process with little real understanding of the law and no litigation experience. Many complete the family court process with only a limited understanding of what occurred and with a willingness to defy court orders unless they are made clearly aware of the consequences of ignoring a court order.

---

cases, *not* in the sense that judges should be therapists, but rather in the sense that even when focusing exclusively on the decisions made by judges, it is important to 'study the effects of law and the legal system on the behavior, emotions and mental health of people.' This is the definition of 'therapeutic jurisprudence' provided in *Black's Law Dictionary*, 9th ed., *sub verbo* 'therapeutic jurisprudence.'

11   Under the *Divorce Act*, R.S.C. 1985, c. C.3 (2d Supp), s.11(1)(b), the judge granting a divorce has an obligation to ensure that reasonable arrangements have been made for the support of a child whose parents are getting a divorce. Under Rule 35.1 of the Ontario *Family Law Rules*, any person seeking a custody or access order is required to complete a detailed form about their children, parenting history, and involvement in issues of domestic violence. This recognizes that the court needs 'up-to-date and accurate information' to make an order and suggests that the judge has an independent duty to the child before an order for custody or access. See Ontario, *Family Law Rules*, r. 35.1. Section 146 of the *Child and Family Services Act* RSO 1990, c. C.11, requires a judge to make a determination that an adoption is in a child's 'best interests' before making an order for adoption.

C. Problems in the Family Justice System

There is a range of concerns about the inefficiency and ineffectiveness of family justice in Ontario, including issues of expense, lack of accessibility, complexity, and delay. There are related concerns about difficulties in enforcing family orders, especially those relating to control of behaviour, such as restraining orders and access orders. Further, some critics charge that the family justice system, and professionals in what is sometimes pejoratively called the 'divorce industry,' may increase the level of hostility between separated parents and the expense of divorce, thereby undermining the interests of children and their parents.[12] There is certainly some validity to these concerns, with respect to both systemic issues and individual professionals who may be failing to deal appropriately with cases. While high conflict is not *caused* by the family justice process, the legal and extralegal responses of separated partners and their professional advisers can heighten *or* reduce conflict.

It is also essential to recognize that only a minority of family cases can be classified as 'high conflict,'[13] given that only a fraction of them result in any form of judicial decision making and only a small portion of them – common estimates are 2 to 5 per cent – result in a full trial.[14] In many

---

12 The concept of the 'divorce industry' is used by critics, especially those who are dissatisfied with their treatment in the legal system. This term is used almost exclusively by 'men's rights advocates' to characterize professionals such as family lawyers, judges, custody assessors, and mediators. The 'solution' proposed by these critics is usually some form of self-representation, often with an invitation to purchase some Internet-sold services to help with this undertaking. See, for example, 'Great Divorce Advice: Winning Strategies for Men,' http://www.greatdivorceadvice.com.

13 The term 'high conflict separation' was popularized in academic and professional circles by Janet Johnston in the early 1990s to describe a subset of separating families characterized by repeated court appearances and high levels of mistrust and hostility. See Janet R. Johnston, 'High-Conflict Divorce' (1994) 4 The Future of Children 165. There is no single definition for the 'high conflict separation' and hence there are no reliable statistics on its incidence. However, it is clear that a majority of separations are not high conflict and that within a couple of years of separation, not more than 10 to 20 per cent of cases involve significant conflict. Only 2 to 5 per cent of family separations result in a trial, although exhaustion, lack of resources, and even intimidation may explain the paucity of trials.

14 While there are no reliable data on judicial resolution rates, it is commonly estimated that less than 5 per cent of civil and family cases go to trial in Ontario. One Canadian study of family law lawyers found that 14 per cent of their family cases were resolved by a judge after an interim hearing or trial. See Joanne J Paetsch *et al.*, *The Child-Centred Family Justice Strategy: Baseline Data from Family Law Practitioners*

high-conflict cases, it is the unreasonable, antagonistic behaviour of one parent – or often both – that leads to delay, expense, and the frustration of the legal process. Usually, by the time a case gets to trial, a number of professionals – including lawyers and members of the judiciary – have tried to steer the parties towards a settlement, but one or both parties have rejected these efforts to settle.[15] In many high-conflict cases, one or both parties are abusive or personality disordered and make unreasonable demands on the other parent or on the children. Even if a settlement or judicial resolution is achieved, an unreasonable or abusive party may refuse to comply or may seek variation as soon as one proceeding is completed, adding to the frustration, delay, and expense.

In some studies (such as the recent Law Commission of Ontario report[16]) and media accounts, individuals who have been involved in the family justice process state that they have been frustrated by the 'system' and the professionals in it, apparently without recognizing how they may have contributed to the situation and forgetting that they may have ignored professional advice to settle. As recently noted by a group of Australian forensic child psychologists:

> It is well documented that the population of litigants who reach the end stages of the family law process have particular qualities. It is a special person who is prepared to fight to the death for what is often a pyrrhic victory and who resists a more sensible resolution from the available alternatives … some parents seem to go through 'separation psychosis' where their behaviour is irrational … Often parents find it difficult to recognize their own personalities and behaviours during and after their separation.[17]

It is very important to appreciate that while separation and divorce are invariably emotionally traumatic, and often economically dislocating, a majority of Ontario cases involving family disputes are resolved reasonably well. The parties, often acting with the assistance of lawyers,[18]

(Department of Justice Canada, 2005), http://www.justice.gc.ca/eng/pi/fcy-fea/lib-bib/rep-rap/2005/biflp-dbpdf/pdf/biflp-dbpdf.pdf.

15 See, for example, Noel Semple, 'Judicial Settlement-Seeking in Parenting Disputes: Consensus and Controversy,' Conflict Resolution Quarterly (forthcoming, 2012).

16 LCO, *Voices, supra* note 2.

17 Jennifer Neoh, Vicent Papaleo, and Simon Kennedy, 'Run for the Hills: Why Would You Specialise in Family Law Assessment?' (2010) 32 *InPsych* 14 [Neoh, 'Run for the Hills'].

18 Statistics Canada, *Navigating Family Transitions: Evidence from the General Social Survey*

and possibly a mediator or a judge, reach a reasonable, fairly expeditious settlement of the issues outstanding between them. They usually
comply with the terms of their agreement, perhaps seeking to vary relevant provisions relating to the children as circumstances change, but
they are able to do this with limited professional involvement, or even
on their own. Parties to these cases often involve the court system in
some limited fashion, such as applying for an uncontested divorce and
filing an agreement as the basis of a consent order, but they do not have
contested hearings. An increasing amount of information and advice
has become available to assist former spouses and parents in restructuring their relationships after separation, and there is an increasing
trend among parents to agree to some form of joint decision making
('joint legal custody') or shared parenting. This usually does *not* mean
equal time with each parent, but rather significant time and involvement of both parents in the lives of their children.

A central goal of reforming the family justice process is to resolve
more cases in this type of non-litigious, less expensive fashion than
happens at present. There have already been significant developments
in the family justice system – such as the emergence of collaborative
family law – that facilitate the settlement of cases without having to
resort to litigation. These types of developments are to be encouraged.

One of the challenges in reforming the family justice system is that
parenting arrangements and justice process responses that are desirable
and should be encouraged for the lower-conflict majority of separated
parents are inappropriate for higher-conflict cases or where there are
domestic violence concerns. High-conflict cases need to be dealt with
in a different fashion from the lower-conflict majority of cases. There
is a critical need for early identification of the nature of the dispute
and the issues involved in it if there is to be an efficient and effective
response – hence the importance of 'triage' in discussions about family
justice reform.

There are cases where one parent, usually the father, has little or no
involvement with the children. Often in these cases, the parents have
not married or lived together. If the uninvolved parent has income, he
will typically be pursued for child support, though he may have only a

---

(Ottawa, 2007) provides a study in which 78 per cent of those going through separation or divorce and having a lawyer were either very satisfied or satisfied with the
assistance they received from their lawyer, and the major sources of dissatisfaction
were high costs and slow progress.

limited and diminishing role in the child's life, having effectively abandoned the child and become a 'ghost dad.'[19] In some of these cases, the attenuation of the relationship with the child is due to difficulties in effecting visitation, or it reflects communication difficulties between the parents. Legal and social responses that improve relationships and communication between parents can result in children having better relationships with both parents and improve the child's social, emotional, and economic outcomes. This usually involves parental education or mediation;[20] but in many cases, there is little scope for the family justice system to increase the engagement of parents who have chosen to be absent from the lives of their children.

Thus, the central problems for the family justice system involve cases in which parents do not come to a reasonably fair and expeditious resolution of their separation issues and a child-focused restructuring of their future parenting relationship. In some of these cases, the parents lack access to the services or information that would assist them in achieving such an outcome; in other cases, one or both parents may be too angry, abusive, distrusting, emotionally wounded, personality disordered, or involved in substance abuse to allow for such a resolution.

II. The Four Pillars

A. Information for Separating Spouses: The First Pillar

Separation has profound social, psychological, economic, and legal implications for adults and children. The more those who are experiencing this process understand its effects on themselves and their children, the better they can deal with its associated challenges. The establishment of court-connected information and education programs has been a significant aspect of reforming the family justice process in many jurisdictions.[21] While these programs do not have a standardized

---

19 Sarah Hampson, 'Ghost Dad, Not Deadbeat,' *Globe and Mail,* 17 January 2008.
20 See Andrew Schepard and James W. Bozzomo, 'Efficiency, Therapeutic Justice, Mediation, and Evaluation: Reflections on a Survey of Unified Family Courts' (2003) 37 Fam LQ 333.
21 For developments in the United States and a review of research studies on the effectiveness of these programs, see Susan L. Pollet and Melissa Lombreglia, 'A Nationwide Survey of Mandatory Parent Education' (2008) 46 Fam Ct Rev 375; and Tamara Fackrell, Alan Hawkins, and Nicole Kay, 'How Effective Are Court-Affiliated Divorcing Parents Education Programs?' (2011) 49 Fam Ct Rev 107 [Fackrell, 'Education

content, they typically provide basic information about the legal process and different methods of dispute resolution, with some emphasis on the value of settlement and non-adversarial dispute resolution, as well as some information about the emotional effects of separation on children. The programs are usually two to six hours, though some are longer and address 'skill building' with the intent of improving communication and parenting.[22]

Court-connected information programs serve a number of important objectives; in particular, they promote the use of alternative dispute resolution[23] and efforts by parents to reduce children's exposure to conflict.[24] These programs also provide an introduction to the family justice process for the growing number of unrepresented family litigants.[25] Making attendance mandatory for those who wish to access the family courts is the first of the four pillars of Ontario family justice reform.[26] Attendance at a session co-taught by a lawyer and a mental health professional or mediator is to precede an initial appearance in court, with exceptions for urgent cases where the safety of children or their removal from the jurisdiction is at issue.

A number of American studies[27] and two Canadian studies have

Programs']. For a review of programs in Alberta, see Joanne J. Paetsch *et al.*, *High Conflict Intervention Programs in Alberta: A Review and Recommendations* (Canadian Research Institute for Law and the Family, Alberta Justice, 2007). For proceedings in British Columbia, the Alberta Court of Queen's Bench (a six-hour course), and the Family Division of the Supreme Court of Nova Scotia, attending the parenting education program is mandatory for separating and divorcing parents prior to receiving a court order.

22 K.R. Blaisure and M.J. Geasler, 'The Divorce Intervention Model' (2000) 38 Family & Conciliation Courts Review 501.

23 Ontario Ministry of the Attorney General, *1998 Unified Family Court Expansion in Ontario: A Proposal to the Federal Department of Justice* (1998).

24 Andrew Schepard and Stephen W. Schlissel, 'Planning for P.E.A.C.E.: The Development of Court-Connected Education Programs for Divorcing and Separating Families' (1995) 23 Hofstra L Rev 845.

25 *Report of the Ontario Legal Aid Review: A Blueprint for Publicly Funded Legal Services*, vol. 1 (1997).

26 Proof of attendance is already mandatory at some court sites, including the Superior Courts in Toronto, Milton, Brampton, and Ottawa. By the summer, these requirements will be province-wide.

27 See Susan L. Pollet & Melissa Lombreglia, 'A Nationwide Survey of Mandatory Parent Education' (2008) 46 Fam Ct Rev 375; Fackrell, 'Education Programs,' *supra* note 21; and Amanda Sigal *et al.*, 'Do Parent Education Programs Promote Healthy Postdivorce Parenting? Critical Distinctions and a Review of Evidence' (2011) 49 Fam Ct Rev 120.

found that parents generally report satisfaction and modestly improved parenting skills as a result of taking such a program. The research also suggests that the greatest value is for those parents who have the least conflict.[28] While these programs can be valuable, they have the least impact on the higher-conflict cases, which take up a disproportionate amount of professional and court time and which have the highest social costs.

Given the low cost, the lack of possible negative effects, and the potential positive effects for children, the introduction of Mandatory Information Programs is a good initiative, but there needs to be more research on the value and cost-effectiveness of these programs, especially in terms of the justice system and potential conflict. The present Ontario plan requires attendance at only a single two-hour session with a limited standardized content, and is appropriately referred to as 'information' rather than 'parenting education.' The research suggests that it would be preferable to have at least two sessions of two or three hours each: the first for a general introduction and including issues of domestic abuse and the effects of divorce on children; and the second exploring options for dispute resolution and including an introduction to mediation and collaborative family law. Each session could be divided into two parts: the first part for all litigants, the second just for those with children. An optional third session to focus more on skills related to post-separation parenting would also prove helpful.

B. Identification of Cases and Referral: 'Triage' and the Second Pillar

The 'second pillar' of Ontario's family justice reform is an improved intake system, which includes establishing services that allow for the early identification of the matters in dispute, the level of conflict, and the risk of future violence, as well as referrals to community services that can address non-legal issues. One objective of the intake process is to expedite access to a lawyer and court hearings for high-risk cases. The parties in cases that are not high-risk – a majority of cases – are to be informed about the value of mediation services and non-adversarial dispute resolution, including negotiation.

There is growing international recognition of the value of a 'triage

---

28 Brenda L. Bacon and Brad McKenzie, 'Parent Education after Separation/Divorce: Impact of the Level of Parental Conflict on Outcomes' (2004) 42 Fam Ct Rev 85; and Shelley M. Kierstead, 'Parent Education Programs in Family Courts: Balancing Autonomy and State Intervention' (2011) 49 Fam Ct Rev 140.

model' of family justice rather than the traditional 'tiered approach.'[29] The tiered model has all cases follow a similar route through the court system until they are resolved either by settlement or by trial. The process generally starts with a referral to lawyers for negotiation or to mediation; from there, it moves to attempts at judicial settlement, then to assessment and perhaps appointment of child's counsel, and then, if necessary, to trial. A triage model provides for an initial assessment of the case and early access to the most appropriate method of dispute resolution. It is intended to provide more efficient and faster dispute resolution and to prevent parents and children from becoming engaged in intrusive processes that are unlikely to resolve their case.

Some jurisdictions, such as Connecticut, have a comprehensive and fairly sophisticated model of family justice triage, with trained court-affiliated staff interviewing all family litigants at the time of court filing and referring cases to the most appropriate government-funded or -subsidized program, which might involve mediation, counselling intervention, and comprehensive custody assessment.[30] The Connecticut model has a court-affiliated staff person who serves a gatekeeping function, rationing and optimizing the use of scarce publicly funded resources.[31] In Alberta, Family Court counsellors offer an intake service for unrepresented individuals. They can provide information and referrals to various government-funded or -subsidized services, assist in the preparation of court documents, or draw up an agreement that reflects terms that the parents have negotiated.

Ontario has had no formal system of triage, though case identification and gatekeeping do occur. For example, the Office of the Children's Lawyer (OCL) undertakes a limited form of triage, deciding which of

---

29 Peter Salem, 'The Emergence of Triage in Family Court Services: The Beginning of the End for Mandatory Mediation?' (2009) 47 Fam Ct Rev. 371 [Salem, 'The Emergence of Triage']. The movement towards a triage model is an implicit rejection of mandatory mediation and has provoked some controversy: see Hugh McIsaac, 'A Response to Peter Salem's Article, "The Emergence of Triage in Family Court Services: A Beginning of the End for Mandatory Mediation"' (2010) 48 Fam Ct Rev 190; Steve Baron, 'A Response to Salem: Common Sense' (2010) 48 Fam Ct Rev 195; and Peter Salem, 'A Distinction Without Much of a Difference: Response to Steve Baron and High MacIsaac' (2010) 48 Fam Ct Rev 201.

30 Salem, 'The Emergence of Triage,' *supra* note 29 at 380. The intake staff make a 'recommendation' to the parties about the most appropriate service, but they can appeal to a judge for an order for access to a different government-funded service.

31 Peter Salem, Debra Kulak, and Robin Deutsch, 'Triaging Family Court Services: The Connecticut Judicial Branch's Family Civil Intake Screen' (2007) 27 Pace L Rev 741.

the cases referred to it by court order it will accept and whether to offer the services of a clinical investigator, or a lawyer for the child, or both. Mediators are also expected to perform a limited gatekeeping function, identifying cases where mediation is not appropriate because of domestic violence or power imbalance concerns. Family lawyers in private practice may also engage in a kind of triage for their cases, identifying lower-conflict cases that might benefit from a collaborative resolution and distinguishing those that should begin with a demand letter from those where there should be an immediate court application.

Perhaps most significantly from the perspective of the justice system, at present some Ontario judges perform informal triage. At case conferences and interim motions, experienced family judges may encourage a couple to try mediation if that seems appropriate; or if conflict seems higher, they may suggest that an assessor be involved or order a referral to the OCL. If there is very high conflict, a judge may direct that there be case management of all court activity or an expedited trial date. But this type of judicial triage is undertaken with limited information and depends on the initiative of the individual judge.

There is an important reality for family justice that must be accounted for in any jurisdiction, especially where litigants have few or no resources to access dispute resolution services: cases tend to be resolved by the use of free or subsidized resources. Lawyers, mediators, custody assessors, and judges at the pre-trial stages often perform overlapping functions – meeting with parents, engaging in an evaluation of the case, providing suggestions for settlement and opinions about the range of likely outcomes at trial, and attempting to facilitate a negotiated settlement. However, presently in Ontario, parties with a disagreement only have assured access without charge to the courts;[32] understandably, parties without legal representation will tend to make use of this 'free resource,' even though from a societal perspective judges are by far the most expensive dispute resolvers and in many cases may not be the most effective.

Some versions of the Four Pillars proposals call for the government to hire highly skilled and trained mental health professionals, called case assessment coordinators (CACs). A meeting with a CAC would

---

32 In the Superior and Family Courts there are filing fees, but there are none in the Ontario Court of Justice. In some jurisdictions, the basic fees have been increased, but there the court filing fees include a right to make use of public mediation or other services that may facilitate resolution without additional charge.

be required before court documents could be filed (except for cases of urgency – for instance, where domestic violence is alleged).[33] The CAC would perform an initial assessment and make appropriate referrals. These CACs would be especially important for cases where individuals lacked representation, but meetings would be required even for those *with* legal representation. There are significant challenges to the establishment of a province-wide network of CACs to perform a real triage function. The development of methods to accurately assess cases and refer them to the appropriate service is still in its infancy, though significant work is being done to develop triage instruments.[34] Further, these professionals would have significant responsibilities and would require graduate level education in mental health or social work as well as a fairly sophisticated knowledge of family justice dispute resolution.

The qualifications required for this type of position are dependent on the role that a CAC would be expected to play, which in turn would be dependent on the nature of the family justice process in Ontario. If a system were established with a range of government-provided or -subsidized services, including mediation, crisis intervention, enhanced legal advice, and assessment, then the efficient and effective use of such services would clearly be improved by having a skilled professional perform a gatekeeping function and by requiring that those who wish to use these services be screened and referred to the most appropriate service. Absent a broad range of government-subsidized court-affiliated services, the 'triage' function would have little utility for litigants who lack resources to purchase services. For those who are represented by counsel, requiring an individualized consultation with a court staff person or CAC before allowing an application to the court would be both an unnecessary use of public resources and an inappropriate intrusion into the solicitor–client relationship.

Rather than the elaborate and comprehensive CAC model, the Ontario government extended its more modest program using information and referral coordinators (IRCs),[35] who were previously only

33 Landau, *Home Court Advantage, supra* note 4.
34 Michael Saini and Rachel Birnbaum, 'Unraveling the Label of "High Conflict": What Factors Really Count in Divorce and Separated Families' (2007) 51 Ontario Association of Children's Aid Societies Journal 14; and Rachel Birnbaum and Michael Saini, 'A Pilot Study to Establish Reliability and Validity: The Dimensions of Conflict in Separated Families' (2007) 51 Ontario Association of Children's Aid Societies Journal 23.
35 Similar services are provided in Alberta by Family Court Counsellors; for a generally positive assessment of the work of these counsellors, see Joanne J. Paetsch *et al., High*

at the seventeen Unified Family Court sites, to family courts throughout the province. The IRCs provide procedural and substantive legal information, make referrals, and offer limited assistance with completion of forms. In addition to IRCs, Ontario has established a Family Court Support Worker (FCSW) program to assist victims of family violence in getting urgent access to the courts. FCSWs are mainly employed by community agencies to provide support for victims of domestic abuse as they navigate the family court system. The FCSW provides those who identify as victims with information about the family court process and help to document the history of abuse for use in court, as well as making referrals to specialized services and supports in the community. The FCSW can also help with safety planning related to court appearances and victims to court.

Although IRCs do not perform a full triage function, they provide a voluntary form of triage and referral, and government provision of this type of service is likely to result in more efficient use of expensive court time, as well as assisting unrepresented individuals to understand and make use of the family justice system. The FCSW program is also intended to perform a triage function, facilitating access to appropriate protective services, including those available only by court order, for cases where there is the greatest risk. The biggest concerns at present relate to the qualifications and resourcing of the IRCs and FCSWs. Until it is clear that they have adequate resources, staff time, and training, it would not be appropriate to make a meeting with them mandatory or to expand their role to include a potentially very important, but challenging, mandatory triage function.

C. Mediation: Part of the Third Pillar

The increasing use of mediation over the past three decades has resulted in important improvements in the family dispute resolution process. For lower-conflict couples, a negotiated settlement facilitated by a mediator is certainly less expensive than litigation and more likely to meet their needs than a resolution imposed by a judge. Further, helping parents achieve their own mediated settlement has the 'transformative potential' to help them establish a constructive co-parent-

---

Conflict Intervention Programs in Alberta: A Review and Recommendations (Canadian Research Institute for Law and the Family, Alberta Justice, 2007).

ing arrangement; the parents may be helped to develop the skills and relationship to make their future plans on their own as their circumstances change, thereby reducing future demand on family justice services.

Despite the value of mediation, some of the rhetoric and research about family mediation overstates its value.[36] Proponents of mediation often base their claims about its value on a comparison of those who have chosen mediation with those who have chosen to litigate. This comparison, however, fails to take into account the fact that couples who choose mediation tend to be lower conflict than those who choose to litigate. The real comparison for most cases is not between mediation and a trial, but between mediation and a settlement negotiated by lawyers, or, for those without counsel, a settlement that a judge is likely to effect through the conferencing process. The systemic cost advantages of mediation are significantly reduced in such comparisons, and if mediation is mandatory and the costs of unsuccessful mandated mediations are included, those advantages may disappear.

There is a widespread recognition that family mediation cannot and should not resolve all cases. Instances where there are serious and ongoing power imbalances – for example, because of domestic violence or substance abuse issues – may not be suitable for mediation; while mediation may well result in a 'settlement' in such cases, a vulnerable party will very likely be exploited. There are also cases where the emotional state of one or both parties (or their personality disorders) causes them to be intransigent, making it impossible to achieve a reasonable and fair mediated settlement.

Further – and perhaps most significantly, given present fiscal realities in Ontario – the 'transformative' effect of mediation is most likely to be achieved through a mediation process that is relatively resource intensive and that allows sufficient time to properly address issues, especially if there is a higher level of conflict. There is, for example, promising research from Australia about the value of 'child-inclusive mediation' for improving both relationships between the parents and

---

36 For surveys of some of the limitations of the mediation and research rhetoric, see Salem, 'The Emergence of Triage,' *supra* note 29; and Joan B. Kelly, 'Family Mediation Research: Is There Empirical Support for the Field?' (2004) 22 Condlict Resolution Quarterly 3.

parent–child relationships, but this model of mediation requires highly skilled mediators with a sound knowledge of child development issues and is more resource intensive than traditional mediation.[37]

The Ontario government clearly appreciates the value of encouraging the use of mediation, not only for parents and children but also for the family justice system. Its support for mediation is manifested through various government educational efforts, and most significantly through the extension of mediation services to all family court sites as part of the Four Pillars reforms. These services offer some access to free mediation services in the courthouse on the day of a court attendance, as well as longer periods of subsidized 'off-site' mediation for lower and middle income clients. In addition to government-subsidized mediation services for low and middle income Ontario citizens, private mediators provide family mediation services for those with higher incomes.[38]

One of the most controversial policy questions about family justice in Ontario is whether, as was suggested at one point by Chief Justice Winkler and others, mediation should be 'mandatory' before a case can proceed through the courts.[39] Some American states have mandatory mediation for family cases. In 2006, as part of a major, resource-intensive package of reforms, Australia introduced a requirement that litigants must make a 'genuine effort' at mediation before an application can be made to the family courts, subject to certain exceptions – for example, if there are significant domestic violence concerns. Further, every case involving children was to be allotted three hours of mediation free of charge, and at a subsidized rate based on income thereafter. There was significant initial enthusiasm about these reforms in Australia, and there

---

37 Australian Government, Attorney-General's Department, *Children Beyond Dispute: A Prospective Study of Outcomes from Child Focused and Child Inclusive Post-Separation Family Dispute Resolution* by Jennifer E. McIntosh, Caroline M. Long, and Yvonne D. Wells (2009).

38 See, e.g., website of Ontario Association of Family Mediators, http://www.oafm.on.ca.

39 Judy Van Rhijn, 'Chief Justice Expands on Proposals to Redesign Family Law System: Winkler Undaunted by Mandatory ADR Critics,' *Law Times*, 8 November 2010, http://www.lawtimesnews.com/201011087841/Headline-News/Chief-justice-expands-on-proposals-to-redesign-family-law-system. For support for this idea, see, for example, Alfred A. Mamo, Peter G. Jaffe, and Debbie G. Chiodo, *Recapturing and Renewing the Vision of the Family Court* (2007), http://www.crvawc.ca/documents/Family%20Court%20Study%202007.pdf.

was an initial drop of 18 per cent in cases filed in the family courts.[40] However, due to government funding cuts, there will soon only be one hour of free mediation, which may have an effect on court filings.[41]

One lesson to be taken from the Australian experience is that it may not be possible in family cases to enforce a 'genuine effort' to mediate requirement. While parties can be required to *attend* mediation sessions, it is not uncommon for one or both parties to attend mediation with unrealistic expectations and with an unwillingness to compromise. In theory, a mediator in Australia can refuse to give an intransigent party a certificate of having made a 'genuine effort' to mediate; in practice, however, mediators will give any party who attends a mediation session the required certificate, thus allowing them to enter the family court process.[42] This is in part a reflection of the difficulty of determining whether a person has made a *'genuine* effort' to mediate as well as a result of the fact that refusal to give the certificate can (understandably) itself be challenged in court, dragging a mediator who refuses to issue a certificate into the litigation process. More fundamentally, it reflects an appreciation by Australian mediators that a significant number of family disputes cannot be settled by this process because of the inflexibility of one or both litigants.

The extension of government-supported mediation throughout Ontario in 2011 was a significant development. There is clearly value in educating individuals about the advantages of mediation, whether at mandatory individualized information sessions – which is the requirement in Quebec for family litigants with issues related to children (except in cases of family violence) – or through the mandatory information programs in Ontario. However, the experience in Australia raises real doubts about whether family litigants can be meaningfully mandated to attempt mediation. Further, there is no clear empirical evidence that government financial support for mandatory mediation is a good use of limited public resources. If, as would be likely, litigants were required to pay for mandatory mediation, this requirement would

---

40 See Patrick Parkinson, 'Parenting after Separation: The Process of Dispute Resolution in Australia' (2010) 330 Ritsumeikan Law Review 110.

41 Patricia Karvelas, 'Cuts to Send Family Battles Back to Court,' *The Australian,* 13 May 2010, http://www.theaustralian.com.au/news/nation/cuts-to-send-family-battles-back-to-court/story-e6frg6nf-1225865755234.

42 Hilary Astor, 'Making a "Genuine Effort" in Family Mediation: What Does It Mean?' (2008) 22 Austl J Fam L 102.

be a barrier to access to justice for those with limited resources, and would be exploited by some as a tactic to delay or increase costs to the other party.

Given the tendency of litigants – especially those who are self-repre-sented – to use resources that can be accessed without charge, there is a good argument that increasing the availability of free or significantly subsidized mediation services would decrease pressure on the courts and result in overall cost savings. Properly managed, the provision of more mediation services throughout Ontario might well result in cost savings to the justice system. However, in the absence of good research that such action would result in cost savings, making mediation man-datory for family cases is not justified at this time. The real issue in Ontario is not whether the government should be making mediation mandatory for family litigants, but rather how much government financial support there will be to ensure adequate voluntary access to mediation, and what measures will be in place to ensure that mediators are skilled and effective.[43] Present government plans, for example, do not provide support for access to the more effective but costly child-inclusive mediation, which has the greatest potential to change the atti-tudes and behaviours of high-conflict parents.

Related to the establishment of mediation services has been the intro-duction of the dispute resolution officer (DRO) project at the Superior Courts in Toronto, Brampton, Milton, and Newmarket. The *Family Law Rules* allow parties (whether represented or not) on motions to vary a family order in those locales to meet with a DRO before the case goes before a judge. The DROs are volunteer senior family law practitioners who meet with the parties and their counsel, if represented, to investi-gate settlement options and determine whether the file is ready to go before a judge. Such early evaluation of cases by a neutral third par-ty can facilitate what are essentially mediated settlements or at least narrow the issues in dispute. While there are always concerns about the sustainability and quality of services provided by volunteers, and research is needed to establish the cost-effectiveness of this project for

---

43 Mediators are required to have Accredited Mediator designation from the Ontario Association of Family Mediators or equivalent credentials. Funding is provided for an average of eight hours per case, including intake interviews. Subsidies are provided for single clients with a gross annual income below $60,000, or for a cli-ent with two dependants and an income below $70,000 a year. Ontario, *Request for Proposals for Family Mediation and Information Services,* No. OSS-079340, issued 21 Sep-tember 2010.

both parties and for the justice system, the DRO project certainly has the potential to facilitate settlements and reduce costs.

D. *Improving Access to Legal Services: Another Part of the Third Pillar*

Lack of access to appropriate legal services related to family disputes has repeatedly been identified as a major problem for litigants[44] and the family courts. It has been estimated that more than 50 per cent of all custody and access litigants in Ontario have no legal representation,[45] resulting in delays in the court process and placing further strain on judges and court staff as they try to help those who are without representation cope with the demands of the justice process. Lack of representation raises the prospect that the interests of children and adults may not be properly protected in the court process. The present eligibility criteria make Legal Aid Ontario accessible only to the very poorest Ontarians – those on Social Assistance or working at minimum-wage jobs.

Some individuals choose to represent themselves because they think they will do as good a job as a lawyer or because they have a desire to personally confront their former partners in court. Some may be concerned that having lawyers may increase the adversarial nature of the process. However, it is clear that the vast majority of those without lawyers in the family justice process are unable to afford the cost of legal services and are ineligible for legal aid.[46] The process of separation and

---

44 Law Society of Upper Canada, *Listening to Ontarians: Report of the Ontario Civil Legal Needs Project* (Toronto: Ontario Civil Legal Needs Project Steering Committee, 2010), http://www.lsuc.on.ca/media/may3110_oclnreport_final.pdf. See also Jamie Baxter, Michael Trebilcock, and Albert Yoon, 'The Ontario Civil Needs Project: A Comparative Analysis of the 2009 Survey Data,' *supra* this volume.

45 Barbara Landau *et al.*, OBA Family Law Section, ADR Institute of Ontario, and Ontario Association of Family Mediators, *Family Law Process Reform: Supporting Families to Support Their Children* (Toronto: Ontario Association for Family Mediation, 2009), http://www.oafm.on.ca/Documents/OBA%20OAFM%20ADR%20Institute%20submission%20Apr%207%2009.pdf at 6. Statistics Canada, *Navigating Family Transitions: Evidence from the General Social Survey* (Ottawa, 2007), reports that just 44 per cent of all those who had recently separated or divorced consulted a lawyer in private practice or at a legal aid clinic.

46 See Rachel Birnbaum and Nicholas Bala, 'Views of Ontario Lawyers on Family Litigants without Representation' (forthcoming 2012), University of New Brunswick Law Journal); and Anne-Marie Langan, 'Threatening the Balance of the Scales of Justice: Unrepresented Litigants in the Family Courts of Ontario' (2005) 30 Queen's LJ 825.

establishing two households is a very significant financial burden, and many are unable to afford a lawyer at this time; often when a lawyer is retained, it is because grandparents are providing assistance, or because the parents are using savings they had earmarked for retirement or for their children's education.

There has been a welcome increase in information available to the public about family law in print and on the Internet, provided by the Ontario government, the Law Society of Upper Canada, and various public legal education organizations and advocacy groups. Unfortunately, significant numbers of family litigants lack the literacy or language skills to make use of these resources. Further, for many of those facing family dissolution, information alone will never be adequate. Family law is substantively and procedurally complex; proper resolution of cases in this area may also require an understanding of the laws governing evidence, taxation, estates, land transactions, and other fields of law, as well as an appreciation of the psychological needs of parents and their children. Resolution of these cases may also require careful investigation of the parties' economic and social affairs. Further, these are cases in which emotions can run high, and it is important for individuals to be provided with objective, knowledgeable, and individualized advice about their specific case; such guidance can help resolve disputes without litigation. Presently in Ontario, judges sitting on family settlement conferences offer some of this individualized legal advice to unrepresented litigants, though in a fashion that is very expensive for the government compared to other means of providing such advice. Also, there are very understandable limitations imposed by the judicial role and by the fact that judges at this stage have incomplete information.

There are a number of measures that can help provide more legal information, advice, and assistance to those facing family law problems. Legal Aid Ontario has extended its family duty counsel, mediation, and advice programs for the very lowest income family litigants, though most of the 'working poor' – let alone middle income Ontarians – are ineligible for legal aid.[47] *Pro bono* legal work and student legal aid can also play a role, but it is important to appreciate the limits of what can be done by volunteers, without charge to clients or cost to the government, and to recognize that the most appropriate legal

---

47 For developments, see Legal Aid Ontario, 'LAO Newsroom,' http://www.lao.on.ca/en/news/default.asp.

advice can only be provided by lawyers with significant experience in this complex field.

There is also scope for an expansion of 'unbundled legal services.'[48] The division of responsibility between lawyers and clients has always been somewhat different in family law than in other areas. With ordinary civil litigation, lawyers once retained are likely to deal with all communications between the parties; by contrast, in family cases there will always be some direct communication between the parties. In lower-conflict cases, lawyers may encourage some limited direct negotiation between the parties about such matters as the details of access arrangements or the division of furniture and other personal property. Even when both parties are represented, they may decide to resolve significant matters on their own, subject to later consultation with their counsel.

The unbundling of legal services is becoming more common in family cases, with lawyers being retained not to provide *all* advice and representation on a family law case, but rather to provide limited advice or to handle specific tasks, such as drafting documents for one stage, or arguing one motion.[49] This is potentially challenging for both lawyer and client, and clearly not as desirable as full representation; but given the high cost of providing legal services and the growing public access to legal information, unbundling of legal services in family cases is a trend that should be encouraged. This type of lawyering requires adjustments by clients, lawyers, judges, and other professionals, and there needs to be clear information provided to clients about both the value of such assistance and the risks they run in doing some of their own work.[50] As in other areas of law, however, family litigants are

---

48 See Samreen Beg and Lorne Sossin, 'Should Legal Services Be Unbundled?', *supra* this volume.

49 See, for example, D.A. Rollie Thompson, 'No Lawyer: Institutional Coping with the Self-Represented' (2001) 19 Can Fam LQ 455; Marguerite Trussler, 'A Judicial View on Self-Represented Litigants' (2001) 19 Can Fam LQ 547; and Lonny L. Balbi, 'Self-Represented Litigants from the Mediator's Perspective: Walking the Line' (2001) 19 Can Fam LQ 583.

50 The Law Society of Upper Canada changed the Rules of Professional Conduct to more explicitly deal with 'limited scope' retainers on 22 September 2011. See Law Society of Upper Canada, '"Unbundling" of Legal Services and Limited Legal Representation: Background Information and Proposed Amendments to Professional Conduct Rules' (22 September 2011), http://www.lsuc.on.ca/WorkArea/Download-Asset.aspx?id=2147483764. See, also, e.g., Elliot A. Anderson, 'Unbundling the Ethical Issues of Pro Bono Advocacy: Articulating the Goals of Limited-Scope Pro Bono Advocacy for Limited Legal Services Programs' (2010) 48 Fam Ct Rev 685.

entitled to legal assistance proportionate to their means, the matters at issue, and their assessment of their own competence and ability to deal with their affairs. Accordingly, they may decide to use this type of limited legal assistance.

While family law cases are generally too complex and important for paralegals to provide full representation, there is some role for expanding the use of non-lawyers in this area, such as in regard to child support. Significantly, there are already government-paid non-lawyer family support workers to assist social assistance recipients with making applications for support (a program that surely pays for itself in terms of helping obtain support payments that reduce social assistance expenditures). Ontario should follow the lead of other provinces, such as Alberta, by establishing a child support recalculation service, largely making use of paralegals, to assist applications to increase (or reduce) child support orders if there has been a change in parental income.

E. Access to Legal Information and Resources for Self-Represented Persons

Although self-representation should not be encouraged, it is a growing reality that cannot be ignored, and self-represented individuals need access to good quality legal information and materials. Further, there is a need for access to such materials for those in the early stages of separation who may later retain counsel, as well as for those who will make use of unbundled legal services. While individuals need to be cautioned about the limitations and dangers of doing their own research and representing themselves, improving access to legal information and resources will improve access to family justice.

The Ontario government has significantly increased the amount of legal and social information available to separating spouses, parents, and in some cases children, through print materials available at the Family Law Information Centres (FLICs) at each court, and especially through the Internet.[51] The expanded network of Information & Referral Cordinators (IRCs) is also playing a role in improving access to this type of material and explaining its utility. Government has a responsibility to do more to provide access to legal materials, and doing so will both improve access to justice and result in more cases being fairly and expeditiously settled with less use of court time. Also, the Law Society

---

51 See, for example, Ontario, 'Forms Assistant,' https://formsassistant.ontariocourt-forms.on.ca/Welcome.aspx?lang=en.

should facilitate access by the public – in particular, self-represented litigants – and by the bar to its growing collection of family law materials, prepared for the bar admission program and continuing education programs. Such materials are, to a limited extent, available at law school libraries and to members of the bar, who can purchase papers online through the Access CLE portal of the Law Society. However, much better access could be provided through the Internet, at a modest fee per paper, in the same way that many scholarly journals now sell single articles to members of the public.[52]

One of the more interesting developments for improving public access to legal information is the creation by DIVORCEmate of a free-access website that allows a determination of basic amounts of child support under the *Child Support Guidelines*, and the range of support under the *Spousal Support Advisory Guidelines*.[53] Users of the site enter such information as the spouses' incomes and number of children and are then provided with the relevant figures. Financial support for the website is provided by subscribing law firms in the locality of a user, with firm names and links appearing on the site.

There is a good argument to be made that the federal and provincial governments should be providing this type of information to the public on a website that is certified as reliable; but for a variety of reasons, including concerns about costs and liability, this has not occurred. DIVORCEmate's initiative is most welcome and illustrates the commercial possibilities for improving public access to legal information. The website has obvious utility for those who are unrepresented and should facilitate the work of the courts and the IRCs. Of course, to properly apply the basic information provided by this website will usually require further, more individualized information and legal knowledge. In that regard, this website emphasizes the importance of

---

52 Noel Semple argues that there should be free access to these materials through the Internet or public libraries. As he notes, these papers are prepared by lawyers, judges, and academics, who are not paid. However, the Law Society incurs considerable expense in organizing the programs where the papers are presented and charges a significant fee for attendance or the purchase of program materials: Semple, 'Cost–Benefit Analysis,' *supra* note 45. In December 2011, the Law Society of Upper Canada approved a plan to initiate development of a pilot online family law platform to organize currently available information and provide a 'first stop' for users requiring assistance with family disputes: see www.lsuc.on.ca.

53 The website is developed by DIVORCEmate and Noel Semple: see http://www.mysupportcalculator.ca.

consulting a lawyer and may well encourage use of unbundled legal services.

One paradox of changes that allow those who are without legal representation to participate more effectively in the family justice system is that these changes may result in an increase in the number of people who decide that they will forgo the expense of retaining a lawyer. However, given the complexity and importance of their cases, no matter how much information is provided to the public, most of those who can reasonably afford legal assistance are likely to continue to hire lawyers for family cases.

F. Streamlining of the Court Process: The Fourth Pillar

Building on the other pillars, and especially triage, is the proposal for earlier identification of more complex or higher-conflict cases that are unlikely to be resolved by negotiation or mediation. Reform of the family court process is needed to allow for more focused judicial attention on these high-conflict cases and for a less costly, earlier trial process for them.

The *Family Law Rules* are complex, especially for the growing number of self-represented litigants, and should be simplified (which likely means giving judges more discretion). At the same time, there are some issues that need to be better addressed in the *Rules*. While detailed discussion of possible changes to the *Family Law Rules* and court procedures is beyond the scope of this paper, some general comments can be made.

One major problem in settling or litigating family cases is the difficulty in getting full and timely disclosure of information. In higher-conflict cases there is a tendency for some parties to try to hide assets or information instead of making full disclosure, as required by the *Family Law Rules*. Inadequate disclosure can be exacerbated in cases where a party is self-represented.[54] Better access to the courts, more case management, and greater use of cost sanctions would help address disclosure problems.

Historically, courts were have been reluctant to award costs in family cases, due to a disinclination to penalize parents whose emotions clouded their judgment and led to unnecessary trials. The reluctance to award costs also reflected the view that there is value to having a full judicial inquiry into the best interests of children. With the introduction

---

54 See, for example, *Poursadeghian v. Hashemi-Dahaj*, 2010 CarswellBC 2740 (WL Can) (CA).

of Rule 24 in 1999, there has been a trend towards ordering unsuccessful litigants in family disputes to pay at least a portion of the legal fees of the successful parties.[55] Still, courts need to be more aggressive in making cost awards in family cases, including at the interim stages,[56] to make clear to those who make unnecessary use of the courts or who refuse reasonable settlement offers that they are wasting the resources of the other party and the public and will be obliged to bear a significant portion of these costs. If a party is able to afford a lawyer but has chosen not to have one, and this appears to have contributed to unnecessary court appearances or litigation, it is especially appropriate to make this party pay the full costs of the other party.

The efficiency of the court process could also be improved by shifting some of the functions now performed by judges to other personnel. Some administrative, procedural, or quasi-judicial functions are now being performed by judges that could be carried out just as well by other court officials, leaving judges with more time to perform the most important and challenging tasks: settlement conferences and trials. In some jurisdictions, notably British Columbia and New Brunswick, there are special Family Law Masters[57] who play a significant role in the family court process. An Ottawa pilot project where Family Law Case Managers carry out some judicial functions has apparently succeeded in reducing delays and making better use of scarce and expensive judicial resources.[58] There may be some scope for expanding the role of Family Law Masters in the family justice process in larger centres – for example, in terms of supervising aspects of the disclosure process, support enforcement, and case management, or dealing with uncontested matters.

III. Developments and Needed Changes Beyond the Four Pillars

The Four Pillars reforms that are being undertaken are significant, but there have been a number of other developments in professional practice that need to be encouraged and reforms that need to be pursued to

---

55 See, for example, *Feng v. Phillips*, [2006] OJ no 1708 (QL) (Sup Ct J) and *M (A.C.) v. M(D.)*, [2003] OJ no 3707 (QL) (CA).
56 See, for example, *JC v. AK*, 2010 ONCJ 455 (available on QL).
57 A Master is a judicial officer who deals with a limited range of procedural and pretrial matters in the Superior Court. Masters are appointed by the provincial government.
58 Carleton County Law Association, Evaluation Subcommittee of the Family Law Bench and Bar Committee, *Evaluation of the Ottawa Family Case Manager Pilot Project: Year Two*, http://www.ccla-abcc.ca/uploadedFiles/Year_Two_Evaluation.pdf.

improve the family justice process in Ontario. Many of these are at least mentioned in some of the articulations of the Four Pillars,[59] but they are now receiving inadequate attention in public, professional, and political discussions about family reform.

A. More Collaborative Family Law

Although not formally part of the Ontario Four Pillars, a relatively recent, important development in the non-litigious resolution of family disputes is 'collaborative family law.' This is a non-adversarial method of resolving disputes that is related to mediation and negotiation but is distinct. At the start of the collaborative process, each party, after getting appropriate legal advice, signs a Participation Agreement which provides that each will use best efforts to settle through negotiation all of the issues at hand.[60] Most significantly, they agree that if they do not settle and therefore take any issue to court, they will each retain lawyers other than those used in the negotiation process; this gives the parties a significant financial incentive to settle.

Lawyers who are involved in collaborative family law cases have special training, are expected to ensure that their clients disclose all relevant information in a timely fashion, and must encourage them to settle the case. The parties often have 'four-way meetings' (both lawyers and their clients present) and typically jointly retain any expert who may be needed – for example, to value property or a pension. Although only an option for cases where both parties can afford to retain counsel, and clearly not suitable for all cases, if the lawyers involved have confidence in each other and the parties have a basic degree of trust and respect, collaborative family law can be a cost-effective way of producing a lasting, fair settlement that will be more acceptable to the parties than a resolution imposed by a judge. While there is always a danger that the party with greater resources (usually the husband) may attempt to exploit the situation to get a favourable agreement, knowing that the costs to the other party of 'starting over' with a new lawyer may be prohibitive, collaborative family law should be encouraged by the Law Society, the government, and the judiciary.

---

59 For the fullest and most widely endorsed version of the Four Pillars, see Landau, *Home Court Advantage, supra* note 4.

60 See Barbara Landau, Lorne Wolfson, and Niki Landau, *Family Mediation, Arbitration, and Collaborative Practice Handbook*, 5th ed. (Markham: LexisNexis, 2009).

In some cases, it may be appropriate for collaboratively trained law-yers to represent the parties without signing a Participation Agreement; this may facilitate a settlement without the risk of increased expenses from having to engage new counsel if an agreement is not achieved.

B. Continuity and Case Management: One Judge for the Family

While most family disputes can and should be resolved outside the court system through such means as collaborative family law or media-tion, there are many cases for which early and effective judicial involve-ment is necessary – in particular, in high-conflict cases or if there are unresolved allegations of violence, substance abuse, or mental health issues. Even if a range of non-court programs are made accessible across Ontario, cases involving high conflict or significant risk will often require significant judicial involvement to resolve disputes and ultimately change the behaviours of the parents.

There is growing recognition in many jurisdictions of the value of having high-conflict and high-risk family cases identified early and dealt with by one judge, who is skilled and knowledgeable in family matters.[61] This principle is reflected in a slogan that has widespread acceptance in jurisdictions where family justice has been significant-ly reformed: 'One judge for one family.'[62] A judge who has continu-ing responsibility for a case can gain knowledge of the family and the dynamics of the case and deal with it more efficiently and, ultimately, at a lower cost to the parties and the state. Further, appearing before the same judge should make parents (and their lawyers) feel more account-able and hence more likely to comply with court orders.

An important aspect of the judge's role as a case manager is that it allows the court to more efficiently carry out the traditional judicial role of decision maker – for example, by resolving all pre-trial disputes about procedural and interim matters (perhaps with the assistance of a designated Family Law Master). In some cases, the role of the judicial case manager will be to persuade or direct parents to engage with serv-

---

61 Hon. Donna J. Martinson, 'One Case–One Specialized Judge: Why Courts Have an Obligation to Manage Alienation and Other High-Conflict Cases' (2010) 48 Fam Ct Rev 180.
62 See Nicholas Bala, Rachel Birnbaum, and Donna J. Martinson, 'Differentiated Case Management for Family Cases: "One Judge for One Family"' (2011), 26 Can J Fam L 339.

ices provided by professionals outside the court system; in other cases, it will be to move a case towards an early trial. Further, the judge can attempt to change the attitudes and behaviours of parents, acting either alone or in conjunction with various service providers. Case management judges can encourage parents to seek counselling or attend educational programs. They can also monitor whether recommendations and court orders have been followed and whether there have been any changes in parental behaviour.

In some high-conflict cases, such as those involving alienation or domestic violence, it may also be important for a judge to remain seized with a case after adjudication, to monitor compliance with the implementation of the court order and, as appropriate, to revise the judicially established plan. Where appropriate and available, post-adjudication case management may involve having mental health professionals or social workers report to the court on a case, or appointing a parenting coordinator to work with a high-conflict couple, as will be further discussed below.

In one of the few published studies involving a control group to empirically assess the effects of reforms in the family justice process, Higgins reported on the Australian Magellan Project, which was established to deal with custody and access cases where there were allegations of child sexual abuse at selected sites.[63] The Magellan Project has a case management team that includes a judge and a family consultant (social worker), who take charge of a case with sexual abuse allegations as soon as it is identified in the pleadings and continue with it until it is resolved, with access to significant coordinated community resources at the early stages. The outcomes were compared to a matched group of cases in other centres that were handled in a more traditional way. The managed cases had significantly fewer court appearances and were resolved significantly faster (10.8 versus 15.4 months). Of course, the Higgins study is not a 'perfect test' of case management, as there were also resource differences between the different sites, but a number of justice system professionals who were interviewed for the research project specifically commented on the value of case management and judicial continuity.[64]

---

63 Daryl J. Higgins, *Cooperation and Coordination: An Evaluation of the Family Court of Australia's Magellan Case-Management Model* (Canberra and Melbourne: Family Court of Australia, Australian Institute of Family Studies, 2007).

64 Australia is also experimenting with another version of case management, the 'Less

Varying forms of case management are being used successfully for some family cases in Ontario, especially where there are Unified Family Courts. In some locales there is a bifurcated form of case management, with one judge dealing with all contested matters and the other dealing with all conferences. In places where there is no Unified Family Court, there appears to be significantly more use of case management for family cases in the Ontario Court of Justice than in the Superior Court. While the *Family Law Rules* provide for case management and there is 'selective case management' for high-conflict cases in the Superior Court, there appears to be institutional resistance in that Court to family law case management. The reluctance of the Superior Court to make more use of case management may in part reflect a continued commitment to having circuiting non-specialist judges. Wide use of case management for family cases is administratively difficult to arrange if judges have a general jurisdiction and may be assigned to sit in many different locales. Further, judges without specialized knowledge and experience may find family case management very challenging.

Ontario would have a more effective and more efficient family justice process if there were more use of case management for high-conflict cases, but this would require some rethinking of judicial roles and administrative structures.

C. Assessments and the Role of Mental Health Professionals in the Justice System

Mental health professionals who have expertise in child development and parenting issues often have a very useful perspective on family cases. At one time it was common for parents involved in litigation regarding children to each retain their own mental health experts to come to court to testify in support of their case. In the late 1970s, however, it became more common for the courts to appoint one expert to

---

Adversarial Trial' (LAT), or what could be called the 'More Inquisitorial Family Litigation Process.' It is used for cases where custody or access is at issue. One judge and one family consultant (social worker) are assigned to a case from first appearance until resolution, and the judge takes a significant role in questioning the parties and deciding what evidence will be called. While this process seems to result in less hostility and a more child-focused process than a traditional adversarial trial, research also suggests that it is more costly for both the government and the parties. See Rae Kaspiew *et al., Evaluation of the 2006 Family Law Reforms* (Melbourne: Australian Institute of Family Studies, 2009) at ch. 14.

assess both parents and meet with the children and to provide a set of recommendations about a parenting plan that would best meet the needs of the children. By meeting with both parents and observing each of them with the children, the court-appointed assessor can gain a better understanding of family dynamics than an expert retained by either side. Having a single expert is also less expensive, and this professional is less likely to be perceived as biased than an expert retained by one of the parties.

In Ontario, for disputes between parents, section 30 of the *Children's Law Reform Act*[65] allows the court to appoint an assessor. That assessor is paid by the parties, with the fees apportioned as the court directs, often to be shared equally. Costs vary but are often in the range of $10,000 to $25,000 for a psychologist or psychiatrist. There is also the possibility under section 112(1) of the *Courts of Justice Act*[66] for a court to make an order requesting that the Office of the Children's Lawyer (OCL) have a 'clinical investigator' (social worker) carry out an 'investigation' and prepare a report; that report, pursuant to section 112(3), 'shall form part of the evidence' at the hearing.[67] The cost of preparing these reports is borne by the OCL (Ministry of the Attorney General). The parties may still retain their own experts to critique or support the recommendations of the court-appointed assessor or the OCL, or to provide added information, but in most cases where there is evidence from a neutral mental health professional, that person is the only expert to testify. Further, when there is a divergence of opinion between a court-appointed expert and a party's retained expert, there is a tendency to prefer the opinions of the court-appointed expert, who has access to both parties and who may be perceived as more objective.

In many cases the parents will voluntarily accept the recommendations of the assessor as the basis for a settlement, resulting in a less expensive and embittered process than if the matter went to trial.[68] Because of the importance of settlements in the resolution of family law disputes, assessments are significant tools for lawyers and parents in determining the chances of success at trial and the merits of settlement

---

65 R.S.O. 1990, c.C.12.

66 R.S.O. 1990, c.C.43.

67 In *ACB v. RB*, 2010 ONCA 714 (available on QL), evidence provided by the OCL indicated that an order for a clinical investigation and/or representation is made in about 60 per cent of all cases in which there is a request from the courts (*ibid.* at para. 5).

68 Clinical investigators from the OCL have a report disclosure process that is intended to facilitate and encourage settlements.

proposals. The family law cases that go to trial after an assessment are likely to be those where experts have divergent views, or where there is a sound basis for challenging the expert's evidence or views, or where a party is acting in an ill-informed fashion (which is more likely if that person is self-represented).

There are certainly cases in which it is appropriate for parents to question the recommendations of an assessor or for a court to disregard the assessor's recommendations. Assessment is not an exact science, and the education, skills, experience, and values of assessors will affect their evaluations and recommendations.[69] Some assessors may lack the experience or qualifications to assess certain types of cases, such as those where there may be issues of parental alienation or domestic violence. There are times when the assessor may have failed to understand or appreciate the facts of a case; and there are, in some cases, concerns about bias or preconceived views of an assessor, notwithstanding that the court has appointed them.[70]

Assessments clearly have value for child-related family disputes, but it is becoming increasingly difficult to find qualified mental health professionals who are willing to do this type of work, which is a problem in itself and which is contributing to the likelihood of lengthy delays when an assessment is ordered. One reason for the shortage of mental health professionals who are willing to perform assessments for family proceedings is that they are often the subjects of unwarranted complaints to their professional bodies by disgruntled family litigants. Not infrequently unfounded complaints are made strategically for the purpose of precluding the expert from testifying in family court, or by personality disordered parents who consider an assessor "biased" for having made negative comments about them. Unfounded complaints are eventually dismissed, but only after often protracted and expensive proceedings for the professional; even so they are a significant factor in driving mental health professionals away from acting as assessors, which increases the delay and expense involved in obtaining assessments.[71] There are a number of different strategies that could address

---

69 Nicholas Bala, 'Tippins and Wittmann Asked the Wrong Question: Evaluators May Not be "Experts," But They Can Express Best Interests Opinions' (2005) 43 Fam Ct Rev 554.

70 Nicholas Bala, 'Expert Evidence, Assessments, and Judicial Notice: Understanding the Family Context' in *Evidence in Family Law Cases*, ed. Harold Niman and Anita Volikis (Aurora: Canada Law Book, 2010), ch. 5-1.

71 See Nicholas Bala *et al., Protecting the Integrity of Family Law Litigation: Preventing*

the problem of unwarranted complaints by family litigants. For instance, professional bodies that regulate assessors should generally investigate a complaint against an assessor only *after* the completion of family proceedings, and they should review the relevant family court decisions to ascertain whether there is a sufficient basis to proceed with the complaint.[72] Family court judges are generally well placed to recognize assessors who have failed to meet minimum professional standards, and their decisions should be considered by regulatory bodies before an investigation is commenced.

In the 1970s and early 1980s, a network of Family Court Clinics was established in Ontario. At the core of this network were four university-affiliated clinics in Toronto, Ottawa, Kingston, and London. These university-affiliated clinics had multidisciplinary teams engaging in education, training, and research, as well as service provision in child welfare, young offender, and custody and access cases. The university-affiliated clinics provided leadership and support for smaller, service-oriented clinics in other centres, as well as for professionals in private practice. They also played a critical role in the education of forensic child and youth mental health professionals.

Over the course of the 1990s, the Family Court Clinic network in Ontario was largely dismantled, through dramatic reductions in the funding of some clinics and termination of funding for others.[73] This resulted in some clinics disappearing altogether, as well as dramatic reductions in staff and services at the others. The university-affiliated Family Court Clinics provided supervised clinical experience and mentoring of the kind that mental health professionals need to complement their academic education so that they can become competent assessors. Unfortunately, the clinics no longer provide the education, training, leadership, support, and research needed for a healthy network of assessors across the province. While some formal educational quali-

---

Vexatious Complaints Against Assessors (2009), http://www.sgmlaw.com/media/PDFs/Famlawassessors.PDF; and Neoh, 'Run for the Hills,' *supra* note 17. See also 'Child-Custody Assessors at Risk: Doctors' Group,' *National Post,* 5 March 2010. There is also a tendency to undertake unnecessarily lengthy and costly 'defensive assessments,' which are more detailed than the case requires but are intended to protect the assessor in the event of a possible complaint to a regulatory body.

72 This is the approach in British Columbia.

73 John S. Leverette, 'Enhancing the Learning Curve in Child and Adolescent Forensic Psychiatry: Inter-Professional Relationships, Resource and Policy Development' (2004) 17 Current Opinions in Psychiatry 391.

fications are a necessary prerequisite for a career as a forensic mental health professional, the specialized clinical experience that only a properly funded, university-affiliated Family Court Clinic can provide is also essential if assessors are to be competent and provide appropriate assistance to the court system.[74]

The generation of Ontario assessors who were educated in the clinic system in the 1980s is now approaching retirement. Unless university-affiliated Family Court Clinics are re-established and properly resourced, within a decade there will be few qualified professionals able to do this work, and it will not be possible to effectively address the shortage of qualified assessors. It would clearly be desirable for the government to work with universities and other agencies to revitalize Family Court Clinics, which would have educational, training, research, and professional-support functions, as well as responsibility for provision of assessment services.

Assessments are expensive, but a good assessment can significantly reduce the likelihood of an even more expensive and embittering trial and, even if there is a trial, an assessment should result in a more child-focused resolution. Judges and lawyers can help reduce the costs of assessments by more clearly identifying the matters in dispute and by ordering assessments that are more focused and hence less expensive.[75] Increased government support for the assessments carried out by the OCL may result in more settlements and certainly reduce costs for litigants, and very likely save court time.

---

74 Beginning in 2011, the University of Toronto School of Social Work has started to offer a six-day (forty-eight-hour) certificate workshop series on custody and access, and a three-day advanced program. While this is a very welcome and badly needed educational initiative, it is not the same as the type of supervised clinical educational experience that was provided by the clinics. See 'Foundations for Conducting Custody Evaluations,' at University of Toronto, Factor-Inwentash Faculty of Social Work, http://www.socialwork.utoronto.ca/conted/workshops/custody.htm. While the clinic system has effectively been dismantled, the clinic in London, Ontario, continues to do research and provide some leadership for service providers: see www.lfcc.on.ca.

75 See, for example, Rachel Birnbaum, 'An Examination of Two Different Approaches to Visitation-Based Disputes in Child Custody Matter' in *Practising Social Work Research: Case Studies for Learning*, ed. Rick Csiernik, Rachel Birnbaum, and Barbara Decker Pierce (Toronto: University of Toronto Press, 2010) at 237; and Rachel Birnbaum and Helen Radovanovic, 'Brief Intervention Model for Access-based Post-Separation Disputes: Family and Court Outcomes' (1999) 37 Journal of the Association of Family and Conciliation Courts Review 504.

D. The Child's Role: The Children's Lawyer and Judicial Interviews

Children are the primary victims of high-conflict separations, and too frequently either their views and perceptions are ignored by parents and professionals, or they are pressured by one parent to express views supporting that parent. It is important for their long-term emotional well-being that children feel that they have been consulted in a sensitive way about the arrangements for their care, though they must not be pressured into taking sides or expressing views that they would rather keep private.

As discussed above, the views of children may be introduced in the mediation process as well as in court through an assessment. In Ontario, the courts may make an order *requesting* that the OCL become involved, with that office deciding whether to provide legal representation, undertake a clinical investigation, provide legal representation with a 'clinical assist,' or not to become involved. The Ontario Court of Appeal has recently affirmed that, once the request is made, it is the OCL, not the courts, that should decide whether and how that office will be involved.[76] This reflects the fact this office has a limited budget and must make decisions about how to allocate its resources.

In Ontario, if a child has a clear preference for residing with one parent, a lawyer appointed for the child will generally advocate based on the child's wishes, though these lawyers must ultimately advocate a position based on their own assessment of what is in the child's interests.[77] If the lawyer believes that the child is 'alienated' and that the views expressed are not independent, that may affect the lawyer's willingness to advocate based on the child's views, though counsel for the child is always to ensure that the court is aware of the child's views.

In practice, a lawyer for the child will often try to encourage the parents to settle their dispute,[78] as the emotional tension associated with a

---

76 *ACB v. RB,* 2010 ONCA 714 (available on QL). Some passages in this judgment suggest that there may still be a narrow residual power, in appropriate cases, for judges to appoint counsel for children.

77 See, for example, Rachel Birnbaum and Nicholas Bala, 'The Child's Perspective on Legal Representation: Young Adults Report on Their Experiences with Child Lawyers' (2009) 25 Can J Fam L 11.

78 The settlement promotion role is reflected in the Office of the Children's Lawyer, *Policy Statement: Role of Child's Counsel* (Toronto: Office of the Children's Lawyer, 2006): '4. Resolution. At all stages of the proceedings, efforts will be made by child's counsel to resolve the disputed issues by communicating with the parties and their counsel, and by attending at settlement meetings and pre-trials.'

trial is very stressful for children, and children often say that their greatest wish is for their parents to stop arguing and get along.[79] This settlement promotion role is important for children, parents, and Ontario's family justice system, and there must be continuing support and recognition for the role played by the OCL. Indeed, there is a real likelihood that if funding for the OCL were increased, a greater number of high-conflict cases would be settled, resulting in savings to the justice system.

While judges in Ontario have traditionally been very reluctant to meet with children who are the subject of disputes between parents, this practice is now common in some other jurisdictions. A relatively brief judicial meeting with a child on one occasion cannot provide the court with a reliable sense of a child's views and perspectives, but it can give the judge some insights about the child. In cases where an assessment has not been completed and no counsel has been appointed for the child, a judge who has met with the child at the interim or conference stage may be able to communicate information to the parents that may help them achieve a settlement.[80] In particular, if – as is commonly the case – the judge reports to the parents about the anguish of the child at the parents' disagreement and the child's desire for a resolution, this may help push the parents towards a settlement, with the result that proceedings are resolved with less expense and bitterness. In cases that go to trial, an assessment by a mental health professional or counsel for the child will provide the court with much fuller and more reliable information about the children and their wishes than a judicial interview. Even in these situations, however, there may also be value for both the child and the court in having the child meet the judge.

E. Supervised Visitation, Parenting Co-ordination, and Court-Directed Interventions

In high-conflict cases there may be an important role for a judicial order to allow for the appointment of mental health or social service professionals who can, hopefully, improve relationships between parents or at least facilitate contact. Ontario has a network of community-based cen-

---

79 The Alberta Institute of Law Research and Reform reported that 90 per cent of the cases in which a lawyer was appointed for the child were settled out of court. See Alberta Law Reform Institute, *Protection of Children's Interests in Custody Disputes: Report No. 43* (Edmonton: Alberta Law Reform Institute, 1984).

80 Rachel Birnbaum and Nicholas Bala, 'Judicial Interviews with Children in Custody and Access Cases: Comparing Experiences in Ontario and Ohio' (2010) 24 Int'l JL Pol'y & Fam 300.

tres that can supervise visits or an exchange of the child. These centres facilitate visits so that estranged, high-conflict parents do not need to have direct contact, and the cost of the services is subsidized by the government for lower income parents. It is certainly preferable for parents to have contact with their children without such professional involvement, but in some cases, especially where there are concerns about spousal or child abuse, or problems related to drug or alcohol abuse, these centres provide a valuable service by enabling post-separation involvement of both parents in the lives of their children. This can be especially important if there are serious but unproven allegations that must be resolved by the justice system before unsupervised contact can be permitted.

In many jurisdictions, it is becoming increasingly common for a parenting coordinator to be appointed to help high-conflict separated parents implement a parenting plan. These professionals are, in effect, performing a mediation role, and in some cases they may also be arbitrating the details of the parenting plan. A number of American states have statutes that allow for the appointment of parenting coordinators, and British Columbia has also enacted such a law.[81] While parenting coordination is only an option for relatively wealthy parents who can afford to engage such services, this is a potentially valuable resource, and the enactment of legislation to allow for the appointment of these professionals might well encourage their use.[82] Available research sug-

---

81 *Family Law Act*, SBC 2011, c.25, s.14 (not yet in force). British Columbia, Ministry of the Attorney General, *White Paper on* Family Relations Act *Reform: Proposals for a New Family Law Act* (2010), at B.C., Ministry of Attorney General, http://www.ag.gov. bc.ca/legislation/pdf/Family-Law-White-Paper.pdf.

82 The Alberta *Court of Queen's Bench Family Practice Notes* allow judges to direct that mental health and child development experts 'intervene' with a family, although appropriate services are available only in Edmonton. See Marguerite Trussler, 'Managing High Conflict Family Law Cases for the Sake of the Children' (2008) 86 Can Bar Rev 515.

The court may direct that neither parent can make an application to the court during the intervention process. The therapy is not confidential, as the team is expected to communicate with the court. The parties do not receive a copy of any letters or reports to the court unless so ordered. The intervention typically involves at least three professionals working with the family: one for each parent and one for the child or children. The parents may at some point be seen together if appropriate. The therapeutic intervention involves different team members meeting with different family members in various combinations to address the issues. This model includes both therapy and assisting the parents to develop a parenting plan through a directive mediation process. There is no public funding and parents are responsible for paying the fees in full by way of a retainer to the team. While expensive, this type of intervention is less costly and more child-focused than a trial. Anecdotal reports

gests that appointment of a parenting coordinator reduces the likelihood of further court filings and ultimately saves private and public
resources.[83]

F. Recognizing 'High End' Privatized Family Justice

One of the interesting developments in family dispute resolution in
Ontario, and especially in the Greater Toronto Area (GTA), has been
the rise of arbitration and 'med/arb' as practical responses to problems
in the justice system for relatively wealthy family law litigants.[84] While
arbitration of disputes has long been common in labour and commercial law, it was only in the 1990s that family law practitioners in Ontario
began to make considerable use of it. Particularly in the GTA, concerns
about delays in the family courts and a lack of specialist family law
judges prompted a number of senior family law practitioners to look
to one another (and sometimes to senior mental health practitioners)
to help resolve disputes, either as mediators or arbitrators. The practice
of med/arb has become quite common. Med/arb involves a mediator who tries to facilitate a settlement; if some issues are not resolved
through mediation, the mediator will then arbitrate those matters.
While there are potential problems with med/arb, it can be an effective
way of resolving family disputes.

Even though the parties have to pay for a dispute resolver in addition to their own lawyers, for wealthier family law litigants, especially
in the Toronto area, private mediation, arbitration, and med/arb are
often preferable to having to resort to public programs and the courts,
as these private processes may well be faster and more predictable,
and are certainly more confidential.[85] For those with significant wealth

---

suggest that this type of intervention is often effective, but there has as yet been no
research on the Edmonton project.

In appropriate cases where there are clients with means and mental health professionals are available, judges in Ontario already have the jurisdiction to order therapeutic intervention for parents and children. There is value to closer collaboration
between the courts and mental health professionals, and it should occur in individual cases, but further research into the various models of court-directed interventions
is needed before Ontario changes its laws.

83 William J Henry, Linda Fieldstone, and Kelly Bohac, 'Parenting Coordination and
Court Relitigation: A Case Study' (2009) 47 Fam Ct Rev 682.
84 See, for example, Stephen Grant, 'Alternate Dispute Resolution in Family Law:
What's Not to Like?' (2008) 27 Can Fam LQ 235.
85 See Semple, 'Cost–Benefit Analysis', *supra* note 45 at ch. IV.

compared to litigation costs, it may be more cost-effective to pay a knowledgeable arbitrator to resolve a dispute rather than rely on a generalist judge to conduct a trial. It is perhaps ironic, though undoubtedly unplanned, that in most major centres in Ontario outside the GTA (e.g., Ottawa, London, Kingston, and Hamilton), even wealthier litigants seem less likely to resort to arbitration or med/arb as they have access to the experienced specialist judges of the Unified Family Courts.

From a public policy perspective, the creation of a 'private family justice system' in the GTA is not totally unproblematic. It is in effect 'two-tiered' justice, with wealthier litigants enjoying access to faster, confidential dispute resolution by professionals who have the specialized knowledge and skill set to deal effectively with family cases. On the other hand, it gets a significant number of cases out of the court system, thus reducing the demands on an already resource-stressed public system. Further, it allows those individuals with means to choose how they will resolve their disputes, and in many cases it results in a mediated settlement that the parties have taken the lead in crafting. The existence of this private family justice system was acknowledged by the Ontario legislature with the enactment of legislation in 2006 that requires those who conduct family arbitration to be members of a regulated profession, undergo domestic violence training, and apply Canadian law; that legislation also makes their decisions enforceable by legal process as well as subject to judicial appeal on the basis of an error of law.[86]

If an adequately rostered Unified Family Court with specialist judges is established in Toronto, it will be interesting to see what effect this will have on the private family justice system in the GTA. Regrettably, this development seems unlikely to occur in the near-term future, and until it does, public policy should continue to recognize and support private approaches to family justice, though without subsidizing them. While this may constitute 'two-tier justice,' we live in an economically tiered society, and even if Toronto gets a UFC, there will continue to be some role for private family dispute resolution in that region and throughout the province.

Many family litigants cannot afford to pay their own lawyers, let alone pay for an arbitrator, and this privatized family justice model is only viable in places where there is a fairly large pool of wealthy clients. There are clearly some advantages to the private processes – advan-

---

86 Bill 27, 2nd Sess., 38th Leg., Ontario, 2006 (assented to 23 February 2006).

tages that should be adopted in the courts. Most notably, given the interests of children, there should be a greater degree of privacy in the family courts. Other jurisdictions, such as Quebec, restrict identification, reporting, and access to court records for family cases – something that should be done in Ontario as well.

G. Unified Family Courts

At present, in many places in Ontario, family proceedings are dealt with at both levels of trial court – the Superior Court and the Ontario Court of Justice – with federally and provincially appointed judges dividing responsibility for family cases while also dealing with non-family cases. This has resulted in inefficiency[87] as well as in duplication of proceedings and services. In Canada, appointing judges who have comprehensive jurisdiction over family matters, including domestic, child welfare, and enforcement issues, requires cooperation between the federal and provincial levels.[88] The first Unified Family Court was established in Ontario in 1977 in Hamilton as a 'pilot program.' It had three central features: comprehensive jurisdiction over family disputes, specialist judges, and court-connected support services. The UFC was slowly extended to seventeen other sites in Ontario. Policy-oriented writing in Canada and elsewhere has strongly advocated the extension of UFCs,[89] and research on UFCs in Canada clearly indicates that this

---

87 In its recent decision in *ACB v. RB*, 2010 ONCA 714 (available on QL), the Ontario Court of Appeal remarked on the inefficiency of not having a Unified Family Court: 'The fact that Toronto does not have a Unified Family Court and that jurisdiction is split between the Ontario Court of Justice and the Superior Court makes *it more difficult for some family matters to be dealt with efficiently.* In a Unified Family Court, it is quite possible that at the same time as the interim custody order was made, the question of possession of the matrimonial home would also have been resolved on an interim basis. It is also possible that the court record concerning the CCAS proceeding would have been available' (*ibid.*, note 4, per Weiler JA [emphasis added]).

88 This is because the *Constitution Act, 1867* (UK), 30 & 31 Vict, c.3, s.96, reprinted in R.S.C. 1985, App II, No. 5, allows only the federal government to appoint judges to deal with matters traditionally within the jurisdiction of the superior courts, including divorce, division of property, and the making of exclusive possession orders. See *Ontario (AG) v. Canada (AG)*, [1982] 1 SCR 62. The provincial government, however, has jurisdiction over the administration of justice, including the court structure and rules, and may appoint judges who deal with child welfare cases and such family issues as support, custody, and access.

89 See, for example, J.G. McLeod, 'The Unified Family Court Experience in Ontario' (2004) [unpublished]; Alfred A. Mamo, Peter G. Jaffe, and Debbie G. Chiodo, *Re-*

model of family justice has the potential to increase the effectiveness and efficiency of the family dispute resolution process.[90]

As reflected in the Four Pillars (and discussed in this chapter), access to a range of legal and non-legal services – including parenting education, mediation, assessments, child representation, legal advice, and triage services – is essential for the most effective resolution of family cases. Having a single court makes it more efficient to offer such services. Further, appointing judges with the specialized knowledge, skill sets, and interests to deal with family cases is facilitated by having this type of court – indeed, specialist judges are necessary if UFCs are to function effectively. Judges with this type of caseload can acquire the interdisciplinary financial, child development, and family relations knowledge to deal most effectively with these cases. Although it is possible to have case management without a unified court, clearly this court structure assists family law case management.

In some smaller locales, judges sitting on the UFC might also deal with other types of cases, so that they are intensively, but not necessarily exclusively, family judges. In larger centres, however, there is more than enough family work to allow for full specialization. A UFC model does not preclude periodic judicial rotation into and out of this court, but such courts are clearly premised on having judges with a significant degree of specialization and interest in family law.

The frustratingly slow pace of extending UFCs in Ontario is, in part, a result of the difficulty in achieving federal and provincial cooperation in making appointments. Until now, there has also been a concern about the cost of funding the support services for new sites. Although the resistance to increased spending has sometimes effectively resulted in resistance to the extension of UFCs, there is no logical reason for this. As the recent extension of family justice services across Ontario demonstrates, services can be extended without UFCs, and UFCs have value even without an extension of services, though clearly having such services available increases the effectiveness and efficiency of a UFC.

There is still some resistance to UFCs among some members of the

---

capturing and Renewing the Vision of the Family Court (2007), http://www.crvawc. ca/documents/Family%20Court%20Study%202007.pdf; and Barbara A. Babb, 'Reevaluating Where We Stand: A Comprehensive Survey of America's Family Justice Systems' (2008) 46 Fam Ct Rev 230.

90 Department of Justice Canada, Evaluation Division, Office of Strategic Planning and Performance Management, *The Unified Family Court Summative Evaluation: Final Report* (Ottawa: Department of Justice Canada, 2009).

judiciary, who are concerned about the administrative and philosophical effects of moving away from a generalist Superior Court. It is important to be realistic about the limits of any family court to solve family relationship problems[91] (and about the limits of any court to solve human problems), and to recognize that the effectiveness of the Unified Family Court will be affected by the judicial and other resources available. The efficiency and efficacy of a UFC compared to the present divided jurisdiction is clear, however, and Ontario can no longer afford a model of family justice that was developed in the nineteenth century.

IV. The Need for a Cultural Shift Among Justice System Professionals

The effectiveness of the family justice process for those who are experiencing separation and divorce depends as much strongly on the attitudes and skills of lawyers and judges as it does on the support services and legal structures in place. The understanding of lawyers and judges about their roles and responsibilities in family disputes has been evolving, but the 'cultural shift' must be deepened and broadened.[92]

Although legal professionals are not psychologists, they must have an understanding of the social and emotional needs of those experiencing separation, as well as an appreciation that attitudes and needs will often change over time as families go through the separation process. Lawyers and judges must have knowledge of child development issues. They must also encourage parents to understand and give priority to the interests of their children, and warn their clients about the harmful effects of conflict on their children. While there will always be a role for courts and the adversarial system in dealing with some cases, legal professionals need to do more to encourage settlement. Lawyers should avoid increasing conflict through the drafting of inflammatory pleadings and affidavits and should carefully consider the effect that their letters and litigation tactics may have on parental relationships and on any children.[93] Family lawyers and judges need to recognize

---

91 On the need for realism about the limits of any 'problem solving court,' including a Family Court, see Jane M. Spinak, 'Romancing the Court' (2008) 46 Fam Ct Rev 258.

92 This change in the culture of family law is an aspect of a broader change in the role of lawyers. See Julie Macfarlane, *The New Lawyer: How Settlement Is Transforming the Practice of Law* (Vancouver: UBC Press, 2008).

93 For an excellent discussion of how the language used in pleadings and affidavits can needlessly exacerbate conflict, see Assistant Chief Judge Victor T. Tousignant, 'Con-

their responsibility in helping clients develop new post-separation parenting attitudes and behaviours. Legally trained professionals need to be comfortable in working with professionals from other disciplines and in making appropriate referrals. There needs to be more and better interdisciplinary collaboration.

While the ultimate responsibility for changing the culture of the practice of family law is on individual professionals, there are collective and systemic measures that can help in this process. Having more specialization can certainly help professionals gain the expertise and understanding to deal more effectively with family cases. Legal educators – both in law schools and for practising professionals – need to provide opportunities for skills development and multidisciplinary education as well as address issues of ethics in family dispute resolution. Providing mentors for new members of the legal profession who want to practise family law is also very important, especially since there are few articling positions that provide exposure to family law.

V. Conclusion: Effecting Change in the Family Justice System

Ontario is in the midst of reforming its family justice processes. The recent extension of family justice services across the province is a most welcome initiative, especially in the current fiscal environment. However, while these are significant steps in the right direction, there needs to be monitoring of the implementation of these reforms. There are concerns that budgetary pressures or too much reliance on volunteer lawyers and law students may result in services of such poor quality that they may do no good and, in some cases, could actually do harm. Further, there are other important matters that do not have direct costs that must be addressed. In particular, there need to be Unified Family Courts and effective family case management throughout the province; these developments can occur without significant added costs; indeed, they should result in resource savings.

Improving access to justice and the efficacy of the process of family dispute resolution is a challenging but critically important task. While more and better research is clearly needed both about the present operation of the family justice system and about innovations that can

---

flict – What's Language Got to Do with it?' (paper prepared for the Legal Education Society of Alberta, 23 and 30 January 2007), at Canadian Bar Association, http://www.cba.org/alberta/main/pdf/Conflict.pdf.

improve family justice, enough is known to begin meaningful reform. Experience from other jurisdictions, notably Australia, suggests that the support of the Family Law Bench and Bar are essential if reform is to succeed, especially if the reforms are to result in a 'cultural shift.' There needs to be involvement of family law judges, lawyers, and other justice system professionals if there is to be meaningful change. This will require the engagement of justice system professionals in the design of reforms; education prior to implementation; ongoing monitoring and research, including from the perspectives of these professionals; and ultimately further reform.

10 Some Reflections on Family Dispute Resolution in Ontario

JUSTICE GEORGE CZUTRIN*

I. Introduction

I generally agree with Professor Bala's excellent, insightful, and, not surprisingly, well-researched paper, and with his conclusions on systematic changes and cultural shifts. I add my own commentary based on my personal judicial perspective, influenced by my experiences as a practising family lawyer in Hamilton, as a sitting judge at the original Unified Family Court in Hamilton, and, since 2007, as a member of the Superior Court Family Team in Toronto.

Wonderful, dedicated, and well-intentioned professionals (including academics and researchers) across disciplines and court staff work in family. They assist the vast majority of families to resolve issues arising from family break-up with or without court intervention. A brief paper, such as this, may appear critical, when in fact it is meant to continue to build on what we do well and look at how we might all do better. For families who are facing challenges and look to the justice system to find answers, we need to find ways to better assist.

The recently adopted Family Law Strategic Plan for the Ontario Superior Court of Justice (the 'Strategic Plan')[1] includes the following definitions:

'Access to justice' [means] providing family court services and processes

---

* The views in this commentary are the author's own and do not necessarily represent those of the court (the Ontario Superior Court of Justice) or the author's colleagues.

1 Superior Court of Justice Ontario, *Family Law Strategic Plan*, 2008.

that are timely, efficient, effective and affordable. The purpose of these services and processes is to resolve family cases in ways that minimize conflict, safeguard the children's best interests, protect the legal rights of all family members, and resolve the issues as early as possible.

'Accessibility' [means that] appropriate judicial resources and family court services should be available at all court locations ... [C]ourt processes should be understandable to all litigants, including the unrepresented, and should promote early, fair and expeditious resolutions.

'Effectiveness' [means that] front end family court services and court processes should be designed to ensure that each court attendance is necessary, meaningful, timely and as comprehensive as possible.

The Strategic Plan sets the following goals:

- appropriate expansion of a fully resourced Family Court branch;
- appropriate judicial complement that meets the needs of all family law litigants;
- availability of comprehensive front-end family court services to all litigants, both represented and self represented ... [to include] at a minimum ... Family Law Information Centres, Mandatory Information Sessions, Mediation, Legal Aid Services, Supervised Access Centres, and Support Re-calculation services;
- court processes that make sure parties are prepared to have a meaningful appearance before a judge;
- improv[ing] the Family Law Rules where needed, to simplify and streamline proceedings in an effort to provide efficient and timely judicial events;
- appropriate case management ... proportionate to ... children's needs ... complexity, importance of the issues ... family's financial resources. High conflict cases should be identified as early as possible and managed by the same judge wherever possible;
- enhance[d] judicial education;
- improved communications and consultations with judges and other justice partners and stakeholders, regarding ongoing developments, new initiatives and current issues in family law

There is wide support for this plan and its goals. There has, however, been a long history of trying to implement changes, and real challenge in achieving consensus on the details of reform plans. We have to focus on the strengths of our system and look for ways to build on those strengths. While we want to encourage families to resolve issues without necessarily resorting to litigation, we should be careful not to create impediments that prevent timely and appropriate access to justice.

Professor Bala writes that

> members of the judiciary, government officials, and professional organizations have been engaged in extensive discussions about the family justice process, and there is significant consensus about the directions for reform.[2]

In fact, the family justice reform began well before I started law school in 1973. Over the years, while there has been some consensus on what works and what is still needed, differing points of view have slowed reform. These different points of view have come from the vantage points of professionals, individual litigants, policy makers, and judicial officers, all with differing personal experiences, interests, and philosophies. As a result, rather than move ahead on what has proven successful, we continue to repeat studies, taking some steps forward and some in the wrong direction, but seldom make a major commitment to institute change. Such a change would require bold steps and the commitment of necessary resources. We cannot expect to have a system that relies on volunteers and underresourced staff, judges, and courts.

I agree with Professor Bala when he states:

> It is important to be realistic about family disputes and to recognize the strengths of the present system as well as the limitations of any social or legal interventions for dealing with high-conflict situations.[3]

However, I find myself unwilling to accept for families his suggestion that

> [i]t is also important to be realistic about improvements that will require additional resources and to identify changes that can be undertaken without corresponding increases in spending ... However, in the present fiscal

---

2 Nicholas Bala, 'Reforming Family Dispute Resolution in Ontario: Systemic Changes and Cultural Shifts,' *supra* this volume, 272.

3 *Ibid.*, 273.

environment, it seems unlikely that there will be a commitment of significant additional government resources for the family justice system in the
near future beyond those already announced.[4]

I applaud the Attorney General's interest in improving Family Justice. The recent announcement of the addition of resources to all courts
is very significant. I hope that it is the beginning of a trend.
Professor Bala accurately remarks:

> The broad support for the Four Pillars may in part reflect the fact that there
> has never been complete agreement about some important details of the
> plan, which has allowed different supporters to each cite their own pre-
> ferred version.[5]

II. The Importance of Unified Family Courts

It is my personal perspective that priority should be given to a properly
structured and resourced province-wide Unified Family Court (UFC);
this would provide a solid foundation on which all other changes,
including the securing of the additional pillars, can be built. Priority
should also be given to the commitment that this will be achieved within a specific and reasonably short period.
It is important to learn lessons from the history of the Unified Family
Court as we move forward:

- the original jurisdiction (including young offenders and criminal
  matters involving family members),
- case management innovation,
- court and community-connected services (including mediation and
  assessments),
- early triaging, simplified forms and rules, and assistance for those
  who could not afford legal fees.

Justice David Steinberg's 1981 book *Family Law in the Family Courts*[6] is

---

4 *Ibid.*
5 *Ibid.*, 272.
6 Second edition (Toronto: Carswell, 1981–6). This book looks at the Provincial Court
  (Family Division) and the then one and only Unified Family Court in Ontario and
  Canada, created by the Ontario Unified Family Court Act on 1 July 1977.

worthy of study and review. It contains the court's original philosophy and the original UFC rules, including this one:

- Rule 4: These rules shall be construed liberally so as to secure an inexpensive and expeditious conclusion of every proceeding consistent with a just determination of the proceeding.

Sadly, many lawyers in Ontario do not even know what a Unified Family Court is. I hear the same discussions and ideas of the past, previously rejected for valid reasons. The court should not be two-tiered. It should be a court with comprehensive jurisdiction and specialized judges who all have the authority and jurisdiction of a Superior Court judge. We should not have to say to any family: 'Sorry you are in the wrong court, UFC has jurisdiction, or OCJ has jurisdiction, or SCJ has jurisdiction, but I do not.' Families should not have to be going through the divorce process or determination of their property issues before one judge, while at a different court another judge is dealing with their child protection, default, or variation issues. One court should decide all Hague Convention cases that deal with family matters. There should be no confusion about the appeal process, which court families need to go to, or which court offers which services.

III. Pressing Short-Term Issues to Address

As Ontario moves towards a province-wide single model of family justice with the Unified Family Court, we also need to continue with urgency to address the following issues.

1. *We need to develop new ways of providing legal advice and legal services to all families.*

(a) The self-represented litigant poses a very significant challenge that we must accept as a reality, while looking for solutions to assist all involved. There is no perfect alternative to a properly represented party. Not being properly represented impacts all parties to the case (represented or not), the court, and any alternative dispute resolution process employed. It affects court staff, witnesses, and other cases in the system. When a judge takes time to explain process and law and to intervene to ensure fairness, the represented may feel that they are not being treated fairly. While the examination of why individuals choose to be without counsel is important, it is beyond the scope of my remarks. The decision to proceed without a lawyer is not only financial. There is a critical and urgent need for parties to receive legal advice and proper representation and for a collaborative dialogue to address this urgent and critical need.

(b) Self-help kits, material, the Internet, and videos do not replace a well-informed family lawyer giving advice and properly representing parties. Some materials intended to inform a person, who then chooses to proceed without counsel, may create more problems rather than help. Popular media may provide inadequate or irrelevant information. How to disclose evidence, present a case, call a witness, and interpret the law is not easily taught in a short time frame, in particular when someone is attempting to understand and look for solutions for their own personal issues.

(c) If a party chooses to proceed without counsel, we need to provide the best possible education, assistance, and tools, while always encouraging legal representation and advice.[7] These tools include information regarding what will be required at each court attendance and what the process looks like, including courtroom decorum. Judges now spend a lot of time explaining to unrepresented parties the process, what should be focused on as relevant, and the inadequacy of disclosure, materials, and the presentation of the

---

7 See ABA Coalition for Justice, *Report on the Survey of Judges on the Impact of the Economic Downturn on Representation in the Courts (Preliminary)* (12 July 2010), at http://www.americanbar.org:

> The overwhelming consensus at 86% is that the courts would be more efficient if both parties were represented. Contrary to the popular belief that lawyers slow the wheels of justice, the court views advocates as an efficiency within an adversarial system. (14)
>
> Our system of justice is based on an adversarial model. It also has a sophisticated set of rules and procedures that allow it to operate. For it to operate most efficiently, each party should be represented by counsel. When parties are not represented, we now have direct evidence that those who are not represented actually hurt their cause by doing so. However, they are not always damaged because the judge will often work to prevent an injustice from happening in many cases. The judge recognizes that in doing so they may appear to compromise the impartiality of the court. Such an appearance can have a long term negative impact on the court.
>
> When parties are represented, the system is more just and more efficient. Judges think that the best solution is to find ways to get more people representation when they appear in court. (15)

evidence.[8] This sort of information should be provided as early as possible and to the extent possible prior to court appearances.

(d) The Law Society, lawyers, and the courts should engage in a dialogue about how to formalize the reality of limited scope retainers. The court is already faced with lawyers who attend for limited purposes and with series of changes in representation. We need to address how best to deal with this shift, not only to assist the court to find ways to adapt to this change, but more importantly to help families.

(e) We might want to consider assigning space in the Family Law Information Centres to a roster of lawyers who are knowledgeable in family law and who are prepared to offer services at reduced rates and at additional off-site locations without the impediment of subject or financial eligibility restrictions. I was impressed by Sue Talia's presentation about limited scope retainers at this past year's Federation of Law Societies National Family Law Conference. Legal Aid may want to consider taking another look at delivering either contributory certificates or reduced rate retainers and hourly rates.

(f) Parties who are not fully informed about their rights in law and about available court processes and services, whether resolving their disputes privately or with the assistance of mediators, arbitrators, or a judge, are a concern. Resolution should not be in the absence of proper and relevant disclosure. Parties should have the right to know a reasonably fair range of outcomes consistent with the law. We should not look to divert for the sake of diversion.

(g) In Toronto (now spreading to other locations), we have been blessed by the efforts of the family bar and by the Dispute Resolution Officer services they have provided to the Superior Court. While the statistics are kept manually, I asked Ross Davis, chair of the Toronto program, about the number of self-represented parties participating in the program and their impact. Reviewing the data for 2009 and 2010, he found, not surprisingly, that settlement rates were dramatically lower where both parties were self-represented.

2. *We need to encourage and do more research that is multidisciplinary.* We

---

8 This is not restricted to parties without counsel, but applies to unprepared counsel who have not adapted to new changes and shifts in the family law process culture as well.

need better data entry that will allow better research. This will allow us to speak less anecdotally and more from the strength of facts and valid, independent, reliable research. We might confirm the validity of statistics and what lessons we might learn to improve the process.

I am encouraged by a new initiative called the Court Information Management System (CIMS). CIMS intends to modernize technological support for court operations; enhance electronic court services for the public; and provide enhanced electronic document management as well as court scheduling and financial and automated workflow capabilities. The application should enable the introduction of online court services. The first version of CIMS is expected in the spring of 2012. I hope that it will allow for the collection and analysis of data to answer questions such as these:

- How many cases involve one or more self-represented parties?
- Is there any correlation between self-represented parties and requesting the OCL to consider involvement or settlement rates at various stages (i.e., is there a greater chance of success for settlement with or without counsel, and at what stage)?
- Who are we seeing on motions, and what are the issues? I sense, but cannot validate, that *ex parte*, without-notice motions are more likely brought by self-represented parties. If so, why, and what is the result?
- What combination of factors (e.g., number of self-represented versus represented parties) increases the likelihood and length of trial and possible appeal?
- What influences timely disclosure and a meaningful court attendance?

This type of research should help in determining the effectiveness of the Family Law Rules (the 'Rules'),[9] and in proposing changes to rules, services, and interventions. I asked one of our law clerks[10] to see whether we could mine our daily door sheets for some information. She worked diligently to get a handle on how many self-represented parties we see in family law proceedings at the Toronto Superior Court, and what the outcomes were of different events, conferences, motions, and trials. Her preliminary data, still to be tested and verified, sug-

---

9 O.Reg. 114/99.
10 Kathleen DeBlock.

gest that the rate of settlement decreases as the proportion of unrepresented parties increases. In Case Conferences, Settlement Conferences, Motions, and Trial Management Conferences, 64 per cent of litigants were represented, while 36 per cent were unrepresented. In Trials and Appeals, 49 per cent of litigants were represented, while 51 per cent were unrepresented.[11]

3. *We need to implement the family law rules and apply them as they were intended.* The 1999 Rules were first applicable at UFC and OCJ sites, where there were largely family specialist judges and Rule 39 or 40 clerks to assist in case management. The Rules came in at the time of the last expansion of the Family Court. They were intended to promote and encourage resolution, limit motions, encourage front-end disclosure, and provide early judicial intervention without the exchange of accusatory affidavits.

While the Rules Committee is always looking for ways to improve the Rules, I would suggest that it is in the application and implementation of the Rules that we have faced challenges. The Rules were intended to alter the culture and bring about a systematic change from an emphasis on the adversarial process to an emphasis on resolution.

- The language of the Rules was intended to be plain. For example, interim orders became 'temporary,' and *ex parte* became 'without notice.' The intention was to simplify. I believe we need better material to explain the Rules and their process rather than wholesale changes. We also need consistency in application and approach.
- Not everyone has accepted, adapted to, or adopted the new culture and Rules (in fact, some continue to ignore them), and some have not shifted away from the traditional roles of the adversarial process. Some courts remain overwhelmed with long lists of conferences, without enough time to do effective interventions, particularly if parties and counsel are not prepared or have not followed the Rules or accepted the objectives.[12]
- Over time, change has occurred and the promise of early judicial intervention has proven effective. In some locations, motion num-

---

11 This research was collected from all Toronto Superior Court family law door sheets from the beginning of November 2009 through to the end of October 2010.
12 The objectives of the Rules can be found in Family Law Rules, O.Reg. 114/99, ss.2(2)–2(5).

bers have gone down, trials are fewer, and cases resolve or are tried earlier.

- We need research to confirm under what conditions the Rules are working and the objectives met.
- We must find ways to ensure timely, relevant, and necessary disclosure. Either by Rule, auto orders, or legislation, we need to make sure that disclosure is ordered as soon as possible so that every court attendance can lead to resolution or a neutral evaluation. We should not need a motion or to wait for a case conference to have a necessary disclosure order made, a valuation ordered, property preserved, or status quo maintained.

Based on lessons learned, a Unified Family Court and courts insisting on Rules compliance would go a long way to promote the objectives of the Rules.

4. *We need a child support recalculation service.*

5. *We need to establish a dedicated and well trained and resourced specialized family staff to support the process.* This staff needs to be familiar with the process and must be given the tools and resources to provide the judges, lawyers, and parties with ready access to a well-organized file at all times. Our present staffs are dedicated but are also overburdened and without adequate resources, while being asked to provide process and legal information.

6. *We need better designed and resourced motions, conference, and court rooms to provide safety and security for all.* Courtrooms should have video and audio conferencing and video witness capacity. All the rooms should be equipped with modern technology to allow better access to information and the use of electronic information, including exhibits, briefs, and other material. We need to be able to do more online. We need to be able to better record and access to improve efficiency. I am optimistic that CIMS and new or retrofitted courthouses will address these issues.

7. *We need to offer support in more languages at all court sites.*

8. *We need judicial support officers (an enhanced and dedicated Rule 39 or 40 clerks) who can make sure cases are judge-ready.* They could do so by ensuring that required documents are filed, disclosure is complete, and

parties or counsel know what to expect and what is expected from them so that a judge can either help settle or decide the issues in dispute. We should not have lists with cases that are not ready to proceed and thus blocking access to those who are ready.

9. *We need to support the Children's Lawyer and look for ways of accessing more assessors in a timely manner.*

10. *We need to look at Family Court Clinics to offer custody and parenting assessments and perhaps therapeutic assessments.* Many professionals are reluctant to be involved in highly conflictual and litigious cases for fear of being dragged into the process. We need more supervised access centres that also offer education and therapeutic interventions to address the issues that have required supervision.

11. *We need to develop the ability to triage cases.* Furthermore, we need to identify and make available timely services that are identified to meet the needs of families.

12. *We need to encourage law schools to offer courses and programs that train family lawyers.* This branch of law requires skills of a different kind – ones that aim at effective dispute resolution. So such courses and programs would need to provide students with knowledge of family law rules and procedure, child development, psychology, accounting, and tax. The goal is not that family lawyers become experts in all areas, but that they be alive to the issues and the necessary resources. There should be more offers of joint degrees or multidisciplinary training.

13. *We need to consider the advantages of family teams.* Since my transfer to Toronto, I have been impressed by the family team concept, where judges are assigned to the family team for longer periods, only do family cases for their rotation, have no more than five conferences per day, have trial management conferences generally the week before the scheduled trial, and have trials that occur generally in under six months after being scheduled at a settlement conference. While not a Unified Family Court with comprehensive jurisdiction, the family team concept and adequate judicial resources allowing for reasonable time for conferences promises to maximize opportunities for meaningful attendances.

14. *We need to seek solutions that are not a financially and emotional repetition of attempts without some continuing benefit of moving towards resolution for families.* Solutions should be along a continuum so that families are not required to incur the increased financial and emotional costs of continually starting over. Professionals need to work together, and the effort may cross professional boundaries and the work of individual ministries and institutions. It requires a holistic effort.[13]

---

13 See Barbara A. Babb, 'Reevaluating Where We Stand: A Comprehensive Survey of American Family Justice' (2008) 46 Family Ct Rev. 230 at 232: 'UFCs embrace the notions of therapeutic jurisprudence and an ecological, holistic approach to the family's problems [with] specially trained and interested judges who address not only the legal issues … but also the family's nonlegal needs, such as substance abuse, mental health issues, or domestic abuse. A therapeutic and ecological UFC model allows for the resolution of legal, personal, emotional, and social disputes with the aim of improving the well-being and functioning of families and children.'

11 Access to Justice for Small Amount Claims in the Consumer Marketplace: Lessons from Australia

JUSTIN MALBON

1. Introduction

This paper addresses the problem of small amounts claims in the marketplace for consumer goods and services. A small amount claim is an amount that could potentially be obtained by a successful (legal) claim for loss suffered but that is insufficient to justify actually pursuing the claim because of the risks and potential costs involved. Because these risks and costs are generally so substantial, the dollar amount of a small amount claim can be significant. The loss from abandoning the claim is borne by individual consumers, as well as by society and the economy. Individuals suffer loss through forgone compensation for shoddy goods or services. Society loses through sub-optimal consumer participation in the marketplace, because consumers mistrust firms; through regulatory failure, in the form of firms not complying with their legal obligations, because they enjoy an effective immunity from legal action; and through a misallocation of resources in the supply of substandard goods and services.

The small amounts claims problem arises from what is in effect a denial of access to justice, a right to which all members of a democratic society are entitled. The rule of law and the concomitant provision of access to justice are not simply of aesthetic appeal to the chardonnay-drinking chattering classes; they are essential to holding governments and corporations to account, which in turn builds public trust in institutions and holds corruption in check. Rothstein tells a story that in November 1997 he was invited to Moscow to deliver a lecture to Russian academics, politicians, and bureaucrats about the Swedish civil service. After his lecture, a Russian tax official asked why it was that Swedes paid their taxes and Russians did not. The Swedish government receives 98 per cent of the taxes that Swedish taxpayers are required to pay, while Russians pay 26 per cent. The reason why Russians do not pay their taxes, it seems, is because, although they do want publicly funded services such as health care, education, pensions, defence, and so forth, they correctly assess that most other taxpayers do not pay their taxes, and that even if they did, a significant proportion of the money would go to corrupt officials. It would appear, then, that in Russia trust in the system is in short supply.[1] An effective taxing regime therefore needs a strong rule of law, which in turn can forge a more trusting society.

Arguably, democratic states are better than authoritarian states at producing generalized trust because they are better at restricting the use of coercion, which in turn enhances rather than undermines trust.[2] The reason why people obey the law in general is that they believe the laws are enforced fairly. It is becoming evident that there is a correlation between a nation applying a weak rule of law and its poor socioeconomic performance.[3] Research shows that good governance leads to improved rule of law, which, along with the provision of access to justice, helps increase a nation's GDP.[4] A country with a strong rule of law 'has less corruption, protected and enforceable legal rights, due process, good governance and accountable government.'[5] A strong rule of law provides an economic as well as a general social payoff through a more trusting and harmonious society. Canada and Australia have both been ranked by the World Bank over the past decade as being in the 95th percentile regarding indicators for the quality of the rule of law.[6]

---

1 Bo Rothstein, 'Trust, Social Dilemmas, and Collected Memories; On the Rise and Decline of the Swedish Model' (2000) 12 *Journal of Theoretical Politics* 477 at 478.

2 Eric Uslaner, 'Tax Evasion, Trust, and the Strong Arm of the Law' in *Tax Evasion, Trust, and State Capacities*, ed. Nicholas Hayoz and Simon Hug (Bern: Peter Lang AG, 2007) at 19.

3 United Nations Development Programme, *Human Development Report 2003, Milliennium Development Goals: A Compact among Nations to End Human Poverty* (New York: Oxford University Press, 2003), http://hdr.undp.org/en/media/hdr03_complete.pdf, cited in Commonwealth of Australia, Attorney-General's Department, Access to Justice Taskforce, *A Strategic Framework for Access to Justice in the Federal Civil Justice System* (Canberra, 2009) at 3 [Access to Justice Taskforce].

4 *Ibid.* at 2.

5 *Ibid.* at 1.

6 Daniel Kaufmann, Aart Kraay, and Massimo Mastruzzi, *Governance Matters VIII: Aggregate and Individual Governance Indicators 1996–2008,* Policy Research Working Paper 4978 (Washington: World Bank Development Research Group Macroeconomics and Growth Team, 2009) at 92.

Both nations are also strong economies. However, there is little room for complacency. The rule of law is part reality, in terms of procedures and systems for the provision of justice, and part perception, in terms of the members of society believing they are being treated fairly. Within the marketplace there are rising consumer expectations about being provided fair redress and access to justice. In Part II below, a rationale is offered for a broad definition of 'justice' in the consumer marketplace.

Access to justice is an important mechanism for holding institutions and firms to account and for prompting them to improve the quality and efficiency of their service delivery. A recent Australian Government report noted that justice institutions 'enable people to protect their rights against infringement by government or other people or bodies in society, and permit parties to bring actions against government to limit executive power and ensure government is accountable.'[7] A central challenge for governments is to give people affordable access to justice institutions. Part III of this paper outlines the relative success and the continuing challenges faced by the Victorian Civil and Administrative Tribunal (VCAT) in providing affordable access to justice for consumers. Ontario has recently adopted a 'clusters' approach to dealing with inefficiencies arising from a proliferation of tribunals.[8] Victoria's super-tribunal approach offers an interesting contrast to Ontario's approach.

Access to justice in the consumer marketplace is not only an issue of government concern – it is also of interest to firms in the marketplace. They benefit from improved access to justice through greater consumer trust, which in turn stimulates greater consumer participation in the market, leading in turn to increased economic activity – a virtuous cycle. Because firms benefit from improved access to justice, it can be reasoned that they should bear some of the cost of providing access, which admittedly is passed on to consumers through the increased cost of goods and services. Firms in Canada, Australia, and other countries voluntarily provide access to justice in some marketplaces by instituting internal complaints processes and free consumer access to industry-run external dispute resolution schemes – generally in the form of industry-run ombudsman schemes. There may be some instances, however, where it is not enough to rely on industry to take the initiative so that it is necessary for government to mandate participation in such a scheme. This is the case with the financial advisory industry in

---

7 Access to Justice Taskforce, *supra* note 3 at 2.
8 See text at note 39, *infra*.

Australia, where federal legislation compels advisers to obtain a financial services licence. One of the licence conditions requires the licensee to institute an internal complaints-handling system and become a member of an approved external dispute settlement scheme. All financial advisers are members of the industry-funded Financial Ombudsman Scheme. The operation of the scheme is described in Part IV of this paper. Mandatory membership in an external dispute settlement scheme has recently been extended to financial institutions such as banks and mortgage brokers. This is also briefly described below.

The cost of access to the courts is a significant issue. Lord Woolf noted in his *Access to Justice* report that 'the problem of cost [of litigation] is the most serious problem besetting our litigation system' and that 'the unaffordable cost of litigation constitutes a denial of access to justice.'[9] One means of giving consumers access to courts is through a robust class action regime. Australia, like Canada, has permitted class actions for some time. An interesting Australian development is the growth of litigation funding companies, which are established for the sole purpose of funding class actions. The growth and operation of litigation funding companies is outlined in Part V of this paper.

II. Justice in the Consumer Marketplace

The consumer marketplace is a locus in which the interests of two key parties, namely consumers and firms, are mediated. Although governments play a key role in the regulation of the marketplace, by setting the rules of the game, they ought not to be solely responsible for providing marketplace 'access to justice,' broadly defined. Both firms and consumers have a vested interest in market fair play, though justice is not only a marketplace concern: it is, according to Rawls, the first virtue of social organizations.[10] Of course, an unscrupulous player can take

---

9 U.K., Lord Chancellor's Department, *Access to Justice: Interim Report to the Lord Chancellor on the Civil Justice System in England and Wales* by Lord Woolf (London, June 1995), chapter 25 at para. 1 and chapter 3 at para. 13, http://www.dca.gov.uk/civil/interim/woolf.htm. See also Martin Gramatiko, 'A Framework for Measuring the Costs of Paths to Justice' (2008) 2 *Journal Jurisprudence* 111 at 112; and Barbara Baarsma, Flóra Felsö, and Kieja Janssen, 'Regulation of the Legal Profession and Access to Law: An Economic Perspective,' SEO Economic Research Commissioned by the International Association of Legal Expenses Insurance (Amsterdam, 2008).

10 John Rawls, *A Theory of Justice* (Cambridge, MA: Belknap Press of Harvard University Press, 1971) at 3.

advantage of a corrupt and unfair market, but a fair marketplace is in the enlightened self-interest of the majority of players and in the interests of society more generally.

A fair marketplace has a number of characteristics: firms are trusted, and there is a high degree of consumer confidence and participation. Trust is gained in part through consumers believing they will be treated fairly if there are failures (as perceived by the customer) in the firm's provision of its goods or services – for example, delays, errors in delivery, or failure to honour promises.[11] 'Justice' has a broader meaning for marketplace consumers than it does for lawyers and jurisprudential scholars. As Konovsky observes, 'justice'

> strikes a chord with anyone who has experienced disrespect. In business organizations, considerations of fairness appeal to managers, employees, and other organizational stakeholders who see fairness as a unifying value providing fundamental principles that can bind together conflicting parties and create stable social structures.[12]

The injustice caused by a service failure can be redressed in various ways, depending on the circumstances. The firm might have a returns policy of immediately replacing a defective good recently purchased by a customer; it may provide some form of compensation for delayed flights and lost luggage; or it might provide an internal dispute resolution process in the case of more complex service delivery, such as banking and financial services.

Interesting research is being undertaken into consumers' perceptions of justice in relation to the purchasing of goods and services from firms. Studies suggest that service failures do not necessarily lead to customer dissatisfaction because most consumers accept that things can sometimes go wrong.[13] What *can* deeply affect consumer perceptions and emotions is how the firm responds to the service failure. Konovsky believes that consumers' perceptions of justice are critical

---

11 David Bejou and Adrian Palmer, 'Service Failure and Loyalty: An Exploratory Empirical Study of Airline Customers' (1998) 12 *Journal of Services Marketing* 7 at 11.

12 Mary Konovsky, 'Understanding Procedural Justice and Its Impact on Business Organizations' (2000) 26 *Journal of Management* 489 at 489 [Konovsky, 'Understanding Procedural Justice'].

13 Ana Belén del Río-Lanza, Rodolfo Vázquez-Casielles, and Ana Díaz-Martín, 'Satisfaction with Service Recovery: Perceived Justice and Emotional Responses' (2009) 62 *Journal of Business Research* 775 [del Río-Lanza, 'Satisfaction with Service Recovery'].

to understanding their reaction to a conflict situation.[14] Service failure is a typical example of a conflict situation.[15] Perceived injustice triggers emotional responses as well as cognitive appraisals about a firm.[16] Rather unsurprisingly, a number of studies have found that low levels of perceived justice correlate to high levels of negative emotions (anger, fury, enragement, annoyance, sadness) as well as low levels of positive emotions.[17]

Some studies have disaggregated perceptions of justice into the dimensions of distributive, procedural, and interactional justice. These categories differ from the legal and jurisprudential comprehension of them. *Distributive* justice in this context refers to the way in which the firm assigns resources to rectify and compensate for a service failure – for example, by refunding money, providing a replacement good, or offering a discount for further purchases.[18] *Procedural* justice refers to the steps taken by members of the firm to deal with a complaint, and *interactional* justice to the way in which staff have interacted with the customer regarding the complaint. This latter relates to staff accessibility, speed in dealing with the matter, the control the firm exercises over the process of handling the matter, and the firm's flexibility in adapting to a customer's needs.[19]

According to a study by Maxham and Netemeyer, procedural justice has little impact on consumer satisfaction in the context of banking and new home construction services, but it does have a significant impact in relation to online purchases of electronic equipment.[20] It seems that while a quick response to complaints about service failure does not trigger positive emotions toward the firm, a slow response *does* trigger negative ones. In other words, consumers expect a quick response as a matter of course and react negatively to a slow response. In this sense,

14 Konovsky, 'Understanding Procedural Justice,' *supra* note 12 at 492.
15 del Río-Lanza, 'Satisfaction with Service Recovery,'*supra* note 13 at 776.
16 Konovsky, *supra* note 12 at 492.
17 Discussed in Konovsky, 'Understanding Procedural Justice,' *supra* note 12.
18 *Ibid.*
19 *Ibid.*
20 James Maxham III and Richard Netemeyer, 'Firms Reap What They Sow: The Effects of Shared Values and Perceived Organizational Justice on Customers' Evaluations of Complaint Handling' (2003) 67 *Journal of Marketing* 46 at 58. See also James Maxham III and Richard Netemeyer, 'Modelling Customer Perceptions of Complaint Handling over Time: The Effects of Perceived Justice on Satisfaction and Intent' (2002) 78 *Journal of Retailing* 239.

there is a basic expectation of procedural fairness.[21] So, the sympathetic handling of a complaint will positively affect a customer's attitude towards the firm.[22]

Other research indicates that procedural justice and interactional justice may have a stronger influence than distributive justice in terms of consumers' reactions to a firm and their willingness to continue dealing with it.[23] A study by del Río-Lanza *et al.* of the mobile phone sector found that procedural justice has a dominant role in explaining customer satisfaction for two reasons: first, procedural justice has the strongest direct effect on satisfaction; and second, procedural justice is the only dimension that exerts both a direct effect on satisfaction and an indirect one (via emotions).[24]

Generally speaking, a firm that responds to consumer complaints by implementing a well-designed and well-implemented complaint management system can expect to benefit from increased consumer satisfaction and loyalty, along with improved internal company well-being.[25] An effective and easy-to-use complaint management system can also result in employees feeling more in control and suffering less stress.[26]

Negative consumer sentiment towards a firm can cause reputational damage to the firm, leading to loss of market share and consequent financial loss.[27] The history of a consumer's past interactions with a firm informs the consumer about the firm's trustworthiness.[28] The past dealings raise expectations about future dealings, besides generating

---

21 del Río-Lanza, 'Satisfaction with Service Recovery,' *supra* note 13 at 776.
22 *Ibid.* at 777.
23 *Ibid.*
24 del Río-Lanza, 'Satisfaction with Service Recovery,' *supra* 13 at 779.
25 Leonard Berry and A. Parasuraman, *Marketing Services: Competing Through Quality* (New York: Free Press, 1991), cited in Torben Hansen, Ricky Wilke, and Judith Zaichkowsky, 'Managing Consumer Complaints: Differences and Similarities among Heterogeneous Retailers' (2010) 38 *International Journal of Retail and Distribution Management* 6 at 6–7 [Hansen, 'Managing Consumer Complaints'].
26 Michael Matteson and John Ivancevich, *Managing Job Stress and Health* (New York: Free Press, 1982).
27 See Heski Bar-Isaac, 'Imperfect Competition and Reputational Commitment' (2005) 89 *Economics Letters* 167; Gary Bolton, Elena Katok, and Axel Ockenfels, 'How Effective Are Online Reputation Mechanisms? An Experimental Investigation' (2004) 50 *Management Science* 1587; Ernst Fehr and Klaus Schmidt, 'A Theory of Fairness, Competition, and Cooperation' (1999) 114 *Quarterly Journal of Economics* 817; and Johannes Hörner, 'Reputation and Competition' (2002) 92 *American Economic Review* 644.
28 Paul Resnick, Richard Zeckhauser, Eric Friedman, and Ko Kuwabara, 'Reputation Systems' (2000) 43 *Communications of the ACM* 45 at 46 [Resnick, 'Reputation Systems'].

likely opportunities for retaliation if one of the parties misbehaves. Axelrod describes these expectations as the 'shadow of the future.'[29] Resnick *et al.* propose that an effective reputation system depends on at least three properties:

1 Long-lived entities that inspire an expectation of future interaction;
2 Capture and distribution of feedback about current interactions (such information must be visible in the future); and
3 Use of feedback to guide trust decisions.[30]

Studies confirm that a firm can gain considerable value by developing a good reputation and being trusted in the marketplace.[31]

The Internet has added to the ways in which firms can suffer reputational damage because it gives consumers the capacity to engage in what Schwartz describes as cyber-griping.[32] 'Cyber-griping' is where a consumer or a former employee maintains a website devoted to criticizing a company or group.[33] Social media sites on the Web, including Facebook and Twitter, offer additional and easily accessible means for cyber-griping. Schwartz notes that

[a]ccording to Jack West, former president of the American Society for Quality, the service industry, especially manufacturers of automobiles, computers, and appliances, is witnessing a marked decline in consumer satisfaction. As consumers become increasingly disgruntled, they become more empowered, finding ways to inform both the company of their experiences as well as fellow consumers. Thus, consumers are taking to the 'information superhighway' in record numbers to publicise their complaints and draw attention to companies' poor products and services by establishing websites.[34]

---

29 Robert Axelrod, *The Evolution of Cooperation* (New York: Basic Books, 1984).
30 Resnick, 'Reputation Systems,' *supra* note 28 at 47.
31 Peter Roberts and Grahame Dowling, 'Corporate Reputation and Sustained Superior Financial Performance' (2002) 23 *Strategic Management Journal* 1077.
32 Jonathan Schwartz, 'Making the Consumer Watchdog's Bark as Strong as Its Gripe: Complaint Sites and the Changing Dynamic of the Fair Use Defence' (2006) 16 *Albany Law Journal of Science and Technology* 59 [Schwartz, 'Consumer Watchdog's Bark'].
33 Hansen, 'Managing Consumer Complaints,' *supra* note 25.
34 Schwartz, 'Consumer Watchdog's Bark,' *supra* note 32 at 66.

Before the Internet, consumers had fewer opportunities to raise complaints because of the difficulty of gaining access to redress and also because of the attitude of many firms, which was largely to ignore complaints.[35] E-mails, blogs, Facebook, and Twitter have increased the opportunities for griping about firms, educational institutions, and government. In other words, we are now in a world where perceived injustice will not simply be internalized and borne with stoicism and resignation; now consumers can vent their frustrations online. This has placed increasing pressure on both governments and firms to establish systems for dealing with injustice instead of simply assuming that most people will do little or nothing about unjust treatment.

In summary, although Canada and Australia enjoy a strong rule of law, there are few grounds for complacency. The consumer marketplace is an important field for the operation of the rule of law. It plays a significant role in our day-to-day lives and forms an essential component of our overall economy. It is therefore in our social and economic interests to ensure the optimum operation of a fair and efficient marketplace by meeting consumer expectations about access to 'justice,' broadly defined.

To fully comprehend the dimensions of consumer marketplace access to justice issues, it is necessary to understand the marketplace's systems for providing justice as well as the ways in which consumers themselves define 'justice' and 'fairness.' This requires broadening the definition of justice to incorporate the insights gained from the research discussed above into consumer understandings of, and responses to, perceived injustice and unfairness. A broader comprehension of marketplace justice leads to the insight that governments and firms need, for their own survival, to understand and respond to consumer expectations about receiving justice in the marketplace. Providing improved access to justice is potentially very expensive. Paradoxically, increasing public expectations about better access to justice sits alongside resistance to paying higher taxes or prices to fund the improvements. This confronts governments with the challenge of improving access to justice at the lowest possible cost to the public purse. In responding to the challenge, governments need to do the following:

1 strive for low-cost means of attaining access to justice to reduce overall costs to taxpayers and consumers;

---

35 *Ibid.* at 67.

2 look for ways to share the cost of providing access to justice with marketplace firms, or have firms pay the full cost on the ground that the potential benefits to firms from an access to justice scheme are direct and significant; and

3 reduce the costs to government of supervising firms' conduct by lessening the burden placed on corporate and consumer regulators.

There are at least three possible ways of responding to these challenges, namely by

1 providing access for small claims and credit claims to low-cost formal justice systems such as tribunals;

2 requiring firms to become members of independent industry-funded dispute resolution systems in appropriate circumstances; and

3 enhancing access to the courts by improving the incentives for class actions.

The Australian experience on these three fronts is discussed in Parts III through V with particular reference to the Victorian Civil and Administrative Tribunal (VCAT), the industry-funded Financial Ombudsman Service (FOS), and the emergence of litigation funders to support class actions.

III. The Victorian Civil and Administrative Tribunal

A number of Australian states have introduced a tribunal that operates as a 'one-stop shop' or 'super-tribunal' that, among other things, deals with small amounts claims. The following account focuses on the Victorian Civil and Administrative Tribunal (VCAT). VCAT was established in 1998 and is apparently the world's first amalgamated civil and administrative super-tribunal. If imitation is a signifier of success, then the VCAT model has been at least a moderate success, with Western Australia and Queensland along with the Australian Capital Territory also establishing super-tribunals along the lines of the VCAT model. The U.K. has also established a super-tribunal, in 2007, known as the First-Tier Tribunal, which covers a wide range of jurisdictions including mental health, social security, and pension reviews, along with consumer credit, but not small claims more generally.[36]

---

36 See *Tribunals, Courts, and Enforcement Act 2007* (U.K.)

VCAT was established by a (radically) 'conservative' government that made bold reforms during its term in office, which included implementing an extensive privatization program. On formation, the jurisdictions of a wide range of state tribunals were amalgamated into VCAT, and other jurisdictions have since been added. This tribunal now deals with matters such as residential tenancies, small claims, consumer credit, guardianship, freedom of information, domestic building disputes, professional and industry regulation, liquor licensing, anti-discrimination, motor car traders licensing, prostitution control and licensing, travel agents, land valuation, and planning and environment.

The establishment of a single large tribunal was in part a response to the exponential growth in the number of tribunals in Victoria. The result was 'a perplexing mosaic of tribunal jurisdictions' that was confusing to lawyers, laypeople, and public servants alike.[37] In addition, the jurisdictional boundaries between the various tribunals were often arbitrary. Before VCAT, problems included an unproductive duplication of administrative infrastructure, the potential for capture of tribunals by interest groups, differences in procedures, inconsistent approaches to similar legal issues, poor service delivery to people living outside metropolitan areas, and an unduly narrow specialization in tribunal members' skills.[38]

Ontario has taken a more measured approach to these shortcomings by recently introducing the *Adjudicative Tribunals Accountability, Governance and Appointments Act*,[39] which, among other things, has introduced a 'clustering' arrangement to gain institutional efficiencies. The Act allows two or more adjudicative tribunals to be designated as a 'cluster' and for the appointment of an executive chair to be responsible for the cluster. The first cluster to be established under the Act was the Environment and Land Use Planning Cluster, which includes the Ontario Municipal Board, the Board of Negotiation, the Assessment Review Board, and the Environmental Review Tribunal. It is too early yet to judge the success of this approach. It is interesting, then, to consider the effectiveness of Victoria's super-tribunal approach after a decade of operation.

In 2008, Victoria's Attorney General asked VCAT's president, Justice

---

37 Kevin Bell, *One VCAT: President's Review of VCAT* (Melbourne: Victorian Civil and Administrative Tribunal, 2009) at 11 [Bell, *One VCAT*].
38 *Ibid.*
39 S.O. 2009, c.33.

Kevin Bell, to undertake a review of the tribunal with a focus on access to justice as well as operational and jurisdictional issues. His report, titled *One VCAT*, was published in November, 2009.[40] The *One VCAT* report identifies a number of concerns, including these:

1 problems accessing the tribunal experienced by people in outer-suburban Melbourne and rural Victoria;
2 underuse of the tribunal by residential tenants;
3 poor utilization of the tribunal by what the report describes as 'culturally and linguistically diverse' members of the community, and indigenous communities;
4 difficulties experienced by self-represented persons;
5 a perception of 'creeping legalism,' which is undermining public confidence in the tribunal; and
6 insufficient community education about the tribunal's role.[41]

Despite these shortcomings, VCAT is a highly active and productive body. It deals with cases at an average cost to the government purse of $450 per case.[42] During the period 2008–9, it finalized 81,000 matters on a budget of $35 million. The tribunal has a relatively large number of decision makers, or 'members,' with 44 full-time members and 180 sessional members and a support staff of 200. The tribunal's president is a Supreme Court judge. The two vice-presidents are County Court judges. These high-level appointments give the tribunal a substantial degree of authority.

VCAT has general public support, and there appears little doubt that the community considers it to be beneficial. However, operating an institution of this size and within its budget constraints creates a number of challenges. In addition, the process of amalgamating so many different pre-existing tribunals into a single body created problems of institutional unity, coherence, and organizational effectiveness in the early stages, and some of these institutional and cultural differences persist.

A constant challenge identified in the *One VCAT* report is to balance the objectives of cost-effectiveness and fair decision making. The report notes that VCAT is a tribunal and not a court,

---

40 Bell, *One VCAT, supra* note 37. The following account draws on this report.
41 *Ibid.* at 2–3.
42 *Ibid.* at 2.

but it is also an independent part of the system of justice, not a government department. VCAT operates within a paradigm of justice that is appropriate for a tribunal, but justice is still its objective. This is a fundamental feature of its operating model.[43]

Nevertheless, the quality and consistency of tribunal decisions have been the subject of some criticism. In response, the report proposes improved institutional support for tribunal members, particularly part-time members. It also recommends that a process be established for internal reconsideration of decisions to allow first-instance errors in decisions to be corrected; that questions of law be referred to the president; and that the tribunal be given power to issue guideline judgments to reduce future errors and to help improve internal consistency in decision making. The report sees guideline judgments not as a substitute for appeals but rather as a mechanism for addressing significant issues of general application.[44] Multiple parties and interested persons or organizations could be heard for the purposes of issuing a guideline judgment. The report notes that guideline judgment systems operate successfully in tribunals in Canada and the U.K.[45] The report also recommends the creation of an appeals division within VCAT, to avoid the need for appeals to the Supreme Court.[46]

Criticisms have been levelled against the quality of some of the tribunal's decisions; however, it needs to be recognized that if the only alternative available to small amounts claims litigants is a high-quality but prohibitively expensive court system, they are being offered in effect no access to justice at all. That said, parties are entitled to expect that their disputes will be dealt with by reference to objective, ascertainable, and universally applicable standards, with like cases decided alike and with reasonable consistency and predictability in decision making.[47]

VCAT faces a problem which many Australian courts complain about, and that is the difficulty of dealing with self-represented litigants. A further and related problem, also not confined to VCAT, is the difficulty of obtaining sufficient and reliable evidential material from self-representing parties. The apparent opposite problem can also be

---

43 *Ibid.* at 37.
44 *Ibid.* at 62.
45 *Ibid.* at 61.
46 *Ibid.* at 31.
47 *Ibid.* at 39.

faced by a tribunal when it is presented with a mass of letters, e-mails, and other documentation, much of which is often irrelevant or repetitive. With self-represented litigants, tribunal members have the heavy burden of obtaining a coherent account of each party's argument and locating the supporting evidence, without the assistance of counsel. Despite the difficulties, the report recommends that there be a positive duty on the tribunal to assist all parties; that an in-person coordinator be appointed for litigants; that the powers and duties of the principal registrar be enhanced; that *pro bono* legal services be expanded; and that a self-representation civil law service be established.[48]

VCAT's size presents challenges but also offers considerable advantages by enabling the attainment of economies of scale to lower the overall cost of administrative support, as well as by giving the tribunal flexibility in assigning resources to areas where they are most needed. For instance, the tribunal is able to identify more complex matters and have them dealt with by more senior members.

Doubtless, reforms promoting greater access to justice will after a time further raise community expectations about the nature and quality of the justice system. These enhanced expectations are to be embraced. Courts and their attendant legal practitioners have over the centuries acquired a reputation for elitism and for operating as some kind of privileged and secretive high priesthood. These perceptions may have developed at a time when the courts – or at least Chancery – were heavily populated by members of the clergy, and they are reflected in the savage depictions of the legal profession by Shakespeare, Dickens, and others. The report stresses that the tribunal was established for its users and the community, not the other way around.[49] Community consultations in the lead-up to the report revealed that many users, especially self-represented parties, felt disempowered by their experience in the tribunal, with some feeling a loss of personal dignity, autonomy, and respect. According to the report, these reactions lie 'behind the intense criticism of "creeping legalism," which is often expressed in emotional terms.'[50] The report concludes that this problem should be recognized and acted upon.[51]

The report notes that, to an increasing degree, individuals expect

---

48 *Ibid.* at 44.
49 *Ibid.* at 49.
50 *Ibid.* at 51.
51 *Ibid.*

public institutions to be efficient, responsive, and competent in the performance of their functions and that VCAT is no exception.[52] It adds that individuals expect to be treated with respect, and this implies not just politeness but also accountability, transparency, and due attention paid their complaints.[53] It goes on to say:

> Contemporary society is relatively well educated, but there are groups suffering from disadvantage and even illiteracy; it is socio-economically diverse, with significant numbers of people in [culturally and linguistically diverse and indigenous] communities; it is highly connected by mass-communication systems, yet there are groups who are lonely and disengaged; transport systems are well developed, but distance remains a tyranny for people outside the main population centres in the city and the country; new technology offers great potential for overcoming some of these problems, although not everyone can use or get it and there is no substitute for personal service by a real human being; and people and businesses need access to the means of resolving civil and administrative disputes, yet may encounter many barriers of various kinds in doing so.[54]

In summary, VCAT provides low-cost access to justice across a wide range of jurisdictions, including small claims and consumer credit complaints. The tribunal is heavily used by the public. Its size enables it to use its resources more efficiently than a disaggregated number of separate tribunals would allow. However, the super-tribunal model presents a number of challenges, not the least of which is consistency in decision making and avoidance of creeping legalism.

IV. The Financial Ombudsman Service

Industry-operated ombudsman schemes have been in place for a number of decades in Canada and Australia. One interesting development in Australia is the mandatory requirement for persons providing financial advice to retail (non-professional) investors to become members of an industry-funded external disputes resolution scheme, which is itself required to meet standards laid down by the government.

Canada has a number of industry-operated ombudsman services,

---

52 *Ibid.* at 46.
53 *Ibid.*
54 *Ibid.*

including the Canadian Ombudsman for Banking Services and Investments (OBSI), OmbudService for Life and Health Insurance (OLHI), and the General Insurance Ombudsman (GIO). In addition, the Financial Consumer Agency of Canada (FCAC) was established by the federal government in 2001 to strengthen oversight of consumer issues, expand consumer education in the financial sector, and monitor financial institutions' compliance with voluntary codes of conduct. Section 157 of the *Bank Act*[55] provides that directors of banks must manage or supervise the management of the bank's business and affairs and requires them to establish procedures for dealing with complaints. This, in effect, requires banks to establish internal dispute resolution systems.

Many Canadian banks and financial institutions are members of the industry-run external dispute resolution provider, OBSI. Recommendations made by OBSI regarding the complaints it deals with are not binding on either party, although it claims on its website to have an excellent record regarding acceptance of its recommended settlements by both firms and clients.[56] In 2009, all of its final recommendations for compensation were accepted by firms. As mentioned above, the FCAC plays an oversight role in monitoring firms' compliance with their consumer obligations, including their handling of consumer complaints. However, the FCAC itself does not have a mandate to resolve or provide redress on individual consumer complaints and, in contrast to the position in Australia, membership in industry ombudsman schemes is voluntary.

Australia also has a number of industry-run ombudsman schemes, including the Financial Ombudsman Service (FOS) and the Telecommunications Industry Ombudsman. FOS is an amalgamation of a number of pre-existing industry-run ombudsman and consumer dispute resolution schemes. In July 2008, the Insurance Ombudsman Service, the Financial Industry Complaints Service, and the Banking and Financial Ombudsman Service were combined to form the FOS. This was done to achieve economies of scale and to provide greater public visibility for these dispute resolution services. FOS received nearly a quarter of a million phone inquiries from consumers in 2008–9. In that same period it received nearly 20,000 new dispute applications. It employs 134 full-time and 78 part-time staff, including members of the panels.[57]

Despite the amalgamation, the organization retains internally distinct

---

55 S.C. 1991, c.46.
56 See Ombudsman for Banking Services and Investments, http://www.obsi.ca.
57 http://www.fos.org.au.

terms of reference for managing disputes, which largely conform to the jurisdictions of the pre-amalgamation organizations. Consequently, complaints against financial institutions such as banks are dealt with by FOS staff members, who recommend appropriate ways to resolve the disputes. Complaints against financial planners, life insurers, income protection insurance, and stockbrokers, on the other hand, are often ultimately dealt with by a panel of three decision makers, if the monetary amount is within prescribed amounts. The panel consists of a full-time FOS staff member, who may be a retired judge, magistrate, or senior legal practitioner, along with a member appointed on the recommendation of consumer organizations and another member appointed on the recommendation of industry members of the scheme.

Financial disputes can be resolved by conciliation where both parties agree. Otherwise disputes over a certain amount within the jurisdiction of FOS are resolved by a panel. The process is conducted by correspondence, which is to say that each party puts its case in writing with supporting documentation. The panel makes its decision on the basis of the documentation. A panel decision is binding upon the industry member and (generally speaking) cannot be appealed. A decision is not binding on the consumer. The service is free to consumers and is paid for by industry members through a combination of a general levy and a fee payable for a particular dispute.[58]

At face value, firm membership in the FOS and other industry-run ombudsman schemes is voluntary. There are, however, a number of significant mandatory elements to the schemes, particularly in relation to the provision of financial services. The Australian Securities and Investments Commission (ASIC) must approve the ombudsman scheme; it also sets the standards that the ombudsman scheme applies to resolve disputes.[59] FOS is by far the largest single independent industry-run consumer complaints service. There are two other small schemes for credit societies. In practice, all financial planners and financial institutions (except credit societies) are members of FOS. Because of the size and credibility of FOS, ASIC tends not to closely monitor and report on its activities, although it does maintain a watchful eye to ensure that the organization operates appropriately.

The federal government instituted major reforms regarding the pro-

---

58 www.fos.org.au/centric/home_page/members/apply_for_membership/financial_services_providers.jsp?str=fees+member.

59 See *Corporations Act 2001* (Cth), s. 912A *et seq.*, discussed *infra*.

vision of financial services with the introduction of a package of amendments to the *Corporations Act 2001* (Cth), and the introduction of the *Australian Securities and Investments Commission Act 2001* (Cth). The net effect has been that a person or organization providing financial services advice is required to hold a licence. A licensee has a statutory obligation to provide its services to retail investors in an efficient, honest, and fair way (s. 912A *Corporations Act*), as well as to provide the client with specified information about recommended financial products (ss. 941A and 941B). Section 912A also obliges the licensee to ensure that its representatives are adequately trained and that adequate risk management systems are in place. In addition, the licensee is required to establish an internal dispute resolution procedure that complies with standards and requirements made or approved by the regulator, ASIC. The licensee must also become a member of an external dispute resolution scheme approved by the regulator. As a result, financial planners and advisers are in effect required to join FOS. Members of FOS are required to comply with its constitution, rules, and terms of reference as a condition of membership. The FOS dispute resolution procedures themselves must comply with regulatory requirements. The net effect is that a mandatory external and independent dispute resolution process is available to resolve consumer complaints free of charge to the consumer.

Thus, the Australian government provides a mandatory system of access to justice in the consumer marketplace – a system that is fully funded by industry. Arguably, this benefits both consumers and industry. Consumers benefit from having ready and free access to justice (though ultimately they pay for this benefit through increased prices), and this in turn improves their confidence in the marketplace. Industry benefits from an enhanced reputation, which in turn leads to more consumer activity in the marketplace than would otherwise be the case.

More recent legislative reforms require mortgage brokers and financial institutions to hold a licence, and a condition of the licence is membership in an external dispute resolution scheme. There is also an obligation on licensees to examine whether a potential borrower has a capacity to repay the loan for which he or she is applying.[60] Consumer credit complaints must also be dealt with by an independent external dispute resolution scheme. This requirement is likely to further expand the jurisdiction of FOS.

---

60 *National Consumer Credit Protection Act* 2009 (Cth), Chapter 2.

V. Litigation Funding for Class Actions

Class actions are an important mechanism for dealing with the small amount claims problem. Firms gain an effective immunity from legal action where the harm done to an individual consumer is too small to justify the consumer taking legal action. However, small individual losses in aggregate may sometimes be substantial.[61] If action is not taken to recover these amounts, there may be a significant economic loss to the community and an increase in the provision of substandard consumer goods and services and other poor corporate behaviour. There is therefore a very real social interest in facilitating consumer class actions.[62] In addition, a democratic society should guarantee its citizens access to redress in a real rather than merely a theoretical sense. Indeed, the Supreme Court of Canada in *Western Canadian Shopping Centres Inc v. Dutton* observed that without class actions, 'the doors of justice remain closed to some plaintiffs, however strong their legal claims.'[63]

Of interest in the Australian context is the existence of litigation funding companies, which help stimulate a high number of class actions, relative to other countries.[64] These companies will fund class actions for selected cases in return for a substantial share of any payouts to liti-

---

61 Matthew Good offers the following example: 'Consider the following scenario: a bank unlawfully deducts one half of one cent from the accounts of 1,500,000 customers each month for 15 years. Customers complain, but the bank refuses to return the funds. Over time, customers might lose a few dollars each, but the loss to each individual is so minimal as to be almost meaningless. Nevertheless, the bank unlawfully profits to the tune of more than $1,000,000': 'Access to Justice, Judicial Economy, and Behaviour Modification: Exploring the Goals of Canadian Class Actions' (2009) 47 *Alberta Law Review* 185 at 186 [Good, 'Access to Justice'].

62 The Supreme Court of Canada held in *Western Canadian Shopping Centres Inc v. Dutton* [2001] 2 S.C.R. 534 at paras. 27–29 that class proceedings are intended to further three goals: judicial economy; access to justice; and behaviour modification. See also *ibid.* at 186.

63 *Western Canadian Shopping Centres Inc v. Dutton* [2001] 2 SCR 534 at para. 28.

64 The overall proportion of class action cases, however, is relatively small. Since 1992, an average of fourteen class actions have been initiated each year in Australia, representing less than 1 per cent of Federal Court actions. In fact, there has been a decline in the number of class actions over the period since 1992. According to Morabito, 51 per cent of class actions commenced do not continue, or do not continue as a class action: Vincent Morabito, *An Empirical Study of Australia's Class Action Regimes: First Report – Class Action Facts and Figures*, vol. 1 (Department of Business Law and Taxation, Monash University, 2009) at 30 [Morabito, *Class Action Regimes*].

gants. Two major law firms are actively engaged in class actions, which are usually funded by litigation funding companies. Some Australian jurisdictions prohibit contingency fee arrangements. Ironically, this bar has helped prompt the development of litigation funders. The funders are not constrained from entering into contingency payment agreements. This was confirmed in the Australian High Court decision of *Campbells Cash & Carry v. Fostif*. [65] In *Fostif,* the defendants argued that litigation funding was an abuse of process; the law had long prohibited the funding of legal actions by third parties on the basis that it amounts to champerty, maintenance, and barratry. [66] However, the court rejected the argument, with Kirby J. going so far as to say that the 'importance of access to justice, as a fundamental human right which ought to be readily available to all, is clearly a new consideration that stimulates fresh thinking about representative or "grouped" proceedings.' [67] Kirby J. further observed that

> [t]o lawyers raised in the era before such multiple claims, representative actions and litigation funding, such fees and conditions may seem unconventional or horrible. However, when compared with the conditions approved by experienced judges in knowledgeable courts in comparable circumstances, they are not at all unusual. Furthermore, the alternative is that very many persons, with distinctly arguable legal claims, repeatedly vindicated in other like cases, are unable to recover upon those claims in accordance with their legal rights. [68]

In *Fostif*, the appellants sold tobacco products as wholesalers to supermarkets and other retailers. They had about 21,000 customers. The price of the goods sold to the retailers included a tax payable to the State government that was later found to be unconstitutional. A subsequent court decision ruled that the retailers could recover from the wholesalers the invalid taxes they had not remitted to the State taxing authority. Despite requests from retailers, wholesalers largely ignored their demands for repayment of the money. The litigation funder, Firmstones Pty Ltd, instituted the 'tobacco licence fee recovery project' in which it engaged solicitors and approached retailers so as to take court action on

---

65 [2006] HCA 41, 229 CLR 386 [*Fostif*].
66 *Jeffery & Katauskas v. SST Consulting*, [2009] HCA 43, 239 CLR 75 at para. 25.
67 *Fostif, supra* note 65 at para 145.
68 *Ibid.* at para 120.

their behalf to recover the tax amounts. Quick agreement was reached between the wholesalers and a number of large retailers in 2001. In 2002, in an action funded by IMF Australia (another litigation funder), 9,500 small retailers brought action against Philip Morris and British American Tobacco, Australia. The matter was settled, with the retailers receiving a refund of 105 per cent of the licence fees and IMF receiving 30 per cent of the refund. Meanwhile, Firmstones acted for Shell and nine hundred other retailers. It was this claim that led to the High Court action. Kirby J. noted that 'it is a fair inference that, but for the foregoing proceedings, the residual wholesalers would not have refunded the outstanding invalid licence fees to the retailers concerned.'[69] In other words, to extract the refunds, litigation was necessary.

Litigation funders typically enter into agreements with potential litigants in which it is agreed that the fund will receive between one-third and two-thirds of the proceeds. The fund then retains a law firm that agrees to conduct the litigation for the fund on the basis of the 'normal' rules governing the legal profession. The funder retains a broad discretion to conduct litigation as it sees fit. The lawyers can, however, charge an 'uplift fee' if the litigation is successful.[70]

IMF (Australia) Ltd is a litigation funder that listed on the Australian stock exchange in 2007 with a $35 million float. It tends to hire the law firm Maurice Blackburn for its class action litigation. Another Australian law firm heavily involved in class actions is Slater & Gordon, the world's first publicly listed law firm. It tends to undertake actions funded by Comprehensive Legal Funding LLC, a Texas-headquartered company that recently opened an office in Melbourne. On its website, Comprehensive claims that it will consider funding any case that has legal merit, including class actions involving securities, product liability, or employment law.[71]

Through its website Slater & Gordon is presently inviting potential claimants to register involvement with a number of class actions. The cases include actions on behalf of shareholders and small investors relating to failed investment companies. Other actions include an action on behalf of travel agents against Qantas and six other airlines to recover commissions on allegedly wrongly imposed fuel surcharges.

---

69 *Fostif, supra* note 65 at para 112.
70 Stuart Clark and Christina Harris, 'The Push to Reform Class Action Procedure in Australia: Evolution or Revolution?' (2008) 32 Melb.U.L.R. 775 at 789.
71 See Comprehensive Legal Funding, http://www.comprehensivelegalfunding.com.

Slater & Gordon is also involved in the class action against the pharmaceutical company Merck, which withdrew its product Vioxx from the market on 30 September 2004 after the company's own study found that people who had taken a dosage of 25 mg for eighteen months or more faced a higher risk of heart attacks and strokes.

IMF Australia is presently taking action against Australian banks for allegedly overcharging their customers about $5 billion in penalty and late fees over the past six years. The fees are generally imposed if a customer's bank account exceeds an agreed overdraft limit, the customer's cheque bounces, or the customer is late in repaying a monthly loan or credit card debt. The fees typically range between $25 and $60 on each transaction. IMF is using its website to sign up claimants. It alleges that the fees and charges exceed a reasonable pre-estimate of the loss to the financial institution and are therefore an unlawful penalty.[72]

However, a degree of caution needs to be exercised in assessing the consumer benefits to be gained from litigation-funded class actions. There is a risk that the relevant law firms and litigation funders, under pressure to maximize returns for the shareholders, will insist on taking an unduly large proportion of any successful claim, in some cases rendering the return to the consumer relatively insignificant. Of course, the risk and expense borne by the funder can be quite high, so it is reasonable to expect that it will want a good return on its investment. Nevertheless, the Australian government needs to keep a close eye on the activities of litigation funders to ensure that they do not unfairly exploit class action plaintiffs.

As indicated above, the emergence of litigation funding in Australia has been prompted in part by the prohibition of contingency fee arrangements in some jurisdictions. There is no similar prohibition in Canada. A survey undertaken in 2009 reported a total of 332 class actions being undertaken in Canada during the spring of that year, the vast majority (if not all) of which were undertaken on a contingency fee basis.[73] Clearly, class actions are popular in Canada, despite the absence of litigation funders. However, in the recent Ontario case *Dugal v. Man-*

72 A. Ferguson and M. West, 'Fee Gouging: Banks Face Huge Class Action' *Sydney Morning Herald*, 12 May 2010.
73 J. Kalajdzic, 'Consumer (In)justice: Reflections on Canadian Consumer Class Actions' (2010) *Canadian Business Law Journal* 356 at 359. This contrasts with the 241 class actions filed with the Australian Federal Court between 2002 and 2009; see Morabito, *Class Action Regimes*, vol. 1 at 24.

ulife Financial Corporation,[74] the court approved a third-party funding arrangement under which an Irish company, Claims Funding International plc, agreed to indemnify the plaintiffs against costs in return for a 7 per cent share of any award or settlement. This case may signal the rise of litigation funding in Canada and makes the Australian experience apposite. One possible advantage of third-party litigation funding is that it indemnifies the plaintiffs and their lawyers, thereby shifting the risks of losing an action to the funder. This in turn allows the plaintiffs' lawyers to focus their attention on prosecuting the case rather than on the costs and risks of the action.

VI. Conclusion

Effective access to justice is an essential component of the rule of law. Enhanced access to justice in the consumer marketplace offers improved economic and social outcomes through greater consumer confidence in the market and increased consumer activity. Consumer expectations about being treated fairly and justly in the marketplace are increasing, just as their capacity to voice opinions about bad service and unjust treatment is being enhanced by the Internet. Governments and firms that fail to take due account of these increasing expectations as well as consumers' capacity to express dissatisfaction at not having these expectations met do so at their peril. These rising expectations may not necessarily be visible to governments and their policy advisers unless they appreciate the community's understanding of, and expectations about, 'justice.' The community's understanding is, in some respects, broader than that of a lawyer or jurisprudential scholar. Consumers sometimes experience 'injustice' as a deep emotional response to being treated unfairly. Insights from empirical research by scholars interested in consumer behaviour and expectations in the marketplace are important in this regard. With a broader understanding of consumer comprehensions and expectations about justice, we can start to think more creatively about possible ways of catering to them.

An effective policy and legislative response requires more nuanced and varied approaches than, for instance, simply widening the doors of the courts (in the metaphorical sense) and increasing legal aid budgets, as important as these initiatives are. It requires, among other things, enlisting marketplace firms in the provision of access to justice. Their

---

74 2011 ONSC 1785 (Ont.Sup.Ct).

enlistment is appropriate as they are often the beneficiaries of a marketplace where consumers feel they will be treated justly and fairly. Firms benefit from greater consumer confidence and participation in the marketplace.

Building on these thoughts, this paper has discussed Australian developments aimed at improving consumer access to justice. These developments provide some interesting comparisons with Canadian approaches. The Australian experience suggests ways of providing cheap and effective access to justice in the consumer marketplace, including the establishment of 'super-tribunals,' mandating firm membership in approved industry-run external dispute resolution schemes, and enhancing consumer access to class actions.

12 Challenges in Small Claims Court Design: Does One Size Fit All?

SHELLEY MCGILL

I. Introduction

The small claims court holds a unique place in access to justice theory;[1] often hailed as the 'People's Court,' it purports to offer individuals an informal, fast and inexpensive public forum for resolution of small disputes.[2] Within this aggressive mandate, the court is charged with the responsibility of satisfying the access *and* justice needs of disputants. In addition to access to justice objectives, the court has other responsibilities, such as enhancing government efficiency within the administration of justice as a whole and offering effective business debt collection. In sum, the expectations for small claims courts are numerous and varied, involving individual, public, government, and business interests.

Unfortunately, all too often reality falls short of expectations and Canadian small claims courts struggle to meet their many conflicting objectives.[3] Across the country, provinces take differing approaches to system design in the valiant effort to fulfil their complicated mandates.[4]

---

1 Shelley McGill, 'Small Claims Court Identity Crisis: A Review of Recent Reform Measures' (2010) 49 Can. Bus. L.J. 213 at 214–17 [McGill, 'Identity Crisis'] (describing a multidimensional strategy).
2 Sean C. McGuire and Roderick A. Macdonald, 'Small Claims Court Cant' (1996) 34 Osgoode Hall L.J. 509.
3 See, for example, Jacob Ziegel, 'Canadian Consumer Law and Policies 40 Years Later: A Mixed Report Card' (2010) 50 Can. Bus L.J. 259 at 291–2 (lamenting failure to serve the consumer); and *Civil Justice Review, Supplemental and Final Report* (Toronto: Ministry of the Attorney General, 1996) at 93 [*Civil Justice Review*] (citing unclear objectives as a barrier to reform).
4 McGill, 'Identity Crisis,' *supra* note 1 at Appendix 1.

This paper examines the plight of the small claims court in three contexts. First, the inherent conflict between the requirements of access and those of justice are demonstrated through an examination of common system characteristics with a view to focusing attention on the complexity of small claims court system design and the impossibility of meeting all expectations.[5] Procedurally, one size does not fit all. Next, the paper shines light on the absence of access to justice characteristics in the small claims court's post-judgment phase. Often little more than a mirror image of the superior court model, post-judgment processes lack the easy, fast, and inexpensive features that are standard in the pre-judgment process. The post-judgment phase is arguably the most important and sensitive part of the system, and reforms are needed to bring an access to justice perspective into its design.[6] Finally, the paper considers recent external pressures that have been brought to bear on the small claims court by emerging dispute resolution forums and players.[7] Recommendations for more effective integration are made.

If the small claims court is to remain a vital component in an overall access to justice strategy, it must evolve and respond to the internal and external pressures placed upon it. With identified priorities, integrated processes, and a holistic view of dispute resolution through collection, the small claims court can continue to make a valuable contribution to access to justice.

II. Conflicting Priorities and the Challenge of System Design

Although access to justice is not synonymous with access to the courts,[8]

---

5 Content in this part drawn from McGill, 'Identity Crisis,' *supra* note 1.
6 Content drawn from Shelley McGill, 'Is It Worth the Paper It's Written On? The Search for an Improved Model for Small Claims Court Judgment Enforcement,' paper presented to the 2010 Conference of the Southeastern Academy of Legal Studies in Business, Charleston, 13 November 2010; subsequent revision published as 'Is It Worth the Paper It's Written On? Examining Small Claims Court Judgment Enforcement in Canada and the United States' (2011) 17 *Journal of Legal Studies in Business* 22.
7 Content drawn from Shelley McGill, 'Who Should Protect the Consumer? The Eroding Role of the Small Claims Court,' paper presented to the 40th Annual Workshop on Commercial and Consumer Law, Toronto, 16 October 2010 (unpublished).
8 McGill, 'Identity Crisis,' *supra* note 1 at 215–17 (describing the relationship); see also *Listening to Ontarians: Report of the Ontario Civil Legal Needs Project* (Toronto: Ontario Civil Legal Needs Project Steering Committee, 2010) at 19 [OCLN] (82 per cent of respondents considered the 'courts an important way for ordinary people to protect their rights').

it is the oft cited rationale for the small claims court.[9] Access and justice, although interrelated, have different objectives: access focuses on reducing barriers to use, and justice focuses on the substantive and procedural fairness of the resolution. Often access to justice initiatives advance one or other of these components, but the small claims court is assigned both tasks. The now common cant[10] reflects access objectives in its references to 'easy and inexpensive' processes, whereas justice priorities are reflected in sworn evidence, public adjudication,[11] wide appeal rights, and motions to set aside. Inherent conflict arises when efforts are made to design an informal quick process that still retains enough formality to yield fair and accurate results. How much justice should be sacrificed in the interests of access?[12] This question involves balance and proportionality, and the answer inevitably defines the priority of the court.

Added to this already conflicted environment are several other objectives.[13] The small claims court acts as a flagship for the entire justice system. Litigants may judge the effectiveness of the entire administration based upon their experiences in this court. As well, the government faces cost limitations in delivering the judicial system and not surprisingly looks to the small claims court for efficiencies. Finally, the commercial marketplace needs a forum to collect its minor debts; without this facility, the public would absorb such losses through higher prices generally. These goals further complicate the already conflicted access to justice priorities.

---

9 See, for example, *Grover v. Hodgins*, 2011 ONCA 72, [2011] O.J. No. 310 at paras. 45–9 [*Grover*]; Ontario Superior Court of Justice, Chief Justice Heather Smith, 'Ontario's Overview of Two Approaches to Keeping Litigation Costs in Check,' paper presented to the Into the Future: The Agenda for Civil Justice Reform conference of the Canadian Forum on Civil Justice, 1 May 2006 at 2, http://cfcj-fcjc.org/docs/2006/smith-en.pdf.

10 McGuire and Macdonald, 'Small Claims Court Cant,' *supra* note 2 (coining the phrase).

11 See George Adams, 'The Small Claims Court and the Adversary Process, More Problems of Function and Form' (1973) 51 Can. Bar Rev. 583 at 592 (defining adjudication).

12 Robert Goldschmid, British Columbia Ministry of the Attorney General, 'The Civil Justice Reform Context Behind British Columbia's Expedited Litigation Rule and the Small Claims Court Jurisdictional Limit Increase' (Victoria: Ministry of the Attorney General, 2005) at 5, http://www.ag.gov.bc.ca/justice-reform-initiatives/publications/pdf/Goldschmid.pdf; *Grover*, *supra* note 9 at para. 46 (suggesting convenience and accessibility should be the priorities of the court).

13 *Civil Justice Review*, *supra* note 3 at 93.

The recent survey of the civil legal needs of Ontarians concluded that access to justice cannot be delivered in a one-size-fits-all model,[14] and this is also true for small claims court system design. It is not possible to design one system that meets all goals for all disputes and all stakeholders. The challenge is evident in the examination of some typical characteristics of the court.

A. Eligibility of Disputes (Size vs Type)

The complexity of managing multiple objectives is visible in the seemingly simple task of defining eligible disputes. Virtually all Canadian and U.S. systems set a maximum monetary value for eligible disputes, ranging in Canada from $5,000 to $25,000, with half the provinces at $20,000 or above.[15] Although high limits are often defended with 'improving access' rationales,[16] they may actually be motivated by the government efficiency objective. High limits trigger downloading of high court backlogs to the lower court, the inflation of claims that would be advanced in the small claims court in any event, and the resurgence of abandoned claims.[17] To further encourage downloading, most Canadian jurisdictions expressly empower litigants to waive any excess above the small claims limit, and this brings even larger disputes within the small claims court jurisdiction.[18] Naturally, the concept of large is relative and changes over time, but the dramatic increase in the Ontario limit[19] cannot be justified on purely inflationary grounds[20] and

---

14 OCLN, *supra* note 8 at 4.

15 McGill, 'Identity Crisis,' *supra* note 1 at Appendix 1.

16 Higher limits give more disputes (and possibly more disputants) access to the quick, inexpensive, and simplified process.

17 *Civil Justice Review, supra* note 3 at 93 (citing backlog reduction as objective); Hon. Coulter A. Osborne, *Civil Justice Reform Project Summary of Findings and Recommendations* (Toronto: Ministry of the Attorney General, 2007) at 17–18 (projecting volume if limit increased); Peter Adams *et al., Evaluation of the Small Claims Program,* vol. 1 (Victoria: Ministry of Attorney General of B.C., 1992) at ii (reporting that claims came 'out of the woodwork' after limit increase), cited in Manitoba Law Reform Commission, *Review of the Small Claims Court* (Winnepeg: Manitoba Law Reform Commission, 1998) at 32–3, http://www.gov.mb.ca/justice/mlrc/reports/099.pdf.

18 See, for example, N.L.R. 52/97, Rule 3(4).

19 Ontario's limit rose from $6,000 to $10,000 in 2001 and to $25,000 in 2010.

20 Between 2001 and 2009, Ontario's annual consumer price index ranged from a low of –2 per cent to a high of 2.2 per cent; Statistics Canada Consumer Price Index Ontario Summary (2005–9), http://www40.statcan.gc.ca/l01/cst01/econ09g-eng.htm;

must reflect a change in priorities for the court. When monetary limit is the dominant criterion and the limit is set relatively high, the obvious objectives are government efficiency, with access trumping justice. The inevitable side effects of high limits include increased fees,[21] more legal representation,[22] and longer trials – all usually considered barriers to access. When more money is at stake, the procedures must reflect the higher jeopardy, and therefore systems tend to become more formalized.[23] Similarly, litigants can hardly be denied the right to legal representation when faced with potential liability of $25,000 plus costs and interest. Quebec is the only province that prohibits legal representation and correspondingly keeps its monetary limit relatively low, at $7,000. [24] Similarly, low limits are prevalent in the United States, where lawyers are often excluded.[25] British Columbia takes a tiered approach, essentially creating a small claims court within small claims court; in that province, claims are streamed by value and formality increases with the value of the claim.[26]

Although Canadian courts restrict eligibility of a few types of disputes, subject matter is not at the core of the access decision. By contrast, the Australian state of Victoria adopts dispute type as its major eligibility criterion. The Victorian Civil and Administrative Tribunal (VCAT) defines eligibility based upon the subject matter of the dispute, not its monetary value.[27] Dispute value remains relevant to determine

Statistics Canada Consumer Price Index Historic Summary (2000–4), http://www40.statcan.gc.ca/l01/cst01/econ150b-eng.htm. See also Marvin A. Zuker, *Ontario Small Claims Court Practice 2001–2002* (Toronto: Thomson Rueters, 2001) at lxxxiii (making the inflation argument relating to the $10,000 limit).

21 McGill, 'Identity Crisis,' *supra* note 1 at n106.

22 *Civil Justice Review, supra* note 3 at 99.

23 For example, with Ontario's increased limits came mandatory settlement conferences for all claims (1 July 2006), service of witnesses lists and document discovery (R. 13.03(2) O. Reg. 78/06).

24 Arts. 953, 959 C.C.P.

25 See, for example, California (attorneys not allowed, limit is $7,500) and Arizona (attorneys not allowed, limit is $2,500). The median monetary limit across the United States is $4,250: Bruce Zuker and Monica Herr, 'The People's Court Examined: A Legal and Empirical Analysis of the Small Claims Court System,' (2003) 37 U.S. F. L. Rev, 315, 318.

26 B.C. Reg. 263/93, Rule 9.2; Small Claims Court Pilot Project (B.C. Reg. 360/07), creating four processes.

27 Disputes over goods or services supplied in trade or commerce, and relating to residential or retail tenancies, may be advanced by individuals, consumers, businesses, or companies regardless of their value. Victoria Civil and Administrative Tribunal

type of hearing, entitlement to legal representation, and cost awards.[28] In effect, increased formality is reserved for the higher-valued claims and the modest-level claims are protected from the formalization that comes with high limits. This graduated value approach is an attractive way to satisfy the differing objectives of the court. Ontario's retreat from graduated-value features[29] should be reconsidered in light of recent limit increases.

B. Eligibility of Disputants

Much of the criticism of the small claims court involves the characteristics of the users. Some complain that parties do not reflect the demographics of society generally,[30] that the poor are not accommodated,[31] or that businesses dominate as plaintiffs.[32] The reality is that only Quebec restricts access to the court by disputant characteristics, prohibiting corporations and businesses.[33] The obvious conclusion is that access to justice for any particular group is not the priority of remaining Canadian small claims courts; rather, ensuring access for *all* claimants with *modest-sized* disputes is the goal.[34] Therefore, evaluation based upon disputant characteristics is at odds with the apparent priority of system designers.

Rules 2008, S.R. No. 65, r. 2.03(3), Sch. 1, Part 2. For further discussion of the VCAT, see Justin Malbon, 'Access to Justice for Small Amount Claims in the Consumer Marketplace: Lessons from Australia,' *supra* this volume.

28 See Victorian Civil and Administrative Tribunal, Civil Disputes – Small Claims Hearings, http://www.vcat.vic.gov.au.

29 Until the mid 1990s, Ontario had graduated fees. See O. Reg. 585/91 (claims under $100 cost $9.05 to issue, under $500 for $16.20 and over $1,000 for $31.70 [$3,000 limit]). When first introduced in the early 2000s, settlement conferences were only mandatory for claims over $2,000. Appeals remain controlled by the value of the dispute but at such a modest level (claims over $500 since the 1970s increased to $2,500 on 1 January 2011 by O. Reg. 440/10) that it is hardly exclusionary. Awardable costs remain capped by claim value (15 per cent); *Courts of Justice Act*, R.S.O. 1990, c. C-43, s. 29.

30 McGuire and Macdonald, 'Small Claims Court Cant,' *supra* note 2 at 545–7.

31 *Ibid.* at 510.

32 Ziegel, 'Canadian Consumer Law and Policies,' *supra* note 3 at 292; Adams, *supra* note 11 at 608-609 (citing 4 earlier studies, discussing Terence G. Ison, 'Small Claims' (1972) 35 Modern L. Rev. 18); Suzanne E. Elwell and Christopher Carlson, 'The Iowa Small Claims Court: An Empirical Analysis' (1990) 75 Iowa L. Rev. 433, 484.

33 Art. 953 C.C.P. Ontario indirectly targets business with frequent user fees; see *infra* note 42.

34 See Adams, 'The Small Claims Court and the Adversary Process,' *supra* note 11 at 611 (concluding not intended to serve one type of disputant).

Allowing business plaintiffs access to the small claims court can be defended on consumer protection, commercial market efficiency, and historic grounds. Forcing business to take its disputes to a more expensive, complicated, or slower forum does not serve the interests of the consumer defendant or the public at large. Consumers will be placed in higher jeopardy and unable to defend without representation. Even for undefended actions, increased costs ultimately will be borne by the consumer. If business decides against pursuing the debt in the higher court, the public will suffer as the losses are recouped through higher prices generally. Efficient functioning of the commercial marketplace requires an effective debt collection mechanism.[35] Providing this mechanism is a recognized historic objective of the Canadian small claims court.[36]

Streaming is a possible compromise. British Columbia has introduced a separate track for business debt collection, with streamlined procedures. It is unclear whether this separate track for business is more effective than generally available streamed options in Ontario. Clerks in Ontario may sign judgment for undefended claims involving any liquidated damages.[37] Also, where the amount of indebtedness or terms of payment are the only issues in dispute, Ontario litigants may be redirected to a 'terms of payment hearing' rather than trial.[38] Eligibility is not defined by disputant type or dispute size; rather, the substance of the defence determines access.

C. Legal Representation

Another very controversial feature in system design is whether to allow legal representation. In sharp contrast to Quebec's prohibition of lawyers, Ontario seems to be encouraging legal representation by removing the cap on legal fees specifically[39] and by equalizing cost entitlement for

---

35 Georg Haibach, 'The Commission Proposal for a Regulation Establishing a European Small Claims Procedure: An Analysis' (2005) 4 E.R.P.L. 593 at 594; see also Zuker and Herr, 'The People's Court Examined,' *supra* note 25 at 316 (reporting significant economic impact).

36 Adams, 'The Small Claims Court and the Adversary Process,' *supra* note 11 at 605–8 (tracing the history and acknowledging that the majority of cases are from business).

37 O. Reg. 258/98 Rule 11.02(1).

38 O. Reg. 258/98 Rule 9.03(1–7). The hearing focuses on reasonableness of terms and ability to pay; judgment is not entered unless default occurs.

39 In 2006, the $300 limit on lawyer's representation fees was removed. Paralegals were considered ineligible for representation fees; subsequent amendments set paralegals'

lawyers and paralegals. This seems a natural fairness and justice reaction to the increased limit that has raised the stakes and formalized the process. Not surprisingly, VCAT takes a tiered approach to the right to legal representation, allowing lawyers only for claims over $10,000; but most importantly, the cost of the lawyer is not passed on to the unsuccessful litigant.

The impact of the loser-pays rule in small claims court will be discussed more fully below, but suspension of the rule for legal fees is a possible compromise between the access and justice features of the court. Forcing a reluctant litigant to attend unrepresented seems unfair and a denial of natural justice, but forcing the other party to pay for the personal choice of the represented party is at odds with the inexpensive character of the court and significantly raises the stakes.

D. Fees and Costs

Fees charged by the court and costs awarded to the litigants[40] combine to determine whether or not the system is inexpensive. The determination cannot be made in isolation. Expense is relative and it raises the obvious question 'compared to what?' The answer is not clear – compared to the cost of superior court individual actions? arbitration? class actions? the size of the dispute? the means of the disputant? Ontario seems divided on the answer. The 15 per cent cap on total costs suggests a 'size of dispute' comparative. However, flat fees that apply equally to all disputes rebut such a presumption and suggest an alternative comparative.

Fee increases have been quite dramatic over the past decade and are usually defended based on both higher limits and higher court cost comparatives.[41] Ontario long ago abandoned a graduated fee scale based on value of claim and adopted a single issuing and set-down fee

---

fees at 50 per cent of lawyers' fees. As of 2011, there is no limit for either lawyer or paralegal fees subject only to the general cap of 15 per cent exclusive of disbursements: O. Reg. 440/10. The *Civil Justice Review* of 1996 suggested lawyers should be limited in what they can charge their clients for small claims court work; *supra* note 3 at 101–2.

40 Unrepresented litigants may also request $500 as compensation for inconvenience and expense irrespective of the value of their claim. O. Reg. 440/10, s. 5 amending Rule 19.05.

41 See, for example, Smith, 'Ontario's Overview of Two Approaches,' *supra* note 9.

irrespective of the claim's value.[42] Without graduated fees, the lower-end claims quickly become economically unfeasible to pursue, even for those with means. Who will sue to recover $200 when it costs $75 to issue the claim, $20 to serve it, and $100 to set it down for trial? The need for the class action is born.

Fee waivers[43] focus on the means of a disputant and partly address the concern over access for the poor. Unfortunately, poor litigants remain in considerable jeopardy because of the 'loser pays' rule. This should be revisited, if not for all purposes then certainly in the area of representation costs. VCAT rejects loser pays for all claims under $10,000 and for most over. In sharp contrast, Ontario uses 'loser pays' as a tool to encourage settlement[44] and to punish bad behaviour.[45] Even the 15 per cent cap can be exceeded to punish unreasonable behaviour.[46] The small claims court was never contemplated as a high-stakes game where litigants are punished for having their day in court. A loss should mean that the loser must pay what is owed, without an added penalty for trying to defend. Such a concept speaks to the government efficiency need to discourage trials and keep trial lists at manageable and timely levels; this is understandable, but it is inconsistent with accessibility and justice concerns. How can unrepresented litigants be punished for failing to accurately value their claims? Costs should not be used as a weapon to extort submission in the people's court.

E. Procedural Features and Formality

Just and fair decision-making models are neutral, accurate, and transparent, and outcomes are correctable.[47] Typical justice features of formal court proceedings include pleadings, pre-trial disclosure, public adjudicative formats, sworn evidence, settlement conferences, and appeals. The Ontario small claims court system adopts this standard

---

42 Fees are increased by volume; they are higher for plaintiffs who issue more than ten claims per calendar year. See O. Reg. 432/93, s.1(3), Sch. 1.
43 Fees charged for issuing and defending a claim may be waived by the clerk or deputy judge for eligible litigants as defined: O. Reg. 2/05, *infra* note 132.
44 Costs awarded against a losing party may be doubled for failing to accept a reasonable settlement offer: O. Reg. 258/98, Rule 14.07(1).
45 Inserting a setdown fee after the settlement conference and doubling eligible cost awards: *supra* note 43.
46 *Courts of Justice Act*, R.S.O. 1990, c. C-43, s.29.
47 McGill, 'Identity Crisis,' *supra* note 1 at 219.

format, albeit with some modifications.[48] Forms are simplified although numerous,[49] disclosure is limited although mandatory,[50] hearsay rules are relaxed, and trial dates are expedited.[51] Appeals and new trials remain widely available.[52] The same process is applied to all defended claims, and all steps are user driven.[53] What justice compromises are appropriate to advance the access goals of speed, finality, and low cost remains a question of balance and proportion that cannot and should not be answered the same way for all claims.

As in other provinces,[54] Ontario courts are encouraged to apply proportionality principles to questions of procedural justice,[55] but again, there are multiple proportionality considerations: speed, expense, dispute size, and issue complexity. The small claims court is only expressly asked to consider the most expeditious and least expensive interpretation of its rules.[56] Such case-by-case assessment lacks the predictability and certainty necessary for easy use. The flexibility to deal with certain cases differently should not be left to the discretion of the individual judge. Litigants should enter the system with an understanding of the proceedings available to them and should not have avenues foreclosed or expanded on a case-by-case basis.

Both British Columbia and VCAT tier the available processes based upon the value of the dispute, increasing the formality of the proceedings for higher values. However, dispute value does not always determine

---

48 As do most Canadian small claims courts, to varying degrees. Consider Quebec's no lawyers or corporate plaintiffs, and also B.C.'s varying streams for mediation.

49 O. Reg. 78/06 (forty forms).

50 Witness lists and document lists before settlement conferences: O. Reg. 258/98, Rules 13.02(7), 13.03(2).

51 Time line for settlement conference and trials: O. Reg. 258/98, Rule 13.01(3), 11.1.01, 17.02(2).

52 Appeal eligibility changed from $500 to $2,500 on 1 January 2011; Default Judgment may be set aside and even trial *de novo* may be ordered based upon new evidence: O. Reg. 258/98, Rules 17.01(4), 17.04(1).

53 Undefended claims do not require a settlement conference and may go to judgment without an assessment hearing if the claim is one of liquidated damages: O. Reg. 258/98, Rule 11.02.

54 Goldschmid, 'The Civil Justice Reform Context,' *supra* note 12 (proportionality in B.C.); *Ontario Rules of Civil Procedure*, R.R.O. 1990, Reg. 194 Rule 1.04(1) as am. by O. Reg. 436/10 [*Ontario Rules*].

55 *Ontario Rules*, *supra* note 54, Rule 1.04(1.1) (the court shall make orders and give directions that are proportionate to the importance and complexity of the issues, and to the amount involved, in the proceeding).

56 O. Reg. 258/98, Rule 1.03.

complexity, so the more formalized proceedings should also be available for complicated issues and multiparty proceedings. The less formal process should be preserved for low-valued simple disputes. Naturally graduated fees and cost rules should match the tiered processes.

Multiple processes would be a significant sea change for Ontario, given its trend toward standardization, and would be administratively challenging; but such an approach could accommodate a wider range of objectives than the current one-size-fits-all model.

F. System Evaluation

Nowhere is the confusion over the role of the small claims court more evident than in the evaluation of its performance. Is it fast? Is it cheap? Is it easy to use? Does it handle volume? Are litigants happy with outcomes? Are outcomes consistent with the law and one another? Who uses the system? Is there compliance? All of these questions find their way into discussions of the court's effectiveness.[57] In the current one-size-fits-all model, there is no single criterion that enables a fair assessment of the court's performance.[58] Before meaningful evaluation can take place, clear priorities must be set, and sacrifices are inevitable. Ontarians continue to see the courts as an important forum for protection of their rights,[59] so it is important that the small claims court respond their needs.

III. Post-Judgment Phase

Access to justice considerations are relevant to more than just the pre-judgment features and design of the small claims court; they must also be reflected in the design of the post-judgment process. To be considered just or fair, a dispute resolution process must be capable of actually *resolving*, ending, or concluding the dispute. No dispute can be considered completely resolved until outstanding obligations are met. Therefore, a dispute resolution process must incorporate mechanisms

---

57 Patry, *Evaluation of the Nova Scotia Small Claims Court, infra* note 62; McGuire and Macdonald, 'Small Claims Court Cant,' *supra* note 2; Ison, 'Small Claims,' *supra* note 32.

58 One example of an integrated approach to system assessment comes from HALT, an American legal reform organization. It arrives at a single grade by assessing six criteria, with varying weights assigned to each. See McGill, 'Identity Crisis,' *supra* note 1 at 224–5.

59 OCLN, *supra* note 8 (while 82 per cent say courts are important, only 66 per cent say the justice system is fair).

that ensure compliance with outcomes. If outcomes are left unfulfilled, the process will be perceived as unfair to participants and reflect badly upon the whole justice system.

The challenge of post-judgment design is greater in the small claims court context than in superior courts because the judgment amounts are, by definition, small, making the creditor less willing to spend time or money on judgment collection and diminishing the debtor's interest in resolving it. In this context, access considerations suggest a need for easy-to-use, inexpensive, efficient processes that respect the circumstances, sensitivities, and interests of all participants. Cumbersome or expensive features are of little assistance to unrepresented parties. Affected stakeholders extend beyond the immediate small claims court litigants to include third-party garnishees and other disputants referred to the small claims court to collect outstanding administrative tribunal orders or arbitral awards.[60] Unfulfilled judgments impact the general public with higher costs for goods and services and undeterred bad behaviour. Finding a fair balance between divergent creditor and debtor interests, between the needs of the system provider and the interests of the public, is the challenge.

Wide creditor dissatisfaction and high rates of judgment non-compliance are common failings of the post-judgment collection process.[61] One study of the Nova Scotia Small Claims Courts reported that complaints about enforcement were the most common topic among survey respondents, with more than 63 per cent of creditors reporting difficulty collecting their judgments.[62] In Prince Edward Island, government concern over low compliance prompted an Auditor General review of the post-judgment process.[63] On the debtor's side, Ontario has only recently modified its seemingly harsh debtor contempt penalty of a possible forty-day jail term.[64]

The effectiveness of the standard collection tools – garnishments or

---

60 *Residential Tenancies Act*, S.O. 2006, c. 17, s.210; *Arbitration Act*, S.O. 1991, c. 17, s.56(8); *Statutory Powers and Procedures Act*, R.S.O. 1990, c. S.22, s.19(1), (3).

61 Auditor General of Prince Edward Island, 'Report of the Auditor General to the Legislative Assembly' (Charlottetown, 2008) at 70–91, http://www.assembly.pe.ca/auditorgeneral/ag_report2008.pdf.

62 Marc W. Patry, Veronica Stinson, and Steven M. Smith, *Evaluation of the Nova Scotia Small Claims Court: Final Report to the Nova Scotia Law Reform Commission* (Halifax: St Mary's University, 2009) at 82, 85.

63 Patry *et al.*, *supra* note 62.

64 Effective 1 January 2011, length of incarceration is reduced from forty to a maximum of five days: O. Reg. 440/10, s.7(6).

writs of seizure and sale – is largely dependent on the ability of the creditor to first identify or locate debtor assets. Although high cost and complicated user-driven models are significant impediments, nothing is collected without reliable debtor financial information. From the debtor's perspective, a willingness to voluntarily participate or comply may logically be connected to confidence that the system will treat them with respect, sensitivity, and fairness[65] – all hallmarks of access to justice. The debtor must see the court not as a mere extension of the creditor but rather as a neutral overseer empowered to balance the interests of both parties. Creditors should not be allowed to indiscriminately use the information and tools at their disposal without checks and balances to protect debtors from abuse. To that end, this part of the paper focuses on the accessibility and effectiveness of the information-gathering and debtor-accommodation aspects of the process as a means of building creditor and debtor trust and participation.

A. Information Gathering

The Ontario system is typical of others across the country: creditors are entitled to summon defaulting judgment debtors before the court to examine them under oath as to their financial ability to pay.[66] This is a user-driven model: the creditor takes out the appointment, pays the fee, finds the debtor, serves the notice, attends the hearing, asks the questions, and acts on the obtained information. Ontario has struggled with how to handle a debtor's failure to appear at the examination. Prior to 2006, failure to appear triggered a contempt hearing and a possible forty-day committal.[67]

In 2006, concern about the power of a deputy judge to punish *ex facie* contempt led to the transfer of the contempt hearing to the Superior Court.[68] The result was a slower, longer, and more formal process that

---

65 Jennifer Long, 'Compliance in Small Claims Court: Exploring the Factors Associated with Defendants' Level of Compliance with Mediated and Adjudicated Outcomes' (2003) 21(2) *Conflict Resolution Quarterly* 139 at 150 (linking voluntary compliance to perceptions of fairness).

66 O. Reg. 258/98, Rule 20.10.

67 For a history of contempt committal power, see McGill, 'Identity Crisis,' *supra* note 1 at n. 194.

68 The Ontario small claims adjudicator is a part-time deputy judge appointed from the practising bar for renewable terms of three years. See O. Reg. 78/06, amending O. Reg. 258/98, Rule 20.10(11). A distinction is drawn between the constitutional pow-

creditors found not worth pursuing.[69] Amendments, effective in 2011,[70] have returned control of the contempt hearing to the small claims court but with much reduced power to commit – a maximum of five days. The desired judgment debtor (JD) examination may once again be completed in conjunction with the contempt hearing if the debtor appears, furthering the substantive goal – information gathering.

There are still significant barriers to access in Ontario's user-driven approach to information gathering. It is labour intensive for both creditor and debtor; it takes time and money; it can be complicated; and at the end of the day, it may be ineffective. Barriers could be reduced by adopting a more court-driven and user-friendly model that is initiated earlier in the process. U.S. systems provide some insight.

New York City has a well-developed albeit still user-driven approach to information gathering. Information subpoenas may be served on debtors or on *anyone* with information about the debtor's finances.[71] Once served, accurate written responses must be filed with the court at no cost to the creditor, under threat of contempt penalties.[72] Although the subpoena must be requested and served by the creditor, the obligation to provide information is more easily satisfied when the response is by written submission rather than by personal attendance. The wide power to demand information from *anyone* believed to have knowledge gives the creditor a much more powerful tool than is currently available in Canada. Only a reasonable belief that a person has information is required in order to obtain the subpoena.[73]

The New York court also maintains an index of unsatisfied judgments,[74] and business debtors who have three or more debts on the list may be sued by unsatisfied judgment creditors for triple the damages.[75] To defend, the business must establish that it has insufficient resources

---

ers of a deputy judge to deal with *in facie* and *ex facie* contempt. See McGill, 'Identity Crisis,' *supra* note 1 at 239–42, 246–8.

69 Superior Court judges did not complete the JD exam if the debtor appeared, rather they rescheduled another date in small claims; McGill, 'Identity Crisis,' *supra* note 1 at n197 (citing usage statistics for Waterloo Region).

70 *Good Government Act*, S.O. 2009, c. 33, Sch. 2, amending *Courts of Justice Act*, R.S.O. 1990, c. C.43 s.30 (enforcement procedures proclaimed in force 1 January 2011).

71 N.Y. C.P.L.R. § 5224 (2006); N.Y. City Civ. Ct. Act, § 1812(d) (2006).

72 N.Y. City Civ. Ct. Act §1812(d) (2006); N.Y. C.P.L.R. §§ 5224, 2308(b) (2006).

73 Concern over abuse is legitimate as the creditor need not disclose the basis for the reasonable belief and the burden is on the subpoenaed party to challenge its existence.

74 N.Y. City Civ. Ct. Act § 1811(d) (2006).

75 *Ibid.*, § 1812(b).

to pay the outstanding judgments. This provides an alternative way for the creditor to obtain the necessary financial disclosure. Although one would hardly characterize the commencement of an entirely new action as easy compliance, this novel approach is worth noting and does provide creditors with a way to distinguish the impoverished business debtor from the deceitful one. The New York court must advise the local or state licensing authority of any defaults or treble award.[76] The database also adds value to the pre-judgment process; a plaintiff can assess his or her chances of collecting based on the defendant's payment history. A database will provide creditors with useful information throughout the pre- and post-judgment processes.

The Ontario model expects a creditor to wait to see if the judgment is paid voluntarily prior to gathering information. This is not the case in Florida or Arizona, where information gathering begins at the point of granting judgment. At the moment of judgment, a creditor may request or the court may, on its own initiative, inquire into the financial condition of the 'soon-to-be' debtor.[77] Creditors may learn valuable information at this very early stage without the need to wait for default, re-serve the debtor, and re-attend at court. In default proceedings, Florida courts include the demand for information in the judgment and set the time limit for return of the financial disclosure form.[78] The post-judgment steps of separately issuing and serving information subpoenas are bypassed. Although it may be less likely that an absentee party will return the demanded information, it moves the process more quickly to contempt proceedings when the initial demand is contained in the judgment.[79]

California takes an even more court-driven approach to information gathering. All debtors are required to complete a financial information form[80] within thirty days of the entry of the judgment. Any *wilful* failure to do so may be considered contempt of court and attract punishment, including arrest.[81] There is no need for a creditor to request the exer-

---

76 *Ibid.*, §§ 1812(c), 1813(b). Licensing authority to consider revocation or suspension of licence.

77 Fla. Sm. Cl. R. 7.210; Ariz. Rev. Stat. § 22-524.

78 Fla. Sm. Cl. R. 7.221(a).

79 Fla. R. Civ. P. Form 1.982 (contempt notice); same remedies as are generally available in the higher courts (Fla. Sm. Cl. R. 7.220).

80 Judgment Debtor's Statement of Assets Form – S.C. 133; Cal. Civ. Proc. Code §§ 116.620a, 116.830. Form must be provided to the creditor.

81 Cal. Civ. Proc. Code § 116.830(d).

cise of court discretion. It is a mandatory requirement triggered by the granting of judgment.

The contempt powers available in the New York, Florida, California, Arizona, and Nevada small claims courts include commitment to jail for failure to respond to a written information demand.[82] Only the Nevada contempt procedures are divided into *ex facie* and *in facie* processes.[83] The distinction seems to focus on objectivity, not the relative status of the adjudicator.

Although the current Ontario model contemplates written disclosure as part of the judgment debtor examination, Ontario's written form only supplements the mandatory personal attendance.[84] The information-gathering demand could be more easily complied with if written submission replaced personal attendance, at least initially. Incomplete or false disclosures could trigger the more onerous obligation to attend. Early court-initiated demand, possibly as part of the trial notice process, could ensure that information was available for disclosure at the conclusion of the trial. Ontario's recent return of contempt hearings to small claims court control should be expanded to expressly cover the failure to comply with written information demands. These early court-initiated processes could make Ontario's information-gathering process easier to use and to satisfy.

B. Debtor Accommodation

Similar concerns relating to ease of compliance, early intervention, and user- versus court-driven initiatives exist in the context of debtor accommodation. Ontario's post-judgment process contains some safeguards limiting the harshness of the garnishment and seizure tools, including caps on wage garnishments.[85] As well, the court may make a payment order following a JD examination, suspending creditors' rights provided that the debtor remains in compliance.[86] The court may also consolidate multiple small claims court judgments under one com-

---

82 See, for example, Sarasota Clerk of Circuit Court and County Comptroller, 'Small Claims,' http://sarasotaclerk.com/default.asp?Page=70.
83 Nev. Rev. Stat. § 22.030.
84 New Ontario requirements – debtors must serve form on creditor, and bring to exam a copy for court and supporting documentation: O. Reg. 440/10, s.6.
85 *Wages Act*, R.S.O. 1990, c. W.1, s.7(2).
86 O. Reg. 258/98, Rules 20.10 (7)(8), 20.02. General power to impose payment terms and times: *Courts of Justice Act*, R.S.O. 1990, c. C.43, s.28.

bined payment order, providing some relief for a debtor subject to multiple collection efforts by different creditors.[87]

The perceived weakness in the system lies in the court's inability to vary the outstanding balance owing to creditors or to control intimidating or harassing conduct by collection agencies communicating outside the court process. Consumer protection measures outside the small claims court process exist to address these concerns. Under bankruptcy legislation, a consumer may file a proposal reducing the original indebtedness in exchange for voluntary repayment.[88] The Ministry of Consumer Services has a complaints process available to consumers affected by the harassing behaviour of collection agents.[89]

Why not also authorize the small claims court to address these concerns, in a form of one-stop shopping for consumer debtors? The answer may lie in the court's *dispute size* rather than *disputant type* focus and in the limited jurisdiction of the court. The major constitutional barrier to expanding the small claims court debt consolidation and reduction power is that bankruptcy and insolvency are matters of federal jurisdiction and that previous provincial initiatives have been found *ultra vires* of a province.[90] Controlling out-of-court collection agency behaviour is also a lack-of-authority issue; most small claims courts lack the power to grant equitable relief – injunctive, *mandamus*, or declaratory relief is not awarded. Orders may deal only with the payment of money or with the transfer of property.[91] These limitations often mean that the court cannot address struggling consumer debtors' concerns in any comprehensive way.

Florida and Nevada have empowered their courts to impose payment arrangements simultaneously with granting judgment.[92] If the court is persuaded, it may further accommodate the debtor's circumstances by staying entry or execution of the judgment. Relief does not

---

87 *Ibid.*, Rules 20.09, 20.10 (1–7).
88 *Bankruptcy and Insolvency Act*, R.S. 1985, c. B-3, ss.66.11–66.4 (consolidation), ss.217–42 (consumer proposals maximum $250,000).
89 *Infra* notes 148–50.
90 *Reference re Validity of Orderly Payment of Debts Act, 1959 (Alta.)*, [1960] S.C.R. 571, 23 D.L.R. (2d) 449.
91 *Grover, supra* note 9 at paras. 21, 49 (finding that the Ontario Small Claims Court has authority to grant equitable relief only where the relief requested is a payment of money or a transfer of property).
92 Fla. Sm. Cl. R. 7.210; Nev. Justice Court Rules of Civ. Proc. C. XII, R. 97. Ontario deputy judges have general authority to order payment terms, *supra* note 86.

depend upon debtor awareness; the court may invoke the process or initiate a stay on its own. Debtors and creditors leave the trial with a full resolution in hand – with the outcome on the merits as well as a plan for collection in place.

The above-described judgment database also has a debtor protection aspect. Debtors are not left at the mercy of the creditor's calculation of indebtedness; instead they can rely on a court-maintained record. To this end, Florida requires that creditors file a satisfaction of judgment form when the debt is paid in full. The PEI Auditor General's report has also recommended this step to ensure the integrity of the court record. California has gone one step further by creating a civil cause of action against creditors and their agents who fail to file the required satisfaction piece.[93] Although debtors must initiate the action, it is a major step in empowering debtors within the process and ensuring the accuracy of the court record. Another debtor accommodation application of the database relates to debt payment consolidation. A list of unsatisfied judgments affecting the subject parties could easily be generated for the judge at the conclusion of every trial. With this court-driven initiative, the debtor would not need to request consolidation of other outstanding orders or even be aware of the possibility.

The Ontario model could benefit from enhanced power to delay entry of a judgment on debtor accommodation grounds and from access to an unsatisfied judgment database. Existing powers to stay an order or impose payment terms are general discretionary measures, not part of the trial process.[94] Imposing a responsibility on the court to collate all outstanding orders and to consider the debtor's circumstances at the point of entering judgment would make it less user driven. No doubt assigning the court these extra tasks will increase trial time, but the reduced number of appearances may ultimately net an overall efficiency gain.

IV. External Impact on the Small Claims Court System

This part of the paper looks beyond the internal goals and features of the court to the surrounding environment and external developments that also impact the court's ability to meet its goals and advance its access to justice objectives. Two external access to justice developments

---

93 Cal. Civ. Proc. Code § 116.850 (c), (d).
94 *Supra* note 86.

– the growth of alternative forums and the expanded nature of representation – overlap with traditional small claims court turf. In the context of alternative forums, consumer arbitration and class actions target monetarily small consumer disputes, ordinarily within the small claims court genre. In addition, the expanded availability of representation through paralegals, credit counsellors, and collection agencies has changed the dynamics of the small claims courtroom, making third-party representation feasible for typically unrepresented litigants. System designers must acknowledge these developments, accommodate their strengths and weaknesses, and consider the advisability of encouraging or discouraging their use.

A. Consumer Arbitration

In today's marketplace, it is common for standard-form consumer contracts to include arbitration clauses that redirect plaintiff consumers away from class actions and small claims court towards private arbitration. Many dispute the genuineness of the practice, suspecting that business is merely employing the clause as a tactic to discourage consumers from advancing claims.[95] The usual arbitration advantages of party autonomy[96] seem hollow when the choice of arbitration is imposed on unaware consumers as part of 'a take it or leave it' decision to purchase. Consumer usage statistics support the *business tactic* theory, as few consumers resort to arbitration and most continue to see courts as important to the protection of their rights.[97] The U.S. statistics, available as a result of regulation of the industry,[98] indicate that virtually all arbitrations are initiated by business and that the vast majority

---

95 Myriam Gilles, 'Opting Out of Liability: The Forthcoming Near-Total Demise of the Modern Class Action' (2005) 104 Mich. L. Rev. 373 at 378; Shelley McGill, 'Consumer Arbitration Clause Enforcement: A Balanced Legislative Response' (2010) 47 American Bus. L.J. 361 at n. 1 [McGill, 'Clause Enforcement']; *Griffin v. Dell Canada Inc.* 2010 ONCA 29 at para. 30.

96 Andrew Little, 'Canadian Arbitration Law after *Dell Computer Corp. Union des Consommateurs*' (2007) 45 Can. Bus. L.J. 356 at 375–81.

97 OCLN, *supra* note 8 (as to importance of courts); *infra* notes 99–100 (as to consumer usage).

98 Providers must post their disputant usage, outcome, and repeat player data. *See* McGill, 'Consumer Arbitration Clause Enforcement,' *supra* note 95 at 388–90 (highlighting public reporting requirements imposed upon consumer arbitration providers under Cal. Civ. Proc. Code §§ 1280 – 1298.8).

proceed on a default basis.[99] Similarly one-sided usage statistics have been cited by Canadian and American courts.[100] Arbitration's lack of popularity with consumers could relate to unfamiliarity with the process, unknown or high costs, and bias in favour of business.[101]

Across Canada, judicial reaction has been mixed. Applying the general policy in favour of arbitration,[102] some courts have enforced the 'choice' of arbitration and have restricted court jurisdiction. Other courts have doubted the appropriateness of the forum and preferred class actions over private arbitration.[103] The Supreme Court of Canada first signalled its support for consumer arbitration agreements in the Quebec case *Dell Computers v. Union des consommateurs*,[104] without speaking to the common law provinces' practice of integrating the clause enforcement decision with the class action certification process.[105] In the Supreme

---

99 Public Citizen, *The Arbitration Trap: How Credit Companies Snare Consumers* (Washington: Public Citizen, 2007) at 15, http://www.citizen.org/documents/ArbitrationTrap.pdf (finding only 118 out of 33,948 consumer arbitrations conducted by the National Arbitration Forum (NAF) were initiated by consumers, also finding very high business success rate). See NAF, 'California CCP 1281.96 Reports,' http://www.adrforum.com/main.aspx?itemID=563&hidebar=False&navID=188&news=3. Others suggest that high business use and success in consumer arbitration is consistent with court usage: Christopher Drahozal and Samantha Zyontz, 'Creditor Claims in Arbitration and in Court,' (2011) 7 Hastings Bus. L.J. 77.

100 *Scott v. Cingular Wireless* [2007] 161 P.3d 1000 at 1007 (Wash.) (finding not a single arbitration initiated against Cingular by the consumer between 2001 and 2007); *Smith v. National Money Mart Co.*, [2007] O.J. No. 46, at para. 132 (certification hearing, S.Ct.J.) (finding class proceedings preferable because no consumer had ever initiated arbitration against National Money Mart and it even used the courts for its collections).

101 Gilles, 'Opting Out of Liability,' *supra* note 95.

102 Little, 'Canadian Arbitration Law,' *supra* note 96 at 357–62.

103 See for example, *Smith v. National Money Mart Co.*, [2005] O.J. No. 4269 (QL), 258 D.L.R. (4h) 453 (C.A.); *Mackinnon v. National Money Mart Co.*, [2004] B.C.J. No. 1961 (QL), 2005 W.W.R. 233 (BCCA).

104 2007 SCC 34, [2007] 2 S.C.R. 801 [*Dell*] (considering the mandatory stay of a class action prior to certification and holding that the arbitrator must first decide on the validity of the arbitration clause). See also *Rogers Wireless Inc. v. Muroff*, 2007 SCC 35, [2007] 2 S.C.R. 921 (applying *Dell* and holding that consumer arbitration clauses are not inherently unconscionable).

105 This process of refusing a stay application until after it was determined if a class action was the preferable vehicle derives from *Mackinnon 2004, supra* note 103, and has been followed by courts in Ontario and Saskatchewan. Any certification would automatically render the arbitration clause inoperative. After the release of *Dell, supra* note 104, it was reconsidered and overruled in *Seidel v. Telus Communications Inc.* 2009 BCCA 104, 304 D.L.R. (4h) 564, leave granted, 2009 CanLII 61381 (S.C.C.)

Court's recent decision *Seidel v. Telus Communications Inc*,[106] the majority held that, absent legislative intervention to the contrary, consumer arbitration agreements contained in contracts of adhesion are enforceable. Legislative intention to intervene can be found in the explicit or implicit text,[107] context, and purpose of the subject province's consumer protection legislation. The *Seidel* decision will result in a patchwork of positions across the country.

Legislatures are starting to recognize the risks associated with consumer arbitration and in particular, pre-dispute agreements contained in contracts of adhesion.[108] Some Canadian provinces limit enforcement of pre-dispute consumer arbitration agreements,[109] and the U.S. Congress has considered several similar bills, recently holding hearings over the proposed *Arbitration Fairness Act* of 2009.[110] Both nations are contemplating the choice of arbitration remaining alive only through post-dispute agreements. Around the world, many jurisdictions also restrict or regulate consumer arbitration.[111]

(heard and reserved 12 May 2010). Supreme Court decision released 18 March 2011, *infra* note 106.

106   2011 SCC 115 (involving a one-side mediation/arbitration clause obligating only the consumer (not Telus) to use arbitration).

107   *Ibid.* This was the major point of disagreement in the Supreme Court's 5–4 split decision. The majority considered that a legislative intention to exclusively assign the rights and remedies provided for in s.172 of the *British Columbia Business Practices and Consumer Protection Act* SBC 2004, c.2 (BPCPA) to the provincial Supreme Court was implicit in the text, context, and purpose of the legislation. The arbitration clause amounted to a waiver of the s.172 rights and was therefore void under s.3 BPCPA (paras. 2, 5–6, 40). The minority concluded that the public policy in favour of arbitration demanded that only express restrictions of arbitration should operate to block its use. They found no express restriction in the combined reading of ss. 3 and 172 of the BPCPA and warned that the majority opinion represented hostility towards the use of arbitration (paras. 101–3).

108   Standard form agreements, including arbitration clauses, are prepared in advance by the business and submitted to the consumer at the point of purchase; clauses may even be added later online: see *Kanitz v. Rogers Cable Inc.*, [2002] 58 O.R. (3d) 299. The *contra proferentem* rule applies to the interpretation of arbitration clauses: *Seidel*, *supra* note 105 at para. 47.

109   *Consumer Protection Act*, 2002, S.O. 2002, c. C.30, Sch. A, ss.7–8; *Consumer Protection Act*, R.S.Q. c. P-40.1, s.11.1. Alberta's legislation requires ministerial approval of all consumer arbitration clauses: *Fair Trading Act*, RSA 2000, c.F-2, s.16.

110   H.R. 1020, 111th Congr. (2009) (would have invalidated pre-dispute arbitration agreements in consumer, employment, and franchise agreements). See also *Arbitration Fairness Act of 2011*, H.R. 1873, 112th Cong. (2011), s.987.

111   McGill, 'Consumer Arbitration Clause Enforcement,' *supra* note 95 at 391–412 (referencing various strategies adopted around the world).

Perhaps the most stunning development in the consumer arbitration environment is the recent withdrawal of the big U.S. arbitration providers from the consumer debt collection market.[112] The expressed reason was the high rate of non-participating consumers; however, there is no doubt that concern over arbitrator neutrality in the face of the repeat player effect[113] also influenced the decision.[114] Since it is common for consumer arbitration clauses to designate the specific provider, there is new uncertainty as to the interpretation of existing clauses.[115] Will a court force a consumer to use a different arbitrator from that designated in the agreement? It is possible that not-for-profit providers could fill the void in the marketplace and offer the coveted neutrality. In many communities, the Better Business Bureau (BBB) offers business-to-consumer mediation and arbitration services in a not-for-profit and ostensibly more neutral environment.[116] Costs to consumers are minimal, and arbitrators are volunteers or are working for a modest honorarium. Still, it seems unlikely that the BBB could handle any significant volume, and it does not proceed without participation of both parties.

Small claims court system designers must respond to this fluid consumer arbitration environment. At its peak, the consumer arbitration

---

112 In July 2009, NAF and the American Arbitration Association (AAA) announced that they would no longer conduct consumer arbitrations arising from pre-dispute agreements. See NAF, Press Release, 'National Arbitration Forum to Cease Administering All Consumer Arbitrations in Response to Mounting Legal and Legislative Challenges' (19 July 2009), http://www.adrforum.com/newsroom. aspx?itemID=1528; see also AAA, Notice, 'Notice on Consumer Debt Collection Arbitrations' (19 October 2010), http://www.adr.org/sp.asp?id=36427.

113 Generally understood to mean that business as the party most likely to repeatedly use the arbitration forum is more likely to be successful. For an evaluation of the repeat player effect in employment arbitration, see Lisa Blomgren Bingham, 'Employment Arbitration: The Repeat Player Effect' (1997) 1 Employee Rts. & Employment Pol'y J. 189.

114 Days prior to NAF's announcement, the Minnesota Attorney General commenced a lawsuit against NAF, claiming it failed to disclose to consumers its affiliation with major debt collection and credit card companies and that it carried a pro-business bias into the outcomes. NAF's withdrawal was part of the settlement of this lawsuit. See also Public Citizen, *The Arbitration Trap, supra* note 99 at 2, 32–3 (finding that in NAF arbitrations, MNBA won 94 per cent of the time over consumers and suggesting that a pro-business bias was the reason).

115 *Dell, supra* note 104 at para. 55.

116 See, for example, Better Business Bureau for Mid Western and Central Ontario, 'BBB Dispute Resolution Process' (2011), http://www.kitchener.bbb.org/sitePage. aspx?site=160&id=74e956b6-d82d-4cfa-9e87-2312e1b5bdbc.

initiative had the potential to divert a significant portion of plaintiffs' claims away from small claims courts and class actions. In its current state, the impact will be much smaller, though uneven across the country. Consumers in provinces without legislation will see their right to individually advance their claims in small claims court foreclosed,[117] and even in provinces with protective legislation, the mere presence of the arbitration clause may deter consumers, who are unaware of its unenforceability. Empowering legislation should expressly preserve the small claims court forum for consumer causes of action (statutory and common law), notwithstanding the existence of a pre-dispute arbitration clause contained in a contract of adhesion. Clear retroactive priority of subject matter jurisdiction must be articulated so that general arbitration legislation, the competence–competence principle, and pre-existing arbitration clauses do not combine to oust the court's jurisdiction.[118]

Consumer arbitration should also be addressed during the collection phase. Under general arbitration legislation, disputants are entitled to file their awards with the relevant civil court and avail themselves of the collection remedies offered by the public system.[119] Legislative definitions should make it clear that once an award is filed,[120] it is subject to all the debtor relief provisions for consolidation or arrangements to pay, as discussed more fully above. Once within the court system, all debtors should be offered full accommodation.

Finally as noted above, many consumers do not defend debt collection arbitrations, resulting in default awards. Currently, enforcement of these awards may also be pursued through the small claims court; this should not continue. Consumer participation as a prerequisite to

---

117 Most cases on arbitration clause enforcement focus on the loss of collectivity; *supra* note 95. It seems assumed that where the matter is an individual claim, the arbitration agreement will prevail and the action will be stayed under the mandatory stay provisions of the relevant arbitration legislation. See, for example, *Arbitration Act, 1991*, S.O. 1991, c.17, s.7; *Seidel, supra* note 105 at para. 42.

118 Conflicting jurisdiction provisions exist in Brazil and New Zealand; McGill, '''Consumer Arbitration Clause Enforcement,' *supra* note 95 at 408–9. The competence–competence principle requires that matters as to jurisdiction of the arbitrator over a dispute and validity of the clause are to be first determined by the arbitrator, unless a pure question of law is at issue with only a superficial involvement of undisputed facts. See *Seidel, supra* note 105 at para. 29.

119 See, for example, *Arbitration Act, 1991*, S.O. 1991, c.17, s.50.

120 See O. Reg. 258/98, Rules 20.09, 20.10(1)(7) (currently 'orders as to the payment of money' undefined).

the court enforcement of an arbitral award would be a natural access to justice measure.[121] Only consumer atonement to the arbitration process should trigger court enforcement of its outcome. Alternatively, the same procedures in place to set aside a default judgment should be available to restrict access to collection.[122]

B. Class Actions

Some suggest that business's defensive move to consumer arbitration was triggered by the growth in consumer class actions;[123] improving access to justice and creating economies of scale for small disputes were among the expressed reasons for the creation of class actions.[124] Procedurally, two fee-related factors made consumer class actions economically attractive: contingency fees[125] and ever-increasing small claims court fees.[126] The latter is the most relevant to the discussion at hand.

Under the current fee model discussed above, there is an ever-expanding group of claims that are not worth pursuing individually, even in small claims court, because the value of the dispute, although within the jurisdiction of the court, does not warrant the cost of processing it.[127] Most problematic are disputes involving only a few hundred dollars, not usually considered worth the time and money to pursue even when one has the means.[128] Such claims may not be advanced at

---

121 Japan considers a consumer's failure to appear at the arbitration to be cancellation of the arbitration agreement: Chusai Ho [Arbitration Law], Law No. 138 of 2003, Supplemental Provisions art. 3 (Japan), translation available online at Japan Commercial Arbitration Association, http://www.jcaa.or.jp/e/arbitration-e/kisoku-e/kaiketsu-e/civil.html.

122 Ontario litigants may set aside a default judgment if there is a meritorious defence, a reasonable explanation for default, and a quick request. Rule 11.06, 17.01(4).

123 Gilles, 'Opting Out of Liability,' *supra* note 95 at 378. Only Prince Edward Island lacks class action legislation.

124 *Western Canadian Shopping Centres Inc. v. Dutton*, 2001 SCC 46 at para. 28, (CanLII), 2 S.C.R. 534 [*Western Shopping Centres*] (deterring bad defendant behaviour was the third).

125 Ontario contingency fee timeline of 1992 for class proceedings and 2004 generally: *Class Proceedings Act*, S.O. 1992, c.6, s.33. Ontario was the last province to approve individual contingency fees. See *Contingency Fee Agreements*, O. Reg. 195/04 s.7.

126 *Supra* notes 29, 42, 45.

127 See Ontario Law Reform Commission, *Report on Class Actions* (Toronto: Ministry of the Attorney General, 1982) at 119–22. See also *Western Shopping Centres, supra* note 124.

128 In Ontario, it costs $75 to issue a claim and $100 to set the matter down for trial. For a general discussion of fees charged in various small claims courts, see McGill,

all unless a class action is available. Class actions may also be preferred over individual small claims court actions when the complications of the problem, formidability of the defendant, or the expertise necessary to prove the claim make it a daunting task to take on alone. Collectivity seems like the only viable way to litigate such matters. Given these realities, class actions make a valuable contribution to the larger access to justice picture,[129] but they are not without limitations.

It is not the aim of this paper to provide an exhaustive review of the pros and cons of consumer class actions; however, there are some negatives that are in direct contrast to the strengths of the small claims court. These include the risk of negative cost awards, limited availability,[130] and slow processing time. Although contingency fees have, for the most part, removed concerns about the cost of the plaintiff's own counsel, a class action loss could expose the representative plaintiff to a staggering adverse cost award – not something too many consumers would want to risk for a small potential recovery.[131] In addition, the class action process is not a quick one; time-consuming preliminary steps on the road to certification mean that class members must be patient. Finally, wide access to redress is not guaranteed; the representative plaintiff must find a lawyer who is willing to process the claim or, alternatively, may have the claim foreclosed by a concluded class action without sharing in the compensation.[132] Many class actions are driven by law-

---

'Identity Crisis,' *supra* note 1 at 231–4. Even costs concerns associated with adverse cost awards, counsel, or paralegal fees and settlement offer penalties appear modest compared to those faced by a representative plaintiff in a class proceeding.

129 Ziegel, 'Canadian Consumer Law and Policies,' *supra* note 3 at 293.

130 Jasminka Kalajdzic, 'Consumer (In)justice: Reflections on Canadian Consumer Class Actions' (2010) 50 Can. Bus. L.J. 275 at 278–9 (reporting a total of 332 pending Canadian class actions). See Ward K. Branch, *Class Actions in Canada*, looseleaf (Aurora: Canada Law Book), ch. 22.10 (reporting a total of 271 certification hearings in Ontario, 90 certifications, and 120 settlements as of March 2010).

131 *Kerr v. Danier Leather Inc.*, 2007 SCC 44, [2007] 3 S.C.R. 331 at para. 60–71 (upholding large cost award against unsuccessful representative plaintiff). Individual claim members are protected from cost awards except as to proceedings for their individual claims and those are confined to the small claims court tariffs if applicable: *Class Proceedings Act*, *supra* note 125, ss.31(2), (3). Funding options are available through the Law Foundation of Ontario; see 'About Us,' http://www.lawfoundation.on.ca/cpcabout.php; and sometimes lawyers agree to indemnify representative plaintiffs: see Chief Justice Warren K. Winkler and Sharron D. Matthews, 'Caught in a Trap: Ethical Considerations for Plaintiff's Lawyer in Class Proceedings,' http://www.ontariocourts.on.ca/coa/en/ps/speeches/caught.htm.

132 *Class Proceedings Act*, *supra* note 125, s.26(4) (award may not necessarily be paid to

yers rather than plaintiffs and yield little compensation for the actual class members.[133]

The small claims court can address some of the class action limitations, not only with graduated fees for small individual claims, caps on negative cost awards, and improved affordability for low-income litigants through fee waivers,[134] but also through the collective management of similar claims. There is discretion to consolidate common claims or to join actions and trials for matters dealing with similar facts or legal issues.[135] This discretion could be exercised to offer some economies of scale to small claims court litigants, albeit on a far more modest level than class proceedings.[136]

Although joining of actions is most often considered in the context of claim splitting by a single plaintiff,[137] it is not confined exclusively to such situations. Two different employees, each with multiple claims

---

class members particularly when class members are unidentifiable or fail to make claims). See Christopher R. Leslie, 'The Significance of Silence: Collective Action Problems and Class Action Settlements' (2007) 59 Fla. L. Rev. 71 at 120 (reporting shockingly low participation rates by consumers in U.S. class actions). In such cases, remaining awards may be paid to other organizations that could indirectly benefit the class or right the perceived wrong. It is beyond the scope of this paper to review the limitations of cy-près distributions. See Kalajdzic, 'Consumer (In) justice,' *supra* note 130 at 287–91.

133 Ziegel, 'Canadian Consumer Law and Policies,' *supra* note 3 at 294–6; Kalajdzic, 'Consumer (In)justice,' *supra* note 130 at 280–1, 287–91.

134 In Ontario, fee waivers may be granted by the clerk or the deputy judge upon the filing of proof of need: *Administration of Justice Act*, R.S.O. 1990, c. A.6, ss.4.3, 4.4; O. Reg. 2/05; O. Reg. 671/05.

135 See *Courts of Justice Act*, R.S.O. 1990, c. C.43, s.138 (avoid multiple proceedings), s.25 (hear matters in summary way); O. Reg. 258/98, Rule 13.05 (consolidate overlapping matters after settlement conference), Rule 1.03(1) (most expeditious and least expensive determination); O. Reg. 258/98, Rule 2.01 (vary rules to secure just determination of the real dispute), Rule 1.03(2) (remedy lack of authority through analogy to Superior Court rules).

136 *Class Proceedings Act*, *supra* note 124, ss.1, 31(3) (expressly excluding small claims court, although preserving cost scale).

137 Business debt collectors sometimes separate claims by invoice to remain under the monetary limit. Once issued, the plaintiff seeks to have all claims tried together. Defendants attack the splitting, seeking to have claims consolidated and forcing the defendant to abandon excess over the jurisdiction. Alternatively, the consolidated claim is transferred to the higher court. See, for example, *Aitchison v. Nordson Canada Ltd.*, (1990) 1 W.D.C.P. 2d 3 (Ont. Prov. Ct. (Civ. Div.)), [1989] O.J. No. 2285; *Lysiak v. Re/Max Cataract City Ltd.*, (1989) W.D.C.P. 202 (Ont. Prov. Ct. (Civ. Div.)), [1988] O.J. No. 2693 (QL).

against a common employer, had their split claims consolidated and their remaining single claims tried together in *Roberts v. S.G. Transport Ltd.*[138] In *Kent v. Conquest Vacations Co.*[139] the Divisional Court upheld the finding that each vacationer was a separate party to the contract, entitled to a separate breach of contract claim, and that they could avail themselves individually of the full monetary jurisdiction of the court; this was not sacrificed when they consensually joined their claims.[140] Provided the issues disclosed in the pleadings are sufficiently similar, multiple plaintiffs may decide to join their actions; or, the small claims court has the discretion to make such an order. Admittedly, this discretion has not been exercised often to date and plaintiffs will likely be unaware of other similar actions or of the possibility of joining with them. Still, whether and how the joinder or consolidation discretion could be applied to group monetarily small claims is worthy of study as the future of small claims court is mapped.

C. Third-Party Representation

Two recent developments have changed the nature of litigant representation in Ontario. Internally, the 2010 limit increase to $25,000 has made it more lucrative for legal representatives to participate.[141] Externally, the regulation of paralegals, although part of a wider access to justice and quality-control measure, has directly impacted the small claims courts. There are now more than 2,700 paralegals in Ontario[142] offering litigants a wide choice of representation, at least theoretically, at different price points.[143] The Ontario government is overtly encouraging the use of paralegals in the small claims court with the recent change to the assessment of representation fees;[144] paralegals and lawyers are now

---

138 [1998] 26 C.P.C. (4h) 343 (P.E.I. S.C.(T.D.)), [1998] P.E.I.J. No. 12 (QL) (dealing with twenty-five different small claims court claims and two different plaintiffs).

139 [2005] 136 A.C.W.S. (3d) 831 (Ont. Div. Ct.), O.J. No. 312 (CanLII).

140 *Ibid.* at paras. 4–9.

141 Cost awards are capped based on the amount claimed not recovered: See *Courts of Justice Act, supra* note 46.

142 OLCN, *supra* note 8 at 70.

143 The OCLN reports that only one in ten respondents used a paralegal and that among users only 62 per cent indicated that they were satisfied with the quality of the service: *ibid.* at 36. Troubling results compared with a satisfaction rate for lawyers of 81 per cent: *ibid.* at 35.

144 While lawyers were eligible for 15 per cent of the claimed amount, paralegals and students at law were eligible for only 50 per cent of that amount per Rule 19.04(2); O. Reg. 78/06 s.39, repealed by O. Reg. 440/10, s.3.

eligible for the same fees. Legal representation adds formality, creates a power imbalance with unrepresented litigants, and generates slower and more expensive proceedings.[145] These developments are moving the court towards a more formal justice-based initiative.

Creditors and debtors also involve third parties in the post-judgment process. In addition to lawyers and paralegals, some creditors hire collection agencies[146] to represent them on a fee-tied-to-recovery basis. Other creditors completely assign their judgment to a collection agency, giving the agency seizure of the matter.[147] Although the national scene is dominated by a few big organizations,[148] presently there are more than 190 agencies registered in Ontario alone, each employing many more individuals as collectors.[149] Unfortunately, there is wide discontent. Over the past five years, the Ministry of Consumer Services has received more consumer complaints about collection agencies than about any other industry.[150] The high number of complaints reflects a lack of confidence in the industry, as well as questionable practices.

In the post-judgment phase, third-party representation may actually frustrate the proceedings. Rarely does a creditor appear for an examination if it has a third-party representative; there is no obligation to attend or send settlement instructions. This means that an immediate response to a payment proposal is less likely and that debtors may leave the examination without a voluntary payment plan in place. Second, creditor expectations for the amount of recovery may rise because they now need to cover the third-party collection costs. Finally, the court

---

145 The court may not exclude a representative licensed under the *Law Society Act* even if incompetent – *Courts of Justice Act, supra* note 46, s.26.

146 *Collection Agencies Act*, R.S.O. 1990, c. C.14, s.1(1).

147 Quebec excludes collection agencies and any organization not a primary party to the contract: *Code of Civil Procedure*, R.S.Q. c. C-25, art. 953.

148 National players include Total Credit Recovery, Portfolio Management Solutions Inc., and Financial debt Recovery Ltd.

149 The Ministry of Consumer Services website, http://www.sse.gov.on.ca/mcs/en/Pages/default.aspx, discloses the number of agencies but not the number of individual collectors. Only forty-four agencies are members of the Ontario Society of Collection Agencies, a voluntary professional organization devoted to integrity and professionalism in the industry: http://www.oscagencies.com.

150 In 2009, the Ministry of Consumer Services received 4,764 complaints about collection agencies and debt collectors, the most of any industry and a five-year high: 'Top 10 Consumer Complaints,' http://www.sse.gov.on.ca/mcs/en/Pages/Top_Ten_Complaints.aspx. Complaints may be filed electronically to the director. At date of writing, only eight collection agencies were recorded on the ministry's 'Consumer Beware List': http://www.consumerbeware.mgs.gov.on.ca/catsct/start.do.

has limited ability to control the behaviour of the third-party organization outside the courtroom; follow-up calls and potentially harassing behaviour are beyond the scope of small claims court remedies, especially as they relate to non-parties.[151] Debtors looking for this protection from the court must be told to complain to the government.[152]

On the consumer side, debt counselling agencies sometimes advise, if not appear with, the debtors involved in JD examinations. The Ontario Association of Credit Counselling Services has more than twenty-seven not-for-profit member agencies.[153] It is unclear how these various types of organizations affect the debtor's substantive ability to pay, but it is likely that debtors appearing without their advisers will be unwilling to respond to a payment proposal without first reviewing it with them (and rightly so).

Several modifications could facilitate meaningful resolution when third-party representatives are involved post-judgment. First, require both the party and the adviser to appear at the JD examination. Such a requirement is not without precedent; the current practice in Ontario settlement conferences requires parties *and* their representatives to participate in the conference.[154] This ensures a full canvassing of settlement options during the conference without stretching out the discussion over the following weeks. The judgment debtor process would similarly benefit from both the creditor and debtor being in a position to advance and respond to payment proposals. Arguably, such a requirement is more important at this point in the life cycle of the dispute, as the parties are less likely to voluntarily engage in constructive dialogue outside the courtroom.

---

151 Limited equitable relief is available in the small claims court: *Grover, supra* note 9 at para. 49; McGill, 'Identity Crisis,' *supra* note 1 at 242–3. The Ontario court is empowered to exclude incompetent representatives (other than lawyers or paralegals); however, the tone of the provision speaks to behaviour during the proceeding, not outside the courtroom, and the constitutional limitations surrounding *ex facie* contempt would cast doubt on its use to control out of court behaviour: *Courts of Justice Act*, R.S.O. 1990, c. C.43, s.26.

152 Anyone can file a complaint about a collection agency with the registrar under *Collection Agencies Act, supra* note 146, ss.12–16.2. See Ziegel, *supra* note 3 at 287–90 (as to failings of complaints process).

153 Ontario Association of Credit Counselling Services website, http://www.oaccs.com/main.html. Debt counselling agencies are not subject to registration in Ontario and come in for-profit and not-for-profit models.

154 O. Reg. 258/98, Rule 13.02 (either actual attendance or reachable for instructions by phone or video).

Second, the court needs the power to award declaratory and injunctive relief that would control collection agency behaviour, restrict collection calls, and force corrective action for wrongful credit reporting. A California-style civil cause of action should be created against creditors who violate the court-ordered behaviour or who fail to comply. Given the high level of discontent with collection agency behaviour, civil liability may bring some much needed accountability to the industry.

It appears that pre- and post-judgment third-party representation is the new reality in the Ontario small claims court. The court should be empowered to manage the representation so that it does not frustrate the process.

V. Conclusion: Recommendations for Reform

Identifying priorities among the many competing objectives of the small claims court will make design and proportionality decisions easier, more predictable, and more transparent. The multipronged mission of the small claims court defies a single strategy, and consideration should be given to tiered processes that expand the justice components with the value of the claim. Graduated fees and modifications to loser-pays rules could control the cost of the process and use of legal representation.

The post-judgment process would better reflect access to justice priorities if it adopted information-gathering and debtor-accommodation measures that ease compliance, intervene earlier in the process, assign the court rather than users carriage, and ensure integrity of the system.

Initially, written information gathering should be preferred over personal attendances. Prior to trial, forms could be forwarded to litigants on the court's initiative and returned at trial. All parties could be ready to discuss payment arrangements immediately following trial without waiting for default or a subsequent attendance. Courts should be directed to solicit additional information as needed and should also accommodate debtors' circumstances by consolidating indebtedness, imposing a single payment schedule, and suspending collection tools and interest accrual.

Courts should maintain public databases of unsatisfied judgments. The accuracy of the information could be protected if creditors were obligated to file a satisfaction document and were liable for damages for default. Lists of outstanding judgments should be generated for trial so that the judge is ready to consider consolidation to assist a sincere debtor managing multiple creditors.

Finally, system designers must recognize the impact of external developments, including class actions, consumer arbitration, and third-party representation. Rules should be interpreted to allow economies of scale through joinder and consolidation of small claims court actions. Pre-dispute arbitration clauses should not be allowed to foreclose consumer access to the court, and post-judgment enforcement systems should only be available to assist collection of defended arbitral awards. The reality of third-party representation throughout the pre- and post-judgment processes must be anticipated with attendance requirements, cost limits, and behaviour control measures.

Expectations for the small claims court are numerous and varied, complicating system design and evaluation. External pressures, as well as the access and justice needs of stakeholders, require a move away from the current one-size-fits-all model.

PART 7

Creating Change and Reform of the Judicial System

13 Growing Legal Aid Ontario into the Middle Class: A Proposal for Public Legal Expenses Insurance

SUJIT CHOUDHRY, MICHAEL TREBILCOCK, AND

JAMES WILSON

I. Introduction

The legal aid system in Ontario is not working, particularly with respect to access to justice in civil matters. Financial eligibility requirements remain frozen at extremely low levels and have been steadily eroded by inflation, leaving increasing numbers of people ineligible for publicly paid legal assistance. The range of services covered prioritizes criminal law and family law and, except for some legal aid clinics, does not extend to employment law, consumer law, and debtor/creditor law. In combination, this means that publicly funded legal aid cannot meet many of the most pressing legal needs of middle income Ontarians. Moreover, private markets, as currently structured and regulated, have not bridged this gap in access. Market rates for legal services continue to rise, and representation by legal counsel is unaffordable for a majority of Ontarians. As a result of these pressures, staggering numbers of Ontarians are attempting to navigate an increasingly complex civil justice system without any or adequate legal assistance, and they feel increasingly alienated from the system. The Chief Justices of Canada and of Ontario have independently referred to this state of affairs as a 'crisis' for the legal system.[1]

---

1 Hon. Warren K. Winkler, Chief Justice of Ontario, 'Civil Justice Reform – The Toronto Experience' (The Warren K. Winkler Lectures on Civil Justice Reform, delivered at the Faculty of Law, University of Ottawa, 12 September 2007); Tracy Tyler, 'Access to Justice a "Basic Right": Country's Top Judge Says the System's High Cost Is an "Urgent" Problem That Must Be Addressed, But Lawyer's Recent Accusations of Money Grubbing among his Peers Won't Help, Chief Justice Says' *Toronto Star,* 12 August 2007.

Many of the solutions to this crisis that have been proposed to date have taken the basic financial architecture of the legal aid system as it currently exists but would increase funding significantly. This would serve a number of goals: it would maintain existing levels of services by providing significantly enhanced compensation to lawyers who take on legal aid cases and thereby ensure the future of the legal aid bar; and it would also expand both eligibility and the areas of law covered.[2] In our view, increasing public funding for legal aid on the scale required to serve the civil justice needs of the middle class, on a sustainable basis, is an economic and political non-starter. In this paper, we propose a different solution to the system's failings: to grow Legal Aid Ontario (LAO) into the middle class by grafting public legal expenses insurance onto the existing program of publicly funded legal services for low income Ontarians. Adapting the acronym for legal expenses insurance, LEI, we term this a proposal for public LEI. This proposal would respond directly to the institutional, political, and market challenges that beset access to justice.

The first (and central) challenge to reform is institutional: the disarticulation of the justice system and its component parts, which are strongly independent – beginning with the courts, which are self-administered, and the legal profession, which is self-governing. In our justice system, no single institution is responsible for the whole and therefore no single institution can establish the financial and regulatory incentives that will drive down costs for publicly paid legal services while ensuring that the most acute legal services needs of Ontarians are met. We assume therefore that effective reform will have to involve the creation of new institutional capacities and a corresponding realignment of incentives to make cost-effective legal services viable. The principal mechanisms we propose for accomplishing these objectives are enhanced purchasing power for the public payer for legal aid services, and improved information about the system as a whole. We propose to enhance LAO's capacity along both these dimensions. Indeed, one of the principal advantages to locating a public LEI program within an existing institution, LAO (as opposed to creating a new public corporation, or facilitating the growth of private markets for LEI), is that LAO, as the dominant purchaser of legal services in Ontario, could use public LEI to achieve the purchasing power it needs to require lawyers to

---

2 Ontario Ministry of the Attorney General, *Report of the Legal Aid Review 2008* by Michael Trebilcock (2008) [Trebilcock Report].

innovate in how they deliver these services, and to institute innovative structures for the delivery of services on its own. Grafting the program onto LAO as it currently exists will enable the program's administrators to maximize economies of scale and scope while fostering institutional complementarities. Our proposal that taxpayers and lawyers can participate in the program as a matter of choice will help maintain the competitive pressures necessary to ensure that the program is able to guarantee services at low cost while continuing to innovate.

With improved data, LAO would be assisted in overcoming the institutional fragmentation that is a barrier to reform. It is striking how little information we have, in contrast to other public services (e.g., health care), about the operation of the justice system. Accordingly, meaningful reform will have to include improvements in the way we gather and disseminate information about the system (to scholars, practitioners, and the public) – for example, through the creation of an arm's length agency to augment the work of independent scholars and organizations currently engaged in the collection and analysis of this kind of information. These data, in turn, would help empower LAO to lead an evidence-based discussion of justice sector reform.

The second challenge is political. Middle income earners currently have very little stake in legal aid because their only involvement in the system is as taxpayers as opposed to participants. Accordingly, we assume that there is very little likelihood that politicians will direct significant new funding into the system in order to target the civil justice needs of middle income earners on an ongoing basis. Indeed, in the contest for increased public funding, legal aid has consistently lost out to those public programs that cater to the middle class, especially health care and education. Legal aid, to ensure its political viability, needs to expand its scope to encompass the middle class. This new set of stakeholders in the legal aid system will champion its ongoing viability, which will benefit the poor in two ways: (1) by providing political incentives that will maintain and even marginally improve public funding in the face of competing budgetary pressures, and (2) by enhancing LAO's existing institutional capacities by providing direct financial support to LAO through premiums. Program contributions from higher income Ontarians can help pay for services provided to lower income Ontarians by funding common organizational infrastructure.

The third challenge concerns the operation of markets. The markets for legal services generally and for private LEI in particular are characterized by failures of information in addition to other shortcomings.

On the demand side, ordinary consumers of legal services have very little capacity to anticipate what their needs may be in regard to legal services or to evaluate the quality of services on offer when those needs become acute. LEI is an effective means of spreading the risk of legal contingencies, recognizing that consumers are generally reluctant to pay for insurance, again, because it is hard to anticipate the legal contingencies that will affect them. On the supply side, the gap between what legal services cost and what most Ontarians are able to pay means that many lawyers lack the financial incentives to serve low and middle income consumers. With respect to LEI, problems of adverse selection (high-risks disproportionately seek insurance) and moral hazard (once insured, individuals may have incentives to engage in protracted or speculative litigation) may render comprehensive private insurance extremely expensive. These forms of market failure, and the lessons we draw from the European market for LEI (which has been fostered, in significant part, by state intervention), weigh in favour of an insurance model for legal services, and a public rather than a private model. In our model, every Ontarian would be enrolled as a matter of default but would be free to 'opt out'; conversely, lawyers would not be enrolled by default but would be free to 'opt in' on a case-by-case basis (as they currently do in the LAO certificate system). In other words, as a matter of default, the program would provide strong incentives for participation while preserving the freedom of participants to choose private alternatives.

A public insurance model for legal services would enable us to mitigate these institutional, political, and market impediments to access to justice. It would be a means of pooling the resources of the system's diffuse and heterogeneous clients and using their collective demand for legal services to drive down the costs of legal services, by funnelling demand through a dominant purchaser of legal services: institutional consolidation on the demand side would offset institutional fragmentation on the supply side. Financed by taxpayer premiums, the model would be financially self-sustaining. In addition, LEI located in LAO would serve as a platform for political mobilization: rejuvenated with a mandate and the resources to serve a wider consumer base at low cost, LAO could lead discussions about the reform of the system in a way that current institutions advocating access to justice cannot.

Our fundamental assumption is that access to justice is a 'basic right' for all Canadians. Some range of legal services should be provided to all citizens on a non-means-tested basis. But in order to realize the right to access to justice, we must pay careful attention to questions of institutional design and the political and economic incentives those institutions create. In order for reform to succeed, it must be motivated by moral considerations but approached with a strategic mindset. The basic calculus is this: if we continue to expect middle income Ontarians to financially support, through their tax dollars, a legal aid system for the poor, we would be wise to offer them a material stake in the well-being of the system, in as transparent a manner as possible – by linking their financial stake in the system to legal services that meet their most acute needs. Creating a public legal expenses insurance program is one way to accomplish this objective. In companion research, our colleagues have found that the most acute, unmet civil legal needs for middle income Ontarians arise in the areas of family law, employment law, and consumer and debtor/creditor law.[3] Accordingly, we propose a public LEI program that would target these needs. At the same time, we take the position that all of the program's participants (taxpayers on the demand side; lawyers on the supply side) should be free to favour market alternatives if they choose: taxpayers would be free to 'opt out' of a program in which they are enrolled by default, while lawyers would be encouraged to 'opt in' on a case-by-case basis.

We advance our proposal as follows. In Part II,we elaborate on our diagnosis of the challenges posed by the disarticulation of the justice system into 'contending autonomies' and on the incentives of the system's major players that may pose barriers to reforming the system. In Part III, we build the case for increasing LAO's fiscal and informational leverage in the justice system using a public LEI program, by describing how LEI works and the case for a public model based on the need for state intervention to foster private markets for LEI in other jurisdictions. In Part IV, we describe the key features as well as the benefits of a public LEI program: it could empower LAO and its partners to innovate in the delivery of cost-effective legal services in Ontario, in conjunction with an arms-length body empowered to gather the information about the system that we will need to evaluate these innovations. In Part V, we conclude.

---

3 University of Toronto Faculty of Law, Middle Income Access to Civil Justice Initiative, Background Paper by the Steering Committee, http://www.law.utoronto.ca/documents/conferences2/AccessToJustice_LiteratureReview.pdf [Background Paper].

II. The Reform Challenge: Contending Autonomies and Diffuse Consumers

Regarding the obvious question of 'who is in charge?' of the administration of justice in Ontario, the facts reveal disconcertingly that the answer is 'everybody and nobody.' Thus our diagnosis of the justice system's failings begins with the observation that our legal system is defined by the autonomy of its major players and by the difficulty of aligning incentives to reform among them.

We begin with the constitutionally protected independence of the judiciary and the professional autonomy of lawyers (which may also have a constitutional foundation). Broadly speaking, in the name of judicial independence, judges have historically resisted state oversight of courts administration – for example, the Ontario Integrated Justice Project.[4] Likewise, lawyers typically resist oversight of their management of cases due to concerns that this will affect solicitor–client relations by constraining the lawyer's professional judgment and the client's liberty to instruct counsel. Indeed, the independence of both lawyers and judges is layered, because individual lawyers and judges work independently of each other while forming, as groups, self-governing institutions that are largely independent of state oversight. Thus, the collective resistance to accountability and oversight is compounded by the individual independence of judges and lawyers.

Lawyers and judges, however, are not the only 'contending autonomies' that shape the justice system. Indeed, we can extend the characterization of independence to the Law Society of Upper Canada, university-based law schools, community legal clinics, and LAO itself (which is an arm's length agency of the government), as well as the provincial and federal governments. The independence of these institutions from one another allows each of them, to a greater or lesser extent, to avoid shouldering responsibility for reforming the system. For example, the Law Society as the self-regulating body for the legal profession has historically found itself in a conflict of interest position vis-à-vis widening access to the supply of legal services, due to the pro-

---

4 See, for example, *2003 Annual Report of the Office of the Provincial Auditor of Ontario*, http://www.auditor.on.ca/en/reports_en/en03/403en03.pdf; Sandford Borins, 'New Information Technology and the Public Sector in Ontario: A Report to the Panel on the Role of Government' (June 2003), http://www.law-lib.utoronto.ca/investing/reports/rp12.pdf.

fession's historical perception that allowing paralegals, volunteers, and clinics to provide legal services will erode the monopoly of lawyers to provide these services. The vigorous debate in Ontario over the licensing of paralegals usefully illustrates this point.[5] Law schools do not see themselves, necessarily, as preparing their students for careers in service to lower and middle income Ontarians, in the areas of family, employment, and consumer and creditor/debtor law. LAO is a quasi-independent agency, though it may still find itself under pressure to align its policies and goals with the expectations of the Attorney General (financial and otherwise), and though its regulatory authority is subject to oversight by the Lieutenant Governor in Council (indeed, to a large extent LAO's regulatory authority in respect of legal aid services is concurrent with the provincial government's).[6] Community legal clinics are fiercely protective of their institutional autonomy, often operating at the behest of community-based boards of directors and resisting LAO oversight. Finally, either level of government may act autonomously of the system as a whole, where they are not under consistent pressure to internalize the costs of their policy decisions – decisions that increase the burden on the legal aid system without commensurate investments in the system or cost sharing. A well-known example is the provincial government's 'guns and gangs' policy, which has had enormous cost implications for LAO and has resulted in the diversion of resources toward its big case program and away from other criminal matters. Changes to the refugee determination system by the federal government have likewise had implications for LAO expenditures.

We have so far surveyed the institutional barriers against reform on the supply side of the legal services equation. On the demand side, there is another set of public choice issues. The consumers of legal services in general are a diffuse, heterogeneous, and disorganized group and face information and collective action problems in organizing themselves and articulating their concerns in so many different fora.[7] The situation

---

5 See generally, Julia Bass and Paul Saguil, 'The Authorized Provision of Legal Services by Non-Lawyers: Paralegals and Others,' in *Canadian Legal Practice – A Guide to the 21st Century*, ed. Adam Dodek (LexisNexis Canada, 2009).

6 See *Legal Aid Services Act*, 1998, S.O. 1998, c.26, s.97.

7 As Trebilcock has observed, '[C]onsumers of professional services including legal services may be ill-equipped to diagnose or identify the precise nature of the problem they are confronting, which may require professional services. Even if they can identify the problem or need, they may be ill-equipped to choose an appropriate service provider, to exercise meaningful judgement over the appropriate service

is somewhat more complex with respect to legal aid. The fact that the program is targeted at the very poor has generated a politics in which the financing of publicly funded legal services is viewed as part of the bundle of social services targeted at the poor (e.g., welfare or public housing). Thus, in addition to provider organizations (e.g., the Criminal Lawyers' Association, the Association of Legal Clinics of Ontario), anti-poverty groups also advocate increased public funding for LAO. By contrast, the exclusion of the middle class from the scope of legal aid means that it is not an influential voice for reform.

Any discussion of the reform of publicly funded legal services has to acknowledge these issues. With respect to the supply of legal advice and representation, for example, it is clear that lawyers can respond to market pressures on an individual basis to reduce costs and explore alternative means of providing legal services (especially where practitioners work together in a firm or other arrangement to rationalize services and reduce costs). Nonetheless, the gap between what most legal services cost and what lower and middle income Ontarians are able to pay means that without the intervention of a dominant payer for publicly paid legal services, there is no institutional purchaser to provide lawyers with the financial incentives to address the needs of this underserved clientele. Even where these services are purchased by the state, we see that it is very difficult to practise-manage lawyers, who exercise considerable autonomy in respect of legal aid services and who are not required to use least-cost methods of providing advice to ensure that public money goes farthest. As Trebilcock has noted, LAO 'has often faced a certain amount of resistance to change from its service providers, which has undoubtedly hampered some of its attempts to be innovative.'[8] As a result of this, he laments that 'beyond the increased use of staff delivery systems, LAO has not been particularly innovative in service delivery.'[9] Untested (or undertested) possibilities include more selective membership on legal aid panels, block fees, and triaging

---

procedure and to monitor effectively performance by the service provider of the relevant procedure thereafter, and the time and cost associated therewith.' See Michael J. Trebilcock, 'Regulating the Market for Legal Services' (2008) 45 Alta. L.R. 215, at 217 [Trebilcock, 'Regulating the Market for Legal Services']. See also Ontario Civil Legal Needs Project, *Listening to Ontarians – Report of the Ontario Civil Legal Needs Project* (May 2010), http://www.lsuc.on.ca/media/may3110_oclnreport_final.pdf [*Listening to Ontarians*].

8 Trebilcock Report, *supra* note 2 at 83.
9 *Ibid.*

(i.e., using staff paralegals or lawyers to handle routine matters before directing clients toward specialized practitioners).

In other words, in a system defined by these competing autonomies, a poorly financed payer for legal aid services has very little leverage. This is even truer of the individual consumer. We appreciate that lawyers who work for legal aid certificates are under considerable pressure to establish efficient practices in their own interest, and that they remain under professional obligations with respect to their standard of practice. Nonetheless, we believe we can achieve a sea change in the cost-effective delivery of legal services by empowering LAO – through a public legal expenses insurance program – to require lawyers and other legal service providers to innovate in how they deliver these services, and by instituting innovative structures for the delivery of services on its own.

III. The Case for (Public) Legal Expenses Insurance

In this section, we describe how LEI works, emphasize the merits of LEI generally, and set out the difficulties associated with encouraging consumers to embrace LEI in the marketplace. Accordingly, we suggest that public LEI (with an opt-out provision) merits attention as a possible solution to private market shortcomings in Ontario.

A. What Is LEI?

LEI provides coverage for unexpected and costly events ('legal accidents') that require the policy holder to consult a lawyer or other legal service provider or resort to the judicial system. LEI plans provide coverage for legal expenses, including litigation costs, in contrast to prepaid plans, which guarantee legal assistance for more predictable events (such as drafting wills or real estate conveyances).[10] 'Stand-alone' LEI plans are generally more expensive than 'add-on' plans, which are linked to other insurance policies, such as home or auto insurance,[11] or are an element of employee group benefit plans. Plans may be pur-

---

10 See Paul Vayda and Stephen Ginsberg, 'Legal Services Plans: Crucial Time Access to Lawyers and the Case for a Public–Private Partnership,' *supra* this volume [Vayda and Ginsberg, 'Legal Services Plans'].

11 For example, automotive liability insurance in Ontario covers litigation costs arising from claims on the policy.

chased 'before the event' (BTE) or, at a premium, 'after the event' (ATE) in order to manage unpredictable legal costs arising from an existing legal problem. LEI typically uses panels of law firms to which clients are referred. LEI providers have considerable leverage to set the terms of service. For example, a 2002 survey-report sponsored by the Nuffield Foundation describes how a number of insurers in the United Kingdom exercise their leverage to enforce service standards with respect to panel firms (in the personal injury context):

> With an attractive quantity of personal injury work to refer, LEI insurers across the market are in a powerful position to negotiate favourable terms with panel firms. These include shorter contracts, tendering processes and the requirements that firms adopt a certain quantity of fixed fee claims in addition to receiving the more lucrative personal injury work ... Firms were expected to adhere to specific service standards and were monitored through annual or bi-annual file audit.[12]

The report also notes that 'a small number of firms said that audits were more theoretical than real as they involved the insurer in unnecessary expense and administration,' but we do not take this as a theoretical criticism of the model.[13]

B. The Current Availability of LEI in Canada

LEI is currently available in Canada but not widely used. The consumer market for LEI in Ontario is served by a single insurer:[14] in 2010, DAS, a German company, began to offer plans in provinces, including Ontario. Media reports indicate that DAS's plans for individuals

---

12 Pamela Abrams, 'In Sure Hands? Funding Litigation by Legal Expenses Insurance: The Views of Insurers, Solicitors, and Policyholders' (University of Westminster, 2002) at 9 (copy on file with the authors).
13 *Ibid.*
14 Sterlon Underwriting Managers Ltd. provides LEI to corporations and professionals. See http://www.sterlon.com. Prepaid LEI plans have been available in Ontario since 1999 on a personal or household basis through an American company called Prepaid Legal Services ('PPLS'). See https://www.prepaidlegal.com. LEI has also been made available to some labour unions for their members. For example, the Canadian Auto Workers Union ('CAW') and the Power Workers Union ('PWU') both provide LEI plans to their members. See CAW Legal Services Plan, http://www.cawlsp.com; PWU Protection Plan, http://www.pwu.ca/protection_plan/legal_expense.php.

could cost under $500 per year and provide up to $100,000 in coverage per claim, including litigation costs, but that the plans would exclude family law cases.[15] Quebec is the exceptional market in Canada; there, approximately twelve companies offer LEI plans for individuals and families, at premiums ranging between $35 and $90 per year. Coverage includes both telephone legal assistance and coverage for the costs of legal representation. The insured can generally select their own lawyer and legal strategy, with the lawyer being paid by the insurer at below-market rates. Coverage generally does not include services for family law matters, criminal charges, and pre-existing matters, and it is usually limited to $5,000 per dispute and $15,000 per year.[16] As a result of significant promotion by the Barreau of Quebec, approximately 10 per cent of Quebec residents are covered by LEI plans (although this is arguably a disappointing result, as we discuss below).[17] The European market for LEI is significantly more developed than in Canada, although highly variable from country to country, for reasons set out below.[18]

C. Why Public LEI? What Kind of Public LEI?

Our review of the literature suggests that the supply of and demand for LEI is highly responsive to state intervention to mitigate market failure. Indeed, barring ideal conditions, the private adoption of LEI may not occur on a significant scale without state intervention. On the supply side, state intervention may be required to ensure a sizeable and well-diversified risk pool – for example, by making LEI compulsory – or to help make the costs of litigation as predictable as possible – for example, by requiring adherence to costs tariffs. On the demand side, the need for state intervention may arise from a number of sources: consumer cognitive bias (i.e., the inability of consumers to consider the

---

15 Tracey Tyler, 'Firm to Offer Up to $100,000 Legal Coverage for $500,' *Toronto Star*, 7 October 2009, http://www.thestar.com/news/gta/article/706635. See also DAS, http://www.das.ca.

16 Barreau du Québec, 'Legal Protection Insurance: For a Greater Access to Justice' (1999).

17 Tracey Tyler, 'New Insurance Makes Lawyers Affordable,' *Toronto Star*, 18 August 2008, http://www.thestar.com/article/480287.

18 See, generally, riad / International Association of Legal Expenses Insurance, 'The Legal Protection Insurance Market in Europe' (June 2010), http://www.riad-online.net/430.0.html.

true risks of legal contingencies), the complexity of LEI policies (which may be difficult to sell on their own, or to distinguish in their substance and limitations from the other policies to which they are added), and cost.[19]

Among these considerations, the issue of cost may be determinative. Even for the middle class, the costs of LEI may be prohibitive. Kilian and Regan have found that in Germany (where LEI has been widely adopted and the plans are generally affordable), the distribution of private LEI associated with household insurance policies is largely consistent with income distribution: 'the least priority seems to be given to LEI if only limited financial resources are available.'[20] As a consequence, the authors expect that it would be 'very difficult' for governments to substitute private LEI for publicly funded legal aid.[21] Indeed, while the lowest income earners in this case would qualify for legal aid in Germany (which may explain their reluctance to purchase insurance), the authors nonetheless caution that

---

19 For instance, Germany is Europe's largest LEI market (approximately 44 per cent of German households have coverage and about 25 per cent of all lawyer fees are paid by LEI plans); but Kilian and Regan advise that LEI 'has only been able to flourish [in Germany] because the most important conditions of insurance theory are met by the German legal system.' For example, speculative funding of attorney fees is forbidden, legal aid is available only on the basis of stringent merits and means tests, and neither lawyers nor non-lawyers are allowed to offer legal services pro bono. On the supply side, costs and court fees are calculated based on a statutory scale of fees based on the monetary value of the dispute. Consequently, uncertainty in relation to fees is reduced from the outset of the litigation. The risk pool is 'mainly a historic achievement' but is sizeable. We note that some authors characterize Germany as an example of a jurisdiction where LEI has flourished without state intervention, but the above list of factors belies that assertion; the conditions for LEI to flourish are a product of legislative choices. See Matthias Kilian and Francis Regan, 'Legal Expenses Insurance and Legal Aid – Two Sides of the Same Coin? The Experience from Germany and Sweden' (2004) 11 *International Journal of the Legal Profession* 233 [Kilian and Regan, 'Legal Expenses Insurance']. In another notable example, the well-established private market for LEI in Sweden can also be attributed, at least in part, to strong government support: beginning in the 1960s, the public legal aid regime was supplemented by free (government-sponsored) LEI for a limited set of civil law issues, provided to the public through private home insurance policies. The government cut back public support for LEI in the 1990s. See Francis Regan, 'The Swedish Legal Services Policy Remix: The Shift from Public Legal Aid to Private Legal Expenses Insurance,' 30 J.L. & Soc'y 49 2003 [Regan, 'The Swedish Legal Services Policy Remix'].

20 *Ibid.* at 243.

21 *Ibid.*

cutting back legal aid budgets with the hope that those included by legal aid in the future will take out insurance cover is a rather optimistic approach. It seems to be more likely that a fair number of those losing legal aid cover would be left totally unprotected against the expense of legal services.[22]

In the face of these concerns, Kilian and Regan observe that 'the crucial [policy] question is how citizens can be convinced to take out insurance cover instead of relying on legal aid (or other ad hoc funding mechanisms).'[23] The obvious solution is to make LEI compulsory – that is, to link LEI with other forms of compulsory personal insurance, such as automobile liability insurance.[24] Nonetheless, this is a not a solution that legislatures have adopted (although Kilian suggests that some have considered it).[25] This is likely the case because mandatory LEI is a political non-starter, taking into account the likely resistance from consumer groups.[26]

If mandatory legal insurance is not an option, what are the alternatives?[27] Marketing private LEI is not a complete answer. It stands to reason that legal service insurance policies 'are not typically sold to marginalized groups of the society whose jobs are threatened, or who are facing eviction from housing,' or who are otherwise at risk.[28] As we argue below, mandatory public LEI (which would be difficult to achieve politically) and purely voluntary LEI (which would be inefficient) do not exhaust the range of possibilities. There is a third option, an opt-out regime, which we detail shortly.

---

22 *Ibid.*

23 *Ibid.* at 236.

24 *Ibid.* See also, Regan, 'The Swedish Legal Service Policy Remix, *supra* note 19.

25 Matthias Kilian, 'Alternatives to Public Provision: The Role of Legal Expenses Insurance in Broadening Access to Justice: The German Experience,' 30 J.L. & Soc'y 31 2003 at 35.

26 Kilian also suggests that the 'legal risks have not been regarded as serious enough, in personal or economic terms, to introduce compulsory LEI in either England or Germany.' See *ibid.*

27 Depending on the jurisdiction, barriers to entry for private LEI firms can be removed – for example, the U.K. will soon allow non-lawyers to invest in legal practices – but the same underlying issues that we have indentified will remain unless the state intervenes. See Ministry of Justice (U.K.), 'Alternative Business Structures Fact Sheet' (9 June 2008), http://www.justice.gov.uk/publications/abs-fact-sheet.htm.

28 Edward Blankenburg, 'Private Insurance and the Historical "Waves" of Legal Aid' (1993) 13 *Windsor Yearbook of Access to Justice* 185 at 199.

D. Objections to LEI

Quite aside from how broad participation could be ensured, the efficacy of private LEI has been doubted on the basis of adverse selection and moral hazard. We take the view, supported by the literature,[29] that concerns about the abuse of these programs can be addressed in their design. For example, some services that lend themselves to abuse (such as traffic infractions) could be exempted entirely from coverage. Alternatively, co-payments could be introduced for those services.

IV. How a Public LEI Program Might Work in Ontario

As far as we are aware, the idea of public LEI has not been considered in Ontario. Nonetheless, in our view, an opt-out public LEI program should be considered here. The ideal conditions for private LEI to flourish do not exist in Ontario, and we doubt the efficacy of attempting to engineer a market for this product from scratch (although we acknowledge the need to experiment with policies that would complement the public–private mix of LEI offerings that we advocate below). Second, the legal services needs that LEI would address here are not suitable for the obvious alternatives, such as class actions and contingency fees. Neither of these mechanisms is suitable for the kinds of personal civil matters that are pressing and acute in Ontario (although the latter might be ideal for potentially lucrative litigation such as personal injury claims). In the remainder of this paper we provide a thumbnail sketch of the logistics involved in creating a public LEI program – who and what services would be covered, and how it would be paid for. We also flesh out the benefits to creating a public LEI program: it would increase the purchasing power of LAO in relation to the private bar, so that it could lead the reform discussion and innovate in its own right. We also discuss the critical importance of information to the reform effort.

A. The Mechanics of a Public LEI Program in Ontario

The basic model for the program we advocate is that all taxpayers are enrolled by default, although free to 'opt out,' while lawyers have to

---

29 See, for example, Kilian and Regan, 'Legal Expenses Insurance,' *supra* note 19 at 242–3.

'opt in' on a case-by-case basis. In the remainder of this part we explain how premiums would be established (on an actuarial basis), how services would be included (on the basis of consultation), why extra-billing would not be permitted, and how the program would be financed and administered (by premiums, through LAO). We close with a comment on the handling of problem participants.

(1) *The importance of competition and shared institutional capacities.* Our proposal for the mechanics of the program, outlined in more detail below, is based on two assumptions: the need to foster competition in the marketplace for innovative, low-cost legal services; and the value of economies of scale and scope among public institutions. We take the view that these assumptions can be balanced in a productive tension. We have suggested that grafting the program onto LAO as it currently exists will enable the program's administrators to maximize economies of scale and scope while making the most of what LAO and a public LEI program would have in common – that is, the institutional capacities that would be necessary to administer and provide legal services directly to LAO's existing clients as well as to the new clients of a public LEI program (e.g., billing clients and the training and management of staff lawyers and paralegals). Given the choice between grafting a public LEI program onto LAO as it currently exists (or linking it with LAO as an affiliate institution)[30] and creating a new institution from scratch, we prefer the former. Our position raises an immediate objection: if LAO as it currently exists has failed to innovate, how can a larger version of the same organization be expected to succeed? We answer this objection, in part, by stressing the importance of competition. For the reasons set out below, we propose that taxpayers and lawyers be free to participate in the program as a matter of choice. In other words, the program's participants will have an 'exit' option, not merely a 'voice' option (as in the public health care system), as a means of expressing their preferences. This will help maintain the competitive pressure on a public LEI scheme that will be necessary to ensure that the program is able to guarantee high-quality services at low cost while continuing

---

30 Compare the relationship between LSUC and the Lawyers' Professional Indemnity Company ('LAWPRO'), the insurance company that provides professional liability insurance to lawyers in private practice in Ontario. LAWPRO was incorporated in 1990 by LSUC but has operated independently since 1995, with its own management and Board of Directors. See http://www.lawpro.ca.

to innovate (indeed, innovation will be imperative to the success of the program, from a competitive standpoint). This is just one of the reasons why we take the view that an 'opt out / opt in' approach for taxpayers and lawyers, respectively, is so critical to the model for public LEI that we are proposing.

(2) *Consumers opt out*. We have suggested that state intervention is needed to encourage lower and middle income Ontarians to embrace LEI. However, we do not believe that mandatory public LEI is the answer, for political reasons but also because a public LEI program cannot provide complete coverage for the needs of Ontarians and private alternatives should be encouraged for those who can afford them. Indeed, we expect that wider public awareness of the benefits of public LEI will help spur the development of the private LEI market for legal services that are not covered by the LEI scheme, or for private LEI for add-on services or as a comprehensive, competitive alternative to public LEI. Accordingly, we take the view that the program's participants (taxpayers) should be free to opt out of the program in favour of market alternatives.

We note that an opt-out approach (rather than an opt-in approach) is consistent with a recent shift in policy-making thinking, whereby 'default' policy options are designed to promote socially beneficial outcomes.[31] This approach is based on social science research into the ration-

---

31 See Richard H. Thaler and Cass R. Sunstein, *Nudge: Improving Decisions About Health, Wealth, and Happiness* (New Haven: Yale University Press, 2008). The authors, calling themselves 'libertarian paternalists,' introduce this concept with (among others) a stylized illustration of the University of Chicago's annual benefits enrolment process. Each year, employees are invited to choose whether to enrol in, and how much to contribute to, various benefits plans – for example, health insurance entitlements, flexible spending accounts for health insurance, and retirement savings accounts. For the sake of simplicity, the authors contrast the effect on the employees of setting the 'default' option at 'back to zero' or 'same as last year.' The authors suggest that 'libertarian paternalists would like to set the default by asking what reflective employees … would actually want.' For instance, employees would probably prefer to retain their entitlement to heavily subsidized health insurance; accordingly, the default option for this entitlement should be 'same as last year.' If the default was 'back to zero,' then an employee who missed the deadline for enrolment in any given year would be seriously disadvantaged. Selecting the default options for the other benefits involved more nuanced analysis. Because they involved discretionary spending, it probably made sense to set the default options at 'back to zero' for contributions to flexible spending accounts for health insurance and retirement savings accounts. Nonetheless, contributions for the retirement savings accounts could be cancelled at any time; accordingly, it might make sense to set the default option for that benefit at

ality of personal judgments and decisions; the evidence suggests that people do not typically analyse the costs and benefits of every choice they make but are instead prone to accept the status quo. Recognizing this yields the possibility that default policy options across a wide spectrum of regulatory activity can be used to promote health and well-being and to avoid the social cost of underutilization of services or benefits, while preserving freedom of choice – for example, in the pension reform context.[32] Indeed, the Province of Quebec has recently announced its commitment to developing a Voluntary Retirement Savings Plan (VRSP) for Quebec workers (i.e., those who are not already covered by an employer-sponsored pension plan), predicated on these same basic principles. In order to ensure the participation of a large number of workers so that they benefit from low-cost pension plans, eligible workers would be enrolled by default, with the freedom to opt out; the opt-out model has been proposed as a key feature of the plan's design.[33]

An opt-out approach to public LEI could help Ontarians avoid the social cost of legal underrepresentation. Indeed, our proposal that Ontarians be enrolled in a public LEI program by default appears to be supported by public opinion data and the experience of other provinces, which (we suggest) indicates that consumers are unable to accurately evaluate the potential likelihood and costs of legal contingencies. For example, the recent Report of the Ontario Civil Legal Needs Project (*Listening to Ontarians*), a survey of low and middle income Ontarians, found that more than two-thirds of respondents (67 per cent) said they would not be interested in obtaining LEI, the majority of whom (56 per cent) did not believe they would need it, and nearly one-third of whom

---

'same as last year.' The underlying assumption in this illustration is that not everyone who is eligible for these benefits will actually go through the process of making these selections every year. Thus, a set of rational default options – thoughtfully designed 'choice architecture' – can minimize the cost of this kind of failure. Working from this premise, the authors highlight the cognitive biases that impact personal decision making, and propose a wide range of default interventions, in both the private and public sectors, that could be designed to 'nudge' citizens toward choices that reflect their presumed self-interest, without significantly burdening their freedom to choose otherwise. See *ibid*. at 1–14.

32 See Keith Ambachtsheer, 'Pension Reform: How Canada Can Lead the World,' C.D. Howe Institute (18 November 2009), http://www.cdhowe.org.

33 Government of Quebec, '2011–2012 Budget: A Stronger Income Retirement System – Meeting the Expectations of Quebecers of Every Generation' (2011) at 3.2, http://www.budget.finances.gouv.qc.ca/.

thought it would be too expensive.[34] Similarly, despite the efforts of the Barreau in Quebec (i.e., despite a five-year, $2 million campaign to promote LEI through a website, hotline, television advertising, and pamphlets distributed in lawyer's offices), citizens of that province have not widely embraced private LEI.[35] We take the view that findings along these lines cannot be taken at face value but rather should be understood as reflecting our systematic myopia in regard to forecasting the value of insurance for legal services. Indeed, *Listening to Ontarians* found that the main reason (42 per cent) most people cited for not seeking out legal assistance for a legal problem 'was their perception that legal assistance would cost too much or that they could not afford a lawyer.'[36] If we are wrong in our assumptions, and if a majority of taxpayers are genuinely determined not to obtain coverage for legal expenses, then they would remain free to opt out of the program we are proposing. Nonetheless, we expect that a policy shift whereby Ontarians were automatically enrolled in a program that would potentially yield more benefits to them at a lower cost than anticipated (by statistical measures) could yield a sizeable pool of program participants who would elect to remain in the program as they discovered its substantial benefits.

Taking the view that an 'opt out' approach is essential to the integrity of a public LEI program, we acknowledge the possibility that participants will do precisely that, and we stress the need to manage premiums and coverage carefully to ensure that participants realize (and recognize) true value for premiums. We propose the following institutional architecture in which this fine-tuning will take place.

(3) *Lawyers opt in.* Lawyers would not be enrolled in the program by default but rather would be free to opt in on a case-by-case basis (i.e., one file at a time). This is how lawyers currently participate in the existing LAO certificate system, in order to maintain a mix of LAO and non-LAO clients. The goal would be to extend the same model to lawyers under public LEI. Lawyers available to take public LEI files would identify themselves on publicly accessible lists or websites by area of competence and location (as is the case at present with lawyers willing to accept legal aid certificates).

---

34 Ontario Civil Legal Needs Project, *Listening to Ontarians, supra* note 7 at 39.
35 Luis Millan, 'Legal Insurance: While Europeans Have Embraced the Concept, Canadians Remain Cool to Pre-paid Legal Services,' *Lawyers Weekly*, 1 May 2009.
36 Ontario Civil Legal Needs Project, *Listening to Ontarians, supra* note 7 at 39.

We expect that by pooling a large number of taxpayer contributors, LAO would be able keep the cost of premiums down while offering competitive rates for legal services, thereby attracting a sizeable cadre of lawyers to accept public LEI mandates at different stages of their careers. Indeed, we expect that, owing to the nature of the oversight that LAO will adopt in relation to public LEI mandates, a number of lawyers will establish themselves as proficient and reliable partners to LAO in the program. At the same time, because lawyers rely on a mix of institutional and individual clients paying different rates depending on the nature of the legal services they require, preserving maximum freedom of choice for lawyers in the program (i.e., to accept or decline public LEI mandates on a case-by-case basis) will enable more lawyers to participate on business terms that they can manage.

(4) *Premiums*. The rates for premiums should be established on the basis of actuarial calculations. In our view, the alternative approach – tying premiums to ability to pay (i.e., establishing premiums on actuarial principles but adjusting them up or down to take into account a modest cross-subsidy between higher and lower income participants) – would raise the untenable possibility that the middle class would opt out of the program, thereby eroding its financial basis. From the standpoint of optics, we assume that middle income consumers would be sceptical of the benefits of a redistributive program for LEI, for the same reason that private markets for LEI have yet to flourish here: taxpayers undervalue it. From an economic perspective, we assume that a public LEI program that is not established on actuarial principles would face competitive pressure, at least in the long run. We assume that higher income participants would eventually opt out of a redistributive program in favour of lower-cost private alternatives, or abandon LEI altogether.

We acknowledge the possibility that if premiums are not cross-subsidized, they will be perceived as too high by middle and lower income Ontarians; accordingly, in the next section we propose that discrete services targeting their particular needs should be included. Nonetheless, we emphasize that if a high number of low income Ontarians decided to opt out of the program (because of the cost of premiums) while remaining ineligible for legal aid (because it is directed at the very poor), this would serve as a powerful signal to government that legal aid coverage should be expanded. In other words, legal aid and public LEI are complements, not substitutes.

(5) *Lawyer remuneration and included services.* Generally, stakeholders – including lawyers and consumers – should negotiate rates for lawyer remuneration and schedules for included services in a manner akin to how tariffs and schedules are maintained in the Ontario Health Insurance Plan (OHIP), which involves stakeholders in an ongoing process of review.

In terms of the obvious imperative to establish rates for services that are reasonably attractive to lawyers, we stress that a public LEI program would benefit lawyers simply by consolidating demand. This could have a pronounced impact on small firms and sole practitioners in particular, and especially on lawyers working in underserviced communities (including rural communities), by helping ensure a steady supply of clients who have historically faced hurdles to finding a lawyer. Moreover, a strategic approach to lawyer remuneration might be used to augment the program's impact on underserved markets (i.e., by area of law as well as geographically). For example, rates for family law lawyers could be adjusted upwards, on a comparative basis, to encourage young lawyers to take family law mandates.

We assume that services should be offered in respect of acute civil justice needs (e.g., family law, employment law, consumer and debtor/creditor law), which could be identified on the basis of empirical evidence (e.g., consumer surveys). We assume that this would exclude, on a category basis, strongly subjective causes of action, such as defamation. As a matter of substance, the program's administrators should be able to exercise the discretion to screen claims on a merits basis, to ensure that unmeritorious claims (including claims brought in apparent bad faith) are unfunded.

We also stress that our proposal that the program be non-mandatory places particular pressure on the program's stakeholders to develop a 'menu' of services that are easy to understand and place a value on, to ensure that the program is able to meet the diverse expectations and needs of its participants.[37] In particular, given that we have proposed that premiums not be cross-subsidized, an obvious concern is that lower income Ontarians will opt out of the program because they consider the premiums too costly. Accordingly, we take the view that popular

---

37 See, e.g., Ontario Civil Legal Needs Project, *Listening to Ontarians, supra* note 7, regarding the imperative to differentiate between the legal services needs of different consumers (including low- and middle-income consumers).

services should be included. For example, we propose the inclusion of high-demand legal services that are usually associated with prepaid legal services plans, such as the drafting of wills, powers of attorney, and real estate conveyances. We acknowledge that including these services in an insurance program runs counter to one basic view of insurance (i.e., that we purchase coverage for low-probability but high-risk events, rather than commodity-type services). Nonetheless, we agree with Vayda and Ginsberg that basic legal services can have a preventative function in relation to more complex legal problems (e.g., valid wills help avoid the social costs of intestacy), and we might justify including these services in a public LEI scheme on this basis alone.[38] In any event, we assume that LAO could purchase a high volume of these services at low cost by pooling the resources of all of the program's participants. Thus the program could include highly valued discrete benefits to participants, who might be encouraged to remain in the program on that account alone.

(6) *Extra-billing*. We take the view that lawyers who accept public LEI mandates should not be allowed to negotiate higher rates with their clients on top of insured rates ('extra-billing'). Under the LAO certificate program, a lawyer who accepts a certificate cannot bill above the hourly rate or the total overall billing cap. We would extend the same system to public LEI, for at least two reasons. First, we expect that higher effective rates for public LEI services would undermine public confidence in the value of contributions to the program (regardless of the services that are included in relation to a given case). Second, we assume that the great majority of cases should be able to be handled within the constraints established by LAO. For example, the program could require the unbundling of services to maximize the potential for self-help, and its rates and coverage could be designed to create incentives to settlement, in areas of law where these approaches have been found to be particularly effective. We emphasize that if a high number of lawyers decline to opt into the program (because of the rate of remuneration), this would serve as a powerful signal to LAO that fees for services should be adjusted.

(7) *Financing*. The administrative apparatus for the program as well as

---

38 See Vayda and Ginsberg, 'Legal Services Plans,' *supra* note 10.

its initial funding would have to be provided through public seed funding. From that point forward, the program would be financed through individual taxpayer premiums rather than out of general tax revenues (i.e., through paystub withholding or the personal income tax filing process). A premium would have the benefit of notifying the taxpayer of her contribution, which is consistent with our objective that she see a dedicated revenue base and identifiable benefit in a plan for which she is eligible and that she be allowed to opt out of the program.

(8) *Administration.* We have already suggested that a public LEI program be grafted onto LAO as it currently exists in order to maximize its existing institutional capacities. Here we acknowledge the corresponding need for LAO to develop new capacities to support the administration of a public LEI program, as well as the importance of good governance in the oversight of the institution's proposed expanded mandate. Professional management in key roles must be ensured, as well as effective board oversight.

(9) *Problem participants.* We have acknowledged that the program's financial integrity could be undermined by adverse selection or moral hazard. As stated above, we take the view (supported in the literature) that LEI programs can be designed to accommodate the risk of abuse – for example, through exclusions of services and the introduction of co-payments.[39] Here, we note another form of potential abuse: consumers of legal services who 'opt out' of and strategically rejoin the program, timing their contributions to coincide with litigation. This form of abuse could be curtailed by imposing mandatory waiting periods before benefits, once cut off, are resumed, as well as exclusions of coverage for 'pre-existing' cases as appropriate. Finally, we acknowledge the potential need to exclude certain abusers of the program altogether – on the supply as well as the demand side. LAO should have the capacity to review and, as necessary, bar vexatious litigants as well as incompetent lawyers from the program.

---

39 We note, in support of this view, the finding of the Ontario Civil Legal Needs Project that '[p]eople do not need, or want, full legal representation to solve every civil legal issue they encounter,' and 'a significant proportion of middle income Ontarians can afford to pay for some legal services.' See Ontario Civil Legal Needs Project, *Listening to Ontarians, supra* note 7 at 56.

B. The Benefits: LAO Purchasing Power and the Impetus to Reform

An opt-out public insurance scheme benefiting lower and middle income Ontarians, targeting their most acute needs, located in LAO, would have three key benefits: (1) LAO would enjoy increased leverage with respect to the private bar, to lower costs and enforce service standards in relation to publicly paid legal services; (2) LAO would enjoy increased funding to innovate in how it delivers legal services in its own right; and (3) with increased funding and a broadened mandate, LAO would be empowered as a focal point – for members of the community, lawyers, and policy makers – to advocate for innovations to enhance access to justice across the justice system as a whole.

(1) *LAO and the private bar.* An increase in purchasing power derived from a public LEI program could strengthen LAO's efforts to control costs – efforts such as practice-managing legal services provided by the private bar, as well as requiring lawyers who accept LEI mandates to innovate in how they deliver these services. Because LAO is already the dominant purchaser of legal aid services in criminal law matters, we can highlight its existing capacities in this regard – for example, the capacity of LAO's Quality Service Office to develop standards of practice for panels, through a consultative process,[40] and the willingness of LAO to partner with elite panels in the context of its big case management program. This development was emphasized in LAO's submissions to the Lesage-Code review of large and complex criminal case procedures,[41] where LAO identified 'significant opportunities to improve the effectiveness and efficiency of complex criminal cases in Ontario.' These opportunities included encouraging more of Ontario's best lawyers to accept legal aid certificates; establishing high panel standards for counsel acting in serious criminal cases; establishing protocols, rules, and expectations for counsel accepting these certificates; requiring defence lawyers to be more accountable for their decisions and budgets; ensuring that LAO provide more valuable input on the

---

40 See LAO, http://www.legalaid.on.ca/en/about/qualityservice.asp.
41 See LAO, 'Submission to the Lesage / Code Review of Complex Criminal Cases' (20 June 2008), http://www.legalaid.on.ca/en/publications/downloads/advisorygroups/transform-major_lesage-code.pdf [LAO Submissions]. For the consideration of these proposals in the final report, see Ministry of the Attorney General, *Report of the Review of Large and Complex Criminal Case Procedures* by Patrick J. LeSage and Michael Code (2008) at 95–120, http://www.attorneygeneral.jus.gov.on.ca.

largest and most complex cases; ensuring that LAO governs the program more effectively and that it can track the costs and progress of the cases better; and providing more ongoing monitoring and analysis of cases as they progress.[42] We assume that a similarly robust approach to public LEI mandates could be adopted, as appropriate.

(2) *Innovation within LAO.* By providing a mandate for LAO to provide cost-effective legal services in a limited number of areas, a public LEI program could spur LAO's own reform efforts in the areas where delivery innovations have been identified as having real potential. Public LEI in the areas of family law, employment law, and consumer and debtor/creditor law could provide impetus for creating staff offices, as well as online resources, and for pursuing an integrated service delivery model in relation to relevant clusters of problems.[43] Innovations could be introduced along the legal services spectrum – a spectrum that includes public legal education and information, advice from non-lawyers, summary advice, brief services and referrals, duty counsel, and unbundled legal services.[44] We note, as Trebilcock observed in his Legal Aid Review, that LAO has already taken initial steps in many respects[45] but a great deal of work is yet to be done. What is needed now, in our view, is the infusion of funding, focus, and political traction that a public LEI program, targeting the needs of the middle class, can provide.

(3) *LAO as advocate for evidence-based reform.* LEI located in LAO would serve as a platform for political mobilization: rejuvenated by a mandate and the resources to serve a wider consumer base at low cost, LAO could lead discussions about the reform of the system in a way that current institutions advocating access to justice cannot. In particular, it could lead evidence-based discussions about reform, which it currently does not.

We take the view that the potential for reform would be augmented

---

42 LAO Submissions, *ibid.* at 4–5.
43 See Trebilcock Report, *supra* note 2 at 109.
44 See Background Paper, *supra* note 3.
45 For example, LAO has been examining ways to make applications for legal aid and access to the legal aid system easier for potential clients via the Internet; developing technological innovations that reduce administrative burdens both for certificate lawyers and for the system itself; and improving the quality of legal aid services in the province by introducing minimum panel standards and a mentoring program. See Trebilcock Report, *supra* note 3 at iii.

by the creation of an arm's length legal services information institute, whose mandate would be to gather information about the justice system for use by LAO, lawyers and judges, policy makers, and academics. A fruitful comparison can be drawn between the legal system and the health care sector (especially the hospital sector), in which a culture of information gathering provides a basis for accountability and service improvement across the system.[46] In particular, these sectors are in the process of adopting systematic quality assurance and risk management programs, whose purpose is to proactively monitor the quality of medical care by drawing on medical audits, utilization reviews, tissue and death reviews, and incident reports. These serve as triggers for corrections of practice deficiencies as well as for more systemic reviews. A key institution in this regard is the relatively new Canadian Institute for Health Information (CIHI), a national, not-for-profit independent organization that focuses on promoting cooperation among major health care stakeholders and on providing Canadians with essential statistics and analyses about their health and the health care system.[47] CIHI also coordinates national health information standards to ensure

---

46 We note that a number of important concerns with respect to the quality and the use of data in the health care sector have been raised in the literature. In the words of one recent report, there is 'a great deal of ambiguity about who is being held accountable, for what, to whom, and with what (if any) consequences or rewards for performance and improvement.' The principal carrots and sticks appear to be financial rather than qualitative. Authors have also noted problems with data quality and with aligning indicators across different levels of the system. The fact remains, however, that information gathering is a deeply entrenched element of the system. The authors of a recent report on public reporting in health care affirm this view, citing 'an irreversible trend toward public disclosure as the public increasingly demands more accountability,' not only because of perceived as well as real deficiencies in quality of care, 'but also because it "is philosophically desirable in democratic societies."' See Jack Wallace, Gary F. Teare, Tanya Verrall, and Ben T.B. Chan, 'Public Reporting in the Quality of Healthcare: Emerging Evidence on Promising Practice for Effective Reporting' (7 September 2007), Canadian Health Services Research Foundation (CHSRF) at 4–5, http://www.chsrf.ca/migrated/pdf/evidenceBoost/Public_Reporting_E.pdf; 'Accountability Agreements in Ontario's Health System: How Can They Accelerate Quality Improvement in Enhanced Public Reporting' (July 2008), Ontario Health Quality Council (OHQC); and Ontario Joint Policy and Planning Committee White Paper at 14–16, http://www.ohqc.ca/pdfs/accountability_agreements_in_ontario-july_31_2008.pdf.
47 See generally, Office of the Auditor General of Ontario, *2006 Annual Report* (2006), s.3.08 at 179, http://www.auditor.on.ca/en/reports_2006_en.htm; for more information about CIHI, see: http://www.cihi.ca.

that the measurements are comparable and meet the same quality requirements.

The legal profession must move aggressively in a similar direction. With the exception of institutions such as the Canadian Forum on Civil Justice,[48] we have no equivalents in the legal system to the various private and public institutions doing the work of data collection and analysis in the health care sector. We echo Trebilcock's observation that consumers of legal services are not interested in the quality of service inputs *per se* (i.e., the education of lawyers and judges) but rather in the quality of service outputs (advice, representation, adjudication),[49] and the fact remains that we lack sufficient data about the system to evaluate these outputs and require corresponding improvements. Information provides leverage for accountability and reform, and the absence of information about the justice sector makes reform much more difficult. With better data, stakeholders will be empowered in reform-oriented discussions with government, and LAO – newly empowered to speak for the middle class – would have a central role to play in this discussion.

V. Conclusion

We have proposed that we fundamentally reconsider how legal aid services are paid for and provided to lower and middle income Ontarians. Our basic premise is that at least some legal services should be provided to a larger group of Ontarians and that the cost of providing these services should be financed through an optional public insurance scheme, with the result that LAO would enjoy greater purchasing power in relation to legal aid services in Ontario. LAO could thereby impose strict conditions with respect to the deployment of those services, with the goal of containing costs by requiring lawyers and other legal service providers acting for clients under a public LEI mandate to innovate, while instituting innovative structures for service delivery in its own right. We strongly resist the notion that any proposal for reform should be relied on as a silver bullet or a panacea, but we hope a frank discussion of the merits of a public LEI scheme targeting Ontarians' most pressing needs will open up new possibilities for discussion.

---

48 See Canadian Forum on Civil Justice, http://cfcj-fcjc.org.
49 Trebilcock, 'Regulating the Market for Legal Services,' *supra* note 7 at 226.

PART 8

The Options Papers

Middle Income Access to Justice: Policy Options with Respect to Family Law

NOEL SEMPLE AND CAROL ROGERSON*

I. Introduction

Family law problems are the civil legal issues that are experienced most frequently by Ontarians.[1] Roughly 75,000 new family proceedings are commenced every year in the province's courts.[2] The justice system that these people encounter has substantial strengths but also notable weaknesses. For example, 45.7 per cent of lower- and middle-class Ontarians who resolved a family justice problem within the past three years reported that the process by which they did so was 'unfair.'[3] These problems persist despite continuous and well-intentioned reform efforts. Within the past few years alone, there have been several major policy reports focused on family dispute resolution procedure.[4] The provincial government introduced legislative reforms in

* We gratefully acknowledge the assistance provided by Chantal Morton, Khalid Janmohamed, and Angelina Ling. This paper should be read in conjunction with Nicholas Bala, 'Reforming Family Dispute Resolution in Ontario: Systemic Changes and Cultural Shifts,' *supra* this volume.

1 R. Roy McMurtry *et al.*, *Listening to Ontarians: Report of the Ontario Civil Legal Needs Project* (Toronto: Ontario Civil Legal Needs Project Steering Committee, 2010) at 21, http://www.lsuc.on.ca/media/may3110_oclnreport_final.pdf, accessed 8 December 2010.

2 Ministry of the Attorney General (Ontario), *Court Services Division Annual Report 2008–2009* (Toronto: Ministry of the Attorney General, 2009) at 32.

3 *Civil Legal Needs of Lower and Middle-Income Ontarians: Quantitative Research* (Toronto: Environics Research Group, 2009) at 49, Law Society of Upper Canada, http://www.lsuc.on.ca/media/may3110_oclnquantitativeresearchreport.pdf, accessed 8 December 2010.

4 For example, Alfred A. Mamo, Peter G. Jaffe, and Debbie G. Chiodo, *Recapturing and*

2009 intended to strengthen judicial oversight of parenting matters.[5] Meanwhile, jurisdictions such as British Columbia and Australia have been actively pursuing more ambitious reforms.[6] Australia's 2006 legal reforms were accompanied by more than $400 million in new funding for mediation, counselling, education, and other services for separated families.[7]

In Ontario, the most recent effort has been the 2010 'Four Pillars' policy initiative introduced by the provincial government in response to an influential report.[8] In order to assess the Four Pillars and explore options for the future, the University of Toronto Faculty of Law working group on Access to Justice convened stakeholder consultations with family justice system leaders in June 2010 and February 2011. These produced a number of innovative reform ideas, along with a

Renewing the Vision of the Family Court (Toronto: Ministry of the Attorney General [Ontario], 2007), Centre for Research and Education on Violence against Women and Children, http://www.crvawc.ca/documents/Family%20Court%20Study%20 2007.pdf, accessed 8 December 2010 [*Mamo Report*]; Law Commission of Ontario, *Voices from a Broken Family Justice System: Sharing Consultation Results* (Toronto, 2010), http://www.lco-cdo.org/en/family-law-process-consultation-results, accessed 8 December 2010 [LCO, *Consultation Results*; OBA Family Law Section, ADR Institute of Ontario and Ontario Association of Family Mediators, *Family Law Process Reform: Supporting Families to Support Their Children* (Toronto: Ontario Association for Family Mediation, 2009), http://www.oafm.on.ca/Documents/OBA%20OAFM%20 ADR%20Institute%20submission%20Apr%207%202009.pdf, accessed 8 December 2010 [OBA, *Supporting Families*].

5 *Family Statute Law Amendment Act, 2009*, S.O. 2009, c.11. Custody and access applications, even those brought on a consensual basis, must now be accompanied by affidavits in a prescribed form. Transfers of custody to non-parents now require criminal and child protection record checks.

6 *Family Law Amendment (Shared Parental Responsibility) Act 2006* (Cth) (Australia); *White Paper on Family Relations Act Reform: Proposals for a new Family Law Act* (Victoria: Ministry of Attorney General [British Columbia], 2010), http://www.ag.gov. bc.ca/legislation/pdf/Family-Law-White-Paper.pdf, accessed 8 December 2010 [*B.C. White Paper*].

7 The 2005–6 Commonwealth budget announced AU $397 million, and an additional $55.6 million was allocated in 2007–8. See *Family and Community Services and Centrelink: 2007–08 Budget Initiatives* (Canberra: Commonwealth of Australia, 2007), http://www.budget.gov.au/2007-08/ministerial/html/dotars-16.htm, accessed 8 December 2010.

8 Barbara Landau *et al.*, *Final Report and Recommendations from the Home Court Advantage Summit (22–23 November 2009)* (Toronto: Ontario Bar Association, ADR Institute of Ontario, and Ontario Association for Family Mediation, 2009), Ontario Bar Association http://www.oba.org/en/pdf/011-0022_Family%20Law%20Process%20 Reform%20Report_final_web.pdf, accessed 8 December 2010.

palpable sense of frustration that is also evident in much of the existing literature.

The general consensus among stakeholders was that the Four Pillars reforms are a step in the right direction but that investment of new government resources is required if they are to fulfil their promise. Very little new funding came with the new reforms,[9] and this was a source of frustration for some focus group participants.[10] This paper will make the case that public spending on family mediation, triage, and legal aid actually can be an 'investment' in the strict sense of the word. These expenditures on early family dispute intervention can yield equal or greater savings to the taxpayer, besides offering proven and substantial benefits to family litigants and their children. This paper will also urge caution in terms of grafting new initiatives and programs onto the system without considering that system's overall design and complexity.

This paper begins by discussing the limited role of prevention and statutory reform in family law access to justice debates. The next four sections correspond to the Four Pillars reforms whereby the Attorney General intends to make family justice 'faster, cheaper, and less confrontational.'[11] The pillars are as follows:

1 Providing early information for separating spouses and children through parenting information classes.
2 Assessing parties and directing them to appropriate and proportional services using a triage approach.
3 Facilitating greater access to legal information, advice, and alternative dispute resolution processes
4 Developing a streamlined and focused family court process.[12]

---

9 Cristin Schmitz, 'Top Judge Proposes Fee Court-Based Mediation, AG Says "No Money,"' *Lawyers Weekly*, 8 October 2010.

10 For an articulation of this scepticism, see Lisa Cirillo, 'Ontario's Family Law Process Reform: Promises And Pitfalls,' *AFCC Ontario Newsletter*, Fall 2010. Others have proposed ideas for funding the system, such as a dedicated tax on marriage licences or a new provincial lottery. Tracey Tyler, 'Tax Marriage to Help Pay for Divorce, Lawyers Say,' *Toronto Star*, 28 September 2010.

11 Chris Bentley, *Access to Justice for Ontarians Podcast Transcript: 29 September 2010* (Toronto: Ministry of the Attorney General [Ontario], 2010), http://www.attorney-general.jus.gov.on.ca/english/AG_podcasts/Transcripts/20100929_access_justice_transcript.asp, accessed 8 December 2010.

12 *Ibid.*

The final section of this paper addresses family legal service delivery, which, although related to pillar 4, is better treated as a distinct and essential 'fifth pillar' for building a better family justice system.

The Middle Income Access to Civil Justice Project has focused on employment, consumer, and debtor/creditor law along with family law. These fields were chosen because they feature many of the same access to justice issues and solutions. However, it is important to identify a distinguishing feature of the access to justice debate in family law: prevention and substantive law reform are less emphasized than they are in other areas, while design and delivery of responsive services is the focus of debate.

Many legal problems can be partially or entirely prevented. Disputes over mortgages or consumer contracts can be forestalled through mandatory disclosure or cooling-off periods.[13] Litigation over workplace disputes can be prevented through the provision of information to employers and employees.[14] Richard Susskind's oft-cited metaphor reflects a consensus about the superiority of prevention over cure: 'clients prefer to have a fence at the top of a cliff rather than an ambulance at the bottom.'[15]

Some family law disputes – such as those regarding child protection or adoption – may be preventable. However, the overwhelming majority of family litigation in Ontario arises from divorce and the dissolution of conjugal relationships. These phenomena were at one time considered preventable problems,[16] but the consensus today is that they are inevitable and not even invariably regrettable.[17] In contrast to other areas in which providing information might help people avoid legal problems altogether, stakeholders have generally accepted that widespread divorce and relationship dissolution are inevitable.[18]

---

13 Anthony Duggan and Iain Ramsay, 'Front-End Strategies for Improving Consumer Access to Justice' *supra* this volume [Duggan and Ramsay, 'Front-End Strategies'].

14 *Judith McCormack and Azim Remani,* 'Middle-Income Access to Justice: Policy Options with Respect to Employment Law,' *infra* this volume ['Middle-Income Access to Justice'].

15 Richard E. Susskind, *The End of Lawyers?: Rethinking the Nature of Legal Services* (Oxford: Oxford University Press, 2008) at 224.

16 A vestige of this idea can be found in the *Divorce Act*, R.S.C. 1985, (2d Supp.), c.3, at ss.9(1)(a) and (b).

17 E. Mavis Hetherington and John Kelly, *For Better or for Worse: Divorce Reconsidered* (New York: W.W. Norton, 2002).

18 Nor was there stakeholder support for a return to the era of restrictive divorce laws and other impediments to divorce. However, some participants said that a better understanding of the implications of divorce might deter some people from taking this step.

Canadian family law likewise no longer seeks to prevent relationship breakdown; it seeks instead to fairly apportion its economic consequences and to protect the interests of children. Family law procedure aims to bring about these goals while minimizing the cost in time, money, and interpersonal conflict. To adopt the terms of Susskind's metaphor, the goal is not to build a fence to stop divorce. If the end of an intimate relationship is a trip from the top of a hill to the bottom, the goal is to find routes that involve not cliffs but rather walkable paths.

Also, doctrinal law reform seems less important in the family law field than it does in some others. While access to justice advocates continue to propose substantive new legal requirements in debtor/creditor and employment law,[19] proposals to amend the substantive provisions of our family law statutes were conspicuously absent in the stakeholder consultations, as they have been in most of the literature. Canadian family law doctrine was dramatically transformed in the final third of the twentieth century, with the need for clear rules to encourage settlement and discourage litigation as one of the explicit goals;[20] there is little remaining demand for substantive reform.[21] Nor for the most part does the discussion focus on family law 'procedure' in the traditional sense of the applicable court rules and procedural precedents. Instead, the live debates centre on alternative dispute resolution mechanisms and services for individuals with family law problems.

II. Pillar 1: Information

The first pillar of the Attorney General's reform plan entails providing more information to litigants, primarily through group classes for family litigants. Attendance at these 'parenting information sessions' has been made mandatory for parties to divorce proceedings in several communities,[22] and the Attorney General recently announced that this

---

19 Duggan and Ramsay, 'Front-End Strategies,' *supra* note 13; Smith, 'Middle Income Access to Justice,' *infra* this volume.

20 Examples include the introduction of no-fault divorce, matrimonial property rules that include a strong presumption of equal division of matrimonial property, child support guidelines, and the Spousal Support Advisory Guidelines.

21 The one exception might be custody and access laws; some argue that the language of custody and access creates a 'win–lose' mentality that fosters conflict and recommend new legislation using the language of parental responsibility.

22 These are Brampton, Milton, Newmarket, and Ottawa. The classes have been man-

program will be extended across the province.[23] The three-hour mandatory sessions review the effects of separation and divorce on families and children, legal issues, alternatives to litigation, and the court process. Participation in a longer, six-session course will be optional.[24] The new courses will be delivered by volunteer mental health professionals and lawyers.[25] Information and Referral Coordinators will also be made available in all Ontario family courts to 'help direct and connect potential litigants to services in the community that assist with family breakdown.'[26] In addition, enhancements will be made to existing information services that provide literature about family law and procedure to litigants.

A. Stakeholder Consultations

Stakeholders recognized that the family justice system can be enormously confusing to those entering it, exacerbating an already emotionally fraught and difficult situation. There was agreement that litigants who are better informed about the interaction of the law with family life might make better decisions in resolving these problems. While the obvious focus was on the need for guidance at the early stages of separation as people enter the family justice system, it was also acknowledged that information about marriage and cohabitation contracts, which are signed during intact intimate relationships, could help some people plan for the possibility of relationship breakdown and help prevent interpersonal conflict arising from it. Stakeholders emphasized the need to provide family law information in as many of the Ontario's

---

datory at Toronto's Superior Court for a number of years. Similar classes are available on a voluntary basis at other Ontario courts.

23 Chris Bentley, 'Family Law Reform Underway,' *Briefly Speaking (Ontario Bar Association)*, December 2010, http://www.oba.org/PDFs/brieflyDecember2010_web.pdf, accessed 8 December 2010. As of 1 September 2011, mandatory attendance at information programs is required by Rule 8.1 of the *Family Law Rules*, O. Reg. 114/99.

24 Judy Van Rhijn, 'Four Pillars to Resurrect a Broken System,' *Canadian Lawyer*, August 2010, http://www.canadianlawyermag.com/Four-pillars-to-resurrect-a-broken-system.html, accessed 8 December 2010.

25 Katie Wood, 'Family Justice Reform Report,' *OBA Matrimonial Affairs*, September 2010, Ontario Bar Association, http://www.oba.org/En/Family_en/newsletter_en/PrintHTML.aspx?DocId=42359#Article_9, accessed 8 December 2010.

26 Ministry of the Attorney General (Ontario), 'Family Law Reform in Ontario,' 9 December 2010, http://news.ontario.ca/mag/en/2010/12/family-law-reform-in-ontario.html, accessed 8 December 2010.

most spoken languages as possible. They also questioned whether it is feasible to introduce high-quality parenting information sessions across the province while paying the session leaders only small honoraria. It was agreed that many people need personalized legal services in addition to information.[27]

B. From the Research

Legal information, as opposed to personalized legal service, means materials or presentations that are available to the public at large or to all family litigants. While a fired employee or evicted tenant may not recognize that she holds legal rights, most Canadians know that the law assigns rights and duties after a marriage ends. Convincing people that they have legal needs and issues is therefore less of a challenge than it is in other areas, although it remains a problem in some communities. However, popular awareness of family law must be supplemented by accurate and timely legal information for those who seek it out.

Investments in legal information can be a very cost-effective way to help people with family justice problems. Educational texts, videos, websites, and podcasts are relatively inexpensive to produce and can be reproduced and disseminated almost for free. Perhaps in part because they are cheaper than providing personalized services, many jurisdictions have allocated public resources to legal information programs. Ontario has a variety of Web-based resources, as well as Family Law Information Centres (FLICs) with hardcopy materials in most courts that hear these matters.[28]

The 2007 *Mamo Report* evaluated the FLICs in Ontario's Unified Family Court sites, and two recent documents cover similar initiatives in British Columbia.[29] There are several points of consensus among

---

27 See section VI.A, below.

28 The ministry website lists sixty-seven FLIC locations, with coordinators available at seventeen of them. Ministry of the Attorney General (Ontario), 'Family Law Information Centre (FLIC) Locations,' http://www.attorneygeneral.jus.gov.on.ca/english/family/infoctr_locations.asp, accessed 8 December 2010.

29 *Mamo Report, supra* note 4; John Malcolmson and Gayla Reid, *BC Supreme Court Self-Help Information Centre: Final Evaluation Report* (Vancouver: B.C. Supreme Court Self-Help Information Centre, 2006), http://justiceeducation.ca/themes/framework/documents/SHC_Final_Evaluation_Sept2006.pdf, accessed 8 December 2010 [*Vancouver Evaluation*]; Ministry of the Attorney General (B.C.), *Nanaimo Family Justice Services Centre Implementation Phase Evaluation: Final Report* (Victoria: Focus Consul-

these three evaluations of family legal information provision. All three reported high levels of satisfaction among users, generally above 80 per cent.[30] Relatively high numbers of users were not yet involved in a court process at the time they accessed the facilities.[31]

However, users did not generally perceive legal information as a complete substitute for personalized legal services.[32] At the Nanaimo Family Justice Hub, which offers both a 'resource room' and access to family justice professionals, almost all of the visitors wanted to meet with a professional. Likewise, in Vancouver, 'the overwhelming majority of service providers and users identified the in-person, hands-on assistance as being a crucial feature of the service.'[33] In the new Australian system, Family Relationship Centres educate and inform the parties and also facilitate settlement through mediation. They explain and assist in developing parenting plans, advise separating parents on options for equal or substantially shared time, and provide referrals.[34]

The evaluation literature also raises doubts about the ability of legal information materials to help those with limited education. The evaluation of the Vancouver self-help pilot project found that 39 per cent of the users had a college diploma or university degree – a disproportionately high share relative to the population.[35] Likewise, among the Nanaimo users, 61 per cent had some post-secondary education.[36] It may be that less educated people, who are generally less able to pay for legal services, are also less willing or able to use generalized legal information, which may not therefore be a functional alternative to investments in personalized legal services for these people.

There are innovative and cost-effective ways to provide legal information with some of the benefits of personalized legal services. For

---

tants, 2008), http://www.ag.gov.bc.ca/justice-reform-initiatives/publications/pdf/ FJSCFinalReport.pdf, accessed 8 December 2010 [*Nanaimo Evaluation*].

30 *Mamo Report, supra* note 4 at 56; *Vancouver Evaluation, ibid.* at 44; *Nanaimo Evaluation, ibid.* at 24.

31 *Mamo Report, supra* note 4 at 53; *Vancouver Evaluation, supra* note 29 at 32.

32 Mary Stratton, *Some Facts and Figures from the Civil Justice System and the Public* (Toronto: Canadian Forum on Civil Justice, 2010) at 27, http://cfcj-fcjc.org/docs/2010/ cjsp-ff-en.pdf, accessed 8 December 2010.

33 *Vancouver Evaluation, supra* note 29 at 48.

34 Rae Kaspiew *et al.*, *Evaluation of the 2006 Family Law Reforms* (Melbourne: Australian Institute of Family Studies, 2009) at 4, http://www.aifs.gov.au/institute/pubs/fle, accessed 8 December 2010.

35 *Vancouver Evaluation, supra* note 29 at 26.

36 *Nanaimo Evaluation, supra* note 29 at 47.

example, Nova Scotia has followed the lead of an English group in creating a 'divorce fair' that provides information and services to prospective divorcees.[37] Websites are also available that calculate personalized child and spousal support entitlements based on the user's inputs.[38]

The social science literature is cautiously optimistic regarding the impact of parenting information sessions. One metastudy found that they increase settlement;[39] another concluded that they have a variety of other positive effects.[40] Participant satisfaction generally seems to be high.[41] However, the literature has demonstrated that these classes have only a 'small, non-significant effect' on relitigation,[42] and it has not yet established which of the myriad existing forms of parenting education are most effective.[43] One survey of Ohio family court litigants found that respondents were significantly less satisfied with divorce education programs than they were with other court-adjunct services such as mediation.[44] The *Mamo Report* noted that voluntary parenting information sessions in Ontario's unified family courts are

---

37 Donalee Moulton, 'All's Fair in Love and Divorce,' *Lawyers Weekly*, 19 February 2010; Will Pavia, 'Divorce Fair Eases the Pain of Splitting,' *The Times (London)*, 16 March 2009.

38 Department of Justice (Canada), 'The Federal Child Support Guidelines: Step-by-Step,' http://www.justice.gc.ca/eng/pi/fcy-fea/lib-bib/pub/guide/index.html, accessed 8 December 2010. A similar initiative for spousal support is being developed; see http://www.divorcemate.com/library/Newsletter66.pdf, accessed 7 December 2011.

39 Desmond Ellis and Dawn Y. Anderson, 'The Impact of Participation in a Parent Education Program for Divorcing Parents on the Use of Court Resources: An Evaluation Study' (2003) 21 *Conflict Resolution Quarterly* 169.

40 Tamara A. Fackrell, Alan J. Hawkins, and Nicole M. Kay, 'How Effective Are Court-Affiliated Divorcing Parents Education Programs? A Meta-Analytic Study' (2011) 49 Fam. Ct. Rev. 107.

41 Shelley Kierstead, 'Parent Education Programs in Family Courts: Balancing Autonomy and State Intervention' (2011) 49 Fam. Ct. Rev. 140; Susan L. Pollet and Melissa Lombreglia, 'A Nationwide Survey Of Mandatory Parent Education' (2008) 46 Fam. Ct. Rev. 375.

42 Fackrell *et al.*, 'How Effective Are ...?', *supra* note 40 at 114.

43 Pollet and Lombreglia, 'A Nationwide Survey,' *supra* note 41. But see Amanda Sigal *et al.*, 'Do Parent Education Programs Promote Healthy Postdivorce Parenting? Critical Distinctions and a Review of the Evidence' (2011) 49 Fam. Ct. Rev. 120; and Fackrell *et al.*, 'How Effective Are ...?', *supra* note 40 at 115–16 for new research insights on this question.

44 Randall W. Leite and Kathleen Clark, 'Participants' Evaluations of Aspects of the Legal Child Custody Process and Preferences for Court Services' (2007) 45 Fam. Ct. Rev. 260 at 265. On a satisfaction scale of 1 to 7, divorce education programs generated a mean score of 3.51. Mediation was rated 5.68.

not very well attended,[45] which suggests that litigants themselves are not entirely convinced of their value. Some have suggested that these sessions need to be made available in a wider range of languages and that the information should be customized for different groups of litigants.[46]

C. Policy Options

1 Carefully select mandatory information program session leaders and subject matter. Moving beyond the 'honorarium' system for compensating session leaders might help attract the most competent staff. This could pay off by reducing the number and increasing the competence of self-represented family litigants.
2 Consider expanding the sessions to four to six hours, with the final half required only for parents.[47]
3 Introduce a curriculum in high school that teaches young people about relationships and conflict management.[48]
4 Disseminate information in multiple languages and various formats (visual, audio, text). Information can be targeted not just to families in the process of dissolution or reformation but also to those that are forming or intact.[49] It could include information on cohabitation and prenuptial agreements, conflict resolution, parenting skills, and so on. It might be provided after the government receives notice of

---

45 *Mamo Report, supra* note 4 at 55.
46 Cirillo, 'Ontario's Family Law Process Reform,' *supra* note 10; LCO, *Consultation Results, supra* note 4 at 56; OBA, *Supporting Families, supra* note 4 at 12.
47 Bala, 'Reforming Family Dispute Resolution In Ontario,' *supra* this volume.
48 Regarding the potential of high school education in this regard, see Andrew Schepard, 'Parental Conflict Prevention Programs and the Unified Family Court: A Public Health Perspective' (1998) 32 Fam. L.Q. 95; and Robert E. Emery, 'Interparental Conflict and Social Policy' in *Interparental Conflict and Child Development: Theory, Research, and Applications*, ed. John H. Grych and Frank D. Fincham (New York: Cambridge University Press, 2001) 417 at 430. Regarding the potential place for such material in the current Ontario secondary school curriculum, see Noel Semple, *Cost–Benefit Analysis of Family Service Delivery: Disease, Prevention, and Treatment* (Toronto: Law Commission of Ontario, 2010) at 32, http://www.lco-cdo.org/family-law-process-call-for-papers-semple.pdf, accessed 8 December 2010 [Semple, *Disease, Prevention, and Treatment*].
49 For example, unlike Ontario, Justice Québec publicizes information about cohabitation contracts on a website. See Justice Québec, 'De Facto Spouses,' http://www.justice.gouv.qc.ca/english/publications/generale/union-a.htm, accessed 8 December 2010.

'triggering events,' such as the registration of a marriage or child-birth.[50]

5 Advertise services and resources already available through community-based organizations, as well as government offices and the websites for courthouses and legal clinics. There is evidence that Ontarians are largely unaware of many free sources of legal information.[51]

6 Either the Law Society or local bar associations should explore the possibility of 'divorce fairs' such as the one organized in Nova Scotia as a vehicle for facilitating access to information about separation and divorce.

III. Pillar 2: Triage and Early Intervention

The Attorney General's second pillar is a 'new intake issue identification approach,' often referred to in the literature as 'triage.'[52] Duty counsel and other staff will help parties identify the issues in their family dispute and direct them to the appropriate services.[53] Systems of this nature have been introduced in Milton and Brampton. All Ontario family courts will soon also have Information and Referral Coordinators, who will direct people to community services.[54]

A. Stakeholder Consultations

The main emphasis of stakeholders, with respect to preventative strategies that might reduce legal needs, was on early and appropriate intervention in family problems to prevent the escalation of conflict and to reduce the subsequent demands on the legal system. There was much discussion of triage or 'case assessment' as a crucial part of the family justice system, with many issues raised both with respect to who should perform it and what factors should be taken into account. It was noted that judges currently perform informal triage in family court, although some stakeholders observed that this may not be the most

---

50 Susskind, *The End of Lawyers?*, *supra* note 15 at 241.
51 McMurtry *et al.*, *Listening to Ontarians*, *supra* note 1 at 28.
52 Bentley, *Access to Justice for Ontarians*, *supra* note 11.
53 Van Rhijn, 'Four Pillars to Resurrect a Broken System,' *supra* note 24.
54 Ministry of the Attorney General (Ontario), 'Backgrounder: Family Law Reform in Ontario (11 March 2011),' http://www.attorneygeneral.jus.gov.on.ca/english/news/2011/20110311-dv-bg.asp, accessed 8 December 2010.

efficient use of expensive judicial time and that earlier intervention as part of the intake process would be more appropriate.

Family problems are not exclusively legal in nature. Stakeholders therefore underscored the importance of triage or case assessment in providing litigants with knowledge of and access to a range of services, including psychological and financial counselling, as well as to methods of dispute resolution, such as mediation and collaborative law, that focus on the reduction of conflict. Stakeholders stressed that parties with limited resources will use those services that are state-subsidized, as courts are now, and that other services must be provided on similar terms to be effective in reducing demand on courts and judges.

Stakeholders focused on the need to develop appropriate triage mechanisms to determine whether a case might be appropriately resolved outside the court system. It was suggested that low-conflict cases might be suited to resolution without judicial involvement, whereas those involving domestic violence or dramatic power imbalances between the parties might require full court intervention. Where ADR is ineffective, it may only delay case progression.

Reference was made to the fact that researchers and practitioners in Ontario and abroad are developing interview-based triage tools for family cases, with a particular focus on measuring conflict. However, other stakeholders were quick to make the point that level of conflict is not the only factor in determining the appropriate response and that legal complexity, safety, and urgency are just as important as conflict. Stakeholders suggested that empirical research was required to accurately determine the kinds of cases requiring judicial intervention before implementing a triage system; they also emphasized the need to ensure that triage systems do not inappropriately restrict access to courts. An effective system of triage or case management may be difficult to implement without additional public funding.

B. From the Research

Jurisdictions with mediation programs are increasingly adopting systems that seek to channel individuals to the most appropriate dispute resolution options.[55] Scholars agree that at a minimum, the presence of

---

55 Peter Salem, 'The Emergence of Triage in Family Court Services: The Beginning of the End for Mandatory Mediation?' (2009) 47 Fam. Ct. Rev. 371. In particular, there is substantial evidence that high-conflict couples are not as well served by traditional facilitative mediation. See Glenn A. Gilmour, *High-Conflict Separation*

domestic violence is highly relevant in assessing the suitability of mediation, and that at least some cases of this nature should be 'screened out.'[56] However, as consultation participant Lisa Cirillo pointed out in a recent paper, there is an important difference between screening and triage. Whereas 'screening is focused on identifying the presence of red flags, a triage process is broader and includes both identifying and prioritizing the family's needs.'[57] Ontario court mediators already engage in screening. Whether the minister's second pillar will fund true triage systems is unclear.

Investments in triage may pay for themselves by permitting savings in courtroom staff. To make this case, the *Supporting Families* report analysed the cost of hiring a Case Assessment Coordinator to conduct triage and consultations with litigants at the 47 Sheppard East Family Court in Toronto.[58] The cost of such a program included a salary of $55,000 to $70,000 per year, plus administrative costs.[59] The benefit would be one-hour consultations with 1,500 clients per year, leading to the diversion of 500 additional cases to mediation.

The *Supporting Families* report did not determine how much money this would save the province, but other data permit a rough calculation. Extrapolating from Ministry of the Attorney General figures, roughly 64 per cent of cases in family mediation would achieve full settlement and an additional 17 per cent would achieve partial settlement.[60] If removing 320 cases (0.64 multiplied by 500) from a court's docket and reducing the number of issues in an additional 85 (0.17 multiplied by 500) would eliminate the need for a new judge, then the ministry could save money by hiring Case Assessment Coordinators in lieu of new judges. Clearly, this simplistic calculation excludes numer-

---

and Divorce: Options for Consideration (Report # 2004-FCY-1E) (Ottawa: Department of Justice [Canada], 2004) at 36, http://www.justice.gc.ca/eng/pi/fcy-fea/lib-bib/rep-rap/2004/2004_1/index.html, accessed 8 December 2010). For a recent Canadian experiment with triage, see 'New Brunswick Unveils Family Law Pilot Project,' *Lawyers Weekly*, 26 February 2010.

56 Salem, *ibid.*; Kaspiew *et al.*, *Evaluation of the 2006 Family Law Reforms*, *supra* note 34 at E4.

57 Cirillo, 'Ontario's Family Law Process Reform,' *supra* note 10.

58 OBA, *Supporting Families*, *supra* note 4 at Appendix C.

59 The total estimated cost was between $100,050 and $132,250 in the first year, and somewhat less in subsequent years.

60 Ministry of the Attorney General (Ontario), *Court Services Division Annual Report 2005/2006 and 2007/2008* (Toronto, 2009) at 30, http://www.attorneygeneral.jus.gov.on.ca/english/about/pubs/courts_annual_05_06/Court_Services_Annual_Report_FULL_EN.pdf, accessed 8 December 2010.

ous monetary and non-monetary costs and benefits associated with the two alternatives. For example, therapeutic early intervention can produce savings beyond the most immediate efficiencies in the courtroom. A large-scale English survey found that over half of relationship breakdown and domestic violence problems led to 'stress-related ill health.'[61] Ill health imposes substantial costs on the taxpayer, especially in jurisdictions with state-funded care, such as Ontario. If early interventions into high-conflict family problems reduce ill health, they may be investments that pay for themselves through savings in the health care system.

C. Policy Options

1 Collect information about the paths that different types of family disputes take through the system and about what happens to the families after they leave court. Data of this nature might allow reliable predictions of which cases will be well served by which responses. It could also allow better-informed decisions regarding which cases require full legal representation and which do not.
2 The Ministry of the Attorney General should adopt or develop family triage or case assessment tools for use across the province and to this end should consider interview-based triage tools for family cases that researchers and practitioners in Ontario and abroad are developing. Many of these focus on measuring conflict, on the theory that appropriately assessing the level of conflict is the key to determining the appropriate response. However, as stakeholders have cautioned, complexity, safety, and urgency are just as important as conflict. Triage staff should also offer referrals to a range of non-legal services.
3 Rigorously evaluate models for implementing triage and mediation. One option is the case assessment coordinator, a dedicated *triageur* as proposed by the *Supporting Families* report.[62] A dedicated *triageur* may perform this function most effectively. However, this adds yet

---

61 Pascoe Pleasence, Nigel J. Balmer, and Alexy Buck, 'The Health Cost of Civil-Law Problems: Further Evidence of Links Between Civil-Law Problems and Morbidity, and the Consequential Use of Health Services' (2008) 5 *Journal of Empirical Legal Studies* 351. See also Paul R. Amato, 'The Consequences of Divorce for Adults and Children' (2000) 62 *Journal of Marriage and the Family* 1269.
62 OBA, *Supporting Families, supra* note 4.

another stage to the already complex system, and it could also require hiring and training an entirely new cadre of professionals.

4 An alternative is to have mediators perform triage, screening out those who are inappropriate candidates for mediation and directing them to other services. Litigants may thereby receive the benefits of dealing with one process rather than two. This model may also save public expense. As in Australia, Ontario mediators might be given the power to issue 'certificates' giving parties expedited access to court if mediation was inappropriate or was sabotaged by the other party.[63]

5 Recognize that effective triage requires access to a range of appropriate services, the cost of which must be subsidized to the same extent as judicial services if the intention is to reduce demand on courts.

IV. Appropriate Dispute Resolution

Attorney General Chris Bentley has described the third pillar as encouraging various forms of alternative dispute resolution, including arbitration and collaborative family law.[64] However, mediation appears to be the central element in this pillar. The Attorney General recently announced that state-subsidized mediation services will soon be expanded to all Ontario courts hearing family matters.[65]

A. Stakeholder Consultations

Appropriate/alternative dispute resolution (ADR) includes all techniques other than adjudication and bipartite negotiation. Use of ADR was supported by stakeholders inappropriate cases. For some families, mediation might be very effective, save money and time, and end in a much speedier resolution with buy-in from all parties. Some participants proposed that resources currently earmarked for the court system be refocused on mediation. Collaborative family law (CFL) can

---

63 *Family Law Act 1975*, (Cth) (Australia), section 60I ('Attending Family Dispute Resolution Before Applying for Part VII Order').

64 Bentley, *Access to Justice for Ontarians, supra* note 11; Van Rhijn, 'Four Pillars to Resurrect a Broken System,' *supra* note 24.

65 Ministry of the Attorney General (Ontario), 'Families Will Benefit from Justice Improvements,' http://news.ontario.ca/mag/en/2010/12/families-will-benefit-from-justice-improvements.html, accessed 8 December 2010.

also be effective as a means of avoiding expensive and draining litigation.[66] However, consultation participants said it is especially important that cases involving domestic violence not be directed out of the traditional court system. Litigants experiencing domestic violence were among vulnerable groups identified as needing full legal representation. Vulnerable litigants need advocates' assistance in navigating the legal system.

B. From the Research

Mediation, in which a neutral third party seeks to bring about a voluntary settlement, is probably the oldest and best established form of ADR in the family justice sphere. Family lawyer Phil Epstein recently estimated that 60 per cent of Ontario families going through relationship dissolution use some form of mediation.[67] Mediation is available on a subsidized or free basis in some Ontario courts[68] and is also provided by private sector practitioners. Mediators are still mostly non-lawyers,[69] although this is changing in some jurisdictions.[70]

Government investments in mediation might 'pay for themselves' by reducing the need for judges.[71] If the health care system invests in low-cost preventative and community health initiatives to reduce the need for high-cost emergency wards, a similar logic may support mediation to reduce the need for high-cost adjudication and judicial case conferences. Judges earn in excess of $250,000 per year,[72] whereas a family

---

66 For a description of CFL, see Pauline H. Tesler, 'Collaborative Law: What It Is and Why Lawyers Need to Know About It' (1999) 2008 *American Journal of Family Law* 215, Collaborative Family Law of Utah, http://www.collaborativefamilylawofutah.com/articles/whatandwhy.html, accessed 8 December 2010.

67 Linda Diebel, 'Unqualified Mediators Prey on Broken Families,' *Toronto Star*, 14 January 2008) at A1.

68 Ministry of the Attorney General (Ontario), 'Family Mediation Services,' http://www.attorneygeneral.jus.gov.on.ca/english/family/mediation.asp, accessed 8 December 2010.

69 Jay Folberg, Ann Milne, and Peter Salem, *Divorce and Family Mediation: Models, Techniques, and Applications* (New York: Guilford Press, 2004).

70 Edward Kruk, 'Practice Issues, Strategies, and Models: The Current State of the Art of Family Mediation' (1998) 36 Fam. Ct. Rev. 195.

71 They might also reduce the demand for publicly funded personal legal representation, insofar as mediators allow the parties to resolve their disputes alone, whereas they would otherwise require lawyers to negotiate on their behalf.

72 Semple, Semple, *Disease, Prevention, and Treatment, supra* note 48 at 65.

mediator with a Masters of Social Work would be paid between $53,000 and $80,000 per year.[73] If hiring two mediators increased the settlement rate sufficiently to eliminate the need for one judge, doing so would save public funds.

That family mediation produces settlement is beyond doubt. Court-adjunct mediation in Ontario produced full or partial settlement in 81 per cent of cases in 2009–10.[74] While some of these cases might have settled without mediation, research has established that most non-mediated cases require at least some court intervention.[75] In Australia, the introduction of Family Relationship Centres providing free mediation was largely credited for a decrease in the total number of child-related family law court applications from 19,188 in 2004–5 to 14,549 in 2008–9.[76]

Of course, the purpose of justice system reform is not simply to pinch pennies but to do justice as well. A proper comparison of triage-plus-mediation to its alternatives would have to take into account the quality of justice provided in terms of outcomes, process impact on the parties, and a variety of other factors. Resolutions negotiated by competent lawyers may be as good as or better than mediated resolutions,[77] although the reality is that most Ontarians cannot afford competent family lawyers.[78] In the family law context, some scholars have suggested that mediated resolutions are likely to leave women with less

---

73 Legal Aid Ontario, 'Family Mediator for Greater Toronto Region of Legal Aid Ontario,' http://www.legalaid.on.ca/en/careers/lao-122-10.asp, accessed 8 December 2010.

74 Ministry of the Attorney General (Ontario), *Court Services Division Annual Report 2009-2010* (Toronto, 2009) at 31, http://www.attorneygeneral.jus.gov.on.ca/english/about/pubs/courts_annual_09/Court_Services_Annual_Report_FULL_EN.pdf, accessed 8 December 2010. While full settlement rates were not provided in the most recent annual report, past versions of this report indicate that between 60 and 65 per cent of cases that enter family mediation are completely settled therein. See Ministry of the Attorney General (Ontario), *Court Services Division Annual Report 2005/2006 and 2007/2008* (Toronto, 2009) at 30, http://www.attorneygeneral.jus.gov.on.ca/english/about/pubs/courts_annual_05_06/Court_Services_Annual_Report_FULL_EN.pdf, accessed 8 December 2010.

75 Robert E. Emery, David Sbarra, and Tara Grover, 'Divorce Mediation: Research and Reflections' (2005) 43 Fam. Ct. Rev. 22 at 25.

76 Kaspiew *et al.*, *Evaluation of the 2006 Family Law Reforms*, *supra* note 34 at 305.

77 For example, Martha J. Bailey, 'Unpacking the Rational Alternative: A Critical Review of Family Mediation Movement Claims' (1989) 8 Can. J. Fam. L. 61.

78 See section VI.B, below.

than their legal entitlements.[79] However, empirical research has not generally supported this theory.[80]

One Ohio study using family litigant surveys found that both men and women were substantially more satisfied with court-adjunct mediation than they were with lawyers and judges.[81] The review of Australia's new mandatory mediation system reached a similar conclusion.[82] A recent meta-analysis aggregated empirical comparisons of mediation and litigation in terms of the litigants' satisfaction with the process and outcome as well as the processes' impact on their relationship and likelihood of future litigation.[83] The unambiguous conclusion was that 'mediation has been shown quantitatively to be superior to litigation in dealing with divorce cases.'[84] In sum, family mediation is supported by a body of empirical evidence that none of the newer and more fashionable ADR innovations such as collaborative family law or arbitration can come close to matching.

Enthusiasm for family mediation has led some to suggest that participation should be mandatory. Ontario's Chief Justice Warren Winkler recently made such a proposal.[85] The 2005 B.C. Working Group report proposed mandatory participation in either mediation or collaborative processes,[86] although this recommendation was not adopted in the 2010 White Paper. Australia is among the jurisdictions in which mediation is a mandatory precursor to court appearances for most litigants, and

---

79 Sandra A. Goundry, Rosalind Currie, and Yvonne Peters, *Family Mediation in Canada: Implications for Women's Equality* (Ottawa: Status of Women Canada, 1998) at 41, http://dsp-psd.pwgsc.gc.ca/Collection/SW21-30-1998E.pdf, accessed 8 December 2010.

80 Mary G. Marcus *et al.*, 'To Mediate or Not to Mediate: Financial Outcomes in Mediated Versus Adversarial Divorces' (1999) 17 *Mediation Quarterly* 143; Carol Bohmer and Marilyn L. Ray, 'Effects of Different Dispute Resolution Methods on Women and Children after Divorce' (1994) 28 Fam. L.Q. 223.

81 Leite and Clark, 'Participants' Evaluations,' *supra* note 44 at 265.

82 Kaspiew *et al.*, *Evaluation of the 2006 Family Law Reforms*, *supra* note 34 at 7.

83 Lori Anne Shaw, 'Divorce Mediation Outcome Research: A Meta-analysis' (2010) 27 *Conflict Resolution Quarterly* 447.

84 *Ibid.* at 461.

85 Tracey Tyler, 'Chief Justice Urges Forced Family Law Mediation,' *Toronto Star*, 15 September 2010, A1.

86 B.C. Justice Review Task Force, *A New Justice System for Families and Children: Report of the Family Justice Reform Working Group to the Justice Review Task Force* (Vancouver: Justice Review Task Force, 2005) at 39, http://www.bcjusticereview.org/working_groups/family_justice/final_05_05.pdf, accessed 8 December 2010 [JRTF, *New Justice*].

that country's experience may offer some insights. Family dispute resolution practitioners may issue certificates excusing people from the mandatory mediation requirement owing to violence, among other reasons.[87] All other family litigants must attend at least one mediation session. While the reforms originally forbade lawyers to attend mediation sessions at the FRCs, in 2009 this policy was reversed.[88] When Australia made family mediation mandatory, it also pledged $200 million to provide these services on a free and subsidized basis.[89]

There are ongoing concerns that the process for screening out families with potential violence or abuse from mediation is not reliable enough.[90] The recent Law Commission of Ontario (LCO) consultations revealed scepticism regarding the effectiveness of mandatory mediation.[91] The concerns raised related, among other things, to parties' inability to attend for health reasons, lack of child care, risks of missing work, or lack of funds for travel to the sessions.[92]

Mediation is only one type of family ADR,[93] which is a broad field in which new ideas and techniques continue to evolve. *Family law arbitra-*

---

87 *Family Law Act 1975, supra* note 63. For a critique of this system, see Bala, *supra* note 47; and Alastair Nicholson, 'Family Law in Australia 2009: Troubling Changes,' *Unified Family Court Connection,* Fall 2009, University of Baltimore School of Law, http://law.ubalt.edu/downloads/law_downloads/FALL%202009%20UFC%20NL.pdf, accessed 8 December 2010.

88 Helen Rhoades, 'Mandatory Mediation of Family Disputes: Reflections from Australia' (2010) 32 *Journal of Social Welfare & Family Law* 183 at 185.

89 *Implementation of the Family Relationship Centres Initiative* (Canberra: Australian National Audit Office, 2006), http://www.anao.gov.au/director/publications/auditreports/2010-2011.cfm?item_id=C420F6AA1560A6E8AA1F19D38258E9E6, accessed 8 December 2010.

90 *Ibid.* at 14–15. Concerns about domestic violence are part of a broader feminist critique of mandatory mediation that focuses on the potential for power imbalances to create exploitative or unjust results. See, for example, Trina Grillo, 'The Mediation Alternative: Process Dangers for Women' (1991) 100 Yale L.J. 1545; and Penelope E. Bryan, 'Killing Us Softly: Divorce Mediation and the Politics of Power' (1992) 40 Buff. L. Rev. 441.

91 See, for example, Judy Van Rhijn, 'Chief Justice Expands on Proposals to Redesign Family Law System,' *Law Times,* 8 November 2010, http://www.lawtimesnews.com/201011087841/Headline-News/Chief-justice-expands-on-proposals-to-redesign-family-law-system, accessed 8 December 2010.

92 LCO, *Consultation Results, supra* note 4 at 14.

93 Anne-Marie Ambert, *Divorce: Facts, Causes, & Consequences,* 3rd ed. (Ottawa: Vanier Institute of the Family, 2009) at 671, http://www.vifamily.ca/sites/default/files/divorce_facts_causes_consequences.pdf, accessed 8 December 2010; Salem, 'The Emergence of Triage,' *supra* note 55 at 371.

tion is a dispute resolution option that has been recognized in Ontario law.[94] Arbitration may be combined with a prior mediation phase in a hybrid known as 'Med-Arb.' While it offers significant advantages to litigants,[95] it is significantly more expensive than mediation and primarily serves a relatively wealthy niche market. *Online resolution* of family disputes has been the subject of some experimentation and scholarship.[96] Finally, a *custody and access assessment* conducted by the Office of the Children's Lawyer or by a private practitioner might be considered a form of ADR, insofar as these assessments often lead to voluntary settlement.[97]

C. Policy Options

1 The mediation participation rate might be increased very substantially without making attendance compulsory. Reducing the cost and increasing the visibility of courthouse mediation could have this effect. Moreover, the *Mamo Report* found that judges very seldom refer litigants to mediation,[98] and if they were to do so many litigants might willingly comply.

2 Regulate family mediators, in order to ensure high-quality service.[99] Regulation could also help ensure that mediators are aware of and respond appropriately to domestic violence and power imbalance concerns. The B.C. White Paper proposed that mediators and other

94 *Family Arbitration*, O. Reg. 134/07.

95 Marion Boyd, *Dispute Resolution in Family Law: Protecting Choice, Promoting Inclusion* (Toronto: Ministry of the Attorney General [Ontario], 2004), http://www.attorney-general.jus.gov.on.ca/english/about/pubs/boyd, accessed 8 December 2010) at 35 et seq.

96 John Zeleznikow and Andrew Stranieri, 'Split-Up: An Intelligent Decision Support System Which Provides Advice upon Property Division Following Divorce' (1998) 6 *Journal of Law and Information Technology* 190; Susskind, *supra* note 15 at 219; Louise Ellen Teitz, 'Providing Legal Services for the Middle Class in Cyberspace: The Promise and Challenge of On-Line Dispute Resolution' (2001) 70 *Fordham Law Review* 985.

97 Janet R. Johnston, 'High-Conflict Divorce' (1994) 4 *The Future of Children* 165; Michael A. Saini, 'Evidence Base of Custody and Access Evaluations' (2008) 8 Brief Treat. Crisis Interven. 111.

98 *Mamo Report, supra* note 4 at 23.

99 Diebel, 'Unqualified Mediators,' *supra* note 67. Family mediation expert Desmond Ellis, who has welcomed Chief Justice Winkler's call for mandatory mediation, has also said that government regulation of mediators should accompany its introduction. See Desmond Ellis, 'Call for Mediation Applauded,' *Toronto Star,* 20 September 2010, Social Policy in Ontario, http://spon.ca/call-for-mediation-applauded/2010/09/21, accessed 8 December 2010.

alternative family dispute resolution professionals be regulated by the province.[100]

V. Pillar 4: Streamlining the Court Process

Under this heading, the primary reform initiative that the Attorney General has mentioned is a new Court Forms Assistant. This tool, found on the ministry website, asks users questions and then uses the information to produce court-ready forms.[101] Another recently announced court reform is the expansion of the Dispute Resolution Officer (DRO) program. DROs are volunteer senior lawyers who perform quasi-mediatory and issue-narrowing work in case conferences.[102] The DRO program has been extended from its Toronto base to four new communities.

A. Stakeholder Consultations

The stakeholders were clear on the need for courts as part of the family justice system. They generally opposed replacing judges with non-lawyer decision makers on a wholesale basis. Stakeholders said that courts should offer an array of services and dispute resolution options in addition to adjudication. However, they preferred the Unified Family Court, rather than an administrative tribunal, as a model.

One theme that emerged from the stakeholder consultations was the need for expertise on the part of decision makers involved in the family law system. 'One family one judge' – the idea that a single family law case ought to be overseen by a single judge – was strongly supported by stakeholders. However, there was scepticism as to its feasibility. At the very least, stakeholders were strongly of the view that a judge who presides over a particular stage of a case ought to leave notes on the matter for subsequent judges.[103]

---

100 *B.C. White Paper, supra* note 6 at 20–1.
101 Ministry of the Attorney General (Ontario), 'Ontario Court Forms Assistant,' https://formsassistant.ontariocourtforms.on.ca, accessed 8 December 2010.
102 Heather Smith, Michael Brown, and Francine Van Melle, *Dispute Resolution Officer Program Pilot Project in the Superior Court of Justice in Brampton, Milton, and Newmarket: Practice Direction* (Toronto: Superior Court of Justice [Ontario], 2010), Judges' Library, http://www.ontariocourts.on.ca/scj/en/notices/pd/disputeresolution.htm, accessed 8 December 2010. On 29 November 2010, this DRO system was extended to Barrie.
103 The family court file review conducted as part of the *Mamo Report* found that information in the files was often incomplete: *supra* note 4, at 86.

Stakeholders were asked to comment on the recent Australian reforms that introduced a more inquisitorial process for adjudicating child-related disputes, called the less adversarial trial (LAT). They noted that a more activist judiciary might create adjustment and other challenges but that it might also be useful in streamlining court processes. Some stakeholders were concerned that the recent reforms to parenting affidavits were simply making the system more complex, to no real benefit. It was also suggested that procedural requirements such as case conferences can be unduly cumbersome if used inappropriately.[104]

Stakeholders saw merit in giving non-judicial officials authority over some decisions, such as child support recalculation. Some commented that the Ontario system is very judge-heavy and that straightforward issues could be dealt with by non-judicial officials. For example, the Toronto DRO program has twenty to thirty lawyers sitting one day per month on a *pro bono* basis to hear motions, mainly those involving modification of support orders. The DROs dispose of approximately 72 per cent of the cases before them and narrow the issues in many others. The DROs are clearly effective, and the willingness of the private bar to donate services is admirable; however, some stakeholders asked whether the demand for this type of service indicates a need for broader reform.

B. From the Research

Whatever progress is made with mediation and innovative legal service delivery, authoritative decision making will remain a necessary element of the system. The Law Commission of Ontario has highlighted the importance of expertise among authoritative neutral decision makers responding to family law problems.[105] Expertise in this context includes facility with the *Family Law Rules* and the applicable statutes and case law. However, it may also require an understanding of the relevant social issues such as domestic violence, power dynamics, high conflict, and race and disability.

The literature has identified a number of reform options for public

---

104 According to Ontario Chief Justice Warren Winkler, there is a widespread sentiment that 'there are too many' case conferences, 'and they are too expensive.' Winkler would replace case conferences with mandatory mediation: Van Rhijn, 'Chief Justice Expands on Proposals,' *supra* note 91.

105 LCO, *Consultation Results, supra* note 4 at 12.

sector responses to family challenges. Family law civil procedure rules could be amended to curtail excessive litigation,[106] deal with parenting issues before financial issues,[107] or otherwise temper the party-controlled, adversarial model.[108] Reducing the number of judges involved in the average case is usually considered a laudable goal.[109] However, there is a tension in the literature between inquisitorial models of family justice and the classic adversarial approach.[110]

Judges could be assigned permanently as family court specialists so as to develop expertise.[111] The 2005 B.C. Working Group report recognized the dangers of judicial burnout created by this practice area, but nonetheless endorsed the appointment of new permanent family specialist judges.[112] It is also possible to obtain some of the same benefits by ensuring that those who hear family law matters devote a substantial proportion of their working time to matters of this nature.[113] The *Mamo*

---

106 Noel Semple, 'Whose Best Interests? Custody and Access Law and Procedure' (2010) 48 Osgoode Hall L.J. 287.

107 Michelle Zeitler and Samantha Moore, *Children Come First: A Process Evaluation of the Nassau County Model Custody Part*, New York State Office of Court Administration, 2008, http://www.courtinnovation.org/_uploads/documents/Children_Come_First.pdf, accessed 8 December 2010.

108 Australia is among the jurisdictions to have experimented with more inquisitorial methods in children's cases. Evaluations have generally been positive. See Jennifer E. McIntosh, Hon Diana Bryant, and Kristen Murray, 'Evidence of a Different Nature: The Child-Responsive and Less Adversarial Initiatives of the Family Court of Australia' (2008) 46 Fam. Ct. Rev. 125.

109 For example, Carol Flango, H. Ted Rubin, and Victor Eugene Flango, *How Are Courts Coordinating Family Cases?* (Williamsburg: National Center for State Courts, 1999); and *Mamo Report*, *supra* note 4. However, there are also procedural justice reasons why a judge who conducts pre-trial conferences (which often include promoting settlement) should not also adjudicate the matter if it comes to trial.

110 For example, Gerald W. Hardcastle, 'Adversarialism and the Family Court: A Family Court Judge's Perspective' (2005) 9 UC Davis J. Juv. L. & Pol'y 57; Dan Goldberg, 'Judicial Interviews of Children in Custody and Access Cases: Time to Pause and Reflect,' paper presented at conference on Family Law: The Voice of the Child, Law Society of Upper Canada, Toronto, 10 March 2010; Rollie Thompson, 'The Evolution of Modern Canadian Family Law Procedure: The End of the Adversary System? Or Just the End of the Trial?' (2003) 41 Fam. Ct. Rev. 155.

111 OBA, *Supporting Families, supra* note 4.

112 JRTF, *New Justice, supra* note 86 at 103.

113 For a literature review on the costs and benefits of judicial specialization, see Canadian Bar Association Task Force on Court Reform in Canada and Law for the Future Fund, *Report of the Canadian Bar Association Task Force on Court Reform in Canada* (Ottawa, 1991).

Report also recommended that judges be appointed to family court for terms lasting at least four to six months.[114]

In Ontario, the term 'unified family court' (UFC) refers to a court in which judges can both grant divorces and apply provincial family legislation.[115] There are currently eighteen UFCs in the province. Because divorce is a federal power under the *Constitution Act, 1867* while other family law issues are under provincial jurisdiction, UFCs can only be created by federal–provincial agreement.[116] More broadly, UFCs are defined in the literature as courts that meet as many of a family's needs as possible within one building.[117]

While UFCs have generally received broad support, there are sceptics who caution that they are not panaceas.[118] A recent evaluation found that Canadian UFCs are more likely than other family courts to have mediation, support services, and specialized family judges available.[119] However, it did not find that UFCs resolve the average case in a speedier or less adversarial fashion than other courts.[120] As part of

---

114 *Mamo Report, supra* note 4 at 86.

115 *Ibid.* at 114.

116 *Constitution Act, 1867,* s.91(26).

117 James W. Bozzomo and Andrew Schepard, 'Efficiency, Therapeutic Justice, Mediation, and Evaluation: Reflections on a Survey of Unified Family Courts' (2003) 37 Fam. L.Q. 332. In the United States, UFCs almost invariably also deal with juvenile delinquency and 'status offences' such as truancy.

118 Scholars and reports supporting the extension of unified family courts include Federal and Provincial Territorial Family Law Committee, *Report on Custody and Access and Child Support: Putting Children First* (Ottawa: Department of Justice [Canada] 2002) at xiii, http://www.justice.gc.ca/eng/pi/fcy-fea/lib-bib/rep-rap/2002/flc2002/pdf/flc2002.pdf, accessed 8 December 2010). For a more sceptical view, see Jeffrey A. Kuhn, 'A Seven-Year Lesson on Unified Family Courts: What We Have Learned Since the 1990 National Family Court Symposium' (1998) 32 Fam. L.Q. 67 at 77–8. A 2007 survey of Canadian family lawyers produced an interesting result. Although 'almost three-quarters of the survey respondents (72 percent) who do not have Unified Family Courts in their jurisdiction said they would like to see them established ... less than half of the respondents agreed or strongly agreed that Unified Family Courts have positive consequences.' Joanne J. Paetsch, Lorne D. Bertrand, and Nicholas Bala, *The Child-Centred Family Justice Strategy: Survey on the Practice of Family Law in Canada* (Ottawa: Department of Justice Canada, 2007) at vi, http://www.justice.gc.ca/eng/pi/fcy-fea/lib-bib/rep-rap/2007/ccfjs-sjfae/co.html, accessed 8 December 2010.

119 Evaluation Division, Office of Strategic Planning and Performance Management, *The Unified Family Court Summative Evaluation Final Report* (Ottawa: Department of Justice [Canada], 2009) at 33, http://www.justice.gc.ca/eng/pi/eval/rep-rap/09/ufc-tuf/ufc.pdf, accessed 8 December 2010) [*UFC Evaluation*].

120 *Ibid.* at 40–3.

its 2006 reforms, Australia notably departed from the UFC model by transferring mediation away from courts and into Family Relationship Centres.[121]

The Dispute Resolution Officer (DRO) program is an example of delegating family law decision-making authority to professionals other than judges. Another example is the Ottawa Family Case Manager, who presides over case conferences and motions and exercises many judicial powers.[122] Judges could be authorized to delegate authority to parenting coordinators, who typically have authority over minor parenting disputes arising after an order or agreement.[123] Some jurisdictions have subdivided decision-making authority even further. In the New York City Family Court, Court Attorney Referees have authority in custody and access cases while Support Magistrates hear child support and paternity matters. Specialized decision makers may (1) increase efficiency by conserving judges' expensive time for the cases that are most in need of it, and (2) allow decision makers to develop more expertise in specific areas. On the other hand, this approach is clearly a departure from the principle of 'one family, one judge,' and as such may expose families to a more time-consuming and arduous procedure.

Others have proposed more dramatic reforms to family law decision making. Lesley and Brenda Jacobs recently argued in a consultation paper for the LCO that family legal services should be delivered within 'multidisciplinary centres' inspired in part by modern health care facilities.[124] Some have suggested that administrative tribunals would

---

121 The rationale for this is that family disputes are 'essentially relationship problems rather than legal ones' and are therefore 'better suited to community-based interventions' rather than court-based ones. See Kaspiew *et al.*, *Evaluation, supra* note 34 at 4. For a critical response to this reform, see Nicholson, *supra* note 87.

122 *Family Law Rules*, O. Reg. 114/99, R. 42; Robert Beaudoin, remarks presented to conference Home Court Advantage: Creating a Family Law Process That Works, Toronto, Ontario, 22–3 November 2009, at 40–3, http://www.oba.org/en/pdf/011-0022_Family%20Law%20Process%20Reform%20Report_final_web.pdf, accessed 8 December 2010).

123 Christine A. Coates *et al.*, 'Parenting Coordination for High-Conflict Families' (2004) 42 Fam. Ct. Rev. 246; AFCC Task Force on Parenting Coordination, 'Parenting Coordination: Implementation Issues' (2003) 41 Fam. Ct. Rev. 533. The *B.C. White Paper* proposed giving judges this power: *supra* note 6 at 16.

124 Brenda Jacobs and Lesley Jacobs, *Multidisciplinary Paths to Family Justice: Professional Challenges and Promising Practices* (Toronto: Law Commission of Ontario, 2010), http://www.lco-cdo.org/en/family-law-process-call-for-papers-jacobs, accessed 8 December 2010.

be better suited than courts to dealing with family disputes.[125] Government agencies already play a leading role in child support enforcement and could be entrusted with more authority in the family law sphere.[126]

There is substantial merit in the pillar 4 agenda of streamlining court processes. A valuable reminder of the byzantine complexities of the existing system came in the personal account of A. Arshad that recently appeared in the *Canadian Forum on Civil Justice News and Views*.[127] This document should be required reading for those interested in the experience of self-represented litigants. Ms Arshad is a university-educated single parent earning less than $15,000 per year. She wanted the right to make all decisions for her child, given that the child's father lived abroad. Knowing that she needed legal advice, she began with Internet searches and a visit to a student legal clinic. What followed was a six-month odyssey involving eight distinct services and agencies, conflicting instructions, and multiple circular referrals before she was granted a sole custody order. Arshad's matter was unopposed and legally straightforward; self-represented litigants with complex and high-conflict cases face additional hurdles such as case conferences and the OCL intake process.

The system that Arshad confronted is the result of many generations of procedural reforms. Most of the reforms have added new require-

---

125 Kathy Carmichael, *New Directions: Divorce and Administrative Law* (Ottawa: Department of Justice [Canada], 1999), Canadian Forum on Civil Justice, http://cfcj-fcjc. org/clearinghouse/drpapers/divorce.htm, accessed 8 December 2010; Michael Cochrane, 'The Flaw in Family Law,' *The Mark*, 4 May 2009), http://www.themarknews. com/articles/153-the-flaw-in-family-law, accessed 8 December 2010. For an opposing view upholding the role of courts in family law, see Hon Diana Bryant, 'Speech to the Inaugural Family Law System Conference,' Old Parliament House, Canberra, 19 February 2009, http://www.ag.gov.au/www/agd/rwpattach.nsf/alldoc/8166F1E08FB CEBF0CA2575EE007BCF54/$file/Plenary%20Session%201%20-%20Speech%20-%20 Hon%20Diana%20Bryant%20QC.pdf, accessed 8 December 2010.

126 For example, in Ontario, the Family Responsibility Office (FRO). Ontario Ministry of Community and Social Services, 'About the Family Responsibility Office,' http:// www.mcss.gov.on.ca/en/mcss/programs/familyResponsibility, accessed 8 December 2010. See also Statistics Canada, *Maintenance Enforcement Programs in Canada: Description of Operations, 1999/2000, Catalogue no. 85-552-X* (Ottawa: Statistics Canada, 2002), http://dsp-psd.pwgsc.gc.ca/Collection-R/Statcan/85-552-XIE/0010085-552-XIE.pdf, accessed 8 December 2010. Regarding the potential role of the Canada Revenue Agency, see Semple, *Disease, Prevention, and Treatment, supra* note 48 at 77.

127 A. Arshad, 'A Self-Represented Family Litigant,' *Canadian Forum on Civil Justice News and Views* (Fall 2007) at 12, http://cfcj-fcjc.org/docs/2007/newsviews10-en. pdf#page=7, accessed 8 December 2010.

ments and offices to the system without removing anything.[128] For all their merits, the Four Pillars are also of this nature. The streamlining pillar could be expanded into a ground-up rebuild of the family justice system. For example, a system architect starting from scratch would probably unify the mediatory functions that are currently performed by at least four different groups.[129] Triage, whereby the government decides what resources to allocate to a case, is done at the Office of the Children's Lawyer (OCL), at Legal Aid Ontario, and by the new triage officers described in pillar 2. It seems likely that both government expense and litigant aggravation could be reduced if each family were subjected to only *one* triage process.

C. Policy Options

1 Redesign the Ontario family justice system from the ground up. Identify all of the necessary services and functions, and unify them in a smaller group of new offices and processes that would replace those currently existing.
2 Expand the unified family court system across the province. As an intermediate step, larger centres could group family law specialist judges in a single court as a 'team.' This model is currently used in Toronto.
3 Increase judicial specialization in family court – for example, by imposing a minimum period of appointment to family court or by appointing more judges with family law experience.
4 Reduce the number of judges involved with a file; move towards 'one family, one judge.'
5 Give judges training and a mandate for a more inquisitorial style of conducting family law proceedings, either in all family law cases or in those involving children.
6 Introduce an administrative procedure for recalculating child support after changes in income.[130]

---

128 This is unsurprising. Each office and procedure has its own constituency, which will vigorously oppose its abolishment. Removing something therefore has a much higher political cost than adding something.
129 Court-adjunct mediators, case conference judges, DROs, and Office of the Children's Lawyer employees.
130 Provisions authorizing a child support recalculation service were added to Ontario's *Family Law Act* in late 2009, but these remain unproclaimed. (*Family Law Act (Ontario)*, R.S.O. 1990, c.F.3 at s.39(1).)

7 Authorize judges to delegate authority to parenting coordinators or enforce decisions made by parenting coordinators.
8 Use intake and education reforms to increase the likelihood that self-represented litigants will appear in court with the necessary information and documents. As in Alberta, court staff might be trained to help litigants fill out forms and draft memoranda of agreement.[131] Providing these services would result in a more efficient use of court time and judicial resources.

VI. Legal Service Delivery

A. Stakeholder Consultations

The provision of legal *services* (as opposed to legal *information)* involves personalized advice and representation. Although not mentioned in the Four Pillars, legal services are an essential element of the system. Many of the stakeholders were of the view that information and education are not enough. Many people involved in family law disputes need more ready access to individualized legal services. While stakeholders recognized that professionals other than lawyers might usefully play a larger role in resolving family law disputes, there was also agreement that lawyers with expertise in family law play an important role. This role is essential in protecting the interests of vulnerable parties and managing high-conflict cases, but also in shaping parties' expectations and facilitating efficient dispute resolution. Stakeholders commented on the growing numbers of self-represented litigants and the difficulties this posed for opposing counsel and judges, while noting that self-represented litigants were a diverse group and that not all were in financially constrained circumstances.

In its recent report, the Ontario Civil Legal Needs Project urged a rethinking of the model of full legal representation and suggested that in some cases 'unbundling' of legal services (also called partial legal representation or limited scope retainers) could offer significant benefits.[132] It is fair to say that the focus group participants had mixed views about unbundling. Many cautioned that cases involving vulnerable and

---

131 Nicholas Bala, 'Reforming Family Dispute Resolution in Ontario: Systemic Changes and Cultural Shifts,' *supra* this volume.
132 McMurtry *et al., Listening to Ontarians, supra* note 1 at 56–7. See also Samreen Beg and Lorne Sossin, 'Should Legal Services Be Unbundled?', *supra* this volume.

high-conflict parties required full representation and that unbundled legal services would at best only be appropriate for a relatively small group of fairly sophisticated middle income parties. Many participants noted the complexity and drawn-out nature of family law disputes and expressed concern about the lack of time to develop relationships with clients purchasing unbundled services, and the errors that might be made as a result of a lack of trust. The concerns raised in the discussion of unbundling included the fact that lawyers may be providing advice and assistance based on inadequate information, and may find it difficult to abide by professional and ethical obligations.

Judges with family law expertise were seen as the primary solution to the problems raised by self-represented parties. However, others were of the view that self-represented parties are a permanent feature of the family justice system and that if some form of limited representation were available and utilized by those who are currently unrepresented it could contribute to the more efficient operation of the family justice system. Concern about liability issues was seen as a major deterrent to limited representation in the current regulatory context, and the Law Society of Upper Canada was urged to take leadership and provide guidelines on limited representation.

Although the discussion of legal expense insurance was not extensive, the focus group yielded a positive review of the Canadian Auto Workers' legal services plan – the only such plan in Canada – which provides twelve hours of legal services in a family law matter, with subsequent time billed at a somewhat reduced hourly rate. The twelve hours, while limited, was viewed as very helpful to parties in resolving their family law problems; in some cases, further legal services were purchased on an unbundled basis.[133]

B. From the Research

Ms Arshad's experience is a reminder of the essential value of personalized legal services.[134] A competent lawyer or paralegal could have been her agent and guide through the process, making the experience vastly less difficult. The Ontario Civil Legal Needs telephone survey confirmed the continuing need for face-to-face legal services, despite

---

133 See Paul Vayda and Stephen Ginsberg, 'Legal Services Plans: Crucial-Time Access to Lawyers and the Case for a Public–Private Partnership,' *supra* this volume.
134 Arshad, 'A Self-Represented Family Litigant,' *supra* note 127.

the increasing prevalence of and reliance on legal information.[135] In this regard, an emphasis on triage and mediation does not by any means eliminate the need for personalized legal services.[136]

Today, most family legal services are offered by licensed lawyers, who bill by the hour and who are subject to the Law Society of Upper Canada (LSUC) *Rules of Professional Conduct*.[137] Services provided in this way are very satisfactory to many clients,[138] and the rise of collaborative family law demonstrates the continued potential for innovation within the family law bar.[139] Access to justice initiatives in the context of traditional full legal representation include JusticeNet and the Law Society's Lawyer Referral Service.[140] The Office of the Children's Lawyer provides free legal representation to some children involved in custody and access cases.[141] Within courthouses, duty counsel and volunteer law students are sometimes available to assist.[142]

However, a very large proportion of Ontarians enter the family law system without the benefit of any personalized legal services whatsoever. Somewhere between 40 and 70 per cent of Ontario family litigants are unrepresented.[143] The high and unpredictable cost of legal services

---

135 McMurtry *et al., Listening to Ontarians, supra* note 1 at 59.
136 In some cases and some jurisdictions, lawyers attend family mediation with their clients. See, for example, Craig A. McEwen, Nancy H. Rogers, and Richard J. Maiman, 'Bring in the Lawyers: Challenging the Dominant Approaches to Ensuring Fairness in Divorce Mediation' (1995) 79 Minn. L. Rev. 1317 at 1357. Even if they do not, legal advice is a valuable complement to mediated settlements.
137 Rule 2 in *Rules of Professional Conduct* (Toronto: Law Society of Upper Canada, 2000), http://www.lsuc.on.ca/WorkArea/linkit.aspx?LinkIdentifier=id&Item ID=10272, accessed 8 December 2010.
138 McMurtry *et al., Listening to Ontarians, supra* note 1 at 46.
139 See footnote 66, *supra.*
140 JusticeNet puts low-income individuals in touch with lawyers willing to provide services for a reduced fee. See http://www.justicenet.ca, accessed 8 December 2010. See also Christopher Guly, 'New Lawyer Directory Seeks to Make Justice More Accessible to Middle Class,' *Lawyers Weekly,* 26 February 2010. The LSUC service offers a free thirty-minute consultation with a lawyer. Law Society of Upper Canada, 'Lawyer Referral Service,' http://www.lsuc.on.ca/public/a/faqs-lawyer-referral-service, accessed 8 December 2010.
141 *Courts of Justice Act*, R.S.O. 1990, c. C.43, s.89.
142 Pro Bono Students Canada, 'Family Law Project' (FLP), http://www.probonostu-dents.ca/programs/court-and-tribunal/flp-by-province, accessed 7 December 2011. http://www.probonostudents.ca/en/programs/court-tribunal/family-law-project, accessed 8 December 2010.
143 OBA, *Supporting Families, supra* note 4 at 6. The Department of Justice recently reviewed 1,435 case files from family courts in ten Canadian cities. In only 25 per cent

is the primary reason for this phenomenon.[144] Legal Aid Ontario (LAO) continues to offer certificates for legal representation to some family litigants. However, the income cut-off for certificate eligibility is only $12,000 gross per year for a single individual.[145] In order to provide services to more people, LAO's Family Law Division appears to be emphasizing less comprehensive and expensive services, such as those offered by duty counsel and clerks.[146]

The argument for civil legal aid has been made in terms of ideals such as basic procedural fairness and preserving the legitimacy of the justice system.[147] In addition, however, government expenditures on civil legal aid may be investments that create savings in the long run. There are two ways in which this could occur. First, parties represented by lawyers may be more likely to settle their dispute at an early stage.[148] Self-represented family litigants may be particularly unwilling or unable to personally discuss settlement – for example, in cases of domestic violence or high conflict. Providing legal representation to these individuals can allow them to negotiate through agents and thereby settle a dispute that would otherwise end up in court. Second, in those disputes

---

of the cases were both parties represented by counsel. In 44.1 per cent of the cases, neither party was represented. These figures produce an overall self-representation rate of 60 per cent. *UFC Evaluation, supra* note 119 at 19.

144 D.A. Rollie Thompson and Lynn Reierson, 'A Practicing Lawyer's Field Guide to the Unrepresented' (2002) 19 C.F.L.Q. 529 at 529–30; Anne-Marie Langan, 'Threatening the Balance of the Scales of Justice: Unrepresented Litigants in the Family Courts of Ontario' (2005) 30 Queen's L.J. 825 at 832.

145 Sheilagh O'Connell, 'Legal Aid Ontario: New Models of Family Law Service and Practice Management in the New World' (slides presented to Association of Family and Conciliation Courts, Ontario Chapter Second Annual General Conference), Toronto, 12–13 October 2010, at 12, AFCC Ontario, http://www.afccontario.ca/OConnellonLegalAidOntario.pdf, accessed 8 December 2010.

146 *Ibid.,* at 16 and 27.

147 Mary Jane Mossman, Karen Schucher, and Claudia Schmeing, *Comparing and Understanding Legal Aid Priorities* (Association of Community Legal Clinics of Ontario, 2009), SSRN, http://ssrn.com/abstract=1640533, accessed 8 December 2010; Michael Trebilcock, *Report of the Legal Aid Review* (Toronto: Ministry of the Attorney General [Ontario], 2008) at 61 *et seq.*, http://www.attorneygeneral.jus.gov.on.ca/english/about/pubs/trebilcock/legal_aid_report_2008_EN.pdf, accessed 8 December 2010.

148 PricewaterhouseCoopers, *Economic Value of Legal Aid: Analysis in Relation to Commonwealth Funded Matters with a Focus on Family Law* (Brisbane: Legal Aid Queensland, 2009) at v; National Legal Aid, http://www.nla.aust.net.au/res/File/Economic%20Value%20of%20Legal%20Aid%20-%20Final%20report%20-%206%20Nov%202009.pdf, accessed 8 December 2010.

that do end up in court, legal representation can lead to speedier and more efficient adjudication. Self-represented litigants generally require more time to present the evidence and argument that the court requires, and judges must often take time to educate them.

Looking outside the province, one finds innovative ideas for facilitating family legal service delivery. Services of a limited nature may be provided along with information and education in self-help facilities for self-represented litigants. This model, which was proposed by a 2005 B.C. report, has been manifested in the new Nanaimo Family Justice Services Centre.[149] Another intriguing model is the Law Society of Manitoba's Family Law Access Centre. This centre subsidizes lawyers' fees for those with family law problems and incomes between $35,000 and $60,000. The Law Society pays the lawyers at a reduced rate of $100 to $160 per hour. The clients then repay the Law Society on a monthly basis over time. This initiative has proven very popular, with demand substantially outstripping the available funds.[150]

Unbundling is one way to make legal services more flexible and affordable without new government money.[151] In addition to lowering costs, unbundling may also respond well to the needs of the modern family litigant.[152] However, this practice model also creates unique ethical and competence challenges.[153] The LSUC is currently considering changes to the *Rules of Professional Conduct* that would address unbun-

149 JRTF, *New Justice, supra* note 86 at 29; *Nanaimo Evaluation, supra* note 29. Legal Aid Ontario appears to use a similar model in its new Family Law Service Centres in the Toronto area. See O'Connell, 'Legal Aid Ontario,' *supra* note 145 at 15–17.

150 Anu Osborne, 'Centre Offers Working Poor Affordable Family Law Services,' *Lawyers Weekly*, 24 September 2010.

151 For a series of papers on unbundling of family legal services, see the special issue of the *Family Court Review* (40, no. 1) published in January 2002. Unbundling of family law services is not a new idea, despite the recent surge of interest in Ontario. See Forrest S. Mosten, 'Unbundling of Legal Services and the Family Lawyer' (1994) 28 Fam. L.Q. 421. On unbundling more generally, see Beg and Sossin, 'Should Legal Services Be Unbundled?', *supra* this volume.

152 McMurtry *et al.*, *Listening to Ontarians, supra* note 1 at 44–6; Michael Robertson and Jeff Giddings, 'Legal Consumers as Coproducers: The Changing Face of Legal Services Delivery in Australia' (2002) 40 Fam. Ct. Rev. 63 at 72-73.

153 Elliot A. Anderson, 'Unbundling the Ethical Issues of Pro Bono Advocacy: Articulating the Goals of Limited-Scope Pro Bono Advocacy for Limited Legal Services Programs' (2010) 48 Fam. Ct. Rev. 685. In the family law context, concerns have been expressed about lawyers exacerbating situations of violence or abuse or failing to fulfil the *Divorce Act* requirement to discuss reconciliation, mediation, and negotiation with their clients. *Divorce Act*, R.S.C. 1985, (2d Supp.), c.3, s.9.

dled legal service delivery;[154] B.C. has already done so.[155] In order to embrace unbundling, lawyers must have certainty that courts will allow them to withdraw after completing the agreed-upon services.[156]

Legal insurance might make family law services more affordable.[157] As described above, members of the Canadian Auto Workers are covered by legal insurance that includes family law. A 'divorce insurance' product recently became available in the United States.[158] However, family law is excluded from the coverage of the only private sector legal insurance product currently offered in Ontario.[159] Moreover, even in Europe, where legal expense insurance is much more pervasive, family law is rarely covered.[160] Contingency fee arrangements, like legal insurance, are impeded by the nature of family disputes. Specifically, it is difficult to define the 'winning conditions' under which the contingency fee would be paid, and creating this incentive to 'win' for the lawyer might have deleterious effects.[161] Third-party financing for

---

154 Law Society of Upper Canada, '"Unbundling" of Legal Services and Limited Legal Representation: Call for Input,' http://www.lsuc.on.ca/unbundling, accessed 8 December 2010. The amendments were passed in September 2011, see http://www.lsuc.on.ca/unbundling, accessed 7 December 2011.

155 Jim Varro, 'Unbundling' of Legal Services and Limited Legal Representation: Background Information and Proposed Amendments to Professional Conduct Rules (Toronto: Law Society of Upper Canada, 2010) at 6, http://www.lsuc.on.ca/WorkArea/Download-Asset.aspx?id=2147483764, accessed 8 December 2010. The B.C. reforms were made pursuant to the following report: Doug Munro, Limited Retainers: Professionalism and Practice (Report of the Unbundling of Legal Services Task Force (Vancouver: Law Society of British Columbia, 2008), http://www.lawsociety.bc.ca/publications_forms/report-committees/docs/LimitedRetainers_2008.pdf, accessed 8 December 2010.

156 M. Sue Talia, Roadmap for Implementing a Successful Unbundling Program (Des Moines: American Judicature Society, 2005) at 3, http://www.ajs.org/prose/South%20Central%20Notebook%20Contents/Tab%206/Roadmap%20for%20Implementing.pdf, accessed 8 December 2010.

157 McMurtry et al., Listening to Ontarians, supra note 1 at 39; Trebilcock, Report of the Legal Aid Review, supra note 1477.

158 Jennifer Saranow Schultz, 'Divorce Insurance (Yes, Divorce Insurance)' New York Times, 6 August 2010, http://bucks.blogs.nytimes.com/2010/08/06/divorce-insurance-yes-divorce-insurance, accessed 8 December 2010.

159 DAS Canada, 'Products and Services: FAQs,' http://www.das.ca/html/products/FAQs.asp, accessed 7 December 2011; http://www.das.ca/html/products/consumers/FAQs.asp, accessed 8 December 2010.

160 Matthias Kilian and Francis Regan, 'Legal Expenses Insurance and Legal Aid – Two Sides of the Same Coin? The Experience from Germany and Sweden' (2004) 11 Int'l. J. of the Legal Profession 233.

161 Mavis Maclean, 'No House, No Fee – Conditional Fee Arrangements in Divorce' (1999) 29 Fam. Law 245.

divorce litigation does exist in the United States, but this is generally only an option for the wealthiest litigants.[162]

There are substantial regulatory impediments to the provision of innovative and affordable civil legal services in Ontario. The time may be ripe to re-evaluate the regulatory environment from a consumer welfare point of view.[163] It is worth asking whether the status quo law school curriculum and the LSUC's licensing process are both necessary and sufficient preparation for offering family legal services. The Law Society has seen fit to prohibit paralegals from offering almost all family law services – a controversial decision that is contrary to the landmark *Cory Report* on paralegal practice.[164] Canada's Competition Bureau recently made a compelling case that paralegals should not be prohibited from offering legal services unless 'compelling evidence of demonstrable harm to the public' is present.[165] The bureau also noted the 'obvious conflict of interest' that arises from allowing lawyers to regulate paralegals, who are their potential competitors.[166] Families might also be well served by closer working relationships between lawyers and other professionals.[167] While the Law Society does permit multidisciplinary practices involving lawyers and others, it imposes onerous and perhaps unnecessary restrictions upon them, and they are quite rare in Ontario.[168]

---

162 Binyamin Appelbaum, 'Taking Sides in a Divorce, Chasing Profit,' *New York Times*, 4 December 2010.

163 This task was begun by Michael Trebilcock and Lilla Csorgo, 'Multi-Disciplinary Professional Practices: A Consumer Welfare Perspective' (2001) 24 Dalhousie L.J. 1.

164 Peter de C. Cory, *A Framework for Regulating Paralegal Practice in Ontario: Report* (Toronto: Ontario Ministry of the Attorney General, 2000); Carol Goar, 'Family Courts Filled with Litigants and No One to Guide Them,' *Toronto Star*, 10 November 2010.

165 *Self-Regulated Professions: Balancing Competition and Regulation* (Ottawa: Competition Bureau [Canada], 2007) at 70, http://www.bureaudelaconcurrence.gc.ca/eic/site/cb-bc.nsf/vwapj/Professions%20study%20final%20E.pdf/$FILE/Professions%20study%20final%20E.pdf, accessed 8 December 2010.

166 *Ibid.* at 69.

167 Lynn M. Akre, 'Struggling with Indeterminacy: A Call for Interdisciplinary Collaboration in Redefining the "Best Interest of the Child" Standard' (1992) 75 Marq. L. Rev. 628; Linda D. Elrod and Milfred D. Dale, 'Paradigm Shifts and Pendulum Swings in Child Custody: The Interests of Children in the Balance' (2008) 42 Fam. L.Q. 381; Andrew Schepard, *Children, Courts, and Custody: Interdisciplinary Models for Divorcing Families* (New York: Cambridge University Press, 2004).

168 Law Society of Upper Canada, 'By-Law 7: Business Entities. Adopted by Convocation on May 1, 2007; most recently amended April 30, 2009' (2007); and idem, 'Rules of Professional Conduct. Adopted by Convocation on June 22, 2000; most recently

C. Policy Options

1 Amend the *Rules of Professional Conduct* to encourage multidisciplinary practices and/or the provision of unbundled legal services.
2 Review Law Society regulations that make it more difficult and/or
   more expensive to provide family law services.
3 License paralegals to provide family law services. If demonstrably
   necessary in order to protect the public, paralegal practice in this
   area could be limited to certain categories of case (e.g., only child
   support and parenting disputes, or only uncontested matters).
4 Increase access to short consultations with lawyers. A variety of
   methods should be explored, including provision of legal aid duty
   counsel for all unrepresented litigants, subsidizing the cost of short
   consultations as part of the services offered by family information
   centres, or simply providing a roster of lawyers available (for payment) for short consultations through family information centres.
5 Implement public legal expense insurance, including coverage of
   family law.[169]

VII. Conclusion

The family law stakeholder consultations provided a valuable opportunity to reflect on the Four Pillars reforms to the Ontario system. The
general view was that the Four Pillars are sound in principle but may
not support the weight of expectations unless reinforced by new public
money. The literature that this paper reviewed suggests strongly that
certain types of spending in this system can pay for themselves or even
yield gains by reducing overall social costs. Hiring mediators and/
or *triageurs* has demonstrable potential to produce out-of-court settlements that are satisfactory to all parties as well as cheaper to the state.
Recruiting trained and compensated professionals to deliver parenting
education classes and conduct case conferences, as opposed to relying
on volunteers, may be necessary in order to consistently realize the
courtroom savings that these initiatives promise while extending them

---

amended June 25, 2009' (2000). See also Trebilcock and Csorgo, 'Multi-Disciplinary
Professional Practices,' *supra* note 1633.

169 Sujit Choudhry, Michael Trebilcock, and James Wilson, 'Growing Legal Aid Ontario
into the Middle Class: A Proposal for Public Legal Expenses Insurance,' *supra* this
volume.

across the province. Civil legal aid, accompanied by reforms that make market-provided legal services more affordable, might make the system both fairer and cheaper.

This paper has also identified a tendency to attach new reforms and offices to the system without considering the complexity of the entire structure, and the challenges this presents to novice litigants such as Ms Arshad. The Attorney General has proposed to build four new pillars to support the roof that is Ontario family justice. However, a maze of columns, of various classical orders and in various states of repair, is already beneath this structure. The minister might consider the case for demolishing and rebuilding it from the ground up, with new materials and a new blueprint.

Appendix: Organizations and Individuals Consulted

Professor Carol Rogerson, University of Toronto Faculty of Law (Chair)
Lee Akazaki, Ontario Bar Association
Professor Nick Bala, Queen's University Faculty of Law
Carol Barkwell, Luke's Place
Marion Boyd, Bencher, Law Society of Upper Canada
Caroline Brett, Law Student, Pro Bono Family Law Project
Lisa Cirillo, Downtown Legal Services
Justice Marion Cohen, Ontario Court of Justice
Kenneth Cole, Epstein Cole LLP
Justice George Czutrin, Superior Court of Justice
Justice Gloria Epstein, Court of Appeal for Ontario
Professor Russell Engler, New England Law
Philip Epstein, Epstein Cole LLP
Howard Feldman, Lawyer
Aaron Franks, Epstein Cole LLP
Justice Stephen Goudge, Ontario Court of Appeal
Claire Hepburn, Downtown Legal Services
Emily Hubling, Law Student, Pro Bono Family Law Project
Judith Huddart, Dranoff & Huddart
Patricia Hughes, Law Commission of Ontario
Barbara Landau, Cooperative Solutions Inc.
Julie Lassonde, Consultant
Alfred Mamo, McKenzie Lake Lawyers LLP
Mary Marrone, Income Security Advocacy Centre
Gillian D. Marriott, Pro Bono Law Alberta

Wendela Napier, Canadian Auto Workers Legal Services Plan
Anne-Marie Predko, Ministry of the Attorney General
Noel Semple, Ph.D Candidate, Osgoode Hall Law School
Victoria Smith, Lawyer
Professor Rollie Thompson, Schulich School of Law, Dalhousie
    University

Middle Income Access to Justice: Policy Options with Respect to Employment Law

JUDITH MCCORMACK AND AZIM REMANI

I. Introduction

The complex role of work in the lives of individuals presents a number of unique challenges for access to justice in the area of employment law. With over 17 million people working in Canada,[1] the pool of individuals with potential legal needs is substantial, and the proportion of daily life spent at the workplace contributes to the likelihood that problems will arise. Moreover, the stakes involved for employees are often high. Employment is the 'primary means of distributing income in Canada,'[2] and its impact on the life of an individual extends to non-economic issues as well. As the Supreme Court of Canada has observed:

> Work is one of the most fundamental aspects in a person's life, providing the individual with a means of financial support and, as importantly, a contributory role in society. A person's employment is an essential component of his or her sense of identity, self-worth and emotional well-being.[3]

Loss of employment – often the occasion on which legal assistance is sought – has been described by the Court as a 'traumatic event,'[4] and

---

1 Statistics Canada, *Labour Force Characteristics*, http://www40.statcan.gc.ca/l01/cst01/econ10-eng.htm.
2 Canadian Centre for Policy Alternatives, *Labour Law's Little Sister: The Employment Standards Act and the Feminization of Labour* by Judy Fudge (Ottawa: Canadian Centre of Policy Alternatives, 1991) at 2 [CCPA, *The Employment Standards Act*].
3 *Reference Re Public Service Employee Relations Act (Alta.)*, [1987] 1 S.C.R. 313 at 368 (dissent of Dickson, C.J. subsequently adopted by the Court in other cases, including http://scc.lexum.org/en/1992/1992scr1-986/1992scr1-986.pdf
4 *Wallace v. United Grain Growers Ltd.* (1997), 152 D.L.R. (4th) 1 (S.C.C.) at para. 95.

others have noted that it can have a profoundly negative impact on both employees and their families.[5] Such loss is also associated with entry into poverty[6] and can trigger cascading legal problems in the areas of debtor/creditor, eviction or foreclosure, and family law. For these and other reasons, discharge from employment has been referred to by courts and tribunals as the 'capital punishment' of the workplace,[7] and employment law problems have been identified as some of the most prevalent and serious legal concerns among the middle income population.[8]

Despite this, middle income Ontarians often encounter considerable difficulty in gaining access to the legal system in this area as a result of the complexity of the law, the costs of legal representation and procedures, lack of knowledge about their rights, and a host of other barriers. The purpose of this paper is to develop policy options to improve the accessibility of the civil justice system for those seeking to resolve employment problems. With this in mind, Part II of the paper provides a brief overview of employment law in Ontario, while Parts III through V offer a discussion of some of the problems faced by individuals in obtaining access to the legal system, focusing on issues that emerged

---

5 A. Gladstone, 'Settlement of Disputes over Rights,' in *Comparative Labour Law and Industrial Relations in Industrialized Market Economies*, ed. R. Blanpain and C. Engles (Cambridge, MA: Kluwer Law International, 1998) 503 at 511 [Gladstone, 'Disputes over Rights'].

6 Statistics Canada, *The Ins and Outs of Poverty in Advanced Economies: Poverty Dynamics in Canada, Germany, Great Britain, and the United States* (Ottawa: Statistics Canada, 2005) at 14, http://www.statcan.gc.ca/access_acces/alternative_alternatif.action?l=eng&loc=http://www.statcan.gc.ca/pub/75f0002m/75f0002m2005001-eng.pdf&t=The%20Ins%20and%20Outs%20of%20Poverty%20in%20Advanced%20Economies:%20%20Poverty%20Dynamics%20in%20Canada%20Germany%20Great%20Britain%20and%20the%20United%20States.%20(Income%20Research%20Paper%20Series).

7 See, for example, *Brien v. Niagara Motors Ltd.*, [2008] O.J. No. 3246 at para. 220.

8 See, for example, *Listening to Ontarians: Report of the Ontario Civil Legal Needs Project* (Toronto: Ontario Civil Legal Needs Project, 2010) at 21. Common employment problems include those involving wages owed, health and safety concerns, unfair disciplining by employers, harassment, unfair dismissal, benefits denied, and employment insurance claims: Ab Currie, *The Legal Problems of Everyday Life: The Nature, Extent, and Consequences of Justiciable Problems Experienced by Canadians* (Ottawa: Department of Justice Canada, 2007), http://justice-canada.net/eng/pi/rs/rep-rap/2007/rr07_la1-rr07_aj1/rr07_la1.pdf [Curry, *The Legal Problems of Everyday Life*]. For the purposes of this paper, middle income Ontarians are defined as those whose household income is too high for them to qualify for Legal Aid certificates, but too low for them to be able to afford to hire lawyers to represent them in civil law matters.

from stakeholder consultations,[9] relevant literature, and other sources. Those issues fall into three categories: the front-end prevention of employment law problems, the operation of employment standards regimes, and dispute resolution fora for employment law matters. Under each of these headings, we have synthesized stakeholder consultations, literature survey findings, and other sources to generate policy options for improving access to the civil justice system in the area of employment law. Finally, Part VI offers a brief coda on the relevance of collective bargaining regimes in this context.

II. Employment Law in Canada and Ontario

One of the threshold difficulties for individuals with employment law problems is the variety of legal regimes, fora, and processes that may apply. Most employees in Ontario fall under provincial regulation, which includes the *Employment Standards Act, 2000*[10] (*ESA*), the *Occupational Health and Safety Act*,[11] the *Workplace Safety and Insurance Act*,[12] and the *Labour Relations Act, 1995*.[13] However, federal counterparts to most of these statutes[14] govern a smaller number of employees within federally regulated industries,[15] and there are a number of other legislative instruments that apply to federal and provincial civil servants and employees in particular sectors.[16] Also relevant are federal and provincial human rights statutes,[17] as well as a large body of common

---

9 Consultations took the form of a focus group held in Toronto on 18 May 2010, follow-up discussions with various stakeholders, and the Employment Law Workshop held as part of the Middle Income Access to Justice Colloquium on 10–11 February 2011 by the Faculty of Law, University of Toronto. Stakeholders consulted included private lawyers representing employees or employers, arbitrators, mediators, and staff from legal clinics, government, and other organizations.

10 S.O. 2000, c.41.

11 R.S.O. 1990, c. O.1.

12 S.O. 1997, c.16.

13 S.O. 1995. c.1.

14 *Canada Labour Code*, R.S. 1985, c. L-2; *Government Employees Compensation Act*, R.S. 1985, c. G-5.

15 Such as airlines, banks, telecommunications, the federal civil service, post offices, and interprovincial railways. See, for example, http://www.labour.gov.on.ca/english/es/pubs/factsheets/fs_general.php.

16 See, for example, *Hospital Labour Disputes Arbitration Act*, R.S.O. 1990, c. H-14; *Pay Equity Act*, R.S.O. 1990, c. P–7; *Police Services Act*, R.S.O. 1990, c. P-15; *Ambulance Services Collective Bargaining Act, 2001*, S.O. 2001, c.10.

17 *Human Rights Code*, R.S.O. 1990, c. H-19; *Canadian Human Rights Act*, R.S. 1985, c. H-6.

law employment jurisprudence on wrongful dismissal. Each of these regimes has its own jurisdiction, processes, and fora, and an employment law problem will often engage more than one.

For example, an employee who is fired after experiencing a workplace injury may have varying and overlapping remedies under one or more of the *Employment Standards Act, 2000*, the *Workplace Safety and Insurance Act*, the *Occupational Health and Safety Act*, the *Human Rights Code*, and the common law. If the employee is unionized, other remedies may be available, either in addition or instead, and the *Labour Relations Act, 1995* may be implicated. If the employee works in a federally regulated industry, another set of statutes will apply, except that the federal government uses the provincial Workplace Safety and Insurance Board to provide compensation and rehabilitation programs. Conversely, employment insurance and other programs are provided federally to provincially regulated employees.

The differences between these regimes may also be significant; federally regulated employees have the right to challenge unjust dismissals and seek reinstatement, while dismissed provincially regulated employees are generally limited to monetary claims for lack of notice and to related claims such as unpaid wages.[18] Similarly, wrongful dismissal suits have been largely reserved for employees with higher salaries who have both the income losses and the means to make civil action worth pursuing, while *ESA* claims tend to involve lower-paid employees and can encompass violations of the statute beyond termination and severance pay. Moreover, the damages awarded in wrongful dismissal cases at common law are substantially greater than the termination payments available under the *ESA*.

Some of the relevant statutes are also lengthy and confusing – the *ESA* has some 142 sections, the *Workplace Safety and Insurance Act* 183, and the *Canada Labour Code* 267, and there are usually associated regulations. Most employees will find it difficult to sift through these various avenues on their own to ascertain which are available, required, or most likely to yield appropriate redress.

The rationale for this multiplicity of regimes is not always self-evident, even apart from the duplication related to constitutional imperatives. Three of the provincial statutes listed above, for example,

---

18 *Canada Labour Code, supra* note 14, ss. 240–6; *Employment Standards Act, 2000, supra.* There are some circumstances where reinstatement is possible under the *ESA* (e.g., under s. 74.17(1), but these are rare.

are encompassed within one federal statute, although even the latter provides different processes for different types of employment matters. We will return to this issue in Part V; for the moment, it is sufficient to note that this cluttered legal landscape contributes to the difficulty of gaining access to applicable rights and remedies.

III. The Prevention of Employment Law Problems

A. Stakeholder Consultations

The general perception among stakeholders was that the types of employment law problems normally addressed in employment standards, human rights, or wrongful dismissal claims are difficult to prevent because they often arise from unique interactions among individuals.[19] There may, however, be ways in which they might be mitigated. In particular, some problems may arise because employers are simply unaware of their legal obligations to employees; these problems, it was suggested, could be avoided or reduced by educating employers in regard to their duties under relevant statutes.[20] In support of this proposition, it was noted that the Human Rights Legal Support Centre frequently succeeded in preventing imminent terminations by calling employers to inform them of their legal responsibilities.[21] Various methods of educating employers were considered, including the types of website information, interactive tools, and information kits currently provided to both employers and employees by the Ministry of Labour Employment Standards Program (ESP),[22] as well as the ESP informa-

---

19 We note that there are a number of ways to analyse the employment law context in broader, more structural terms, but the consultations were oriented to discussions of individual claims.

20 Presumably the education of both employers and employees on their rights and responsibilities constitutes an access-to-justice goal in itself, but it is considered here in terms of its prophylactic potential.

21 The Human Rights Legal Support Centre (HRLSC) reports a high success rate in assisting callers who believe their employers are preparing to terminate them; such calls make up a portion of the approximately 104 to 136 employment-related calls that the HRLSC receives daily. It may be that the impact of this kind of assistance is due in part to factors beyond merely the provision of information; employers are also likely to take into account that the employee in question appears to have access to a legal advocate.

22 See, for example, Ontario, Ministry of Labour, http://www.labour.gov.on.ca/english/es/pubs/brochures/br_compliance.php and http://www.labour.gov.on.ca/english/es/eop/survey.php.

tion telephone lines, which receive some 500,000 calls annually.[23] The ESP also participates in training sessions offered to businesses by other ministries.

Similarly, the provision of information to employees with respect to their rights and obligations was also considered useful in the context of prevention. While employees have admittedly less control over workplace decisions and events, better-informed employees might more capably assert their rights, depending on the circumstances.[24] With respect to how employment law information might best be communicated to employees, stakeholders noted that employers were required by the *ESA* to post information about statutory rights and obligations in the workplace in the form of mandatory (and in some cases, multilingual) notices.[25] However, it was also suggested that compliance with this requirement was the exception rather than the rule. Other forms of distribution were discussed, including making pamphlets and materials available through community centres, public libraries, and other sites.

At the same time, some stakeholders observed that simply making such information available might be too passive a technique for reaching target audiences effectively. Instead, it might be more appropriate to provide information and training to community organizations and other types of intermediaries who interact with specific employee groups. These intermediaries could be equipped, for example, with basic information about the ESP website and other employment law resources to facilitate their clients' access to this information. Some stakeholders commented that community legal clinics in Ontario often provide such training or information workshops, but that these activities are limited by resource issues. There was general consensus that any education initiatives would have to be designed in ways that accounted for the language and literacy barriers that many employees face.[26]

Stakeholders also supported the incorporation of employment law topics into high school curricula. Some employers and schools already

---

23 Stakeholder consultation, 18 May 2010.
24 But see the discussion in Part IV with respect to the reluctance of employees to file claims during the tenure of the employment relationship.
25 *ESA, supra* note 10, s.2.
26 See, for example, Karen Cohl and George Thomson, *Connecting across Language and Distance: Linguistic and Rural Access to Legal Information and Services* (Toronto: Law Foundation of Ontario, 2008). We also note in this connection that some of the information on the ESP website is provided in twenty-three languages.

seek employment law information from the ESP with respect to cooperative education placements – a fact that might indicate existing demand for this sort of curriculum component. Employment law education efforts aimed at high school students might be particularly effective, since the result would be to disseminate information to individuals at a key point – that is, at or around the time they first join the workforce. It was suggested that approaching an employment law curriculum module from a human rights perspective might have particular appeal for school boards and that an engaging approach would not have to be lengthy or intensive. The goals would be relatively modest; students might not retain much in the way of specific details about the law, but alerting them to the existence of basic workplace rights and mechanisms for redress might enable them to seek further information if they encountered employment law problems subsequently.

Other timely sources of information were discussed as well, including the provision of information or directions to the ESP website on the back of the Record of Employment or other mandatory forms required at the point of termination or hiring. In general, it seemed likely that effective education initiatives would require a multipronged approach that encompassed a variety of techniques, vehicles, and sites.

Apart from the education of employers and employees, stakeholders considered whether internal mediation processes might offer some degree of prevention or at least reduce the incidence of employment problems escalating or proceeding to litigation. Examples included the internal procedures sometimes used by larger employers as a means of resolving employee complaints; these systems can provide opportunities for discussion, the airing of concerns, and in some cases mediation. In particular, an external mediator can often assist in conditioning the expectations of parties, providing them with some perspective on their positions, and facilitating settlement. However, to the extent that these mechanisms are within the discretion and control of the employer, employees may lack confidence in them, and stakeholders pointed out that they would not likely address more significant problems, such as where an employer intends to dismiss an employee.

B. Literature Review and Discussion

The importance of educating employers and employees on their respective rights and obligations was considered in *Fairness at Work – Federal Labour Standards for the 21st Century*, the report of the Arthurs Commission, which reviewed the employment standards provisions contained in Part III of *the Canada Labour Code*.[27] The Arthurs Commission identified ignorance as a likely factor in non-compliance with statutory obligations, particularly for small employers, and noted that '[t]he best prospects for securing compliance with labour standards involve programs to educate workers and employers concerning their rights and responsibilities under [labour legislation].'[28] Among other things, the commission recommended providing information to employers and employees through pamphlets, toll-free numbers, websites, and training for workers, employers, and their advocates.[29]

The implicit value of such employment law information is also reflected in the widespread use of information websites across jurisdictions (see, for example, Australia,[30] New Zealand,[31] and the United Kingdom[32]). The ESP website offers a particularly good example of the use of interactive tools and calculators.[33] Admittedly, websites and other vehicles tend to rely on the initiative and ability of individuals to seek this information out, which may render that information more marginal or at least reduce its reach and efficacy. A more effective approach might be to mainstream and routinize the delivery of employment law information in a number of different ways.

For example, the fact that most employees are still clustered at physical workplaces of varying sizes[34] offers unique opportunities for the dissemination of information – opportunities that may not be available in other areas of law. This is clearly the rationale behind the *ESA* requirement of mandatory posters in the workplace, as well as various post-

---

27 Canada, Human Resources and Skills Development Canada, Federal Labour Standards Review Commission, *Fairness at Work – Federal Labour Standards for the 21st Century* (Gatineau: Human Resources and Skills Development Canada, 2006), http://www.hrsdc.gc.ca/eng/labour/employment_standards/fls/pdf/final_report.pdf [*Arthurs Commission Report*].

28 *Ibid.* at xiv and 195.

29 *Ibid.* at 195.

30 http://www.fairworkaust.com.

31 http://ers.govt.nz/publications/index.html.

32 http://www.direct.gov.uk/en/Employment/index.htm.

33 Ontario, Ministry of Labour website, *supra* note 22.

34 Despite the trend to home work, over 80 per cent of Canadian employees had a usual place of work outside the home in 2006: Canadian Council for Health and Active Living at Work, *A Statistical Profile of Canadian Workplace Characteristics*, 31 March 2009, http://www.cchalw.ca/english/info/MappingofCanadianIndustriesreport1.pdf at 2.

ings directed by the Ontario Labour Relations Board and the Human Rights Tribunal of Ontario in specific situations.[35] The fact that some stakeholders reported low levels of compliance in regard to the *ESA* poster does not necessarily negate the value of this delivery approach, since it reflects a broader enforcement problem (discussed in Part IV of this paper) that must be addressed in any event.

It is worth noting that there are two types of postings contemplated by the *ESA:* the mandatory posting of substantive information about the Act, which is required of all employers; and postings directed by an employment standards officer for specific employers relating to the administration and enforcement of the *ESA* or investigation and inspection reports.[36] These latter postings are generally used only in the context of proactive inspections; for example, officers have the power to require postings that indicate an employer has violated the Act and the orders made as a result – but they rarely if ever do so. A remedial posting of this nature is considered a normal form of relief for unfair labour practices under the *Labour Relations Act, 1995,*[37] and while not all of the reasons for such postings will apply in an employment standards context, the central purpose – that is, to convey to employees that their employer cannot violate legislation with impunity – is highly relevant.

Another method of mainstreaming and routinizing the delivery of employment law information would be to integrate it into current licensing and regulatory requirements. For example, a new employer might be required to participate in a short online workshop on the *ESA* before registering a business, qualifying for a business licence, or obtaining a business tax number. Employees in regulated employment sectors might be required to participate in corresponding exercises in order to qualify for relevant occupational licences. Integrating this kind of education into existing requirements offers the advantage of using current structures to maximize compliance, rather than requiring additional enforcement measures.

At the same time, any prerequisites of this nature should be designed to avoid the imposition of unrealistic burdens on both employers and employees, while still reflecting the importance of minimum standards

---

35 For example, the OLRB uses workplace posters to notify employees of applications for certification and decertification, and both the OLRB and the Human Rights Tribunal of Ontario order postings as remedies for violations of their respective statutes.

36 *ESA, supra* note 10, ss. 2, 93.

37 See, for example, *Call-a-Cab Limited* [1991] OLRB Rep. April 448.

legislation. In this context, incorporating information or directions to resources into existing pre-printed government forms offers an additional method of bringing such information to the attention of workplace parties – a method that is both universal and relatively simple for workplace parties to manage.

Turning to the idea of incorporating employment law topics into high school curricula, we observe that this concept is not novel; an 'aggressive campaign' to provide information on employment rights in high schools was proposed twenty years ago, specifically in regard to the employment standards regime in Ontario.[38] Without dismissing either the challenges of secondary school curriculum development or the many competing factors involved, the notion that Ontarians should be taught something about employment rights seems consistent with the high proportion of the population that will be employed for at least some part of their adulthood, and the multifaceted importance of work referred to earlier.

At the same time, it is evident that education is not a panacea for employment law problems. The complexity of the employment law landscape means it is difficult to develop information materials that are both accurate, and concise and clear enough to be of meaningful practical assistance to employers and employees. This is particularly true across legal regimes. As noted previously, the ESP website does provide good materials and tools with respect to the *ESA*, and other tribunals such as the Workplace Safety and Insurance Board and the Human Rights Tribunal of Ontario have useful information on their websites as well. Nevertheless, employees who need advice with respect to the range of available avenues to pursue and the respective benefits and drawbacks of each in relation to their particular circumstances are unlikely to find it on public websites.

This may reflect some untapped potential for providing interactive legal tools that span the different employment law regimes, perhaps guiding an employee or employer through a series of steps to identify relevant or applicable law and remedies. At the same time, even the best of such tools are likely to have some unavoidable weaknesses because of the degree of contingency, fluidity, novelty, contextuality, and complexity characterizing many legal problems. The issue here, then, touches on a more fundamental dilemma with respect to the inherent shortcomings of legal information as a substitute for skilled legal advice.

---

38 CCPA, *The Employment Standards Act, supra* note 2 at 101.

Some of the other limits of legal information as a preventative instrument have more to do with specific features of the employment law context. Employers may have economic or other motives for violating legislation, and even knowledgeable employees may be discouraged from asserting or enforcing their rights by the unilateral control that employers exercise over the workplace, or by the attendant potential for reprisals, about which more will be said in Part IV.[39] This means that legal information is best seen as one element of a broader access to justice strategy in this area.

For similar reasons, internal employer processes may be limited in their utility. An employee who feels mistreated by an employer may not view a process controlled by that same employer as offering effective remedies. While France does require employers to hold a conciliation meeting with an employee before any dismissal for personal reasons (as opposed to economic layoffs),[40] 72 per cent of French workers have a union or analogous body at the workplace, and the employee is represented at such a meeting by a union or other agent.[41] Similarly, claims in Germany will normally go through an internal conciliation process before being filed at a Labour Court, but these are handled by Works Councils, which are non-union bodies for employee representation that are mandatory for employers with more than five employees.[42] Such structures may provide a counterweight to the employer's unilateral control of the workplace and make more balanced outcomes available, or at least heighten the confidence of employees in the process. In any event, this does mean that the efficacy of such in-house conciliation is difficult to compare with stand-alone employer procedures where employees are not represented.

More promising for the Ontario context are proactive mediation serv-

39 Workers' Action Centre, *Working on the Edge* (Toronto: Workers' Action Centre, 2007), http://www.workersactioncentre.org/!docs/pb_WorkingOnTheEdge_eng.pdf at 69 [WAC, *Working on the Edge*].
40 Roger Blanpain *et al.*, *The Global Workplace: International and Comparative Employment Law – Cases and Materials* (Cambridge: Cambridge University Press, 2007) at 438 [Blancpain, *The Global Workplace*].
41 European Industrial Relations Observatory Online, *France Industrial Relations Profile*, http://www.eurofound.europa.eu/eiro/country/france_4.htm (EIRO); see also *ibid.* at 438.
42 Blancpain, *The Global Workplace*, at 394. Note that employees must opt to form such Works Councils; the mandatory element is that where a Works Council exists, employers must deal with it.

ices provided by impartial and independent bodies such as the U.K.'s Advisory, Conciliation, and Arbitration Service (ACAS), which among other things offers early workplace mediation for disputes between individual employees and employers.[43] ACAS also makes available authoritative information and advice about employment law and best workplace practices, and this, too, may have potential for reducing employment conflicts. While such services require funding, it is reasonable to think they will also reduce public costs; a review of the economic impact of individual mediation services provided by ACAS cites savings to taxpayers of £71½ million as a result of fewer cases proceeding to hearings.[44] Similarly, an evaluation of a pre-claim mediation pilot project by ACAS identified net savings to the public purse of £83,382; in other words, the costs of providing the service were outweighed by savings – for example, from fewer claims and hearings.[45]

Currently, ESP officers in Ontario do provide varying degrees of mediation in the course of the employment standards process, but these settlement efforts are only available after a claim has been commenced. One of the goals of early mediation is to avoid the necessity of such claims being filed at all.

C. Policy Options

1 Develop a high school employment law module focused on basic employment rights and enforcement mechanisms in an engaging and relevant manner, to be integrated into existing high school courses (e.g., Civics, Law or Career Studies).[46]

---

43 United Kingdom, *ACAS, Promoting Employment Relations and HR Excellence: Mediation,* http://www.acas.org.uk/index.aspx?articleid=2008.

44 United Kingdom, National Institute of Economic and Social Research, *A Review of the Economic Impact of Employment Relations Services Delivered by Acas* by Pamela Meadows, 2007, http://www.acas.org.uk/CHttpHandler.ashx?id=743&p=0 at 6.

45 United Kingdom, Institute for Employment Studies, *Pre-Claim Conciliation Pilot – Evaluation Summary Report* by Ann Denvir *et al.,* 2009, http://www.acas.org.uk/CHttpHandler.ashx?id=1079&p=0 at 9.

46 We note in this regard that the University of Toronto Faculty of Law has acquired considerable expertise in the creation and delivery of law-related curricula to high school students through its LAWS program, a project of the Faculty and the Toronto District School Board, as well as the Faculty's Youth Summer Program. Other sources of expertise and curricular resources include the Ontario Justice Education Network, which offers programming and materials about the justice system to high school students.

2 Develop a range of educational programs and information for both employers and employees on their respective rights and obligations, to be delivered in a variety of formats and languages by different organizations and intermediaries at various sites, including both general and remedial postings in the workplace. Such programs and information should also be integrated into current licensing and regulatory requirements and mandatory forms.

3 Develop a pilot project offering early mediation services by an independent and impartial body to minimize the escalation of employment problems to litigation.

IV. Employment Standards Regimes

A. Stakeholder Consultations

As noted above, the ESA prescribes minimum employment standards in Ontario in regard to working conditions such as wages, hours of work, overtime, pregnancy leave, and termination and severance pay.[47] The Act is designed to protect employees from the harm that can result from their unequal bargaining power.[48] Enforcement takes place primarily through claims made to the ESP and appeals to the Ontario Labour Relations Board (OLRB). Some 24,000 claims are filed each year, with approximately 21,000 of these receiving a decision from the ESP. Of those complaints receiving a decision, some 3,000 are appealed to the OLRB, with between 200 and 300 of these appeals brought by employees and the remainder by employers; approximately 80 per cent of appeals are settled through mediation provided by the OLRB.[49]

Concern was expressed in stakeholder consultations with respect to how effectively the *ESA* is being enforced: at the time, the ESP had a backlog of approximately 10,000 *ESA* claims investigations, with priority being assigned to breaches viewed as more serious. Explanations for this backlog include the introduction of electronic claim filing (an initiative that began four years ago and that roughly doubled claim intake)[50]

---

47 *ESA, supra* note 10.
48 *Machtinger v. Hoj Industries Ltd., supra* note 3 at 22.
49 Stakeholder consultation, 18 May 2010.
50 Approximately 70 to 80 per cent of claims are filed online, 8 per cent by mail, and the rest via facsimile.

and the introduction of Service Ontario filing.[51] In this sense, such a backlog represents successful initiatives to make claims filing easier, without sufficient resources being allocated to the processing and adjudication of the resulting volume of cases. The impact at the time, however, was that the waiting period between the filing of a claim and the first contact with parties by the ESP was approximately six months, with another six months elapsing before a meeting was scheduled that might result in an order.[52]

Since the initial stakeholder consultation, the ESP has announced the creation of an Employment Standards Task Force to eliminate the backlog, together with plans to expedite the intake, investigation, and decision-making process more generally. Currently, the backlog is closer to 3,400 claims, with new claims reaching the second stage in approximately two months.[53]

Concern was also expressed by some stakeholders in regard to whether the *ESA* provides sufficient substantive protection for employees. A majority were of the view that *ESA* prescriptions for minimum notice of termination for employees (or pay in lieu thereof) were inadequate.[54] More specifically, employees may be entitled to a much longer notice period (and equivalent damages) at common law than those prescribed by the *ESA*. While this might suggest an incentive to shift claims from the more accessible procedures at the ESP to a less accessible court process for wrongful dismissal suits, these entitlements may not be large enough to make retaining a lawyer for a wrongful dismissal suit economically feasible. However, although stakeholders recognized that short minimum notice periods were problematic, they also expressed concern that longer notice periods might make smaller

---

51 Service Ontario filing allows employees to file *ESA* claims at any one of seventy-two Service Ontario locations, rather than only eighteen MOL offices, as was the previously the case.

52 Stakeholder consultation, 18 May 2010.

53 Stakeholder consultation, February 2011; and see Ontario, Ministry of Labour, *Employment Standards Task Force*, http://www.labour.gov.on.ca/english/es/pubs/is_estf.php.

54 Notice of termination or pay in lieu thereof requirements are set out in Part XV of the *ESA*, *supra* note 10. Employers must provide employees with a minimum period of advance notice of their terminations. If employers wish to terminate employees immediately, employees must be paid a sum equal to the wages they would have earned during the required notice period. Severance pay is also available in certain circumstances under Part XV as well.

businesses liable for payments they could not afford.[55] Yet they also pointed out that most employers want clarity, certainty, and predictability, and such notice periods might be less costly than defending a wrongful dismissal suit.

A majority of stakeholders were also of the view that the current cap of $10,000 on the orders of employment standards officers[56] could not be justified. The *ESA* is minimum standards legislation, and either employees were entitled by statute to certain payments or they were not; if they were, they should be able to recover the full amount of their entitlement.

B. Literature Review and Discussion

Historically, employment standards legislation has been conceptually marginal; the original assumption was that collective bargaining would be the principal means of establishing working conditions and that minimum standards would have only a collateral role.[57] Such laws were to operate as both a floor for collective bargaining and as a safety net for those employees who, for one reason or another, did not have union representation. However, collective bargaining is now a 'threatened norm' as a result of declining rates of unionization, with the result that employment standards regimes that were intended as fallback schemes have become the dominant mode of regulating employment conditions.[58] Among other things, the effect has been that minimum standards designed as floors are now functioning as if they were optimal – or at least appropriate – endpoints. This may explain in part some of the inadequacies of the legislation described below.

From an access to justice perspective, a major concern with the *ESA* involves the downloading of the Act's enforcement to employees. At its inception, the statute was generally enforced through random or targeted inspections initiated by employment standards officers;[59] however,

---

55 Among other conditions, the *ESA* stipulates that severance pay is only owing to employees whose employers have a payroll of $2.5 million or more. See *ESA, supra* note 10 at s.64.

56 *Ibid.*, s.103(4).

57 CCPA, *The Employment Standards Act, supra* note 2 at 5.

58 *Ibid.* at 7 and 19.

59 See, for example, a reference to this by the Hon. D.A. Bales, Minister of Labour, in the Legislative Assembly, *Legislative Debates (Hansard)*, Twenty-Eighth Legislature, 1968, vol. 3 at 3740, http://www.archive.org/details/v3hansard1968ontauoft.

investigations are now performed primarily in response to complaints by employees against employers. A 2004 report by Ontario's Auditor General found that despite the high rate of *ESA* violations uncovered by proactive inspections, the ESP had essentially abandoned this form of activity – a state of affairs that had been identified by the Auditor General as early as 1991.[60] By 2008–9, the ESP had increased the number of proactive inspections conducted annually to 2,135,[61] but this figure represents only approximately 0.7 per cent of workplaces in Ontario.[62] The fact that the same ministry conducted 66,230 inspections under the *Occupational Health and Safety Act* in 2008–9 provides an illuminating contrast.[63] With respect to federally regulated employees, the Arthurs Commission found that in 2005–6, 87 per cent of federal inspectors' time was dedicated to reactive rather than proactive functions.[64]

Relying on employees to enforce employment standards legislation through individual claims appears to be problematic. The Auditor General found that approximately 90 per cent of *ESA* complaints against employers are brought by employees after they leave their employment,[65] and noted that 'current employees are generally reluctant to file claims for fear of losing their jobs, despite the protection of employee rights that exists in the Act.'[66] As a result, the Auditor General concluded that the Ministry of Labour's protection of the rights of currently employed workers was inadequate.[67] The Arthurs Commission observed that 92 per cent of complaints at the federal level were filed by employees who were no longer employed in the same workplace,[68] and that employees may refrain from filing complaints out of ignorance, because of fear of retaliation by employers, or because they are with-

---

60 Ontario, Office of the Auditor General, *2004 Annual Report – 3.09 Employment Rights and Responsibilities Program*, http://www.auditor.on.ca/en/reports_en/en04/309en04.pdf at 240 [OAG, *2004 Report*].

61 Ontario, Ministry of Labour, *Investigations and Inspections Statistics*, http://www.labour.gov.on.ca/english/es/pubs/enforcement/investigations.php.

62 Based on the Auditor General's estimate that 300,000 employers operate in Ontario: OAG 2004 Report, *supra* note 60 at 242.

63 Ontario, Ministry of Labour, *Enforcement Statistics*, http://www.labour.gov.on.ca/english/hs/pubs/enforcement/index.php.

64 *Arthurs Commission Report, supra* note 27 at 212.

65 OAG, *2004 Report, supra* note 60 at 242.

66 *Ibid.*

67 WAC, *Working on the Edge, supra* note 39 at 50.

68 *Arthurs Commission Report, supra* note 27 at 192.

out the necessary resources or stamina to obtain redress.[69] The concerns of employees in this regard include not only the risk of discharge but also the myriad of other ways in which employers can make work life unpleasant.

This reluctance on the part of employees to file claims is not new; a similar problem was identified in Ontario in 1987.[70] Nor is it limited to Canada – in the United Kingdom, 76 per cent of complaints by employees against employers are brought after employees leave employment, and an additional 17 per cent of complaints are brought by employees who leave employment after they make their claims.[71]

In this context, a recent amendment to the *ESA*[72] requiring employees to notify their employers of violations and the amount of wages owed before they are permitted to file claims has been the subject of criticism. Ostensibly aimed at fostering settlement, commentators allege that it will create additional barriers for employees seeking remedies for unpaid wages and other breaches of the legislation.[73] More generally, strategies that seem intuitively reasonable in other legal contexts can fail in this area because of the vulnerability of employees and the power imbalance in the workplace.[74]

The fact that employees are unlikely to file claims while they are employed means that the *ESA* is operating largely as a mechanism focused on the termination of employment rather than on regulating working conditions during its currency.[75] The weaknesses of a complaint-driven process may also be one reason that the rate of non-compliance with employment legislation on the part of employers is significant. The Arthurs Commission pointed to 1997 findings in

---

69 *Ibid.*
70 CCPA, *The Employment Standards Act, supra* note 2 at 18.
71 U.K., Department of Trade and Industry, *Better Dispute Resolution – A Review of Employment Dispute Resolution in Great Britain* by Michael Gibbons (London, 2007), U.K. Department for Business, Innovation, and Skills, http://www.berr.gov.uk/files/file38516.pdf at 10, 15. [DTI, *Better Dispute Resolution*].
72 Ontario, Legislative Assembly, *Open for Business Act*, Bill 68, 39th Legislature, 2nd Session, 2010, http://www.ontla.on.ca/web/bills/bills_current.do?locale=en.
73 Nicholas Keung, 'Employment Bill Stymies Complaints Against Employers, Critics Say,' *Toronto Star*, 3 August 2010, http://www.ontla.on.ca/web/bills/bills_current. do?locale=en; David Doorey, 'Bill 68: When Did Discouraging Workers to File ESA Complaints Become Public Policy in Ontario?', http://www.yorku.ca/ddoorey/lawblog/?p=2003.
74 Professor Kerry Rittich, interview, 14 July 2010.
75 CCPA, *The Employment Standards Act, supra* note 2 at 95.

the federal government's Labour Standards Evaluation survey to the effect that 25 per cent of federally regulated employers were not in compliance with most obligations under Part III of the *Labour Code*, and that 75 per cent were not in compliance with at least one provision; these findings were also supported by the 2005 Statistics Canada Federal Jurisdiction Workplace Survey.[76] The commission also noted that these figures likely understated the degree of non-compliance because the methodology used was based on employer self-reporting.[77] In the provincial sphere, the Auditor General found that proactive inspections of high-risk business sectors revealed breaches of the Act in regard to unpaid wages, overtime pay, and public holidays at rates ranging from 40 to 90 per cent, depending on the sector.[78]

Another problem identified in the literature is that even where *ESA* complaints are made and payment orders are issued, collection rates are low. The Auditor General found that on average, approximately 40 per cent of employers pay the amounts owed voluntarily[79] and that collection agencies are assigned to collect the remainder. In 2004, these agencies had a collection rate of approximately 15 per cent.[80] Similarly, in 2005–6 it was estimated that of the $37 million owed to workers, $21.3 million (58 per cent of monies due) was not collected.[81] Unless employers agree voluntarily to pay workers, wages largely go unpaid: in the fourteen years between 1989–90 and 2002–3, 71 per cent of wages that the ESP ordered employers to pay remained uncollected, amounting to approximately $500 million in unpaid wages.[82]

Both federally and provincially, employers in breach of their statutory obligations are liable to prosecution. A violation of the *ESA* is punishable by up to twelve months in prison and fines ranging from

---

76 *Arthurs Commission Report, supra* note 27 at 192–3; WAC, *Working on the Edge, supra* note 39 at 46.

77 *Ibid.* at 192.

78 OAG, *2004 Report, supra* note 60 at 242.

79 *Ibid.* at 246.

80 *Ibid.* at 240.

81 WAC, *Working on the Edge, supra* note 39 at 58.

82 Juana Berinstein and Mary Gellatly, *Effective and Enforced Employment Standards for Improved Income Security – Brief to the Task Force on Modernizing Income Security for Working-Age Adults*, http://www.workersactioncentre.org/!docs/pb_Effective&Enforced-eng.pdf [Berinstein and Gellatly, *Income Security for Working-Age Adults*].

$50,000 to $500,000, depending on the circumstances.[83] For the most part, however, the ESP does not exercise these prosecutorial powers; rather, to the extent that it prosecutes at all, it usually proceeds by way of tickets with set fines of $295 plus costs and victim fine surcharges.[84] Similarly, the Arthurs Commission noted the twenty-year moratorium on prosecutions at the federal level.[85]

Few proactive inspections by the Ministry of Labour to uncover violations, minor penalties when violations are uncovered, and reluctance among employees to file *ESA* claims together mean that the cost to employers of violating the *ESA* is low.[86] The Auditor General also noted that a lack of punitive action against employment standards violators may be encouraging non-compliance.[87] Others have observed that, in essence, 'employers have a financial incentive to violate the Employment Standards Act in Ontario.'[88] Similar observations have been made elsewhere – for example, in Greece, where the labour inspectorate 'seldom issues fines, and, when it does, they are usually very small and not effective as a deterrent ... As a result, the mechanisms to resolve individual labour disputes in Greece have proven to be extremely inadequate.'[89]

From an access to justice perspective, the shifting of enforcement to individual employees has the anomalous effect of requiring employees to enforce a statute that is premised on their own vulnerability. It also generates a need for individual legal assistance and representation that might otherwise be unnecessary. This in turn gives rise to other questions in regard to the locus of responsibility for implementing remedial or protective legislation, including the extent to which victims of violations should bear the costs of ensuring compliance. In one sense, enforcement of the *ESA* has been privatized in a way that transfers the task to those who are least likely to be able to pursue it effectively.

---

83 *ESA, supra* note 10, s. 132.
84 In 2008–9, for example, a vast majority of the 480 prosecutions undertaken for *ESA* violations were by way of tickets. Ontario, Ministry of Labour, *Convictions Archive*, http://www.labour.gov.on.ca/english/es/pubs/enforcement/archive.php.
85 *Arthurs Commission Report, supra* note 27 at 187.
86 Kent Elson, 'Taking Workers' Rights Seriously: Private Prosecutions of Employment Standards Violations,' (2008) 26 Windsor Y.B. Access Just. 329 at 332.
87 OAG, *2004 Report, supra* note 60 at 240.
88 CCPA, *The Employment Standards Act, supra* note 2 at 99.
89 Eurofound, *Individual Disputes at the Workplace: Alternative Disputes Resolution* by John Purcell, http://www.eurofound.europa.eu/eiro/studies/tn0910039s/tn0910039s.htm at 9 [Purcell, *Individual Disputes*].

It is worth noting that in other circumstances where such responsibility has been allocated to individuals, legal resources have also been made available to them. Recent reforms to the *Human Rights Code* in Ontario were coupled with a statutory commitment to establish and fund the independent Human Rights Legal Support Centre, which provides free legal services to complainants.[90] Similarly, the *Workplace Safety and Insurance Act* provides for the funding of the Offices of the Worker and Employer Adviser, which provide free legal services to employees and employers respectively in regard to *WSIA* matters.[91] This approach is not widespread, however, and the fact that the transfer of enforcement responsibilities under the *ESA* occurred incrementally over a number of decades has rendered it less visible.

At the same time, shifting the primary burden of enforcement back to the ESP has a significant cost component. It has been suggested that such expenditures could be funded through levies or penalties for defaulting employers; this would have the effect of internalizing costs of compliance rather than externalizing them to the public purse.[92] Currently, costs and victim fine surcharges are payable under the *Provincial Offences Act*,[93] and administrative costs are payable under the *ESA*,[94] but these are relatively minimal. In contrast, fines for employers convicted of violations of the *Occupational Health and Safety Act* amounted to over $14 million in 2008–9,[95] suggesting that similar fines under the *ESA* could be a substantial source of funding.

Other models of internalized funding already exist in this area; for example, the Workplace Safety and Insurance Board is funded by experience-rated employer premiums related to health and safety records.[96] The WSIB model, which is primarily geared to the funding of substan-

---

90 *Human Rights Code, supra* note 17, s.45.11-18.
91 *Workplace Safety and Insurance Act, supra* note 12, s.176.
92 Professor Brian Langille, interview, 16 July 2010. Professor Langille points to the former Employee Wage Protection Program and the *Workplace Safety and Insurance Act* as examples of self-funded schemes. See also Berinstein and Gellatly, *Income Security for Working-Age Adults, supra* note 82.
93 R.S.O. 1990, c. P-33, s.60 and 60.1.
94 See, for example, *ESA, supra* note 10, s.103(2).
95 Ontario, Ministry of Labour, *Enforcement Statistics,* http://www.labour.gov.on.ca/english/hs/pubs/enforcement/index.php.
96 Ontario, Workplace Safety and Insurance Board, Coverage and Premiums, http://www.wsib.on.ca/en/community/WSIB/230/ArticleDetail/24338?vgnextoid=5f167 96cc342c210VgnVCM100000469c710aRCRD&vgnextchannel=104d7de3827d6210Vgn VCM1000000e18120aRCRD.

tive benefit payments and programs for injured workers, is not without problems,[97] but it is suggestive of other possibilities. Other examples include an Australian experiment with a model for wage protection in insolvency situations that was partially funded through a payroll tax that excluded small employers.[98] In any event, the costs of shifting compliance back to the ESP must be weighed against both the substantial wage losses and the enforcement costs borne by employees under the current system.

Turning to the issue of the length of minimum notice periods for termination, the *ESA* provides for mandatory notice or pay in lieu of notice ranging from one week to eight weeks, depending on an employee's length of service.[99] The formula involved is roughly one week per year of service, in contrast to wrongful dismissal jurisprudence, where one month per year of service is common, although frequently characterized by courts as not a 'rule of thumb.'[100] Moreover, a long-service employee is at a particular disadvantage under the *ESA*, since termination after even thirty years of service involves only eight weeks of notice. A similarly placed employee may be entitled to approximately thirty months of notice in a wrongful dismissal action, although it must be kept in mind there are other differences between these legal regimes as well.

As noted previously, however, wrongful dismissal suits are frequently beyond the reach of lower or middle income employees, both because the jurisprudence tends to be oriented towards higher echelons of employment and because civil actions in amounts over $25,000 must be pursued through the more traditionally formal procedures of the Superior Court of Justice. Even actions in Small Claims Court now involve a large number of rules and forms that are likely to be inexpli-

---

97 Among other things, premiums geared to injury rates create an incentive for employers to underreport injuries. See HR Compliance Insider, *Injury Reporting and the Risk of Liability for Workers' Compensation Fraud*, 2009, http://www.hrcomplianceinsider.com/tag/ontario-workplace-safety-and-insurance-board.

98 Canada, Parliamentary Research Branch, *Protecting Employee Wages in Bankruptcy* by Margaret Smith, http://dsp-psd.pwgsc.gc.ca/Collection-R/LoPBdP/BP/prb0134-e.htm#2. Wage Guarantee Schemes (txt).

99 *ESA, supra* note 10, s.57. Note that there are also *ESA* severance pay provisions for employees in certain circumstances – for example, layoffs of fifty employees or more or employers with payrolls of 2.5 million or more: ss.63–66.

100 *Bardal v. the Globe and Mail* (1960), 24 DLR 2d 140.

cable to the layperson, together with delays of up to one year before trial.[101]

From an access to justice perspective, a dual process system that provides stronger substantive rights through the more cumbersome, lengthier, or expensive process is problematic. Whether the purpose of termination pay is to provide an opportunity to seek alternative employment, cushion employees against the adverse effects of economic dislocation, or compensate them for the loss of their 'investment' in employment,[102] it is a little difficult to rationalize such disparate results. This is particularly true given that shorter notice periods have a compounding effect for less well-paid employees; since the amount of pay in lieu of notice is already tied to their lower wage levels, shorter notice is doubly disadvantageous.

Such notice periods under the *ESA* may be contrasted with those of other jurisdictions: for example, one to twelve weeks in the United Kingdom,[103] four weeks to seven months in Germany,[104] one to twenty-four months in Greece,[105] one to six months in Sweden,[106] up to twenty-four months in Finland, and so forth. Even the severance pay provided under the *ESA* is capped at twenty-six weeks, rather than eight, although it is only payable where a worker has been employed for five years or more and in situations where at least fifty employees are being terminated on the permanent discontinuance of a business, or the employer has a payroll of at least $2.5 million.[107]

The importance of the *ESA* notice periods is heightened by the absence of protection from termination without just cause – protection that is provided by some other jurisdictions. Federally regulated employees in Canada have a statutory right to reinstatement and damages for unjust

---

101 See, for example, Ontario, Ministry of the Attorney General, *Rules of the Small Claims Courts,* http://www.e-laws.gov.on.ca/html/regs/english/elaws_regs_980258_e.htm.
102 *Rizzo & Rizzo Shoes Ltd. (Re),* [1998] 1 S.C.R. 27 at para. 2.
103 *Employment Rights Act* 1996, c.18, s.86.
104 Blancpain, *The Global Workplace, supra* note 40 at 399.
105 Christina Vlachtsis, 'Greece,' in *The Comparative Yearbook of International Business, Special Issue 2006: Employment Law,* ed. Daniel Campbell and Antonida Alibekova (Salzburg: Centre for International Legal Studies, 2006) at 301–2 [Vlachtsis, 'Greece'].
106 Leif Ramberg, 'An Introduction to Swedish Employment Law,' http://www.law-europe.com/documents/men_04_practice_03_09.pdf at 3.
107 *ESA, supra* note 10, s.65.

or unfair dismissal,[108] as do employees in the United Kingdom[109] and Australia.[110] Other jurisdictions require a variety of threshold standards such as real and serious cause (France),[111] justifiable cause (Mexico),[112] just cause (Sweden),[113] or enumerated grounds (Hungary)[114] (Norway)[115] (Spain)[116] (Germany)[117]; and employees in Greece can challenge 'abusive dismissals.'[118] In contrast, under the *ESA* the existence of cause for dismissal will disentitle an employee to termination pay, but there is no general right to challenge a discharge on the basis of lack of just cause or to obtain damages or reinstatement in such circumstances. As a result, termination pay in lieu of notice assumes greater salience.

The concern with respect to the economic impact of longer notice periods on smaller employers is difficult to address, given the variability of such impacts and the absence of empirical evidence in regard to the effect of any proposed increase. It has also been argued in the context of labour flexibility that inadequate employment standards operate to externalize business costs to employees and the public purse.[119] Following this logic, larger termination payments might represent the appropriate return of such costs to employers. Alternatively, one proposal for ameliorating the impact of severance costs on smaller employers would be to impose a payroll levy on all employers,[120] with the effect of distributing the impact on a proportional basis. In any event, the fact that small employers are currently liable for considerably longer notice periods in wrongful dismissal actions provides a useful perspective when it comes to contemplating legislated increases.

Yet another problem in regard to employment standards regimes is that they are generally based on a traditional model of full-time, per-

---

108 Canada Labour Code, *supra* note 14, ss.240–6.
109 *Employment Rights Act 1996*, c.18, s.94.
110 International Labour Organization, XVIIIth Meeting of European Labour Court Judges, 2010, National Reports, http://www.ilo.org/public/english/dialogue/ifpdial/downloads/judges18/natreport.pdf at 4 [ILO, *2010 Judges' Meeting*].
111 Blancpain, *The Global Workplace, supra* note 40 at 437.
112 *Ibid.* at 222.
113 ILO, *2010 Judges' Meeting, supra* note 110 at 78.
114 *Ibid.* at 32.
115 *Ibid.* at 55.
116 *Ibid.* at 74.
117 Blancpain, *The Global Workplace, supra* note 40 at 399–400.
118 Vlachtsis, 'Greece'*supra* note 105 at 303.
119 *The Employment Standards Act, supra* note 2 at 22.
120 *Ibid.* at 88.

manent employment that no longer characterizes many employment relationships. Entitlements such as termination, severance and vacation pay, and leaves of absence (including pregnancy and parental leave), for example, are often calculated based on continuous lengths of service, with the result that they may not apply to non-standard and precarious workers, despite the fact that intermittent periods of work for a single employer may add up to a considerable length of service.[121] The Arthurs Commission noted that 32 per cent of the Canadian workforce works in non-standard employment arrangements such as part-time, temporary, agency, and self-employment.[122] The *ESA* has been amended to extend some of these rights to employees of temporary agencies,[123] but many others are still excluded. This has been described as the 'passive deregulation' of the workplace.[124]

If the *ESA* represents minimum employment standards, excluding such employees from its protection is problematic. Indeed, the Arthurs Commission observed that precarious workers might be particularly vulnerable, not only because legal protection with respect to their employment relationships is limited, but also because even where they have such benefits, 'they often lack the means, confidence or knowledge to enforce their rights.'[125] As well, precarious employment disproportionately affects women, racialized groups, younger workers, and immigrants[126] and has been associated with low earnings, negative physical and mental health outcomes, adverse impacts on personal and community relationships, and limited access to education and training.[127]

The chronic instability of precarious work and the various economic and personal costs to employees require a broader discussion than is

---

121 *Arthurs Commission Report, supra* note 27 at 238.
122 *Ibid.* at 231. See also Curry, *The Legal Problems of Everyday Life, supra* note 8, with respect to the growth of non-standard work in the context of justiciable legal problems; and Richard P. Chaykowski, Canadian Policy Research Networks, 'Non-Standard Work and Economic Vulnerability,' 2005, http://cprn.org/documents/35591_en.pdf [Chaykowski, 'Vulnerability'].
123 *ESA, supra* note 10, Part XVIII.1.
124 Berinstein and Gellatly, *Income Security for Working-Age Adults, supra* note 82.
125 *Arthurs Commission Report, supra* note 27 at 28.
126 Chaykowski, 'Vulnerability,' *supra* note 122 at 80; and Law Reform Commission of Ontario, *Vulnerable Workers and Precarious Employment,* 2010, at 40-24, http://www.lco-cdo.org/VulnerableWorkersBackgroundPaper-December2010.pdf [LRCO, *Vulnerable Workers*].
127 *Ibid.* at 42–5.

possible here.[128] Nevertheless, recent amendments to the *ESA* in regard to temporary workers suggest that the extension of minimum standards protection to precarious workers may be less complex than otherwise supposed. While such changes are unlikely to fully address the issues related to this phenomenon, there seems little doubt that they would have a significant and positive impact on the employees involved.

C. Policy Options

1 Shift the primary burden of enforcement of the *ESA* back to the ESP, to be implemented in the form of speedy proactive inspections and prosecutions and prompt and effective collections. Compliance and collection mechanisms should be integrated with existing requirements; for example, the annual renewal of various types of licences should be declined where there are outstanding payment orders. The costs of the ESP's enforcement activities should be funded from penalties and fines levied on offenders.
2 Lengthen the notice periods for termination in the *ESA* and eliminate the $10,000 recovery cap.
3 Amend the provisions of the *ESA* to ensure that precarious workers have benefits and protections that are similar to those of other employees.

V. Dispute Resolution Fora for Employment Law Matters

A. Stakeholder Consultations

Throughout the stakeholder consultations, there was general agreement that a single legal forum to adjudicate all employment law matters was desirable – one that would encompass not only *ESA* claims but wrongful dismissal suits and human rights claims as well. Currently, *ESA* claims are filed with the ESP, wrongful dismissal actions with either the Small Claims Court or the Superior Court depending on the amount claimed, and human rights claims with the Human Rights Tribunal of Ontario, although courts also have the jurisdiction to apply the

---

128 We note that the Law Commission of Ontario has embarked on a more comprehensive review of the legal protections afforded to vulnerable and precarious workers; see http://www.lco-cdo.org/en/content/vulnerable-workers.

Human Rights Code in the course of wrongful dismissal suits.[129] Stakeholders pointed out that employees are unlikely to consider their problems in segregated legal categories and that employers normally wish to limit their liability by disposing of all matters relating to a particular employee at the same time.

Stakeholders held different opinions on whether such a single forum should be a court or a tribunal; the majority, however, favoured a court. Regardless of the designation, key characteristics of the forum might include specialized expertise in employment law on the part of judges or adjudicators; standing procedures to accommodate self-represented litigants (as opposed to the *ad hoc* measures currently used); duty counsel; and the generation of a consistent body of jurisprudence. While consolidation of regimes was viewed positively, stakeholders generally felt that including WSIB matters would be difficult, given the degree of specialization and the medical nature of many of the issues involved. In addition, caution was advised given the tendency of governments to amalgamate or cluster tribunals for reasons that might be inimical to access to justice – for example, relating to incursions into the independence of adjudicators. The importance of retaining the faster and more informal *ESA* processes was emphasized as well; consolidation should not operate to impede or decrease accessibility. This might suggest the virtues of a two-track system akin to the one employed by the Human Rights Tribunal of Ontario for transition cases, where a claimant could opt for a faster and more informal hearing for 'fact fight' cases, or, alternatively, for a more traditional hearing for cases involving complex legal issues or expert evidence. On the other hand, there was some concern that a two-track system might itself produce disparities with respect to the quality of justice.

Stakeholders also had mixed views on the promulgation of guidelines for the length of notice in wrongful dismissal cases in a manner similar to those of the federal Child Support Guidelines in family law. A number felt that a 'legislate notice, litigate cause' regime would not be flexible enough to encompass the wide variety of circumstances in such cases, and that clients – especially those who were better paid or held more senior positions – did not want formula solutions. These

---

129 See *Tranchemontagne v. Ontario (Director, Disability Support Program)*, [2006] 1 S.C.R. 513. Whether ESP officers or the OLRB have jurisdiction to apply the *Human Rights Code* under the *ESA* (as opposed to the OLRB's jurisdiction under the *Labour Relations Act, 1995)* is less clear.

views may also be related to the concerns noted earlier with respect to the inadequacy of *ESA* notice provisions. To the extent that the *ESA* represents a model of legislated notice, it may not be one that inspires confidence, given the disparity between its provisions and wrongful dismissal awards.

Some stakeholders suggested that costs awards in wrongful dismissal cases should be structured to provide some incentive for lawyers to take cases, although concern was also expressed that the prospect of paying another party's costs could deter potential plaintiffs from bringing meritorious claims to court. Contingency fees might also play a role in making the cost of legal representation more manageable for some litigants, although there was a feeling among stakeholders that such fee arrangements are sometimes used by lawyers to take advantage of clients with 'sure thing' claims. Increased magisterial or inquisitorial powers on the part of judges and adjudicators might also work in tandem with unbundled services; most stakeholders indicated that they provided *pro bono* summary advice and that they might be willing to draft claims, for example, as a discrete service, but that an effective forum would still be necessary to provide assistance to unrepresented litigants.

The Human Rights Legal Support Centre currently provides a wider range of unbundled services in the sense that its staff will not only give summary advice but also 'ghost-write' pleadings and provide coaching or other preparation for mediation sessions and hearings. This is not without hazards; among other things, claimants they have assisted behind the scenes have on occasion been held to a higher procedural standard than other unrepresented claimants by the Human Rights Tribunal of Ontario.

Stakeholders also expressed concern about the interactions among the various legal regimes. Under the *ESA*, employees must choose between an employment standards claim and a wrongful dismissal suit and are not permitted to proceed with both.[130] However, they have only fourteen days after filing a claim to elect a civil action instead and withdraw the claim. This election has significant implications given the differences in the amounts recoverable and the costs associated with them. The majority view was that the fourteen-day period was insufficient to allow employees to make informed decisions in this regard.

---

130 *ESA, supra* note 10, s.96.

B. Literature Review and Discussion

Dispute resolution mechanisms can generally be divided into four categories: the traditional court system, labour courts, quasi-judicial administrative agencies, and arbitration processes.[131] Various jurisdictions employ combinations of these four categories in determining employment law disputes. Below are quick snapshots of other employment fora and procedures which together provide a context for considering those in Ontario. These brief descriptions are necessarily incomplete but are nevertheless useful in providing a broader perspective.

(1) *Australia.* Fair Work Australia (FWA) is the country's national workplace relations tribunal that among other things enforces minimum employment standards and determines employment termination matters. Members of FWA are trained in alternative dispute resolution techniques such as conciliation, mediation, and arbitration.[132] Wrongful dismissal applications are first conciliated, but if a resolution is not reached, FWA determines the matter; if a wrongful dismissal is found to have occurred, reinstatement or compensation for the employee may be ordered.[133] The FWA regime also includes the Fair Work Ombudsman, whose function is 'promoting harmonious, productive and cooperative workplace relations and ensuring compliance with Commonwealth workplace laws.'[134] In performing this function, the Ombudsman operates as a single point for information about Australia's workplace relations system; educates employees on their workplace rights; investigates complaints and suspected violations of workplace laws, awards, and agreements; and litigates to enforce workplace laws and to deter wrongdoing.[135] In 2009–10, 85 per cent of termination applications were completed within eighty-seven days of filing.[136]

(2) *France.* Disputes with respect to individual labour contracts are filed

---

131 Gladstone, 'Disputes over Rights,' *supra* note 5 at 505.
132 Australia, Fair Work Australia, *About Dispute Resolution*, http://www.fwa.gov.au/index.cfm?pagename=disputeabout.
133 Australia, Fair Work Australia, *The Unfair Dismissal Application Process*, http://www.fwa.gov.au/index.cfm?pagename=dismissalsprocess.
134 Australia, Fair Work Ombudsman, *Our Role*, http://www.fwo.gov.au/About-Fair-Work-Ombudsman/Pages/Our-role.aspx.
135 *Ibid.*
136 ILO, *2010 Judges' Meeting, supra* note 110 at 18.

with the *Conseils de Prud'hommes* (Labour Courts), which employ a simplified, informal system. This includes a conciliation stage before a panel of representatives from employer and employee groups and, where the matter is not settled, a hearing before four lay adjudicators, who have also been designated by these constituencies. Decisions are reached by a majority vote.[137] As noted previously, terminations for personal reasons require a conciliation meeting even before the employee is discharged,[138] and terminations for economic reasons require various types of consultations with employee representatives.[139] Decisions of the *Conseils* can be appealed to the *Cour d'Appel* and/or the *Cour de Cassation*, depending on the amount claimed; cases involving lower amounts are judicially reviewed, while an appeal for a case with a higher claim involves a trial *de novo*.[140] In 2009 the average length of time for the completion of a case before the *Conseils de Prud'hommes* was seven months.[141]

(3) *Germany.* In Germany, labour inspectorates in each state conduct workplace inspections and enforce protective employment rules.[142] Individual claims can also be filed with local Labour Courts, which 'aim to be speedy, simple and inexpensive' and which have exclusive jurisdiction over most employment disputes.[143] As noted previously, termination claims go first to a conciliation process before Works Councils in each workplace; these are mandatory for employers with more than five employees.[144] However, local Labour Courts also include an initial conciliation step for cases more generally as well.[145] Subsequent hearings are presided over by tripartite panels that include employer and employee representatives and are designed to accommodate unrepresented parties.[146] Decisions can be appealed to a state Labour Court,

---

137 Blancpain, *The Global Workplace, supra* note 40 at 435–6.

138 *Ibid.* at 438.

139 *Ibid.* at 441–3.

140 *Ibid.* at 435–6.

141 XII Meeting of European Labour Court Judges, *Do We Need Labour Courts?* M. Pierre Sargos, http://www.ilo.org/public/english/dialogue/ifpdial/downloads/lc_05/hungary_1.pdf.

142 Manfred Weis, 'Germany' in *Employment and Industrial Relations in Europe*, ed. Michael Gold and Manfred Weiss (The Hague: Kluwer Law International, 1999) at 71.

143 'Individual Disputes,' *supra* note 89 at 5.

144 'The Global Workplace,' *supra* note 40 at 416–17.

145 Purcell, *Individual Disputes, supra* note 89 at 5.

146 Werner Blenk, ed., *European Labour Courts: Current Issues* (Geneva: ILO, 1989) at 19; Blancpain, *The Global Workplace, supra* note 40 at 429.

and from there to the Federal Labour Court if certain criteria are satisfied.[147] At any point, the parties may submit a dispute to arbitration.[148]

(4) *Mexico.* Minimum standards enforcement in Mexico takes place both through labour inspectors who conduct workplace inspections and through complaints-based adjudication, and employers are subject to fines for violations.[149] Claims in Mexico go to *Juntas de conciliation y artitrage* (Conciliation and Arbitration Boards), where the process begins with a mediation stage. Subsequent hearings are presided over by lay judges[150] and must be 'conducted with a maximum of economy, concentration and simplicity.'[151] Workers are entitled to free public legal assistance in these proceedings.[152] Generally speaking, decisions of the *juntas* are final.[153]

(5) *New Zealand.* In New Zealand, employers and employees are first expected to attempt to resolve problems in their employment relations between themselves.[154] If employers and employees are unable to reach a resolution in this manner, the parties may engage in mediation at no cost or a labour inspector can investigate problems related to minimum employment rights.[155] If a resolution still cannot be reached through these channels, the parties may apply to the Employment Relations Authority (ERA) for determination of the issue. The ERA focuses on the merits of the case rather than on its technical, legal details; for decisions on important or complex questions of law, the matter may be referred to the Employment Court.[156] The Employment Court exists to deter-

---

147 *Ibid.* at 401.
148 Nigel Foster and Satish Sule, *German Legal System and Laws*, 4th ed. (Oxford: Oxford University Press, 2010) at 601.
149 Canada, Human Resources and Skills Development Canada, *Review of Public Communication CAN 2003-1*, http://dsp-psd.pwgsc.gc.ca/collection_2008/hrsdc-rhdsc/HS24-13-2005E.pdf at 72.
150 Danielle Venn, OECD, Directorate for Employment, Labour, and Social Affairs, *Legislation, Collective Bargaining and Enforcement: Updating the OECD Employment Protection Indicators*, Working Paper No. 89 at 2.
151 Blancpain, *The Global Workplace, supra* note 40 at 235.
152 *Ibid.* at 234.
153 *Ibid.* at 235.
154 New Zealand, Department of Labour, *Resolving Employment Relationship Problems* (flow chart), http://www.ers.dol.govt.nz/problem/employment-relationship.pdf.
155 *Ibid.*
156 *Ibid.*

mine cases involving employment disputes, particularly challenges to ERA decisions and questions of legal interpretation.[157] The ERA may also direct parties to mediation at any point during its investigation.

(6) *United Kingdom*. In the United Kingdom, employment tribunals determine disputes between employees and employers, including unfair dismissal claims. The employment tribunals are less formal than courtrooms[158] and have target time frames for disposing of cases.[159] They also provide general information on their processes in various languages, such as Cantonese, Hindi, and Polish.[160] The employment tribunals offer judicial mediation as a form of alternative dispute resolution. Sixty-five per cent of mediated cases are settled on the day of mediation, and a number of cases are settled subsequently as a result of the momentum created by mediation.[161] Mediation may produce outcomes that cannot be ordered in the standard tribunal hearing process, such as employment references.[162] This mediation service is in addition to the ACAS conciliation services.[163]

For Ontario, the insights to be gleaned from this set of brief descriptions include a general emphasis on speed, informality, conciliation, and specialized decision makers. These characteristics could be said to apply to the ESP process, with the exception of speed, although recent improvements in this regard offer some reason for optimism. Wrongful dismissal suits are a different matter: the Superior Court of Justice is a highly formal process, Small Claims Courts normally lack mediation mechanisms, and neither can be considered speedy, at least for contested cases. This lack of speed is of particular concern; expedition tends to be more important for termination cases, where employees

---

157 New Zealand, Ministry of Justice, *Employment Court*, http://www.justice.govt.nz/courts/employment-court.
158 U.K., Tribunals Service – Employment, *About Us*, http://www.justice.gov.uk/guidance/courts-and-tribunals/tribunals/employment/index.htm.
159 U.K., Tribunals Service – Employment, *About us – Charter Statement*, http://www.justice.gov.uk/guidance/courts-and-tribunals/tribunals/employment/index.htm.
160 U.K., Tribunals Service – Employment, *Publications – Alternative Formats*, http://www.employmenttribunals.gov.uk/Publications/alternativeFormats.htm.
161 U.K., Tribunals Service – Employment, *Employment Tribunals (England and Wales) – Judicial Mediation*, http://www.employmenttribunals.gov.uk/Documents/Publications/JudicialMediationEnglandandWales.pdf.
162 *Ibid.*
163 *Ibid.*

and their dependents may be without income and where delays may lead to increased private losses as well as public costs in the form of social assistance.

Both types of courts also require cases to be heard by generalist judges, with no requirement for specialized expertise in employment law; the result is a significant degree of inconsistency in the jurisprudence.[164] This is problematic not only in terms of the quality of decision making but also because consistency and certainty are associated with high rates of settlement.[165]

However, the channelling of employment claims into a single, specialized forum raises issues with respect to the synchronization of the various legal regimes involved. The *ESA* is a detailed legislative code of minimum standards and is both conceptually and functionally quite distinct from the common law of wrongful dismissal. Conversely, the latter incorporates doctrines and principles that are foreign to the purposes and provisions of the *ESA*. If specialized judges or adjudicators are to determine both statutory and common law entitlements, the relationship between the two is likely to come into sharper focus.

This means that consolidation into one forum may also offer an opportunity for a more comprehensive review and reorganization of the employment law landscape. In essence, the various statutes and the common law in this area have evolved in a relatively segregated manner, and integration, rationalization, and simplification appear to be overdue.

C. Policy Options

1 Consolidate employment law claims into a single forum with the following characteristics:

- Easy access to multilingual information and instructions
- Choice of methods for initiating claims, including online filing with template coaching
- Court/tribunal staff assistance in drafting claims and explaining procedures
- Duty counsel

---

164 Stakeholder consultations, 18 May 2010.
165 See, for example, *Consolidated Bathurst Packaging Ltd.* [1983] OLRB Rep. December 1995 at 2001.

- Routine mediation by staff mediators
- Speedy, simplified procedures with statutory time requirements (e.g., hearings or trials must occur and decisions must be delivered within specific periods of time)
- Judges/adjudicators with specialized expertise in employment and human rights law
- Hearing/trial protocols designed to accommodate unrepresented litigants, including magisterial processes
- Possibility of a two-track system where parties can choose either simplified hearings for standard notice length cases, or more formal trials for more complex cases

2 In the longer term, explore merging the various legal regimes to produce a coherent, simplified body of law.

VI. Collective Bargaining Regimes

It is difficult to consider access to justice in the employment law context without at least some discussion of the provincial and federal collective bargaining regimes set out in the *Labour Relations Act, 1995* and Part II of the *Canada Labour Code* respectively.[166] While public discourse on such regimes is often divided, a look at them from an access to justice viewpoint indicates that they provide self-funded solutions to most of the access problems identified in connection with this area of law. Some of these features are also present in the various Works Council and other employee representation structures found in some Western European countries, but for the sake of brevity, the description that follows will focus on collective bargaining in Ontario.

Generally speaking, the purpose of collective bargaining is to address the vulnerable position of employees in the employment relationship and their lack of individual bargaining power.[167] In 2007, the Supreme Court of Canada found that collective bargaining was a fundamental right protected by Section 2(d) of the Charter of Rights and Freedoms and held that this right reaffirmed the Charter values of dignity, personal autonomy, equality, and democracy, giving workers the ability to exercise some control over 'a major aspect of their lives.'[168]

---

166 *Labour Relations Act, 1995, supra* note 13; *Canada Labour Code, supra* note 14.

167 See, for example, Chaykowski, 'Vulnerability,' *supra* note 122 at 1.

168 *Health Services and Support – Facilities Subsector Bargaining Assn. v. British Columbia,* [2007] 2 S.C.R. 391 at paras. 40, 82, 85, and 86.

From an access to justice perspective, these regimes first provide opportunities for front-end arrangements to minimize the incidence of employment law problems. They do so by establishing mechanisms for the periodic negotiation of collective agreements, which include terms and conditions tailored to the needs of the specific workplace.[169] Typically, such negotiations include a consideration of problems that have arisen over the life of the previous agreement, as well as proposals for new provisions to resolve those and other problems that the parties anticipate may arise in the future. They also establish wages, benefits, and other employment rights, which are generally (although not always) superior to more static statutory minimums. Many collective agreements create labour–management committees to discuss workplace issues during the term of the agreement as well.

With respect to knowledge of employment law, at least some information about workplace rights is usually disseminated to employees by their unions, and compliance with the collective agreement is monitored by shop stewards or other departmental representatives, who normally receive some form of training in this regard. Enforcement is handled through internal grievance procedures that are aimed at encouraging settlement, coupled with binding arbitration to determine unresolved disputes.[170] Arbitrators are generally selected and paid for by the employer and the union[171] and will often provide mediation services as well. They are also legislatively empowered to apply employment-related statutes in the course of arbitrations with the effect of consolidating different regimes into one forum.[172]

Representation at arbitration is provided to employees by union representatives or lawyers, who are paid for by the union. The result is akin to a form of legal insurance, in that employees pay annual dues to the union, which then provides representation in the justice process should the need arise. The union also provides both advocacy and a protective buffer for vulnerable employees who would otherwise be reluctant to make claims during the term of their employment.

Finally, it is worth noting that least one union has negotiated into its collective agreements an express form of pre-paid legal insurance

---

169 See, for example, *Labour Relations Act, supra* note 13, ss. 16, 59 and 17–36, *Canada Labour Code, supra* note 14, ss.48–50.
170 *Labour Relations Act, supra* note 13, ss. 48–50, and *Canada Labour Code, supra* note 14, ss.57–66.
171 *Ibid.* Arbitrators are also appointed in some circumstances.
172 *Ibid.*

that provides employees with legal advice and representation in matters beyond the workplace, including family law, criminal law, and real estate transactions.[173]

Of course, this highly simplified and abbreviated description does not take into account the full complexity of collective bargaining regimes or their broader social, economic, and regulatory implications. Even in access to justice terms, a host of other issues are at play, including the delays and judicialization that have come to characterize many arbitration processes and the fact that unions have carriage of grievances rather than employees. Nevertheless, the point of this brief canvas is not to consider the merits of collective bargaining more generally or to examine its operation in any detail. Rather, it is to provide a glimpse of these regimes through an access to justice lens, and to note those features that are relevant to the current project.

Appendix: Organizations and Individuals Consulted

Jas Basra, DAS Insurance Canada
Arleen Huggins, Partner, Koskie Minsky LLP
Lisa Loader, Staff Lawyer, Community Legal Clinic - Simcoe, Haliburton, Kawartha Lakes
Katherine Laird, Executive Director, Human Rights Legal Support Centre
Professor Brian Langille, Faculty of Law, University of Toronto
Michele Leering, Community Advocacy and Legal Centre
Daniel Lublin, Partner, Whitten & Lublin LLP
Julie Matthews, Community Legal Education Ontario
Natalie McDonald, Partner, Grossman, Grossman & Gale LLP
David Mossop, Community Legal Assistance Society, B.C.
Murray Murphy, Law Society, Prince Edward Island
Elaine Newman, Newman Arbitrations
Professor Pascoe Pleasence, University College, London
Professor Kerry Rittich, Faculty of Law, University of Toronto
Rebecca Sandefur, American Bar Association
The Honourable Warren K. Winkler, Chief Justice of Ontario
Loreta Zubas, Partner, Zubas & Milne

---

173 Canadian Autoworkers Legal Services Plan, http://www.cawlsp.com/home.htm: see Paul Vayda and Stephen Ginsberg, 'Legal Services Plans: Crucial Time Access to Lawyers and the Case for a Public-Private Partnership,' *supra* this volume.

Middle Income Access to Justice: Policy Options with Respect to Consumer and Debtor/Creditor Law

ANTHONY DUGGAN, AZIM REMANI, AND DENNIS KAO

I. Introduction

Problems involving consumer and debtor/creditor law have consistently been identified as some of the most prevalent legal concerns among the lower and middle income population.[1] Ontarians consistently have difficulty accessing the legal system to address these concerns due to a lack of awareness (1) of their rights with respect to various consumer transactions, and (2) of the mechanisms available to vindicate these rights. Other hurdles include literacy barriers, legal process costs, and a variety of other factors considered below. This paper develops policy options for improving access to the civil justice system for lower and middle income Ontarians seeking to resolve consumer and debtor/ creditor disputes. The discussion addresses issues under four general headings in consumer protection and debtor/creditor law that were

---

1 For the reasons explained in Michael Trebilcock, Anthony Duggan, and Lorne Sossin, 'Introduction,' *supra* this volume, this volume as a whole is concerned particularly with improving access to justice for middle income earners. This paper has the same focus, as its title indicates, although much of the discussion is relevant to lower income earners as well. Common consumer problems include those involving repairs, large purchases, service provision, product safety, and insurance claims; common debt problems include those related to disputes over bills, collecting money owed, collection agencies, unfair refusal of credit, and bankruptcy: Ab Currie, *The Legal Problems of Everyday Life: The Nature, Extent, and Consequences of Justiciable Problems Experienced by Canadians* (Ottawa: Department of Justice Canada, 2007), http:// justice-canada.net/eng/pi/rs/rep-rap/2007/rr07_la1-rr07_aj1/rr07_la1.pdf. For the purposes of this paper, middle income Ontarians are defined as those whose household income is too high for them to qualify for Legal Aid certificates, but too low for them to be able to afford to hire lawyers to represent them in civil law matters.

raised during stakeholder consultations: consumer protection legislation enforcement and consumer education; consumer credit and bankruptcy, consumer proposals, and credit counselling; alternative dispute resolution mechanisms for consumers; and consumer redress within the traditional court system. Parts II through V of this paper present the findings from consultations with various stakeholders and a broader literature review.[2] The paper concludes with policy options for increasing access to justice with respect to consumer and debtor/creditor law.

II. Consumer Protection Legislation Enforcement and Consumer Education

A. Stakeholder Consultations

Ontario's Consumer Protection Act[3] (CPA) has provisions relating to unfair practices, general consumer rights, consumer rights in certain agreements (e.g., time shares, Internet agreements, direct agreements), credit agreements (including credit cards), and leasing. Ontario's Ministry of Consumer Services (MCS) also regulates many other areas of a more sectoral character, including payday loan companies, motor vehicle dealers, real estate, and the travel industry. Some of these responsibilities have been delegated to various administrative authorities.[4]

In 2009 the ten most common complaints made to the MCS involved the following:

1 collection agencies/debt collectors (4,764)
2 home repairs/renovations (2,468)
3 motor vehicle purchases/sales (1,710)
4 appliances (1,134)
5 credit reporting (1,127)
6 home furnishings (1,109)

---

2 Consultations were made in the form of a focus group and follow-up discussions with various stakeholders (see Appendix for a listing of all organizations and individuals consulted). The literature review sections of this paper are based on surveys of the academic literature as well as such informational sources as government websites.
3 *Consumer Protection Act*, S.O. 2002, c.30, Sch. A [*CPA*], ServiceOntario e-Laws, http://www.e-laws.gov.on.ca/html/statutes/english/elaws_statutes_02c30_e.htm.
4 See http://www.sse.gov.on.ca/mcs/en/Pages/Consumer_Protection_Legislation.aspx and http://www.sse.gov.on.ca/mcs/en/Pages/Delegated_Administrative_Authorities.aspx.

7 motor vehicle repairs (1,098)
8 health and fitness clubs (1,094)
9 energy brokers (1,044)
10 telephone/long distance (939)[5]

No business is legally obligated to rectify consumer complaints made to Ontario's Consumer Protection Bureau[6] (CPB). However, under the CPA, businesses that opt not to resolve complaints made to the CPB are liable to be placed on the publicly available 'Consumer Beware List.' Before a consumer can file a complaint with the CPB, she must have tried to resolve the dispute with the business involved in the complaint. If the consumer is not satisfied after discussion with the business, she may submit a formal complaint to the CPB. The CPB will mediate between the consumer and the business and attempt to reach a mutually acceptable resolution. If this is not possible, the consumer may be advised to consult with legal counsel. The CPB usually attempts to mediate disputes within its jurisdiction; however, various factors – such as the amount in dispute[7] and the vulnerability of the complaining consumer – may affect a decision by the CPB to mediate.[8] Many of the businesses against which complaints are filed do not utilize e-mail or facsimile technology, so the CPB must communicate with them through traditional mail service; this can cause delays that make resolutions more difficult to reach. Telephone mediation is not common, as a more formal process is required to comply with the provisions governing the Consumer Beware List and the possibility of a future investigation or prosecution of the business involved in

---

5 Ontario, Ministry of Consumer Services, *Top 10 Consumer Complaints (2009)*, Top 10 Complaints Archive, http://www.sse.gov.on.ca/mcs/en/Pages/Top_Ten_Complaints.aspx. Some of these categories of complaints do not necessarily fall within the MCS's purview: complaints pertaining to motor vehicle sales/purchases and repairs are properly directed to the Ontario Motor Vehicle Industry Council; complaints regarding energy brokers are properly directed to the Ontario Energy Board; and complaints regarding telephone/long distance providers are properly directed to the Commissioner for Complaints for Telecommunications Services. Typically, complaints received by the MCS in these areas will be redirected to the proper authority.
6 The Consumer Protection Bureau is operated by the Consumer Protection Branch of MCS.
7 The CPB will not usually mediate disputes over small amounts, although it may do so in cases where several small complaints have been made against a single business.
8 There are twelve staff at the ministry whose principal responsibility is mediation of consumer complaints.

the dispute. Between 1 January 2009 and 30 July 2010, the CPB recovered approximately $846,000 through its mediation efforts. Other, less quantifiable resolutions that are considered successes for consumers are the termination of calls from creditors; the removal of incorrect information from credit files; and the proper delivery of goods or services.

Consumer credit complaints under the *Consumer Reporting Act*[9] (*CRA*) are also considered by the CPB. Typically, such complaints are associated with data errors, bankruptcies that have not been removed from consumers' credit files,[10] and debts whose legitimacy is disputed. With respect to this last category of cases, the issue of a debt's legitimacy is often difficult to address once the debt has been passed to a collection agency because this is not the agency's concern. Two other concerns relate to the *CRA*'s requirement that consumer reporting agencies adopt procedures to ensure the accuracy and fairness of its reports[11] and that they investigate consumer complaints of inaccurate or incomplete information within a reasonable time.[12] More specifically, it is unclear what constitutes fair information or a reasonable time within which credit reporting agencies ought to complete a consumer complaint investigation. Contraventions of the *CRA* are referred to the Registrar of Consumer Reporting Agencies for review and follow-up.

Similarly, the CPB is responsible for Part VII of the *CPA*, 'Credit Agreements,' although few complaints are made under this part. Some stakeholders speculated that this may be in part due to the difficulty that consumers experience in navigating the *CPA*.

Another common problem in consumer credit law pertains to credit charge-backs. A credit charge-back occurs when funds are credited back to a consumer's account after an allegation of, for example, fraud or defective goods or services received. Often consumers do not realize

---

9 *Consumer Reporting Act*, R.S.O. 1990, c. C33 [*CRA*]. The *CRA* outlines what information a consumer reporting agency can report and how the information can be used; it also protects consumers from the use of outdated or inaccurate information. See Ontario, Ministry of Consumer Services, *More Information on the Credit Reporting Act*, http://www.sse.gov.on.ca/mcs/en/Pages/Personal_Finance_Credit_Reporting_Act.aspx.

10 The *CRA* prohibits consumer report agencies from reporting 'information as to the bankruptcy of the consumer after seven years from the date of the discharge except where the consumer has been bankrupt more than once.' See *ibid.* at s.9(3)(e).

11 *Ibid.* at s.9(1).

12 *Ibid.* at s.13(1).

that they may request a charge-back until after the prescribed period for such a request has expired, generally around 120 days. Contrast this with the federal consumer protection regime in the United States, where there is a statutory right to charge-backs. In Canada, charge-backs are a matter of banks' accommodating credit card holders based on contractual agreements between banks and credit card companies, rather than agreements between banks and card holders; that is, charge-back provisions are found in contracts between banks and credit card companies, not in contracts between banks and card holders.

Consumer protection concerns are often best addressed by educating consumers on their rights and obligations before they enter into transactions, but it is unclear whether this goal is being met. The MCS website contains a variety of consumer education materials, including a listing of consumer rights by subject,[13] a Consumer Protection Survival Guide, and a searchable version of the Consumer Beware List. These materials are in plain English[14] and are intended to promote dispute avoidance by educating consumers *ex ante* on their rights with respect to specific transactions. There are three concerns regarding the accessibility of these materials: (1) the channels through which consumers may become aware that these materials even exist; (2) accessibility limitations related to Internet access; and (3) literacy barriers that may prevent some consumers from accessing the materials at all.

First, consumers generally do not contemplate the risks associated with a given transaction until those risks have materialized in a dispute; this is a social perspective that ought to be accounted for in consumer protection initiatives. Consumers tend to view transactions more as commodities than as agreements with attached legal rights and obligations. Even where transactions have a more obviously legal element to them (e.g., loan signings), consumers rarely read the relevant documentation that explains, for example, complaint resolution mechanisms. It is unclear how the MCS promotes its website so as to encourage consumers to educate themselves on transactions before commencing them.

---

13 See the *What Are My Rights?* menu at Ontario, Ministry of Consumer Services, *Consumer Protection, Consumer Education, Consumer Information*, http://www.sse.gov. on.ca/mcs/en/pages/default.aspx. Subject headings include 'Auto Repair Warranties,' 'Big Ticket Items,' and 'Door-to-Door Sales.'

14 Some materials are available in other languages, such as Italian, Korean, and Punjabi.

Second, citizens who do not have access to an Internet connection cannot access the MCS's website. Further, of the citizens who do have Internet access, many utilize a relatively slow, dial-up connection. Slower Internet connections restrict the online content that users may view within a reasonable time or at all.

Third, some consumers may not possess the basic literacy or language skills to read plain English materials, though these materials are certainly more consumer-friendly than standard credit agreements or legislation such as the *CPA*. Moreover, any individual's comprehension level can be reduced by the stress that is often associated with transactions such as loan signings or defaults.

These accessibility limitations may be overcome in part by live presentations, which the MCS offers. In the past four or five years, the MCS has delivered approximately seven hundred presentations to businesses; and in the past year or so, it has delivered approximately two hundred presentations on consumers' rights to groups such as newcomers to Canada. The MCS sometimes attempts to educate businesses on consumers' rights as a part of its complaints mediation process. Businesses that want to be responsible commercial citizens and consumers who are the target of education efforts are two groups with little in common and whose needs therefore must be considered separately. It might be useful to create brochures that include information on various consumer transactions from across ministries and to distribute these brochures to businesses when they are starting up. Targeting consumers is more difficult because effective access points are more difficult to identify; for example, the MCS has printed information calendars but is unsure of where to distribute them.[15] It might be useful to identify consumers according to their life stages and to target specific groups with information that is likely to prove pertinent to their consumer habits. For example, the Ministry of Education is in the midst of developing a financial literacy high school curriculum.

B. Literature Review

(1) CONSUMER EDUCATION

There appears to be a lack of consumer education in Canada. For exam-

---

15 The calendars contain such information as how to identify fraudulent currency, how to protect oneself from identity theft, and consumer rights generally and is available in a variety of languages on MCS's website: *Smart Consumer Calendar 2010*, http://www.sse.gov.on.ca/mcs/en/Pages/Smart_Consumer_Calendar.aspx.

ple, the newly rebranded Consumer Protection BC found that only 1 per cent of respondents in B.C.'s 2009 Public Awareness Survey, when unprompted, would go to this organization for help if they had a consumer protection problem.[16] The Ontario Motor Vehicle Industry Council (OMVIC), which is responsible for maintaining a fair, safe, and informed marketplace in the motor vehicle dealer industry, found that only 17 per cent of Ontarians were aware of OMVIC in 2009.[17] These organizations have taken measures to increase consumer awareness and knowledge. For example, Consumer Protection BC's advertising and rebranding efforts, combined with B.C.'s efforts in formal education, are useful first steps towards enhancing consumer education in that province. OMVIC has undertaken a consumer awareness project that targets schools and media and that is building partnerships with key stakeholders.[18] A recently released report by the federal government's Task Force on Financial Literacy deals with the learning issue in some depth in the context of consumer financial transactions; it recommends, among other things, the appointment of a Financial Literacy Leader to coordinate national learning strategies; the formation of an advisory council on financial literacy; and the development of a range of educational initiatives aimed at improving consumers' financial skills and knowledge.[19]

The experiences of other jurisdictions offer insights into several possible initiatives. In 2009, the OECD Committee on Consumer Policy produced a report titled *Promoting Consumer Education: Trends, Policies, and Good Practices*.[20] The report includes detailed accounts of initiatives in over a dozen countries and breaks down consumer education strategies into three useful categories: (1) formal education, (2) lifelong learning, and (3) targeted education. Formal education refers to learning through

---

16 Consumer Protection BC, *2009 Annual Report* (2010) at 10.

17 OMVIC, *2009 Annual Report* (2010) at 20. Tarion, Ontario's new home warranty protection program, suffers from a similar problem. Tarion, *2007 Annual Report* (2008) at 11 (15 per cent of Ontarians were aware of Tarion in 2007).

18 OMVIC, *ibid.* at 5–8, 19–20. The industry-funded Commissioner for Complaints for Telecommunications Services (CCTS) has also sought to increase consumer awareness. CCTS, *2008–2009 Annual Report* (2009) at 3; CCTS, 'Developing Public Awareness' (2009).

19 Task Force on Financial Literacy, *Canadians and Their Money: Building a Brighter Financial Future* (December 2010), Financial Literacy in Canada, http://www.financialliteracyincanada.com.

20 OECD, *Promoting Consumer Education* (2009) [OECD, *Consumer Education*], http://www.oecd.org/document/47/0,3343,en_2649_34267_42279215_1_1_1_1,00.html. Thanks to Professor Iain Ramsay of University of Kent Law School for this source and others.

a program of instruction in an educational institution or adult training centre or in the workplace, and is generally recognized by a qualification or a certificate.[21] Most countries integrate consumer education into related subject areas in primary and secondary education. Common topics include consumer rights and obligations, personal finance, and social issues.[22] According to the OECD study, European experience suggests that consumer education is 'little used' in the classrooms, even though more than 50 per cent of school curricula include it and even though it 'has more influence in second and third level studies, included in one or more subjects or as horizontal subject matter.'[23]

Lifelong learning covers all purposeful learning activity 'from the cradle to the grave' that aims to improve the knowledge and competencies of all individuals who participate in learning activities.[24] Some countries have adopted this strategy in their legislative or strategic frameworks, and many other countries have pursued this approach on a *de facto* basis.[25] These programs tend to focus on (1) developing understanding of basic education needs for different age groups; (2) exploring how education can be structured to build knowledge cumulatively, over time; and (3) providing for adults who have not benefited from previous education opportunities.[26] Targeted education, the most common approach to consumer education among the countries included in the OECD study, targets specific needs, with the focus on particular consumer groups or issues.[27] Popular issues include fraud and scams, misleading practices or confusing information, financial literacy, and identity theft.[28] The focus here is often on vulnerable groups, such as young children, the elderly, persons with mental, chronic, or debilitating illnesses, ethnic minorities and immigrants, rural residents, the unemployed, tourists, and temporary residents.[29]

---

21 *Ibid.* at 11.
22 *Ibid.* at 14. Some countries use teaching methods built around everyday life and the interests of students. *Ibid.* at 16–17. Also important are programs designed to supplement the school curriculum, for example, an educational game that provides students with information on Danish law on the sale of goods. *Ibid.* at 15–16, 183.
23 *Ibid.* at 18. See also common challenges with consumer education in schools generally. *Ibid.* at 184.
24 *Ibid.* at 11.
25 Japan, Korea, and Hungary have lifelong strategies. *De facto* programs exist in Spain and elsewhere. *Ibid.* at 22–4, 131.
26 *Ibid.* at 183.
27 *Ibid.* at 182.
28 *Ibid.* at 29, 184–5.
29 For examples, see *ibid.* at 27–8.

Many countries have engaged in campaigns to educate consumers about specific market-related issues using publications, television, websites, conferences, courses, and seminars. Materials used in campaigns 'need to be easily understood and accessible if the campaigns are to be successful.'[30] The U.S. government has recognized this issue in the context of its overall online communication strategy and is attempting to improve the design and navigability of its websites.[31] In Canada, the Office of Consumer Affairs has created the Canadian Consumer Information Gateway, an ambitious early attempt at a consumer education clearinghouse.[32] Unfortunately, the website appears to be in need of a major renovation.[33]

The following challenges and recommendations are highlighted by the OECD report:[34]

- *Objectives.* In most countries, consumer education strategies are not well defined; rather, countries often develop initiatives in an *ad hoc* manner to address specific problems.
- *Approach.* The report favours adapting principles from all three 'categories' (lifelong learning, formal education for schoolchildren, and targeted education for emerging problems and vulnerable consumers).
- *Communication.* The report finds that it is not clear 'to what extent consumers are aware of the wealth of material that is available [on

---

30 *Ibid.* at 185. Examples: the U.S. government's campaign to educate consumers about identity theft, centred on a website as its one-stop national resource; and Turkey's use of a popular live TV program focusing on consumer issues, including a call-in feature.

31 The Federal Web Managers Council was created to cure this problem: 'Many agencies focus more on technology and website infrastructure than improving content and service delivery.' Federal Web Managers Council, *Putting Citizens First: Transforming Online Government* (November 2008) at 1.

32 It involved a partnership of over four hundred entities. http://consumerinformation.ca/app/oca/ccig/html.do?page=aboutUs&language=eng.

33 See, for example, their alleged 'Consumer Challenge of the Week' for the week of 17 October 2010, discussing Organic Food Labelling: Canadian Consumer Information Gateway, http://consumerinformation.ca/app/oca/ccig/consumerChallengeOfTheWeek.do?language=eng. The links on the Web page to other Government of Canada websites do not work. In addition, it appears to have more links than content. For example, most if not all of the tools and calculators link to other websites. See, for example, 'Tools & Calculators,' http://consumerinformation.ca/app/oca/ccig/search.do;jsessionid=0001mvHMkR98a0joa6Je2g6NH1E:N0NVMRVB9?language=eng&currentPage=tools&topic=CAT15.TOPICS.ROOT.

34 OECD, *Consumer Education, supra* note 20, at 188–9.

the Internet].' It suggests that more work be done to find effective ways to link consumer-related information, noting that the clearing-houses some countries have developed are a good first step.[35]

- *Cooperation and coordination.* There is significant national coordination and cooperation but a lack of *cross-border* cooperation and coordination.[36]
- *Lack of self-motivation.* Educational institutions, educators, and the educated are not always sufficiently motivated to find consumer education opportunities and information.

(2) FEDERAL CONSUMER PROTECTION LAWS

Overview. The interaction between federal and provincial consumer protection legislation and oversight reflects the division of powers in the *Constitution Act, 1867* and case law on the relationship between the relevant federal powers (e.g., trade and commerce, banking, criminal law) and the relevant provincial powers (property and civil rights).[37] Most provinces have a core consumer protection statute (e.g., Ontario's *Consumer Protection Act*) and a host of industry-specific statutes.[38] The federal landscape is less centralized. Major statutes include the *Food and Drugs Act,* the *Weights and Measures Act,* the *Consumer Packaging and Labelling Act,* the *Hazardous Products Act,* and the *Motor Vehi-*

---

35 See, for example, the OECD's International Gateway for Financial Education, http://www.financial-education.org. The OECD's concern about public awareness is well founded. The U.S.-based Quantcast, which measures U.S. Web traffic, ranks the U.S. government's OnGuardOnline website 35,620 (approx. 45,900 visitors per month): Quantcast, http://www.quantcast.com/onguardonline.gov. By comparison, Quantcast ranks *The Consumerist* blog 2,602 in total U.S. Web traffic with approximately 748,000 U.S. visitors per month.

36 See, for example, the OECD's International Network on Financial Education (INFE), created to help promote awareness of the importance of financial education worldwide: *OECD Project on Financial Education and Its International Network on Financial Education* (2009).

37 See, for example, *Constitution Act, 1867* (UK), 30 & 31 Vict., c.3, ss.91(2), 92(13); Jacob Ziegel, 'Canadian Consumer Law and Policies Forty Years Later: A Mixed Report Card' (2011) 50 Can Bus LJ 259 at Part II. See also *Prebushewski v. Dodge City Auto (1984) Ltd,* [2005] 1 SCR 649 at paras. 34–5. The relative weakness of the trade and commerce power has led some courts to rely on the criminal law power, including for the *Hazardous Products Act,* R.S.C. 1985, c.H-3, and *Food and Drugs Act,* R.S.C. 1985, c. F-27. See *Reference re Firearms Act,* [2000] 1 SCR 783 at para. 29.

38 For a non-exhaustive list, see http://www.sse.gov.on.ca/mcs/en/Pages/Consumer_Protection_Legislation.aspx.

cle Safety Act.[39] The former Department of Corporate and Consumer Affairs became part of Industry Canada in 1995. Industry Canada has the statutory mandate to 'promote the interests and protection of Canadian consumers.'[40] Although this responsibility is not limited to Industry Canada, Industry Canada's Office of Consumer Affairs (OCA) is entrusted with the general protection of consumers.

Office of Consumer Affairs. The OCA is a relatively small unit of Industry Canada and appears more focused on information gathering, research promotion, and coordination.[41] To accomplish this, the OCA partners with consumer organizations, the OECD, standards organizations, and other Canadian government agencies and ministries (via the Consumer Measures Committee (CMC)). It produces or co-produces several online consumer resources, including the *Consumer Handbook* and the Canadian Consumer Information Gateway.[42] It also offers several policy resources, including periodic Consumer Trends reports on marketplace developments, a database of consumer policy publications, and a Consumer Research Post e-Bulletin (i.e., a newsletter).[43]

Competition Bureau. The federal Competition Bureau, an independent agency within Industry Canada, plays an important role in consumer protection. Its primary aim is to ensure that Canadians benefit from a competitive marketplace that promotes innovation and competitive prices. The Bureau operates under the assumption that competition is

---

39 Most of these statutes were enacted in the 1960s and 1970s. See Ziegel, *supra* note 37 at Part I.
40 *Department of Industry Act*, S.C. 1995, c.1, s.5(i).
41 See Ziegel, *supra* note 37 at Part I and the OCA's description of itself at http://www.ic.gc.ca/eic/site/oca-bc.nsf/eng/ca00038.html. The OCA has an annual budget of around $6 million and only twenty-two full-time employees.
42 The OCA has a significant amount of content on its own website as well, but some of it is outdated. For example, its cellphone plan guide is four years old: http://www.ic.gc.ca/eic/site/oca-bc.nsf/vwapj/Guide_english_final.pdf/$FILE/Guide_english_final.pdf.
43 For example, the most recent Consumer Trends publication was in Winter 2010 on mobile commerce: Office of Consumer Affairs, Industry Canada, *Mobile Commerce – New Experiences, Emerging Consumer Issues* (Winter 2010), Industry Canada, http://www.ic.gc.ca/eic/site/oca-bc.nsf/vwapj/Mobile_Commerce_mobile-eng.pdf/$FILE/Mobile_Commerce_mobile-eng.pdf. Many of the consumer policy publications in its database were funded by the OCA and written by consumer organizations or academics.

good for both business and consumers. It investigates 'anti-competitive practices,' including various unfair or deceptive business practices such as false or misleading representations, deceptive marketing, and price fixing.[44]

Financial Consumer Agency of Canada. The Financial Consumer Agency of Canada (FCAC) was established in 2001[45] and given the general mandate of 'working to protect and inform consumers of financial services.'[46] Its core functions are (1) educating consumers about financial products and services; (2) building financial literacy skills in consumers so that they can use information on financial products and services; and (3) ensuring that federally regulated financial institutions comply with relevant consumer legislation by providing requisite disclosure.[47] As with the OCA and the Competition Bureau, its website provides a substantial amount of information as well as links to other relevant provincial and federal entities. Notably, its website is reasonably clean and effective and has some useful and easy-to-use calculators for consumers.

Other relevant federal bodies. The three organizations just described are the primary federal offices responsible for consumer protection, but many other federal ministries and offices play an important role. For instance, Transport Canada is responsible for motor vehicle safety, and Health Canada (with the Canadian Food Inspection Agency) is responsible for product safety.[48] The Canada Mortgage and Housing Corporation, a national housing agency, assists lower income Canadians

---

44 'Competition Bureau – Our Legislation,' http://www.competitionbureau.gc.ca/eic/site/cb-bc.nsf/eng/h_00148.html. More specifically, these issues are legislated for in the *Competition Act*, R.S.C. 1985, c. C-34; *Consumer Packaging and Labelling Act*, R.S.C. 1985, c. C-38; *Textile Labelling Act*, R.S.C. 1985, c. T-10: 'What Is the Competition Bureau?', http://www.competitionbureau.gc.ca/eic/site/cb-bc.nsf/eng/h_00125.html.
45 Established by the *Financial Consumer Agency of Canada Act*, S.C. 2001, c.9.
46 The FCAC's specific mandate is laid out in *ibid.* at ss.3(2)–(3).
47 Financial Consumer Agency of Canada, 'Helping Canadians Make Informed Financial Decisions,' http://www.fcac-acfc.gc.ca/eng/publications/HelpingConsumers/FCAC_Brochure-eng.pdf. See further, Anthony Duggan and Iain Ramsay, 'Front-End Strategies for Improving Consumer Access to Justice,' *supra* this volume.
48 On motor vehicle safety: Transport Canada, Road Safety and Motor Vehicle Regulation, 'Guidelines on Enforcement and Compliance Policy,' http://www.tc.gc.ca/eng/roadsafety/tp-tp12957-menu-173.htm. On product safety, Health Canada, 'Consumer Product Safety,' http://www.hc-sc.gc.ca/cps-spc/index-eng.php.

in finding affordable housing and provides mortgage loans to home buyers.[49] Measurement Canada is responsible for 'ensuring the integrity and accuracy of measurement in the Canadian marketplace.'[50]

Federal–provincial interaction. The provinces and the federal government interact formally on consumer affairs through the Consumer Measures Committee.[51] The CMC occasionally sets up working groups to study consumer issues, presumably with the aim of enacting legislation across Canadian jurisdictions or developing non-legislative solutions.[52] The committee also produces the *Canadian Consumer Handbook*, which lists federal, provincial, and territorial consumer affairs offices and consumer groups and also directs consumers who are looking for information on particular consumer protection topics to the appropriate authority.[53] Based on the information listed in the handbook,[54] there are overlapping responsibilities in several areas, including the following: unfair or deceptive business practices (the Competition Bureau and provincial consumer affairs offices);[55] products and services (mostly provincially regulated, but Health Canada and the Canadian Food Inspection Agency are responsible for product safety); and financial services (the FCAC regulates consumer aspects of federally regulated financial institutions, whereas provincial regulators, such as the Financial Services Commission of Ontario, regulate provincially regulated financial institutions).[56]

---

49 Canada Mortgage and Housing Corporation, *Annual Report 2009* (2010) at 1.
50 Measurement Canada, at Industry Canada, http://www.ic.gc.ca/eic/site/mc-mc.nsf/eng/home. It is responsible for the *Weights and Measures Act* and other measurement-related legislation.
51 Consumer Measures Committee, 'About the CMC,' http://cmcweb.ca/eic/site/cmc-cmc.nsf/eng/h_fe00013.html.
52 Consumer Measures Committee, 'CMC Working Groups,' http://cmcweb.ca/eic/site/cmc-cmc.nsf/eng/h_fe00016.html.
53 Consumer Measures Committee, *Canadian Consumer Handbook*, http://www.consumerhandbook.ca.
54 See the categories in the sidebar.
55 See, for example, Ontario, *CPA*, *supra* note 3, ss.14–19.
56 An interesting case working its way through the court system suggests that some financial services provided by a federally regulated institution may be provincially regulated (in this case, credit cards). *Marcotte c. Banque de Montréal*, 2009 QCCS 2764, 11 June 2009, Gascon J., as cited in Ziegel, 'Canadian Consumer Law and Policies,' *supra* note 37.

III. Bankruptcy, Consumer Proposals, and Credit Counselling

A. Bankruptcy and Consumer Proposals

(1) STAKEHOLDER CONSULTATIONS

Bankruptcies in Canada are governed by the Bankruptcy and Insolvency Act.[57] They are overseen by the Office of the Superintendent of Bankruptcy Canada (OSB) and are conducted through private trustees, who are responsible for disposing of debtors' assets and distributing payments to creditors. In Canada, 116,381 consumers filed for bankruptcy in 2009;[58] 46,521 of these bankruptcies originated in Ontario.[59] The result of bankruptcy proceedings is a discharge that relieves individuals of their outstanding debts[60] – a process that is typically completed about nine months after the filing date.[61] In Ontario, trustees are entitled to recover approximately $1,800 from debtors' estates before any payments are made to creditors.[62] Debtors who cannot afford this charge, or who make other arrangements for payment, may be denied access to the bankruptcy system. As an alternative to bankruptcy, debtors may file a consumer proposal, which is an agreement made between a debtor and her creditors regarding repayment obligations.[63] The con-

---

57 R.S.C. 1985, c. B-3
58 Canada, Office of the Superintendent of Bankruptcy, *Statistics in Canada – 2009 (Table 2: Insolvencies Filed by Consumers)*, Industry Canada, http://www.ic.gc.ca/eic/site/bsf-osb.nsf/eng/br02347.html [IC, *Bankruptcy Statistics 2009*]. This figure represents a 28.4 per cent increase from the 90,610 bankruptcies filed in Canada in 2008.
59 *Ibid.* This figure represents a 28.5 per cent increase from the 36,200 bankruptcies filed in Ontario in 2008.
60 There are some exceptions to this relief; for example, student loans are not forgiven in cases of bankruptcy unless the bankruptcy is filed at least seven years after the debtor ceased being a part- or full-time student. See Office of the Superintendent of Bankruptcy, *Student Loans and Bankruptcy*, Industry Canada, http://www.ic.gc.ca/eic/site/bsf-osb.nsf/eng/br02057.html.
61 The process may be longer for filers with higher incomes or larger income tax accounts due.
62 See *Bankruptcy and Insolvency General Rules*, CRC c. 368, s.128, Department of Justice, http://laws.justice.gc.ca/en/C.R.C.-c.368/FullText.html [DOJ, *Bankruptcy Rules*], which sets out the fees a trustee make recover from a bankrupt's estate in a summary administration.
63 In 2009, 35,331 consumer proposals were filed in Canada (a 40.3 per cent increase over the number of proposals filed in 2008), 20,414 of which originated in Ontario (a 43.3 per cent increase over the number of proposals filed in 2008). See IC, *Bankruptcy Statistics 2009, supra* note 588.

sumer proposal process is typically more expensive than a bankruptcy filing,[64] and its failure rate is approximately 39 per cent.[65]

(2) LITERATURE REVIEW

The 2002 *Final Report* of the Personal Insolvency Task Force (PITF) found that 'the Canadian insolvency system was basically sound and in need of incremental, rather than fundamental reform.' [66] But it also noted that 'no systematic program of research was designed and implemented' in making this finding.[67] Except for considering a streamlined bankruptcy process for indigent debtors – a process that was ultimately abandoned as impractical – the PITF did not directly address concerns surrounding the accessibility of Canada's bankruptcy system.[68]

A 2007 paper by Professors Stephanie Ben-Ishai and Saul Schwartz discusses bankruptcy among poor debtors and makes recommendations to improve the accessibility of Canada's bankruptcy scheme for this population.[69] The paper includes findings from interviews with bankruptcy trustees, who reported that clients who could not afford to pay their bankruptcy fees were, in the words of one trustee, 'people who live a marginal existence, on social assistance, living in government-subsidized housing and with no prospects for changing this around.'[70] Ben-Ishai and Schwartz report that poor debtors need access

---

64 See DOJ, *Bankruptcy Rules, supra* note 622, , s.129, which sets the fee for consumer proposals at $1,500, plus 20 per cent of the moneys distributed to creditors, in addition to counselling, filing, and registrars' fees and provincial and federal sales taxes for goods and services.

65 Anthony Duggan, 'Consumer Bankruptcy in Canada and Australia: A Comparative Overview' [2006] *Annual Review of Insolvency Law* 857 at 881 [Duggan, 'Comparative Bankruptcy'].

66 Personal Insolvency Task Force, *Final Report* (Ottawa: Industry Canada, 2002) at 7–8 [*PITF Report*].

67 *Ibid.* at 11.

68 *Ibid.*

69 Stephanie Ben-Ishai and Saul Schwartz, 'Bankruptcy for the Poor?' (2007) 45 Osgoode Hall LJ 471 at 473 [Ben-Ishai and Schwartz, 'Bankruptcy for the Poor']. Ben-Ishai and Schwartz define 'poor debtors' as 'debtors seeking bankruptcy who cannot pay the fees associated with filing and who seem unlikely to attain anything but a low income for the foreseeable future.' This group is differentiated from so-called no-income, no-asset (NINA) debtors who have no non-exempt assets (assets that are required to be liquidated in bankruptcy filings) or surplus income to be paid into their bankruptcy estates. An estimated 70 to 80 per cent of bankruptcies in Canada are filed by NINA debtors, but most of these debtors are able to pay normal trustee fees.

70 *Ibid.* at 473.

to the bankruptcy system for two reasons. First, although many poor debtors may be judgment-proof, calls from credit collectors may still disrupt their lives. Second, despite the assumption that lower income groups do not qualify for enough credit for them to become overindebted, enough lower income families have some type of debt to suggest that poor debtors may require access to the bankruptcy system.[71]

Trustees' own reports notwithstanding, there is no way to determine how many debtors either do not approach a bankruptcy trustee or are turned away because they cannot afford trustees' fees. Trustees surveyed by Ben-Ishai and Schwartz reported that fee flexibility is common[72] but not universal; thus, poor debtors' geographic locations may affect how readily they can access the bankruptcy system.

The Office of the Superintendent of Bankruptcy administers the Bankruptcy Assistance Program (BAP), which is supported by trustees who volunteer to be placed on the program's roster. The program assigns trustees to administer the files of debtors who have been turned away from at least two trustees because the debtors cannot afford normal trustee fees.[73] There is no fixed fee for BAP files, though the median trustee fee in the set of BAP cases analysed by Ben-Ishai and Schwartz was $1,594.[74] BAP is infrequently used; only about 1 per cent of cases

---

71 *Ibid.* at 475–6. For example, one of four families in the lowest income decile (less than $12,500 annually) has credit card debt. It is also noted that families in the lowest income decile are the most likely to hold student loans, which cannot be discharged by a bankruptcy filing. Thus, it might make financial sense for members of the lowest income decile to file for bankruptcy to eliminate their other financial obligations and focus repayment efforts on their student loans.

72 *Ibid.* at 479–80. For example, in 1994, Halifax-area trustees agreed as a group that they would act for debtors filing for bankruptcy who could not afford standard fees; as of September 2006, debtors who could not afford standard trustee fees were being asked to pay a reduced fee of $250. As of September 2006, a similar agreement existed among trustees in Edmonton, where debtors who cannot afford standard trustee fees are asked to pay a reduced fee of $450, an amount equivalent to trustees' out-of-pocket expenses in these cases.

73 *Ibid.* at 480. For a complete listing of eligibility criteria for the BAP, see Canada, Service Canada, *Bankruptcy Assistance Program*, http://www.servicecanada.gc.ca/eng/goc/bankruptcy_assistance.shtml.

74 *Ibid.* at 481. Ben-Ishai and Schwartz analysed all summary administration bankruptcies for which a Statement of Receipts and Disbursements (SRD) was submitted electronically in 2006 (29,279 bankruptcies). SRDs include all of the receipts and disbursements arising from a given consumer bankruptcy, including trustee fees, voluntary payments by debtors, and dividends paid to creditors: *ibid.* at 512. Bankruptcies involving assets whose realizable value does not exceed $1,000, after

analysed by Ben-Ishai and Schwartz (304 of 29,279)[75] had been administered under the program.[76]

In the United States, there is statutory provision for persons filing for bankruptcy to have certain costs waived;[77] there is no corresponding provision in Canada. Opponents of such an allowance assert that no-cost bankruptcy proceedings would decrease the total fees collected by the bankruptcy system, require screening mechanisms for illegitimate waiver applications, and encourage unnecessary and improper bankruptcy filings.[78] A 1994 pilot project in six judicial districts studied the effect of waiving the $175 filing fee for individual Chapter 7[79] debtors; it concluded that 11 per cent of successful fee waiver applicants would not have filed for bankruptcy without the waiver, but that only a 'small fraction' of the filing increases observed during the period could be attributed to the pilot project.[80] Thus, the fee waiver program may have increased access to the bankruptcy system for poorer debtors.[81] Further support for a fee waiver program may be found in two empirical studies of Canadian bankruptcies; these suggest that a majority of filings in the country are made by people who cannot, rather than will not, pay their debts.[82] Interviews of trustees conducted by Ben-Ishai and Schwartz suggest that trustees are intermediaries who can restrict access to the bankruptcy system by debtors seeking to abuse it. A report

---

secured creditors' claims are deducted, are eligible for streamlined summary administration procedures. Most bankruptcies filed by poor debtors are summary cases: Ben-Ishai and Schwartz, 'Bankruptcy for the Poor,' *supra* note 69 at 512.

75 *Ibid.* at 480. Ben-Ishai and Schwartz also noted that in regions where agreements exist among trustees for providing access to the bankruptcy system to poor debtors, trustees will sometimes administer bankruptcies themselves rather than refer clients to the BAP. Thus, a more accurate measure of the number of poor debtors filing for bankruptcy might be the number of cases with receipts less than $500. In Ben-Ishai and Schwartz's set of non-BAP bankruptcies, 1,056 (3.5 per cent) of files had receipts of less than $500.

76 Jacob Ziegel has commented similarly that the BAP program is in practice used very little: see Ziegel, 'Indigent Debtors and Financial Accessibility of Consumer Insolvency Regimes' [2004] Ann Rev Insolvency L 499 at 501 [Ziegel, 'Indigent Debtors'].

77 Ben-Ishai and Schwartz, 'Bankruptcy for the Poor,' *supra* note 69 at 486–7.

78 *Ibid.*

79 *Bankruptcy*, 11 USC §§ 701–84. Chapter 7 of the USC governs liquidations, the most common form of bankruptcy in the United States. See Ben-Ishai and Schwartz, 'Bankruptcy for the Poor,' *supra* note 69 at 486, note 58.

80 *Ibid.* at 488.

81 *Ibid.*

82 *Ibid.* at 484.

from a subcommittee of the PITF submitted that, given Canada's current employment of private trustees in bankruptcy proceedings, a shift toward a public trustee office would be 'politically infeasible.'[83] As well, in contrast to the American administrative process, the Canadian bankruptcy system includes a judicial discharge process that permits opposition to discharge in cases of abusive filings.[84] Another barrier that American debtors face in filing for bankruptcy is the attorneys' fees associated with the processes; such fees range approximately from US\$500 to \$2,000.[85]

In Australia, overindebted individuals may file for bankruptcy under section 55 of the *Bankruptcy Act* 1966 (Cth) or Part X of the *Bankruptcy Act*. A majority of bankruptcy filings in Australia proceed through the Official Trustee, and where the debtor has no funds in her estate, no payment is made to the Official Trustee.[86] Part X proceedings involve lawyers and are more complex and expensive; proceedings under s.55 are, for the poorest debtors, effectively funded by the public purse. Bankruptcies under s.55 are typically discharged after three years. This asymmetry may create a bankruptcy system that gives preference – in the form of earlier discharges – to debtors wealthy enough to file under Part X.

B. Credit Counselling

(1) STAKEHOLDER CONSULTATIONS

Credit counselling is a financial management and literacy program for debtors that includes repayment plan negotiations with creditors. Repayment plans developed in credit counselling programs typically entail 100 per cent principal repayment over three to five years. Credit counselling organizations also engage in efforts to prevent overindebtedness. Fees for credit counselling are not public, although they may be up to \$100 per month; these fees may be waived for clients who cannot afford them. Despite the possibility of such fee waivers, some stakeholders expressed concern that credit counselling, like bankruptcy filings and consumer proposals, is not a financially viable solution for poor debtors.

Debtors who complete a consumer proposal and debtors who complete a credit counselling program receive the same credit rating, despite

---

83 *Ibid.* at 502
84 *Ibid.* at 485.
85 Ziegel, 'Indigent Debtors,' *supra* note 76 at 506.
86 Ben-Ishai and Schwartz, 'Bankruptcy for the Poor,' *supra* note 69 at 490.

the fact that consumer proposals typically only require approximately 30 per cent of debts to be repaid.[87] This seems unfair, given findings from studies which suggest that credit counselling graduates may have subsequent credit histories up to 30 per cent better than the general population. Approximately 200,000 Canadian debtors completed a credit counselling program in 2009; and while the repeat rate for bankruptcy generally is approximately 10 per cent of files, less than 1 per cent of debtors who complete a credit counselling program file for bankruptcy. Although any debtor may contact a credit counselling agency to discuss program options, credit counselling is only *mandatory* after a debtor has filed for bankruptcy. This fact may be related to a broader problem, which is that consumers are unaware of their options for dealing with overindebtedness and of the implications of filing for bankruptcy.

Some stakeholders argue that consumers should receive a free copy of their credit report annually from each of Canada's two major credit bureaux;[88] this would provide them with ongoing knowledge of their credit files and their credit usage patterns. It is possible that the gross income-to-debt ratio used by creditors to determine consumers' creditworthiness is outdated; a net-income-to-debt ratio might provide a more realistic or prudent indication of how much credit any given consumer can manage. Finally, despite the increasing prevalence of consumer debt problems, there is no publicly funded debt advice agency in Ontario or Canada to assist consumers. Such an office might be helpful, particularly in developing prophylactic approaches to the problem of overindebtedness.

(2) LITERATURE REVIEW

Bankrupts in Canada are currently required to complete two credit counselling sessions as a part of the larger filing process.[89] This credit counselling program has been criticized as too brief to provide effective financial education; moreover, it increases the cost of filing for bankruptcy.[90] Mandatory counselling as a part of the bankruptcy filing process also presupposes that bankruptcies are a result of financial mismanage-

---

87 A similar concern was noted in the *PITF Report*, supra note 66 at 47, and in Insolvency and Trustee Service Australia, *Report on the Review of Debt Agreements Under Part IX of the Bankruptcy Act 1966* (2006) at ¶48. Both of these are reported in Comparative Bankruptcy, *supra* note 65 at 880.

88 Equifax and Transunion.

89 Duggan, 'Comparative Bankruptcy,' *supra* note 65 at 888.

90 *Ibid.* at 889–90. Credit counselling fees are $85 per individual session or $25 per group session: DOJ, *Bankruptcy Rules, supra* note 622, s.131.

ment, though empirical evidence suggests that many bankruptcies are actually caused by events outside of debtors' control, such as family disruption and unemployment.[91] Studies to date have suggested that mandatory credit counselling has had little influence on debtor behaviour.[92]

Iain Ramsay has drawn a distinction between bankruptcy regimes in which most of the work is done by professionals and those in which public agencies play a significant role.[93] According to Ramsay, public and publicly funded agencies typically have no financial incentive to promote bankruptcy over other alternatives to overindebtedness because such agencies' compensation, in contrast to that of private trustees, does not depend on commencing bankruptcy proceedings.[94] In England and Wales, publicly funded debt advice agencies play a major role in the countries' bankruptcy regimes – a fact that might explain why informal debt arrangements appear to be used more often in those jurisdictions than in Canada.[95] In 2004, there were 50,597 formal bankruptcies and an estimated 72,500 debt agreement plans in England and Wales; in the same year, there were 109,928 formal bankruptcies and an estimated 8,000 debt management plans in Canada, excluding Quebec.[96]

IV. Alternative Dispute Resolution Mechanisms for Consumers

A. Stakeholder Consultations[97]

(1) OMBUDSMAN FOR BANKING SERVICES AND INVESTMENTS

Consumers may submit banking services and investment disputes to the Ombudsman for Banking Services and Investments (OBSI) for

---

91 Saul Schwartz, *Counselling the Overindebted: A Comparative Perspective* (report prepared for the Office of the Superintendent of Bankruptcy, December 2005) at 3–4.

92 Saul Schwartz, 'The Effect of Bankruptcy Counselling on Future Creditworthiness: Evidence from a Natural Experiment' (2003) 77 Am Bankr L Rev 257.

93 Iain Ramsay, 'Functionalism and Political Economy in the Comparative Study of Consumer Insolvency: An Unfinished Story from England and Wales' (2006) 7 Theor Inq L 625 at 666 [Ramsay, 'Consumer Insolvency'], as discussed in Duggan, 'Comparative Bankruptcy,' *supra* note 65 at 893.

94 Ramsay, 'Consumer Insolvency,' *supra* note 93 at 664.

95 Duggan, 'Comparative Bankruptcy,' *supra* note 65 at 893.

96 Ramsay, 'Consumer Insolvency,' *supra* note 93 at 650–1.

97 This section's discussion of alternative dispute resolution mechanisms in Ontario is not intended to be exhaustive, but rather to provide a brief overview of some such mechanisms available in the province.

resolution, although this office is intended to operate as a forum of last resort. From one perspective, the OBSI's resolution success rate is almost 100 per cent: only one of the office's recommendations has been refused in its fourteen years of operation. However, the OBSI currently has a complaint backlog of approximately five months. The OBSI's complaint-handling structure for banking services complaints is more mature than its system for investment complaints,[98] and the banking industry has fewer participants than the investment industry, which makes cooperation between the former industry and the OBSI easier.

In 2007, the OBSI implemented a more rigorous triage program to uncover complaints with no merit as well as meritorious claims in which the involved firm was amenable to a resolution. The purpose was to enable a focus on complaints most in need of investigative resources. Consumers often bring complaints to the OBSI without first attempting to resolve them with the business against which they are filing. Approximately one in every ten complaints submitted to the OBSI becomes a full case file; the remainder are referred back to the business in question. This may indicate that consumers are simply not educated on the appropriate procedures for resolving various complaints. Few of the complaints referred back to businesses ever reach the OBSI again. Until recently, the OBSI did follow up on these complaints. It found generally that they had been resolved. Recent capacity constraints, however, have made this follow-up impossible.[99] Consumers learn of the OBSI's existence from their provincial legislators, their friends and neighbours, Yellow or Blue Page directories, government websites, and Internet searches. The MCS website, however, does not provide a link to the OBSI's website; this is because the OBSI is viewed as a last resort for dispute resolution rather than as a resource that consumers ought to be readily directed to access. Anecdotally, many complaints received by the OBSI are submitted by newcomers to Canada and by elderly consumers.

Two factors facilitate the OBSI's successful operation: (1) the banking and investment industry is comprised of few members, which makes

---

98 Examples of complaints from banking services consumers include allegations of debit and credit card fraud; examples of complaints from the office's investment-side operations include those involving alleged provision of unsuitable investment advice. The OBSI began handling banking services complaints in 1996 but did not commence its investment-side operations until 2002.

99 For example, complaint volume increased by approximately 200 per cent between 2007 and 2009.

interactions among them and the OBSI relatively simple (e.g., decisions by the OBSI may be anticipated by industry members); and (2) the OBSI has more flexibility in dispute resolution processes than, for example, a statutory regime would allow. One challenge the OBSI faces is consumer complaints that focus on a fundamental injustice in the relationship between debtors and creditors. Such complaints sometimes cannot be satisfied by the restitution recommendations that the OBSI is authorized to make – for example, some consumers want the firm complained about to be punished.

(2) LICENCE APPEAL TRIBUNAL

Ontario's Licence Appeal Tribunal (LAT) is a consolidated appeal body charged with claims and licensing appeals under twenty-two statutes.[100] Claims appeals involve complaints by specific consumers, whereas licensing appeals, such as licence revocations and suspensions, may or may not involve consumers. For example, a regulator may propose not to renew a registrant's licence based on consumer complaints made against the registrant or on its general failure to meet compliance requirements. The LAT's discretion with respect to remedies is governed by each of the statutes under which it has jurisdiction. Although the LAT is another access point for consumer complaints, it is an expensive process; to illustrate, complainants must take time off work to appear and must also pay for representation if they desire it.

(3) TARION WARRANTY CORPORATION

Tarion Warranty Corporation, Ontario's warranty program for new homes, is an example of a consumer redress system that employs alternative dispute resolution mechanisms. Tarion has implemented customer service policies and standards for the residential construction industry in Ontario, based on extensive research with consumers and

---

100 Among the statutes under the LAT's jurisdiction are the *Collection Agencies Act*, R.S.O. 1990, c. C-14; *CPA, supra* note 3; and the *CRA, supra* note 9. For a complete listing of the statutes within the LAT's jurisdiction, see Ontario, Licence Appeal Tribunal, *Annual Report 2008–2009* (Ontario: Licence Appeal Tribunal, 2009) at 4, http://www.lat.gov.on.ca/english/news/pdf/LATAnnualReport2008-2009English.pdf. Effective 1 January 2010, the *Motor Vehicle Dealers Act* has been replaced by the *Motor Vehicle Dealers Act, 2002*, S.O. 2002, c.30, Sch. B, though some cases under the old statute are still being processed. Since the annual report's drafting, the *Payday Loans Act, 2008*, S.O. 2008, c.9 has also come under the LAT's jurisdiction.

ongoing consultation with the Ontario Home Builders' Association.[101] New home warranty protection is provided for two years by builders and for five years after by Tarion.[102] There is a tension, however, between the integrity of the program and its total claim funding pool – one severe defect in a large, multiple-dwelling structure could exhaust the fund.

B. Literature Review

(1) CANADIAN MOTOR VEHICLE ARBITRATION PLAN

The Canadian Motor Vehicle Arbitration Plan (CAMVAP) is a cross-Canada arbitration program for complaints about recently purchased new cars. It is funded by vehicle manufacturers based on their market share and past CAMVAP experience. It is composed of fifteen members with voting rights: two manufacturers' associations, a dealer's association, the Consumers' Association of Canada, and provincial and territorial governments.[103] It handled 285 cases in 2009 (92 per cent of which went to arbitration), representing about 0.019 per cent of potentially eligible vehicles. Most cases were from Ontario, Alberta, and Quebec. CAMVAP acknowledges in its Annual Report that '[a]wareness of the program remains an issue' but suggests that CAMVAP is working because manufacturers are using notice of a CAMVAP case in their customer satisfaction processes.[104]

According to the Annual Report, manufacturers are not involved in selecting arbitrators to the CAMVAP roster. When a case is to go to arbitration, the Provincial Administrator selects three names from the roster in the consumer's home community and the consumer selects one to conduct the hearing.[105] It is not clear how much information a consumer has on shortlisted arbitrators. Most parties in arbitration hearings are self-represented, despite the fact that cases have become more complex over the years.[106] CAMVAP is mostly able to hold hearings near the con-

---

101 Tarion Warranty Corporation, *Warranty Service*, http://www.tarion.com/Warranty-Protection/Statutory-Warranty/Pages/default.aspx.
102 Tarion Warranty Corporation, *Protecting Statutory Warranty Rights*, http://www.tarion.com/Warranty-Protection/Statutory-Warranty/Pages/Protecting-Statutory-Warranty-Rights.aspx.
103 CAMVAP, *2009 Annual Report* (2010) at 11.
104 *Ibid.* at 5.
105 *Ibid.* at 11–12. The Administrators are generally the Better Business Bureaux.
106 In 2009, consistent with past years, 89 per cent of manufacturers appeared alone

sumer's home community, and lists more than 450 locations where it held hearings in 2009.[107] In 2009, consumers were 'successful' in 62 per cent of the 263 arbitrated cases.[108] Success is based on whether the manufacturer was found to be liable – that is, whether the consumer won an award. Three remedies are available to the consumer: buyback by the manufacturer, repair cost/reimbursement, or out-of-pocket allowances up to $500.

(2) ONTARIO MOTOR VEHICLE INDUSTRY COUNCIL

The Ontario Motor Vehicle Industry Council (OMVIC) enforces the *Motor Vehicle Dealers Act*, which registers motor vehicle dealers and salespeople in Ontario. It is an industry-run body that handles, *inter alia*, complaints between consumers and dealers.[109] In this area, its strategy is to provide a 'no-cost service for consumers and dealers as an alternative to litigation whenever possible.'[110]

Complaints can be submitted by phone or online. Customers are generally encouraged to settle disputes directly with the dealer. A complaint file typically takes a few days to resolve, but some more complex files can take months. The most common complaints relate to liquidated damages, misrepresentation, vehicle condition, contract disputes, and Safety Standards Certificates. In 2009, OMVIC's compliance team handled 1,562 disputes.[111] The complaint process appears to be more informal than CAMVAP's, and OMVIC cannot force the dealer to settle. However, it states that in 'many instances, OMVIC's involvement often results in a settlement without the purchaser having to bring the dealer to court.'[112] Consumers may appeal OMVIC's handling of their complaint to the Appeals Committee of OMVIC's Board of Directors.[113]

---

and 58 per cent of consumers appeared alone (31 per cent appeared with a family member). Case completion now takes on average 70.54 days for single-hearing cases and 81.6 days for multiple-hearing cases. *Ibid.* at 8–10.

107 *Ibid.* at 8–10.

108 *Ibid.* at 6. This excludes the twenty-two cases settled prior to hearing or prior to the arbitrator making an award. According to this Annual Report, these results are consistent with the past several years.

109 OMVIC, 'More on OMVIC,' http://www.omvic.on.ca/omvic/who_we_are/who_we_are_more_info.htm.

110 OMVIC, *2009 Annual Report* (2010) at 9.

111 *Ibid.* at 16–17.

112 OMVIC, OMVIC Complaints Process Acknowledgement Form, http://www.omvic.on.ca/pdf/Complaints%20Process%20Acknowledgement.pdf.

113 OMVIC, *2009 Annual Report, supra* note 110 at 17, 22. Note that the Appeals Com-

The committee 'may suggest further lines of inquiry, but cannot direct further action be taken.'[114]

(3) COMMISSIONER FOR COMPLAINTS FOR TELECOMMUNICATIONS SERVICES

The Commissioner for Complaints for Telecommunications Services (CCTS) is designed 'to resolve consumer and small business complaints about retail telecommunications services, including wireless, local and long distance telephone, and internet access services.'[115] It is a private, not-for-profit corporation funded by the telecom industry, as required by the CRTC. Its first commissioner was appointed in August 2008. It appears to have support from some telecommunications service providers (TSPs), and some appear to be cooperative in ensuring that consumers are aware that they can make complaints to the CCTS.[116] In 2008–9, most complaints related to billing issues, contract disputes, or service delivery.[117]

In the initial phase of its complaints process, the CCTS effectively gives TSPs twenty business days to handle consumer complaints.[118] If the TSP reports that the complaint is unresolved, the CCTS will strive to mediate the dispute. Complaints that feature challenging or complex issues are generally investigated first, but the complaint may be dismissed at any point if the CCTS finds that the TSP has 'taken reasonable steps to resolve the complaint, even if this resolution is not acceptable

---

mittee consists of five directors: four representing dealers and one consumer representative, who is a representative appointed by the Minister of Consumer Services.

114 *Ibid.* at 17.

115 CCTS Brochure, http://www.ccts-cprst.ca/wp-content/uploads/2010/01/eBrochure-en.pdf. Several government agencies regulate certain aspects of the telecommunications industry, which chip away at the commissioner's overall mandate (e.g., false or misleading advertising, pricing of services, privacy violations, telemarketing or unsolicited messages). CCTS, 'Mandate,' http://www.ccts-cprst.ca/en/complaints/mandate. Note that the CRTC is currently undertaking a review of the CCTS; CRTC, 'Review of the Commissioner for Complaints for Telecommunications Services: 8665-C12-201007229,' http://www.crtc.gc.ca/PartVII/eng/2010/8665/c12_201007229.htm.

116 For example, under Rogers's 'Contact Us' page, CCTS is listed under the 'Making a Complaint' section. Rogers, 'Contact Us,' https://www.rogers.com/web/content/contactus.

117 CCTS, *2008–2009 Annual Report* (2009) at 19.

118 *Ibid.* at 6. The CCTS forwards all complaints in its scope to TSPs for resolution. TSPs are 'asked' to report back to the CCTS on the complaints' status within twenty business days.

to the consumer.'[119] Upon completing an investigation, the CCTS may make a written recommendation for resolution, which may be rejected by either the customer or the TSP. It can force the TSP to take, or refrain from taking, an action; to make an apology; or to pay monetary compensation up to $5,000. Finally, the commissioner will make a final decision based on reasons for the recommendation and, if available, the customer's or the TSP's reasons for rejecting it. The TSP cannot reject the decision. The customer is entitled to reject the decision without sacrificing the usual legal rights and remedies. If the customer accepts the decision, it becomes binding on the TSP.[120] Most complaints are resolved before investigation. In 2008–9, the CCTS issued only forty-eight recommendations and made six final decisions.[121]

(4) ASSESSMENT

Michael Trebilcock has suggested that most consumers with legal grievances have small-scale complaints that might best be handled outside the traditional court system, in order to avoid the costs, delays, stress, and general unpleasantness associated with structured adversarial processes.[122] Dispute resolution mechanisms outside the court system may range from company-level and industry-wide dispute resolution processes to private-sector and governmental agencies with broader mandates, such as consumer protection bureaux and Better Business Bureaux.[123] Trebilcock notes that in addition to resolving complaints, these dispute resolution fora ought to publish a record of complaints received and their outcomes. Such records would enhance the operation of reputational markets and might illuminate complaint trends that suggest areas where preventive regulatory change might be effected.[124]

A 1999 British study found that 'courts and ombudsmen play a mini-

---

119 For example, TSP acted reasonably in fulfilling its obligations under its contract or made a reasonable settlement offer.
120 *Ibid.* at 6–7.
121 *Ibid.* at 14–15. In 2008–9, the CCTS opened 3,214 complaints, resolved 1,968 complaints before investigation, and resolved or closed 748 in investigation. Note that the numbers may not add up because files may not have been completed when the report was compiled.
122 Michael J. Trebilcock, 'Rethinking Consumer Protection Policy' in *International Perspectives on Consumers' Access to Justice*, ed. Charles E.F. Rickett and Thomas G.W. Telfer (Cambridge: Cambridge University Press, 2003) 68 at 85.
123 *Ibid.* at 86.
124 *Ibid.*

mal role in the resolution of consumer disputes';[125] in 40 per cent of the cases observed in this study, consumers did not appear to take further action if two-party attempts to resolve the complaint failed. Thus, effective complaint resolution mechanisms at the company level might be important for consumers.[126] With respect to complaints made even at this level, however, members of the lowest income groups might lack the social attributes associated with socio-economic position – for example, confidence – and therefore be underrepresented among complainants.[127]

Industry-wide dispute resolution schemes such as specialist tribunals and ombudsman offices employ decision makers who are familiar with the industries in which they operate. These decision makers do not require as much background information on cases as non-specialized judges – a fact that tends to make tribunal and ombudsman office hearings comparatively shorter and cheaper.[128] Furthermore, such industry-specific schemes can often promote dispute avoidance more effectively than courts as industry participants come to anticipate case outcomes. To operate effectively, however, tribunals and ombudsman offices must avoid, and be seen to avoid, industry capture or bias.[129] There is also a possibility that industry dispute resolution schemes may be anti-competitive in that their rules might discourage new market entrants or innovation.[130] Finally, it may be more costly to run multiple industry-specific dispute resolution schemes than to run one Small Claims Court system.[131]

Mediation of consumer disputes via consumer agencies such as consumer protection bureaux can facilitate mutually acceptable resolutions between consumers and businesses, in contrast to adjudicative resolution processes that impose decisions on consumers and businesses.[132] A concern associated with this sort of mediation, however, is the tension

---

125 Iain Ramsay, 'Consumer Redress and Access to Justice' in *ibid.* 17 at 28–9 [Ramsay, 'Consumer Redress'].
126 *Ibid.* at 28.
127 *Ibid.*
128 Anthony J. Duggan, 'Consumer Access to Justice in Common Law Countries: A Survey of the Issues from a Law and Economics Perspective' in Rickett and Telfer, *supra* note 122 , 46 at 62 [Duggan, 'Consumer Access to Justice'].
129 *Ibid.*
130 *Ibid.*
131 *Ibid.*
132 *Ibid.* at 60.

between the consumer protection bureau's consumer advocacy and mediation functions; it may be difficult for mediators to perform either of these functions adequately without losing credibility in the eyes of consumers or businesses, or both.[133]

V. Consumer Redress within the Traditional Court System

A. Small Claims Court[134]

(1) STAKEHOLDER CONSULTATIONS

Concerns associated with the current Small Claims Court system include problems serving linguistic minorities and unrepresented litigants. First, parties who require a language interpreter must pay for the service themselves;[135] this additional cost may serve as a barrier to parties' initiating or defending an action in Small Claims Court. More generally, Small Claims Court documents and forms are often too complex even for litigants who do have English proficiency. Second, unrepresented litigants may cause delays in the system if court processes must be explained to them. These litigants may also not understand relevant substantive law and consequently fail to raise arguments that would be obvious to trained counsel. Duty counsel are not always on hand at Small Claims Court locations to assist unrepresented litigants; and small claims judges, as impartial adjudicators, are limited in the assistance they can offer unrepresented litigants without giving rise to an apprehension of bias. At the same time, it has been suggested anecdotally that approximately one-third of parties to small claims actions appear with paralegal representation and that this representation may slow down proceedings as well. A possible reform to address these concerns might be a movement toward a small claims system that more resembles the Australian model, in which adjudicators take on a more inquisitorial role in eliciting information from parties and in which legal representation for parties is banned.

Other concerns regarding the current Small Claims Court system

---

133 *Ibid.* at 61.
134 This section should be read in conjunction with Shelley McGill, 'Challenges in Small Claims Court System Design: Does One Size Fit All?', *supra* this volume.
135 Parties do not have to fund their own English, French, or visual interpretation. See Ontario, Ministry of the Attorney General, *Before Making a Claim in Small Claims Court*, http://www.attorneygeneral.jus.gov.on.ca/english/courts/scc/b4aClaim. asp [MAG, *Small Claims Fees*].

relate to the issuance of default judgments,[136] the short time for deliberations before reasons are delivered, and court fees. Presently, a default judgment may be issued against a defendant without any guarantee that she even understands the claim she has been served with. These concerns are exacerbated by the fact that default judgments may be for amounts up to $25,000 and are difficult to reverse. Regarding reasons for judgment, Small Claims Court decisions are currently given on the same day that the matter is heard. While this procedure may be expeditious, giving judges more time to prepare their reasons might allow them to more thoroughly address parties' arguments; this may be crucial in providing the assessment of their arguments that consumers expect from the court system and that is integral to their sense that justice has been served. Finally, potential plaintiffs with meritorious claims might not be able to afford the fees associated with commencing small claims actions. For example, it costs $75 to file a Small Claims Court claim and $100 to fix a trial date for it.[137]

(2) LITERATURE REVIEW

Small Claims Courts seek to reduce the costs of citizens' access to the justice system by relaxing the rules and procedures associated with the traditional court system.[138] The extent to which Small Claims Courts differ from traditional courts varies across jurisdictions. Ontario's small claims regime can be contrasted with some Australian models where there is a greater divergence from traditional court procedures in favour of less formal dispute resolution mechanisms.[139] Some particularly striking features present in the small claims regimes of various Australian states include fora where consumers but not traders may bring claims; legal representation is banned; there are no rights of appeal; and referees, rather than being bound by rules of evidence, may inform themselves in any manner they see fit.[140]

In Quebec's Small Claims Court system, 'lawyers are barred, corporations may not use the process, judges play an activist role, and the

---

136 A default judgment is a judgment in favour of the plaintiff after the defendant fails to respond to a summons or appear before a court as required.

137 MAG, *Small Claims Fees, supra* note 135.

138 Duggan, 'Consumer Access to Justice,' *supra* note 128 at 58.

139 *Ibid.*

140 *Ibid.* at 58–9. Similar characteristics for a small claims court system were proposed for England and Wales in U.K., Consumer Council, *Justice Out of Reach – A Case for Small Claims Courts* (London: HMSO, 1970).

court provides advice and assistance for the lay litigant.'[141] Despite this progressive model, however, a study of a Small Claims Court in Montreal found that the court continues to be used by well-educated, wealthier males who are running unincorporated businesses and who are making claims for goods and services not paid for by consumers, rather than by consumers making claims for defective products and services.[142] Thus, it is possible that attempts to broaden access to the Small Claims Court system have simply increased access to the system for groups who already use it.[143] Similar findings with regard to the demographic characteristics of claimants as were made in the Montreal study were reached in a study of the English Small Claims Court system, where it was noted that ordinary people are more likely to appear as defendants.[144]

A study of Small Claims Courts in the United States found that there was often a disconnect between what litigants wanted from the legal system and what it actually provided – for example, litigants often misunderstood the court's power to punish opposing parties and often found that their hopes of telling their stories were in conflict with the court's need for efficient claims processing.[145] The authors of the study concluded that 'the law often defines the problems of ordinary people in a manner that may have little meaning for them and that does not offer them the remedies they desire.'[146]

Shelley McGill, who is a Deputy Judge of the Ontario Small Claims Court, has discussed the system's internal developments and relevant external developments. Internally, 'multiple conflicting goals and poorly defined priorities have led to the adoption of counter-productive strategies and an unclear mission for the small claims court.'[147] She

---

141 Ramsay, 'Consumer Redress,' *supra* note 125 at 36.
142 S.C. McGuire and R.A. MacDonald, 'Small Claims Court Cant' (1996) 34 Osgoode Hall LJ 509, discussed in Ramsay, 'Consumer Redress,' *supra* note 125 at 36–7.
143 Ramsay, 'Consumer Redress,' *ibid.* at 37.
144 John Baldwin, *Small Claims in the County Courts in England and Wales: The Bargain Basement of Civil Justice?* (Oxford: Clarendon Press, 1997), discussed in Ramsay, 'Consumer Redress,' *ibid.* at 36.
145 John M. Conley and William M. O'Barr, *Rules versus Relationships: The Ethnography of Legal Discourse* (Chicago: University of Chicago Press, 1990), discussed in Ramsay, 'Consumer Redress,' *ibid.* at 37.
146 *Ibid.*
147 Shelley McGill, 'Who Should Protect the Consumer? The Eroding Role of the Small Claims Court' (working paper prepared for the 40th Annual Workshop on Commercial and Consumer Law, October 2010) at Part I, summarizing Shelley McGill,

observes that Small Claims Courts often strive to address far too many objectives and interests, including the interests of a wide variety of disputants and stakeholders; access-related objectives such as lowering costs and reducing formality, complexity, and delay; and judicial objectives of fairness, finality, and compliance. She suggests that attempting to meet all of these expectations is unrealistic, and she recommends that Small Claims Courts each develop their own clear mandate and objectives and openly make choices of 'priority and proportionality.'[148]

She also argues that the Small Claims Court is still the most widely and easily accessible forum for most consumer disputes, despite several significant developments that have reduced the impact of Small Claims Courts on consumer protection, including consumer class actions, consumer arbitration clauses, the use of debt collection and counselling agencies in post-judgment processes, and the availability of debt consolidation and consumer proposals under the *Bankruptcy and Insolvency Act*. She advances eight recommendations for reforming small claims courts to complement these developments, including the following:[149]

- Preserve right to individual action in Small Claims Court even in the face of a pre-dispute consumer arbitration agreement.
- Promote modest collective management of similar cases in Small Claims Court.
- Allow the court to control the behaviour of external collection agencies.

B. Class Actions

Class actions may improve access to the civil justice system for low to middle income Ontarians by allowing consumer claims that could not be pursued individually to be brought before a court in aggregate. However, there is little information available on the effectiveness of

---

'Small Claims Court Identity Crisis: A Review of Recent Reform Measures' (2010) 49 Can Bus LJ 213 ['Small Claims Identity Crisis']. See also Shelley McGill, 'Challenges in Small Claims Court Design: Does One Size Fit All?,' *supra* this volume.

148 McGill, 'Small Claims Court Identity Crisis,' *ibid.* at 250–1.

149 McGill, 'Who Should Protect the Consumer,' *supra* note 146 at Part V (Concluding Recommendations). She also refers to the recent Ontario Civil Legal Needs report, concluding that 'access to justice is no longer a one size fits all approach; different strategies must be employed to meet the wide variety of civil legal needs.' *Ibid.* at Part V. See also Ontario Civil Legal Needs, *Listening to Ontarians* (May 2010).

class actions in improving access to the civil justice system. The Canadian Bar Association (CBA) maintains a repository of class actions filed, but submission to it is voluntary and anecdotal evidence suggests that many parties to class actions do not include information about their claims on the website. Data are not available to indicate the number of class actions in Ontario that are commenced, certified, or settled outside of court, nor is information available on how many members of class actions receive settlement notices or cheques. Also, with respect to class actions that are settled outside of court, data are frequently not available to indicate the value of settlements or what percentages of these sums are ultimately available for distribution to consumers after legal fees are paid.

A study conducted by Jasminka Kalajdzic at the University of Toronto on class actions within thirteen law offices found that fewer than 25 per cent of the 332 class actions considered were client-initiated.[150] Smaller claims may thus be excluded from the class action system because counsel will naturally be drawn to cases involving either larger classes or larger claims per class member.[151] Further, only approximately 10 per cent of actions considered were 'consumer' cases, a category 'involving criminal interest, fees and currency exchange rates.'[152]

Some stakeholders argued that plaintiffs' and defendants' counsel ought to be required to report the rate at which their clients are successful in bringing or defending class actions. It was also suggested that literacy issues should be considered by judges who approve claim notices: complex language should not serve as a barrier to consumers' claiming their awards. A further concern is the increasing trend toward paying smaller per-member claims in aggregate to a charitable cause – a *cy près* order – to avoid the high administrative costs associated with administering such awards individually; this trend may be deterring consumers from bringing actions that involve relatively small claims per each class member. Finally, it was suggested that perhaps government agencies should proactively bring class actions against defendants as a method of regulation that encourages responsibility and reform on the part of defendants. With respect to this last suggestion,

---

150 Jasminka Kalajdzic, *Access to Justice for the Masses?: A Critical Analysis of Class Actions in Ontario* (LLM Thesis, University of Toronto Faculty of Law, 2009) [unpublished].
151 *Ibid.*
152 *Ibid.*

the study noted above found that little information is available about the extent to which class actions benefit from government investigation to unearth causes of action and evidence to support them.[153]

VI. Policy Options

The following policy options are based on the foregoing stakeholder consultations and literature review:

1 *Increase consumer education.* Consumer education initiatives can address a number of the problems identified above, ranging from consumers' not being aware of their substantive rights to their not being aware of how to vindicate them. Particular emphasis should be placed on reaching consumers *before* they commence transactions, with the aim of reducing the prevalence of consumer problems and their associated costs. Education efforts could also promote measures to prevent consumers' overindebtedness and to improve debtors' awareness of their options for coping with financial difficulties.[154]

2 *Develop a centralized consumer protection information access point.* A variety of provincial and federal offices provide consumer protection support online and by other means. Within the parameters of federal and provincial jurisdictions, efforts should be coordinated to develop an as near as possible one-stop, plain-language information access point for consumers.[155]

3 *Consider establishing neighbourhood advice centres based on the U.K. Citizens Advice Bureau model.*[156] A pilot program would be a good way to start, using existing facilities such as local legal aid clinics as the base, and drawing (as the U.K. system does) on volunteer support.

4 *Reduce the costs associated with bankruptcy filings for lower income debtors.* Ways of reducing or eliminating the costs of accessing the bankruptcy system for middle income consumers ought to be explored,

---

153 *Ibid.*
154 See, further, Anthony Duggan and Iain Ramsay, 'Front-End Strategies for Improving Consumer Access to Justice,' *supra* this volume.
155 *Ibid.*
156 See Roger Smith, 'Middle Income Access to Justice: Implications of Proposals for the Reform of Legal Aid in England and Wales,' *supra* this volume.

with an emphasis on solutions that are feasible in conjunction with Canada's current private trustee system.

5 *Explore the possibility of establishing a consumer dispute resolution process outside the court system.* The CPB's current mediation program could be expanded to provide a more publicized and robust means of consumer dispute resolution.

6 *Reform Small Claims Court procedures.* Simplify, shorten, and reduce the number of forms; introduce a graduated value system under which the formality of the proceedings would vary depending on the amount in dispute; streamline the post-judgment enforcement process; modify the loser-pays-costs rule.[157] (As a more radical alternative, consider establishing a consumer claims tribunal along the lines of the Australian model.)

7 *Improve evaluation of the effectiveness of class actions.* It is difficult to propose meaningful reforms in the absence of more detailed information about consumer class actions – in particular, information about the number of actions commenced, how many are certified, settlement rates, and claim take-up rates. Information with respect to these matters should be required for submission to the Canadian Bar Association's class action repository.

Appendix: Organizations and Individuals Consulted

Anthony Duggan, Professor, University of Toronto Faculty of Law (co-chair)
Michael Trebilcock, Professor, University of Toronto Faculty of Law (co-chair)
Barbara Allan, Coordinator, Consumer Services Bureau, Consumer Protection Branch of the Ontario Ministry of Consumer Services
Gordon Baird, Partner, McCarthy Tétrault LLP
Stephanie Ben-Ishai, Associate Professor, Osgoode Hall Law School, York University
Susan Charendoff, Senior Investigator, Banking Services, Ombudsman for Banking Services and Investments, Ontario Ministry of the Attorney-General
Barbara Duckitt, Director, Consumer Protection Branch of the Ontario Ministry of Consumer Services

---

157 For these and other proposals, see Shelley McGill, 'Challenges in Small Claims Court Design: Does One Size Fit All?,' *supra* this volume.

Trevor Farrow, Professor, Osgoode Hall Law School
Elizabeth Herrema, Assistant General Counsel, Royal Bank of Canada
Jeff Hirsh, Law Society of Manitoba
Jasminka Kalajdzic, Assistant Professor, University of Windsor Faculty
     of Law
Vishnu Kangalee, Manager, Consumer Services Bureau, Consumer
     Protection Branch of the Ontario Ministry of Consumer Services
Aubrey LeBlanc, Member of Board of Directors, Consumers Council of
     Canada
Jennifer Leitch, Volunteer, Law Help Ontario
Shelley McGill, Deputy Judge, Ontario Small Claims Court
Justin Malbon, Professor, Faculty of Law, Monash University
Douglas Melville, Ombudsman for Banking Services and Investments
Gina Papageorgiou, Deputy Judge, Ontario Small Claims Court
Iain Ramsay, Professor, Faculty of Law, University of Kent
Henrietta Ross, Executive Director, Canadian Association of Credit
     Counselling Services
Lorne Sossin, Dean, Osgoode Hall Law School
Lynda Tanaka, Chair, Licence Appeal Tribunal
Laura Watts, National Director, Canadian Centre for Elder Law; Staff
     Lawyer, British Columbia Law Institute
Jacob Ziegel, Professor Emeritus, University of Toronto Faculty of Law

Select Bibliography

I. General and Empirical Studies

Access Across America: First Report of the Civil Justice Infrastructure Mapping Project. Chicago: American Bar Foundation, 2011. Draft provided on 5 August 2011 by Rebecca Sandefur.

Alberta Rules of Court Project. *Self-Represented Litigants: Consultation Memorandum 12.18.* Edmonton: Alberta Law Reform Institute, 2005.

Amato, Paul R. 'The Consequences of Divorce for Adults and Children' (2000) 62 J. Marriage Fam. 1269.

American Bar Association. *Legal Needs and Civil Justice: A Survey of Americans.* Chicago: American Bar Association, 1994.

Asia Consulting Group Limited and Policy 21 Limited. *Consultancy Study on the Demand for and Supply of Legal and Related Services.* Hong Kong: Department of Justice, 2008.

Balmer, Nigel J. 'Research Methods for Legal Empowerment and Access to Justice.' Paper presented at the symposium 'A Decade of Bottom-up Legal Development Cooperation: A Socio-Legal Perspective on the State of the field,' University of Amsterdam, 7–8 February 2011.

Bass, Julia, W.A. Bogart, and Fredrick Zemans, eds. *Access to Justice for a New Century: The Way Forward.* Toronto: Law Society of Upper Canada / Irwin Law, 2005.

Barendrecht, Maurits, Peter Kamminga, and Jin Ho Verdonschot. 'Priorities for the Justice System: Responding to the Most Urgent Legal Problems of Individuals' (2008) Tilburg University Legal Studies Working Paper No. 002/2008.

BC Legal Services Society. *Civil Hub Research Project: Needs Mapping* by Gayla Reid and John Malcolmson. Vancouver: Legal Services Society, 2007.

British Columbia, Ministry of the Attorney General. *Nanaimo Family Justice Services Centre Implementation Phase Evaluation: Final Report by Focus Consultants*. Victoria: Focus Consultants, 2008.

Buck, Alexy, Nigel Balmer, and Pascoe Pleasence. 'Social Exclusion and Civil Law: Experience of Civil Justice problems among Vulnerable Groups' (2005) 39:3 Soc. Pol'y & Admin 302.

–. 'Do Citizens Know How to Deal with Legal Issues? Some Empirical Insights' (2008) 37:4 Journal of Social Policy 661.

Canadian Forum on Civil Justice. *Alberta Self-Represented Litigants Mapping Project: Final Report* by Mary Stratton. Edmonton: Canadian Forum for Civil Justice, 2007.

Clark, Charles and Emma Corstvet. 'The Lawyer and the Public: An A.A.L.S. Survey' (1938) 47 Yale Law Journal, 1272.

Consortium on Legal Services and the Public. *Report on the Legal Needs of the Low- and Moderate-Income Public*. Chicago: American Bar Association, 1994.

Coumarelos, Christine, Zhigang Wei, and Albert Z. Zhou. *Justice Made to Measure: New South Wales Legal Needs Survey in Disadvantaged Areas*. Sydney: Law and Justice Foundation of New South Wales, 2006.

Curran, Barbara A. *The Legal Needs of the Public: The Final Report of a National Survey*. Chicago: American Bar Association, 1977.

Currie, Ab. 'A National Survey of the Civil Justice Problems of Low and Moderate Income Canadians: Incidence and Patterns' (2006) 13 International Journal of the Legal Profession 217.

–. 'Civil Justice Problems and the Disability and Health Status of Canadians' (2007) 21 J.L. & Soc. Pol'y 31.

–. 'The Legal Problems of Everyday Life' in *Access to Justice*, ed. Rebecca L. Sandefur. Bingley: Emerald, 2009.

–. 'Lives of Trouble: Criminal Offending and the Problems of Everyday Life.' Paper presented at the ILAG conference, Wellington, 1–3 April 2010.

Department of Justice Canada. *The Legal Problems of Everyday Life: The Nature, Extent, and Consequences of Justiciable Problems Experienced by Canadians* by Ab Currie. Ottawa: Department of Justice Canada, 2007.

Dignan, Tony. *Northern Ireland Legal Needs Survey*. Belfast: Northern Ireland Legal Services Commission, 2006.

Ellickson, Robert C. *Order without Law: How Neighbors Settle Disputes*. Cambridge, MA: Harvard University Press, 1991.

Engler, Russell. 'Connecting Self-Representation to Civil Gideon: What Existing Data Reveal about When Counsel Is Most Needed' (2010) 37 Fordham Urb. L.J. 37.

Environics Research Group. *Civil Legal Needs of Lower and Middle-Income Ontarians: Quantitative Research*. Toronto: Environics Research Group, 2009.

Felstiner, William, Richard Abel, and Austin Sarat. 'The Emergence and Transformation of Disputes: Naming, Blaming, Claiming ...' (1981) 15 Law & Soc'y Rev. 631.

Gallant, André. 'The Tax Court's Informal Procedure and Self-Represented Litigants: Problems and Solutions' (2005) 53:2 Can. Tax J. 333.

Galanter, Marc. 'Why the "Haves" Come Out Ahead: Speculation on the Limits of Legal Change' (1974) 9 Law and Society Review 95.

Genn, Hazel. *Paths to Justice: What People Do and Think about Going to Law*. Oxford: Hart, 1999.

Genn, Hazel, and Alan Paterson. *Paths to Justice Scotland: What People in Scotland Do and Think about Going to Law*. Oxford: Hart, 2001.

Ginsberg, Stephen. 'Legal Services Plans in the Year 2020' in *Access to Affordable and Appropriate Law Related Services in 2020*, ed. W.A. Bogart. Toronto: Canadian Bar Association, 1999.

GfK Slovakia. *Legal Needs in Slovakia II*. Bratislava: GfK Slovakia, 2004.

Gramatikov, Martin. 'Multiple Justiciable Problems in Bulgaria' (2008) Tilburg University Legal Studies Working Paper No. 16/2008.

–. *Justiciable Events in Bulgaria*. Sofia: Open Society Institute, 2010.

Greiner, D. James, and Cassandra Wolos Pattanayak. 'What Difference Representation? Offers, Actual Use, and the Need for Randomization' (2011) 121 Yale L.J. [forthcoming].

Hadfield, Gillian K. 'Higher Demand, Lower Supply? A Comparative Assessment of the Legal Resource Landscape for Ordinary Americans' (2010) 37 Fordham Urb. L.J. 129.

Hetherington, E. Mavis, and John Kelly. *For Better or for Worse: Divorce Reconsidered*. New York: W.W. Norton, 2002.

Houseman, Alan W. 'The Future of Legal Aid: A National Perspective' (2007) 10 U.D.C. L. Rev. 35.

Ignite Research. *Report on the 2006 National Survey of Unmet Legal Needs and Access to Services*. Wellington: Legal Services Agency, 2006.

Jacob, Herbert. 'The Elusive Shadow of the Law' (1992) 26 Law & Soc'y Rev. 565.

Johnsen, Jon. 'Studies of Legal Needs and Legal Aid in a Market Context' in *The Transformation of Legal Aid: Comparative and Historical Studies*, ed. Francis Regan *et al*. Oxford: Oxford University Press, 1999. 205.

Kritzer, Herbert M. 'To Lawyer or Not to Lawyer: Is That the Question?' (2008) 5 J. Empirical Legal Stud. 875.

Langan, Anne-Marie. 'Threatening the Balance of the Scales of Justice: Unrepresented Litigants in the Family Courts of Ontario' (2005) 30 Queen's L.J.825.

Landau, Barbara, *et al. Final Report And Recommendations from the Home Court Advantage Summit (November 22–23, 2009).* Toronto: Ontario Bar Association; ADR Institute of Ontario; Ontario Association for Family Mediation, 2009.

Law Commission of Ontario. *Voices from a Broken Family Justice System: Sharing Consultations Results.* Toronto: Law Commission of Ontario, 2010.

Law Foundation of BC. *Civil Legal Needs Research Report* by Carol McEown. Vancouver: Law Foundation of BC, 2009.

Legal Services Corporation. *Documenting the Justice Gap in America: The Current Unmet Civil Legal Needs of Low-Income Americans,* 2nd ed. Washington: Legal Services Corporation, 2007.

–. *Making Legal Rights a Reality.* London: Legal Services Commission, 2006.

Lewis, Philip. 'Unmet Legal Needs' in *Social Needs and Legal Action,* ed. Pauline Morris, Richard White, and Philip Lewis. Oxford: Martin Robertson, 1973.

Linguistic and Rural Access to Justice Project. *Connecting across Language and Distance: Linguistic and Rural Access to Legal Information and Services* by Karen Cohl and George Thomson. Toronto: Law Foundation of Ontario, 2008.

Mamo, Alfred A., Peter G. Jaffe, and Debbie G. Chiodo. *Recapturing and Renewing the Vision of the Family Court.* Toronto: Ministry of the Attorney General (Ontario), 2007.

Marshall, Anna-Maria. 'Idle Rights: Employees' Rights Consciousness and the Construction of Sexual Harassment Policies' (2005) 39 Law & Soc'y Rev. 89.

Mayhew, Leon. 'Institutions of Representation: Civil Justice and the Public' (1975) 9 Law & Soc'y Rev. 389.

McMurtry, R. Roy, *et al. Listening to Ontarians: Report of the Ontario Civil Legal Needs Project.* Toronto: Ontario Civil Legal Needs Project Steering Committee, 2010.

Michelson, Ethan. 'Climbing the Dispute Pagoda: Grievances and Appeals to the Official Justice System in Rural China' (2007) 72 Am. Sociol. Rev. 459.

Michelson, Ethan. *Popular Attitudes towards Dispute Processing in Urban and Rural China.* Oxford: Foundation for Law, Justice, and Society, 2009.

Miller, R.E. and A. Sarat. 'Grievances, Claims, and Disputes: Assessing the Adversary Culture' (1981) 15 Law & Soc'y Rev. 525.

Moorhead, Richard and Peter Hurst. *Improving Access to Justice.* London: Civil Justice Council, 2008.

Mossman, Mary Jane, with Karen Schucher and Claudia Schmeing. 'Comparing and Understanding Legal Aid Priorities: A Paper Prepared for Legal Aid Ontario' (2010) 29 Windsor Rev. Legal Soc. Issues 149.

Mulherin, Geoff, and Christine Counmarelos. 'Access to Justice and Disadvantaged Communities' in *Transforming Lives: Law and Social Process*, ed. Pascoe Pleasence, Alexy Buck, and Nigel Balmer. Norwich: TSO, 2007.

Murayama, Masayuki. 'Experiences of Problems and Disputing Behaviour in Japan' (2007) 14 Meiji Law Journal 1.

Nova Scotia Department of Justice. *Self-Represented Litigants in Nova Scotia: Needs Assessment Study*. Halifax: Department of Justice Court Services, 2004.

Ontario, Ministry of the Attorney General. *Civil Justice Reform Project: Summary of Findings and Recommendations* by Honourable Coulter A. Osborne. Toronto: Ministry of the Attorney General, 2007.

−. *Report of the Legal Aid Review 2008* by Michael Trebilcock. Toronto: Ministry of the Attorney General, 2008.

Pleasence, Pascoe. *Causes of Action: Civil Law and Social Justice*, 2nd ed. London: Legal Services Commission, 2006.

Pleasence, Pascoe, and Nigel Balmer. 'Understanding Advice Seeking Behaviour: Findings from New Zealand and England, Wales' in *Empirical Studies of Judicial Systems*, ed. K. Huang. Taipei: Academia Sinica, 2009.

Pleasence, Pascoe, Nigel J. Balmer, and Alexy Buck. 'The Health Cost of Civil-Law Problems: Further Evidence of Links between Civil-Law Problems and Morbidity, and the Consequential Use of Health Services' (2008) 5 J. Empirical Legal Stud. 351.

Pleasence, Pascoe, Nigel J. Balmer, and Stian Reimers. 'Horses for Courses? People's Characterization of Justiciable Problems and the Use of Lawyers' in *The Future of Legal Services, Emerging Thinking*. London: Legal Service Board, 2010.

Pleasence, Pascoe, *et al.* 'Civil Law Problems and Morbidity' (2004) 58 J. Epidemiology and Community Health 552.

−. *Civil Justice in England and Wales: Report of the 2007 English and Welsh Civil and Social Justice Survey*. London: Legal Services Research Centre, 2008.

Rickett, Charles E.F., and Thomas G.W. Telfer, eds. *International Perspectives on Consumers' Access to Justice*. Cambridge: Cambridge University Press, 2003.

Sandefur, Rebecca L. 'The Importance of Doing Nothing: Everyday Problems and Responses of Inaction' in *Transforming Lives: Law and Social Process*, ed. Pascoe Pleasence, Alexy Buck, and Nigel Balmer. London: TSO, 2007. 112.

−. 'Access to Civil Justice and Race, Class and Gender Inequality' (2008) 34 Annual Review of Sociology 339.

−. 'The Fulcrum Point of Equal Access to Justice: Legal and Non-legal Institutions of Remedy' (2009) 42 Loy. L.A. L. Rev. 949.

–. 'The Impact of Counsel: An Analysis of Empirical Evidence' (2010) 52 Seattle J. for Soc. Just. 51.

Sandefur, Rebecca L., ed. *Access to Justice. Sociology of Crime, Law and Deviance Series*. Bingley: Emerald/JAI Press, 2009.

Sarat, Austin. '"The Law Is All Over ...": Power, Resistance, and the Legal Consciousness of the Welfare Poor' (1990) 2 Yale J.L. & Human. 343.

Saskatchewan, Ministry of Justice and Attorney General. *Unrepresented Litigants' Access to Justice Committee: Final Report*. Regina: Ministry of Justice and Attorney General, 2007.

Silbey, Susan S. 'After Legal Consciousness' (2005) 1 Annual Review of Law and Social Science 323.

Stratton, Mary, and Travis Anderson. *Social, Economic, and Health Problems Associated with a Lack of Access to the Courts*. Edmonton: Canadian Forum on Civil Justice, 2006.

Tenant Duty Counsel Program. *Toronto East Representation Pilot Project Report* by Gene Filice. Toronto: Advocacy Centre for Tenants Ontario, 2006.

Trubek, David M., *et al. Civil Litigation Research Project: Final Report*. Madison: University of Wisconsin Law School, 1983.

Van Velthoven, Ben, and Marijke ter Voert. 'Paths to Justice in the Netherlands: Looking for Signs of Social Exclusion.' Leiden: Leiden University Department of Economics, 2004.

Rt. Hon. Lord Woolf. *Access to Justice: Final Report to the Lord Chancellor on the Civil Justice System in England and Wales*. London: Her Majesty's Stationery Office, 1996.

II. Self-Help, Education, and Information

Bachmann, Steve. 'Access to Justice as Access to Organizing' (2002) 4 Journal of Law and Social Challenges 1.

Bacon, Brenda L., and Brad McKenzie. 'Parent Education after Separation/Divorce: Impact of the Level of Parental Conflict on Outcomes' (2004) 42 Fam. Ct. Rev. 85.

Banks, Cate, Rosemary Hunter, and Jeff Giddings. *Australian Innovations in Legal Aid Services: Balancing Cost and Client Needs*. Nathan: Griffith University, 2006.

Conference of State Court Administrators. *Position Paper on Self-Represented Litigation*. Arlington: Government Relations Office, 2000.

Eggert, Kurt. 'Lashed to the Mast and Crying for Help: How Self-Limitation of Autonomy Can Protect Elders from Predatory Lending' (2003) 36 Loy. LA. L. Rev. 693.

Ellis, Desmond, and Dawn Y. Anderson. 'The Impact of Participation in a Parent Education Program for Divorcing Parents on the Use of Court Resources: An Evaluation Study' (2003) 21 Conflict Resolution Quarterly 169.

Emery, Robert E. 'Interparental Conflict and Social Policy' in *Interparental Conflict and Child Development: Theory, Research, and Applications*, ed. John H. Grych and Frank D. Fincham. New York: Cambridge University Press, 2001. 417.

Fackrell, Tamara A., Alan J. Hawkins, and Nicole M. Kay. 'How Effective Are Court-Affiliated Divorcing Parents Education Programs? A Meta-Analytic Study' (2011) 49 Fam. Ct. Rev. 107.

Federal Labour Standards Review Commission. *Fairness at Work – Federal Labour Standards for the 21st Century*. Gatineau: Human Resources and Skills Development Canada, 2006.

Kierstead, Shelly. 'Parent Education Programs in Family Courts: Balancing Autonomy and State Intervention' (2001) 49 Fam. Ct. Rev. 140.

Goldschmidt, Jona. 'The *Pro Se* Litigant's Struggle for Access to Justice: Meeting the Challenge of Bench and Bar Resistance' (2002) 40 Fam. Ct. Rev. 36.

Greacen, John M. 'An Administrator's Perspective: The Impact of Self-Represented Litigants on Trial Courts – Testing Our Stereotypes against Real Data' (2002) 41 Judges J. 32.

Kaspiew, Rae, *et al. Evaluation of the 2006 Family Law Reforms*. Melbourne: Australian Institute of Family Studies, 2009.

Langan, Anne-Marie. 'Threatening the Balance of the Scales of Justice: Unrepresented Litigants in the Family Courts of Ontario' (2005) 30 Queen's L.J. 825.

Leite, Randall W., and Kathleen Clark. 'Participants' Evaluations of Aspects of the Legal Child Custody Process and Preferences for Court Services' (2007) 45 Fam. Ct. Rev. 260.

Pollet, Susan L., and Melissa Lombreglia. 'A Nationwide Survey of Mandatory Parent Education' (2008) 46 Fam. Ct. Rev. 375.

Ramsay, Iain. 'Consumer Redress Mechanisms for Defective and Poor Quality Products' (1981) 21 U.T.L.J. 117.

Rekaiti, Pamaria, and Roger Van den Bergh. 'Cooling-Off Periods in the Consumer Laws of the EC Member States: A Comparative Law and Economics Approach' (2000) 23 Journal of Consumer Policy 371.

Sato, Iwao, *et al. Citizens Access to Legal Advice in Contemporary Japan: Self-help, Negotiation, and Third-Party Advice Seeking*. Paper presented at the Law and Society Association Conference, Berlin, 26 July 2007.

Schepard, Andrew. 'Parental Conflict Prevention Programs and the Unified Family Court: A Public Health Perspective' (1998) 32 Fam. L.Q. 95.

Schepard, Andrew, and Stephen W. Schlissel. 'Planning for P.E.A.C.E.: The Development of Court-Connected Education Programs for Divorcing and Separating Families' (1995) 23 Hofstra L. Rev. 845.

Schwartz, Saul. 'Can Financial Education Improve Financial Literacy and Retirement Planning?' IRPP Study No. 12. Montreal: Institute for Research on Public Policy, 2010.

Semple, Noel. *Cost-Benefit Analysis of Family Service Delivery: Disease, Prevention, and Treatment.* Toronto: Law Commission of Ontario, 2010.

Sigal, Amanda, *et al.* 'Do Parent Education Programs Promote Healthy Post-Divorce Parenting? Critical Distinction and a Review of the Evidence' (2011) 49 Fam. Ct. Rev. 120.

Stratton, Mary. *Some Facts and Figures from the Civil Justice System and the Public.* Toronto: Canadian Forum on Civil Justice, 2010.

Task Force on Financial Literacy. *Canadians and Their Money: Building a Brighter Financial Future.* Ottawa: December 2010.

Thompson, D.A. Rollie. 'No Lawyer: Institutional Coping with the Self-Represented' (2001) 19 Can Fam. L.Q. 455.

Thompson, D.A. Rollie, and Lynn Reierson. 'A Practicing Lawyer's Field Guide to the Unrepresented' (2002) 19 C.F.L.Q. 529.

Trussler, Marguerite. 'A Judicial View on Self-Represented Litigants' (2001) 19 Can Fam L.Q. 547.

Williams, Toni. 'Empowerment of Whom and for What? Financial Literacy Education and the New Regulation of Consumer Financial Services' (2007) 29 Law and Policy 226.

III. The Role of Non-Lawyers and Paralegals

Cory, Peter de C. *A Framework for Regulating Paralegal Practice in Ontario: Report.* Toronto: Ontario Ministry of the Attorney General, 2000.

Engler, Russell. 'And Justice for All – Including the Unrepresented Poor: Revisiting the Role of Judges, Mediators, and Clerks' (1999) 67 Fordham L. Rev. 1987.

–. 'Ethics in Transition: Unrepresented Litigants and the Changing Judicial Role' (2008) 22 Notre Dame J.L. Eth. & Pub. Pol'y 67.

Law Society of Upper Canada. *Report to the Attorney General of Ontario on the Implementation of Paralegal Regulation in Ontario.* Toronto: Law Society of Upper Canada, 2009.

Moorhead, Richard, Alan Paterson, and Avrom Sherr. 'Contesting Professionalism: Legal Aid and Nonlawyers in England and Wales' (2003) 37 Law & Soc'y Rev. 765.

Paetsch, Joanne J., *et al. High Conflict Intervention Programs in Alberta: A Review and Recommendations.* Canadian Research Institute for Law and the Family, Alberta Justice, 2007.

IV. The Delivery of Legal Services

2006 Edward V. Sparer Symposium, *Civil Gideon: Creating a Constitutional Right to Counsel in the Civil Context* (2006) 15 Temp. Pol. & Civ. Rts. L. Rev. 697–800.

An Obvious Truth: Creating an Action Blueprint for a Civil Right to Counsel in New York State (2009) 25 Touro L. Rev. 1–539.

Anderson, Elliot A. 'Unbundling the Ethical Issues of Pro Bono Advocacy: Articulating the Goals of Limited-Scope Pro Bono Advocacy for Limited Legal Services Programs' (2010) 48 Fam. Ct. Rev. 685.

Baarsma, Barbara, Flóra Felsö, and Kieja Janssen. 'Regulation of the Legal Profession and Access to Law: An Economic Perspective.' SEO economic research commissioned by the International Association of Legal Expenses Insurance, Amsterdam, 2008.

Bhabha, Faisal. 'Institutionalizing Access-to-Justice: Judicial, Legislative, and Grassroots Dimentions' (2007) 33 Queen's L.J. 139.

Bolger, William A., Jeffrey K. Anderson, and Thomas P. Chiancone. *The Cost of Personal Legal Services: A National Study.* Washington: National Resource Center for Consumers of Legal Services, 1988.

Charn, Jeanne. 'Legal Services for All: Is the Profession Ready?' (2009) 42 Loy. L.A. L. Rev. 1021.

Carabash, Michael. 'A Better Mousetrap?' (2009) 12 Canadian Forum on Civil Justice 20.

Derocher, Robert J. 'Access to Justice: Is Civil Gideon a Piece of the Puzzle?' (2008) 32 A.B.A. B. Leader 11.

Devlin, Richard. 'Breach of Contract?: The New Economy, Access to Justice, and the Ethical Responsibilities of the Legal Profession' (2002) 25 Dalhousie L.J. 335.

Echols, Robert. 'The Rapid Expansion of "State Access to Justice Commissions"' (2005) 19 Mgmt. Info. Exchange J. 41.

Engler, Russell. 'Approaching Ethical Issues Involving Unrepresented Litigants' (2009) 43 Clearinghouse Rev. 377.

–. 'Connecting Self-Representation to Civil Gideon: What Existing Data Reveal about When Counsel Is Most Needed' (2010) 37 Fordham Urb. L.J. 37.

–. 'Pursuing Access to Justice and Civil Right to Counsel in a Time of Economic Crisis' (2010) 15 Roger Williams U. L. Rev. 472.

–. 'Shaping a Context-Based Civil Gideon from the Dynamics of Social Change' (2006) 15 Temp. Pol. & Civ. Rts. L. Rev. 697.

–. 'Towards a Context-Based Civil Gideon through Access to Justice Initiatives' (2006) 40 Clearinghouse Rev. 196.

Farley, Alicia M. 'An Important Piece of the Bundle: How Limited Appearances Can Provide an Ethically Sound Way to Increase Access to Justice for Pro Se Litigants' (2007) 20 Georgetown Journal of Legal Ethics. 563.

Fedorak, Jeanette. 'Unbundling Legal Services: Is the Time Now' (2009) 12 Canadian Forum on Civil Justice 14.

Hadfield, Gillian K. 'The Price of Law: How the Market for Lawyers Distorts the Justice System' (2000) 98 Mich. L. Rev. 953.

Hogan, Lindsay E. 'Current Developments 2007–2008: The Ethics of Ghostwriting: The American Bar Association's Formal Opinion 07-446 and Its Effect on Ghostwriting Practices in the American Legal Community' (2008) 21 Georgetown J. of Legal Ethics 765.

Kritzer, Herbert. 'Fee Regimes and the Cost of Civil Justice' (2009) 28 Civil Justice Quarterly 1.

Justice Johnson Jr., Earl. 'Three Phases of Justice for the Poor: From Charity to Discretion to Right' (2009) 43 Clearinghouse Rev. 486.

Law Society of British Columbia. *Report of the Unbundling of Legal Services Task Force, Limited Retainers: Professionalism and Practice*. Vancouver: 2008.

Law Commission of Ontario. *Best Practices at Family Justice System Entry Points: Needs of Users and Responses of Workers*. Toronto: Law Commission of Ontario, 2009.

–. *Voices from a Broken Family Justice System: Sharing Consultations Results*. Toronto: Law Commission of Ontario, 2010.

Legal Aid Ontario. *2007 Annual Report*. Toronto: Legal Aid Ontario, 2007.

Luban, David. *Lawyers and Justice: An Ethical Study*. Princeton University Press, 2008.

Marvy, Paul. '"To Promote Jurisprudential Understanding of the Law": The Civil Right to Counsel in Washington State' (2006) 40 Clearinghouse Rev. 180.

Marvy, Paul, and Debra Gardner. 'A Civil Right to Counsel for the Poor' (2005) 32:3 A.B.A. Hum. Rts. 8.

Ministry of Justice. *Proposals for the Reform of Legal Aid in England and Wales*. London: TSO 2010.

Mosten, Forrest S. 'Unbundling of Legal Services and the Family Lawyer' (1994) 28 Fam. L.Q. 421.

Munro, Doug. *Limited Retainers: Professionalism and Practice: Report of the*

Unbundling of Legal Services Task Force. Vancouver: Law Society of British Columbia, 2008.

Ontario Civil Legal Needs Project. *Listening to Ontarians – Report of the Ontario Civil Legal Needs Project.* Toronto: The Ontario Civil Legal Needs Project Steering Committee, 2010.

Pastore, Clare. 'The California Model Statute Task Force' (2006) 40 Clearinghouse Rev. 176.

PricewaterhouseCoopers. *Economic Value of Legal Aid: Analysis in Relation to Commonwealth Funded Matters with a Focus on Family Law.* Brisbane: Legal Aid Queensland, 2009.

Regan, Francis, and Jon Johnsen. 'Are Finland's Recent Legal Services Policy Reforms Swimming against the Tide of International Reforms?' (2007) 26 Civil Justice Quarterly 341.

Robbins, Ira. 'Ghostwriting: Filling in the Gaps for Pro Se Prisoners' Access to the Courts' (2010) 23 Georgetown J. of Legal Ethics 271.

Robertson, Michael, and Jeff Giddings. 'Legal Consumers as Coproducers: The Changing Face of Legal Services Delivery in Australia' (2002) 40 Fam. Ct. Rev. 63.

Rothermuch, John. 'Ethical and Procedural Implications of "Ghostwriting" for Pro Se Litigants' (1999) 67 Fordham L. Rev. 2687.

Sachs, Stephen H. 'Keynote Address: Seeking a Right to Counsel in Appointed Civil Cases in Maryland' (2007) 37 U. Balt. L. Rev. 5.

Sandbach, James. *No Win, No Fee, No Chance: CAB Evidence on the Challenges Facing Access to Injury Compensation.* London: Citizens Advice, 2004.

Seron, Caroll, Martin Frankel, and Greg Van Ryzin. 'The Impact of Legal Counsel on Outcomes for Poor Tenants in New York City's Housing Court: Results of Randomized Experiments' (2001) 35 Law & Soc'y Rev. 419.

Sossin, Lorne. 'The Public Interest, Professionalism, and Pro Bono Publico' (2008) 46 Osgoode Hall L.J.131.

Special Issue: A Right to a Lawyer? Momentum Grows (2006) 40 Clearinghouse Rev. 163–293.

Susskind, Richard. *The End of Lawyers? Rethinking the Nature of Legal Services.* Oxford: Oxford University Press, 2008.

Talia, M. Sue. *Roadmap for Implementing a Successful Unbundling Program.* Des Moines: American Judicature Society, 2005.

Trebilcock, Michael J. 'Regulating the Market for Legal Services' (2008) 45 Alta. L.R. 215.

–. *Report of the Legal Aid Review.* Toronto: Ministry of the Attorney General, 2008.

Trubek, David M., *et al*. 'The Costs of Ordinary Litigation' (1983) 31 UCLA Law Review 72.

United Kingdom, Ministry of Justice. *Proposals for the Reform of Legal Aid in England and Wales*. Consultation Paper CP 12/10. London: HMSO, 2010.

Varro, Jim. *'Unbundling' of Legal Services and Limited Legal Representation: Background Information and Proposed Amendments to Professional Conduct Rules*. Toronto: Law Society of Upper Canada, 2010.

Yerbich, Thomas J. 'Testing the Limits on Unbundled, Limited Representation' (2004) American Bankruptcy Institute Journal 8.

Zorza, Richard. 'Access to Justice: The Emerging Consensus and Some Questions and Implications' (2011) 94 Judicature 156.

–. 'Discrete Task Representation, Ethics, and the Big Picture: Toward a New Jurisprudence' (2002) 40 Fam. Ct. Rev. 19.

V. Legal Insurance Plans

Blankenburg, Edward. 'Private Insurance and the Historical "Waves" of Legal Aid' (1993) 13 Windsor Y.B. Access Just. 185.

Kilian, Matthias. 'Alternatives to Public Provision: The Role of Legal Expenses Insurance in Broadening Access to Justice: The German Experience' (2003) 30 J.L. & Soc'y 31.

–. 'Legal Expenses Insurance – Germany's Funding Concept as a Role Model' in *After Universalism: Re-engineering Access to Justice*, ed. Richard Moorhead and Pascoe Pleasence. Oxford: Blackwell Publishing, 2003. 31.

Kilian, Matthias, and Francis Regan. 'Legal Expenses Insurance and Legal Aid – Two Sides of the Same Coin? The Experience from Germany and Sweden' (2004) 11 Int'l J. Legal Prof. 233.

Law Society. *Access to Justice Review: Final Report*. London: Law Society, 2010.

U.K., Ministry of Justice. *Proposals for the Reform of Legal Aid in England and Wales*. Consultation Paper CP12/10. London: HMSO, 2010.

–. *Review of Civil Litigation Costs: Final Report by Lord Justice Jackson*. Norwich: HMSO, 2010).

VI. Contingency Fees and Class Actions

Branch, Ward K. *Class Actions in Canada* (looseleaf). Aurora: Canada Law Book.

Clark, Stuart, and Christina Harris. 'The Push to Reform Class Action Procedure in Australia: Evolution or Revolution?' (2008) 32 Melb.U.L.R. 775.

Duggan, Anthony J. 'Consumer Access to Justice in Common Law Countries:

A Survey of the Issues from a Law and Economics Perspective' in *International Perspectives on Consumers' Access to Justice*, ed. Charles E.F. Rickett and Thomas G.W. Telfer. Cambridge: Cambridge University Press, 2003. 46.

Gilles, Myriam. 'Opting Out of Liability: The Forthcoming Near-Total Demise of the Modern Class Action' (2005) 104 Mich. L. Rev. 373.

Kalajdzic, Jasminka. 'Consumer (In)justice: Reflections on Canadian Consumer Class Actions' (2010) 50 Can. Bus. L.J. 275.

Kritzer, Herbert M. *Risks, Reputations, and Rewards: Contingency Fee Legal Practice in the United States*. Stanford: Stanford University Press, 2004.

Maclean, Mavis. 'No House, No Fee – Conditional Fee Arrangements in Divorce' (1999) 29 Fam. Law 245.

Moorhead, Richard. 'An American Future? Contingency Fees, Claims Explosions, and Evidence from Employment Tribunals' (2010) 73:5 Modern Law Review 752.

–. 'Contingency Fees in England and Wales: Access to Justice in Employment Tribunals.' Paper presented to the International Legal Aid Group Conference, Wellington, New Zealand, 3 April 2009.

Morabito, Vincent. *An Empirical Study of Australia's Class Action Regimes: First Report – Class Action Facts and Figures*, vol. 1. Department of Business Law and Taxation, Monash University, 2009.

Trebilcock, Michael. 'The Case for Contingent Fees: The Ontario Legal Profession Rethinks Its Position' (1989) Can. Bus. L.J. 360.

VII. Informal Complaint Systems

B.C. Justice Review Taskforce. *A New Justice System for Families and Children: Report of the Family Justice Reform Working Group to the Justice Review Taskforce*. Vancouver: Law Society of British Columbia, 2005.

Bingham, Lisa Blomgren. 'Employment Arbitration: The Repeat Player Effect' (1997) 1 Employee Rts. & Employment Pol'y J. 189.

Dewees, Don, David Duff, and Michael Trebilcock. *Exploring the Domain of Accident Law: Taking the Facts Seriously*. New York: Oxford University Press, 1996.

Lacoursière, Marc. 'Le consommateur et l'accès à la justice' (2008) 49(1) C. de D. 97.

Landau, Barbara, *et al. Home Court Advantage – Creating a Family Law Process That Works: Final Report and Recommendations from the Home Court Advantage Summit*. Submission to the Attorney General of Ontario, 27 September 2010.

Little, Andrew. 'Canadian Arbitration Law after Dell Computer Corp. Union des Consommateurs' (2007) 45 Can. Bus. L.J. 356.

McGill, Shelley. 'Consumer Arbitration Clause Enforcement: A Balanced Legislative Response' (2010) 47 American Bus. L.J. 361.

Public Citizen, *The Arbitration Trap: How Credit Companies Snare Consumers*. Washington: Public Citizen, 2007.

Ramsay, Iain. 'Consumer Redress and Access to Justice' in *International Perspectives on Consumers' Access to Justice*, ed. Charles E.F. Rickett and Thomas G.W. Telfer. Cambridge: Cambridge University Press, 2003. 17.

Rogerson, Carol, and Rollie Thompson. *Spousal Support Advisory Guidelines*. Ottawa: Department of Justice Canada, 2008.

Schwartz, Jonathan. 'Making the Consumer Watchdog's Bark as Strong as Its Gripe: Complaint Sites and the Changing Dynamic of the Fair Use Defence' (2006) 16 Albany Law Journal of Science and Technology 59.

Trebilcock, Michael J. 'Rethinking Consumer Protection Policy' in *International Perspectives on Consumers' Access to Justice*, ed. Charles E.F. Rickett and Thomas G.W. Telfer. Cambridge: Cambridge University Press, 2003. 69.

VIII. Mediation

Australia, Attorney-General's Department. *Children beyond Dispute: A Prospective Study of Outcomes from Child Focused and Child Inclusive Post-Separation Family Dispute Resolution* by Jennifer E McIntosh, Caroline M. Long, and Yvonne D. Wells. Australian Government: Attorney-General's Department, 2009.

AFCC Task Force on Parenting Coordination. 'Parenting Coordination: Implementation Issues' (2003) 41 Fam. Ct. Rev. 533.

Ambert, Anne-Marie. *Divorce: Facts, Causes, and Consequences*, 3rd ed. Ottawa: Vanier Institute of the Family, 2009.

Astor, Hilary. 'Making a "Genuine Effort" in Family Mediation: What Does It Mean?' (2008) 22 Austl J Fam L 102.

Bailey, Martha J. 'Unpacking the Rational Alternative: A Critical Review of Family Mediation Movement Claims' (1989) 8 Can. J. Fam. L. 61.

Balbi, Lonny L. 'Self-Represented Litigants from the Mediator's Perspective: Walking the Line' (2001) 19 Can. Fam. L.Q. 583.

B.C. Justice Review Task Force. *A New Justice System for Families and Children: Report of the Family Justice Reform Working Group to the Justice Review Task Force*. Vancouver: Justice Review Task Force (British Columbia), 2005.

Blaisure, Karen R., and Margie J. Geasler. 'The Divorce Intervention Model' (2000) 38 Family & Conciliation Courts Review 501.

Boyd, Marion. *Dispute Resolution in Family Law: Protecting Choice, Promoting Inclusion*. Toronto: Ministry of the Attorney General (Ontario), 2004.

Bohmer, Carol, and Marilyn L. Ray. 'Effects of Different Dispute Resolution Methods on Women and Children after Divorce' (1994) 28 Fam. L.Q. 223.

Bozzomo, James W., and Andrew Schepard. 'Efficiency, Therapeutic Justice, Mediation, and Evaluation: Reflections on a Survey of Unified Family Courts' (2003) 37 Fam. L.Q. 332.

Bryan, Penelope E. 'Killing Us Softly: Divorce Mediation and the Politics of Power' (1992) 40 Buff. L. Rev. 441.

Coates, Christine A., et al. 'Parenting Coordination for High-Conflict Families' (2004) 42 Fam. Ct. Rev. 246.

Cohen, David, and Peter Finkle. 'Consumer Redress through Alternative Dispute Resolution and Small Claims Court: Theory and Practice' (1993) 13 Windsor Y.B. Access Just. 81 at 113.

Emery, Robert E., David Sbarra, and Tara Grover. 'Divorce Mediation: Research and Reflections' (2005) 43 Fam. Ct. Rev. 22.

Evaluation Division. Office of Strategic Planning and Performance Management. The Unified Family Court Summative Evaluation Final Report. Ottawa: Department of Justice (Canada), 2009.

Federal and Provincial Territorial Family Law Committee. Report on Custody and Access and Child Support: Putting Children First. Ottawa: Department of Justice (Canada), 2002.

Folberg, Jay, Ann Milne, and Peter Salem. Divorce and Family Mediation: Models, Techniques, and Applications. New York: Guilford Press, 2004.

Gilmour, Glenn A. High-Conflict Separation and Divorce: Options for Consideration. Report # 2004-FCY-1E. Ottawa: Department of Justice (Canada), 2004.

Goundry, Sandra A., Rosalind Currie, and Yvonne Peters. Family Mediation in Canada: Implications for Women's Equality. Ottawa: Status of Women Canada, 1998.

Grant, Stephen. 'Alternate Dispute Resolution in Family Law: What's Not to Like?' (2008) 27 Can Fam. L.Q. 235.

Grillo, Trina. 'The Mediation Alternative: Process Dangers for Women' (1991) 100 Yale L.J. 1545.

Johnston, Janet R. 'High-Conflict Divorce' (1994) 4 The Future of Children 165.

Kelly, Joan B. 'Family Mediation Research: Is There Empirical Support for the Field?' (2004) 22 Conflict Resolution Quarterly 3.

Kruk, Edward. 'Practice Issues, Strategies, and Models: The Current State of the Art of Family Mediation' (1998) 36 Fam. Ct. Rev. 195.

Kuhn, Jeffrey A. 'A Seven-Year Lesson on Unified Family Courts: What We Have Learned Since the 1990 National Family Court Symposium' (1998) 32 Fam. L.Q. 67.

Marcus, Mary G., *et al*. 'To Mediate or Not to Mediate: Financial Outcomes in Mediated versus Adversarial Divorces' (1999) 17 Mediation Q. 143.

McEwen, Craig A., Nancy H. Rogers, and Richard J. Maiman. 'Bring in the Lawyers: Challenging the Dominant Approaches to Ensuring Fairness in Divorce Mediation' (1995) 79 Minn. L. Rev. 1317.

Office of Consumer Affairs, Industry Canada. *Market Driven Consumer Redress and Legal Issues: Case Studies* by David Clarke and Kernaghan Webb. Ottawa: Industry Canada, 2002.

Ontario Bar Association, Family Law Section, ADR Institute of Ontario and Ontario Association of Family Mediators. *Family Law Process Reform: Supporting Families to Support Their Children* by Barbara Landau *et al*. Toronto: Ontario Association for Family Mediation, 2009.

O'Shea, Paul. 'Underneath the Radar: The Largely Unnoticed Phenomenon of Industry Based Consumer Dispute Resolution Schemes in Australia' (2004) 15 Australian Dispute Resolution Journal 156.

–. 'The Lions Question Applied to Industry-Based Consumer Dispute Resolution Schemes' (2006) 25:1 The Arbitrator and Mediator 63.

Paetsch, Joanne J., Lorne D. Bertrand, and Nicholas Bala. *The Child-Centred Family Justice Strategy: Survey on the Practice of Family Law in Canada*. Ottawa: Department of Justice Canada, 2007.

Paetsch, Joanne J., *et al*. *High Conflict Intervention Programs in Alberta: A Review and Recommendations*. Canadian Research Institute for Law and the Family, Alberta Justice, 2007.

Parkinson, Patrick. 'Parenting after Separation: The Process of Dispute Resolution in Australia' (2010) 330 Ritsumeikan Law Review 110.

Rhoades, Helen. 'Mandatory Mediation of Family Disputes: Reflections from Australia' (2010) 32 J. Soc. Wel. & Fam. L. 183.

Saini, Michael A. 'Evidence Base of Custody and Access Evaluations' (2008) 8 Brief Treat. Crisis Interven. 111.

Salem, Peter. 'The Emergence of Triage in Family Court Services: The Beginning of the End for Mandatory Mediation?' (2009) 47 Fam. Ct. Rev. 371.

Shaw, Lori Anne. 'Divorce Mediation Outcome Research: A Meta-analysis' (2010) 27 Conflict Resol. Q. 447.

Smith, Heather, Michael Brown, and Francine Van Melle. *Dispute Resolution Officer Program Pilot Project in the Superior Court of Justice in Brampton, Milton, and Newmarket: Practice Direction*. Toronto: Superior Court of Justice (Ontario), 2010.

Teitz, Louise Ellen. 'Providing Legal Services for the Middle Class in Cyberspace: The Promise and Challenge of On-Line Dispute Resolution' (2001) 70 Fordham L. Rev. 985.

Tesler, Pauline H. 'Collaborative Law: What It Is and Why Lawyers Need to Know About It' (1999) 2008 Am. J. Fam. L. 215.

Zeleznikow, John, and Andrew Stranieri. 'Split-Up: An Intelligent Decision Support System Which Provides Advice upon Property Division Following Divorce' (1998) 6 Int'l J.L. & I.T. 190.

IX. Tribunals

Bell, Kevin. *One VCAT: President's Review of VCAT*. Victorian Civil and Administrative Tribunal, Melbourne, Australia, 2009.

Carmichael, Kathy. *New Directions: Divorce and Administrative Law*. Ottawa: Department of Justice Canada, 1999.

Drahozal, Christopher R., and Samantha Zyontz. 'Creditor Claims in Arbitration and in Court' (2011) Hastings Business Law Journal 77.

Eugene, Clark E. 'Small Claims Courts and Tribunals in Australia: Development and Emerging Issues' (1990–91) U. Tasm. L. Rev. 201.

Giddings, Jeff, Merran Lawler, and Michael Robertson. '"It's More Like Judge Judy" – Self-Help in a Hybrid Legal Forum.' Paper presented to the International Legal Aid Group Conference, Wellington, New Zealand, 2 April 2009.

Gramatiko, Martin. 'A Framework for Measuring the Costs of Paths to Justice' (2008) 2 Journal Jurisprudence 111.

McCormack, Judith. 'The Price of Administrative Justice' (1998) 6 C.L.E.L.J. 1.

Saumier, Genevieve. 'Consumer Dispute Resolution: The Evolving Canadian Landscape' (2007) 1(4) Class Action Defence Quarterly 52.

United Kingdom, House of Commons Library. *The Tribunals, Courts and Enforcement Bill [HL]*. Research Paper 07/22 by Alexander Horne, Philip Ward, and Vincent Keter. London: House of Commons Library, 2007.

X. Case Management and Other Reforms

Adams, George. 'The Small Claims Court and the Adversary Process: More Problems of Function and Form' (1973) 51 Can. Bar Rev. 583.

Adams, Peter, *et al. Evaluation of the Small Claims Program*. Victoria: Ministry of Attorney General of British Columbia, 1992.

Akre, Lynn M. 'Struggling with Indeterminacy: A Call for Interdisciplinary Collaboration in Redefining the "Best Interest of the Child" Standard' (1992) 75 Marq. L. Rev. 628.

Alexander, K., and N. Moloney, eds. *Law Reform and Financial Markets*. Cheltenham: Edward Elgar, 2011.

B.C. Justice Review Task Force. *Proposed Rules of Civil Procedure of the British*

Columbia Supreme Court: Questions and Answers. Vancouver: Law Society of British Columbia, 2008.

B.C. Ministry of the Attorney General, Justice Services Branch. *The Civil Justice Reform Context behind British Columbia's Expedited Litigation Rule and the Small Claims Court Jurisdictional Limit Increase* by Bob Goldschmid. Victoria: B.C. Ministry of the Attorney General, 2005.

Bryant, Diana, Jennifer E. McIntosh, and Kristen Murray. 'Evidence of a Different Nature: The Child-Responsive and Less Adversarial Initiatives of the Family Court of Australia' (2008) 46(1) Fam. Ct. Rev. 125.

Elrod, Linda D., and D. Dale Milfred. 'Paradigm Shifts and Pendulum Swings in Child Custody: The Interests of Children in the Balance' (2008) 42 Fam. L.Q. 381.

Flango, Carol H., Ted Rubin, and Victor Eugene Flango. *How Are Courts Coordinating Family Cases?* Williamsburg: National Center for State Courts, 1999.

Haibach, Georg. 'The Commission Proposal for a Regulation Establishing a European Small Claims Procedure: An Analysis' (2005) 13 E.R.P.L. 593.

Hardcastle, Gerald W. 'Adversarialism and the Family Court: A Family Court Judge's Perspective' (2005) 9 UC Davis J. Juv. L. & Pol'y 57.

Higgins, Daryl J. *Cooperation and Coordination: An Evaluation of the Family Court of Australia's Magellan Case-Management Model.* Canberra, Melbourne: Family Court of Australia, Australian Institute of Family Studies, 2007.

Institute for the Advancement of the American Legal System and American College of Trial Lawyers Task Force on Discovery and Civil Justice. *21st Century Civil Justice System: A Roadmap for Reform Pilot Project Rules.* Denver: Institute for the Advancement of the American Legal System, 2009.

–. *Final Report on the Joint Project.* Denver: Institute for the Advancement of the American Legal System, 2009.

Jacobs, Brenda, and Lesley Jacobs. *Multidisciplinary Paths to Family Justice: Professional Challenges and Promising Practices.* Toronto: Law Commission of Ontario, 2010.

Long, Jennifer. 'Compliance in Small Claims Court: Exploring the Factors Associated with Defendants' Level of Compliance with Mediated and Adjudicated Outcomes' (2003) 21 Conflict Resolution Quarterly 139.

Manitoba Law Reform Commission. *Review of the Small Claims Court.* Winnipeg: Manitoba Law Reform Commission, 1998.

McGill, Shelley. 'Who Should Protect the Consumer? The Eroding Role of the Small Claims Court.' Working paper prepared for the 40th Annual Workshop on Commercial and Consumer Law, University of Toronto, Munk Centre for International Studies, 16 October 2010.

–. 'Small Claims Court Identity Crisis: A Review of Recent Reform Measures' (2010) 49 Can. Bus. L.J. 213.

McGuire, Sean C., and Roderick A. Macdonald. 'Small Claims Court Can't' (1996) 34 Osgoode Hall L.J. 509.

McIntosh, Jennifer E., Hon. Diana Bryant, and Kristen Murray. 'Evidence of a Different Nature: The Child-Responsive and Less Adversarial Initiatives of the Family Court of Australia' (2008) 46 Fam. Ct. Rev. 125.

Ontario Civil Justice Review. *Civil Justice Review: Supplemental and Final Report.* Toronto: Ontario Civil Justice Review, 1996.

Patry, Marc W., Veronica Stinson, and Steven M. Smith. *Evaluation of the Nova Scotia Small Claims Court: Final Report to the Nova Scotia Law Reform Commission.* Halifax: St Mary's University, 2009.

Salem, Peter, Debra Kulak, and Robin Deutsch. 'Triaging Family Court Services: The Connecticut Judicial Branch's Family Civil Intake Screen' (2007) 27 Pace L. Rev. 741.

Schepard, Andrew. *Children, Courts, and Custody: Interdisciplinary Models for Divorcing Families.* New York: Cambridge University Press, 2004.

Schepard, Andrew, and James W. Bozzomo. 'Efficiency, Therapeutic Justice, Mediation, and Evaluation: Reflections on a Survey of Unified Family Courts' (2003) 37 Fam. L.Q. 333.

Sedona Conference Working Group 7, Sedona Canada. *The Sedona Canada Principles: Addressing Electronic Discovery.* Sedona: The Sedona Conference, 2008.

Semple, Noel. 'Whose Best Interests? Custody and Access Law and Procedure' (2010) 48 Osgoode Hall L.J. 287.

Sossin, Lorne. 'ADR and the Public Interest.' Paper presented to the Canadian Forum on Civil Justice Conference, Into the Future, Montreal, 2 May 2006.

Tavender, E. David. 'Personal Reflections on ADR Reforms.' Paper presented to the Canadian Forum on Civil Justice Conference, Into the Future, Montreal, Quebec, 2 May 2006.

Thompson, Rollie. 'The Evolution of Modern Canadian Family Law Procedure: The End of the Adversary System? Or Just the End of the Trial?' (2003) 41 Fam. Ct. Rev. 155.

Trebilcock, Michael, and Lilla Csorgo. 'Multi-Disciplinary Professional Practices: A Consumer Welfare Perspective' (2001) 24 Dalhousie L.J. 1.

Walker, Janet, and Garry D. Watson. 'New Technologies and the Civil Litigation Process Common Law General Report.' Paper presented to the XIIIth World Congress of the International Association of Procedural Law, Salvador de Bahia, Brazil, 16–20 September 2007.

Winkler, Warren K. 'Access to Justice Mediation: Panacea or Pariah?' 2007 16(1) Canadian Arbitration and Mediation Journal 5.

Zeitler, Michelle, and Samantha Moore. *Children Come First: A Process Evaluation of the Nassau County Model Custody Part.* New York: New York State Office of Court Administration, 2008.

Ziegel, Jacob. 'Canadian Consumer Law and Policies 40 Years Later: A Mixed Report Card' (2010) 50 Can. Bus L.J. 259.

Zuker, Bruce, and Monica Her. 'The People's Court Examined: A Legal and Empirical Analysis of the Small Claims Court System' (2003) 37 U.S.F. L. Rev. 315.

Index